# THE BLOOMSBURY HANDBOOK TO SYLVIA PLATH

# THE BLOOMSBURY HANDBOOK TO SYLVIA PLATH

*Edited by Anita Helle, Amanda Golden,
& Maeve O'Brien*

BLOOMSBURY ACADEMIC
LONDON • NEW YORK • OXFORD • NEW DELHI • SYDNEY

BLOOMSBURY ACADEMIC
Bloomsbury Publishing Plc
50 Bedford Square, London, WC1B 3DP, UK
1385 Broadway, New York, NY 10018, USA
29 Earlsfort Terrace, Dublin 2, Ireland

BLOOMSBURY, BLOOMSBURY ACADEMIC and the Diana logo
are trademarks of Bloomsbury Publishing Plc

First published in Great Britain 2022
Paperback edition published 2024

Copyright © Anita Helle, Amanda Golden, Maeve O'Brian and contributors, 2022

The editors and contributors have asserted her right under the Copyright, Designs
and Patents Act, 1988, to be identified as Authors of this work.

For legal purposes the Acknowledgements on p. vii constitute an extension of this copyright page.

Cover design: Rebecca Heselton
Cover image © Donald Cheney, *Plath in Rome*, 1956

All rights reserved. No part of this publication may be reproduced or transmitted
in any form or by any means, electronic or mechanical, including photocopying,
recording, or any information storage or retrieval system, without prior
permission in writing from the publishers.

Bloomsbury Publishing Plc does not have any control over, or responsibility for, any
third-party websites referred to or in this book. All internet addresses given in this
book were correct at the time of going to press. The author and publisher regret any
inconvenience caused if addresses have changed or sites have ceased to exist,
but can accept no responsibility for any such changes.

A catalogue record for this book is available from the British Library.

A catalog record for this book is available from the Library of Congress

ISBN: HB: 978-1-3501-1922-2
PB: 978-1-3504-1966-7
ePDF: 978-1-3501-1924-6
eBook: 978-1-3501-1923-9

Series: Bloomsbury Handbooks

Typeset by Integra Software Services Pvt. Ltd.

To find out more about our authors and books visit www.bloomsbury.com
and sign up for our newsletters.

# CONTENTS

List of Illustrations — viii
Notes on Contributors — ix
Acknowledgments — xiv
Note on the Cover — xvi
Abbreviations — xvii

Introduction: Approaching Sylvia Plath in the Twenty-First Century — 1
*Anita Helle*

## Part I  New Cultural and Historical Contexts

1  Plath as Punch Line — 17
   *Jonathan Ellis*

2  "Get bathrobe and slippers and nightgown & work on femininity":
   Sylvia Plath, Self-Identity, and Sleepwear — 31
   *Rebecca C. Tuite*

3  Psychiatric Disability and Asylum Fiction: From *The Snake Pit* to
   *The Bell Jar* — 43
   *Elizabeth J. Donaldson*

4  Sylvia Plath's Cambridge — 53
   *Di Beddow*

5  Plath in Space: Feeling the Chill of the Void — 63
   *Tim Hancock*

6  Spectral Traces, Places, and Sylvia Plath — 75
   *Gail Crowther*

7  <maniacs.> of the Heterotopia: Citizen Critics and Marginalia in Library
   Copies of Sylvia Plath — 83
   *Christine Walde*

8  "God's Lioness" and God's "Negress": The Feminine and the Figure
   of the African American in Plath — 93
   *Jerome Ellison Murphy*

9  Centering Whiteness: Sylvia Plath's Literary Apprenticeship — 101
   *Maeve O'Brien*

| 10 | The Child Reading: Female Stereotypes and Social Authority in Sylvia Plath's Children's Stories<br>*Lissi Athanasiou-Krikelis* | 111 |
|---|---|---|
| 11 | Lucent Figs and Suave Veal Chops: Sylvia Plath and Food<br>*Lynda K. Bundtzen* | 125 |

## Part II  Affiliations, Influences, and Intertextualities

| 12 | Sylvia Plath's Greek Tragedy<br>*Holly Ranger* | 139 |
|---|---|---|
| 13 | "Yeats I like very very much": Sylvia Plath and W. B. Yeats<br>*Gillian Groszewski* | 153 |
| 14 | The Law of Similarity and the Law of Contact: Sylvia Plath, Ted Hughes, and Sympathetic Magic<br>*Katherine Robinson* | 165 |
| 15 | "I am a miner": Long Poems and Literary Succession in *Ariel* and *Crow*<br>*Jennifer Ryan-Bryant* | 177 |
| 16 | "Not Mrs. Hughes and Mrs. Sillitoe": Sylvia Plath and Ruth Fainlight in the 1960s<br>*Heather Clark* | 187 |
| 17 | Beelines: Reading Plath through Edith Sitwell and Carol Ann Duffy<br>*Marsha Bryant* | 199 |
| 18 | Medusa's Metadata: Aurelia Plath's Gregg Shorthand Annotations<br>*Catherine Rankovic* | 211 |
| 19 | "I may hate her, but that's not all": Mother–Daughter Intimacy in the Plath Archive<br>*Janet Badia* | 219 |

## Part III  Media and Pedagogy

| 20 | Plath and Media Culture<br>*Nicola Presley* | 233 |
|---|---|---|
| 21 | "I imagine that a man might not praise it as much": Reception of "Three Women" and Plath's BBC-Recorded Poetry<br>*Carrie Smith* | 243 |
| 22 | Sylvia Plath's "Three Women": Producing a Poetics of Listening at the BBC<br>*Nerys Williams* | 255 |
| 23 | Sylvia Plath's "The Jailor" as Radical Feminist Text<br>*Bethany Hicok* | 267 |

| | | |
|---|---|---|
| 24 | Archival Pedagogy: Curating Edna O'Brien's Sylvia Plath Television Play<br>*Amanda Golden* | 279 |
| 25 | Feminist Recovery, Service Learning, and Community Engagement in a Sylvia Plath Studies Undergraduate Seminar<br>*Julie Goodspeed-Chadwick* | 289 |

**Part IV  Editing the Archives**

| | | |
|---|---|---|
| 26 | Sylvia Plath in the Round<br>*Karen V. Kukil* | 299 |
| 27 | "They will come asking for our letters": Editing *The Letters of Sylvia Plath*<br>*Peter K. Steinberg* | 307 |

| | |
|---|---|
| BIBLIOGRAPHY | 316 |
| INDEX | 340 |

# ILLUSTRATIONS

1   Still from *The Snake Pit*. [Film] Directed by Anatole Litvak. 20th Century Fox, 1948 — 47

2   Detail of "Lady Lazarus" from first edition library copy of *Ariel* from Western Libraries. Photographed by Christine Walde — 84

3   Detail from the chapbook *<maniacs.>* (2017). Photographed by Christine Walde — 88

4   "Revealing the Roots of Sylvia Plath" by Rebekah Geevarghese and Uzma Patel. Image of Digital Project Homepage — 286

# CONTRIBUTORS

**Lissi Athanasiou-Krikelis** is Associate Professor of English and Director of Interdisciplinary Studies at New York Institute of Technology. Her research interests include postmodern metafiction in children's and adult literature, and her articles have appeared in the *Journal of Modern Greek Studies*, *The Lion and the Unicorn*, *Children's Literature Quarterly*, *Bookbird*, *International Research in Children's Literature*, and *Narrative*.

**Janet Badia** is Dean of the College of Liberal Arts and Professor of Women's Studies at Purdue University Fort Wayne. She also served as longtime Director of the Women's Studies Program at Purdue Fort Wayne from 2009–21. She is the author of *Sylvia Plath and the Mythology of Women Readers* (2011) and co-editor of *Reading Women: Literary Figures and Cultural Icons from the Victorian Age to the Present* (2005). Her research interests include the history of women's reading and the reception of American women's writing since the 1950s.

**Di Beddow** wrote her Ph.D. dissertation on the Cambridge period of Sylvia Plath and Ted Hughes at Queen Mary University, London. Her particular interest is in place and poetry. She is a Cambridge resident and a retired English teacher. She has published work on the *English and Drama Blog* for the British Library and in *The Ted Hughes Society Journal*. She has also published on the Rose Library's *Scholar Blog* after gaining an Emory University researcher's award.

**Marsha Bryant** is Professor of English and Distinguished Teaching Scholar at the University of Florida. She is the author of *Women's Poetry and Popular Culture* and *Auden and Documentary in the 1930s*, and her recent work on Plath appears in the journal *Feminist Modernist Studies*. Bryant is Associate Editor of *Contemporary Women's Writing* and has contributed to the collections *The Classics in Modernist Translation*, *The Many Facades of Edith Sitwell*, and *Popular Modernism and Its Legacies*.

**Lynda K. Bundtzen** is Herbert H. Lehman Professor of English, Emerita at Williams College. She is the author of *Plath's Incarnations Woman and the Creative Process* (1989) and *The Other* Ariel (2001).

**Heather Clark** is Professor of Contemporary Poetry at the University of Huddersfield and the author of *Red Comet: The Short Life and Blazing Art of Sylvia Plath*, which was a finalist for the Pulitzer Prize, the National Book Critics Circle Award, and the *LA Times* Book Prize, and the winner of the Slightly Foxed Prize for Best First Biography. She is also the author of *The Grief of Influence: Sylvia Plath and Ted Hughes*, a CHOICE Outstanding Academic Title; *The Ulster Renaissance: Poetry in Belfast 1962–1972*; and the forthcoming *Sylvia Plath: A Very Short Introduction*.

**Gail Crowther** is an independent writer and researcher. She is the author of *Three-Martini Afternoons at the Ritz: The Rebellion of Sylvia Plath and Anne Sexton* (2021) as well as *The Haunted Reader and Sylvia Plath* (2017). She has co-authored two books, *These Ghostly Archives: The Unearthing of Sylvia Plath* (2017) and *A Year's Turning: Sylvia Plath in Devon* (2016). She has also written several chapters, essays, and articles about Sylvia Plath and Anne Sexton.

**Elizabeth J. Donaldson** is Professor of English and Associate Dean at New York Institute of Technology, where she teaches courses in American literature and directs the Medical Humanities minor program. Her edited books include *The Madwoman and the Blindman: Jane Eyre, Discourse, Disability* (2012) and *Literatures of Madness: Disability Studies and Mental Health* (2018). She has published essays on LSD-inspired disability-immersion experiences of schizophrenia, mental illness in graphic medicine and comics, antipsychiatry in Lauren Slater's memoirs, and physiognomy and madness in *Jane Eyre*. She is currently co-editing a neurodiversity collection for MLA Press with M. Remi Yergeau, Diana R. Paulin, and Ralph Savarese.

**Jonathan Ellis** is a Reader in American Literature at the University of Sheffield. He is the author or editor of *Art and Memory in the Work of Elizabeth Bishop* (2006), *The Cambridge Companion to Elizabeth Bishop* (2014), *Letter Writing Among Poets* (2015), *Reading Elizabeth Bishop: An Edinburgh Companion* (2019), and *Elizabeth Bishop in Context* (2021). His nonfiction essays have appeared in *The Letters Page*, *The Tangerine*, and *The Manchester Review*. He is currently finishing a book on Letters for Oxford University Press.

**Amanda Golden** is Associate Professor of English at New York Institute of Technology. She is the author of *Annotating Modernism: Marginalia and Pedagogy from Virginia Woolf to the Confessional Poets* (2020) and the editor of *This Business of Words: Reassessing Anne Sexton* (2016). She is currently co-editing *The Poems of Sylvia Plath* with Karen V. Kukil. Golden has also published in *Modernism/modernity*, *Woolf Studies Annual*, and *The Space Between: Literature and Culture, 1914–1945*.

**Julie Goodspeed-Chadwick** is an IUPUI Chancellor's Professor of English and Women's, Gender, and Sexuality Studies; Indiana University Bicentennial Professor (2019–21); and Director of the Office of Student Research at Indiana University-Purdue University Columbus (IUPUC). Her books include *Modernist Women Writers and War: Trauma and the Female Body in Djuna Barnes, H. D., and Gertrude Stein* (2011) and *Reclaiming Assia Wevill: Sylvia Plath, Ted Hughes, and the Literary Imagination* (2019). With Peter K. Steinberg, she is the co-editor of *The Collected Writings of Assia Wevill* (2021).

**Gillian Groszewski** has published essays on "Ted Hughes and Emily Dickinson" in *Ted Hughes: from Cambridge to Collected* (2013) and on "Structuralist and Poststructuralist Readings of Ted Hughes's Poetry" in the *New Macmillan Casebook* on Hughes (2014). Groszewski works on Plath, Hughes, and midcentury poetics more broadly. She teaches English in London.

**Tim Hancock** is a Lecturer in English at Ulster University, specializing in modernism and twentieth-century poetry. He has published journal articles and chapters on the writing of

T. S. Eliot, Mina Loy, Robert Lowell, Seamus Heaney, Paul Muldoon, and John Betjeman, as well as a book on the last of these, *John Betjeman: Making Light* (2021).

**Anita Helle** is Professor of English at Oregon State University, where she served as inaugural Director of the School of Writing, Literature and Film. Her areas of specialization include archival criticism and theory, twentieth-century literature and photography, and medical humanities. Her essays on Plath and on midcentury poets appear in *Sylvia Plath in Context* (2019), *Representing Sylvia Plath* (2011), *The Oxford Handbook of the Elegy* (2010), *This Business of Words: Reassessing Anne Sexton* (2016), *Feminist Theory and Criticism: A Norton Reader* (2007), and *Robert Lowell in Context* (forthcoming). She is the editor of *The Unraveling Archive: Essays on Sylvia Plath* (2007).

**Bethany Hicok** is a Lecturer in English at Williams College. She is the author of *Degrees of Freedom: American Women Poets and the Women's College, 1905–1955* (Bucknell, 2008) and *Elizabeth Bishop's Brazil* (University of Virginia Press, 2016); editor of *Elizabeth Bishop and the Literary Archive* (Lever Press, 2020); and co-editor of *Elizabeth Bishop in the 21st Century: Reading the New Editions* (University of Virginia Press, 2012). Hicok is also the recipient of a 2017 NEH grant to lead a Summer Seminar for College and University Professors on Elizabeth Bishop and the Literary Archive. She is currently working on a book called *Feminist Futures: Feminist Poetry and Print Culture from 1968–1992*.

**Karen V. Kukil** is a Research Affiliate in English Language and Literature at Smith College, previously curating the Sylvia Plath Collection from 1990 to 2020 and teaching courses on editing Sylvia Plath's correspondence and poetry for Smith's Archives Concentration program. She is the editor of the unabridged *Journals of Sylvia Plath* (2000) and co-editor with Peter K. Steinberg of *The Letters of Sylvia Plath* (2 vols. 2017, 2018) for Faber & Faber in London. Kukil's exhibitions include *"No Other Appetite": Sylvia Plath, Ted Hughes, and the Blood Jet of Poetry* (Grolier Club, 2005) and *One Life: Sylvia Plath* (Smithsonian National Portrait Gallery, 2017–18). Kukil is currently co-editing *The Poems of Sylvia Plath* with Amanda Golden.

**Jerome Ellison Murphy** is a poet, editor, and critic based in New York City. He has published critical work in *The Yale Review*, *LA Review of Books*, *Publishers Weekly*, and *Poets & Writers*. His poetry appears in such journals as *Lit Hub*, *Narrative Magazine*, *The Cortland Review*, *Bellevue Literary Review*, and others. He received his MFA from the Creative Writing Program at New York University, where he currently serves as Manager of Undergraduate Programs.

**Maeve O'Brien** is a Postdoctoral Researcher at the Royal College of Surgeons Ireland. Her research interests include narrative medicine, feminist approaches to archiving, and twentieth-century women's writing. Recent publications include "Delivering Decriminalisation: Alliance for Choice Derry" in *The Road to Decriminalisation* (2021) and "Plath in Devon: Growing Words out of Isolation" in *Sylvia Plath in Context* (2019).

**Nicola Presley** is Senior Lecturer in English Literature at Bath Spa University. She has research interests in women's poetry, feminism, postwar literature, and digital culture and her published work includes articles and chapters on Sylvia Plath, Anne Sexton, William Golding, and Ted Hughes. Her current project is a book on Sylvia Plath, Anne Sexton, and media culture. Nicola is Publicity and Media Manager for William Golding Limited, and Assistant Editor of *Irish Studies Review*.

**Holly Ranger** is an independent scholar and research associate at the Institute of Classical Studies, London, UK. Her work has been published in the *Classical Receptions Journal*, the *International Journal of the Classical Tradition*, and the *Ted Hughes Society Journal*. Her first book, *Sylvia Plath and the Classics*, will appear in the Bloomsbury series *Classical Receptions in Twentieth-Century Writing* in 2024.

**Catherine Rankovic** has published scholarship in *Plath Profiles* and at AureliaPlath. blogspot.com. A writer and editor, Rankovic received her BA in journalism from Marquette University, an MA in English Literature from Syracuse University, and an MFA from Washington University in St. Louis, where she was a Teaching Fellow in Poetry and taught for twenty-one years. She is the author of *Meet Me: Writers in St. Louis* (Penultimate Press). Her Aurelia Plath shorthand transcriptions are posted at Marquette University's online open-scholarship platform, epublications.marquette.edu/aureliaplath.

**Katherine Robinson** is a Ph.D. candidate at Pembroke College, Cambridge where she is researching the influence of early Welsh literature on Ted Hughes's poetry and poetics. Her essays have been published in *Ted Hughes, Nature and Culture* (2018) and *The Ted Hughes Society Journal*, and she has written about Sylvia Plath and other poets for Poetry Foundation. Her poetry, fiction, and translations have appeared in *The London Magazine*, *Poetry Wales*, *Poetry Ireland*, *The Hudson Review*, *The Kenyon Review*, and elsewhere.

**Jennifer Ryan-Bryant** is Professor of English at SUNY—Buffalo State, where she teaches courses in African American literature, gender studies, and poetry. Her recent articles appeared in *The Journal of Popular Culture*, *Radical Teacher*, and MLA's *Approaches to Teaching Pound's Poetry and Prose*. She has also published *Post-Jazz Poetics: A Social History* (2010) and *Turning the Table: Ted Hughes, Sylvia Plath, and Writing between Them* (2021). Current projects include an annotated edition of Wanda Coleman's American sonnets, co-edited with Lizzy Lerud, and a monograph entitled *The Human in This Place: American Literatures of Lynching*.

**Carrie Smith** is a Senior Lecturer at Cardiff University. Her research has focused on archives and creative process. She co-edited a collection titled *The Boundaries of the Literary Archive: Reclamation and Representation* (2013) which draws together archivists and literary scholars to think through the multifaceted nature of archival study. Her monograph *The Page is Printed: Ted Hughes's Creative Process* (2021) makes extensive use of the writer's literary archives.

**Peter K. Steinberg** is an archivist, co-editor of *The Collected Writings of Assia Wevill* (2021), co-editor of *The Letters of Sylvia Plath* in two volumes (2017, 2018), co-author of *These Ghostly Archives: The Unearthing of Sylvia Plath* (2017), and author of *Sylvia Plath* (2004).

CONTRIBUTORS

**Rebecca C. Tuite** is a fashion historian and doctoral candidate at the Bard Graduate Center in New York City, working towards her Ph.D. in Decorative Arts, Design History and Material Culture. She is the author of *1950s in Vogue: The Jessica Daves Years, 1952–1962* (2019) and *Seven Sisters Style: The All-American Preppy Look* (2014).

**Christine Walde** is a writer, artist, and librarian whose work combines library and archival research with interests in experimental prose, poetry, visual poetry, performance, and the visual arts. Creative works specifically related to Sylvia Plath include: *The Black Car* (2011), a chapbook inspired by working with Plath's archive; *<maniacs.>* (2017), an exhibition of marginalia for the Letters, Words, and Fragments Plath symposium (2017); and "Cloud Country," a full-length manuscript that explores Plath and Hughes's 1959 camping trip through Canada. Walde lives and works on Vancouver Island in the Cascadia Bioregion of the Pacific Northwest.

**Nerys Williams** is an Associate Professor in Poetry and Poetics at University College, Dublin. She is the author of *Contemporary Poetry* (2011) and *Reading Error: The Lyric and Contemporary American Poetry* (2007). Williams is also the author of three volumes of poetry: *Sound Archive* (2012), *Cabaret* (2017), and *Republic* (2023). She is currently writing a monograph, *Poets on Air: Producing Poetry at the BBC*, which looks at the collaborative relationship between poets and radio producers at the Third Programme.

# ACKNOWLEDGMENTS

For their support throughout this project, we are grateful to David Avital, Ben Doyle, Lucy Brown, and Laura Cope at Bloomsbury Academic. Curators and Archivists from Smith College, the Rose Manuscript, Archives, and Rare Book Library at Emory University, the Lilly Library at Indiana University, the British Library, and the BBC Written Archives Centre have provided invaluable access to materials. We are immensely grateful to Donald Cheney for generously sharing his photograph for the cover of *The Bloomsbury Handbook* and to Susan Plath Winston, Jennifer Plath, and the Estate of Aurelia Plath for granting permission to quote from Aurelia Plath's annotations. We also thank Ulster University for hosting the Sylvia Plath: Letters, Words, and Fragments conference in 2017, an event where several contributors presented preliminary versions of the chapters in this collection.

Anita Helle wishes to thank her colleagues in the School of Writing, Literature, and Film at Oregon State University State University, especially those who have encouraged and shared conversation about Plath scholarship and teaching through the years – Tracy Daugherty and Marjorie Sandor, poets Karen Holmberg, Jennifer Richter, David Biespiel, and fellow-modernists Elizabeth Sheehan and Neil Davison. For walking breaks, friendship and intellectual sustenance during COVID, enormous gratitude is owed to Mary DeShazer, Elinor Langer, Roger Porter, Sandra Williams, Kay Campbell and members of the Corvallis reading circle – Janet Lee, Rebecca Warner, Susan Shaw, and Vicki Tolar Burton. Near and far, Marsha Bryant, Tracy Brain, and Matthew Roudane have long provided scholarly inspiration and encouragement for the most adventuresome of Plath projects.

Amanda Golden is grateful to her colleagues at New York Institute of Technology, particularly Elizabeth J. Donaldson and Lissi Athanasiou-Krikelis for contributing chapters to *The Bloomsbury Handbook*. Rachel Thomas provided excellent research assistance, generously funded by New York Tech's Institutional Support for Research and Creativity (ISRC) Grants. ISRC Grants were invaluable in completing this project. For their ongoing support, Golden thanks President Henry C. Foley, Provost Junius J. Gonzales, Dean Daniel Quigley, Humanities Department Co-Chairs, Elaine Brown and Katherine Williams, Ermioni Andrea, Hal Burton, Sophia Domokos, Holly Fils-Aime, Eileen Gazzola, Rebekah Geevarghese, Francine Glazer, Jonathan Goldman, Dawn Grzan, Jennifer Griffiths, Kevin LaGrandeur, Loraine Lazarus, John Misak, Christopher Moylan, Uzma Patel, Michael Schiavi, and Karen Wolff. For their inspiration and feedback, Golden is indebted to Jane L. Anderson, Peter Balakian, Marsha Bryant, Heather Clark, Dianna Coppolo, Stephen Coppolo, Michael Coyle, Amy E. Elkins, Gillian Groszewski, Mark Hussey, Emily M. James, Terry Kidner, Margaret Konkol, Karen V. Kukil, Megan Miller, Brian M. Reed, Laura Butler, Peter K. Steinberg, Sarah M. Terry, Janine M. Utell, and Sarah Wider. Finally, Golden has the utmost appreciation for her family: Shirley Goldfine and Louise, Andrew, Vickie, Ben, Molly, Jack, and Kate Golden.

Maeve O'Brien would firstly like to thank Dr. Frank Ferguson and Dr. Thomas Maguire at the School of Arts and Humanities at Ulster University for institutional and personal support in hosting the Sylvia Plath: Letters, Words, and Fragments conference in Belfast in autumn 2017. Thanks are also extended to all at Ulster who assisted with the organization of this hugely stimulating international event. O'Brien is extremely grateful to her parents Peter and Catherine, sister Dervlagh, and her wider circle of friends—in particular, Claire McCay, Dr. Laura Kelly, Méabh Lagan, Niamh Corcoran, Rachel Watters, and Zoë Coleman—all of whom have been a source of inspiration during the development and editing of this book, as well as during COVID-19. The Sylvia Plath community is a vibrant and exciting one to be part of—she is particularly grateful to Dr. Tracy Brain for her kindness and generosity—it has been a privilege to work on this collection that showcases the very best of current scholarship.

## PERMISSIONS

Donald Cheney, for the cover photograph.
The BBC Written Archives Centre, Reading, UK, for quotations in Chapters 21 and 22.
The Lilly Library, Indiana University, Bloomington, Indiana, for quotations from the BBC "Audience Research Report" for Sylvia Plath's "Three Women."
The Estate of Aurelia Plath, for quotations from Aurelia Plath's shorthand annotations in Chapters 18 and 19.

Versions of published essays reprinted with permission:
Bundtzen, Lynda K. "Lucent Figs and Suave Veal Chops: Sylvia Plath and Food." *Gastronomica*, vol. 10, no. 1, Winter 2010, pp. 79–90. Republished with permission of University of California Press Journals.
Murphy, Jerome Ellison. "God's Lionesss and God's Negress: The Feminine and the Figure of the African-American in Plath." *Plath Profiles*, vol. 5, Summer 2012, pp. 169–78.

# NOTE ON THE COVER

In April of 1956, Sylvia Plath was walking in Rome when she recognized her former classmate, Donald Cheney. Years earlier, both had been students at Alice L. Phillips Junior High School in Wellesley Hills, Massachusetts. At the time, Plath was traveling in Rome with Gordon Lameyer, who had also been Cheney's former classmate at the boarding school Choate Rosemary Hall. The cover photograph, previously unpublished, captures Cheney and Plath's visit to what may have been the Borghese Gallery. Plath is animated and attentive in her recently purchased "mackintosh" (*L1* 1156). The photograph distills a moment, one that adds to the materials in Plath's archives and provides a frontispiece for *The Bloomsbury Handbook*, setting a tone for the range of new, lively responses to her life and work that follow.

# ABBREVIATIONS

*Works by Sylvia Plath*
AR   *Ariel: The Restored Edition.* Harper Perennial, 2004.
B    *The Bell Jar.* Harper Perennial, 1999.
CCS  *Collected Children's Stories: Sylvia Plath.* Illustrated by David Roberts. Faber and Faber, 2001.
CP   *The Collected Poems.* Edited by Ted Hughes. Harper & Row, 1981.
J    *The Unabridged Journals of Sylvia Plath.* Edited by Karen V. Kukil. Random House, 2000.
JP   *Johnny Panic and the Bible of Dreams.* Harper Perennial, 2000.
L1   *The Letters of Sylvia Plath: Volume I (1940–1956).* Edited by Peter K. Steinberg and Karen V. Kukil. Faber & Faber, 2017.
L2   *The Letters of Sylvia Plath: Volume II (1956–1963).* Edited by Peter K. Steinberg and Karen V. Kukil. Faber & Faber, 2018.
LH   *Letters Home: Correspondence, 1950–1963.* Edited by Aurelia S. Plath. Harper & Row, 1975.

*Works by Ted Hughes*
TH:CP  *Collected Poems.* Edited by Paul Keegan. 2003. Farrar, Straus and Giroux, 2005.
LTH    *Letters of Ted Hughes.* Edited by Christopher Reid. Faber and Faber, 2007.

*Archives*
BBC              British Broadcasting Corporation Written Archives Centre, Reading, UK
British Library  British Library, London, UK
Lilly            Lilly Library, Indiana University, Bloomington, IN, USA
NYPL             New York Public Library, New York, NY, USA
Rose             Stuart A. Rose Manuscript, Archives, and Rare Book Library, Emory University, Atlanta, GA, USA
Smith            Sylvia Plath Collection (unless otherwise noted), MRBC-MS-00045, Mortimer Rare Book Collection, Smith College Special Collections, Northampton, MA, USA

# Introduction: Approaching Sylvia Plath in the Twenty-First Century

ANITA HELLE

An introduction to *The Bloomsbury Handbook to Sylvia Plath* in this century need not make the case for Plath as a writer of global stature and lasting importance. Plath's poetry, fiction, radio play, autobiographical prose, and private writings are read and studied across the Anglophone world and beyond; her poetry and fiction have been translated into thirty world languages.[1] Given the sustained critical attention Plath has received since the posthumously published first edition of *Ariel* (1965) and the British edition of *The Bell Jar* (1963), readers may well ask what a collection of critical essays at the beginning of the third decade of the twenty-first century proposes to contribute to Plath studies.

As editors, our response to this question begins with fresh archival cargo, the publication of Plath's *Letters, Volumes I: 1940–56* (2017) and *II: 1956–63* (2018), edited by Peter K. Steinberg and Karen V. Kukil. More than with most single authors, advancement of Plath scholarship has centered on the evolving archive, at a time when accelerated changes in digital modes of preservation and rich speculations on archives and cultural memory have expanded possibilities of archival interpretation.[2] In the 2000s, new archival material and published editions added range and depth: first Plath's unabridged *Journals* (2000), then *Ariel: The Restored Edition* (2004), drawings and paintings (*Eye Rhymes*, 2007), voice recordings, an edition of children's writing, the previously unpublished story, *Mary Ventura and the Ninth Kingdom* (2019), and *Letters*. Critical collections, a major biography, and international conferences in each decade have anchored an evolving understanding of how archival findings help readers make meaning.[3] In 2017, scholars from England, the United States, Europe, and North Africa gathered at Ulster University

---

[1] *A celebration, this is*, "Translations." https://www.sylviaplath.info/thumbsnonenglish.html.
[2] For synthesis of recent developments in archival criticism, see Chadwick and Vermeulen, "Literature in the New Archival Landscape," Smith and Stead, eds., *The Boundaries of the Literary Archive*, and Engel and Rutter, eds., "Women and Archives," special double issue.
[3] See Gill, ed., *The Cambridge Companion to Sylvia Plath* (2006); Helle, ed., *The Unraveling Archive* (2007); Bayley and Brain, eds., *Representing Sylvia Plath* (2011); Brain, ed., *Sylvia Plath in Context*; and Clark, *Red Comet* (2020). Plath's celebrity status continues: the fiftieth anniversary of the initial publication of *The Bell Jar* in 2013 was marked by a Salon.com feature on millennials reading Plath (https://www.salon.com/2013/06/12/sylvia_plath_speaks_to_millennials) and a star-studded performance of Plath's poems at London's Royal Festival Hall.

in Belfast to consider how Plath studies might be impacted by the mass of primary sources, cultural references, personal and literary affiliations—the entire web of connections that the full transcripts of over 1,400 known letters represent.[4]

*The Bloomsbury Handbook* is the rare collection in which researchers have had the opportunity to draw upon extensive autobiographical and epistolary writing from both volumes of Plath's *Letters*. Our intention has been to represent a range of methodologies and issues that have developed in response to the challenges of an expanded archive, first conceptualized in theoretical terms by Jacqueline Rose in *The Haunting of Sylvia Plath* (1991) and re-conceptualized during a second stage of debate about Plath's canonicity in *The Unraveling Archive* (2007). Against the backdrop of a large body of prior scholarship, this collection represents both established and emerging approaches—from close readings to new literary geographies of space and place, as well as essays that draw on developing fields (for Plath studies) such as disability studies, critical race studies, periodical studies, food and fashion studies, media and pedagogy.

More than ever, the mass of personal writing belonging to the Plath archive has direct and apparent relevance to the aesthetics, politics, and historicity of her creative work. The descriptive record has thickened. A letter is still just a letter, a crystallization of a moment with a world of detail one cannot hear, see, or touch, but with a mass of personal writing now available, facts adhere and patterns emerge. Similar to midcentury poets such as Elizabeth Bishop, Robert Lowell, Anne Sexton, and Randall Jarrell, Plath redeployed the personal artifact as a medium for not-always personal considerations through processes of allusion, inclusion, exclusions, transformation, transmission, and fictionalization. Her archive, it now appears, includes a great deal of auto-archiving, writing with a consciousness of her futurity and exacting care for the uses of the past. Steven Gould Axelrod's central insight nearly thirty years ago that Plath, more than most writers, saw words as an immediate way to fashion textual identities from the constant threat of the void remains as illuminating now as it did when *Sylvia Plath: The Wound and the Cure of Words* (1992) was written (3–4). Taken as autobiographical prose, Plath's unabridged *Journals*, and now the *Letters*, offer "micro-histories" of a literary oeuvre embedded in materials of everyday life.[5]

If the history of the "Plath archive" as a corpus that stands in for the body of the writer has long been fraught with erasures, removals, and transgressions, partial and misbegotten truths,[6] the more recent history of the Plath archive, encouraged by Frieda Hughes's publication of *Ariel: The Restored Edition*, and more recently by her support for the inclusion of previously unpublished letters in the *Letters*, leans toward greater transparency by supporting ever-more reliable scholarly editions and complete texts.[7] This is an important development: it makes Plath available to broader audiences and enables those who read and write about Plath not only to return to archives as a product, but to consider archivization itself—what is collected, who preserves, and uses it, for

---

[4]Sylvia Plath: Letters, Words, and Fragments, Ulster University, November 10–11, 2017, was preceded by Oxford Conference at the Rothermere American Institute (2007) and Indiana University Plath Conferences in 2002 and 2012. *Plath Profiles*, an interdisciplinary journal, founded by W. K. Buckley at the Oxford Conference, is sponsored by Indiana University Libraries and IU Scholarworks.
[5]See Ginzburg, "Microhistory: Two or Three Things That I Know about It" (10–35). "Micro-histories" as a concept allows for the scripted and performative nature of autobiographical prose.
[6]Rose, *Haunting*, 65–113; Rose's position is that letters themselves are an ultimate form of misrecognition (80).
[7]See Forward, *L1*, xv–xxv.

what purposes—as an ongoing social process. The emphasis on process compels attention to the tangled contexts in which archives are always produced and transmitted through social forces and networks of power.[8] If earlier responses to the Plath archive focused on the gaps in transmission that began with the problem of a posthumous assemblage, the opportunities of conceptualizing the Plath archive in the twenty-first century include the creative challenges of incorporating the marginal archive of notes in library books and teaching materials, assimilating the mass of now-published private writing, acknowledging the role of diverse readerships, and expanding the boundaries of historical and cultural relevance across cultural distances, media forms, and temporalities. Section headings in *The Handbook* represent common rubrics under which scholars consider archives and literature together, but we intend that intertextual echoes and dialogues emerging from overlapping consideration of texts and topics will reverberate across parts.

Debates about the relation of art and life have a long and vexed history in Plath studies. It is fitting that Part I, "New Cultural and Historical Contexts," opens with Jonathan Ellis's overview of the great divides—and the cultural hierarchies underlying them—that have sometimes rendered Plath a too-easy critical punching bag, especially in popular culture, and despite her literary fame. Many of these divides preceded Plath, lodged in the critical infrastructures of a modernism her work borrows from yet simultaneously resists. As Ellis notes, these are divides between lyric as "pure" poetry vs. biographical experience, poem and poet, blackness and whiteness, serious readers and uncritical "followers." Such binary oppositions have been complicated by the popular reception of the "tragic, beautiful, damned" (17) writer whose death has been too often treated as if it readily outstrips poetic achievement. Turning to Plath's poetry, Ellis reads the architecture of Plath's closing one-sentence lines as "punch lines" of a different and interrogative kind, in which Plath's poetic line "punches through" rather than "shak[ing] off" terms upon which the Romantic lyric has depended (28, 22). The process of "unshaming" the Plath lyric from its exposure to everyday life and bodily experience may not be complete, but it is well underway, especially in essays that recognize the varied formations of Plath's readerships.[9] In contrast to Ellis's focus on the mixed expectations that have shaped critical opinion and popular cinema, Christine Walde's research, chapbook, and photographic documentation take seriously Plath readers who have never been deemed worthy of study. These are anonymous "citizen critics" who disrupt the placid surface of the page (and violate proprieties of the lending library) with impassioned marginalia in Plath-authored books in library circulation. Such readers constitute a loosely formed, heterogeneous body by virtue of their common participation in networks constituted by passing of books and inscriptions from hand to hand in heterotopic spaces. Walde's perspective as a librarian helps us see that ordinary readers, too, are "silent witnesses" to histories of reading and writing that continue to shape Plath's legacy.[10]

In "New Cultural and Historical Contexts," we recognize that, as archival boundaries have expanded, there are now many different kinds of archives to be considered. Archives of public and mass culture—from mass-marketed adverts to program records of the British Broadcasting Corporation—are rooted not in the silence of thought in the rare book

---

[8] On the distinction between archival products and processes, see *Shadow Archives*, 33–4.
[9] See White's account of "shame" and the confessional lyric (*Lyric Shame* 95–113).
[10] Edel and Tintner, *The Library of Henry James*, 2; see also Golden, "Sylvia Plath's Library."

room but in the cacophony of public life and social institutions. "Noisy" lines of inquiry erupt where different kinds of media archives and discourses productively intersect, as they frequently do in postmodern frameworks. Rebecca Tuite's exploration of sleepwear as signifier in Plath's letters and journals (part of a larger study on fashion in the fifties) is the first concentrated examination of Plath's sartorial fabrications of femininity to emerge from the study of articles, images, and advertising in 1950s women's magazines, alongside correlative representations in Plath's fictional characters. With food as with fashion, surprising things happen when texts from public and private domiciles collide and comingle. Lynda K. Bundtzen pursues ways by which Plath's letters and journals associate culinary pleasures with other kinds of making—the making of babies, the making of art, the making of distraction, and the "battering out" of "life itself" (*J* 269). Plath's private and public writing assuredly include lavish, sensual, and aesthetic descriptions of food and elaborate menu-planning. The associations are provocative, especially when we consider that the voice Plath and literally millions of other women encountered in the pages of best-selling *Joy of Cooking*—Plath's "blessed Rombauer" (*J* 193)—was the plucky voice of a Depression-era widow whose cookbook retains the aura of scarcity and wartime frugality (in the 1953 edition Plath likely used, there are illustrations of how to flay a squirrel and dress a rabbit).

Although Plath's work has been interpreted through the lens of psychiatric illness, it may be time to acknowledge differential meanings that attach to "mad" identities. When Sandra M. Gilbert and Susan Gubar in their recent volume, *Still Mad: American Women Writers and the Feminist Imagination, 1950–2020* (2021), employ the "madwoman" trope from the nineteenth-century novel to characterize mid-century voices such as those of Plath, Diane di Prima, Joan Didion, and Audre Lorde; they refer to expressively unruly, engaged, angry, and fiery identities, evoking kinship with literary foremothers but through post-Second World War perspectives. In the context of autobiographically informed disability studies, "mad" identities evoke an excruciating history of stigma, shame, and blame that attaches to psychiatric illness.[11] Readers of Plath's unabridged *Letters* may be surprised that they contain little more than a few remarks about Plath's experience with electroshock and institutionalization at McLean Hospital. We may presume she was concerned about the stigma of illness as she resumed her college life at Smith. Although her final letters unmistakably voice horror at facing the harrowing prospect of institutionalization—"return of my madness, my paralysis, my fear & vision of the worst—cowardly withdrawal, a mental hospital, lobotomies" (*L2* 967), Plath's recognized the opportunities for fictionalizing the experiences of the psychiatric patient, a new attitude for a new time. More to the point of literary history, an anti-psychiatric movement forms one hinge of American literature from the late 1940s to the 1970s, as revealed in the growth of novels, plays, and films about asylums, psychiatrists, and psychiatric patients. Elizabeth J. Donaldson's essay provides a focused study of Esther Greenwood's "mad" experience through the framework of disability studies, drawing on Boston University's archives of Mary Jane Ward's *The Snake Pit* in fiction (1946) and Anatole Litvak's cinematic adaptation (1948). Tracing continuities and discontinuities with the writing of psychiatric disability, Donaldson outlines key conventions of gender and genre in *The Bell Jar* and "Johnny Panic and the Bible of Dreams" that mark asylum fiction: hierarchies of the disabled in health care, the "sea" of writhing institutional

---

[11]On reconceptualizing "madness," see Donaldson, "The Corpus of the Madwoman," 99–119.

bodies, memory lapses and eccentricities of disabled "vision," sexual double standards, and destabilized boundaries between psychiatric professional and psychiatric patient.

When carefully historicized, distinctions between Plath as a writer whose work has been approached through feminist readings (and different generations of feminist readings) and Plath as a "feminist" writer grow ever clearer. Bridging culture and media (see Part III), Bethany Hicok explores one setting in which Plath became an avatar of second-wave feminism, pinpointing a moment in 1970 when her poem "The Jailor" ("The Jailer" in *CP*). appeared in *RAT Subterranean News*, a radical left magazine that nourished the Women's LibeRATion movement (as it was called in *RAT*). In 1963, Hughes had submitted "The Jailor" to the liberal establishment journal, *Encounter*. When the same poem appeared in the context of the East Village production with its bold graphics and its anti-imperialist, anti-racist, and anti-sexist rhetoric, readers were invited to make fresh associations with the poem and terror, violence, domestic abuse, and rape—issues that constitute what Barbara Green terms the "performative activism" of second-wave radical feminist periodicals (*Spectacular Confessions*). But it has never been easy to categorize Plath's diverse literary productions in homogeneously narrow ideological terms, across or even within genres. Lissi Athanasiou-Krikelis urges that Plath's narratives for children are worthy of close reading study on their own terms, noting their ideological variety. Whereas the short stories for children reveal Plath's sensitivity to audience and genre expectations, for the most part constructing the child reader as one who should be acculturated into traditional gender norms, Athanasiou-Krikelis argues that "The Bed Book" marks a notable departure from regressive gender roles, with its emphasis on the transformative power of creative imagination.

Archival research takes place not only at institutional and digital sites, but through fleshly encounters with non-institutional places and spaces. In art and life, Plath's orientation to place and space is often paradoxical: a strong sense of "at-homeness" and intense dedication to homemaking, wherever she resided, is set against a highly mobile life, shifting from the Boston-Wellesley axis to Cambridge and later, to Devon-London. Although letters from her last years express a longing to travel, dreaming of more ideal circumstances for writing in Spain, or in Ireland, Plath's writing is seldom world-weary; her need to particularize space and place in language is a constant. Drawing on the writings of phenomenologist Gaston Bachelard and on *These Ghostly Archives* (co-authored with Peter K. Steinberg), Gail Crowther's chapter offers a theoretically informed account of how "living archives" of space and place grow and change over time as material traces revivify past and present connections through different temporalities and shifting perspectives (a habit of composing that Plath pursued herself, in poems written in Brontë country). Such acts of revisitation spark dialogues around shifting notions of "home"; as Crowther's perusal of Plath's domestic spaces in London and in Devon as "living archives" demonstrates, they also involve acts of creative reimagining.

Di Beddow's chapter on Sylvia Plath's Cambridge probes the construction of place and space by mapping walks Plath took between town and countryside as she sought to "make my own Cambridge" (*L1 969*) within and outside the precincts of the university. Plath's psychic landscapes have been previously explored—for example, in Tim Kendall's *Sylvia Plath: A Critical Study* (2001)—but Beddow's psychogeographic approach shows how elemental images of earth, water, and fowl from a regional locale impart a distinctively palimpsestic character to ambulatory poems written in Cambridge. As part of a cluster of essays on space and place, Tim Hancock tackles a different arc of spatial articulation by reconsidering an "insistent set of images in Plath's later poetry that was informed by an awareness of contemporary space exploration" (64). Hancock breaks new ground on the subject of the Cold War atmosphere of Plath's poems that has been explored by Tracy Brain and Robin Peel by bringing a particular sensitivity to spatial sensations of scale and dimensionality wherein Plath expresses feelings of private and personal alienation, the sensation of being "outcast on a cold star" (*J* 519). Historical ironies lurk here. Poets in the 1950s and 1960s were exploring images of space and place as part of a commitment to what Richard Wilbur in his Augustinian revisionism called "the things of this world" (233–4); yet, Plath notably eschewed what she called "headline poetry" (*JP* 98). Hancock illuminates the ways that, as her poet eye roamed the heavens, Plath's late poems reenact Romantic tropes of the negative sublime (the "chill of the void") by dramatizing humankind's first voyages into interplanetary space beyond earth's atmosphere, outer and inner space together.

Plath the historical person is not the avatar or origin of all her literary effects; yet, it is unthinkable that these effects exist outside a web of historically and textually knowable influences, affiliations, and intertextualities represented in Part II, "Influences, Affiliations, and Intertextualities." The work of excavating and tracing Plath's literary affiliations beyond much-discussed links to Anne Sexton and Robert Lowell has been gradual, enriched and complicated by her transatlantic encounters with midcentury literary movements, some of which were only beginning to be named. Plath explicitly named her "ageing giantesses & poetic godmothers" (*J* 360) Marianne Moore and Edith Sitwell, and called out those whom she deemed her competitors. Shadowing these explicit influences are the earlier generation of modernists who were part of Plath's education, as she attended the lectures of Elizabeth Drew (Smith) and David Daiches (Cambridge), studying texts and authors she returned to throughout her life: T. S. Eliot, W. H. Auden, W. B. Yeats, James Joyce, D. H. Lawrence, and Virginia Woolf. In a 1962 interview with the British Council, Plath allies herself with the American poets, Sexton and Lowell, by contrast to contemporary British poets whose lyrics she finds regrettably weighed down by gentility and long tradition.[12] Her public praise for Sexton's emotional depth and transformative craft seems designed to anticipate critical objections to Sexton's bold and direct statements of poetic feeling and to lay the groundwork for work Plath was beginning to produce at the time. But the indictment of contemporary British poetry evidently did not extend to the poet Ruth Fainlight (Sillitoe), the dedicatee of Plath's poem "Elm" (notably without using Fainlight's married name). As Heather Clark notes, Fainlight was one of the only British women poets in Plath's London circles in the early 1960s to be writing and publishing poems that referred to miscarriages, abortions, post-partum anxieties, and ambivalences about motherhood and creative vocation. These were matters that Plath and Fainlight talked out, as Clark shows, in letters and visits, part of a sustained and influential friendship cemented by sharing poems and concerns about poetic vocation. The resonant imagery in Fainlight's "Sapphic Moon" and its influence on "Elm" and "Three Women" offer potent examples of their poetic exchanges.

Yeats's presence as a towering masculine literary figure for Plath has never been in doubt, harkening back to Sandra M. Gilbert's claim in "In Yeats' House" (1982) that Plath is continually resurrected in Yeats's visionary company, and by her self-avowed genuflection to the 'immanence" of Yeats's influence (*L1* 914). In a move that views "influence" as both vertical (in the sense of a canonical inheritance) and horizontal (as a recursive return to an influential voice), Gillian Groszewski brings a close focus to formal strategies to show that Plath returns to Yeats to confront challenges and improve her

---

[12]For a recording of the British Council interview, see: https://www.youtube.com/watch?v=g2lMsVpRh5c.

aesthetic craft not just in the final poems but repeatedly at various stages in her poetic career. In each of these moments of meeting a lyric challenge, Plath brought an exacting ear to Yeats's differential voices, rhythms, and poetic content, from the transposition of the winding stair into the repetitive lines in poetic form to experiments in modeling a more streamlined lyric line. That Plath was also introduced to Yeats at her mother's knee is another potent reminder of Aurelia Plath's prodigious influence on Plath's reading life and her role as an archivist of Plath's work. It should come as no surprise that as myths of the post-Second World War women who left their war jobs to reinvent themselves within the confines of the family home have fallen away, interest in the "Aurelia archive" of Aurelia Plath's life work and influence on her daughter (neither homebound nor part of a privileged class) has expanded.[13] The same Aurelia who wrote a master's thesis on literary tradition in Paracelsus, Renaissance alchemist and founder of homeopathic medicine, later combined ongoing intellectual and literary interests with pragmatic adaptation. Her day job teaching what we might now call technical writing included the arts of stenography. Catherine Rankovic is the first to decode and take seriously the "narrow writing" (*steno* = narrow in Greek) or shorthand notes ("Medusa's Metadata") embodied in 132 Gregg annotations Aurelia Plath used to comment on Plath's publications and her private writing prior to and after her daughter's death. Rankovic's rigorously close focus on nearly fifty years of Aurelia's shorthand annotations argues for the necessity of a more nuanced and multi-dimensional picture of the curatorial role Aurelia assumed in relation to Plath's reading and later through her editing of *Letters Home*. Janet Badia's essay views the Aurelia archive through a wide lens, drawing on the full body of Aurelia's longhand annotations from Smith College and Lilly Library collections, comprising notes written on Plath correspondence, on Plath manuscripts, in library books, on posthumous clippings and publications, and in the expurgated *Letters Home*. Extending Tracy Brain's commentary on the mother–daughter letters, Badia argues that the more complete version of Plath's *Letters* and marginalia together comprise more all-encompassing and complex patterns by which acts of reading and writing constitute mother–daughter intimacies formed of textual bonds, "embraced and resisted" (220).

Multiple facets of Ted Hughes's role as a dominant figure in Plath studies, from his influence on her composing processes to his role in textual editing and archivization, have been treated in Susan Van Dyne's *Revising Life* (on back-to-back writing), Diane Middlebrook's *Her Husband* (on Hughes as editor), Heather Clark's *The Grief of Influence* (the mutual poetic project), and in the visual concordance of Stephen C. Enniss and Karen V. Kukil's catalogue, *"No Other Appetite": Sylvia Plath, Ted Hughes, and the Blood Jet of Poetry* for the 2005 Grolier Club Exhibition. Because the coverage has been ample, and any attempt to make a fair representation of it might eventuate in a different book, we include in "Influences, Affiliations, and Intertextualities" more recent entrants in the business of charting converging lines in Plath–Hughes history. Jennifer Ryan-Bryant frames a convergence around the formal and thematic variations on the postmodern long poem tradition at midcentury, reading Plath's *Ariel* and Hughes's *Crow* manuscripts back-to-back as long poem sequences organized around a fragmented sense of the world and self-reflexive narrators. Katherine Robinson's comparative analysis of Plath's and Hughes's shared literary debt to concepts of "sympathetic magic" begins by tracing Plath's responses to that most influential of modernist anthropological texts,

---

[13]See, for example, *Not June Cleaver*, ed. Meyerowitz.

James George Frazer's *The Golden Bough*, which Plath studied while writing her thesis at Smith, setting Plath's notes against Hughes's reading notebooks in folklore, which also draw on *The Golden Bough*. Robinson's essay establishes a new temporality for a shared literary interest between Plath and Hughes, an interest that long preceded their infamous meeting at the *Saint Botolph's Review* launch party in Cambridge.

Since the 2000s, scholars such as Jo Gill (*Modern Confessional Writing*, 2005; *Anne Sexton's Confessional Poetics*, 2007) and Christopher Grobe (*The Art of Confession*, 2017) have firmly established performance in all its dimensions—bodily, aural, political, historical, intermedial—as a defining feature of midcentury confessional poetry: hence another blow to the presumption of the natural or singularly authentic "breakthrough" voice. Consistent with the growth of interest in media, intermediality, and sonic modernity, scholars on both sides of the Atlantic—from Debra Rae Cohen, Michael Coyle, and Jane Lewty's collection *Broadcasting Modernism* (2009) to David Trotter's monograph *Literature in the First Media Age: Britain Between the Wars* (2013)—have drawn particular attention to the role of radio in challenging textual boundaries and conventional configurations of identity for authors and listeners at midcentury. In Part III, "Media and Pedagogy," Nicola Presley's wide-ranging discussion of Plath's engagement with different forms of media culture sets the stage for a focused consideration in chapters by Carrie Smith and Nerys Williams of how BBC radio in particular becomes culturally significant for Plath. Presley demonstrates that Plath incorporated radio and television as objects and images in short fiction such as "The Wishing Box" (1956) and in later work. Revealing how Plath reflects and subverts popular programming and social discourse on the new media of her era, Presley's essay includes a discussion of Plath's appropriation of superhero figures such as Superman and "The Shadow" from comics and radio.

But what exactly made literature radiogenic for Plath's era? Extrapolating from Cara Lewis's *Dynamic Form: How Intermediality Made Modernism* (2020), this is a question that Plath and her contemporaries would have inherited from modernism's insistence on constituent form in an increasingly saturated marketplace: fusing with literature, form may be "plastic, protean, mortal," expressing dynamism but by no means in utopian or totalizing ways (2). Emily C. Bloom's *The Wireless Past: Anglo-Irish Writers and the BBC, 1931–1968* (2017) demonstrates that by 1940, the BBC had become a dominant aesthetic and institutional platform in the careers of Elizabeth Bowen and Louis MacNeice, among others. Because there is no one-size-fits-all to characterize writerly negotiation with the aesthetic possibilities and institutional imperatives of radio, and because there has been much recent interest in taboos of maternity, we include two case studies on institutional contexts, aesthetics, and reception surrounding the dramatic lyric, "Three Women: A Poem for Three Voices" (1962; 1968), what Carrie Smith calls a "lyrical radio play and extended narrative poem" (249).[14]

Carrie Smith's chapter draws on the BBC Written Archives to give a thick description of the institutional barriers that Plath, similar to other women, faced in proposing productions and writing for high-end BBC's Third Programme (including a less than 2 percent acceptance rate for play proposals). Smith's analysis of the in-house audience research reports the BBC used to assess audience satisfaction with "Three Women" reveals an uneasy politics shaped by gender and class, even as the BBC's most

---

[14] See Moses, "Appendix: The Oral Archive" and Walker, "Plath and the Radio Drama."

experimental cultural channel sought to reach new audiences of women isolated at home, as was Plath in Devon, when she bought a new radio and wrote a proposal for her verse-play. Drawing on contemporary sound theory, poet and critic Nerys Williams locates another source of the "radiogenic" in Third Programme producer Douglas Cleverdon's public lectures and his unpublished treatise, "The Art of Radio." Her essay attends to the sonorous envelope of poetic devices (sound, rhythm, and repeated kernel words) through which "Three Women" achieves lyric intensity. The relationship between form and content in Plath's radio drama augments Cleverdon's belief that the "play of ideas" in feature writing could best reach new audiences through a "poetics of listening" that any contemporary auditor might be able to absorb (258).

Crisscrossing Parts II and III are essays that draw from a Plath archive that has been gradually expanding to include a wealth of material belonging to what Rachel Sagner Buurma and Laura Heffernan have broadly designated as the "teaching archive."[15] To be precise, their definition of the "teaching archive" of modern writers would include artifacts from Plath's education, notes and notebooks from her formal education, as well as curricular and pedagogical notes from her year of teaching at Smith (1957–8). For Amanda Golden in *Annotating Modernism* (2020), Plath's pedagogical notes are especially revealing of her relation to the discourses of modernism when augmented by an attentive focus on marginalia from the modern library she returned to throughout her career. Whereas an earlier narrative of Plath's emergence as a poet constructed an image of Plath discarding the "waste" of a "highly intellectual style of education" she had absorbed as the "model pupil" on the way to acquiring the *Ariel* voice,[16] more recent criticism calls attention to continuities that span her early education at Smith and her later adaptions of modern poetic idioms to the Second World War environment. Langdon Hammer in "Plath's Lives" laid the groundwork for a different way of thinking about Plath and the institutions of poetry by arguing that although Plath struggled to establish her independence from the role of "model pupil," it would be wrong to think that Plath left behind that role entirely (81).

What that model pupil wrought through rigorous habits of note-taking and textual annotations cannot be underestimated. Essays from different sections, in larger scale and granular ways, take up the question of how material artifacts from Plath's critical writing and reading before *Ariel* develop into longer stretches of poetic production. Holly Ranger opens a chapter on "Plath and the Classics" by noting that Plath's immersive study of ancient tragedians at Cambridge, especially Aeschylus and Sophocles, has been understudied in relation to the iconic figure of Electra. Ranger plumbs curricular materials such as Plath's Cambridge Tripos paper on tragedy and a published review on versification of ancient poets, revisiting the "mythological" approach, but without the anti-historicized focus that characterized earlier mythic criticism. Ranger uncovers a subtle yet pronounced critique of the transposition of classical texts into modernist critical discourse through sophisticated and self-reflexive "metapoetic" commentary on canonical tragic figure and forms. "I borrow the stilts of an old tragedy" (*CP* 116), Plath's speaker in "Electra on Azalea Path" protests, both recognizing and swerving from the elevated canon and the conserving culture it represents.

---

[15] For a definition of the "teaching archive," see Buurma and Heffernan, 3–6.
[16] Hughes, Forward, *The Journals of Sylvia Plath*, xiv.

Marsha Bryant (Part II) reframes Plath's place in the continuity of British women poets with a close study of Plath's connections to Edith Sitwell, another influence. Plath assigned both Sitwell and Moore while teaching at Smith and wrote detailed analyses of Sitwell's work in two college papers. Bryant's analysis leads back to Plath's student writing and annotations in the margins of her copy of Sitwell's *The Canticle of the Rose* and forward to the lines of affiliation (literary "beelines") that link Sitwell, Plath, and ultimately the contemporary poems of Carol Ann Duffy to the revised canon of British women poets in *The Bloodaxe Book of Contemporary Women Poets* (1985). Bryant mines Plath's papers on Sitwell, each of which reveals an incisive understanding and appreciation of the texture of Sitwell's poetry—notably the mix of artificial and natural imagery in "The Bee Oracles" and the polar worlds of Sitwell's 1950s atomic poems. Themes and poetic textures from Sitwell, Bryant argues, reveal striking parallels to Plath's poem "Second Winter" and her monumental, late beekeeping poems.

The teaching archive forms a conceptual bridge to the future of Plath studies and to the physical and digital classrooms as sites where Plath's legacy will continue to be revisited and revised. While Plath research has traditionally focused on material artifacts in physical archives, recent innovations in new media and digital humanities increasingly turn toward interdisciplinary projects in which "media" and "pedagogy" are inextricably interwoven. Part III, "Media and Pedagogy," gestures toward the future of Plath studies on and off the printed page. Building on the current speculation that a reinvigorated humanities benefits from more effectively translating our fields through engagement with wider audiences, Julie Goodspeed-Chadwick's narrative of an undergraduate Plath studies course broadens the notion of Adrienne Rich's "politics of re-vision" to cross-institutional and interdisciplinary contexts. Her course on Plath, rooted in service learning and community engagement with library partners, issued invitations to students and a broader public to consider gender justice and canonicity in Plath, Hughes, as well as their portrayals of the overlooked writer in their midst, Assia Wevill. Amanda Golden's chapter offers a case study of how students contribute to the futurity of archives by developing their own narratives of exploration and discovery and sharing them with academic publics. Her essay presents an interpretive project in which students working with Edna O'Brien's projected television play on Sylvia Plath use O'Brien's notebooks and typescripts to gain insight into the act of creation. The creation of a play is also the creation of literary historical knowledge, as one writer (O'Brien) is overheard to be responding to another (Plath). If the nature of archival knowledge is that it always consists of piecing together fragments, inevitably incomplete, Golden concludes that Plath's speaker in "The Colossus" allegorizes that process as she attempts to scale the monument and assemble fragments of her father's memory: "I shall never get you put together entirely" (CP 129).

It is important to acknowledge what *The Bloomsbury Handbook to Sylvia Plath* leaves unfinished, to mark the place where meaning is undone, and gaps become crucial in productive ways. Critical race studies is one such gap, a still-developing field in Plath scholarship. Over twenty years ago, foundational work by Renée R. Curry offered a stunning quantification of racial signifiers in Hughes's edition of Plath's *Collected Poems*:

> Of the 224 poems… a remarkable fifty percent of them (117 poems) use the words "white" and/or "black" as intricate signifiers of power, (im)purity, fear, and thought. Eleven poems address skin color, twelve poems discuss the significance of whiteness,

and fourteen poems refer to peoples other than whites such as Africans, Indians, Latinos, Chinese, and Negroes.

(*White Women Writing White* 125)

Scholarship has not caught up with these representations, although a slender but steady stream of commentary on whiteness, colorism, and Black/white binaries that has been overlooked by a critical and academic environment sometimes hostile to such ideas is beginning to be heard. Vanessa Willoughby deftly rebukes the supposition that "Black girls don't read Sylvia Plath" claiming her "kinship" with Plath: *The Bell Jar* at one time resonated with her personal experiences of mental health struggles that were compounded by racialized barriers to treatment. In previous critical work, Christina Britzolakis has linked the issue of cultural "otherness" to the rationalization of violence in Enlightenment thought; Laura Perry approaches race as part of Plath's obsession with purity in a culture of hygiene. Toni Saldívar has also approached the difficulties of reading Plath through an ethical lens within the postmodern framework in which the artifact offers transcendent power but falls short of pragmatic ends.[17]

One has only to google "Plath and racial representations" to see that racial representation in Plath is now a lively and fraught topic on blogs and websites by ordinary Plath readers who have grappled with the distress of encountering racism and racialized tropes in a beloved writer and have commented outside the lines of formal academic publication.[18] It is time to acknowledge the ways in which serious discussion of Plath's racial stereotyping (Asian, Black, Jewish), her racialized language in *Ariel* poems, the blinkered position of Esther Greenwood in *The Bell Jar*, poised on the verge of a massive eruption of postwar racial tensions in the America of the 1950s and 1960s, is overdue for structural and historical re-examination. We position essays that touch upon racial and racist representations in Plath's poetry across various parts in order to signal that the questions go beyond any singular category. Chapters by Jonathan Ellis and Bethany Hicok acknowledge the cultural embeddedness of Plath studies in issues of race from the 1950s on and raise questions for future study; Maeve O'Brien's and Jerome Ellison Murphy's essays focus more closely on whiteness and Black/white binaries in Plath's poetry and prose. As one approach to decentering whiteness, O'Brien draws on Toni Morrison's methodology in *Playing in the Dark: Whiteness and the Literary Imagination* by studying practices of canon-formation in which representations of the African Americanist presence are "choked in nonblack texts" (17). Her essay imagines the position of the racial "other" through the mechanisms of Plath's education, reading lists, and her engagement with mentors and other poets. O'Brien's interrogation of Plath's obliviousness to her whiteness and the privileges that accompany that racial marker contribute to a more nuanced understanding not only of Plath's performances of self but also our understandings of her era. Poet and critic Jerome Ellison Murphy takes up the subject of racialized poetic tropes in Plath's figurations of the feminine, an approach that leads to nuanced tropological reasoning: Plath renders whiteness serviceable by

---

[17] Britzolakis, "On Daddy"; Perry, "Plath and the Culture of Hygiene"; Saldívar, *Sylvia Plath: Confessing the Fictive Self*, 1–10. See also Miller, "Sylvia Plath and White Ignorance," for a response to Curry.
[18] See Crowther, "The Comforts of Whiteness."

"turning" meanings, so that while "white Godiva" may signify purity and purification, it equally connotes annihilation and death. While Plath's descriptive language of Black/white binaries, as Murphy notes, is neither "journalistic" (94) or rigidly sociological—which may not comfort anyone–they can be described as "distillates" (97) of distorted associations with interior emotional states.

Among archival scenes in modern literary studies, none is more vital, and yet, at times more obscured, than the scene of editors and archivists quietly going about their work. Given controversies that have long swirled around "editing Plath," editorial oversight in an era marked by wider access to a range of her public and private writing has special weight. Jean-Christophe Cloutier, in *Shadow Archives*, argues that collaboration between archivists and researchers and the development of an accompanying battery of surveillance and curatorial techniques characterized the rise of archival specialization in the mid-twentieth century. Cloutier is concerned with the precarity of African American archives, where the gaps and silences of archives have rendered unusual collaborative partnerships especially urgent. In Plath's case, we have had a diffuse archive (Plath's *Letters* alone, according to Peter K. Steinberg, are contained in forty-five different archival sites in the United States and UK) and an author of spectacular visibility—a different historical situation, but with the related problem of building and consolidating cultural capital. For both historical and present-minded reasons, then, it is appropriate that Part IV, "Editing the Archives" concludes with first-person accounts by editors of Plath's *Letters*. Each chapter calls attention to the dynamic ways by which editing of archival material directly and indirectly provides collateral for literary value, past and future. As editor of Plath's unabridged *Journals* and co-editor of the *Letters*, Karen V. Kukil uncovers the editorial motives that have guided making Plath's "multi-dimensional" and "unfettered" voice more available to readers. Her essay demonstrates that Plath's epistolary writing unfolds biographical backstories and illuminates contexts of Plath's poems by detailing "archival, pedagogical, research, and publication projects" that have unfolded from encounters with primary source materials over a period of twenty years of dedication to "walk with grace in the footsteps of Sylvia Plath" (299). Kukil's essay also confirms the close ties between editing and the arts of literary scholarship. Steinberg takes us behind the scenes of the collecting and digital tracking activities involved in the monumental *Letters* project, from sourcing, transcribing, and proofing letters to writing footnotes, building spreadsheets, cross-checking people, places, and events, to the excitement of incidental findings. His claim that the footnotes in Plath's *Letters* serve as a "bibliography" of poems, stories, articles, and school papers underscores the reciprocity of scholarly and archival roles (312).

If there is a single underlying thread to essays in this collection, it is the excitement of an era in which Plath studies is once again revealing its protean shapes and regenerative capacities. Whether digital or virtual, archives develop generative force through a reciprocal process by which materials raise new questions, and the questions in turn provoke new modes and lines of inquiry. In the twenty-first century, Plath archives have become more than paper: they have become histories, subjectivities, quasi-sympathetic identifications of readers, listeners, and publics in the dynamic spaces of multimedia and multidisciplinary study. With Plath, there is no doubt that the archive includes a multitude of stories and anecdotes and that people like hearing them and reading about them. In this collection, the voices include established and new scholarly generations on issues perennially debated, freshly informed and reframed, and topics that have recently come to light as part of reinvigorated humanistic studies. In communicating these perspectives, we stand on the shoulders of many other Plath scholars whose work exemplifies the best of archival research and writing by capturing the beauty, amazement, even the "affective tremor" of scholarly discovery in acts of critical writing.[19]

---

[19]The editors gratefully acknowledge the work of numerous Plath scholars: Steven Gould Axelrod, Sally Bayley, Tracy Brain, Christina Britzolakis, Heather Clark, Kathleen Connors, Gail Crowther, Renée R. Curry, Sandra M. Gilbert, Jo Gill, Luke Ferretter, Langdon Hammer, Tim Kendall, Ann Keniston, Janet Malcolm, Diane Middlebrook, Jan Montefiore, Kate Moses, Deborah Nelson, Robin Peel, Jacqueline Rose, Toni Saldívar, Peter K. Steinberg, Anne Stevenson, Janine M. Utell, Susan Van Dyne, Linda Wagner-Martin, and many others. During the pandemic, a Zoomposium series brought Plath to new audiences and enabled several contributors to present work in progress for this collection. On the affects of archival research and the "tremor" of discovery, see Farge, *The Allure of the Archives*.

# PART I
# New Cultural and Historical Contexts

# CHAPTER ONE

# Plath as Punch Line

JONATHAN ELLIS

According to Marc Spitz, Sylvia Plath is "both a literary and feminist icon and a too-easy punch line. Her outsize sadness and shakiness sometimes upstage her magnificent writing" (59). Oddly enough, in his own book, *Twee: The Gentle Revolution in Music, Books, Television, Fashion, and Film* (2014), Spitz does more or less the same, co-opting Plath into honorary membership of what he calls a Twee Tribe. "When she took the gas in her London kitchen," he concludes his pen-portrait of her life and work, "Plath led a kind of march of the war-scarred into oblivion that would both seal her as a Twee heroine (tragic, beautiful, damned) and afford her followers a vacuum to fill" (61). Literary critics are just as guilty of beginning with Plath's death rather than her artistic achievements. Jeffrey Berman's chapter on Plath in his study *Surviving Literary Suicide* (1999) begins with a diary entry from one of his graduate students that foregrounds the following subjects: "suicide, Smith, free thought, poetry" (137). Berman endorses this free association of nouns by immediately declaring Plath "the most haunting twentieth-century literary suicide" (137). I open with Spitz and Berman's accounts not to endorse them—the image of Plath in both popular culture and literary criticism as a Pied Piper of Suicide is both crass and offensive—but to think about why those who read and write about Plath's work are frequently characterized, explicitly or implicitly, as "followers" rather than "readers." This response to Plath is, unfortunately, a familiar one. Cultural critics and literary scholars, usually male, admit to liking Plath's work but disliking the effect of that work on her, usually female, readers. Thus, a few paragraphs later, while Spitz defends Plath's poems alluding to the Holocaust as written by "a child of World War II and its horror," he simultaneously diminishes their seriousness by stating that she "provides war-haunted voices for those who never served" (59).

One can find versions of this "magnificent" author/shame about her terrible readers divide in popular and scholarly writing about Plath. In Tim Kendall's *Sylvia Plath: A Critical Study*, he attacks critics for losing sight of why Plath was famous in the first place: "her popularity has not always helped to enhance our understanding of her work. … It should not be controversial to assert that the most interesting thing about Sylvia Plath is her poetry" (xi). For Kendall, discussions of mythology and popularity distract us from reading poems. "I have tried to remain as practical as literary criticism allows, using detailed close readings to explain what is characteristic about Plath's poetry and how it changes over time" (*A Critical Study* xi). Kendall's prose is deceptively flat and sober-sounding. Where is the offense here? Surely this is just a call for extended close reading, the in-vogue return to New Formalism popular in the 1990s and 2000s? Perhaps so, and yet I cannot entirely shake off the idea that Kendall, like Spitz, may actively dislike Plath readers, Plath scholars, and, if I am being honest, the majority of Plath's writing.

Plath's prose is conspicuous by its absence from his critical study, so too is her visual art. Tracy Brain's *The Other Sylvia Plath*, published the same year, is more inclusive and wide-ranging, opening with a consideration of the archives and how they change our view of the published poems. Her desire to see "a new edition of the *Collected Poems*, where every poem is transcribed freshly, and checked and double-checked, to ensure that readers have versions that they can rely on" (*The Other Sylvia Plath* 25) is yet to be met. In Kendall's defense, his book was almost certainly finished before the new edition of the *Journals*, edited by Karen V. Kukil, went to press. *Eye Rhymes* did not appear until 2007; Volumes 1 and 2 of the *Letters* were only published recently. Yet, given the starkness of his statements above, I doubt whether any of these publications would have changed his estimation. For him, it is the individual poem that counts. Everything else is secondary, including drafts, manuscript variations, prose, and unpublished work.

I have written elsewhere about the prevalence of such hierarchies, particularly in relation to letters, an art form rarely considered an art form, let alone a literary genre (13–31). Plath's letters, to be specific the letters collected by her mother Aurelia Plath in *Letters Home*, rather than the letters in the new volumes edited by Peter K. Steinberg and Kukil, have often been described as fake or inferior works in relation to the poems, journal entries, and other forms of prose. Kendall hardly mentions them; Spitz doesn't say anything about them at all. Such a position was flawed a decade ago. A cursory reading of *Letters Home* reveals Plath to be an expert mimic and innovator of epistolary prose, even a formulaic note home. Now, with the evidence of her full correspondence, it is indefensible.

Janet Badia's 2011 book, *Sylvia Plath and the Mythology of Women Readers*, helpfully explores the long history behind many of these prejudices, a history that predates the reception of Plath's own work. It is a study not so much of Plath's writing but of writing about Plath, in particular the ways in which the figure of the Plath reader is recycled and replicated in numerous films, television series, novels, and poems. While critics like Spitz and Kendall want to reclaim Plath from her readers who are nearly always depicted as young, misguided women incapable of reading her work properly, Badia wonders how the figure of the Plath reader came to have such a negative reputation in the first place. In so doing, she questions whether continual appeals to "approaching Plath's writings as pure works of literature untainted by the discourse surrounding the author" are, in effect, "literary bullying" (15). One can hear the long and still pervasive legacy of New Criticism here, in particular its treatment of the poem as a self-contained unit, the reading of which requires students to be suspicious of knowledge acquired from fields such as biography, history, or psychology. "We need to recognize," Badia suggests, "that there are many ways of valuing Plath as author, and the first step towards appreciating these different approaches is to understand where our prejudices against certain ways of understanding her originate" (16).

Badia's answer lies at least as far back as the Romantic period when so-called excessive novel reading by women was linked to both illness and madness. "Reading," she observes, "was central to the diagnosis and treatment of hysteria: the wrong reading practices, it was argued, could incline one to the disease, while the right reading could contribute to its cure or prevention" (5). Badia shows the extent to which the Plath reader pathologized by contemporary critics as immature and suicidal is related to the similarly stereotyped nineteenth-century reader of sensational fiction. In both cases, gender is considered to mar judgment.

Let me return briefly to Kendall again as he attempts to separate Plath's poetry from her other writings by appealing to what he calls "Seamus Heaney's belief that poetry cannot be reduced to merely another form of discourse" and so must be read "primarily *as* poetry" ("Preface"). To read poems "primarily *as* poetry" as opposed, say, to read poetry as biography, history, or philosophy sounds harmless enough, but what does it actually mean? It is worth cross-referencing Kendall's words with Heaney's own essay on Plath, "The Indefatigable Hoof-taps," in which he praises "the great appeal" of *Ariel* and its constellated lyrics" (218). "These poems," Heaney writes,

> are the vehicles of their own impulses[.] … They move without hesitation and assume the right to be heard; they, the poems, are what we attend to, not the poet. They are, in Lowell's words, events rather than the records of events, and as such represent the triumph of Sylvia Plath's romantic ambition to bring expressive power and fully achieved selfhood into congruence.
>
> (219)

Heaney loves listening to poets. But what does he hear in Plath's work? "The poems … not the poet."

I am not convinced the line between poem and poet is as clear as Heaney or Kendall would have us believe. The best analogy I can think of for the shifting relationship between author and subject comes from Plath's own poem, "In Plaster" (1961), in which the speaker's broken body is copied, molded, and made "unbreakable" via a plaster-cast before that same cast begins to take on a life of its own. For me, this is a poem that interrogates the modes of critical reading Plath was taught at Smith College in the early 1950s and that she practiced herself when she returned to teach there between 1957 and 1958. As Amanda Golden points out: "Plath's manner in the classroom mirrored the impersonal strategies of the modern writers whom she taught. … Her close readings keep to aesthetic and formal commentary, sizing and dividing up texts into sections and parts, itemizing themes and listing issues" ("Sylvia Plath's Teaching and the Shaping of Her Work" 258). In "In Plaster" Plath reflects on the close and often shameful relationship between biographical experience and lyric poetry, the attempt, particularly on behalf of male critics, to have one without the other. Gillian White's book, *Lyric Shame* (2014), engages with midcentury debates about lyric poetry and subjectivity, what White identifies as an "unspoken but pervasive embarrassment over what poetry is, should be, and fails to be." Thinking about the reception of Anne Sexton's work, she wonders whether "a quintessential Confessional poem has ever existed. The critical tendency has been to displace the shame of the Confessional 'lyric' onto some lesser, inferior, or 'bad' Confessional. But who, what poem, is the quintessential Confessional? Now that some writers affiliated with Language have taken in Sylvia Plath, to whom should one turn as the 'real' Confessional?" (147–8). White's point is not that there is a "good" or "bad" Confessional poem, or "real" and unreal Confessional poets. Such terms say more about the personality of critics than the characters of poems. She is intrigued by why we talk about poems as if we were talking about people. "Poems are ashamed but have no sense of shame," she argues. "What can we make of poetry if we try to unshame it, engaging (new? un-? something other than anti-) lyric readings of it?" (7). Lucy Tunstall's recent work on Plath and the lyric covers similar ground, querying critics like Heaney's focus on poetic "purity" (the word is Heaney's):

> What exactly do we mean by purity? Is it artistic, spiritual or carnal, and how are these aspects connected? How is purity in art bound up with material costliness and the rarefied object? What combinations of register are permissible in a lyric poem, and how are notions of perfection in poetry connected with repression, oppression, neuroticism or tyranny? And not least: what exactly are we looking for when we find transcendence in a poem?
>
> (97–8)

For Tunstall, Plath is not prepared to provide neat answers to these questions. At the same time, her work alerts us through its questions to what Tunstall characterizes as "the potential damage (by intrusion, calcification, domination or commodification) in all lyric poetry, including her own" [103]).

Damage appears an odd word to associate with lyric, even with Plath's lyrics, but I would like to keep it in mind as one of the effects of reading her work. Plath was certainly aware of Romantic and Victorians discourses of lyric purity, of what a poet could or could not say in a poem, particularly if they were a female poet. In the sonnet, "Female Author," exiled to the back of her *Collected Poems* under the heading "Juvenilia," she brings these stereotypes to life, imagining the eponymous author as a Tennysonian woman at a window, absorbed in her own narcissistic concerns and ignorant or indifferent to others' suffering. While she "nibbles an occasional bonbon of sin" or "nurses / Chocolate fancies," actual people are hurting beyond her "rose-papered rooms," the final line of the poem revealing "gray child faces crying in the streets" (CP 301). Plath parodies this image of the female author as decorous and self-absorbed, "lost in subtle metaphor" (CP 301). One could never say this about her own writing! The poem's third-person narrator points out the flaws in the female author's perspective, her narrow focus on what lies inside the room, not outside of it. She hears what the female author pretends not to, widening her frame of reference. Plath could be sharp about other authors, particularly her female contemporaries. Her journals and letters identify such authors as at best mentors to outgrow, at worst rivals to best and outmaneuvre. At the same time, perhaps Plath is also making a more general point about the condition of literary creation of Anglo-American poetry at midcentury. Unlike Heaney (at least in his essays), she does not pretend the poetic space is a pure one. Lyric poetry absorbs impure elements from the author's biography that cannot be entirely cleaned away by rewriting or revision. The reader arrives at the poem with unclean hands as well.

When reading Plath, it is difficult, if not impossible, to forget the two "facts" nearly everybody knows about her even if they have never read a word of her writing: her marriage to Ted Hughes and the manner of her death. I have lost count of the number of times a critic has "found" the biographical Hughes in a poem, often in unlikely places. The same is true of feelings that "foreshadow" her suicide. The page of a Plath poem, whatever poem, is figuratively marked with her and our backstories. How do we read the poem through so much history? In an early poem like "Female Author," this is archly presented via the sight and smell of "hothouse roses" and "festering gardenias" that almost prevent us from breathing for ourselves (CP 301). We have to fight to see the woman underneath it all. In her early work, Plath dramatizes the cost to oneself and perhaps to the poem in attempting to purify one's writing. Whatever else the female author is in the poem, she does not seem especially happy. The thrill of Plath's later work is not just the abandonment of these unwritten rules about what does and does not belong in a poem, but the bravery of telling us she is doing so. She thus has the confidence to begin "Fever 103°" (1962): "Pure? What does it mean?" (CP 231).

If lyric for Plath is a messy business, one that involves the author and reader in complex and frequently uncomfortable positions of power and submission, one would not necessarily know this from the titles of many of her poems. "Mushrooms" (1959), "Tulips" (1961), "A Birthday Present" (1962), and "Balloons" (1963), to pick a poem from each of the last four years of her life, sound deceptively cheery in the list of contents. Plath has a particular gift for lulling us into a false sense of security. By the time we know what the poem is really about, we have been found out. I say "we" and "us" as if we could generalize about the reader when of course this is impossible. How does Plath create such an intimate relationship with the reader? One of the ways is through her frequent use of the second person pronoun, "you." As Tracy Brain points out: "[w]hat is crucial about the second person narrative is that it establishes a relationship between the speaking 'I' and the 'you' who is being addressed. At the same time, it cements a bond between these 'I' and 'you' persona and the reader, who is made to occupy both of these positions at once" ("Sylvia Plath and You" 84). By occupying both of these positions at once, questions of identification and sympathy become tricky. Is the "I" and "you" as inclusive or welcoming as it first appears? This is particularly the case when looking at her use of color in relation to race. The awkwardness of Plath's color-coding has been pointed out by several critics over the years, including Renée R. Curry, Dianne Hunter, and Ellen Miller, though not by as many as one might expect given the prevalence of highly racialized language across her body of writing. Curry counts that in Plath's *Collected Poems*, 117 poems use black and / or white to signify power or fear (*White Women Writing White* 125). As Hunter demonstrates, "Plath's cognitive style tends to divide the world into sharp oppositions" (53), black and white being one of her favorite binaries. Miller defends Plath on the grounds that she "moves beyond simple racial images of white self / black other" and that her poetry "holds whiteness before our eyes so we can at least begin to see and hear it" (144). Plath's lyric might be open to some impurity from outside, but there are limits to her open-mindedness. While images of blackness and whiteness can and do swap associative places in her poetry, neither fixed as negative or positive, the "I" and "you" of the poem rarely, if ever, speak or imagine the world from outside the experiences of a white woman. Critics have rightly examined the legacy of the Holocaust on Plath's imagination,[1] but there is comparatively little research on the legacy of slavery or the presence of the Civil Rights Movement in her writing. Why do we not see these events when we read her poems? Looking away does not mean other equally important historical events and experiences are not there. Teaching *Ariel* recently, I read the title poem aloud. Articulating the n-word is not something I do frequently. Indeed, it is a word I have hardly ever spoken aloud before. I hesitated over the word not because I had never heard it before but because I was unsure if it was right or responsible for me as a teacher to say it, particularly in a classroom. If reading the poems aloud can sometimes feel akin to an act of micro-aggression, or is in fact one, surely failing to acknowledge this fact is the same or worse?

---

[1]There are numerous books and journal articles on Plath and Holocaust poetry, most focusing on a relatively small number of poems, "Daddy" and "Lady Lazarus" being the most frequently cited. For Rose, in 1991, "nothing has produced the outrage generated by Sylvia Plath's allusions to the Holocaust in her poetry, and nothing the outrage occasioned by 'Daddy', which is just one of the poems in which those allusions appear" (205). Gubar, writing a decade after this, detects a similar critical response: "Her appropriation of the voices of Holocaust victims still seems outrageous to those who reject any reasonable affinity or parallelism between Plath's individual suffering and mass murder" (191). Other important analyses of Plath's Holocaust imagery include Banner's "Sylvia Plath and Holocaust Poetry," Narbeshuber's "The Poetics of Torture: The Spectacle of Sylvia Plath's Poetry," and Boswell's "'Black Phones': Postmodern Poetics in the Holocaust Poetry of Sylvia Plath."

Returning to "In Plaster," one notices Plath's commitment to lyric writing as a place where the tyranny of the body's experiences is fought with rather than shaken off and also as a place where the historical body of the American nation, one with its own memories and scars, is exposed to the light. This is the conclusion to the poem when the speaker finally loses patience with the plaster's demands on her energy and time and prepares to prise it off:

> She may be a saint, and I may be ugly and hairy,
> But she'll soon find out that doesn't matter a bit.
> I'm collecting my strength; one day I shall manage without her,
> And she'll perish with emptiness then, and begin to miss me.
>
> (CP 160)

Plath wrote the poem in March 1961 after leaving the hospital, while recovering from an appendectomy. In the next bed there had been a patient in plaster. It was not uncommon for Plath to appropriate the experiences of people close to her, even if it somewhat trampled upon their rights to privacy, as is clearly the case in this instance, though in a letter to her mother written from her hospital bed she defends her conduct thus: "Now I am mobile I make a daily journey round the 28 bed ward stopping & gossiping—this is much appreciated by the bedridden women (most of them are) who regard me as a sort of ward newspaper & I learn a great deal. They are all dying to talk about themselves & their medical involvements" (*L2* 584–5). If Plath saw herself as a hospital journalist in the letter, cheering up twenty-eight bedridden women, in the poem she has become the patient being interviewed, "dying to talk."

A poem, like plaster, takes its shape from experience. It may not need food or sleep, "[b]ut without me, she wouldn't exist" (*CP* 159). And yet, as the composition process develops, the poem-plaster takes on its own shape different to the one imposed on it by the poet. "She stopped fitting me so closely and seemed offish" (*CP* 159). As in other myths of art's creation, the inanimate object becomes live and demands its own identity. Or, as Plath puts it, "[s]he let in the drafts and became more and more absent-minded ... . / Then I saw what the trouble was: she thought she was immortal" (*CP* 159). "Drafts" of air, like drafts of poems, take on a more permanent shape. The proto-poem absorbs life from elsewhere. Before the poet knows it, they have given birth to something that thinks of itself as "immortal."

Body and plaster, life and art, poet and poem. The Romantic lyric, particularly as it was theorized by New Criticism, kept these categories apart. The body of the poet was one thing, messy and mortal; the body of the poem was another, ordered and somehow eternal. Plath's speaker declares that "it must be one or the other of us" as if categories like these could be prised apart. I am not so convinced. And neither is Plath. The title of the poem, "In Plaster," can be read both as an everyday event and as a comment on human existence. After all, one can read any human body as text since each body bears a record of its own injuries and wounds. "The body has memory" (28), declares Claudia Rankine in *Citizen: An American Lyric*. Or, as Ocean Vuong observes in his recent novel, *On Earth We're Briefly Gorgeous*, "trauma affects not only the brain, but the body too, its musculature, joints, and posture" (19). Are we ever *not* in plaster? For Plath, the poem is a space where miracles of recovery and transformation can happen, but only when the wounds have been acknowledged and seen. Lyric cannot magic away the body that gave it life. Significantly, the poem ends on an empty threat on the subject of emptiness. The speaker believes or rather convinces herself to believe (they are not the same thing) that "one day I shall manage without her." The plaster will "perish with emptiness then, and begin to miss me." The dynamics of power have been reversed. The body, who gave the plaster life, now wonders if the plaster will miss her, as if the plaster has more agency, as if the plaster has taken over herself. Does the body have the strength of her convictions to remove the plaster? Or have body and cast, experience and poem, come to depend upon each other for life? In a famous phrase, W. B. Yeats asked, "How can we know the dancer from the dance?" (245). After looking at an uncle's still life of a landscape she also knew well, Elizabeth Bishop wondered at the compression of "life and the memory of it": "Which is which?" (197). Plath's poem finds separation difficult too. Like Yeats and Bishop, she asks not if the poem needs the poet to exist (all three poets accept this proposition), but curiously and uncannily if the poem might miss the poet.

Plath, like Emily Dickinson, frequently writes poems as if she were already dead, or writing in anticipation of that event. Diana Fuss, in a bravura article, calls these "corpse poem[s]" and identifies "Lady Lazarus" as one: "By corpse poem I mean poetry not about the dead but spoken by the dead, lyric utterances not from beyond the grave but from inside it. Abandoning the literary convention of the epitaph, a form of writing that can only be read from outside the tomb, the corpse poem undertakes to bring us inside the tomb" (1–2). The corpse author, in other words, is a ghost-reader of their not-yet-posthumous work years before their literal death. John Keats's "This living hand" is a famous example. In reading poems like "In Plaster," it is important not to sentimentalize or simplify the act of interpreting such writing. Plath knew her body of work could provoke contradictory feelings. In fact, contradictoriness is one of her main poetic subjects. The "I" of the poet and the "she" of the poem represent only "a kind of marriage." Their relationship is "close" but not closed. (The gender of the speaker, for example, is not revealed, a refusal that closes down straightforward readings of the poem in terms of heterosexual relations or traditional male/female subject/muse dynamics.) Interestingly, Plath also appears to predict her posthumous martyrdom. The plaster made out of an "ugly and hairy" life may, she suggests, eventually turn her into "a saint." The two selves do not divide at the end of the poem, however. Their domestic disharmony continues. Although Plath did not foresee in any kind of literal sense the ways in which her body of work would be edited and published after her death, she does provide us with a sophisticated metaphor for how art is formed out of life and then takes on its own existence. Plath's text is also a plaster, something that brings a shattered body together while at the time commemorating the place where that body has been hurt. It is the place where wounds heal but cannot be seen. We can look but not touch the source of pain.

Plath's metaphor explicitly allows for the presence of other people too. After all, a nurse normally applies plaster after an injury has occurred. The poet similarly places her trust in somebody else. What is a good editor if not the person who applies plaster to a misshapen body of words? What is a good reader if not a person who comes on a scene of loss and attempts to make sense of it, even if making sense of it implicates us in the events being depicted?

Being a good reader, not just of formal features one likes, but also of ideological language one hates, necessitates a refusal to turn one's poetic heroes and heroines into saints. As much as I want to read the poem in formal terms, primarily *as* poetry Kendall might say, it is difficult to escape the assumption of racial superiority that is present in the opening lines that read as follows:

> I shall never get out of this! There are two of me now:
> This new absolutely white person and the old yellow one,
> And the white person is certainly the superior one.
>
> (*CP* 158)

The poem continues with image after image of two bodies in a relationship that resembles slavery. I say resemble as if there were some interpretation involved. Is there? These are lines from the poem:

> At the beginning I hated her, she had no personality—
> She lay in bed with me like a dead body
> ..............................
> When I hit her she held still, like a true pacifist
> ..............................
> I patronized her a little, and she lapped it up—
> You could tell almost at once she had a slave mentality.
>
> (*CP* 158–9)

Body and cast swap roles. If at the beginning of the poem, the cast is "[t]his absolutely white person" and "certainly the superior one," as the poem progresses and the cast becomes less white with use and time, it takes on the characteristics of a female body being mentally and physically abused and in the final quotation a Black body that remembers slavery.

I would prefer to skip over these images, but pretending they are not there does more harm than good. As Toni Morrison writes in *The Origin of Others*:

> Descriptions of cultural, racial and physical differences that note "Otherness" but remain free of categories of worth or rank are difficult to come by. … Our tendency to separate and judge those not in our clan as the enemy, as the vulnerable and the deficient needing control, has a long history not linked to the animal world or prehistoric man. Race has been a constant arbiter of difference.
>
> (3)

What does this poem seem to be saying about race? As the cast becomes less white and more black, it loses agency, identity, selfhood. It becomes an object, a passive victim, a slave. What might a defense of such images be? Could one argue that Plath is empathizing with the way in which Black lives were and still are seen as lesser than white lives? Is she at least owning up to white ignorance and white prejudice? Whatever argument one makes, I think it is important to acknowledge the damage of such lines. Plath's language is embedded within a discourse of racial superiority that coincides with and is deeply implicated in Romantic notions of purity. She does not doubt or disown any of these associations, however. Or if she does, it is often too subtle to pin down. Holding "whiteness before our eyes," as Miller suggests, does not necessarily mean that she thinks racial prejudice is wrong.

Plath continues to reflect on the long history of slavery in "The Arrival of the Bee Box" (1962) at the center of which is an astonishing confrontation between an "eye" that is very much coded to be white and a box of enslaved creatures that are repeatedly described as "black":

> It is dark, dark,
> With the swarmy feeling of African hands
> Minute and shrunk for export,
> Black on black, angrily clambering.
>
> (CP 213)

Miller offers an extended close reading of this stanza, partly criticizing Plath's language, partly letting her off the hook. She identifies the main problem as

> an inability to understand the natural black body. In Plath's poem, black bodies are the colonized, whereas the white speaker holds godlike mastery over these irrational maniacs. Plath naturalizes black bodies as primitive, dangerous, excessively sexual. Part of Plath's limitations here are not due to racial prejudice though. Plath displays marked ambivalence about embodiment generally in her poems, particularly her own female body.
>
> (150)

This is a sophisticated, perhaps too sophisticated, defense of what's going on here. While I agree that the female body is a site of terror and trauma across Plath's writing, it is important not to use this as an excuse for racial stereotyping. The box, once open, cannot be shut. In placing her eye to the grid, the poem's speaker re-enacts the gaze of the captain of the slave-ship or slave-owner spying on their possessions. As Miller points out, the angry bees who remind the bee box owner of miniaturized slaves are "primitive, dangerous, excessively sexual." They are colors ("dark, dark"), feelings ("swarmy"), shapes ("Minute and shrunk"), certainly never people. The best we are given is a continent ("African hands"), as if that categorization were enough. But is it?

Banishing Plath's privileged perspectives from her work, or banishing people from reading and talking about them, are both empty gestures predicted by Plath's own writing. Do we really want poetry without poets or poetry without culturally aware readers? It is fascinating how often Plath fills her poems with boxed-in spaces, dead ends, and even dead metaphors. There are several poems that deliberately loop back on themselves and go nowhere, as if drawing attention to their own failure of imagery or narrative. In "The Night Dances," for example, the poem's leaps and bounds encompass a comet's flight but end "Nowhere" (CP 250). It is possible to read such work in aesthetic terms as poems about their own difficult creation, but I take them to be poems about extra-poetic subjects as well. Plath requires readers to join the dots even if it makes us uncomfortable to be talking about what we find there. And if we do not feel uncomfortable by what we find there, perhaps we were too comfortable in the first place. I am reminded of a passage in Ben Lerner's book-length manifesto, *The Hatred of Poetry* (2016), where Lerner reflects upon Marianne Moore's famous statement, "I, too dislike it," the opening line of a short poem called "Poetry." "What kind of art," Lerner asks, "assumes the dislike of its audience and what kind of artist aligns herself with that dislike, even encourages it? An art hated from without and within" (9). Plath, who read Moore closely even as they fell out over the older poet's refusal to endorse her first collection of poetry,[2] frequently writes about poetry in similar terms as a stillborn object that drives the artist-mother "near dead with distraction" (*CP* 142). "These poems do not live," the poem "Stillborn" (1960) begins. "They are not pigs, they are not even fish, / Though they have a piggy and a fishy air" (142). Poems might not be "real" like pigs or fish, but they are close enough to have "a piggy and fishy air." Their mother might wish them dead but they are not. Is this a poem about motherhood or a poem about poetry? Some might wish the figure of Plath to be absent from her poems, particularly the Plath who thinks white bodies more "superior" than Black ones. But, like the pig that's not quite a pig but has a "piggy" air, she will not go quietly. There is always a squeak in the tail.

I began this chapter with Marc Spitz's comment about Plath as "both a literary and feminist icon and a too-easy punch line." For Spitz, Kendall, and even Heaney, Plath is too often a convenient punch bag against which to employ various concealed and unconcealed prejudices aimed not just at Plath's art but at other writers too. What about some of those punch lines? One of the most famous is in Woody Allen's *Annie Hall* (1977) when Alvy berates Annie for owning a copy of *Ariel*. "Aha, Sylvia Plath," he begins. "Interesting poetess whose tragic suicide was misinterpreted as romantic by the college-girl mentality." In Richard Linklater's *Before Midnight* (2013), Plath's death is again invoked by a soon-to-be-quarrelling couple. "Now I know why Sylvia Plath put her head in a toaster," Celine tells Jesse in the build-up to one of contemporary cinema's most visceral arguments. At first glance, these examples sound relatively similar. In *Annie Hall*, as in many articles and book reviews published at the time, the Plath reader is a young woman patronized by a male writer not for her choice of reading matter (Alvy calls her an "interesting poetess") but for misreading her death as "romantic." In *Before Midnight*, Plath's death (rather than life) is still utilized as the punch line, even if Celine gets the method of suicide wrong. Yet the roles have been reversed. In Linklater's film, it is the male writer not the female reader who is insulted by the comparison to Plath and the female partner who gets to put down her husband. Plath has at least become an author both genders have read and can be accused of misunderstanding. If this doesn't seem much of an advance in terms of male/female relations, in particular in relation to male authors and female muses, it is perhaps further than Plath herself imagined in many of her own poems about female writers.

In this spirit, I would like to turn my attention at the end of this chapter to a few of Plath's actual punch lines, of which there are many. In a short essay called "A Comparison," broadcast on the BBC Home Service in July 1962, Plath conceived of the poem *as* a closed hand, its effect identifiably punch-like:

> If a poem is concentrated, a closed fist, then a novel is relaxed and expansive, an open hand: it has roads, detours, destinations; a heart line, a head line, morals and money come into it. Where the fist excludes and stuns, the open hand can touch and encompass a great deal in its travels.
>
> (*JP* 57)

---

[2] For further information on this, see Pollock's article, "Moore, Plath, Hughes, and 'The Literary Life.'"

Plath begins the essay envious of the novelist for having time to do things and space to write about anything. The poet, on the other hand, is in far more of a rush. If the novel is a home, a place, a setting, the poem is more of a feeling, a means of travel, a sense of speed. The poem might begin and end "in one breath" and certainly should last no longer than "about a minute" (57, 56).

Plath's comparison is a convincing, if relatively orthodox, account of the main differences between the novel and the poem. Its binary this-or-that logic doesn't account for experimental or hybrid genres such as the modernist novel, the novella, the prose poem, or the poetic sequence, forms she knew well and in some cases practiced herself. Why make the comparison so stark, the differences between the novelist and poet so artificially and transparently oppositional? One answer might be a practical one: Plath was writing to commission for a radio audience. The BBC was not the place to air her real thoughts on genre. This interpretation is supported by evidence in a letter to Olwyn Hughes from London in which Plath confessed that the broadcasts were "bread & butter stuff" that helped them to pay the bills: "money bleeds away so fast here—the house just devours it: everything from slug killer to thatch insurance to fire extinguishers" (*L2* 785). If we look at the poems Plath was working on at the same time, we discover that she was not writing very much at this point, at least in comparison to the productive final months of the year when the majority of the poems that later constituted *Ariel* were composed. Seen in this context, I wonder whether the comparison she is making—between art that takes time and an art that has no time to waste—is as much about the character of her own poetry, in particular, the dividing lines between *The Colossus* volume and her later writing, as it is about the novel and poem in general. The "open hand" and the "closed fist" might better be seen as analogies for particular forms of poetic writing.

Let us pursue further this notion of a dividing line between different phases of Plath's writing life. Nearly every Plath critic tells a version of the breakthrough story.[3] In fact, "breakthrough" may be one of the most over-used words in Plath criticism. Some discuss breakthrough in relation to a change in form, others to a change in personal circumstances. The first person to tell this story was Plath herself, especially in letters, especially to her mother. Ted Hughes's editing of the *Collected Poems* is another version of this story, separating her career into identifiable "phases" before "her final take-off" (*CP* 16). I prefer Craig Morgan Teicher's account of Plath's changing style and what he terms her "creative surges" (35). For Teicher, there are two major breakthroughs in Plath's career, one in each of her major poetry books, *The Colossus* and *Ariel*. Teicher interprets Plath's breakthroughs as partly breakdowns of poetic form. She had to find subjects "that would push and then exceed the frames of her technique" (37):

> Her art, like a dancer's, is in her ability to carefully and meaningfully choreograph what look like mad flailings. Among the great satisfactions of the *Ariel* poems is their roughness: the roiling that animates Plath's greatest poems is never a chair nor a toy, but a wiry, overgrowing vine, an exploding rock, an utter expulsion of propriety, capacities seemingly beyond her control.
>
> (45)

---

[3]Hammer and James Longenbach have both been critical of the "breakthrough narrative" in discussions of midcentury American poetry. For an overview of these critical debates, see Zuba's "'Poets of the First Book, Writers of Promise': Beginning in the Era of the First Book Prize."

For a long time, I agreed with the idea behind this thesis without seeing how it worked in practice.

Then one day, I began looking at the final lines of Plath's poems and noticed how many of her final lines are single lines. I am tempted to label them punch lines. The first in the *Collected Poems* is "The Thin People" (1957), then "Suicide off Egg Rock" (1959), then "The Beekeeper's Daughter" (1959), then "The Hermit at Outermost House" (1959), then "The Burnt-out Spa (1959), then, after a three-year gap, an avalanche of poems between May 1962 and February 1963, including many of her most iconic lyrics: "Event," "Poppies in July," "The Arrival of the Bee Box," "Medusa," "Lesbos," "The Tour," "Ariel," "The Couriers," "Thalidomide," "Death & Co.," "The Munich Mannequins," and "Mystic." I typed them out to see if there was a pattern:

> And grayer; not even moving their bones. (*CP* 65)
> The forgetful surf creaming on those ledges. (*CP* 115)
> The queen bee marries the winter of your year. (*CP* 118)
> Gulls mulled in the greenest light. (*CP* 119)
> Neither nourishes nor heals. (*CP* 138)
> The dark is melting. We touch like cripples. (*CP* 195)
> But colorless. Colorless. (*CP* 203)
> The box is only temporary. (*CP* 213)
> There is nothing between us. (*CP* 226)
> Even in your Zen heaven we shan't meet. (*CP* 230)
> Toddle on home to tea! (*CP* 238)
> Eye, the cauldron of morning. (*CP* 240)
> Love, love, my season. (*CP* 246)
> Flees and aborts like dropped mercury. (*CP* 252)
> Somebody's done for. (*CP* 255)
> Voicelessness. The snow has no voice. (*CP* 263)
> The heart has not stopped. (*CP* 269)

Plath's final lines are remarkably consistent in their refusal to end neatly. Sometimes this is a matter of linguistic play: they repeat the same word twice as if unsure what it really means. At other times the narrative of the poem is paused half-way through as if another poem is about to begin. I am struck by some of the similes she throws into the final line. "We touch like cripples" is, for example, deliberately provocative. There is a curse-like element too, a heart-in-the-mouth revelation of a secret. What would it be like, I wonder, to be spoken to like that? How would you feel to be told that "there is nothing between us" or that "somebody's done for"? Her punch lines punch through, beyond their literal end on the page and at some imaginary audience that both is and is not present in the poem. It takes a closed fist to do this, one that Plath tested out as early as 1957 but one that she did not properly develop until 1962.

The aim of this chapter has been to move away from the constant focus on Plath as punch line to thinking about the actual form of her lyric poetry, especially the punch lines of her final poems. Plath is the punch line to so many male critics' discussions of modern poetry because of a narrow definition of lyric in terms of purity and transcendence. Plath's lyrics, in contrast to these definitions, are impure and uncomfortable reading experiences because she understood lyric not as an art object separate from the body and life of the poet but as a figurative plaster cast grown in and out of an individual poet's everyday feelings and thoughts. To read Plath closely is to get close not to Plath the person but to the process that transforms good lines into great poems. Such poems are not immune from the prejudices of the historical period, however, in particular in relation to race. The white speakers and implied listeners of her work frequently punch down on Black Americans, including those in extremely vulnerable positions. There is little sympathy in Plath's work for those who do not look and speak like her.

Writing about Plath often becomes writing about other people writing about Plath, not writing about her actual work, including the messy and uncomfortable lives that are found there. Her corpse poems, similarly, are metaphorical burial grounds for more than just Plath's biography. We don't have to look hard to find other skeletons. This chapter has been caught in this conundrum too, the critical equivalent of the bee box grid. Let us hope that the box is only temporary and that we can pay more attention to the bee box's voices soon.

CHAPTER TWO

# "Get bathrobe and slippers and nightgown & work on femininity": Sylvia Plath, Self-Identity, and Sleepwear

REBECCA C. TUITE

One of the most vivid and lasting images from Sylvia Plath's novel, *The Bell Jar* (1963), is of protagonist Esther Greenwood "feeding" her entire wardrobe to the "night winds" from the roof of her Manhattan hotel (*B* 111). While much attention has been paid to both the symbolism of this act and the significance of the garments that she discards, it is the garment that she is left wearing, the only garment not sent "flutteringly" into the urban abyss, that is the most important and most overlooked: Esther's "cornflower-sprigged bathrobe" (*B* 111, 112).[1] With no clothes to wear home the following day, Esther trades this most familiar of flowery robes for a distinctly "unfamiliar" "green dirndl" skirt and "white eyelet blouse" (*B* 112). A thinly veiled account of Plath's own experiences as a *Mademoiselle* magazine guest editor and her subsequent breakdown in the Summer of 1953, *The Bell Jar* contains many real-life parallels, including this bathrobe incident. For both Esther and Sylvia, the cornflower robe was the only part of their wardrobe, and themselves, to be left behind in New York; left to be held and cherished by someone, as opposed to the anonymous "gray scraps" that "were ferried off" by the night winds, "to settle here, there, exactly where I would never know, in the dark heart of New York" (*B* 111). Yet Plath's own relationship with this robe and with sleepwear in general has rarely been explored.

Plath's tendency to wear her cornflower robe regularly around the all-female Barbizon Hotel that June had made quite the impression on the other *Mademoiselle* guest editors, especially Janet Wagner Rafferty, the inspiration for the less sophisticated character Betsy in the novel who swaps her dirndl and blouse for the bathrobe. As Rafferty remembers:

> Well, it was prettier than any bathrobe I had. It was quilted, polyester [or] nylon. And it had little carnations all over it. ... I had noticed her wearing it probably, because we

---

[1] It is notable that April Pelt opens her fashion-centered article with this same "pivotal moment" in her own exploration of "the sartorial dimensions of [Esther's] identity crisis, psychological collapse, and painful rehabilitation." Pelt, too, notes a number of works that exist examining the full gamut of possible symbolic significances that could be attributed to the scene. See Pelt, 13–24.

all wore our bathrobes around The Barbizon. ... Oh yes, I'll never forget the bathrobe. She made me pick something [the morning after the rooftop incident]. ... Well, I gave her something and she wanted to give me something back, when she was leaving. ... And I picked the bathrobe, the nice bathrobe.

(Conversation, September 18, 2017)

Although this incident has become the subject of great autobiographical debate,[2] for Rafferty, the robe has remained a material memory of so many things: their shared experiences that summer living and working in Manhattan, Plath's excellent taste and fine clothes, and even Plath's early opinion that she lacked sophistication (Rafferty once mentioned to Sylvia that the blue carnations dotting the robe were "unnatural," and Plath exclaimed, "Oh *gawd*!" as if entirely exasperated that someone could be unfamiliar with cornflowers) (Conversation, September 18, 2017).[3] For Rafferty, the robe was an intimate reflection of the Plath that *she* knew: Sylvia Plath, the Smith student and *Mademoiselle* guest managing editor who would "giggle a lot," was "the most artistic" and was her (albeit a little snobbish at times) friend (Conversation, September 18, 2017).

Sleepwear is often the clothing of intimacy, of constancy, of friendship and relationships; it can represent comfort, routine, and shared quiet memories. However, sleepwear can also be extraordinarily communicative of how people live and broader ideas pertaining to the social and cultural attitudes that define a time and place. Plath herself gravitated toward sleepwear, personally and professionally, throughout different phases of her life. Sleepwear became yet another way for Plath to navigate, create, perform, challenge, and develop different identities. But it also became a way for her to bring color and emotional resonance to her literary and artistic works. As such, this chapter will examine Sylvia Plath and sleepwear as reflected through three main identities: Sylvia Plath as student, Sylvia Plath as wife and mother, and Sylvia Plath as writer.

## SYLVIA PLATH AND SLEEPWEAR IN CONTEXT

Sylvia Plath came of age when prescribed notions of femininity and traditional gender roles were being widely espoused. Following the Second World War, there was a new "ascendant domestic ideology" that placed women at the center of the home (Rotskoff

---

[2] Aurelia Plath would later deny that the rooftop incident had occurred in real life that summer; see Alexander 115. Rafferty, for her part, has maintained and repeated her recollections of the roof/bathrobe incident, as well as her relationship with Plath more generally in 1953, for many years; see Wagner-Martin, *Sylvia Plath: A Biography*, 100–1; Witchell, p. ST1; Winder, 200; and Rafferty Conversation with author, September 18, 2017. Other *Mademoiselle* guest editors have also corroborated the rooftop incident; see Winder, 199–200. In particular, Ann Burnside Love agreed that the incident happened both "actually and fictionally"; see Love, "The Legend of Plath, the Scent of Roses." Available online: https://www.washingtonpost.com/archive/lifestyle/1979/04/29/the-legend-of-plath-the-scent-of-roses/b62e48b9-ceb3-4cd4-ace2-bee50915e653/; Love qtd. in *Mad Girl's Love Song*, 208. The robe itself has become a significant piece of Plath material culture, and while Rafferty has been largely consistent in her descriptions of it as blue and floral, one anomaly that exists is in the account given to Winder for *Pain, Parties, Work*, where Rafferty describes it as a "green-striped bathrobe" (200). Being unable to assess the bathrobe in its current state, Rafferty has maintained that she wore and used the robe extensively after the swap, and although she likely still has it somewhere, it is not readily available to view; see Winder, 200. Rafferty expressed similar in the telephone conversation with author, September 18, 2017. However, despite this one description deviation and with all due consideration to the many consistent accounts Rafferty has provided over time, as well as weighing the limitations and advantages of oral testimony, the greater significance of the robe in the contexts being considered in this chapter still stands.

[3] For lack of sophistication, see Witchell, p. ST1.

qtd. in *Cambridge Introduction* 26). There was also a renewed cultural focus on the importance of family and what *McCall's* magazine termed "togetherness" (Wiese 27). As Deborah Nelson has explained in her chapter, "Plath, History and Politics," the prevailing notion was that "cultivating the private space of the home made the greatest possible contribution to the US's success in the sphere of Cold War international politics" (qtd. in *Cambridge Introduction* 27). Yet there existed a culture of "mixed messages" for women and as Caroline Smith has suggested, Plath was deeply influenced by "1950s consumer culture, a culture that encouraged women to navigate beyond the private sphere of the home while limiting those options by simultaneously discouraging that navigation" (3, 4). At midcentury, then, sleepwear is especially significant because it is the clothing of the very space that became so contested and contentious for women: the home (and, by extension, spaces that similarly constituted privacy and domesticity).

The US sleepwear industry shifted to meet and, in some cases, create new sleepwear and leisurewear needs in light of these new national ideological shifts.[4] National sleepwear brands grew at an extraordinary rate in the postwar period, both technologically and in terms of design. Brands developed their own synthetic textiles for sleepwear application, including the first "permanently pleated nylon tricot" that could withstand a spin in the new washing machines, and since sleepwear was no longer purely functional nor fully private, sleepwear styles expanded to suit the new lifestyles and leisure pursuits of Americans.[5] New colors, prints, and innovations were developed, major fashion photographers began to partner with sleepwear brands for editorial advertising campaigns, and testament to all of this, sleepwear became a recognized part of the US fashion industry, with Vanity Fair becoming the first lingerie and sleepwear brand ever to win the Coty Award for Fashion Design in 1950.[6] Just as women's ready-to-wear fashion was heavily promoted in women's monthly magazines, so the prescriptive literature on sleepwear appeared ever increasingly in the "slicks" we know Plath devoured.[7] In short stories, and the illustrations that accompanied them, sleepwear garments were coded by character type: for example, the black lace negligee represented the mistress or the promiscuous singleton, while the quilted housecoat was aligned with the dowdy housewife.[8] These images, in conjunction with advertisements, fashion features, and shopping stories, made sleepwear marketing pervasive and impactful.

Plath was interested in fashion and cosmetics as a way to explore her own identity, and attitudes toward women in the 1950s, in performative gestures. She had playful blonde and scholarly brunette personas depending on her mood and ambition, and she would similarly express these identities sartorially (*L1* 807).[9] In 1954, she wrote of the contradictions of these dualities, with specific reference to sleepwear, wondering if one could really be "the urbane and seductive partygoer; the eggs-and-bacon-and-coffee girl

---

[4]Tuite, "Sleepwear in Hollywood Film and Television."
[5]"Success Story: Pleated In," 105; Tuite, "Sleepwear in Hollywood Film and Television."
[6]"Critics Award Honors 1950s Design," 5; Rodengen, 47–57. Note that Vanity Fair is a good case study for these developments, leading the industry in new standards for the sleepwear and lingerie industry within the world of high fashion, but one could also refer to developments in brands like Munsingwear, Van Raalte, and Weldon Pajamas. See "Sleepwear in Hollywood Film and Television."
[7]For "slicks," see *L1* 309, 446, 951. For sleepwear, see "Fashions for the Nicest Hours of the Day," 95–106; Carroll, 146–51.
[8]Rodell, 42–3; Cohen, 26–7.
[9]See also "Sylvia Plath and Fashion," 126–37.

in a housecoat who can also exist somehow on olives, Roquefort and daiquiris while clad in black velvet" (*L1* 661).[10] A concern that would similarly affect her *The Bell Jar* persona, Esther Greenwood, who wondered if her identity as a wife would be simply "getting up at seven and cooking him eggs and bacon and toast and coffee and dawdling about in my nightgown and curlers after he'd left for work to wash up the dirty plates and make the bed" (*B* 84). Although specifically concerned with the wifely identity in these examples, in all stages of her life, Plath instinctively recognized sleepwear for its symbolic and communicative powers, its connection to domestic spaces of family and socialization, and its capacity to shape one's identity at an intimate level.

## SYLVIA PLATH AS STUDENT AND SLEEPWEAR

In June 1954, as Plath geared up for her senior year at Smith College, she sketched a young blonde woman on a letter she was writing to friend (and sometimes-boyfriend), Gordon Lameyer (*L1* 764, fig. 21). Reclined in the upper-left hand corner, with her head resting upon a pillow and her hand supporting her rather glamorously made-up face, she wears a pretty floral nightgown, dotted all about with pink blooms and green foliage, and trimmed at the neck and hem with eyelet lace. Pen in hand, the nib is poised just above the opening salutation to suggest that this is a self-portrait of Plath as she writes this late-night note. As with any self-portrait, it is possible to consider how the artist sees herself, how she wishes to be seen, how that image has been cultivated, and most importantly, what identity or "self" is being portrayed. During these formative years, Plath's relationship with sleepwear was both personal and professional, intersecting with the fashion magazine industry, the sleepwear industry, and college as she shaped her identity as a student, and a young woman, in the early 1950s.

When Plath arrived at Smith, she used sleepwear as a way to not only explore her own identity as a Smith student, understand her peers and her place among them. As such, Plath's engagement with sleepwear as a student can be seen as a powerful example of what Sally Bayley has called "Plath's involvement with constructed forms of femininity reflective of the prescribed social and cultural codes of post-World War II America: the processes of female socialization" ("Costume of Femininity" 183). At Smith, like most women's colleges at the time, the students cultivated a sense of sartorial freedom that was unlike anything many young women had experienced before. Students embraced their own campus clothing traditions that celebrated their status as collegians and their independence, and dormitory attire was the pinnacle of the casual style.[11] As Plath herself noted in a letter to friend Ann Davidow, "I swear no guy would date a Smith gal if he could see the way we look—hair wet, or screwed up in pin curls, old pajamas, knitting needles clicking busily. But in spite of everything, the girls are a pretty sweet lot!" (*L1* 296). Plath embraced the traditions, coming to Smith well-prepared, as one might expect given her habitual reading of magazines like *Seventeen*, *Mademoiselle*, and *Vogue*, with menswear-style robes and pajamas that were *de rigueur* for a Smith student at rest.[12]

Sleepwear also played an important role in assuring Plath's "Smith Self" because it is at the center of her relationship with one-time roommate and lifelong best friend,

---

[10] See also "Costume of Femininity," 197.
[11] Tuite, *Seven Sisters Style*, 40–60.
[12] See Fig. 8 in *J*.

Marcia Brown, of whom Plath once rather brusquely noted, "[s]he remembers two things of me: I always chose books for the color & texture of their covers and I wore curlers and an old aqua bathrobe" (*J* 316). Brown had vivid memories of what would become Plath's lifelong self-care rituals, which often involved the restorative powers of hot baths and fresh nightgowns, recalling,

> [Sylvia had] this long, blond hair ... and every night she got into an aqua blue bath robe, and then she had to put up her hair [using pieces of torn cloth]. And then she put Noxzema on her face, thick Noxzema which I think has one of the worst odors ever. I almost moved out after the first three days just because she smelled so awful.
> 
> (qtd. in *Mad Girl's Love Song* 118)

Brown's observation is more than just a superficial anecdote; in many ways, the robe represents their relationship and Plath becoming the "Smith girl" she had been so excited to be. The robe became witness to what Plath would later call her and Brown's "passionate discussions," their "clear articulate arguments," and it is the garment that represented, in many ways, the *life* they shared in Haven House at Smith College—a year that Plath described as "one of the most vital experiences of my life" (*J* 152).

Plath's dedication to studying and her close relationship with Marcia meant, however, that she had not capitalized on the "female socialization" available to her at Smith ("Costume of Femininity" 183). "I have lived in boxes above, below, and down the hall from girls who think hard, feel similarly, and long companionably, and I have not bothered to cultivate them because I did not want to, could not, sacrifice the time" (*J* 184).[13] Plath continued to strive to secure her own sense of self not only as a student but as a young, educated woman among like-minded individuals.

Plath saw a second chance when she accepted the *Mademoiselle* guest editorship and, as Elizabeth Winder has noted, "shifted her priorities from academics and work to experience and friendships" (12). Acutely aware that she was to be an editor shaping the taste and style of America's young women and that she would be living and socializing in the elegant Barbizon Hotel, she planned a very different sleepwear wardrobe. One month before arriving in New York, Plath wrote to her mother, "I will buy one pair of nice p.j.'s, as I have two blue pairs and a nylon nightgown, and a nice quilted robe, which I need anyway, to go over them" (*L1* 617). Other guest editors remember being woefully ill-prepared for these extra-curricular bonding traditions, as Neva Nelson Sachar, who had forgotten to pack her pajamas, recalled, "at night when groups of us would sit around talking, everyone else would be wearing robes and nightgowns. I had never even owned a robe before" (Winder 11). Thus, Plath was planning specifically for those intimate, communal moments in the shared spaces of the Barbizon, carefully taking note of the way in which her peers presented themselves, dressed, and behaved in a less-public environment while also clearly cultivating a more sophisticated, more traditionally feminine domestic image for herself through sleepwear.

Seemingly crystallizing Plath's growing interest in sleepwear that summer and its continued influence on her developing sense of self was exposure to the exciting sleepwear industry as a professional "insider." The guest editors were invited to a private showing at Vanity Fair, the country's most successful sleepwear and lingerie brand and,

---

[13] See also Winder, 11–12.

of course, *Mademoiselle* advertiser (Winder 191-2). It was a particularly unique moment to witness Vanity Fair's latest offerings: not only were their award-winning advertising campaigns by photographer, Mark Shaw, creating a stir, but this was the year that Vanity Fair debuted their landmark leopard print lingerie and sleepwear: an industry first.[14] First inspired by the abundance of animal prints in the 1953 Paris Spring collections, leopard print bras, pajamas, nightgowns, and robes became a phenomenon, and their advertising emphasized all of the mixed messages typical of the era: these were "exotic jungle beauties to make a girl feel as exciting as a siren in the wilderness" and offered "exotic excitement for the girl with a touch of the primitive in her soul."[15] Although Plath did not attend the showing, her deep engagement with popular and consumer culture coupled with the fact that the other guest editors returned to the Barbizon with their Vanity Fair gifts make it easy to imagine that Plath was particularly struck by the imagery and advertising. This seems especially likely, too, as the messaging promoted by the company appeared to align with the binary dualities of womanhood that Plath was already beginning to identify, in this case, fluttery angels or primitive jungle sirens, "Jungle Beauties" versus "Little Princess."[16]

By Plath's senior year, she was still grappling with the sleepwear industry's promotion of acceptable images of femininity. In 1955, Plath wrote again to Lameyer, telling him that she had purchased "a pink party nylon nightgown that makes me feel I'm going to a prom (you know: I dreamt I went to Guantanamo Bay in my Maidenform nightie!)" (*L1* 858). Maidenform's "I dreamed ... " campaign, which ran from 1949 to 1969, featured models participating in fantasy scenes, from shopping to bullfighting to, in a more ambitious twist, political elections (Fields 194-6).[17] While Maidenform did not actually manufacture sleepwear at that time, it is telling that Plath parodied this image/campaign, with its suggestion of woman as "spectator" and "spectacle," in her own discussion of a flirty nightgown as she continued to grapple with the images of femininity promoted and available to her (Fields 194). Plath's "interactions with advertising extend beyond the stance of parody or satire" ("Plath, Domesticity, and the Art of Advertising" 18), and, as a student, Plath simultaneously rejected the sleepwear industry's promotional image of femininity and yet bought into it, even acting as an intermediary for the industry's message through her *Mademoiselle* position. Sleepwear becomes another example of Garry M. Leonard's observation that Plath, at times, "wishes to speak as a subject against the dehumanizing commodity culture, while at the same time preserving—even improving—her 'feminine' allure as a valuable object within this same culture" (63).

---

[14]"Vanity Fair Lingerie—The Award Winning Campaign," *Mark Shaw Photographic Archive*. Available online: https://markshawphoto.com/fashion-photography/; Art Directors Club, *Annual of Advertising, Editorial, Television Art & Design (1950)*, Vol. 29, 276-77. A good example of one of the Mark Shaw advertisements appears in the issue of *Mademoiselle* that Plath guest edited; see Vanity Fair Advertisement, *Mademoiselle*, August 1953. For Vanity Fair leopard, see Rodengen, 50, 53, 57.

[15]For animal print in the 1953 Paris Collections, see Marshall, Field & Company, "Leopard—Running Wild," 13; "Second Thoughts on the Paris Collections—Fath's Fur-Printed Fleece Coat," 126-7; "The Next Coat Shapes in Fashion—In Fur," 146-7. For advertising copy, see Marshall, Field & Company, "Leopard Print Lingerie by Vanity Fair," p. B3.

[16]Silverwoods Advertisement, "Angels Gilded Here—Vanity Fair," p. C8; Marshall, Field & Company, "Leopard Print Lingerie by Vanity Fair," p. B3; Mandel Brothers Advertisement, "Nylon Tricot Lingerie in Leopard Design & 'Little Princess' Cotton Quilt Robe," 45.

[17]For examples of the Dream Advertisements, see "I dreamed I went shopping ... ," 13; "I dreamed I was a toreador ... ," 4; "I dreamed I won the election ... ," 31.

Thus, Plath's identity as a young, educated woman in the early 1950s was shaped by her engagement with sleepwear, personally and professionally, and these experiences and struggles would inform several literary works that would follow.

## SYLVIA PLATH AS WIFE AND MOTHER AND SLEEPWEAR

Plath explored sleepwear's familial connotations in her artwork, particularly in two collages she created while still at Smith that presented sleepwear as the uniform of a wife and mother (*The Other Sylvia Plath*, 91–3; plates 2 and 3). In both images, Plath pasted a *House & Garden*-style dream kitchen image, one with accents of pink (a color that Tracy Brain described as "the pinkest of 1950s pink" [92]) and the other accented with blue. Alongside the first, she placed a separate image of a woman wearing a pink-red housecoat and complementary fluffy slippers, with neatly coiffed hair and drop earrings, who is mid-step and engrossed in a book and who coordinates perfectly with the kitchen she is placed beside. Alongside the other picture-perfect kitchen, with its blue accents and curtains, is a separate cut-out of a mother and daughter who are beaming at each other in their matching double-breasted blue dressing gowns. In the context of the other collages in this particular scrapbook, they can be seen as an exploration and contestation of American consumer culture, as "dream kitchens" and "Mommy-and-Me" sleepwear were certainly big-business at midcentury.[18] Brain has suggested,

> These figures, Plath implies, are part of the sale: accessories. But neither came with the advert. Plath found them and put them alongside, but not in the pictures; no human beings dirty or disorder what rests inside the perfect frames.
>
> (92)

However the disconnect in these collages between housecoat-clad domestic goddesses and the spaces of domesticity they should traditionally inhabit appears to be more reflective of Plath's own ambivalence about the identities of wife and mother. Thus, these collages can be seen as early evidence of the way in which Plath would engage with sleepwear as a way to question, reject, embrace, and ultimately understand her changing identity as a wife and mother.

Plath had always been especially sensitive to images of women in domestic space, often drawing her mother and grandmother in housedresses while performing exhausting and near-constant housework (*Eye Rhymes*, pl. 5). As Plath began to increasingly consider her own selfhood as a wife and mother, she looked to the clothing that comprised the image of a housewife in magazines: housecoats, dressing gowns, fluffy slippers, and nightgowns with feminine flourishes. The same magazines that likely provided Plath with her collage images were exactly the ones that Plath would read into adulthood, including through her marriage and journey into motherhood, and where such literature consistently linked sleepwear with the identities of wives and mothers, and using such

---

[18]*The Other Sylvia Plath*. For Mommy-and-Me sleepwear, see "Fashions for the Nicest Hours of the Day," 97 and 105; "Nine Nice Reasons for Staying Home," 88 and 91; Cover, *Ladies' Home Journal*, December 1950. See also n. 20.

at-home clothes as the yardsticks by which a successful homemaker could be measured.[19] The most consistent message of sleepwear advertising and magazine features for mothers and wives was: "think of your audience." "It's more important for a wife to look pretty across the breakfast table than across a crowded room" (Norman 187), *Ladies' Home Journal* cautioned, while *Good Housekeeping* reminded readers that a "pretty Mother" has "Proud Little Girls" ("You're the Prettiest Mommy on Earth" 56). *Parents' Magazine* offered the most pointed and ominous counsel that "your children are looking at you," and it was the sight of "mother crisp and morning-bright over the breakfast table" that would rank highly among "the cherished memories to your children, long after they've grown up" (Green and Tucker 111).

Plath appears to have been familiar with such prevailing ideas and did occasionally feel pressure, almost in spite of herself. Although she seemed to believe that her husband, "who sees me sick, ugly, sallow, sneezy & hugs me, holds me," loved her regardless of her domestic style, she would despondently note the occasions when she was "in Ted's woolen bathrobe, my long practical & unlovely peach flannel nightgown & black wool knee socks," essentially self-policing her behavior and appearance at home in such a way as to remain vigilant of her husband and children's perception of her (J 361, 364). Creating a parallel with the way in which, as Deborah Nelson has noted, "Plath works in various poems to unsettle the idea of the home as a place in which to withdraw from scrutiny," sleepwear is configured as another part of the performance of midcentury domesticity ("Plath, History and Politics" 32). In fact, Plath's efforts to establish her wifely/motherly identities became even more forthright, once even chastising her lack of at-home sleepwear womanliness and issuing herself the instruction: "Must get my hair cut next week. Symbolic: get over instinct to be a dowdy lip-biting little girl. Get bathrobe and slippers and nightgown & work on femininity" (J 467). If the deep-seated sense of unhappiness and dissatisfaction that many women experienced at midcentury was called "the problem that has no name" by Betty Friedan, then it seems that sleepwear, clothing that is ostensibly "unseen," most overtly displayed the challenges and frustrations these women faced (57).

However, at times, Plath seemed to experience great satisfaction when her sleepwear lived up to prevailing notions of how a wife "should" look within her home, as if that secured this part of her identity and status. For example, one common suggestion for wifely style was to be both in and of the domestic space. Perhaps best explained by designer Anne Fogarty in her 1959 book, *Wife Dressing*,

> [a] good approach to co-ordination is: Whatever you're buying, keep a picture of the whole in your mind. ... when you're choosing new lounging pyjamas or a hostess gown, conjure up a mental image of how you will look curled up in the big chair near the window or across the tufted bench beside the fireplace.
>
> (71)

As an intensely visual person, Plath instinctually found sleepwear to be a way to not only experiment with patterns and design (she once noted the coordination of the "[p]urple roses on my white flannel nightgown, pink roses on quatre-foil pink ground of

---

[19]Sometimes, this was particularly explicit, as in the following article in which a suburban housewife reports that, thanks to the morning tradition of waving one's husband and children off for the day each morning, "[t]here is great rivalry over who has the prettiest housecoat and any nonconformist who should dare not to appear is considered a very poor homemaker" (Leshan 126–7).

wallpaper" [*J* 311]), but also emotionally revel in her identity, especially when she was a new wife. She once described a scene of such marital bliss, wherein her "gilt bordered" leopard print slippers complemented the subtle sheen of the "blond-brown" coffee table and the "dull inner glow" put forth by the highlights of the "pewter sugar bowl," while her husband rested there alongside her (*J* 327). Thus, Plath's engagement with sleepwear as a performative gesture to assert her identity as a wife suggests a kind of thoughtfulness and a formal attention to the melding of self and home, but also the instability of this connection. The sense of performing the role of the wife through the most intimate sleepwear clothes of home provides the most illuminating example of Nelson's assertion that, for Plath, home's "theatricality indicates that it is not a place of authentic selfhood[.] … The home is as much a place for masks as the theatre of public life" ("Plath, History and Politics" 33).

Interestingly, Plath felt most proud and sure of herself as a mother, not by actually wearing sleepwear in a performative gesture but in the act of *making* sleepwear. From the winter of 1959, Plath expressed a renewed interest in handcrafts more traditionally associated with women, and although she expressed an interest in making children's clothes, she first experimented with making a braided rug (*J* 460; 466; 483). Establishing a generational connection to the handcrafts of women coincided with visits to other young female friends and their babies that prompted Plath to announce that she finally "[f]elt part of young womanhood. … men don't interest me at all now, only women and womentalk" (*J* 466). The following year Plath wrote to her mother detailing her progression to a "new and exciting hobby" of clothes making:

> Yesterday I completely cut out and basted … the little nightgown (in a one-year size.) It is exquisite. … I pinned the nightgown together to see what it would be like & it's a little fairytale thing. … My next purchase I'll save up for is a sewing machine!, I don't know when anything has given me as much pleasure as putting together the flannel nighty for Frieda—the pieces are so little they are very quickly done. … I am awfully proud of making clothes for little Frieda.
>
> (*L2* 522–3)

To make a nightgown for a child was both a product of the time (making children's sleepwear was heavily promoted in women's magazines as a positive motherly activity) and a poignant experience: this is the garment worn by a baby in the quietest, most intimate moments between a mother and a daughter.[20] Thus, Plath embraced sleepwear as a way to validate and confirm her own identity as a mother participating in these emotional and material expressions of motherhood.

In a similar engagement with sleepwear in a non-performative manner, Plath placed sleepwear at the center of family rituals and traditions. On Easter, for example, Plath celebrated by wearing, "my new white nylon nightgown with red roses, very small, embroidered on the collar" (a new nightgown was a special kind of restorative treat for Plath), and by filling "Ted's slippers with a chocolate rabbit & ten tiny chocolate eggs, each wrapped in a different color of tinfoil—green spots on silver, gold mottling, streaked peacock blue. I believe he has eaten them all" (*J* 362). Plath took sleepwear garments

---

[20] "*Good Housekeeping*'s Simplicity Patterns: Make Sweet Sleep-Timers," 277–80; "*Good Housekeeping* Simplicity Patterns: Nighttime Nostalgia," 239–41; O'Leary, 80. Note, too, that in Plath's short story, "Day of Success," a character makes a little nightgown while her child sleeps, see *JP* 87.

that were increasingly coded and charged with broader social, cultural, and gendered significance and restored them, or rather reconfigured them, as expressions of intimacy and shared family experiences, which appeared to be a tonic for Plath as she worked to build her home and her family life.

It is significant that in his poem, "The Shot," Ted Hughes laments that all he could ever truly grasp of Sylvia was "[a] wisp of your hair, your ring, your watch, your nightgown," the most intimate of items that defined Plath as a wife to him (*TH:CP* 1053). These are more than mere totems: a nightgown or a wedding ring are items that strike at the heart of intimate human connections and represent the material culture of daily lives. For Hughes, the nightgown is the fabric of rituals and traditions shared between a man, wife, and a family and, in this case, one of the most representative garments of Plath in her identity as a wife in their day-to-day existence.

Thus, Plath experienced sleepwear in her navigation of her identities as wife and mother as a performative gesture, but often more successfully as a way to reinforce familial traditions and rituals to establish a bond with her children.

## PLATH AS WRITER AND SLEEPWEAR

In Plath's 1962 essay, "A Comparison," the narrator announces,

> How I envy the novelist! … To her, this fortunate one, what is there that *isn't* relevant! Old shoes can be used, doorknobs, air letters, flannel nightgowns, cathedrals, nail varnish, jet planes, rose arbors and budgerigars.
>
> (*JP* 62)

The narrator, possibly Plath herself, envied the novelist who could rely on the abundance of detail even "flannel nightgowns" could tell you about the wearer, and truly take the time to unpack that particular woman's life, mood, emotional state, marital status, rituals—her life. She described the novelist as being gifted a kind of "X-Ray vision" with all the tools at her disposal to tell a story, build a character, and to "pierce" "the psychic interiors of her neighbors" (*JP* 62). In many ways, this describes what happens when we look at Sylvia Plath and sleepwear: in her own private life, in her art, and in her writing, we are given exactly that kind of "X-ray" vision, we get to see midcentury social and cultural expectations and norms, the intimacy of a marriage and family, and the way in which Plath herself gravitated toward sleepwear throughout different phases of her life, through different identities. But this also explains how Plath handled sleepwear as a writer. As Tracy Brain has observed, "Plath's poems and prose forge new patterns[.] … They make us think freshly about what subject matter and forms can be the province of literature" (*The Other Sylvia Plath* 144). As a writer, Plath understood sleepwear's propensity to articulate aspects of a character's private behavior, private relationships, and private worlds, and she parlayed the details of this intimate category of clothing with inventiveness and astute observations into identity, emotional significance, and expressive detail across her writings.

Sleepwear can be seen as a particularly vital way in which Plath achieves her ambition "to write funny & tender women's storys [sic]" (*J* 412).[21] In several of her prose works,

---

[21] See also Leonard, 62–3.

Plath uses sleepwear as a literary device to introduce characters, define different character traits, explore female group dynamics and different national sleepwear traditions—deftly exploring the "tender" emotional elements of women's experience at the midcentury and the broader cultural connotations of sleepwear, while also exploiting the comedy often inherent in sleepwear as a private style made public. In "Stone Boy with Dolphin," for example, sleepwear is used to indicate the humorous cultural differences that protagonist, Dody, an American student in England, notices in her new dormitory: the American students wore "pajamas to breakfast under their bathrobes," while, by contrast, "[a]ll British girls in the college came down fully dressed and starched for their morning hot tea, kippers and white bread" (JP 183).[22] In *The Bell Jar*, too, detailed sleepwear descriptions are used to indicate that Doreen not only wore the most glamorous, sexualized sleepwear styles but was the most daring and experienced young woman in the group. While most of the girls "had starched cotton summer nighties and quilted housecoats, or maybe terry-cloth robes that doubled as beachcoats," Doreen "wore these full-length nylon and lace jobs you could half see through, and dressing gowns the color of skin, that stuck to her by some kind of electricity" (B 5). Interestingly, Plath incorporates sleepwear here both as a character device and as a way to highlight the different feminine "types" that she, the other *Mademoiselle* guest editors, and young women in general, had been exposed to at midcentury, creating a subtle microcosm of the sleepwear industry's contemporary messaging.

Plath employed sleepwear particularly evocatively in her writing at times of extreme intimacy and times of uncomfortable brutality, deploying sleepwear's relationship with the mundane and/or intimate to conjure greater emotional resonance. In the poem, "Morning Song," which includes the lines, "One cry, and I stumble from bed, cow-heavy and floral / In my Victorian nightgown. / Your mouth opens clean as a cat's," the Victorian nightgown becomes the embodiment of a new mother, highly reflective of the pseudo-nostalgia that surrounded the garment's resurgence in popularity at the time Plath wrote the poem (CP 157).[23] Through Plath's poetry, it is aligned with a nurturing image of generational mother–daughter closeness, and, as the garment of a breastfeeding mother, it is emotionally connected to life-giving energy.

By stark contrast, when Esther Greenwood initially considers suicide in *The Bell Jar*, she attempts suicide not only by sleepwear, but by "the silk cord of my mother's yellow bathrobe" (B 158). The stark imagery of the yellow robe cord is compounded by the tortured emotional connection between a mother and a daughter, rendering the belt a twisted metaphor for an umbilical cord. That intimacy is even further corrupted when Esther cannot find a place in the house to hang the rope and then sits "on the edge of my mother's bed and tried pulling the cord tight" (B 159). It is the ultimate rejection of the idealized midcentury "Mommy-and-Me" sleepwear imagery and the suggestion that these at-home garments cultivate an unbreakable bond between a mother and child, and that these roles are the key to happiness and fulfillment for women.

---

[22]Later, Dody rather comically imagines Miss Minchell being exposed in all her sleepwear glory in the middle of the night, "bursting out of her room on the landing between the first and second stair, raging in her red flannel bathrobe, her hair undone for the night from the bun and hanging in a straight black braid down her back" (JP 198–9).
[23]For Victorian Nightgowns, see "*Good Housekeeping* Simplicity Patterns: Nighttime Nostalgia," 239–41; "What Transatlantic Visitors Buy in the USA," 172.

Interestingly, it was not just the content of Plath's writing but her *process* as a writer that remained tied to sleepwear. As a working mother, Plath made a conscious effort to focus on writing in the mornings, and, much like her Smith uniform of robe and typewriter, she stayed in sleepwear to write "on the principle that all housework wait till after noon" (*J* 644). Describing the chaotic scene that would invariably unfold, Plath described how the Nurse and Ted would be rushing upstairs, where she "would be in my pink fluffy bathrobe (over my layers of maternity clothes, for warmth), and … [Nurse D.] would say 'artist's outfit'" (*J* 644), before discovering the neglected housework. This moment is a culmination of the many selfhoods that Plath was attempting to understand: maternity clothes, a frothy and overtly feminine pink robe, furiously typing away in her study with a husband rushing in to meet her. Here, Plath offers an independent interpretation of what sleepwear could represent for a woman, inventing her own rules to fulfill *all* aspects of herself.

Thus, through the "X-Ray" vision that Plath's journals, art, prose, and poetry afford us, we are able to see midcentury social and cultural expectations and limitations, the intimacy of a marriage and family, and the way in which Plath herself understood—and performed a relation to sleepwear—in the formation and exploration of different identities throughout her life.

# CHAPTER THREE

# Psychiatric Disability and Asylum Fiction: From *The Snake Pit* to *The Bell Jar*

ELIZABETH J. DONALDSON

Despite Sylvia Plath's iconic association with mental illness and the overwhelming body of scholarship that interprets her work through her psychiatric history and diagnoses, disability studies approaches which would challenge these pathologized and medicalized readings of Plath have been underexplored. Two notable recent exceptions from the field of feminist disability studies include Rose Miyatsu's "'Hundreds of People Like Me': A Search for a Mad Community in *The Bell Jar*" (2018) and Maria Rovito's "Toward a New Madwoman Theory: Reckoning the Pathologization of Sylvia Plath" (2020). These essays bring novel insights to Plath scholarship by respectively noting the communal within the illness experience and the power of writing and mad identity. Although Maria Farland's "Sylvia Plath's Anti-Psychiatry" (2002) does not explicitly invoke or cite disability scholarship, its subject matter and approach are very much in keeping with projects like Rovito's, which aim to bring mad studies and c/s/x (consumer/survivor/ex-patient) perspectives and history into literary studies.

In this chapter, also from a feminist disability studies standpoint, I place Sylvia Plath's *The Bell Jar* and "Johnny Panic and the Bible of Dreams" within a modern tradition of autobiographically based fiction about psychiatric disability in American literature. It begins with Mary Jane Ward's blockbuster book *The Snake Pit* (1946) and its companion feature film, which were part of a larger change in the discourse of mental illness in the postwar United States. Ward's book, and her later advocacy work, helped to make the hidden world of asylum life more visible to the public and helped to foster empathy for the experiences of people disabled by mental illness. Furthermore, Ward's narrative established literary conventions of asylum fiction that are later reflected in Plath's *The Bell Jar* and "Johnny Panic and the Bible of Dreams." As Luke Ferretter notes, the film version of *The Snake Pit* "may be the most formative influence of all on *The Bell Jar*, in that it provided Plath with a narrative framework not only for her novel but also for the very experience on which the novel is based" (*Sylvia Plath's Fiction* 49). Reading Ward's and Plath's work together from a feminist disability studies perspective reveals the writers' common concerns and similar strategies for critiquing psychiatric care and describing the inner experience of mental illness.

Together these works reveal how writers with mental illness respond to the "spoiled identity" of the asylum patient. Coined by Erving Goffman in *Stigma: Notes on the*

*Management of a Spoiled Identity* (1963), this phrase describes the alienating, harmful effect that stigma has on a person's identity. Goffman's work is a classic text for scholars of disability studies because his concept of stigma became foundational for thinking about disability as a minority identity category. Stigma is fluid and social, Goffman explains; it is ascribed, for example, to addicts, to gay people, to people of color, to the bodies of people with physical disabilities, who are then discredited as a group. People who bear stigma are distinguished from those with "normal" identities, those who do not bear the mark of stigma. For people with mental illness, the stigma of disability isn't always immediately visible or apparent: therefore, this process of stigmatization can be different for those who have the opportunity to pass as "normal" or to experimentally engage with identity categories. Ward and Plath are both writers who found themselves in this sort of position. They are writers with lived experience of mental illness who conduct experiments with disability identity in their work via the use of fictionalized autobiography, pseudonyms, and also with liminal characters who cross the mental health/mental illness divide by moving from psychiatric professional to psychiatric patient.

## *THE SNAKE PIT* AS ASYLUM ICON AND LITERARY CASE STUDY

In May 1941, writer Mary Jane Ward was admitted to New York's Bellevue Hospital as a psychiatric patient. Within three days of her admittance, Ward was transferred upstate to Rockland State Hospital,[1] a sprawling public psychiatric institution 30 miles north of New York City, where she would spend nine months undergoing treatment that included talk therapy, hydrotherapy (cold water wraps), electroshock therapy, and occupational therapy (or, more properly as Ward points out, just plain "work").

This mental health crisis was an extraordinary rupture in Ward's life and was her first psychiatric hospitalization. Preceding her illness, Ward and her husband, Edward Quayle, had moved from Evanston, Illinois, to New York City to focus on their creative endeavors, with Ward at work on her third novel and Quayle, an insurance executive, at work on a theatrical score. Yet life in New York was stressful. They found comparable circles of socialist groups for friendship and political engagement as they had in the Chicago area, but they were also quickly spending their way through their savings. Ward began to have difficulty with her writing and difficulty sleeping. Then things got worse quickly. By the time she was first hospitalized at Bellevue, Ward was experiencing Capgras-like symptoms: she did not recognize her husband. She would later think that he was an imposter. Ward's treatment with electroshock therapy, which was relatively new at the time, seemed to help. At the end of nine months Ward and Quayle were convinced that she had received the maximum benefit that her stay at Rockland could offer. Ward was successfully discharged in the custody of her husband, and the couple repaired back to Evanston. Ward's return home and her recuperation were challenging, but she did recover and she made clever use of these traumatic experiences in her writing. Her psychiatric break and institutionalization would later become the basis for the autobiographical novel, *The Snake Pit*. She lightly fictionalized her experience: her narrator, "Virginia Cunningham," was a married writer who was transferred from Bellevue to the state

---

[1] This is the same hospital Allen Ginsberg later evokes in *Howl*: "I'm with you in Rockland."

hospital "Juniper Hill," where she stayed for one year (rather than nine months) before returning home to Evanston.²

Though Ward struggled to find a publisher for her manuscript—due in part to wartime paper shortages, the disoriented narrator, and the book's difficult subject—once she landed with Random House it was a perfect match. Anticipating its appeal to women readers (editors watched as Ward's unpublished manuscript speedily worked its way through all the women working in their office as leisure reading), Random House invested heavily in the project, choosing it as a 1946 Book-Club-of-the-Month title, which meant an initial print of 100,000 copies. The book made Ward rich.

*The Snake Pit*'s success also pushed Mary Jane Ward into the public eye, especially after the novel was adapted into a feature film directed by Anatole Litvak and starring the popular actor Olivia de Havilland in 1948. The film's depictions of Ward's story are significant because they opened up the psychiatric patient experience to an even wider audience, who previously had limited, if any, knowledge about the closed world of institutional mental health care.

Sylvia Plath was part of that public, and she was deeply affected by the film. Plath makes an explicit connection to *The Snake Pit* in a letter to her long-time correspondent Edward Cohen, dated December 28, 1953. Plath was writing after her first suicide attempt and during her hospitalization at McLean, the well-respected Harvard-affiliated private psychiatric hospital. She has previously noted in this letter that her peer Jane Anderson is also currently in treatment at McLean. Plath tells Cohen:

> When I entered (in the "middle" ward) she [Jane] was in the highest-ranking ward (where I am writing from now); a display of temper, however, involving her breaking several windows, involved her ending up in the "lowest" ward, and I haven't heard from her since. Somehow, all this reminds me of the deep impression the movie "Snake Pit" made upon me about six years ago. I only hope I don't have any serious relapses, and get out of here in a month or two.
>
> (*L1* 657)

As we see in this letter, *The Snake Pit* provides a lens through which Plath can organize her experience. When she refers to Jane's movement from the highest to the lowest ward, she appropriately recalls the film version of *The Snake Pit*. It's an enduring literary roadmap for Plath. In a journal entry years later, Plath writes: "Must get out SNAKE PIT. There is an increasing market for mental-hospital stuff. I am a fool if I don't relive, recreate it" (*J* 495).³

---

²This change in time from nine months to a year in the novel is significant. It avoids the implication that her stay in the institution symbolizes a birth or rebirth. Instead it is a year, a click of the calendar, or the clock. Just time passing. This temporal imagery is also in keeping with Ward's other autobiographically based psychiatric novel, *Counterclockwise* (1969), which is about a subsequent mental health crisis and state psychiatric hospitalization. I discuss this novel briefly in "*The Snake Pit*: Mary Jane Ward's Asylum Fiction and Mental Health Advocacy" (120–2). My discussion of Ward in this chapter draws heavily from my research at the Mary Jane Ward Collection in the Howard Gotlieb Archival Research Center at Boston University.

³Journal entry of June 13, 1959. I am indebted to Amanda Golden for pointing out that Plath was keenly interested in developing marketable material for herself as a professional writer using her asylum experience. For example, in her copy of *The World Within: Fiction Illuminating Neuroses of Our Time*, now housed at the Lilly Library, Plath had underlined in Mary Louise Aswell's Foreword, "That writers today are interested in the more complex, more intense, character of the neurotic personality is undeniable" (viii). She also drew a line beneath the advice that "one password to popularity is psychiatry" (viii). Again, these previous references are beholden to Amanda Golden's extraordinary archival work.

Faithful to the novel, the film version of *The Snake Pit* follows the narrator's rapid transfers into and out of various wards. Juniper Hill's wards are ranked numerically: patients in Ward 1 have the most privileges, better resources, and are expected to be close to discharge. Patients in higher numbered wards—such as Ward 33, the horrific ward that gives the novel its name—have fewer privileges, scant resources, and are less likely to be released. Plath refers to this hierarchy of health in her letter, hoping to maintain her higher-ranking status and avoid relapse and the fall from grace that Jane has suffered.

In *The Snake Pit*, the main character's abrupt and disorienting movement from one ward to another is a recurring and significant pattern: for example, in the book, a chapter might end in one ward with a small crisis moment, and then the next chapter begins mid-conversation in a different ward, while the narrator, Virginia Cunningham, wonders where she is and how she got there. This seemingly haphazard movement from ward to ward reflects the fact that Virginia doesn't know exactly where she is in the system, and she doesn't know if she is progressing, or getting any better. Virginia starts in Ward 3 and then moves to 1, then 2, then 5, then 12, then 8, then 14, and then, finally, to Ward 33.

Obviously, there are significant differences between the lives that Plath and Ward lived and the narratives that the two writers constructed. For the purposes of this collection, it is worth explicitly noting each writer's distinct asylum context: Ward in a larger public state institution with thousands of beds and scores of wards; Plath in a smaller, private university teaching hospital with hundreds of beds and only three wards for women. This is a distinction that was not lost on Plath herself. The imagery of Ward's *Snake Pit* appears again in *The Bell Jar* when Esther imagines what her life would be like if she were to seek institutional psychiatric care:

> They would want me to have the best of care at first, so they would sink all their money in a private hospital like Doctor Gordon's. Finally, when the money was used up, I would be moved to a state hospital, with hundreds of people like me, in a big cage in the basement.
>
> (160)

This image of a horde of people recalls the film's signature snake pit scene, set in the bowels of the asylum (see Figure 1). The camera focuses on Virginia's desperate face and then zooms upwards, as if looking down into an underground well to show Virginia lost in a sea of writhing bodies as dramatic music plays.

I am reading Plath's use of the film *The Snake Pit* as a cautionary tale here. Yet this is perhaps too simplistic. In this extraordinary snake pit scene, as the camera pulls away for the bird's-eye-view shot, the music builds to an uncomfortably loud, chest-vibrating crescendo, which is gently interrupted and alleviated by Virginia's soft voice, speaking to her psychiatrist, Dr. Kik. A close-up of her face slowly comes into focus again as we switch scenes. A noticeably well Virginia is describing a moment of insight that frees her from her madness and metaphorically frees her mind from this pit of despair: she is still institutionalized but is now on her path toward release. At McLean, Plath writes "of the deep impression the movie 'Snake Pit'" made upon her years ago. Critic Rose Miyatsu reads *The Bell Jar* as "a search for a mad community," a search for connections with others with mental illness, for "hundreds of people like me," and notes that Plath's work has in turn shaped a comparable literary community

FIGURE 1  Still from *The Snake Pit*. [Film] Directed by Anatole Litvak. 20th Century Fox, 1948.

in its wake (67). *The Snake Pit* is also part of that mad community, as Plath's 1953 letter explicitly reminds us. Ward's and Plath's stories are literary beacons that simultaneously warn and guide.

## PSYCHIATRY AND PSEUDONYMS: DOUBLES AND DOUBLE STANDARDS

Both Ward and Plath choose to tell their asylum stories via pseudonyms. In *The Snake Pit*, Ward becomes Virginia Cunningham. In *The Bell Jar*, Plath becomes Esther Greenwood. Plath also published under a pen name, Victoria Lucas, when her novel was first printed in England in 1963; editions appeared under Plath's own name years later in 1966. The decision to write about a personal experience of being in a psychiatric hospital under the guise of fiction is certainly understandable considering the stigma surrounding mental illness. In this context, avoiding the pain of discrimination that attends a spoiled identity seems like a reasonable strategy of self-survival.

Yet it's even more complicated than that for Ward. As Catherine Prendergast writes, "[t]o be disabled mentally is to be disabled rhetorically" (57). A diagnosis of mental illness or a history of being a patient in a mental hospital can undermine a person's authority to speak: "If people think you're crazy," Prendergast states, "they don't listen to you" (57). Moreover, the features of an illness itself can be rhetorically disabling: Ward, for example, faced the problem of telling a story that she could only partially recall. The book is "more fantasy than fact," Ward stated in an interview. "I realized I was writing about a place that lived only in the mind of my protagonist," she continued: "Juniper Hill from tubs to tunnel was built and peopled by a mind that was blacked out—so the accuracy is unreliable" (Woods 65).[4] Ward had no recollection of the first several weeks of her hospitalization or the period immediately preceding her breakdown (Martin 8), and this sort of memory loss and disorientation were recurring features of the severe episodes of her illness, independent of any shock therapy (also called electroconvulsive therapy or ECT), which is well-known for its side effect of memory loss. Yet Ward took this problem—"a mind that was blacked out"—and deployed it strategically (Woods 65): her lapses of memory become a source of suspense and a driving force of the plot in *The Snake Pit*. Ward eventually publicly admitted that, yes, the book was based on her experience. She was Virginia Cunningham. Her willingness to make this revelation, at a time when mental illness was rarely discussed in polite conversation, was an act of bravery, and she leveraged the fame from her book and its companion film in her humanitarian work as a public mental health advocate through the 1950s.

Compared to Ward, Plath's identity in *The Bell Jar* is double-wrapped in pseudonyms, with both the pen name, Victoria Lucas, and the character, Esther Greenwood. Plath's typescript draft for the novel at Smith College indicates that Victoria was also an initial name for the protagonist.[5] Plath may have changed the name to avoid libel (*L2* 683).[6] However, it is through the text's exploration of double standards—sexual and medical— that Plath most directly confronts the spoiled identity issues associated with disability.[7] A large part of *The Bell Jar*'s appeal to me has always been the narrator's rebellion against the sexual double standards she faces. Esther's boyfriend is Buddy Willard, a medical student who has the good timing to contract tuberculosis just as Esther is about to break up with him. Buddy is a "hypocrite" in Esther's mind because while she is expected to be a virgin, he has already had sex with a waitress. This sexual double standard is mirrored by a medical double standard that forgives physical illness, but not mental illness. Just as men are allowed to have a sexual history, while women are not; physical illnesses allow

---

[4]Ward's phrase, "from tubs to tunnel," here refers to the tubs where she received hydrotherapy and the underground tunnel system (a common and convenient feature of state asylums in snowy climates) that connected the buildings at Juniper Hill. For a clinical description of Ward's memory loss and her response to electroconvulsive therapy written by her psychiatrist, "Dr. Kik," see Chrzanowski: Ward is M. Q. (Mary Quayle), or Case 2. I am indebted to Ben Harris at the University of New Hampshire for so generously sharing and bringing this source to my attention.
[5]See https://www.bl.uk/collection-items/typescript-second-draft-of-the-bell-jar-by-sylvia-plath
[6]See Brain's discussion of this revision in *The Other Sylvia Plath*. For further details of the publication and reception of the first edition of *The Bell Jar*, see *Red Comet* (851–3). Clark notes that Plath was reading another widely recognized and popular psychiatric novel, Jennifer Dawson's *The Ha-Ha* (1961) at the time of her death.
[7]My discussion here builds on and riffs off of Luke Ferretter's excellent analysis of sexual double standards in *The Bell Jar* in *Sylvia Plath's Fiction*, as well as his medical historical work in "Just Like the Sort of Drug a Man Would Invent."

recovery and acceptance back into the community, while mental illnesses do not. At the end of the novel, when Buddy is recovering from his tuberculosis, but is still too weak to dig his mother's car out of a snow drift, he has the nerve to ask, "I wonder who'll marry you now, Esther?" (*B* 241). As Esther notes, Buddy asks this question "as if to revenge himself for my digging out the car and his having to stand by" (*B* 241). In this scene, Buddy fails to perform the quintessential roadside performative masculine act of tending to a disabled car. (It's also worth noting that Buddy must borrow a shovel: he doesn't even have the right tool for the job.) Moreover, he finds it disturbing to witness Esther's labor and must look off into the distance. The stigma from the mental hospital will stick to Esther's body, Buddy reminds her here, while looking off into the horizon—the image of a free and limitless future for himself.

An important component of Buddy's future is his nascent career as a physician. As Luke Ferretter has convincingly argued, "Plath's portrayal of American medicine. ... prefigures the concerns of the women's health movement" ("Just Like the Sort of Drug" 136). For example, when Buddy takes Esther to a teaching hospital to witness a birth, Esther is horrified by the procedure and by the Twilight Sleep medication that denies women the memory of the pain of childbirth. The birth at the teaching hospital foreshadows the roles Buddy and Esther will play as future physician and future patient, and the gendered dynamic of those roles.[8] Even as Esther leaves the hospital, she realizes that her cure isn't a linear, one-way process: "How did I know that someday—at college, in Europe, somewhere, anywhere—the bell jar, with its stifling distortions, wouldn't descend again?" (*B* 241). As she leaves she is "born twice—patched, retreaded and approved for the road" (*B* 244). The imagery recalls both the teaching hospital and the trapped car and links gender and disability. Esther's mental disability threatens to be chronic and recursive, but, in a scene that recalls a similar exit interview from *The Snake Pit*, she has come to the boardroom dressed in her power suit, ready to face the hospital physicians: "My stocking seams were straight, my black shoes cracked, but polished, my red wool suit flamboyant as my plans" (*B* 243–4).

## LIMINAL FIGURES OF MADNESS

This final part analyzes two boundary-crossing characters in Ward's and Plath's work: Miss Sommerville from Ward's *The Snake Pit* and the narrator from Plath's "Johnny Panic and the Bible of Dreams." In asylum fiction these types of characters—psychiatric health care professionals who become patients—have become generic conventions. For example, in Edgar Allan Poe's "The System of Dr. Tarr and Prof. Fether," Monsieur Maillard, an asylum superintendent, becomes a patient in his own institution. In *The Silence of the Lambs*, psychiatrist Hannibal Lecter winds up in forensic psychiatric care. In *Batman*, psychologist Dr. Harleen Frances Quinzel, under the influence of her patient

---

[8]Esther will also experience the misogynist practice of psychiatry firsthand from the tone-deaf Dr. Gordon, who can't stop mentioning the pretty girls at her college WAC station during the war. More significantly, Esther undergoes a traumatic round of shock treatment under Dr. Gordon. This treatment is juxtaposed with the highly effective and humane shock treatment therapy Esther later receives from her female physician Dr. Nolan, which is often overlooked by readers today. "All the heat and fear purged itself," Esther explains: "I felt surprisingly at peace. The bell jar hung, suspended, a few feet above my head. I was open to the circulating air" (*B* 215). Despite its depiction in the film, shock therapy was also initially frightening but ultimately curative for Mary Jane Ward's narrator in the novel *The Snake Pit*.

the Joker, transforms into Harley Quinn and eventually becomes an inmate at Arkham Asylum herself. In Ward's and Plath's work, these liminal figures reveal the precarious and unstable distinction between normal identity and spoiled identity.

In the film version of *The Snake Pit*, as a large group of new patients enters, Miss Sommerville, the former nurse who does not realize that she is now a patient, complains, "And we're so crowded already. I just don't know where it's all going to end!" Virginia answers, "I'll tell you where it's going to end, Miss Sommerville. When there are more sick ones than well ones, the sick ones will lock the well ones up."[9] In the novel these latter lines are delivered by the no-nonsense nurse Miss Vance, and they lose some of their bold snap in the film version when they are delivered by Olivia de Haviland, Miss Sommerville, as her friend Nurse Vance explained to Virginia earlier, has been ill for a long time:

> She was a good nurse. But she felt things too much. She tried to get some changes made. It was like beating her head against a stone wall. Worse. The damage was more permanent. But maybe she wasn't such a good nurse. Look at it another way. A good nurse can't be any reformer and that's what Sommerville was. A good nurse has got to take orders and get along with what she has at hand. You aren't supposed to get any ideas.
>
> (*The Snake Pit* 260)

Miss Vance links her friend's illness to her efforts to reform the hospital and her emotional investment in her work ("she felt things too much"). These may be "good" qualities but they are not qualities that are compatible with being a "good nurse." Following orders and making do with limited resources, Vance decides, are better, safer options. At the end of the novel as Nurse Vance helps Virginia pack her things, Miss Somerville becomes worried: she needs to unlock the door so Virginia can leave the ward, but she cannot find her key. As a patient on a locked ward, she no longer has access to a key, of course. However, Miss Sommerville still possesses her notebook, and she maintains a roster of all the patients on the ward, where she faithfully and relentlessly tracks everyone's bowel movements. This obsessive recordkeeping bridges her old career as a nurse and her new role as a patient. In the final pages of the novel, Miss Sommerville releases Virginia by erasing her name from her shadow roster: "She held the book out to Virginia. 'See. You're gone'" (*The Snake Pit* 278).

Plath's narrator from the short story "Johnny Panic and the Bible of Dreams" shares Miss Sommerville's unwavering commitment to documenting madness. In "Johnny Panic," the narrator extends her daytime work of transcribing psychiatric patient interviews for her physician boss and produces a second copy of the same material for herself and her other boss, Johnny Panic, or madness itself, by writing at night.[10] The anti-Bartleby, she won't stop writing. In fact, she is so inspired, she no longer needs an original written source: "I am at the point of re-creating dreams that are not even written down at all" (*JP* 160).

---

[9] The idea that "the sick ones will lock the well ones up" may be an allusion to Poe's comic short story "The System of Dr. Tarr and Prof. Fether" (1845), in which the inmates seize control of the asylum.

[10] See Helle for discussion of Plath's work as a medical secretary in the Adult Psychiatric Clinic and detailed description of the electronic transcription device ("Electroshock Therapy and Plath's Convulsive Poetics" 268–71).

"There is a certain spiritual purity about this kind of doctoring," the narrator of "Johnny Panic" claims about her office's talk therapy (159). Yet her workspace is one that is continually subject to the "rude invasions of [the] other clinics" (*JP* 159). There is no physical purity in this crip gothic space. Boundaries are always being penetrated—thresholds, crossed. Tuesdays and Thursdays their offices are used for lumbar punctures. In the mornings the Nerve Clinic patients next door cry for hours. The narrator's quest for privacy in order to read the old record books is impinged upon by the Head Secretary, Miss Taylor, whose lame left leg announces her arrival. The Amputee Clinic is around the corner, and the sounds of strangers' peglegs, mistaken for Miss Taylor, cause the narrator anxiety. When the narrator finally succeeds in cocooning herself into the office overnight with the record books, she is discovered by the Clinic Director, taken through "barren rat tunnels, to an all-night elevator run by a one-armed" man (*JP* 169), up to the Observation Ward for shock treatment. When she enters this space, presumably she becomes a patient herself, part of the bureaucracy of madness in a new way.

The narrator of "Johnny Panic" and Miss Sommerville are both liminal figures who destabilize the boundary between psychiatric professional and psychiatric patient. With Sommerville's character, Ward points to a larger problem of the difficulty of reforming the mental health system and the psychological cost of social reform on activists, which is something she knew all too well. "Johnny Panic" parodies the study of mental illness and psychoanalysis.[11] The narrator of "Johnny Panic" meets a rather flamboyant and terrifying end: "the twenty-story leap, the rope at the throat, the knife at the heart" (172). Yet in true Plath fashion, this character has its double, or verso liminal figure: the asylum librarian from *The Bell Jar*. A former patient, she now works in the asylum. As Esther waits for her exit interview, she thinks about the librarian's life: "Glancing at her—myopic, spinsterish, effaced—I wondered how she knew she had graduated at all, and, unlike her clients, was whole and well" (*B* 243). For both Ward and Plath, writing autobiographical fiction about their asylum experiences became a way to know that they had graduated and that they were relatively whole and well. Ward's and Plath's asylum fiction gave them the vehicle to critique psychiatric care and to describe the inner experience of mental illness.

---

[11]See also Britzolakis, "Dreamwork: Sylvia Plath's Cold War Modernism."

CHAPTER FOUR

# Sylvia Plath's Cambridge

DI BEDDOW

Sylvia Plath arrived in Cambridge in October 1955, having received a prestigious Fulbright Fellowship.[1] She attended Newnham College, one of the women's colleges situated just outside the main university center of the town. Soon after her arrival, she wrote home to her mother that the city "is the most beautiful spot in the world" (*L1* 966). Plath later added: "[A] kind of golden promise hovers in the air along the Cam and in the quaint crooked streets" (*L1* 969). Note that Plath does not pick out the colleges as the source of this potential, but instead the streets and the river, which form a richer source of inspiration for her poetry, both in Cambridge and later in her career. For too long, critics have missed a vital and exciting time in Plath's work; they have been looking at the University of Cambridge, what locals call the "gown" that is recognized worldwide, but Plath was experiencing and reinterpreting the "town," bringing a fresh lens to bear upon nature, her environment, and emotion. For a distinctive source of her poetic inspiration therefore, put simply, they have been looking in the wrong place. Ultimately, Plath's poetry forms a palimpsest of experience of the city beyond the traditional lens of the historic university. She has left us with a collection of poems which fulfilled her early desire: "I must make my own Cambridge" (*L1* 969).

## NEWNHAM AND COLLOQUIAL LANDSCAPES

In Al Alvarez's 1969 article on Plath's "Cambridge Collection,"[2] he describes her process of paring down the inessential in her work until she achieved "utterly authentic simplicity—at once highly disciplined, highly charged and colloquial" (246). This colloquialism develops at a pace during the Cambridge period, specifically in the interpretation of her subject matter, which originates significantly from Plath's immediate environment around Newnham College. During her first year at Newnham, Plath lived in Whitstead, a large, draughty, white house just off the Barton Road and across the playing fields and gardens from the main college. Here the college housed overseas students, so Plath found herself amongst South Africans and fellow Americans as well as one or two home students. She had a room in the eaves on the third floor, which she described in detail

---

[1] A one-year scholarship, renewable for the second year.
[2] The so-called "Cambridge Collection" or "Cambridge Manuscript" was submitted for the English Tripos examinations in May 1957. An optional paper, which could supplement the mandatory examinations, Plath sent in her compilation of poems she entitled "Two Lovers and a Beachcomber." A partial copy is in the Plath Collection at Smith and a full copy in the Alvarez Papers, Add. MS 88589, British Library.

in letters home,³ taking especial delight in its window seat and the view from it: "I can see out into the Whitstead garden to trees where large black rooks (ravens) fly over quaint red tiled rooftops with their chimney pots" (*L1* 966). From Whitstead, Plath would make her way to lectures across a grazing area with small tributaries and sluices, rough pasture, and meadow vegetation, following the old course of the Cam across the Fen Causeway and the Mill Bridge into town. Away from town, she could walk through the Newnham streets or riverside pathways onto Grantchester Meadows. In his own terms, Ted Hughes described this area, often missed by the tourists, in a poem omitted from his final cut for *Birthday Letters* published over forty years after the Cambridge period. Poem "X," or "Cambridge was our courtship,"⁴ describes the Newnham area in a strangely mournful and rather sinister depiction of a place that Hughes cites as important to the couple when they were first in love. From a distance of years of loss and controversy, Hughes sets the landscape in anti-romantic language with melancholy willow trees, pollarded in places, with ducks and swans gliding silently on the Cam that Hughes terms as "slippery" and "lapsing." It is the river which connects the worlds of trade and academia in Cambridge, or "town" and "gown," but the Cam also leads one away from the city and into another setting entirely; the meadows here are the watery world which Plath employs in many of her Cambridge poems; Hughes then remembers and acknowledges the importance of the area in the unpublished "X." He claims it as their own by stating: "That was our place."

## PLATH'S WATERY WORLD

Plath's first depiction of this lesser-known part of Cambridge is seen in "Winter Landscape, with Rooks" (*CP* 21) from February 1956. The poem was inspired by a journey across the water meadows when she caught sight of rooks as she made her way to her "History of Tragedy" seminar on *Macbeth* with Theodore Redpath.⁵ The class was in Grove Lodge on Trumpington Street,⁶ which meant walking through the snow to town. From the initial impression of the birds about the fen, she recreates the landscape, reflecting a state of mind where a swan floats in defiance of the rush of water cascading through the stone sluice in the "millrace." The speaker's mind is "clouded" and unhappy (the poem is of the time Plath had been spurned by Richard Sassoon), and she identifies with the lonely bird, wanting the reflection to be sucked into a world under water and away from the "bleak place" in which she walks. She is tormented with her life passing, "the folding up of the phenomenal world, leaving nothing" (*J* 204). It is as though the world in which she lives is merely some kind of beautiful origami, which tidies itself away unless she can create something from it. Plath finds some consolation to mortality with her writing, creating something new from her experience which is then intended for publication. Using her

---

³Plath to Gordon Lameyer (*L1* 987), Olive Higgins Prouty (*L1* 999), as well as her mother (*L1* 966). She draws the room out in the latter letter and tells much of her daily routine and her home-making activities, buying furniture, prints, flowers, and fruit.
⁴"X" is from Hughes's exercise book labeled "18 Rugby Street." Add. MS 889/8/1/6, British Library.
⁵Plath records in her journal that she was waiting, self-consciously amongst the all-male group, but then a student dashed in to tell them that their lecturer had flu. Plath did not regret her late-night reading of the play, in spite of their teacher's absence, as she gained much from identification with the characters: "who commit suicide, adultery, or get murdered, and I believe completely in them for a while. What they say is True" (*J* 204).
⁶Plath wrote in her journal on February 20, 1956: "Noticed rooks squatting black in snow-white fen, gray skies, black trees, mallard-green water. Impressed" (*J* 203).

observation, she works what she calls a "psychic landscape" (*J* 205) into her poem, following the Romantic topos whereby landscape is employed in revealing the thoughts and feelings of the poet. However, she is not reflecting the awe and wonder of nature, but instead, flaneuse-like, she highlights the local environment. Finding inspiration in the domestic, rather than in the sublime, she expresses a personal psychogeography in her poems. This is also noticeable in Plath's student impressions written up as "Leaves from a Cambridge Notebook" for the *Christian Science Monitor*. She includes a sketch of the rooftops from Whitstead and recounts the presence of "ubiquitous large, black ravens, lurching along the ground or hunching darkly in the trees, muttering perhaps, if one listens closely, 'Never-more'" (17).[7]

In spite of the title, "Winter Landscape, with Rooks," it is the swan that takes center stage, being on the edge of two worlds, both above the water and below. The speaker, though, describes herself as a sullen rook, reminding us of Plath's association with rooks, ravens, and crows being sinister harbingers of unhappiness or death.[8] Meanwhile, paradoxically and magnifying the confusion expressed about the surface world and beneath, "[t]he austere sun descends above the fen," has Plath portraying the sun sinking, but "above" the low horizon. The words "descends" and "above" juxtaposed in this way lend an unreality to the scene, whilst the mythical image of the sun as "an orange cyclops-eye" prefaces the alchemical image of it in "Ariel," and the speaker's ride toward dawn's "red / Eye, the cauldron of morning" (*CP* 21, 239–40).[9] This area of water meadows and the poems that capture it evoke the Cambridge that Plath knew, both the unreal nature of the university and the threat of her self-doubt and otherness, which could lure her into a strange, watery escapism.

## WATER AND EARTH/PLATH AND HUGHES

While part of the pathography around Plath's Cambridge poems derives from the poet herself (she says, for example, that the poems which formed *The Colossus* "quite privately bore [me]"[10]), it is also noticeable that Plath's influence upon Hughes at this time is underrated. Certainly her perception of the local environment contributes much posthumously to *Birthday Letters*,[11] but also to some of Hughes's earlier nature poetry.

---

[7]"Leaves from a Cambridge Notebook." Monday March 5, 1956, 17 and Tuesday March 6, 15. Whilst her reference here is to Poe's *The Raven* and the death of the narrator's wife in the book we are also mindful that Plath was walking to a lecture on *Macbeth* when she is writing this poem. Lady Macbeth describes the king entering her castle to be killed with this bird's symbolism: "The raven himself is hoarse / That croaks the fatal entrance of Duncan / Under my battlements" (*Macbeth* Act 1, Sc 5).
[8]Brain notes this menacing personification and also that Plath changes linguistically in the title for these birds (*The Other Sylvia Plath* 54 and 79n). She alternates rooks and ravens according to the nationality of her audience, although they are not the same species, albeit both members of the crow family.
[9]Lindberg-Seyersted highlights "Winter Landscape, with Rooks" as showing "features that will characterize a great deal of the poetry to come: the color scheme of black, white and red: the theme of loss and frozenness; and the parallel between landscape and human observer" (512).
[10]SP in British Council Interview quoted in "Cambridge Collection," 246.
[11]Nineteen poems of Hughes's collection refer closely to the couple's time and the environment in Cambridge including "Sam" (*TH:CP* 1049–50) which frames itself along "the Barton Road" upon which stood Whitstead. The poem recounts the frightening tale that Plath experienced hanging on to a runaway horse she had hired from the local stables. Plath's 1958 poem, "Whiteness I Remember" (*CP* 102–3), expresses much of the fear of the incident.

Hughes is, for example, clearly influenced by her prolific use of swans as beings caught between two worlds, whether present or past, myth or reality, below or above the water.[12] Heather Clark was one of the first critics to note explicitly that Hughes was very much influenced by Plath as well as *vice versa* (*The Grief of Influence* 49).[13] Clark refers us to Hughes's *Letters* where it is pronounced how he expresses the influence of Plath upon his work when writing from Cambridge to his brother: "As a result of her influence I have written continually and every day better since I met her. She is a very fine critic of my work, and abuses just those parts of it that I daren't confess to myself are unworthy" (*LTH* 46–7).

A Cambridge experience is the focus for such dual writing (where both poets share a theme or respond to each other's work) in Plath's poem "The Lady and the Earthenware Head" (*CP* 69–70) and Hughes's much later poem "The Earthenware Head" from *Birthday Letters* (*TH:CP* 1079–80). Plath had brought with her from Smith a clay likeness that she disliked, but was superstitious about discarding. She was tempted with giving it a grave in the river, but she rejected this because she felt that it would call to her from "watery aspic," like the sirens in the Lorelei legend, "[l]ewdly beckoning" (*CP* 69). Imagining that the head must have fallen from the willow bole in which they placed it in Grantchester Meadows, Hughes recreates it in his poem as Plath's deathly image in the river where it still "kisses the Father / Mudded at the bottom of the Cam" (*TH:CP* 1080). It is only disturbed by strangely ethereal punters making their way to Grantchester and the tourist's "honey / And the stopped clock" (*TH:CP* 1080). Both poems carry the poets' personal intentions but amplify the difference between poetry and Plath's joyful letters about walks the couple took along the Cam at Grantchester Meadows—her beautiful sketches of cattle and willow trees (*Drawings*) and the naive idyll that is commonly gleaned by a superficial reading of Plath's Cambridge work.[14]

The River Cam provides a further point of access for the phantasmagorical underwater world in Plath's poetry when she writes "All the Dead Dears" (*CP* 70–1). This poem shows Plath reflecting on mortality, triggered by the skeleton of a woman, a mouse, and a shrew in the Museum of Archaeology and Anthropology in Cambridge. The coffin was found in 1952 when a housing estate was being built in the north of Cambridge. The stone casket was placed in the museum in Cambridge's Downing Street, but was later removed due to overcrowding. In 2012, the museum was reopened after refurbishment and the skeleton was put back on display (it had been removed because of overcrowding), prompting a telling journalistic response. The newspaper article captures the pathology of much commentary around Plath's poetry as it describes the skeleton of the woman and

---

[12]The "single swan" in "Winter Landscape, with Rooks" (*CP* 21) is also notably present in Hughes's "Swans": "Each swan glued in her reflection" (*TH:CP* 600).

[13]Clark refers us to examples of Plath's editorial authority, for example, on the Faber proof of *The Hawk in the Rain*: "Ted has made some alterations, which I've limited. He would rewrite a poem to eternity and stop the presses" (*L2* 141).

[14]For example, in Uroff's assessment of Plath's Cambridge nature poems: "In general, these poems (the animal / nature poems inspired by Hughes) are weak" (9). Uroff's commentary on "Watercolor" assumes that Plath has written over-enthusiastically. This speaks to the wider argument about the reception of Plath's writing and the widespread desire to see her poetry as authentic, transparently confessional, and autobiographical, rather than performative or meticulously wrought. Hargrove summarizes many of the disparaging critiques of Plath's early work, noting that it was seen largely as an apprenticeship to *Ariel* or as bearing evidence of her tragic end (18–21).

its gnawed ankle bone, presumably damaged by the mouse and the shrew whose skeletons were also found in the coffin:

> The viewing prompted Plath's 1957 poem All the Dead Dears [sic], in which she describes "this antique museum-cased lady" and the "gimcrack" bones of the rodents "that battened for a day on her ankle-bone," and fears that the "barnacle dead," strangers or members of her family will drag her down and suck her life away. Six years later, the poet killed herself.
>
> ("Gnawed Roman Skeleton")

The value of the poem, too often merely seen as a precursor, an omen to Plath's untimely death, is primarily a testament of a poet expressing a very specific sense of place. The exhibit provokes in Plath a vital response to the "[d]ry witness" (CP 70) with the speaker struck by the passage of life and our closeness to death. Layering traces of mirror imagery, family memories, and children's poetry, Plath leads the reader to appreciate the skeleton's full emotional import, giving it a powerful agency.[15]

Earlier drafts of the poem[16] see Plath refining her focus in "All the Dead Dears," removing sections that detract from her poetic intention to center death as a familiar to life, showing her growing strength in editing her work. One omission, though, remains fascinating. In the anthology, *Poetry from Cambridge 1958*,[17] the final stanza, may allude to both the sorry fate of the skeleton's foot and the moors of *Wuthering Heights* and Cathy begging to be allowed in at the window. At the same time, Otto Plath's bees appear to flood the poet's mind (*Poetry from Cambridge* 41):

> And to sanctuary:
> Like the footless woman
> Keening out of the blizzard
> Who flies against the wind when snow
> Hisses, to vamp for bed and board
> In the guise of my sister. Still they'll swarm in.
>
> (*Poetry from Cambridge* 42)

Plath rejects this stanza, though, adhering more closely to her local, earthy inspiration. From this she extracts her acceptance of the relentless passage of the life cycle, weaving in the watery nature of past and present landscapes. In a mirror, the speaker sees her forbears in her own reflection and feels them reaching out "hag hands" to "haul" her into a death where a father floats up to the top of a pond to meet her. The two images, both reflection from the mirror and the underwater nature of the drowning father, forge a strong link to the way in which she described her father's death in the 1962 piece "Ocean

---

[15] Plath's image of "the daft father" under water, for example, chillingly recalls Alfred Noyes's "When Daddy Fell into the Pond" with the Daddy "crawling out of the duckweed" and the quacking "as if they were daft." Referenced originally by Hargrove (114).

[16] Hargrove details an excellent trail of the poem's drafts (112–16), but the note on the exhibit of the woman being off display highlights the 1994 publication of her text.

[17] In a 1959 letter, Plath informs Hughes's parents of the inclusion of both poets' work in this anthology, edited by Levenson (L2 300).

1212-W" (*JP* 21–7) as cutting off her childhood happiness by the sea. In Cambridge, Plath employs her "infant gills" in order to "pierce that looking-glass" (*JP* 21). She reconfigures the dank fen and what is uncovered in its sodden earth into her own poetic environment.

This personal evocation of place in Cambridge remains strong after leaving the city. While poems Plath composed in Cambridge, such as "Resolve," "Winter Landscape, with Rooks," "Black Rook in Rainy Weather," "The Lady and the Earthenware Head," and "All the Dead Dears," evidence that strong sense of place in Plath's poetry, it is a little later that she is able to draw upon her portfolio of past landscapes, including those of the Cambridge period, to greatest effect. Effortlessly matching a past landscape to the mood she is conveying gives us her best-known Cambridge poem.

## WATERCOLOR

Nearly two years after she had left Cambridge, Plath wrote "Watercolor of Grantchester Meadows" in 1959 (*CP* 111–2). The poem is significantly called a painting, a "watercolor." It is a scene described in a watery wash of idyllic beauty, but Plath introduces a darkness, which is hidden beneath the traditional vision of Cambridge. Tracy Brain summarizes this jarring of worlds: "the delicacy of a watercolor is subverted. … Here, only those who don't belong can see the landscape's darker subtext, the predators and prey hiding in the seemingly benign meadows" (*The Other Sylvia Plath* 65). Even in the reflections of the blossom and the willows in the Cam, Plath describes a hidden "[w]orld under the sheer water" (*CP* 112).

The poem begins with a seasonally traditional picture of lambs in a pen and a simile of the spring air "silvered as water in a glass" (*CP* 111), which constrains the world just as the lambs are penned in. We move to the sense of sound, and Plath emphasizes the quiet of the environment, so quiet that the shrew chattering is audible. The tiny birds fit into the Lilliputian world she creates, being "of good color" (*CP* 112), a formal phrase suggesting a Chaucerian tone, reminding us of Plath's reading of "The Wife of Bath's Tale" to the cows grazing here (*L2* 107).[18] The hawthorn, the glassy tones, and the diminution in size of the world are captured after a walk, made on her own on February 8, 1957. In a letter of that date to her mother, Plath describes getting up early and after Hughes had left for work.[19] She

> tramped over a mud-puddled path … meadows shining bright silver-wet in the sun … the dark bare trees along the river framing brilliant green meadows. On my right was a knotty, gnarled hawthorn hedge, red haws bright[.] … There was a sudden flurry of rain, and then the sun shed a silver light over everything and I caught a passing rainbow in a pastel arc over the tiny town of Cambridge, where the spires of King's chapel looked like glistening pink sugar spikes on a little cake.
>
> (*L2* 65)

The miniature nature of the university world emphasizes its artificial nature, and the superficial impression of the landscape as "a country on a nursery plate" (*CP* 112)

---

[18] Plath recited for about twenty minutes, standing on a stile. Hughes writes of this again in "Chaucer" in *Birthday Letters* (*TH:CP* 1075) and recalls "[o]ur Chaucer" twice in "St Botolph's" (*TH:CP* 1051).

[19] The couple was by then living at 55 Eltisley Avenue, a short walk from the Meadows; Hughes was teaching at Coleridge School in Cambridge.

resonates with the iced-buns idealism of the architecture of King's. In the same stanza, the Meadows are "Arcadian green" (*CP* 112), suggesting a bursting spring, but the hawthorn has berries from the autumn and spines, which emerge in winter. However, Plath tells us that the spines are hidden "with white," implying that the Maytime flowers are blousing the hedgerows (*CP* 112). All the seasons appear to be rolled together, and this is where Plath expertly guides us from the romantic idyll of perfect nature and infatuated love toward a darker, more ominous threat which she knows is omnipresent in both nature and romance, whatever the appearance, season, or stage of either. Plath has constructed an idealistic, unreal landscape, alluding to Arcadia. She then knocks down the perfect image by stating simply that it is only the "green" of the meadows to which she refers, not the complete scene. Plath appears to be drawing upon the polarities of nature and their impact on the soul as in the joy of spring, looking back to Chaucer[20] and then forward to Eliot's "April is the cruellest month" in *The Waste Land* (*Complete Poems and Plays* 37).[21]

Although Plath has been criticized for romanticizing an American tourist's view of Cambridge,[22] it is when she leaves the university precincts and the visitor hub that it becomes clear that she is keenly aware of the difference between factual observation and imaginative poetry. In her letters home she cites Rupert Brooke to her mother, conscious that she will associate the place with literature, rather than direct observation:

> I can't describe how beautiful it was to go down the little cobbled streets in the pink twilight with the mists rising from the willows along the river and white horses and black cows grazing in the pastures. remember rupert brooke's poem? well, we had tea by a roaring fire at "the orchard" (where they serve tea under flowering trees in spring) and the "clock was set at ten of three."
>
> (*L1* 986)[23]

But then there is the constructed poem; we are reminded again of Eliot's distinction between experience and poetry where he notes that the original observation or inspiration that triggers the desire to create a poem is transformed into something completely different in the process of writing:

> And what is the experience that the poet is so bursting to communicate? By the time it has settled down into a poem it may be so different from the original experience as to be hardly recognisable.
>
> (*The Use of Poetry and the Use of Criticism* 138)

---

[20] Plath knew Chaucer well and had read him alongside Augustine at Cambridge. In a letter to Hughes in October 1956 she draws together the two and also echoes Eliot's use of Augustine in *The Waste Land:* "All afternoon I'd read about: 'To Carthage I came' [from *The Confessions of Saint Augustine*] and about the cauldron of unholy loves singing. Bless Chaucer; bless the Wife of Bath. Bless the strong loving body" (*Ll* 1280).
[21] Plath's copy of *The Waste Land* at Smith contains evidence of her connection of these two poems and their seasonal references (*Complete Poems and Plays* 37).
[22] See above, Uroff, 92.
[23] The editors of the *Letters* note that Plath misquotes Brooke's "The Old Vicarage, Grantchester" which reads: "Stands the church clock at ten to three? / And is there honey still for tea?" (Healy 96–100). Poignantly, before the famous church clock lines, Brooke looks to Grantchester Meadows as "[d]eep meadows yet, for to forget / The lies, and truths, and pain?" (100).

This is poesis, the creative production of something which has not existed before; it is not biographical authenticity, nor is it a pale imitation of Hughes's nature poetry, a criticism which has been leveled at Plath.[24] "Watercolor of Grantchester Meadows" is a sign of an astute awareness of observed and reimagined things, developed with a remembered perception of a landscape and informed by intense poetic discussion taking place between Plath and Hughes.

## FROM CONSCIOUSNESS TO CREATIVITY

Alvarez summarizes Plath's Cambridge poetry as evidencing "a life led at a considerable pitch of awareness, to an unequivocally creative consciousness" ("Cambridge Collection" 247).[25] Plath articulates this very personal transference of observation and appreciation to creation in another Cambridge poem, "Black Rook in Rainy Weather" (CP 56–7). The poem's speaker does not expect a "miracle" (CP 56). At times, however, the most "obtuse objects" can emit a light and then from a "kitchen table or chair" comes a "celestial burning," which gives what might have been an inconsequential moment a precious importance, allowing her to mark it with her writing (CP 57). This moment of epiphany, when an everyday thing quite suddenly proves to be the inspiration for the poet, is celebrated particularly clearly in "Resolve" (CP 52),[26] with the yellowing leaves and the mist. The poet is looking out of her window, probably in Eltisley Avenue,[27] with the milk float yet to arrive and a single-eared cat washing itself. Having described this scene, Plath announces in the very middle of the poem: "no glory descends" (CP 52). However, after noticing the drops of water on her neighbor's "arched" rose bush, the beauty strikes her, and she does more than simply record the scene, but instead the autumn morning transcends description and becomes a symbol of intent with her resolution that she will impress her academic tutors and she will refuse to fight the wind (CP 52). This volta is marked by the line "o bent bow of thorns" (CP 52). A humble scene with a cat, some milk bottles, and a rose bush release Plath's exceptional, cultured perception of her environment and her psyche in a pathetic fallacy. Reminiscent in mood, as Alvarez notes, of the later "Sheep in Fog" (CP 262) and in the same stretched structure of "Mushrooms" (CP 139), "Resolve" sits on the page and takes the eye from sketching line to decisive declaration comfortably and easily. Alvarez describes how in this poem Plath has captured the mood of "slow autumn melancholy in which inner depression fuses inextricably with the blurred, silent weather outside" ("Cambridge Collection" 301). "Resolve" offers an understanding of Eavan Boland's observation on Plath's poetic authority: "This is no

---

[24]Here is Uroff again: "Plath had caught Hughes's enthusiasm for nature without absorbing his intimacy with and feeling for animals; poems like 'Faun' or 'Watercolour [sic] of Grantchester Meadows' exude a fervency for the subject that exceeds her poetic possession of it" (9).

[25]With the permission of Olwyn Hughes, Alvarez printed four poems in the *Cambridge Review*: "Street Song," "Natural History," "Resolve," and "Aerialist." The introduction to the poems gives a brief biography and bibliography of Plath and notes the poems were in a collection of poetry submitted for the English tripos in the university.

[26]Hargrove places "Resolve" in Fall 1956 (94–5).

[27]Hughes had moved into 55 Eltisley Avenue during the Michaelmas Term of 1956 with Plath coming and going from Whitstead until the end of term when she too moved in.

longer a poet being instructed by nature. This is a poet instructing nature."[28] Brain also economically phrases it: "Plath's writing is very much about the things of this world" (*The Other Sylvia Plath* 6).

One such prosaic thing, a symbol of the university, is the academic gown. Plath describes the tradition to her mother soon after arriving in the city: "To class and everywhere after dark we wear our black university gowns, and although it was rather a nuisance at first, I must admit I feel rather proud of the battered old thing now, and enjoy seeing the gowns flap out bat-like as cyclists spin past" (*L1* 981). Plath takes the gown and relates it to her own experience of the town. The students in "Watercolor of Grantchester Meadows" are "[b]lack gowned, but unaware" that "[t]he owl shall stoop from his turret, the rat cry out" (*CP* 112). As Plath and Hughes used swans figuratively, so the owl connects both again in their poetry set in the landscape of Cambridge. In "The Owl," Hughes describes a walk he made with Plath through the meadows and back along "the Grantchester Road" where he performed his "masterpiece," as he calls it, making a cry of a rabbit in pain to summon the bird (*TH:CP* 1064). Plath was most impressed (as one of Hughes's previous girlfriends, Liz Hicklin, had also been).[29] With this context, it appears that Plath is aware of the violence existing in the perceived Arcadia; as the owl swoops in Plath's poem, so Plath feels the attacks of others keenly. A threatening owl, ready to strike, is used again in the unpublished "Megrims," where Plath lists the horrible things that surprise her protagonist during the day.[30] In the 1958 poem "Owl," the city is not protected from aggressive nature: "Rats' teeth gut the city / Shaken by owl cry" (*CP* 102). It is the black, wing-like cloaks though, as ubiquitous in 1950s Cambridge as the rooks that Plath identifies around Newnham, which turn her critics—academic or literary—into strutting corvids.[31] On the day Plath wrote "Winter Landscape, with Rooks," she also recorded in her journal: "Human rooks which say: Fraud" (*J* 204). In "Resolve," Plath finishes the poem, determined not to disappoint her "twelve black-gowned examiners" (*CP* 52). Plath's Cambridge poems are redolent with the power of landscape and nature, but the imagery employed is personal, allowing her to express through it her astute awareness of the uncertainty and fragility of life, time, and happiness.

Carrying the burden of retrospective knowledge, it is difficult for the reader of Plath's life and work in Cambridge to move beyond the meeting with and marriage to Hughes, followed later with her despair and untimely death. With the weight of this tragic love story, arguably one of the most famous of modern literature, coupled with

---

[28]Boland is commenting on Plath's 1962 poems about her baby Nicholas and how she brings the nursery to the Romantic sublimity of nature. Quoted in *Red Comet*, 797.

[29]Hughes tells the story in "The Owl" in *Birthday Letters*; Plath alludes to it in "Faun" (*CP* 35); Liz Hicklin/Grattidge in Liz Hicklin, "Memories of love, poetry and dancing with Ted Hughes," *AGE* newspaper, Sharon Grey Column, "Correspondence and Papers from Ted Hughes to Liz Hicklin," Add MS 89198, British Library. Liz was a nurse at Addenbrooke's Hospital in Cambridge and dated Hughes between the summers of 1953 and 1955.

[30]The poem was found on a carbon paper in the Lilly Library, and it bears both Plath's Whitstead address and that of Eltisley Avenue. More on this find, which contains the print of typed-up poems for Hughes's *Hawk in the Rain* and two unpublished poems, "Megrims" and "To a Refractory Santa Claus," can be found in *These Ghostly Archives* (41–5).

[31]One recalls Woolf on Cambridge in *A Room of One's Own* (1928), before Plath, when Woolf has the temerity to open a library door in the university: "instantly there issued, like a guardian angel barring the way with a flutter of black gown instead of white wings" (9). Plath's 1954 Hogarth Press copy is held at Smith.

the depth of history of an 800-year-old institution in the very streets in which one walks, it is unsurprising that the living nature of Plath's Cambridge poetry has been so neglected. However, it is Plath's lived experience and perceptive awareness of her surroundings which give us important and powerful poems about the environment of Cambridge.

CHAPTER FIVE

# Plath in Space: Feeling the Chill of the Void

TIM HANCOCK

On April 6, 1958, Sylvia Plath recorded in her journal a "queer nightmare—of seeing a new comet or satellite—round, but conical, with the point behind it like a faceted diamond." Having made a tiny sketch, which looks more satellite than comet,[1] she continues:

> I was up somewhere on a dark high place watching it pass overhead like a diamond moon, moving rapidly out of sight & then, suddenly, there were a series of short sharp jerks & I saw the planet halted in a series of still-shot framed exposures, which for some reason was a sight not granted to the human eye, & at once I was lifted, up, my stomach and face toward earth, as if hung perpendicular in mid-air of a room with a pole through my middle & someone twirling me about on it.
>
> (J 362)

Jacqueline Rose has suggested that the imagery in the latter part of this journal entry implies sexual violence, relating it to Plath's desire to break into "the women's magazines" with suitably sensational short stories (*Haunting* 177). Yet it may be that the novel feeling of suspension recorded here is a sign of its times in another way, as—given the context of skywatching and the planetary snapshots that precede it—the dream appears to have been influenced by pioneering space flight activity. By 1958, the earliest satellites had started to add their evocative beeps to what Plath describes in "Lesbos" as "the staticky / Noise of the new" (*CP* 228). Sputnik 1 became the first man-made object to enter orbit in October 1957; the United States responded to this Soviet first with its own Explorer satellite at the end of January in the following year. These two launches marked the beginning of the space race between the world's two postwar superpowers.[2]

Plath's nightmare offers a nice example, then, of how what's in the air (or in this instance, the ionosphere) at any given time can infiltrate the consciousness and be

---

[1] The sketch most resembles Sputnik 3, which was launched (although it failed to make orbit) later that month. See "Sputnik 3."
[2] See Siddiqi 119–70. The nausea that Plath describes later in this journal entry ("my whole equilibrium went off, giddy, as I spun … screaming, sick," *J* 362) may owe something to the stomach-churning activities of the Reduced Gravity Research Program, instituted by the United States Air Force in 1957 with a view to training future astronauts (see "Zero-Gravity Plane").

transformed there by the mysterious processes of the autonomic imagination. Vividly conveying an impression of the distances of space, its atmosphere modulates from wondering contemplation to tortured helplessness, a feeling that was also to accompany imagery of weightlessness in Plath's journal two months later when she described herself as "suspended in the void, the vacuum" (*J* 396). Once more on October 13, 1959, her mind's eye again projected beyond the earth's atmosphere in order to evoke feelings of impotence and isolation:

> Very depressed today. Unable to write a thing. Menacing gods. I feel outcast on a cold star, unable to feel anything but an awful helpless numbness. I look down into the warm, earthy world. Into a nest of lovers' beds, baby cribs, meal tables, all the solid commerce of life in this earth, and feel apart.
>
> (*J* 517)

Janet Malcolm was attempting to account for what she describes as Plath's "heated self-absorption" when she commented that this poet "felt the chill of the void with ... unnerving intensity" (*Silent Woman* 100). Malcolm's phrase, however, could also be applied to these journal entries, and more broadly to an insistent set of images in Plath's later poetry that, I want to suggest, was most likely informed by an awareness of contemporary space exploration. Plath's writing life coincided with humankind's dramatic first voyages beyond the earth's atmosphere. This chapter will argue that contemplation of the newly traversed heavens transformed her perception of her situation within physical space, the chilly void also providing a metaphorical arena wherein she could express the feelings of existential isolation and emotional abandonment that she experienced toward the end of her life.

Plath acknowledged in interviews the influence that "the 'things of this world'" and "issues of the time" had on her writing ("The Living Poet"; *JP* 98), and her work has increasingly been read in light of the zeitgeist of her age.[3] Rose was among the first to recommend that her corpus be reconceived in the context of its times: describing how this poet engaged with the "most traumatic historical moments when a culture comes to haunt ... itself," she rejected critical responses that "situate the woman inside an exclusively personal struggle to express either the self or the non-self" because "[b]oth seem to remove the woman writer from historical process" (*Haunting* 8, 27). Others have since sought to return Plath's work to this process by observing her responses to the fears and tensions that were generated by the Cold War. Tracy Brain, for example, has discussed the significance of Plath's concern about "the effects of nuclear weapons and fallout on human life and health" (*The Other Sylvia Plath* 13). Deborah Nelson has demonstrated Plath's "extraordinary sensitivity to surveillance and the assault on privacy" peculiar to the age, where boundaries between the public and private became blurred (*Pursuing Privacy* 81). Robin Peel has explored features that reflect her "anxiety about international politics" (*Writing Back* 24), suggesting that "it is time to acknowledge that Plath's assimilation of the terror created by the Cold War atmosphere ... plays a crucial role in her writing" ("Body, Word, and Photograph" 95).

Peel, in particular, is interested in Plath's reactions to events from the early years of the space race. Evidence of her (conscious, rather than dream) awareness of these

---

[3]Most recently and extensively in Brain, ed. *Sylvia Plath in Context*.

developing technologies, and of their potential for artistic application, can be found in her 1960 "Eisenhower collage," where a spherical satellite is pasted in directly below the President's torso. Identifying this as the American *Pioneer V* (launched March 11, 1960), Peel suggests that, partnered by the golf ball behind it, the sphere stands in for one of the POTUS's testicles, thus contributing to the artwork's satirical attack on the macho hubris implicit in American technological power.[4] Elsewhere, he identifies one of the many possible sources for the title "Ariel" as an Anglo-American satellite of that name launched into orbit on April 26, 1962, six months before Plath wrote her celebrated poem. Noting that this piece of space hardware was later damaged by a nuclear test (see "Starfish Prime"), Peel argues that the poem reflects "contemporary anxiety about atmospheric tests," with Plath's arrow as a "kind of ballistic missile that will destroy itself and civilization when it creates the cauldron of the nuclear explosion" (*Writing Back* 196).

In 2002, Peel's suggestion that we should read Plath's corpus "with one eye open on contemporary Cold War discourse" offered a salutary corrective to the kind of ahistorical psychoanalytical speculation that had hitherto dominated readings of her work (*Writing Back* 183), although two riders should be added to his comment. Firstly, not all of the telltale marks left from this period were the residue of terror and trauma. In addition to the nuclear fallout of the age, there was also its less conspicuous background radiation; to borrow an image from "Johnny Panic and the Bible of Dreams," not so much the manifest horrors in the universal reservoir of nightmares as the grains of dirt that "seep in among everything else and revolve under some queer power of their own, opaque, ubiquitous[,]" and "so commonplace it seems silly to mention" them (*JP* 26). As the decade progressed, a fascination with space and space exploration became a ubiquitous part of this cultural background, and it seeped into Plath's discourse. It is there, for example, in a September 1962 letter to her psychiatrist Ruth Beuscher, when (seeking a response) Plath writes that she would "rather just have you say 'shut up' than feel my words dangling in space" (*L2* 816). Secondly, the troubled context of this letter reminds us that, if one eye needs to stay open to Cold War discourse in Plath's writing, then the other must stay open to its more personal emotional agendas, not least what she described as "the hurt and wonder of loving" (*JP* 98). "Ariel" is one of several of the October 1962 poems that Peel links to the Cuban Missile Crisis, doing so in order to support his assertion "that Plath's response to the Cold War and other international events at the historical moment in which her children were born, was as much a catalyst for writing as was the end of her marriage" (*Writing Back* 17).[5] But the creative surge that generated these poems had started well before October 22, which is when John F. Kennedy alerted the world to the presence of Soviet missiles in Cuba ("Radio and Television Address to the American People"). The "state of crisis" that Plath herself identified in a letter to Beuscher on the day before Kennedy's broadcast refers to a breakdown of domestic rather than international relations. When Plath writes in this letter that "everything has blown up, blown apart," but that she still has "enough energy to manage fallout" (*L2* 876), her apocalyptic terminology reflects how matters public and private interact within a writer's mind, as emotional pressures

---

[4]"Body" 82. See Mikulka, "Sylvia Plath on War" for Plath's collage. "Untitled collage, probably 1960," box 21, folder 2, Smith.
[5]The poems are "Ariel," "Lady Lazarus," "Nick and the Candlestick," "Cut," and "Poppies in October" (*Writing Back* 189–98).

repurpose ambient cultural material. In this instance, impending Armageddon provided the imagery, personal distress the motivation.

In the interview where Plath draws attention to her interest in "issues of the time," she went on to say that she saw "headline poetry" as likely to be of no more lasting interest "than the headlines" (*JP* 98). Reconceiving her writing as informed by the background drama of contemporary space exploration should not, then, eclipse its more intimate dimension. As Rose rightly maintains, "[t]he division between history and subjectivity, between external and internal reality, the trials of the world and the trials of the mind, is a false one" (*Haunting* 8), and where Plath is concerned, these two dimensions have a habit of implicating each other. It is possible, for example, to take a lead from Peel's political reading of "Ariel" that sends us back to the trying emotional circumstances that she was going through during the summer of 1962. July 9, which is when the high-altitude nuclear test Starfish Prime put the satellite *Ariel 1* out of action, was a traumatic date for the poet as well as the planet: Plath's suspicions of her husband's infidelity were confirmed on this day by an intercepted phone call. She would almost certainly have been aware of the most powerful man-made explosive device ever detonated in space, but did she clock the coincidence? It may also be worth noting that, on September 10 of that year, *The Times (London)* reported that *Ariel I* had, somewhat miraculously, come back to life ("Ariel Satellite Is Still Working"). Was its resurrection from "stasis in darkness" somewhere in the back of Plath's mind when—a few weeks later—she wrote her own poem of crisis and rebirth (*CP* 239)?

Such questions take us into speculative territory; more demonstrable I think is the broader influence that the contemporary preoccupation with space had on this poet's work. Julia Gordon-Bramer has noted how Plath had "appreciated the stars and stargazing since she was in the sixth grade" (*Fixed Stars* xix), although space imagery is relatively incidental in her early published writing, where the dominant celestial body is the moon, which tends to be co-opted for figurative target practice. A teenage Plath, critiquing her own depiction of "a bulbous moon, which sprouts in the soiled indigo sky," recognized her flair for such "illogical, sensuous description" (*J* 87): elsewhere in her journals the moon is "poised like a picture puzzle that had been broken" and "smaller than a penny blue" (*J* 17, 321). In "Admonitions," it "seems smooth as angel-food," and in "Soliloquy of the Solipsist," it is a "celestial onion" (*CP* 319, 37). As well as whimsical similes, she evidently took pleasure in manipulating perspective, looking alternately through both ends of the telescope, as it were. Sometimes the moon seems unfeasibly close, such as when it "leans down to look" in "Love Is a Parallax" (*CP* 330); sometimes it is inaccessibly distant, as in "Metamorphoses of the Moon":

> Cold moons withdraw, refusing to come to terms
> with the pilot who dares all heaven's harms
> to raid the zone where fate begins,
> flings silver gauntlet of his plane at space,
> demanding satisfaction; no duel takes place:
> the mute air merely thins and thins.
>
> (*CP* 307)

The challenge to a duel here is anachronistic and the plane pre-space race technology; at this stage, as the speaker puts it in the next stanza, "sky" is "absolute" and "won't be drawn closer" (*CP* 307). Not only is there no bridging the gap between earth-bound perceiver and the celestial perceived in this poem, but there is also no real sense of the gap itself: in the last line of this stanza the word "merely" reflects a lack of imaginative engagement with this dimension. This is typical of Plath's early visions of space: there is up there and down here but little attention is paid to the distance that lies between, as the juxtaposed images of 1957's "The Everlasting Monday" also indicate:

> The moon's man stands in his shell,
> Bent under a bundle
> Of sticks. The light falls chalk and cold
> Upon our bedspread.
>
> (CP 62)

Early poems that convey some depth of field, and indeed a traversal of this depth, do so in a self-consciously fanciful manner. "Dialogue En Route" anticipates Roald Dahl's *Charlie and the Great Glass Elevator* in its comic book description of a lift that exceeds its remit, shooting "past the forty-ninth floor / to corral the conundrum of space"; "The Princess and the Goblins," a fairy tale, has its wakeful heroine "leave her bed of fever and ascend / a visionary ladder toward the moon" (CP 309, 333). Slightly later, "The Ghost's Leavetaking" envisages an ascent "toward a region where our thick atmosphere / Diminishes." However, this musing is followed by a dismissive shrug ("and God knows what is there"), and subsequent images of "a stellar carrot" and "cows that moo / And moo as they jump over moons" (CP 90–1) are deliberately frivolous. Evidently, at this point, space was not to be taken too seriously. In a letter to her mother, Plath recalled her panoramic observation from an 830-foot high fire tower one memorable night in April 1954 as "a moving and unifying experience," but this contemplation of "the dark unknown" also brought to mind a comic line from a play she had recently seen: "I don't see nothing but nothing, and then more nothing!"[6]

Extraterrestrial flight was, however, about to move from the realm of fiction into that of reality. The launches of *Sputnik I* and *Explorer* were the most prominent achievements of International Geophysical Year, which, running from July 1, 1957, to the end of 1958, both reflected and amplified the contemporary fascination with space exploration. Such interest manifested itself most obviously in the production and popularity of science fiction movies like *Forbidden Planet* (1956), but evidence of its pervasive nature at this time can be found in many areas of contemporary culture, even academic English studies. I owe a debt for the title of this chapter to William Empson, who playfully entitled his controversial 1957 paper on John Donne's post-Copernican cosmology, "Donne the Space Man," noting in an aside that this poet "was interested in getting to another planet much as the kids are nowadays" (338). Empson argues here that Donne found the new idea of plural worlds within a possibly infinite universe liberating (341). As far as Plath is concerned, Malcolm's word "unnerving" might be a better one for the impression that human penetration of the black vacuum was to make on her imagination. Whimsical projections give way to haunting evocations of emptiness in her later poetry, a development which suggests that pioneering space travel may have drawn her attention and opened her mind to the true scale of things. When combined with the challenging emotional experiences she was going through at this time, this revelation generated an

---

[6] *L1* 732, 734. The play was Tennessee Williams's *Camino Real*.

acute sense of the isolation and fragility of human existence. Sylvia Plath began to feel the chill of the void.

The climax of space activity during this poet's lifetime was the first manned exit from the Earth's atmosphere on April 12, 1961. It is hard to overstate the impact that Yuri Gagarin's 108-minute journey had on the inhabitants of the planet that he orbited. For the great majority of those who flocked to see him on his subsequent world tour, Gagarin's achievement was no sideshow of the Cold War, it was the main event, and he was the beaming embodiment of what had hitherto only been a character from science fiction: the spaceman.[7] There is a reconfiguration and burgeoning of space imagery in the poetry that Plath wrote from May 1961 onwards. Indeed, the change is so distinct that—as far as this aspect of her writing is concerned, at least—it is possible to divide her corpus into two phases: before and after the advent of human spaceflight. The main difference between these phases is one of depth perception. It is doubtful that Plath ever read Mina Loy, but if her early, metaphor-showered moon has something in common with Loy's in "Lunar Baedeker," "pocked with personification / the fossil virgin of the skies" (81),[8] then her later more three-dimensional conceptualization of space recalls another poem by her modernist predecessor, the eighteenth of the "Songs to Joannes":

> Out of the severing
> Of hill from hill
> The interim
> Of star from star
> The nascent
> Static
> Of night.
>
> (60)

Here Loy conceives space as a field of creative potential, something like the Japanese concept of *Ma*, or Laozi's description of the Tao, which "is like the eternal void / filled with infinite possibilities" and "like a bellows ... empty yet infinitely capable" (*Tao Te Ching* 4, 5). Plath, by contrast, would conceptualize this interim as less generative than nullifying, not so much full of potential or infinitely capable as yawningly empty of life and meaning. To enter this space imaginatively would be to confront a distressing sense of isolation and incapacity, "the awful helpless numbness," that she had described in her October 1959 journal entry (J 517).[9] The advent of human spaceflight contributed a potentially infinite $z$-axis to the geometry of Plath's imagination, opening her mind to a hitherto neglected dimension within which her poetry would subsequently strive to find its bearings.

In order to appreciate this change in perspective, we could contrast the flat and artificial imagery of the night sky that opens a pre-Gagarin poem, "On Deck" (from July 1960), where "some few passengers" are described as they "keep track / Of the old star-map on the ceiling" (*CP* 142), to the new deep-field awareness that informs the

---

[7] See Gerovitch 92; Siddiqi 243–98.
[8] I take as coincidental Plath's description of the moon's "pockmarked face" in "Metamorphoses of the Moon" (*CP* 308).
[9] William Empson felt similarly about space: "No reasonable man would want space travel," he writes, "I imagine [Donne] was thankful to get back from the interplanetary spaces, which are inherently lonely and ill-provided" (338, 345).

imagery of two poems written in May 1961, a few weeks after the flight of *Vostok I*. "Insomniac" opens with a characteristically two-dimensional image of the "night" as "only a sort of carbon paper," but this cedes to a recognition that the flimsy world of the page, of print, and of poetic metaphor, only papers over an intimidating vacancy, the existence of which seems to have just been disclosed to the speaker: "the much-poked periods of stars" let in "a bonewhite light, like death, behind all things" (*CP* 163). "Widow" conveys a similarly dismaying sense of this revealed nihility, here described as "that great, vacant estate!":

> The voice of God is full of draftiness,
> Promising simply the hard stars, the space
> Of immortal blankness between stars
> And no bodies, singing like arrows up to heaven.
>
> (*CP* 164)

In both instances, unlike Plath's earlier writing and typical of her later work, the imaginative engagement is less with heavenly objects than with the nothingness which envelops them. This dimension is portrayed as definitively inhospitable and used primarily as an objective correlative for emotional distress (induced by lack of sleep in one poem, bereavement in the other). Plath's imagery had begun to reflect a sense of the true scale and vacancy of our universe.

The poet's eye was still on the heavens when she wrote another astronomical poem two months later in July 1961 (during which month Gagarin was fêted in England—see "Major Gagarin retires"). Plath begins "Stars over the Dordogne" with a panoramic vision of constellations apparently falling to earth as the planet slowly turns. The two-dimensionality of her subsequent description of this French night sky as a "dressy backcloth" for a "luxury" of "scrubbed and self-assured" stars is now deliberately intended to evoke an impression of superficiality (associated with her pampered company), one which is contextualized by the evocation of the "night chill" of the speaker's "home" skies, where

> only the sparsest stars
> Arrive at twilight, and then after some effort.
> And they are wan, dulled by much travelling.
> The smaller and more timid never arrive at all
> But stay, sitting far out, in their own dust.
>
> (*CP* 165)

Here, authenticity is associated with an awareness of the actual distances across which light journeys. As in the two poems written in May, the revelation of true scale is accompanied by a disenchanting feeling of isolation (the stars of New England are "puritan and solitary") and an awareness of human vulnerability ("When one of them falls it leaves a space, // A sense of absence in its old shining place") (*CP* 166). It is this "sense of absence" which marks out Plath's later vision of the heavens. The published version of "The Rival," written during the same month, describes the moon and its female subject as "great light borrowers" (*CP* 166), another flat metaphor that conveys both the phoniness of the speaker's perceived adversary and (by implication) her own depth and genuineness. It is also worth recognizing that an earlier draft of this poem, reprinted in the notes to the *Collected Poems*, situates this counterfeit moon within an expansive, vacuous context: "What good is all that space if it can't draw you off?" (*CP* 291). Somewhat more disconcertingly, the speaker of September 1961's "Wuthering Heights," acutely conscious of her position in physical space and of the "distances" that "dissolve and dissolve" beyond the receding horizon, herself contemplates the possibility of being drawn into the vacuum: when she notes that "the black slots of their pupils take me in," the sheep in this poem appear not only to be observing her but also threatening to absorb her through a black hole into a limitless, indifferent dimension, a journey "like being mailed into space" (*CP* 167).

The imagery of internalized space that opens "The Moon and the Yew Tree," written during the following month, further indicates how a sense of the void was penetrating Plath's consciousness at this time:

> This is the light of the mind, cold and planetary.
> The trees of the mind are black. The light is blue.
>
> (*CP* 172)

It seems likely that this color scheme was influenced by the revelatory new perspective that had recently been gained on the earth's atmosphere: Plath offers a starkly reductive version of Gagarin's well-known description of "the rich color spectrum of the earth" as he saw it through the window of his capsule, the planet "surrounded by a light blue aureole that gradually darkens, becoming turquoise, dark blue, violet, and finally coal black" (qtd. in Young *xi*). In *The Bell Jar*—another product of that spring—a suicidal Esther contemplates the same transition, wondering "at what point in space the silly, sham blue of the sky turned black" (*B* 151). "The Moon and the Yew Tree" takes pains to evoke vertical scale as, following a glance at her "feet," the speaker's eyes describe a trajectory determined by the Yew, which—like a launch vehicle set in the "fumy spiritous mists" of its own steam—"points up" through flowering clouds to the moon (*CP* 173). The speaker of this poem feels that she has "fallen a long way," using cold space imagery to put into a disconcertingly impersonal perspective reassuring ideals of human "tenderness," as represented by warm candlelight and the Marian effigy, "[b]ending, on me in particular, its mild eyes" (*CP* 173). Disillusionment with sentimental ideals is conveyed by the speaker's evocation of a less compassionate maternal figure, the moon, which—dragging "the sea after it like a dark crime"—can be felt to exert its compelling gravitational pull across the cloudy interim (*CP* 173).

Six months later, another tree poem would evoke the same ineluctable force:

> The moon, also, is merciless: she would drag me
> Cruelly, being barren.
> Her radiance scathes me.
>
> (*CP* 192)

In "Elm," what was once a "celestial onion" has now become a terrible white goddess, and "the conundrum of space" has been reconceived as an inescapable coliseum of suffering. However, it is notable that, when the tree attempts to shake itself free of its persecutor, in a similar move to that of "Stars over the Dordogne," Plath reduces the malign female influence to two-dimensionality: "I let her go / Diminished and flat, as after radical surgery." Plath may have been unnerved by the vast neutrality of the universe, but—as is suggested in the first stanza of "Apprehensions" (written the following month)—she acknowledged it as her true home:

> There is this white wall, above which the sky creates itself—
> Infinite, green, utterly untouchable.
> Angels swim in it, and the stars, in indifference also.
> They are my medium.
> The sun dissolves on this wall, bleeding its lights.

(CP 195)

This picture is not reassuring. The imagery of this poem will become progressively more apocalyptic, but already the "bleeding ... lights" of the sun that dissolve onto the exposed skull suggest that there may be fears of radiation exposure hidden in Plath's empyreal vision. As "Starfish Prime" was to demonstrate, the sky glows green when radioactive particles collide with oxygen atoms high in the ozone layer (see Krulwich).

Within a short time, the "cold blanks" of this "medium" (CP 195) would be seared by a heated imagery of velocity and ascension. Plath's great poems of October and November were written during a period of both personal crisis and accelerating space-race activity; where 1961 had seen fifty orbital launches, 1962 saw eighty-two (Krebs). Something of the galvanized, hazardous thrust of this time is caught in the imagery that characterizes the poems of that fall. "Fever 103°" is, as Peel notes, "part rocket launch" (*Writing Back* 220): "I think I am going up / I think I may rise— / The beads of hot metal fly"; in "Mary's Song," "the high // Precipice / That emptied one man into space" where "[t]he ovens glowed like heavens" looks a lot like a launch pad; "Stings" concludes with the vision of a queen leaving "the wax house" to fly, a "red / Scar in the sky, red comet"; the speaker of "Ariel" sets the controls for the heart of the rising sun, "the red / Eye, the cauldron of morning" (CP 232, 257, 215, 240). All of these are images of incandescence but also of space being penetrated and crossed, and the flaring of these projectiles cannot wholly distract the reader from consciousness of the achromatic emptiness that surrounds them, the dark stasis. So the child-like comets described in "The Night Dances," which "[h]ave such a space to cross / Such coldness, forgetfulness," seem vulnerable and forsaken in this context, the heat of fiery red here cooling to a human pink that bleeds its insubstantial trail of light "through the black amnesias of heaven" (CP 250). Space is no longer merely blank, drafty, or indifferent; it is oblivion. The defiant speaker of "Years"— partly a reckless rocketeer with thoughts on "outer / Space," "dying to fly and be done with it" (CP 255)—kicks out against this "great Stasis" and derides contemplative passivity toward its engulfing neutrality:

> O God, I am not like you
> In your vacuous black,
> Stars stuck all over, bright stupid confetti.
> Eternity bores me,
> I never wanted it.

(CP 255)

But the impetuous tone of adolescent rebellion here betrays an ultimate sense of powerlessness and ephemerality in face of such uncompromising authority. In the perspective of eternity, such flights of fancy are short haul.

The language of Plath's last poems suggests that, by late January and early February 1963, the main emotional booster that had been powering these creative flights had burnt itself out. Transcendent, motile imagery of launches, ascensions, and searing passages gives way—in the poem "Sheep in Fog"—to "stillness," a sense of being distanced from "people or stars," and the chilling imminence of envelopment by "vacuous black," as "the far / Fields ... threaten" to let her "through to a heaven / Starless and fatherless, a dark water" (CP 262). Two notes by Hughes in the *Collected Poems* suggest that the earlier death by water meditations, "Full Fathom Five" and "Lorelei," were written partly under the influence of a book (probably *The Silent World*) by Jacques Cousteau, whose pioneering undersea explorations in his "Diving Saucer" could be seen as the submarine equivalent of the first journeys into space, with which they coincided (CP 287). Dark skies and deep waters are blended in these late poems, and both asphyxiating environments threaten to engulf: the "clear eye" of "Child," a "pool in which images / Should be grand and classical," ominously reflects instead a "dark / Ceiling without a star"; the speaker of "Words" looks up to the "fixed stars" of fate "[f]rom the bottom of the pool" (CP 265, 270): the perspective of one who has "fallen a long way." Plath's late memoir of childhood visits to the New England coast, "Ocean 1212-W," also combines these two elements, recasting the metaphor that first appeared in her October 1959 journal entry in order to evoke the dawning sense of existential isolation that had accompanied the birth of her brother:

> As from a star I saw, coldly and soberly, the *separateness* of everything. I felt the wall of my skin: I am I. That stone is a stone. My beautiful fusion with the things of this world was over.
> The tide ebbed, sucked back into itself.
>
> (*JP* 24)

Both the perilous nature of these enveloping elements and Plath's youthful confidence in her own capacity to negotiate this danger are reflected in her subsequent recollection of learning to swim: "I jumped with a side flap of hands; my feet ceased to touch. I was in that forbidden country—'over my head.' I should, according to Mother, have sunk like a stone, but I didn't" (*JP* 26). This passage is followed by an image of effortless ascent through the atmosphere: "The airport across the bay unloosed a blimp. It went up like a silver bubble, a salute" (*JP* 26). There is a degree of wistfulness about this recollection of buoyancy, however, and such blithe gravity-defiance was to be counterpointed in one of Plath's last poems, where the hostile distances of space have the final word. The personified moon of "Edge" embodies the deathly neutrality that the poet had recognized as characterizing the hitherto "forbidden country" over her head (but since Gagarin's flight, no longer forbidden). It is evoked with an icy offhandedness:

> The moon has nothing to be sad about,
> Staring from her hood of bone.
>
> She is used to this sort of thing.
> Her blacks crackle and drag.
>
> (CP 273)

If we agree with Tim Kendall that the famous last line of this poem "may envisage the night sky as a black cloak dragged along the ground by the hooded moon" ("From the Bottom of the Pool" 163), then—whether it refers to theatrical blacks, or a cloak of mourning, or both—this image evokes the burdensome expanse of darkness between two celestial bodies. We have felt the "drag" of gravity across this expanse before in "The Moon and the Yew Tree" and "Elm"; in each case, it suggests the encumbrance of an inescapable and emotionally draining connection. Plath's awareness of the space-in-between finally became intimately bound up with her awareness of the affective ties that bind, whether we want them to or not.

Recalling a night of star watching, a near-sixteen-year-old Sylvia Plath wrote to her German pen pal:

> I felt, somehow, very small and inconsequential in comparison to the endless space of sky, sand and sea. It is an inspiring feeling to be on the edge of the land. I think that the greatness of Nature is somehow healing to the spirit. After dealing with so many problems in world affairs it is comforting to think, for a change, that this world amounts to little more than a speck of dust in the unbelievably huge universe.
>
> (*L1* 134)

A sense of the sheer size of the universe—here gestured to in momentary wonder—would in later years underpin Plath's mature poetic vision, but she would derive little comfort from the perspective that it offered on problematic human affairs, both public and private. As rocket launches guided her attention to the depth of the space in which our planet swims, and extra-terrestrial travel confirmed that this depth was penetrable, Plath's sense of the human situation in the grand scheme of things was transformed and a compelling imagery of alienation emerged.

# CHAPTER SIX

# Spectral Traces, Places, and Sylvia Plath

GAIL CROWTHER

This essay will explore the notion of the living archive, the material places and spaces in Plath's life that she revisited and re-envisioned in her poetry and prose. In contrast to traditional, physical archives, repositories, or libraries, living archives are dynamic spaces subject to change and time.[1] Houses Plath once lived in, places she visited and wrote about, the domestic space surrounding her all feature in an empirical and interpretive sense in some of her most powerful poems and prose. Physical traces remain, and although they can never be fully captured and inhabited by readers or scholars, these traces, however spectral, can lead us to a new understanding of Plath and her creative processes.

"The house," objects, and domestic spaces can be regarded as an archive. Doing so raises several questions. What are the ways in which a researcher can access these spaces and traces? How might speculating on this question help us understand to what degree Plath merged her domestic and creative spaces? When Plath visited the Brontë parsonage at Haworth, she described the writers' home as "a house redolent with ghosts" (*J* 589). Poignantly she records how the sisters touched this or that ("things of everyday life"?)—a wooden cradle, a death couch, a bridal crown, napkin rings, and books—all traces left behind in the black-stone rectory rooms. As readers, we encounter this spectrality in Plath's own work.

Plath's poem "The Detective" depicts a speaker standing listening in an empty room, the barely disguised living room of Plath's own home, Court Green, in Devon. The physicality of the room is captured and frozen in time textually: "There is no body in the house at all. / There is the smell of polish, there are plush carpets. / There is the sunlight, playing its blades, / Bored hoodlum in a red room / Where the wireless talks to itself like an elderly relative" (*CP* 209).[2] The echoing mausoleum of the house quivers with spectrality, with traces of other lives, and the reader sees how Plath has merged her domestic and living space with her poetic output. By using her encounter with the

---

[1] The living archive is a concept first introduced in *These Ghostly Archives* by Crowther and Steinberg. See Chapter 5 in which we argue that "[i]f we see that the archive can be a living, breathing, and moving 'thing,' then it grows and changes and always has a tale to tell. This dynamic nature of the archive is inextricably linked to what gets left behind, what gets preserved, and how these objects persevere in a different time" (88).

[2] We can be certain Plath is writing about her own living room here since this fits both the descriptions she sent home in letters and is visible in photographs taken in December 1962 showing the plush carpets, the red room, and the wireless.

material spaces around her, Plath has plucked her memories and associations and used them in the writing of a poem. The result is that Plath leaves an indelible watermark that we can scrutinize. Archives tell stories, and houses and places tell stories too. They successfully juxtapose stasis and change in such a way that it may be argued a living archive is formed full of traces that often refuse to disappear. They linger and haunt and ultimately aid in the re-creative process of the reader, as well as the writer.

Undoubtedly, though, there are significant differences between a traditional archive and a living archive, and these differences are problematic to theorize. For example, visiting a traditional archive often involves handling physical remains—documents, photographs, realia. There are set rules in each archive: routines, procedures, catalogue numbers, order, files, and folders. A visit requires planning and organization: finding a desk to work, remembering pencil, notepad, laptop. Documents can be transcribed or, in some cases, photographed. What is being explored is, at least in essence, *there*. If the items are old, they may be delicate and contain stains or smudges. Plath's manuscripts often have coffee cup circles or rusted marks where paper clips have held pages together decade after decade. The point is, one purpose of a traditional archive is preservation. This gives it a sense of permanence, perhaps even reliability.

Often visiting a living archive there are fewer tangible traces; in such cases it may become problematic to articulate and theorize origins. Places change, sometimes through design or accident. A house can be altered beyond recognition. Buildings can be razed to the ground and rebuilt. Whole streets can disappear and re-emerge as something completely different. Time impacts on place as do decay, movement, and change. What once was might never be again. What Plath saw in 1962 might be gone forever. In this sense, the living archive contrasts sharply with the permanence and reliability of a traditional archive.

Working in a living archive requires a different approach, a different mindset, and even a different type of research skill because it opens onto the subjectivity and involvement of the perceiving subject. In fact, we could say it reshapes the encounter between the researcher, the author, and the text. What occurs is an opening up of a space for allowing the play of intersubjectivity, and it is this space and the possibilities that occur there that allow new narratives to emerge and new questions to be raised. These narratives and questions will begin to be explored in this essay, as well as offering a framework and discipline for understanding them. The way we access social, cultural, and historical traces becomes less to do with physicality and more to do with what is known in the social sciences as the discipline of sociological hauntings.[3]

Let us take, for example, an artifact from the Smith archive: the cheque stub from Plath's last bank book in December 1962 recording the purchase of her gas stove.[4] Handling this item, we have the immediacy of the "thing" itself. Then we have the actual traces left behind by Plath, her black ink, which she smeared at the bottom of the page.

---

[3]Sociological haunting is an approach best captured by Gordon in her book *Ghostly Matters*, which explores the idea that haunting can be used as a method of sociological research. Drawing on an interdisciplinary approach, Gordon questions and explores the contemporary relationship between experience, knowledge, and power, arguing that haunting can be used to describe that which is no longer present. The ghostly nature of such absence needs exploring itself; what lingers, what are the ways in which the past can inform the present? Gordon argues that "[t]o study social life, one must confront the ghostly aspects of it" (7).
[4]This item is held in the Sylvia Plath Collection at Smith.

As a researcher, one cannot help but engage with this item in several ways. Firstly, there is the factual evidence—the date the stove was purchased and the amount paid. Then there is the ink and the handwriting and the smearing, real traces of Plath's active living that we can see. It is difficult, however, not to experience a certain chill at this. One's imagination comes into play that not only would this be the instrument of Plath's death two months later, but looking at this item retrospectively, we have the omniscience that Plath herself lacked at the time. Even in a traditional archive, a certain amount of imagination and fantasy occurs. This certainly becomes truer when encountering the living archive. An object or a place outside of the institution lends itself to being even more open to imaginative engagement. And this engagement becomes even more powerful if the context of the living archive is one that has been captured in Plath's writing, which mirrors the process of re-creation in Plath's writing.

Perhaps in order to explore these ideas, it is necessary to think in more detail about the nature and role of place, or what Michael Mayerfeld Bell refers to as the "ubiquitous aspect of the phenomenology of place" (813). This statement explores the idea that meaning and intelligibility of place is not completely straightforward, and in fact, even questions the possibility of objectivity. Sociologists Monica Degen and Kevin Hetherington suggest that "any space does not just exist in the present. Its ghosts problematize the issue of time as well as space" (1).[5] The past leaves its imprint, and sites that once held one function can become haunted by what is no longer there. Bell argues that ghosts help constitute the specificity of historical sites.

But interestingly, Bell urges that these ghosts can be both ghosts of the living and the dead, individual and collective, both other selves and ourselves: "[P]laces are in a word personed, even when there is no one there" (813). So, when thinking about the living archive, we might argue that a place is haunted not only by the cultural ghost of Plath, but also by our own lives tracking and tracing her through time, what Bell refers to as a "network of ghosts" (825). If this all seems rather ephemeral (because it is), Nicholas Entrikin suggests that perhaps place is best viewed from points in between the rock of objective generalization and the soft place of subjective particularization, what he calls "the betweenness of place" (cited in Bell 815). This idea allows room for acknowledging that although the living archive resists theoretical closure, it is still possible to offer a meaningful, nuanced approach.

How is it possible though to develop a framework of intelligibility from inhabiting this "betweenness of place"? As Bell rightly points out, "place is a notoriously difficult concept to define, and therefore to pick up and inspect with the mental tweezers of an objective social science" (814). Intangible residues and hauntings are like air motes, and while undoubtedly, certain places can breed a particular atmosphere, the role of fantasy in the observer must not be overlooked. For sociologist Avery Gordon,

> [h]aunting is a constituent element of modern social life. It is neither pre-modern superstition nor individual psychosis; it is a generalizable social phenomenon of great import. To study social life, one must confront the ghostly aspects of it.
>
> (7)

---

[5]The term ghost throughout this essay is used in the sociological sense, best defined by Gordon who sees ghosts as the special merging between the visible/invisible, the dead/living, past/present. She regards the ghost as a social figure "the traffic in the domains of experience that are anything but transparent and referential" (25).

In other words, in order to know ourselves and why we respond in the way we do to certain places we need to explore not only what is visible and there but also what is invisible and gone and how we fill those gaps with narrative and fantasy. While Gordon's claim perfectly describes the elements of contemporary haunting and how, in the present, we can never quite be free from the past, her model does not quite describe the two-way dynamic to haunting. If there are ruptures in linear temporality, then haunting must surely be able to speak to the present and the future as well as the past. We may be haunted by the ghosts of the past, but, equally, we may be haunted by futurities: that which has not yet happened or possibilities that may occur in the future.

How might these ideas about the living archive play out, for example, when the researcher visits a place Plath once lived? One of Plath's former flats can be found at 3 Chalcot Square in London, where she lived from early 1960 to late 1961. There has been almost no alteration to the building since Plath's time there, which becomes evident when comparing the current flat to the floor plan Plath sent her mother in a letter on January 24, 1960 (*L2* 395).[6] Plath's detailed drawing showed the footprint of the flat, location of the rooms, where the bath, toilet, the sink were situated, the boiler in the kitchen, the cooker, cupboards, doors, windows. The same narrow, steep stairs lead into the same rooms with the same layout. Even the stove and boiler are in the same place.

When visiting locations connected to Plath, it can be useful to consider what work she produced in these spaces. In Chalcot Square, Plath conceived of *The Bell Jar*, wrote several short stories such as "Day of Success," and poems such as "Leaving Early," "Zoo Keeper's Wife," and "Morning Song." Plath gave birth to her daughter Frieda in the bedroom of the flat and hosted all sorts of literary dinners there. When she and Hughes moved to Devon in autumn 1961, David and Assia Wevill moved into the flat.

Above Plath's flat was a small attic apartment that the resident, Mary Morton, initially allowed Plath and Hughes to use as their writing space while she was out working during the day. This place featured in one of Plath's poems, "Leaving Early," written in Chalcot Square. To the right of Plath's flat door are the narrow stairs leading up to the attic featured in the poem, "Lady your room is lousy with flowers. … How did we make it up to your attic?" (*CP* 145–6). Inside Plath's flat, directly opposite the front door, is the bedroom, the location of the poem "Morning Song," where the "moth-breath" of the narrator's sleeping child "flickers among the flat pink roses" and "clear vowels rise like balloons" (*CP* 157). Here the poem describes the same wallpaper that Plath sent in sample size to her mother, describing the matching long green curtains and Frieda's crib placed at the side of their bed.[7]

The layout and the descriptions of the bedroom are recognizable from Plath's short story "Day of Success," where the narrator writes:

> Ellen was on her way to the bedroom with an armload of freshly folded nappies when the phone rang, splintering the stillness of the crisp autumn morning. For a moment she froze on the threshold taking in the peaceful scene as she might never see it again—the delicate rose-patterned wallpaper, the forest green cord drapes … the pale pink

---

[6] A color reproduction of this letter also appears in the first set of plates between pages 332–3.
[7] Plath describes her bedroom and furniture in letters to her mother (*L2* 395, 439, 445).

crib. *Please don't let it change* she begged of whatever fates might be listening. *Let the three of us stay happy as this forever.*

(*JP* 185)[8]

In "Zoo Keeper's Wife," a wakeful woman lies resentful in bed, her insomniac mind a jumble of animals that featured in her early days of romance. Plath looked forward to hearing the noises of the zoo animals when she and Hughes moved across from Regent's Park (*L2* 403). The domestic space imprinted itself into Plath's work.

In 2014, on a research visit to explore the resonances of the living archive, I visited 3 Chalcot Square. In letters home to her mother, Plath described the tilting floorboards of the living room. They still tilt. Photographs mailed home show Plath standing in front of the same existing doorway with the same door frame, the same light switches, even the same bumps in the wall. Today, her traces are everywhere. In another letter to her mother, Plath described painting one wall of the kitchen a deep rose color. The current owner told me that they had uncovered beneath layers of wallpaper this same rose-colored paint and pointed to a small corner in the kitchen ceiling where it was visible. It was a peculiar moment. Seeing how Plath observed and transformed her domestic surroundings is powerful, and to visit those same surroundings over fifty years later and see what she had left behind both in the flat and in her work was a moving encounter. This is the living archive telling and revealing its stories.

The left-over, rose-colored paint in the kitchen allows a researcher to engage their fantasy, imagination, and daydreaming. "People need houses to dream, in order to imagine," wrote Gaston Bachelard (viii). With this in mind, we can interpret the poetic imagination not as an echo of the past, but as a past that resounds with echoes. What we do not know is at what depth these echoes will reverberate and then die away (xvi). Seeing the physical traces Plath left behind in her flat supports Bachelard's notion that it is the reverberations (*retentir*) through time of the home, that are "always container, sometimes contained" (viii). The poetics of space and Plath's lingering presence show how her former home "'clings' to its inhabitant and becomes the cell of a body with its walls close together" (Bachelard 46). The place becomes imbued with Plath's presence, and this presence can be conjured in a number of ways.

We can begin to engage in what I have previously termed "surrogate authorship" (*These Ghostly Archives* 93), allowing us to see a place through Plath's eyes and subsequently understand on a practical level how she transformed what she saw into her creative output. This feels a little like being present at the genesis of a poem or a story or a letter. We understand how a certain shape or object captured Plath's imagination and can perhaps see more clearly why she chose a particular word or phrase.[9] These are tangible ways of theorizing the importance of place. But as we move toward the more subjective

---

[8]"Day of Success" also features Mary Morton's attic flat referred to as "Mrs. Frankfort's flat" (*JP* 80–1) with a description of "the steeply angled steps to Mrs. Frankfort's top-floor flat" (*JP* 84) and the explanation that this "middle-aged widow had offered him the use of her flat [for writing purposes] during the day while she was at work" (*JP* 84).

[9]For anyone who has visited North Tawton, this is especially obvious observing the yew tree and the graves in St. Peter's Church which feature in Plath's poems such as "The Moon and the Yew Tree," "Little Fugue," and "Letter in November." The yew tree really does have "fingers" ("Little Fugue" *CP* 187). Equally, the row of headstones which separate Plath's property from the graveyard are perfectly described as "a wall of old corpses" ("Letter in November" *CP* 253).

end of the scale, other equally important factors feature. The traces left behind become part of the very structure of the building. This again opens up a new space: the mix-up of time, and the play between ghosts of the living and ghosts of the dead. Charles Lemert illustrates some of the ways that the dead are not absent from the living, how they are scattered about places and disturb "sober space" (19). Our own ghosts haunt our pasts, places we have been, objects that we have touched. All these ghosts, argue Bell, require a certain level of imagination. We give ghosts to places, we have reasons for conjuring them up, and these reasons have "consequences" (831).

This idea of some sort of ghostly presence was perfectly encapsulated by Plath, who was aware of the role of imagination and how it impacts on what can be found in any given place. Her poem "Two Views of Withens" deals with another sort of house, a ruin, and the difference between a lack and an abundance of imagination when encountering traces left behind. In her life, Plath walked twice to Top Withens, an old farmhouse on the moors above Haworth in West Yorkshire and the alleged inspiration for Emily Brontë's *Wuthering Heights*. Following these visits, Plath wrote an unpublished short story based on the location as well as poems such as "Wuthering Heights" and "November Graveyard" set in Haworth and the surrounding moors.[10]

But "Two Views of Withens" deals directly with daydreaming and expectations of the visitors to the ruin. The exposed, gorse-riddled moors and descending fog reflect the narrator's sense of emptiness and disappointment. She can find no traces here; her imagination stalls. Rather than encountering fictional characters, or the ghost of Emily Brontë plotting her novel, the poem's narrator instead finds "a bare moor" along with "colorless weather," and the farmhouse "low-lintelled, no palace" (*CP* 72). In contrast, her companion reports a much more exciting encounter of "white pillars, a blue sky / The ghosts, kindly" (*CP* 72). This poem exposes the more subjective elements at play when encountering the living archive drawing on color, space, and expectations. The role of fantasy and pre-existing knowledge inform how a person interacts with where they find themselves.

A *Birthday Letters* poem by Ted Hughes, "Wuthering Heights," could read as a meta-poem of Plath's "Two Views of Withens." Place and the house are once again central, as are ghosts, expectations, and traces. Hughes effectively tells the story of Plath conceiving her poem on their visit to Top Withens. Plath's poem offers us a layered interpretation where both Hughes and Plath swap and exchange poetic gazes. Hughes, more than Plath, draws on aspects of the living archive, the interplay between text and place[11]: "The book becoming a map. *Wuthering Heights* / Withering into perspective" (*TH:CP* 1081).

Hughes, too, records the disappointment of place, the struggle of the imagination: "Was that crumble of wall / Remembering a try at a garden?" (*TH:CP* 1081). The poem flits between time, imagining an interplay between Plath and Emily Brontë as Hughes's fantasy explores what each would have made of the other. In a central moment of the

---

[10]Plath used her walk to Top Withens for a number of pieces. An undated, unpublished short story titled "A Winter's Tale" (the manuscript has her Court Green address) was clearly written with a women's magazine in mind and features a love story. Plath also wrote a more journalistic piece for the *Christian Science Monitor* called "A Walk to Withens" published June 6, 1959. She also sketched Top Withens while she was there.

[11]Hughes draws on the living archive repeatedly. There are many poems in *Birthday Letters* that are centered on place, the home, and the notion of haunting, such as "55 Eltisley," "9 Willow Street," "Daffodils," "Perfect Light," "Robbing Myself," and "Red."

poem, we read a description of Plath sitting in the crook of a tree. Hughes writes: "And a poem unfurled from you" (*TH:CP* 1082). Here, the living archive operates on a multi-dimensional level. Hughes recognizes the power of place, the disruption to transparent experience, how ghosts can trouble and disturb, and that time goes both ways: "And maybe a ghost, trying to hear your words, / Peered from the broken mullions / And was stilled" (*TH:CP* 1082). But Hughes also shows how, in the words of Charles Lemert, "[t]he Dead are not exactly absent from the communities of the living" (18). They are, in fact, ever present in our day-to-day space. Their presence serves a purpose as a reminder of our mortality, but equally in a more positive role: "The Dead weigh upon us, not as nightmares, but as life itself[.] … We live among the Dead, and they live among us" (21). In Hughes's case as a presence to converse with, the immediacy of the *Birthday Letters* poems are directly addressed to "you."

The living archive can be seen as a space for considering the role of heritage, remembrance, a space to enter into the process of creative transformation, or even as a self-indulgent space for voyeurism. We can conclude that living archives are "personed" by the living and the dead (Bell 813). It is this haunting that lifts the role of the living archive of being merely biographical or geographical factors.

Avery Gordon explores the idea of places having "rememory" (166). The idea that if a place still exists and one visits, it may be possible to bump into a memory that belongs to somebody else. If one goes there, even if one had never been there when the person was, and stand in the same place, might the event happen again, or become somehow accessible?[12] The places in which Plath lived, wrote, and experienced emotions still exist. For Gordon,

> writ[ing] about invisiblities and hauntings—requires attention to what appears dead, but is nonetheless powerfully alive; requires attention to what appears to be in the past, but is nonetheless powerfully present; requires attention to just who the subject of analysis is.
>
> (42)

Yet, it seems it is these very intangibilities that provide intriguing possibilities for future research.

As a living archive, Court Green in Devon and the town of North Tawton, both of which can be easily revisited, offer a particularly poignant and potent living archive, as I have discovered on numerous research trips. They are immortalized by Plath in her *Ariel* poems. The daffodils in her garden that appear in "Among the Narcissi" still bloom every spring. The lime pollards in her poem "Berck-Plage" still line the bleak cemetery path to Percy Key's grave. The apple trees in her orchard still stretch up the gentle slope of her garden, "Holding their gold-ruddy balls" (*CP* 253). The fingers of the yew tree

---

[12]The first time I visited North Tawton, I was able to navigate the streets from Plath's writing alone. Seeing the landmarks she wrote about was like reliving a memory, although bizarrely, a memory I never had from seeing the place with my own eyes. Gordon refers to this as a "collectively animated world memory … in which you *who never was there* in that real place—can *bump into a rememory that belongs to somebody else*" (166). It is interesting to consider whether the possibility of capturing the place as it was in Plath's time is at the very center of the ephemeral nature of the living archive and ways in which the idea of rememory might be connected to the desire to engage in Plath's authorial process.

wag, the saints remain floating above the pews in St. Peter's Church, and the moon still snags in the branches featured in "The Moon and the Yew Tree." Only Plath is no longer there.[13] But it is the experience of that encounter that lies between something which is both present and absent, both tangible and intangible. That experience is between the researcher and the writer's ghostly remains. This space can be articulated and theorized but also somehow remains a little mysterious. The living archive does not offer us tidy, empirical answers. It remains somewhat beautifully elusive.

---

[13] For reference to these places, see the following poems in *Collected Poems*, "Among the Narcissi" (190), "Berck-Plage" (196), "Letter in November" (253), and "The Moon and the Yew Tree" (172).

CHAPTER SEVEN

# <maniacs.> of the Heterotopia: Citizen Critics and Marginalia in Library Copies of Sylvia Plath

CHRISTINE WALDE

The Library is unlimited and cyclical.
—Jorge Luis Borges, "The Library of Babel"

My first encounter with marginalia in library copies of Sylvia Plath happened when I was studying for my Master's degree in Library and Information Science at Western University in London, Ontario, Canada. As part of my coursework, I was conducting an independent study on the research behaviors of scholars using Plath's archives, and I began thinking about Plath and her readership in a profoundly new way.[1] So when I serendipitously pulled a single first edition of the 1966 Harper & Row *Ariel* from the stacks from the D. B. Weldon Library, I was astounded to see the level of interactivity within its pages. Within the one book, there were coffee rings. Red underlining. Correcting fluid. Blue pen, black pen. Pencil. There was a kind of *violence* to the annotations (see Figure 2). Some pages were entirely missing, just cut out or gone.[2] I soon found my primary research material in plain sight. I learned that no matter where I continued to look—at my local public library branch or in the academic library of the Mearns Centre for Learning-McPherson Library, where I am now a librarian at the University of Victoria—I found multiple copies of Sylvia Plath's primary texts were marked with an array of marginal annotations, similar and dissimilar to the first edition of *Ariel* I had discovered at Weldon Library, which I had mistakenly thought to be an outlier.

After I had graduated from library school and moved across the country, I continued to document these instances of marginalia during my visits to public and academic libraries

---

[1] I was interviewing scholars about their feelings when they encountered Plath's archives, and how their research behaviors had been shaped by these emotional experiences in the archive. "<maniacs.>" highlights a reader's annotation of "The Arrival of the Bee Box" (CP 238).
[2] It was such a remarkable copy I actually tried to buy it from the library, and replace it with a newer, pristine version, but they denied my request. Luckily, as a librarian I know other librarians, and my friend Carey, who worked for Western Libraries at the time, scanned and OCR'd this copy for me.

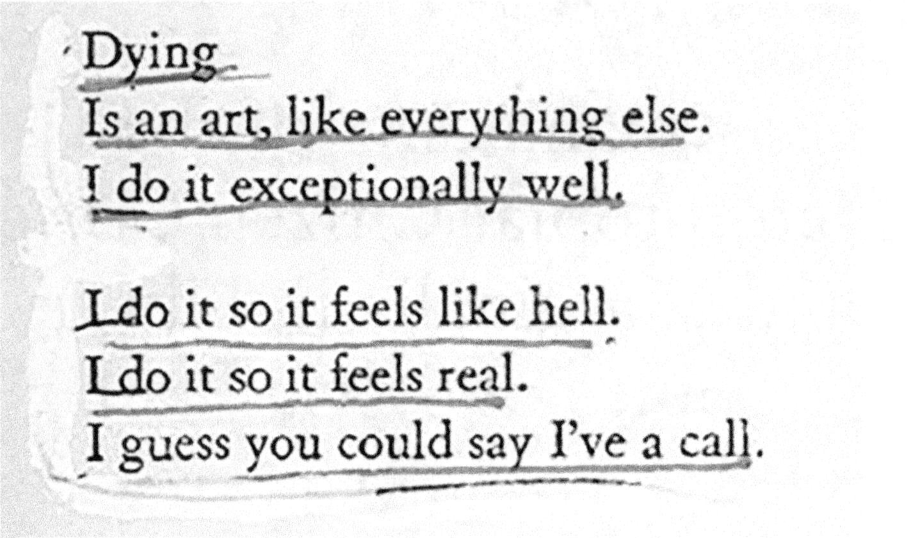

> Dying
> Is an art, like everything else.
> I do it exceptionally well.
>
> I do it so it feels like hell.
> I do it so it feels real.
> I guess you could say I've a call.

FIGURE 2 Detail of "Lady Lazarus" from first edition library copy of *Ariel* from Western Libraries. In this image, one can discern blue and red pen, correction fluid, pencil, and discern marks of erasure, as well as underlining, circling, and written commentary. Photo: Christine Walde.

across Canada and the United States, creating an album of photographs that captured the marginalia examples I had found in Plath's primary texts. The annotations were not just limited to the poetry collections—*Ariel*, primarily, and, in most instances, *Collected Poems*—but were also notable in the pages of *The Bell Jar* and posthumous collections such as *Johnny Panic and the Bible of Dreams*. What I began to see repeatedly—whether the books were from public or academic libraries—was a complex interaction between readers, texts, and books as material artifacts informed and complicated by perceptions of Plath and her celebrity.

But there was something more specific at work. It seemed as though Plath's readers couldn't help themselves from commenting. Their annotations were not only meditative, scholarly contemplations, but they were also quick, impulsive reactions and spontaneous outbursts of words, executed in lead and ink and marker; flourished by drawings of hearts or skulls; spilling out into the margins and the white space of the page. Whether the outcome was incisive lines or loops or dashes—complete with multiple spelling errors, grammatical fluctuations, or other curious demarcations—they were all, in their own way, aesthetic interpretations of the text, spurred by Plath's vivid use of poetic language.[3] Readers were, I began to believe, not only commenting on Plath's writing by making a record of their thoughts and impressions, but they were also, intentionally or unintentionally, in dialogue with each other by authoring themselves in the pages of her work. Some annotations seemed perversely, in a kind of necromancy, to also be

---

[3] I know this because I painstakingly isolated and then traced these annotations and instances of marginalia, in layers, by hand, for a series of composite drawings that examined these clusters of marginalia. By tracing these annotative gestures, I learned how redactive they were.

attempting to talk directly to *her*. I encountered readers who were overjoyed, angered, or impassioned—pleading from the margins and crying out for understanding, justice, salvation, or hope. It seemed that the annotators had preconceptions of Plath's life and art; they read her poems autobiographically and reacted accordingly. That the copies were freely circulating library books, shared publicly among communities of readers over decades of use, made them even more interesting to me as artifacts and records of readership.

I have come to see these annotations as the visual record of what Rosa Eberly identifies as "citizen critics"[4]: ordinary readers engaged in impassioned discourse in the public sphere. As a writer, artist, and librarian whose work combines library and archival research with interests in experimental prose, poetry, visual poetry, performance, and the visual arts, my engagement with this readership resulted in an exploratory body of drawings and a related chapbook.[5] Exploring the topic in this quasi-kinesthetic way not only allowed me to experience the act of making the marginalia itself, but also helped me to understand how the annotations related to reader-to-reader communication, to speculate on conceptual ideas about authority, and engage in speculation on authorship, the book as a material object, the public sphere, and the library as a heterotopia.

Marginalia are not new phenomena. Readers have written in books from the earliest printed works.[6] This was especially true in the Middle Ages since libraries were primarily private collections of kings and clergy and intended almost exclusively for religious use. Books were sacred vessels of the word of the divine, and marginalia operated as a kind of message board of faith, shared between devout borrowers. As books were copied from one version to another, there is evidence of marginalia in many medieval texts: its aesthetic function is both decorative and documentary—simultaneously redactive and additive, creating a visual lore of information that is both idiosyncratic and multiplistic, with many visual and creative dimensions. Often a page can be so heavily annotated that the original text becomes rendered invisible by the anonymous comments that swarm at its edges, competing for the reader's attention and meriting important questions of authority.[7]

In *Marginalia*, H. J. Jackson asserts that while twentieth-century readers may be more inclined to share personal reactions in the margins of texts, they still do "what readers did in the Middle Ages, besides doing much more in the way of recording individual impressions. They mark up books as a way of learning and remember what they contain, and improve them by correcting errors and adding useful relevant information" (60).

It may come as no surprise that, especially in light of her audience of citizen critics, Plath herself was an avid annotator of her personal library. I remember reading the annotations

---

[4]In this instance, and in future references to the public sphere as it pertains to libraries, Eberly defines the citizen critic as a person who produces discourse about issues of common concern from a citizen ethos, and not as an expert. This is an important distinction to make since the annotations that I will be discussing are by citizen critics, not scholars or academics.

[5]The resulting drawings—along with the accompanying chapbook <*maniacs.*>—were shown in an exhibition at the Sylvia Plath: Letters, Words, and Fragments conference in Belfast in 2017.

[6]In Lionel Casson's immensely readable book, *Libraries in the Ancient World*, there is ample historical evidence to suggest that even in Ancient Greek and Roman libraries, annotations were made on copies of scrolls, to suggest new or improved meanings.

[7]An excellent overview and selected reading list of resources related to marginalia—from Roger Stoddard's 1985 book, *Marks in Books, Illustrated and Explained* to Stephen Orgel's *The Reader in the Book: A Study of Spaces and Traces* (2015)—can be found at https://archaeologyofreading.org/further-reading/.

in her dictionary and T. S. Eliot's *The Waste Land* at Smith and being struck by her dazzling and insightful commentary in the margins of these texts. By extension, many of Plath's archival materials—including copies of drafts and pages from her diaries, not to mention her submissions log or even her calendar—include her marginalia, doodles, or sketches. As someone who was skilled in drawing and an aspiring artist, this activity acts as evidence of Plath's own dynamic engagement with the text, the page, and the materiality of the book as object, including her near-obsessive preoccupation with paper.[8]

Similar to many other readers and writers, Plath's own personal annotations leave interesting traces as visual markers on the page, creating paths through her reading and thinking process. Their critical rigor and fierce intelligence are compelling to witness in the margins. Reading her annotations offers important insights into her creative mind and intellectual processes in a way that none of her other primary resources offer. Amanda Golden's excellent study of Plath's annotation practices in *Annotating Modernism* demonstrates how Plath, both as a student, and later, as a teacher at Smith College, annotated. Whether it was underlining or adding marginalia, "Plath made marking books a part of the reading process" (32) to inform both her scholarly and creative natures.[9]

Obviously, annotating books from private collections differs from annotating books from libraries, but the reason *why* people annotate library books is another matter entirely. I want to call attention to this important and integral distinction, because, as I previously mentioned, all the examples I have alluded to here are from *library* copies of Plath's work, from both public and academic libraries. They are free, circulating copies that have usually been held in libraries' collections, often since the date of publication. As a librarian, I'm specifically interested in this intersection between marginalia and the materiality of the library book.

Muhamed Fajkovic and Lennart Björneborn, two Danish librarians from the University of Copenhagen, have argued that in library settings distinctively, readerly marginalia may be regarded as "affordance for reader-to-reader communication." Fajkovic and Björneborn assert that one of the main reasons library users annotate library books is because they can: people write on paper, and since books are printed on paper, this *affords* people the opportunity to write in books. By their very design, and with margins surrounded by printed text, books are made to be inscribed (913). Fajkovic and Björneborn state that marginalia "seem to be physical displays of the mental process of conquering and digesting the matter in the text" (911). This is an important characteristic of responses to Plath's poetry: when confronted by her rich and thick diction, as well as her intense subject matter, readers react accordingly, producing graphic and physical displays of their mental process. It is precisely this "matter in the text" that I am most interested in replicating in my artworks, documenting the physical record of readers as they encounter Plath's writing.

While Fajkovic and Björneborn assert that "annotations are primarily created for personal reasons in studying/reading situations, as mnemonic and structural devices" (912),

---

[8] Plath memorably used the stolen pink Smith writing paper on which the *Ariel* poems were composed (*J*). Her love affair with writing and all its accoutrements extended through every aspect of her life and her work.

[9] My purpose here is not to study Plath's personal annotations, but the behaviors of those citizen critics who have annotated library copies of her primary texts. I mention Plath's own annotations to her personal library here as a way to draw a point of connection between Plath and her readership. While Plath's annotations were scholarly in nature, she is not so dissimilar from her citizen critics in their mutual preoccupation with materiality.

they also postulate that "some of the comments are produced with the explicit awareness of a possible audience, perhaps even with an intention of reaching them" (915). This "awareness" is acutely evident in the margins of library copies of Plath's work: generations of readers talk back to each other about her and her writing, commenting on the work itself, or using the white space to freely conjecture about a wide range of topics using the physical page as a forum. Readers respond to other readers, discussing and debating the previous annotations, creating an intense debate in the margins with Plath's poetry at center stage.

What is interesting is how readers may perceive the notes in a text from prior readers. Since annotations remain anonymous, and because there is no way to date or time-stamp the comments of the other readers, they become a singular entity standing outside or beside or inside the text. While not intending to be a maelstrom, it's evident with certain works — like "Daddy" or "Lady Lazarus," for example — that the marginalia can interfere with the reading of the work. It occupies the reader's imagination, standing in for what they might have thought or, indeed, could have thought, if it weren't for the opinions of others written out before them.

Fajkovic and Björneborn confirmed that seeing another person's annotations was an "interference, an annoyance, irrelevant, sloppy, patronizing, self-promoting" describing it as "a lot like public toilets graffiti," which participants identified as determining "a negative and neutral view of marginalia" (911). Given these conditions of reading, Fajkovic and Björneborn state that marginalia can be a communicative function between communities of readers and can "dramatically change the way we comprehend texts or what kind of reading experience we have" (916). Is it a reaction to this reading experience that precipitated the responses of the other readers to Plath, instead of, perhaps, to her poetry? Who is reading what, and how? Did they feel they needed to "set the record straight" on the poem's meaning? Or censor what they thought was an unpopular opinion?

In this regard, marginalia can not only operate as visual cues but also as aesthetic ones.[10] While underlining was the most common occurrence of marginalia in Fajkovic and Björneborn's survey, followed by vertical lines, summaries, and explanations, there were more uncommon instances, including things such as rough-and-ready translations and doodles. In the annotations I have documented in library copies of Plath's works, I have seen such doodles, including flying hearts, and a skull—even a faceless Gorgon, with a wild stand of snaking hair, pictured beside the title of the poem "Medusa."

Perhaps the most striking graphic illustration I encountered of reader-intervention in a Plath text was an annotated version of "Morning Song," which was accompanied by a flurry of green pen marks, repetitively struck against the page, and clearly drawn by a child.

Such annotations raise provocative questions about readers' encounters with library texts and relationships between books and readers.[11] I immediately asked myself: how

---

[10] I should clarify what I mean by the term "aesthetic" here. It's important to note that this is not a formal notion *per se*, but best understood as an "expressive dimension" of reader annotations. Many thanks to editor Anita Helle for this clarification of terminology.

[11] This calls to mind three of the five laws of library science as purported by Ranganathan: (1) books are for use; (2) every person his/her book; and (3) every book its reader. The assertion that the book somehow has an agency of its own, and that this agency is determined by its readership, is an interesting way of looking at marginalia, since annotations can be construed as permanent evidence of this agency and the reader's temporary "ownership" of the book, which permits the effacement of a book's pages.

FIGURE 3 Detail from the chapbook <*maniacs.*> (2017). In this image, a selected stanza from Plath's poem "Morning Song" has been isolated and removed from the original text, with its marginalia replicated and hand-drawn in successive layers of annotation, and taken from different library copies, using ink, correction fluid, and red and green pen. Photo: Christine Walde.

did the child perceive that writing in books was permissible? Had they seen other people doing it? Had that given them the agency to recreate the behavior they had witnessed? What was the instigating factor that made them choose that first page, with that pen, with that color ink? And how, I wondered, had the majority of the writing come to be executed in a locus of activity around the compounded word "cow-heavy"? Of all the marginalia drawings that I replicated, this was the example that seemed most especially strange and beautiful and ironic, given that the poem is about mothering and children. I especially liked how the marks mirrored the poem's ending and its subject matter: "the clear vowels" rising off the page in an arching crescendo of lines (see Figure 3).

Fajkovic and Björneborn assert that "[o]nce written, marginalia become physical artifacts, whose function is a constant and inseparable part of both the text and the physical book. Only total obliteration of the marginalia, their physical removal if possible, can make them abandon their function completely" (916). In this regard, even when the marginalia is erased or blocked with correction fluid, it has an ephemeral presence. It transforms the poem and its intended effect. Where once there were words, the page appears roughed-up or whitened. It is like a kind of ghost, haunted by what was once said, but which cannot be made legible anymore. This ghostly marginalia in Plath's work, I would argue, has as much presence as its doodled counterpart: but it speaks of a silencing, an intentional interruption or erasure in the life and meaning of the book. Someone has quite literally *had their hand in it*, and this abjective quality informs the reception of the work, as well as its interpretation.[12]

My intention in replicating the Plath marginalia in a series of drawings, by isolating the passages of text in an artistic way, was not only to be guided by these reader responses but also to illustrate and magnify the often profound-and-simultaneously-absurd nature of the public discourse about Plath by her citizen critics. What emerged from this process was a deeper understanding of the books themselves as material objects and vessels of reader-to-reader communication. These library copies were stand-alone historical and material artifacts, marked by the passage of time and its readers in a way that no digital version could illustrate. They had, in short, been *transformed* by the repeated annotations of readers; they bore the evidence of their being both reread and borrowed, over and over again. But why? What was it about these library books that made them so unique?

If we consider annotations of Plath in library books as material objects, we are inevitably drawn to consider the places from which they issue and circulate. With this in mind, I'd like to consider the library as a heterotopia in the Foucauldian sense, as theorized by Radford, Radford, and Lingel (2014), and as "a place one enters with the objective of being transformed" (745)—a place where one has the potential to experience multiple places at once within the same physical space, but in an unreal sense, like looking in a mirror (736).

While order and classification are essential components of a library and integral to its functioning and operations, it is precisely because of this rigor of order that "the disorder and the creativity of the imagination" (Radford et al. 742) is allowed to flourish. The atmosphere of Foucault's mixed, joint experience (Radford et al. 737) is a place of dynamic oppositions where seemingly contradictory forces co-exist along a rarefied threshold of being. In this regard, a library is simultaneously a private and public space, a physical place and an imaginary space, and a realm that embodies all of these elements.[13] The heterotopia of a library permits that habitation, and so, too, do the

---

[12]See Kristeva's definition of abjection here, and the subjective horror one feels when confronted by the corporeal reality between the Self and the Other. If we can think of the book as a mirror to the Self, then marginalia is the Other. Being forced to face annotations could be construed as being traumatic, causing a cognitive dissonance in the reader.

[13]This is Borges's infinite vision in *The Library of Babel*—the same place of rough magic symbolized by Prospero's dukedom-large-enough library in *The Tempest*.

books that inhabit it: "the book is a portal to something or somewhere else, the virtual space inherent in the heterotopia" (Radford et al. 743), extended by the illusions and activities of fantasy the library permits and engenders through its community of users. We must also remember that library books are only ever allowed to be borrowed, not owned, and what goes out must be returned to be recirculated, reborrowed, and reread. As an institution, the library operates within this central function of return, which makes possible the continuous cycle of scholarship, and the discursivity it engenders among communities of borrowers.

In "What is an Author?" Foucault writes that "the initiation of a discursive practice does not participate in its later transformations" and can only refer back to the original work, or as he called it, "the primary coordinates" (20). In this way, Foucault further states, "we can understand the inevitable field of discursivity, for a "return to the origin" (20). Through its discursive nature, marginalia permits readers, as we have seen, not only to witness and/or participate in the poem's interpretation but also to *return* to its origins, to Plath. By returning to these primary coordinates again and again, the book's material transformation—and its capacity to be annotated by its citizen critics—is infinite.

If we can see the marginalia in library copies of books by Sylvia Plath as more than interference, beyond reader-to-reader communications, we should consider the possibility that they are *not* "finished"[14] or stagnant copies; they live on precisely because they are always open to further interpretation, further discursivity. As physical texts, the annotations in library copies of Plath's works offer evidence of citizen critics at work. The books take shape, intertextually, beyond their borders, permitting multiple non-linear readings. Library books with marginalia, I would argue, are infinite or unending—always "open" to their point of origin, their primary coordinates. In this sense, readers, and, indeed, Plath, and the idea of "Sylvia Plath" are transformed and liberated by this concept of return.

There is a powerful connection between Plath's writing and her readership: their combined voltage meets mid-air in a positive and negative charge, seeking a place to strike. In *The Haunting of Sylvia Plath*, Jacqueline Rose states that it is largely impossible to separate Plath's voice from those that speak in her name, standing in effigy for her. "It is this effigy that haunts the culture" (2), Rose concludes—an effigy that must, by extension, include all of the marginalia written about Plath. I would also point out here that "culture" also includes libraries as institutions of learning and research, the acute realization of Habermas's third space.[15]

Reading Plath's work—particularly the *Ariel* poems—Rose asserts, is such an intense experience precisely because Plath evokes a collective memory about the terror of topics such as fascism and Nazism; it is "a fragment of the cultural unconscious that will not go away" (8). As such, this evocation can create a kind of transference between Plath and

---

[14] I am thinking here of Derrida's suggestion in *Of Grammatology* that the book is incomplete as long as writing works toward a finished state, precisely because writing cannot be traced back to an unmediated presence. The process of reading and perceiving the text is open to infinite possibilities.

[15] Jurgen Habermas's theory could be interpreted as being similar to the heterotopia; yet, it exists within the public sphere as a place of social debate, permitting public discourse and intellectual freedom. Libraries are increasingly understood as being "third spaces"; it could be argued that, by extension of their association, the print and digital collections of libraries are also representative of these areas of public debate.

readers, since they dangerously assume that the "I" is *her* speaking, without considering what "I" is, or how many "I"s there might be speaking in a single work.[16] Haunted, haunting readers react, using marginalia to express their feelings, using the book to document their experience.

Whether it is a comment scrawled in the margin, or a repeated word underlined for emphasis, or, as I have seen, each syllable struck through with pencil and every period circled, the effect is the same. The community of citizen critics is informed and emboldened by its previous participants, since each instance of marginalia grants permission to others to add their own opinion. This engenders further discursivity, creating a kind of hive mentality at work in the pages of the book.

These signs are, in short, maniacs—just like the bees Plath describes in her poem "The Arrival of the Bee Box." The word maniac is derived from the ancient Greek *maniokos* (*a "wild excitement"*), but here's the catch with maniacs: in their spontaneous annotations, individuals aren't necessarily aware of taking up this role. They are ignorant of their affliction, protected by it, unaware of the very condition that possesses them. In their collective noise, "the unintelligible syllables" accrue to "a Roman mob, / Small, taken one by one, but my god, together!" (*CP* 213). Similarly, the generations of citizen critics that populate the pages of Plath's works are like drones buzzing at the edges of the pages, building their combs of commentary, feeding young and future readers, carrying forward the dead husks of earlier annotations, transforming the colony.

Increasingly, as digital fluencies shape the way we interact and communicate with one another, new ways of encoding and annotating texts with digital tools present new opportunities for creating communities of global readership, citizen critics, and digital scholarship for the semantic web. With ongoing development in computational ontologies, "Plath_Sylvia" is bound to be reinvented (if it has not been already created) as a SPARQL[17] query, where bots, like worker bees, will trawl her effigy, feeding the machine-learning algorithm that supplies her readers with constant results, and finds new, unforeseen connections in the mycelial network of metadata that exists about her, clustered in electric data clouds, seeking new ground.

For now, annotated physical library copies of Plath's primary texts—and, arguably, every annotated library book—are more than just old, damaged, marked-up books. They are noisy ambassadors of the heterotopia, chaotic neutral containers of information freely circulating among the living and the dead, silently operating between stark worlds of reality and the imagination. As evidence of communication between readers in the margins of these texts, marginalia, it could be argued, go beyond being an affordance, becoming a facilitator of fantastical visions. Operating both inside and outside time, marginalia act as evidence of Foucault's threshold: the signal to the noise that the heterotopia makes possible between readers—a transformative experience that is shared, again and again, among communities of users.

---

[16]"Je est un autre"—I is an other—wrote Rimbaud. I think this is a critically important approach when reading Plath, since her "I" is not a fixed thing; it is a continually evolving and expanding definition of self, both known and unknown.

[17]Considered one of the most important tools of the semantic web, SPARQL (pronounced "sparkle," a recursive acronym for SPARQL Protocol and RDF Query Language) is an RDF query language—that is, a semantic query language for databases—able to retrieve and manipulate data stored in Resource Description Framework (RDF) format. (Definition taken from https://en.wikipedia.org/wiki/SPARQL#cite_note-3).

# CHAPTER EIGHT

# "God's Lioness" and God's "Negress": The Feminine and the Figure of the African American in Plath

JEROME ELLISON MURPHY

This chapter includes reference to and articulations of racism, which some readers may find triggering.

Sylvia Plath's references to race and ethnicity, particularly to Jewish identity, have long been discussed in the context of a poet's license to appropriate such material for personal usage. Plath's depictions of Blackness, however, remain under-discussed, as though the "[n]igger-eye" berries of her signature poem "Ariel" were those of a glaring elephant in the room (*CP* 239). One can condemn Plath's usage of this slur or, at the very least, find it painful or embarrassing to encounter. Some choose to willfully ignore it. Yet why is it there at all? Can we understand the work without it? Plath's work addresses radically individualistic subjects, such as private sexual relationships and the desire of the self for annihilation, operating in a private imaginative sphere with its own consistent symbols, and it might be fruitful here to attempt some of the same critical understanding afforded this poet's other extremist impulses. Rather than avoiding such moments, or condemning them and leaving it there, one might take a more diagnostic approach: linking references throughout Plath's writings for a clearer picture of this poet and the world in which she wrote. Examining the symbolic significance Blackness holds for Plath also contextualizes her other racial references, including whiteness; and without justifying such license, one can trace the associative logic Plath's work uses to portray still-resonating aspects of a mid-twentieth-century American psyche.

"Spain frightened you. Spain / Where I felt at home ... / ... the African / Black edges to everything, frightened you. / Your schooling had somehow neglected Spain. / ... / ... a bobby-sox American," writes Hughes in his collection *Birthday Letters* (*TH:CP* 1068). This depiction of Plath would seem to encapsulate what we know of Sylvia Plath's attitude toward Black Americans from reading her journals; Plath was the middle-class "bobby-sox American" and "academic" poet whose journal entries find the presence of Blacks a silent, somewhat threatening, edge to an existence sanctioned by America's dominant cultural narrative. Recounting an early experience with a fellow farm worker in Dover, Massachusetts, the summer after graduating from high school in 1950, she wrote: "He opened the door, and I stumbled blindly downstairs, past Maybelle and Robert, the little colored children, who called my name in the corrupted way children have of pronouncing things. Past Mary Lou, their mother, who stood there, a silent, dark presence" (J 11).

Indeed, Black people remain a "silent, dark presence" throughout Plath's journals, flickering briefly and infrequently in the passing blurs of description with which she crammed her pages, and usually imbued with this sense of threat or exoticism. Surely the real world was not devoid of Blacks in positions other than spinach pickers, "negro chauffeurs," maids, and "[n]egresses in fruity tropical colors," but this is how her reality as reflected in the journals exclusively perceives them (J 11, 377, 497, 610). In Plath's journals, Blacks occupy positions of servitude or exotic otherness exactly as captured by Hughes in "You Hated Spain." This pattern paves the way for the emotionally heightened hyperreality of *Ariel*, which amplifies the condition of servitude into that of explicit slavery and amplifies the associated sense of threat and otherness.

Rarely, if ever, in her journals does Plath's furiously scribbling pen endeavor to endow these figures with individuality; she writes instead how "all people of the Negro race look alike until you get to know them individually" (J 14). Her rational intelligence perceives them as fellow humans whom one is capable of getting to know individually, but her artistic impulse is to shape them into a symbolic device, the hazardous swam of outsiders who will take their fatal and mysterious vengeance: "Somewhere there will be the people that never mattered much in our scheme of things anyway. In India, perhaps, or Africa, they will rise" (J 32). This perception reminds one of the swarming dark bees of Plath's late "The Arrival of the Bee Box" or "Wintering," both of which emphasize the bees' communal blackness, their otherness, and their implicit threat. When Plath's fully realized later aesthetic refers to an individual Black self, in "Thalidomide," whose horrified speaker contemplates birth defects resulting from a medication once deemed safe for pregnant women, we find an image of alien danger and deception: "Negro, masked like a white, // Your dark / Amputations crawl and appall— / Spidery, unsafe" (CP 252).

Perhaps unsurprisingly, the social perspective found in Plath's journals anticipates at least one poetic gesture emphasizing Africa's distance from her everyday world. During ruminations on American foreign policy in a 1951 college diary entry, she writes: "Hell, I'd sooner be a citizen of Africa than see America mashed and bloody and making a fool of herself. This country has a lot, but we're not always right and pure" (J 46). Clearly, her hyperbolic statement views Africa as a last resort to the unfulfilled moral purity she desires from America. Later, in "The Rival," she will write: "No day is safe from news of you, / Walking about in Africa maybe, but thinking of me" (CP 167). Used as a poetic device, Africa signifies extreme distance, abstraction, from this speaker's everyday life—a life which nonetheless feels a menacing lack of refuge from its distant news.

Plath's use of race as a poetic device becomes, depending how one takes it, either less or more offensive with the understanding that this poet often uses race as representative of inner emotional and imaginative states, rather than in a literal sense, and feels privileged to do so. Identification, or appropriation? Both? Regardless, we can say that in Plath's work, depictions of "race" are neither journalistic nor precisely microcosmic: informed by sociological realities, they are distorted and reordered according to the logic of her interior universe.

Plath's use of the descriptor "Chinese" is one representative case. In "Wintering," there is a dark room that has "[n]o light / But the torch and its faint // Chinese yellow on appalling objects'"; in "Three Women," we find hieroglyphs that "paint such secrets in Arabic, Chinese!" (*CP* 218, 179). In both cases, the word "Chinese" suggests a racialized inscrutability (an all too familiar trope of American Orientalism, viewing East Asian culture and peoples as uniquely exotic and mysterious) and "foreignness" in a deeper sense, that of the poet's inability to properly perceive or comprehend, rather than a literal reference to an ethnic group or that group's language. In a draft of "Lady Lazarus," the speaker wonders if "I may be Japanese," and in "Fever 103°" she feels "my head [is] a moon / Of Japanese paper," in both cases referencing the ash of Hiroshima from which her renewed self will rise in transcendent Phoenix-like form (draft cited in *Writing Back* 192; *CP* 232). In Plath's work, race operates within her system of associative logic, so that races become a lexicon of "code words" for the speakers' interior conditions.

A brief look at Plath's notorious appropriation of Jewish history is useful to understanding her poetry's literal and figurative encodings of Blackness. If, as Stephen Gould Axelrod claims, Plath's introduction to "Daddy" "asserts that the poem concerns a young woman's paralyzing self-division, which she can only defeat through allegorical representation," it is helpful to explore what this self-division entails (*The Wound and the Cure of Words* 52). It may be that "Daddy" primarily concerns not the relationship between a Nazi and a half-Jew, but Plath's relationship to patriarchy ("Every woman adores a Fascist" [*CP* 223]): half belonging to this system, yet only finding her voice when identifying with outsiders and thus beginning "to talk like a Jew" (*CP* 223). The German tongue of the Daddy who stands at the blackboard represents what stifled and paralyzed her about the male canon: "I could hardly speak" (*CP* 223). Axelrod makes the following observation concerning Plath's femininity in relation to her use of racial poetic conceits:

> [H]er formal education had taught her to admire canonized authors who were white and male. ... Plath's personal library reflects this orientation. Her personal anthologies were edited by men [...] and included mostly male poets, virtually none of whom belonged to the ethnic groups with which she tended to identify herself, such as Jews, African Americans, and Asians. Indeed, her library prepares us to understand Plath's identification with minority cultures. In the anthologies and on the book shelves, women also constituted a small and endangered minority.
>
> (*The Wound and the Cure of Words* 36)

Axelrod's argument persuasively presents the possibility that Plath had modeled her literary style on that of male writers, but only found what she considered to be her true poetic voice with the influence of poets like Anne Sexton, who dared write about "taboo" subject matter from a feminine perspective, and that Plath's identification with racial minorities and cultures of Others was deeply informed by her status as a woman. Late works like "Purdah," in which the Indian setting is forcefully linked with segregation by gender, would seem to confirm this idea. Plath's underlying outrage is that, as the song title written by John Lennon and Yoko Ono so forcefully and controversially argued, "Woman Is the N-Word of the World."[1] One need neither share this notion nor endorse this encapsulation of it to grasp Plath's associative logic.

---

[1] In this instance, "n-word" replaces the word in the title of the song.

Although in *Ariel* the speaker often explicitly presents herself as white and associates this color—or lack of color—with a notion of purity, as in the titular poem ("White / Godiva, I unpeel—" [*CP* 239]), such identity is subject to a strange dichotomy, for Plath as often links whiteness with annihilation as with perfection and purity. Even white Godiva in "Ariel" ends in a "[s]uicidal," if creative, dissolve of corporeal transformation (*CP* 239–40). Plath's descriptive language tends to resist categorical interpretation, and indeed it is among her strengths as a poet to make ostensibly simple words such as "black" and "white" bud with multiple meanings, but the whiteness-death trope is consistent from the earlier to the later work. In "Wuthering Heights," the speaker notes: "If I pay the roots of the heather / Too close attention, they will invite me / To whiten my bones among them" (*CP* 167). "Finisterre" similarly finds the sea "[w]hitened by the faces of the drowned" (*CP* 169). "Insomniac" discovers "a bonewhite light, like death, behind all things" (*CP* 163). The famous late poem "Edge" depicts children as "white serpents" in a scene of deadly perfection (*CP* 272). "Words" employs painterly emphasis in describing "[a] white skull, / Eaten by weedy greens" (*CP* 270). Plath often employs "pallor" in this sense. The speaker proposes in "Purdah," "should / The moon, my / Indefatigable cousin // Rise, with her cancerous pallors" (*CP* 242). Needless to say, Plath's speakers rarely find comfort in the female figure of the cold white moon who is "[w]hite as a knuckle and terribly upset" ("The Moon and the Yew Tree") or "[s]taring from her hood of bone" ("Edge") (*CP* 173, 273).

Yet even in "Edge," there is the presence of blackness: "her blacks crackle and drag" (*CP* 273). What is this blackness, and what associates it with death, or with the white moon, which is "used to this sort of thing" (*CP* 273)? How does this blackness relate to the blackness of bees in "Wintering," "[b]lack / Mind against all that white," and in poems such as "The Arrival of the Bee Box" where metaphorical eye melts bees into actual Africans, "[b]lack on black, angrily clambering" (*CP* 218, 213)?

One important solution lies in Plath's use of a whiteness against which what is "colored" is memorably juxtaposed. Though Plath's work often depicts a white self as purified and/ or superior, poems like "In Plaster" dramatize ambivalence about such superiority and perfection. "[T]he white person is certainly the superior one," Plath's speaker asserts (*CP* 158). But "In Plaster" articulates this speaker's discomfort inside her perfect white self, and the speaker, who is "ugly and hairy," plots to get along without that flawless "saint" (*CP* 160). Similarly, Plath's earlier poem, "On the Plethora of Dryads," contrasts the raving of a "white saint" about a beauty "visible only to the paragon heart" with the speaker's own fascination with "[e]very pock and stain" and "eccentric knob and wart" (*CP* 67). Plath's speakers often convey the sense that a paragon, saintly whiteness, indeed "perfection," does not allow for something uglier but truer to life that wants expression. She identifies with a canonized classical whiteness but feels torn by a need to express attitudes—perhaps unpleasant ones, decidedly out of the saint's repertoire—that might be seen as culminating in the speaker's identification with the figure of the Jew, as opposed to that of the Aryan, in "Daddy."

"Whiteness" is also depicted as stifling not only to expression but even to the speaker's life force; this staging is often enacted by placing it in opposition to redness, particularly that of blood. In "Tulips," whiteness contrasts with redness to illustrate the speaker's ambivalence toward life, versus absolute peace and stillness ("The tulips are too excitable, it is winter here"; "[t]heir redness talks to my wound, it corresponds" (*CP* 160–1). Red represents the poet's uncontrollable life force, which exhausts her, but is vital to poetic expression. In "Kindness," "[t]he blood jet is poetry, / There is no stopping it" (*CP* 270).

Similarly, the poem "Cut" captures a flood of poetic inspiration issuing from a "[d]ead white" skin flap (*CP* 235). In "Cut," the stifling or deadening aspect of whiteness is also present in a bandage unsuccessfully attempting to stanch the blood's flow. "The stain on your / Gauze Ku Klux Klan / Babushka / Darkens" (*CP* 235–6). The speaker observes her bandaged finger, suggesting that whiteness's attempt to suppress the creative life force, which has resulted in a flood of associatively connected images, is consonant with violent historical oppression of the Other. Mimicking the running dry of blood, the poem's unstoppable current of description runs dry with the phrases: "Dirty girl, / Thumb stump" (*CP* 236). The choice of language is notable not only in the consistent theme of the taboo feminine ("Dirty girl") versus oppressive whiteness, but in that this white bandage attempting to suppress the lifeblood is explicitly an oppressive Ku Klux Klan uniform—a representative case of Plath's linking of blood and creativity, or taboo poetic truth, with the idea of racial "Blackness."

All these associations seem to suggest that whiteness is as much subject to the poetic license of the poet's ordering imagination, and serves as much for her as a symbolic shorthand, as does blackness: it becomes another "code" by which Plath's speakers stage the particulars of a given psychological scene. This understanding of the serviceability of whiteness could make Plath's use of Blackness (and other racial identifiers) less offensive to some readers, or simply highlight disparities, for there are no equivalent racial slurs to that used in "Ariel." In its theatrical gestures, Plath's poetic imagination is an amoral engine of sociological caricature, depicting racial identities as existential *states*. Without drawing any false equivalences between the actual social status of different racial groups in Plath's time (or ours), one sees how whiteness becomes for Plath another hue in the poetic paintbrush, a distillate of associative meaning.

Alongside her use of whiteness, there is a thematic thread in Plath's work binding blackness with blood; yet blood seems an aspect of blackness, rather than working in opposition to it. In "Blackberrying" the speaker finds "[b]lackberries / Big as the ball of my thumb, and dumb as eyes / Ebon in the hedges, fat / With blue-red juices"; she observes, "I had not asked for such a blood sisterhood; they must love me" (*CP* 168). Not only does the blood-thumb phrasing remind one of "Cut," but the depiction of black berries as black eyes will find a more potent expression in the "[n]igger-eye / [b]erries" of "Ariel." Here, however, the speaker "had not asked for such a blood sisterhood." It is almost as if the poet anticipates here the taboo feminine themes of the unconventional late poetics. Indeed, the voice of her final poetic fury, so unlike that of the poets of her admired canon, is something she "had not asked for" and comes somewhat unexpectedly (*CP* 168). "[T]hey must love me," the speaker speculates, finding unexpected communion in the berries (*CP* 168). Here blackness is "dumb" or voiceless, as in her 1950 journal entry a "silent, dark presence," but seems inextricable from the "taboo" poetic aesthetic of blood, truth, and feminine rage she is developing for herself. It links not only with her conscious minority status as a woman, but as an artist—specifically an artist whose vision encompasses the "ugly and hairy" in life, and not only that which is conventionally beautiful (*CP* 160).

When the speaker of Plath's signature "Ariel" asserts that "[n]igger-eye / Berries cast dark / Hooks— / Black sweet blood mouthfuls, / Shadows," one finds the conceit of blackness/blood in its ultimate compression, using the same loaded racial term employed by John Lennon and Yoko Ono's deliberately controversial "Woman Is the N-Word of the World" (*CP* 239). The term seems deliberately chosen by Plath for its fistlike force, mimetic of violent oppression or abuse, in the same manner that Plath commonly uses code words for their forceful metonymy. Yet if the berries are attempting to cast hooks at Plath's purifying rider, the whitening Godiva, to in some way hinder or injure her, they are also black "mouthfuls" she finds "sweet," as if to link this conception of blackness with poetry—the mouthfuls of poetic lifeblood she discovered in her final months. "I just like good mouthfuls of sound which have meaning," Plath would tell an interviewer (qtd. in *Red Comet* 523).[2] Something about this threatening or injurious blackness is also sweet, alluring, as in "The Arrival of the Bee Box," and "Ariel" propels the speaker into the redness with which blackness has been linked, whose dangerous but liberating life force concludes many of the *Ariel* poems with such indelible power.

"The box is locked, it is dangerous. / I have to live with it overnight / And I can't keep away from it," observes the rapt speaker of "The Arrival of the Bee Box" (*CP* 213). The box is filled with bees described as miniature Africans ("Black on black, angrily clambering" [*CP* 213]). On one level, this metaphor surely describes her poetic inspiration, which provides liberation with a self-destructive sting, linked as it is with repressed rage and the implacable will of a deity alluded to as "The Bee God" by Ted Hughes. In his poem with this title, Hughes interprets Plath's attraction to bees as a connection to the uncanny authority of her lost father: "When you wanted bees I never dreamed / It meant your Daddy had come up out of the well" (*TH:CP* 1140). Hughes seems to suggest that Plath, by exerting a hazardous control over a population of bees as her late father did, once more becomes "The Beekeeper's Daughter." In her 1959 poem of that name, Plath's speaker had viewed flower anthers as "potent as kings / to father dynasties" and found "a queenship no mother can contest" (*CP* 104). In "The Arrival of the Bee Box," evidence for a newfound sense of ownership related to language can be felt in the description of the bee box, particularly the sound made by the bees ("unintelligible syllables" and "furious Latin" [*CP* 213]), and then in the speaker's ambivalent sense of sovereignty over them, which endows her with a godlike status ("I ordered this"; "I am the owner"; "I am not a Caesar. / I have simply ordered a box of maniacs"; "Tomorrow I will be sweet God, I will set them free") (*CP* 212–13).

Plath's reference to a racialized Blackness is repeatedly used in this way, as a poetic device for staging disparities in rank and in agency. In "The Jailer," which finds Plath's speaker at the mercy of a patriarchal presence, the tortured and captive persona observes: "He has been burning me with cigarettes, / Pretending I am a negress with pink paws. / I am myself. That is not enough" (*CP* 226). Here the racial reference is deployed in service of a sense of powerlessness the speaker experiences at the hands of her male captor and shows Plath's (stereo)typical use of the negress as a symbol for the exotic: I am not exotic enough; he must pretend I am something more exotic. This language recalls the journal entry with "negresses in fruity tropical colors" (*J* 610), while the distasteful reference to "pink paws" deploys a stereotyped image of Blackness, particularly feminine Blackness, as not only exotic but primitive, animal, sensual. Such moments in Plath, while painful to encounter, are revealing ones, allowing an intersectional view of how feminist perspectives like that of "The Applicant," which bitterly depicts female objectification, co-exist with Plath's racist tropes (*CP* 221–2). In our own day and time, they would seem to provide a lesson in the blind spots of privilege, and in the perpetuation of oppressive hierarchy by those who deem themselves to be relatively powerless.

---

[2]From an interview conducted by Lee Anderson, April 18, 1958, for the Library of Congress. Audio cassette, box 23, folder 1, Smith.

Yet these pink paws also emphasize vulnerability and delicacy. Plath's relatively infrequent use of pink is not as often discussed as the reds, blacks, and whites that suffuse her poetic palette with such vividness. The early poem "Sow" depicts "pink teats" at which little piglets suckle; the late "Balloons" speaks of an infant's "funny pink world he might eat," a fragile world glimpsed through a balloon which then pops (*CP* 61, 272). It seems only Paradise, to which the speaker of "Fever 103°" ascends, would be hospitable to such delicate entities: "roses, / ... kisses ... cherubim, / ... whatever these pink things mean. / ... / To Paradise" (*CP* 232). Knowing the consistency of Plath's poetic conceits, one feels that a similar sense of delicate vulnerability is inseparable from the exoticism and illicit "otherness" of the blackface imagery in "The Jailer," which dramatizes a state of oppressed femininity (*CP* 226–7).

Though one might be tempted to seek the racial signifier in Plath's each use of "blackness," this would likely overlook other facets of meaning and overburden every usage with automatic connotation. In "Daddy," for example, it seems clear that the "black man who / bit my pretty red heart in two" is intended to be black with devilry and evil, as opposed to racial Blackness. While the associative overlap of these types of blackness is a larger subject than we fully reckon with here, one can say that because Plath frequently plays on culturally shared connotations, certain usages are questionable in this regard, as in "Wintering": "[The bees] ball in a mass, / Black / Mind against all that white" (*CP* 218). Emphasizing Blackness with stark enjambment, Plath in effect italicizes it with a significance that is not entirely clear. Is it simply visual? Is it sociological? Is it wryly theological, implying a "black mass"? She does tell the reader that "[t]he bees are all women," which offers another pairing of blackness with the disempowered status of the feminine (*CP* 218). Yet earlier stanzas describe a room of indeterminate menace, where "the black bunched in there like a bat, no light / But the torch and its faint / Chinese yellow on appalling objects," as the speaker considers that "[t]his is the room I have never been in. / This is the room I could never breathe in" (*CP* 218). The ethnic minority reference, the link to bees (where the blackness bunches like bees that ball in a mass), along with a room described as specifically "at the heart of the house," suggests that these references signify a state of mind, threatening, dark, yet liberating, which the poet had not entered before—the heart of her subject matter. "The room I have never been in" is finally entered, yielding psychological risks represented by swarming female bees, their darkness bristling against the restrictive symbolic whiteness that had stifled her: a whiteness that could also be a visual reference for the white of the page ("Black / Mind against all that white" [*CP* 218]). Indeed, these swarming women "have got rid of the men, / The blunt, clumsy stumblers, the boors," and now "[t]hey taste the spring" (*CP* 218–19, 219).

While Plath's use of Jewishness has clearer links to her conceptions of the occult and the un-Christian, linked in turn with her notion of the ability to create a poetic "magic" (her journals refer to a "witchy Jewess," and "Daddy" refers to a "gipsy ancestress," as well as to trafficking in Taroc cards and "weird luck"), it remains uncertain to what extent the poet associates minority status with her empowerment through art-making (*CP* 223). Hughes's "You Hated Spain" references the voodoo qualities of "the juju land behind your African lips," but this is Hughes's association, not Plath's (*J* 608, *CP* 223, *TH:CP* 1068). It remains mysterious whether the blacks that "crackle and drag" in "Edge" refer to female creative power because they belong to a moon that is "used to this sort of thing," and therefore unfazed at the tableau the "perfected" dead woman has accomplished. Such an explanation hardly seems final, when in Plath's late poems the moon is as often associated with a sense of nullity or barrenness; even in the ambiguous "Elm," the image of a tree letting go of a moon seems consonant with that in "Childless Woman" or "The Munich Mannequins," depicting the launch of ova into barren wombs (CP 163, 259, 262). However, death and creative empowerment are not unrelated in Plath's work (the signature "Ariel" being only one example). Blackness, too, is associated with death, from the vampiric "Daddy" figure to the black telephones in "The Munich Mannequins," "digesting / Voicelessness" (CP 263).

We can say that blackness in Plath's poetic work seems generally linked with a sense of minority status, an oppressed sense of "voicelessness" and ensuing retribution, as well as with Thanatos; and from the berry-hooks cast in "Ariel" to the swarms of Plath's bee sequence, blackness always retains its sense of menace. In her more explicitly racial moments, acting as a white woman of her historical and social milieu, Plath reaches for Blackness as a ready symbol for her own marginalization, a social condition that is on the cusp of self-liberation and a vengeful defiance. And in this same imaginative world, racial whiteness is frequently portrayed as stifling, an oppressive force imposing misguided notions of purity (finding its most literal expression in the Aryan Nazi of "Daddy"). Interrogating such tropes as unchecked acts of imagination, one ponders the perennial tug-of-war between artistic impulse and social conscience. Yet we continue to read Plath because such simple metaphorical correlations are not the whole story; her poetry's thematic threads are inextricable and, at times, variously interpretable. Intriguing strands we might want to preserve are interwoven with unfortunate ones we might like to forget: dense knots of association, resulting in hyperbolic, at times ethically questionable effects, are among Plath's defining traits as a poet.

Finally, the moon in "Edge," with her crackling "blacks," may watch unfazed because she is used to feminine helplessness, Medean drive for retribution, the feminine death-drive: perhaps all three (CP 273). It is impossible to say once and for all what Plath intends by certain recurring associations that at times literally bleed into one another in her poems. One is left like Plath's speaker in "The Detective," a caricature of Doyle's Sherlock Holmes: "There is only the moon, embalmed in phosphorus. / There is only a crow in a tree. Make notes" (CP 209). Such notes will likely provide both creative inspiration and cautionary tale. But Plath's ambiguity of meaning and charged subject matter continue to prompt our critical reassessment of the disturbingly recognizable landscape she depicts in her most fully achieved poetic work.

# CHAPTER NINE

# Centering Whiteness: Sylvia Plath's Literary Apprenticeship

MAEVE O'BRIEN

Nowhere is it timelier and more relevant to examine how the American literary tradition has centered the racialized ideology of whiteness than alongside the work of Sylvia Plath. Within Plath criticism, there has been a significant blind spot regarding the comprehensive investigation of issues pertaining to race and white supremacy in relation to her writings and lived experience. In the 1990s, Malin Walther Pereira's contribution to this conversation offered a close examination of Plath's "bee poems," which prompted critics such as Harold Bloom and Steven Gould Axelrod to offer a cursory acknowledgment of "white colonization" and race as themes present in the same poetic set (*Bloom's Major Poets* 38; *The Wound and the Cure of Words* 36). But it was Renée R. Curry in *White Women Writing White: H. D. Elizabeth Bishop, Sylvia Plath, and Whiteness* (2000) who threw open the door to using critical race theory as a methodological tool by which to examine some of the most important poets of the last century through a racial lens. By and large, in Curry's work, white women writers of the American twentieth century—particularly in the case of Plath—are seen to be wholly ignorant of the privilege of their race (*White Women Writing White* 8). Curry outlines the repeated deployment of "color blindness" whereby white women writers have employed a "selective perception" to remove themselves from their awareness of—and participation in—harmful racist structures that have led to the need for educational curricula to be decolonized and cultural norms to be upended in order to create a fair, diverse, and anti-racist society—something still being fought for at this present moment (*White Women Writing White* 13–14).

Since the 1960s, a key consideration when studying the work of Plath has been grasping how she navigated the multiple barriers and restrictions that impeded her creativity and writing attempts. Critics have analyzed how the posthumous editing of Plath's body of work has imposed narratives that stray from her original vision. In particular, Marjorie Perloff's tracking of the editorial decision-making behind the structuring and reordering of *Ariel* has undoubtedly impacted how we understand her poetry ("The Two *Ariel*s"). Similarly, much has been written about how the restrictive gender roles of Plath's society and culture shaped her desire to pursue a career as a writer.[1] Indeed, Betty Friedan's

---

[1] Jerome Mazzaro is one of many critics who argued that Plath's capacity to pursue writing as a vocation was obstructed by virtue of her gender (220).

groundbreaking text, *The Feminine Mystique* (1963), has often been considered a complimentary text to read alongside Plath's work—not only because of Plath's and Friedan's similar educational backgrounds (both attended Smith College, though Plath did so later)—but because Friedan's work epitomized the barriers Plath's particular demographic of women experienced during the pre-second wave feminist era of the 1950s, where the American government promoted the domestic realm as the epitome of "feminine fulfillment" (61).

However, when discussing the restrictions women writers like Plath experienced in relation to having their work read and published, in general, the critical conversation too often seems to stop with its look back at contexts of second-wave feminism. It is apparent that there is less sustained interest in interrogating the restrictions that Plath and other writers profited *from* by virtue of their race and identity as white women. Consider, for example, Elaine Showalter's 1971 essay "Women and the Literary Curriculum." As one of the most significant feminist essays of its era, Showalter outlined the gendered imbalance that favored male words and work that was evident in education syllabi, literary anthologies, and in literary institutions in general in the United States. In her essay, Showalter posits that the marginalization of women's voices on educational curricula had a negative impact on creative women, women in academia, and women in society in general. She claims that the women of Plath's era did not have "equal opportunity either in the society or in the classroom" and that work by females was largely "ignored, ridiculed or scorned" (Showalter 857). By treating the grouping of "woman" as a rigid monolith, however, Showalter neglects to take into consideration how other identity-markers such as race, sexuality, and class also impacted and impeded creative women from writing and having their work published. Words from poet and critic Denise Riley in 1987 are instructive here, pointing out that "concentration on, and refusal of, the monolithic identity of 'women' is essential to feminism" (35). Riley argued that while "woman" can be a useful descriptive term, it is necessary that the diverse identities that fall under this umbrella term are also outlined. In Showalter's case, refusing to delve into the different identities that exist under the term "woman" is foundationally detrimental to her argument and limits her overall point about the development of educational syllabi to systematically impose barriers upon women writers. Factoring race into Showalter's methodology would add an additional lens whereby questions would be asked as to whether white writers such as Sylvia Plath in some cases benefited from the barriers imposed on Black women and women of color who were doubly creatively disenfranchised due to both their gender and race.

Writing a decade later and marking the beginning of an intersectional critique of language, literature, and identity informed by race, bell hooks made the point that

> the hierarchical pattern of race and sex relationships already established in American society merely took a different form under feminism: the form of women's studies programs being established with all-white faculty teaching literature almost exclusively by white women about white women and frequently from racist perspectives; the form of white women writing books that purport to be about the experience of American women when in fact they concentrate solely on the experience of white women; and finally the form of endless argument and debate as to whether or not racism was a feminist issue.
>
> (166)

Here, hooks asserts that the gains and advances made by women during second-wave feminism did not equate with the advancement of all women. In contrast, the issue of race was often seen by white second-wave feminists as divorced from the fight for women's equity. With this division in mind, it is especially interesting to note the racial disparities evidenced when Plath's poetry became a totemic anthem for the second-wave feminist movement in the United States in the mid-to-late 1960s. Writer Meghan O'Rourke observes that second-wave feminism was "born almost simultaneously with Plath's death" and, as a result, Plath's work gained platform because white women's anger and lived experiences became acceptable alongside this cultural rise of feminism—in a climate where the personal became political (337). For Black women and women writers of color, however, there were fewer such opportunities—and returning to hooks we can deduce that American second-wave feminism largely considered the plight of the woman to be the plight of the *white* women. Indeed, what we can surmise from hooks is that when a door to career advancement opened as a result of feminist gains, more often than not, white women/white structures entered but closed the door behind them. This assertion offers a possible explanation as to the sustained popularity of Plath's work in contrast to why it has taken until recent years for writers of colour to become associated with the so-called "confessional" genre.[2]

It is of course necessary to unpack Plath's relationship with race—and, in particular, her own whiteness—prior to the posthumous evolution of her writing, given that she had no control over how her work would be received, understood, or used. However, a close examination of the material Plath dwells upon in her poems, stories, letters, and journal entries allows us a window into her own understanding of race and its relevance in her life. For example, it is possible to read a subtle and insidious example of white women writers "closing the door" when considering Plath's short critical essay "Context." Written in response to questions posed by *London Magazine* in 1962, Plath observes that "the conservation of life of all people in all places" is of a significant concern to her as a poet (*JP* 66). However, it is somewhat difficult to reconcile Plath's position here when we reflect on the fact that she failed to engage with the issue of race and division in the United States—in a tense and inhumane period in modern American history, prior to Civil Rights Act of 1964.

The presence of white privilege is evident here given that Plath could feasibly consider herself as a person concerned with the conservation of life—yet she largely ignores the Civil Rights Movement and racial disparities of her homeland that were contemporary to her and deeply enmeshed in her history. While it is perhaps unfair to scrutinize "Context" as a sole declaration of Plath's personal and poetic concerns about her self and her society, the scant mention of race issues throughout her poetry, journals, or letters is telling and adds weight to a certain measure of ignorance made possible through white privilege. In Plath's *Letters Volume I*, we see her make cursory mentions of African American friends she made at Cambridge (*L1* 1002), and prior to that, in 1954 Plath wrote in a fetishistic manner about her experience as "the only white girl at an all-Negro party"—declaring that this was an important moment of "action" in her life (*L1* 680). Later, in 1960, when reflecting on the problem of being declined a flat in London because letting agents could

---

[2] Work of this kind has been pioneered by scholars such as Lara Rodriguez, who argues for the inclusion of Black writer Etheridge Knight within this mode. See also Christopher Grobe's discussion of the "unbearable burden of whiteness" as performance in the midcentury confessional modes (37–44).

not abide "children, Nergos or dogs," the major problem Plath dwells on here is the disruption such polities caused her personally (*L2* 503–4).

What is clear, however, is that as Plath professionalized herself as a writer, the literary institutions she concerned herself with and craved acceptance from were deeply bound up in the centering of white voices and texts. Plath carries out the work of centering whiteness in "Context." She approvingly cites an array of white poets such as Robert Lowell and Theodore Roethke, Stevie Smith and Elizabeth Bishop as inspirational contemporaries. By situating herself and her creative ambitions alongside fellow white writers, Plath demonstrates her lack of engagement with and obliviousness of writers of color. Compounded by the fact that, of the twenty-six poets to whom the "Context" question was posed, only one was a writer of color, the Caribbean poet Derek Walcott,[3] the essay and its publication illustrate the prominence of white intellectual perspectives and traditions in Plath's creative world and demonstrate how her literary imagination was racially segregated by virtue of the publications where she submitted her work.

Gayatri Chakravorty Spivak's trenchant critique of literature and education can be used to sharpen the focus on Plath's positioning within the canonical study, providing illumination of the voices, words, and experiences that were invited onto platforms within literary institutions, and those who were not. Spivak discusses how certain narratives of realities are "established as the normative one" (76), explaining how it has been possible for American literature to be categorized and taught as the study of what Shannon Sullivan calls an egalitarian "melting pot" with fabled stories of "the new man" (81). Using Spivak's methodology, a clearer picture of the American dream is formulated when we consider who is conspicuous by their absence in the traditional literary canon. "For the most part," says Toni Morrison, "the literature of the United States has taken as its concern the architecture of a new white man" (14–15). Morrison argues that the mainstream American literary canon is utterly unshaped by African and African American creativity. She insists upon acknowledgment of the existence of a far-reaching, multifaceted, and enduring literary and cultural tradition amongst marginalized communities but argues that these contributions have not been documented or represented by tastemakers, university teachers, and booksellers due to the assumption that non-white cultural expression is "Other," a niche taste, or outside of traditional literary structures. Going further, Morrison details an approach to understanding the contemporary cultural mores of the United States as "literary whiteness"—developing this term as a working praxis by which to understand how literary canons, curricula, and media platforms are curated and created (4). Morrison asserts that by centering the white lived experience, the American literary tradition has been racialized where whiteness is the norm. She reminds us to notice what voices are absent, reminding us to consider presences as much as absences in our readings of contemporary American literature.

For Sylvia Plath, writing and studying under white, male-dominated academic curricula had a profound impact on her creativity—arguably causing her to internalize and reproduce white, patriarchal literary values in an attempt to increase her chances of being published or taken seriously within the male-dominated literary canon. We know that Plath's writing was intrinsically shaped by her education—a key feature of her artistic evolution is the extent to which her academic apprenticeship from her studies as a young

---

[3] See "Putting Sylvia Plath's 'Context' in Context."

child through to her Master's degree at Cambridge shaped her creative mind. Further, meticulous and probing contributions from critics such as Amanda Golden have mapped how Plath's marginalia can be traced to her process as an academic, thinker, and teacher. Because of this connection, it is possible to understand the direct link between the work Plath was taught and the words that ended up on her page. The curricula learned by the impressionable and enthusiastic Plath led to her development of a literary imagination that endured throughout her writing life where white bodies, voices, experiences, and histories were prioritized—with whiteness becoming the center of Plath's creative and intellectual landscape and rendering her a stranger to other linguistic traditions.

Like most schoolchildren and students living and being educated in the United States in the mid-twentieth century, Plath's introduction to English literature was predominately directed by texts written by white men. Biographer Anne Stevenson recounts that Plath's earliest memory of being introduced to poetry was through her mother's reading of "The Forsaken Merman" by Matthew Arnold to her children at bedtime—Plath maintained that hearing this poem ignited her lifelong passion for poetry (9). Additionally, Linda Wagner-Martin has documented the types of novels and thinkers that Plath encountered while participating in an advanced English literature class during her high school years— ranging from "Hemingway, Eliot, Frost, Dickinson, Faulkner, Hardy, Lawrence, Yeats, Joyce, Woolf, Dylan Thomas, much Shakespeare, Plato, Greek drama, Mann" (*Sylvia Plath: A Biography* 43). Fundamental to Plath's adherence to canonical norms was engaging with these white male writers and being mentored by icons of academic male masculinity. Indeed, Plath herself wondered if her attraction to male mentors signified an underlying desire to fill the void created by the loss of her father, writing in her *Journals* in 1951, "[y]ou wonder if the absence of an older man in the house has anything to do with your intense craving for male company and the delight in the restful low sound of a group of boys, talking and laughing" (*J* 64). We can see evidence of this in her work with Wellesley High School English teacher Wilbury Crockett, who taught Plath during the years 1948–50. Luke Ferretter notes that it was under Crockett's tutelage that Plath began to write stories that would "prefigure the concerns of [her] mature work" (3), and in 1951 Plath herself confirmed the lasting impact of Crockett's influence on her creative and intellectual subjectivity in her *Journals*, calling him "the man through high school who fostered your intellectual life" (*J* 65).

Later, as a student at Smith College, Jo Gill notes, Plath continued to encounter and read works almost exclusively by white male thinkers and writers. She "was reading Erich Fromm, Karl Jung, Friedrich Nietzsche, Karl Marx, Henry James, Sherwood Anderson, Nathaniel Hawthorne, Theodore Dreiser, and her college honors thesis analyzed the work of Dostoyevsky" (*Cambridge Introduction* 83). Continuing her trend of seeking out male mentors for her writing, at Smith Plath was taught and influenced by teachers Robert Gorham Davis, Alfred Kazin, and Alfred Young Fisher. She looked to these men for advice and assistance with her creative work. Even in 1957, after Plath had graduated from Smith, she continued to employ their tactics and suggestions in her attempts at writing: "Do it. Like Kazin said," she wrote in her *Journals*, even though in her next thought she acknowledged this advice conflicted with her own writing process, "but for me to break open an idea in summary is at this early stage a life-saving event" (*J* 288). That Plath felt so indebted and devoted to the advice offered to her by men illustrates her desire to fit in and be accepted into the white male-dominated American literary canon. Indeed, despite a cordial relationship with her supervisor Dorothea Krook at Cambridge, Plath's ambivalence toward other women writers and scholars is another aspect of her adherence to canonical male models of literary expression. Gill has posited that "it would be misleading to overlook the value to Plath of a female literary tradition" (*Cambridge Introduction* 18), but by and large her relationship with female contemporaries was at best problematic—oscillating between jealousy and competition. To this end, Al Strangeways has suggested that, in the early years of her poetic apprenticeship, Plath neither sought to identify as a woman writer nor did she look for guidance from them:

> While Plath occasionally views female writers such as Woolf as allies, her frequent attacks both on Woolf and on contemporary women writers implies the existence of an equally anxious relationship with the female literary tradition [...] Conversely, male writers, while sometimes seen as rivals, figure more frequently in her journals as allies: again, perhaps, because Plath sees them as more different from herself, more distant and less threatening and perhaps because she held such male "masters" in greater esteem.
>
> (32–3)

Relevant here is the critique of Sandra M. Gilbert and Susan Gubar, who cite Plath as an example of a women writer who experienced anxiety over the patriarchal lineage of literature, arguing that many women writers found it preferable to replicate "institutionalized and often elaborately metaphoric misogyny" in order to conform and fit in with traditional patriarchal literary norms (*Madwoman in the Attic* 189). Indeed, given the white male-dominated climate and social, cultural, and political expectations of her era, Plath's decision to surround herself with male figures can be read as a pragmatic choice for a young white American woman hoping to write and be published.

Indeed, as her early poetry and short stories account, Plath spent a concerted amount of time attempting to emulate the norms and codes of midcentury American literary practices in her own writing. This is demonstrated most clearly when, in her college years, Plath subscribed to *The Writer* magazine and methodically underlined advice on how to create popular and marketable work that, as Jacqueline Rose has commented, would reinforce typical gender norms (*Haunting* 122). Further, Plath annotated and underlined much of her copy of *The Complete Rhyming Dictionary*, familiarizing herself with the standardized poetic styles and forms. "No one can write poems without engaging with the complex of themes, images, myths, stereotypes, reference points and conventions which are roughly denominated by the word 'tradition'," writes critic Jan Montefiore, "even if a poet knows only the work of contemporaries, she will still be influenced by contemporary conventions of writing" (15). Montefiore's observation here illustrates how deeply embedded elements such as form, structure, and style are to the white, male-dominated literary tradition. By attuning herself to these constructs, especially in her early years as a writer, Plath sought to emulate these traditional and canonical standards in her own writing.

It is interesting to read Plath's absorption of the norms of what bell hooks calls "Standard English" as an inherently political act. Language and expression are at its core devices that have been developed by those who occupy power and in the Western world, prompting Dale Spender to define academic English as a white, male, colonial, and heteronormative institution (11–12). Spender made the claim that marginalized writers such as women struggle to use Standard English as a mode of expression because it has been foisted upon them—it is not a form of communication they have had a hand in creating. Standard English, therefore, caters only to the expression of emotion from white men who espouse qualities of traditional masculine norms. Because men have controlled language and the production of meaning, women "have been unable to give weight to their own symbolic meanings, they have been unable to pass on a tradition of women's meanings of the world" (52). Spender's argument corresponds strongly with thoughts on language by African American writers and thinkers who agree that Standard English can be conceptualized as an imposed barrier that limits expression. bell hooks is salient here, when she states that dictionary definitions, standardized poetic styles, and forms symbolized the "learning to speak against the ruptured and broken speech of a dispossessed and displaced people" (223). What hooks means by this observation is that the superiority of Standard English has too often been mobilized to paper over the nuances, dialects, and linguistic traditions of the working class, of people of color, of queer writers, and of those whose expression of language originates from institutionally prescribed literary norms. With this understanding in mind, it is possible to consider Plath's literary apprenticeship as the replication of traditional and institutional evocations of language—in the hope that emulating such standards would allow her to gain entrance into publishing houses and literary journals, therefore establishing and enhancing her career.

Many critics, including Ted Hughes, have argued that the specter of Otto Plath hangs over the entire breadth of Plath's literary output ("A Picture of Otto," *TH:CP* 1167). Certainly, Otto Plath's legacy as an academic ensured linguistic competence and a strong scholarly work ethic foundational to the Plath family household. We may take as evidence from Plath's poetry and short stories such as "Among the Bumblebees" that she both feared and admired her father for his linguistic prowess. In "Among the Bumblebees," Plath narrates the experience of Alice Denway reflecting on the death of her father—a heroic figure with godlike characteristics, a man whose strength, intellect, and bravery are all-encompassing and cannot be replicated. The alignment of a paternal father figure with power and the declaration that "power was good because it was power" (*JP* 310) shows how deeply rooted the connection between strength and patriarchal structures was embedded in Plath's literary imagination. The father figure's "hard" and "sharp" voice, culminating with his position "like a King, high on a throne" (*JP* 308), is especially important to note, given the pride Alice feels in the superiority and fear her father instilled in his classroom. In this scenario, the male patriarch dominates and directs all methods of thinking, researching, and writing. If, for Plath, father figures represent a goliath of the standardized, stratified norms of linguistic competence valued by canonical culture, Standard English is the language of conquest and domination. Says bell hooks, "in the United States [Standard English] is the mask which hides the loss of so many tongues, all those sounds of diverse, native communities we will never hear … and so many other unremembered tongues" (223). The sharp edges, scolding of women, and thundering voice from Alice's father all represent a specific and traditional model of academic masculinity. Alice's adoration of these characteristics is indicative of the way Plath was educated and offers an insight into the types of attitudes she respected within an educational environment—Plath, too, wanted the power, privilege, and platform assigned to males, and she sought out and was gratified by attention from patriarchal figures.

Indeed, throughout her early writings in particular, Plath variously positions a father figure in canonical roles: in "The Colossus," the patriarch represents a storehouse of lost or shattered monuments, an "oracle" or "mouthpiece" from history, elected to speak by the Gods (*CP* 129). What is clear is that throughout her early writing life, Plath believed she must measure up to the precise normative standards shown by her father. And yet, as

Plath evolved as a writer, so too did her relationship with this notion of Standard English and the norms that dominated early approaches to her craft. For example, in the poem "Daddy," we again see the Otto Plath-inspired imagery of a professor who stands "at the blackboard," but at the end of the poem the speaker recognizes how she "could never talk to you," and her tongue is trapped in a "barb wire snare" in its attempts (*CP* 223). Indeed, Plath's speaker eventually aligns herself with the villagers who "always knew" that the "daddy" figure had restricted them, and they collectively exorcise the patriarch from controlling their words and lives. Taken literally, with all its references to being silenced and the overwhelming repressions of patriarchy, "Daddy" can be read as Plath jettisoning the norms and traditional values she had subscribed to so faithfully in her youth—signifying her desire to negotiate a different way of navigating language to better express her own lived experience. We know that as Plath's personal life fell into disarray in late 1962, there was a significant shift in her writing style where she more clearly wrote from the identity as a woman, a minority, and, at times, a victim—this is seen most significantly in parallels drawn between Plath's speakers and Jewish people who were murdered at the hands of the Nazi regime. That Plath's poetry increasingly self-identified with the experiences and words of the oppressed, persecuted, and marginalized, it is possible she realized that the normative canonical traditions could not fully encompass her desired expression. We can see an exploration of this problem in particular in the poem "Getting There." Here, Plath reflects on the "place" or "thing" she is working toward reaching. The speaker questions "why are there these obstacles" in the way of her journey—and more broadly speaking we may read this as the writer's frustrated attempts to put the words on the page (*CP* 247).

Because of Plath's tragic death at such an early age, in what was the early stages of a lifelong poetry career, we cannot know how possible linguistic and thematic changes would have impacted her work. But taking into consideration the dramatic change between poems written in 1962 and in the January and February of 1963, we have a small insight into creative decisions Plath was making to convey dark, disturbing, and poignant subject matter unlike anything she had previously written. The poems of 1963 are dramatically parsed down from Plath's previous offerings. They are reliant on repeated sounds, a slow pace, and blank textual spaces as much as the words on the page. "Words" offers an example of this technique—the smooth repeated slow "o" sounds found in "stroke," "wood," and "echoes" are situated in a conversation with the blank page spaces and curious line breaks, only to be interrupted by the divisive x in "Axes" and use of exclamation marks which injects the poem with pulses of static (*CP* 270). These experimental poetic formations can be read as Plath's attempts to grapple with the limitations of Standard English and further, the limitations of the masculine canon. She uses unusual structures and turns of expression alongside spatial blankness to allude to a deeper, non-verbal, emotional state. Writing on the cusp of the second-wave feminist movement it is also possible that Plath's awakening to her identity as woman may have led to a more nuanced understanding of the restrictions of language created by white men.

While these creative changes in her writing style may have been predicated on her gender, what did not change however was Plath's centering of whiteness. Even in later poems such as 1962's "Ariel," Plath utilizes the n-word as a descriptor, seemingly unaware of the weight and harm of this word (*CP* 239). Indeed, generally speaking, Plath's creative work echoes an American history plagued by white woman's ignorance and complicity in harm to Black bodies. We see Plath routinely establish darker colors as other, abnormal, and dangerous, while whiteness is normalized as a creative center. Jerome Ellison

Murphy has written of the "racial code" he sees in Plath's work whereby poems such as "In Plaster" operate on a binary oppositional nature where black/white is equated with good/bad tropes (see Murphy's chapter in this volume). Certainly, throughout her career, Plath replicated traditional racist tropes regarding the perceived vulnerability of white womanhood. Early poems such as "Female Author," her novel *The Bell Jar*, and later poems such as "The Arrival of the Bee Box" illustrate a lifelong trend of Othering Black bodies. The "Female Author" is "[p]rim, pink-breasted, feminine" and embodies purity and whiteness (*CP* 301). In "The Arrival of the Bee Box," readers encounter the "dark, dark" and "swarmy feeling of African hands" (*CP* 213). Here, Plath also uses frenetic racist imageries to describe the bees—their "unintelligible syllables" and anger "clambering" and engulfing one another wildly. By comparison, the announcement of white fragility in this poem with the reference to "petticoats" depicts the purity of whiteness against the dark "maniacs" in the box (*CP* 213). Continually, however, whiteness is depicted as central, vulnerable, and pure.

Perhaps the most overt example of the centering of whiteness is seen in Plath's *The Bell Jar* when, following her suicide attempt, Esther Greenwood is in the hospital and encounters an unnamed Black man who is working as a member of the hospital staff. Firstly, the mere presence of a Black man in Plath's literary world is unusual and this really shows up how Plath's creative landscape is prominently white. Straightaway upon encountering the hospital worker, Esther judges the man by focusing on his body—she dehumanizes him and then enacts physical violence by kicking him under the table (*B* 175). Esther notes the "silly way" he smiled, drawing attention to his "gawping mouth" and "big, rolling eyes" (*B* 173). This approach to describing the hospital worker is rooted in racist tropes as Esther suggests he is unintelligent, lazy, and childlike. Indeed, Esther's frequent categorization of the man simply as "negro" sees her establish him as a person without any identity other than his race, and his race renders him abnormal. What we can surmise from the depiction of the hospital worker is that Esther's viewpoint and actions illustrate a deeply rooted sense of difference between white and black personhood. Indeed, Plath's narration of race in *The Bell Jar* instinctively connects with other overtly racist texts from the American canon such as Margaret Mitchell's 1936 novel *Gone with the Wind* and, more contemporary to Plath, Jack Kerouac's 1971 novel *Pic*. Plath can be connected to these texts because all three are white writers who choose to write the spoken words of Black people in a dialect format. This dialect includes purposefully inserted incorrect grammar and misspelled words, ranging from colloquial phrasings such as "[y]ou shouldn't of done that" to slang such as "reely" for "really" and "Miz" for "Miss" (*B* 175). Plath's decision to adopt this writing style can be seen as her weaponizing of language to administer shame and connect stupidity to the Black hospital worker. The lack of eloquence and linguistic clarity afforded clearly shows the endemic racism of Plath's culture as it permeates through into her narrative. It is important to note too that no white person in *The Bell Jar* is dehumanized by virtue of their race—illustrating that Plath's creative world is imbued with the ignorance and prejudice that accompanies white privilege.

Toni Morrison's assertion of the existence of "literary whiteness" speaks to the structural institutional and cultural norms of the United States and the Western world more broadly where white words and white stories are given platform over all other. What remains to be seen is a comprehensive interrogation of the position of whiteness in Plath's poetry and fiction writing. Little to no mention of race in her work does not mean that Plath is exempt from analysis through this lens. Instead, and reflecting back on words cited earlier from Spivak, what is not present in Plath's letters, poems, journals, and other pieces of work is also worthy of note. Plath's obliviousness toward her racial privilege illustrates the extent to which white women of Plath's era were given permission to be oblivious by the white male patriarchy. Plath's own literary imagination was carefully crafted by these constructs, and as a result, her worldview was restricted rendering her unable to see her own whiteness. In conclusion, Curry's conclusion is still relevant: "White women must read black texts to learn—if not to fully understand—what whiteness means to black people and to learn that whiteness exists. And yet, another task exists—that of discovering what whiteness means to white people" ("Daughters of the Dust" 340). Within these discussions and in the arenas being created by anti-racist activists, the work of destabilizing whiteness has begun. Removing it from the center can only be of benefit to destigmatizing and normalizing what was once Othered.

CHAPTER TEN

# The Child Reading: Female Stereotypes and Social Authority in Sylvia Plath's Children's Stories

LISSI ATHANASIOU-KRIKELIS

Sylvia Plath composed two children's stories, "Mrs. Cherry's Kitchen" (1958) and "The It-Doesn't-Matter Suit" (1959); a children's poem, "The Bed Book" (1959); and numerous children's book reviews. These texts have received less critical attention than Plath's poetry and fiction for adults. Further, existing considerations of her writing for children have demonstrated consistent, if limited, theoretical frameworks. Primarily, critics have adopted psychoanalytic, feminist approaches, reading these texts in relation to theories of maternal semiotics associated with Julia Kristeva and Hélène Cixous. In *Out of the Cradle Endlessly Rocking*, Nephie Christodoulides interprets Plath's children's stories as confessional texts, arguing that they reflect a regression to childhood and an examination of the mother–daughter relationship. Aneesh Barai, in "Speaking the Space between Mother and Child: Sylvia Plath, Julia Kristeva, and the Place of Children's Literature," explores Plath's texts through the lens of Plath as a prospective mother. Both Christodoulides and Barai rely on Plath's autobiographical experiences as well as her adult poems and novel, *The Bell Jar*, to interpret her children's fiction. In other words, interpretation of Plath's children's stories has depended on the signifiers found elsewhere in her work. Plath's children's texts have never been examined outside this purview nor from the point of view of a child reader.[1] A close examination of these narratives as specimens of children's texts from the perspective of cultural ideology, I argue, yields a constellation of ideas pertinent to children's literature, such as the dialogic space on the boundaries of the collective and the individual, the child and the adult.

---

[1] Throughout, I use the term child reader to signify the ideal or intended reader constructed by a narrative process. This child reader does not disturb narrative intentions but rather recognizes and follows narrative clues as intended from the adult perspective.

Plath wrote "Mrs. Cherry's Kitchen" in 1958, but the story did not see the light of publication until 2001, when it appeared in Plath's *Collected Children's Stories*,[2] illustrated by David Roberts. The story takes place in a modern-day kitchen with cutting-edge gadgets and two magical pixies who impose order. When the anthropomorphic appliances decide to question their given roles, they turn the kitchen into chaos and inevitably learn that they excel at their prescribed roles only. "The It-Doesn't-Matter Suit," written in 1959, was first published in 1996 with illustrations by Rotraut S. Berner after a manuscript was discovered at Indiana University in mid-1990s (Steinberg, *Sylvia Plath* 7).[3] In this story, a seven-year-old boy wishes to possess a suit to wear for all occasions. When father and siblings repudiate the peculiarly awkward yellow-mustard suit that mysteriously arrives at their home, the suit falls on Max Nix, who is elated to wear it continuously, regardless of what activities he performs. Having been published and illustrated three times, "The Bed Book" is the most popular of the three Plath children's texts: two editions came out in 1976, one illustrated by Emily Arnold McCully and the second by Quentin Blake. Employing no plot and written in poetic verse with a mixture of rhyme schemes, "The Bed Book" describes whimsical beds to excite children's imaginations. Imagery, alliteration, and creative exuberance dominate the verses.[4] Had they been published in the 1960s, the three children's texts would have been undoubtedly cherished by children and parents alike. Nonetheless, it is inconceivable to imagine what criticism they would receive today, had their author not been the young wife and mother poet who captivated the world with her suicide.

As children's texts, the three Plath stories are witty and playful in their use of language, but they differ from each other in their thematic choices. "Mrs. Cherry's Kitchen" and "The It-Doesn't-Matter Suit" appear traditional in gender representation, featuring family settings that conform to patriarchy. Women are stereotypical, engaging in domestic work and tending to the needs of the male characters. Children are subordinate to the adults; they learn to exercise patience and to conform to the rules of those above them. Although patriarchal constructs are both contested and sustained in Plath's adult works, in her children's stories, patriarchy is normalized and, for the most part, appears axiomatic. I attribute Plath's conservativism to a number of reasons. First, "Mrs. Cherry's Kitchen" and "The It-Doesn't-Matter Suit" were written before some of Plath's feminist views emerged, and secondly, Plath seems to write these texts within what she deems as the conventions of the genre as well as within what she perceives as the audience's expectations. "Mrs. Cherry's Kitchen" and "The It-Doesn't-Matter Suit" demonstrate different representations of children's individualism and their integration into the social context. In "Mrs. Cherry's Kitchen," the social environment supersedes individuality; the child is enmeshed in the community and his/her subjectivity is drowned by the subject's

---

[2] While the *Collected Children's Stories* published the title of Plath's story as "Mrs Cherry's Kitchen," it has been changed to "Mrs. Cherry's Kitchen," in *The Bloomsbury Handbook* for US conventions.
[3] "The It-Doesn't-Matter Suit" reappears in Plath's *Collected Children's Stories* (2001).
[4] Most likely, "The Bed Book" and "The It-Doesn't-Matter Suit" were written in the same year, 1959. Steinberg and Kukil note that Plath wrote "The It-Doesn't-Matter-Suit" at Yaddo in 1959 (*L2* xxxvi) and that it was sent to Knopf publisher in September of 1959 (*L2* iv). In his biography of Plath, Steinberg states that the book was written in 1958 (*L2* 7). He suggests that, along with "Mrs. Cherry's Kitchen," Plath wrote "The It-Doesn't-Matter Suit" before she was pregnant, while "The Bed Book" was the only children's book Plath wrote during her pregnancy (*L2* 125).

relation to social responsibility. This image changes in "The It-Doesn't-Matter Suit." Whereas socialization still plays an important role in the child's identity formation, the subjective self is distinctly separated from the social world. In "The Bed Book," Plath abandons the stereotypes and covert didacticism that govern the other two picture books; she openly abandons themes attractive to an adult audience and veers toward topics quintessentially pertinent to the child reader. The poem is itself an escapade away from the adult world of the typical bedroom with its associations for mundane inactivity and boredom where children are asked to quiet down and go to sleep. Although Plath never felt confident in publishing any of her children's stories, she focused her energy on revising "The Bed Book" because she recognized something inarticulately appealing that escapes the other two. "The Bed Book" addresses the child and explores topics a child would indulge in.

When reconsidering Plath's writing for children, the first myth to be dismantled is the proposition that Plath's work demonstrates ideological consistency. In *The Haunting of Sylvia Plath*, Jacqueline Rose stipulates that "[i]t has been the persistent attempt to impose a consistency on [Plath] … which has been so damaging" (10). For Rose, Plath resides within the fissure of binary oppositions from which she emerges: "[Plath] writes at the point of tension—pleasure / danger, your fault / my fault, high / low culture—without resolution or dissipation of what produces the clash between the two" (10). In *Sylvia Plath's Fiction*, Luke Ferretter outlines thematic deviations when comparing poems and prose from the same period. For example, he argues that while Plath explores the pain of love in her lyric poetry during 1954–5, she reserves painful experiences from childhood for her fiction (59). There is diversity in the angle of vision even when she investigates similar topics. During 1958–9—when she wrote the children's stories—Plath uses mental illness in her writing for the first time but again crafts different tapestries according to the genre. Her poetry expresses the speaker's desire for death, whereas her prose is dominated by the heroine's emotions of fear (*Sylvia Plath's Fiction* 75–8). Despite Plath's ruminations upon similar subjects, she oscillates between the binary oppositions within topics of interest. Obsessed with making a name for herself in the literary world but also exercising writing as a vocation, upon which she—as well as Hughes—was financially dependent,[5] Plath often wrote what would appeal to editors and the implied audience. In writing her adult stories, she frequently studied the styles of magazines, producing stories that pander to the magazine's and its audience's needs (*Sylvia Plath's Fiction* 36–7). It should not be surprising, therefore, to find that in "Mrs. Cherry's Kitchen" and "The It-Doesn't-Matter Suit," Plath endorses a patriarchy that she vehemently subverts in poems like "Lady Lazarus" and "Daddy." As Clarissa Ai Ling Lee writes, "[w]hilst struggling with the ardent feminist within her, [Plath] went all out to embrace the ideology of feminineness that has been indoctrinated into the women of her generation."

For the most part, Plath's children's stories do not deviate from canonical art. I use the term *canonical* as employed by Maria Nikolajeva in *Children's Literature Comes of Age*, who borrows it from Russian formalist Yuri Lotman. Lotman argues for two types of art: canonical art, also called "ritual" or "traditional," is based upon canonic systems and prevailing norms, whereas modern art demonstrates violations of the canon

---

[5] In a letter to children's book author and Plath's friend, Ann Davidow Goodman, on April 14, 1959, Plath writes: "So Ted is working on a play—and both of us plan to try our hand at children's books this spring. I hear from reputable sources that children's books are pleasantly lucrative, sell better and longer than most novels" (*L2* 312).

and breakage of conventional patterns (50). Nikolajeva identifies three areas in which children's literature is limited by the canon. The first is subject matter, which dictates themes appropriate for children, the second is character behavior, and the third is the use of appropriate language. Although not explicitly stated by Nikolajeva, these areas are products of another prevailing assumption in children's fiction: in expecting to inscribe positive role models for children, their parents, teachers, and librarians—in other words, those who make literary choices on behalf of the young—literature written for the child anticipates an ideological message in the form of overt or covert didacticism. These norms drive canonical art in children's literature and render it the mainstream form of entertainment for children.[6] Neither Lotman nor Nikolajeva takes issue with the importance of canonical art, while at the same time disputing the idea of one art being superior to the other: "It is, on the contrary, necessary to investigate not only the structure of canonical texts but also the hidden information sources which make a seemingly simple and well-known text a powerful mechanism of human culture" (58). If Plath used to study the styles of magazines to conform to their contours, it is likely that she wrote children's texts by submitting to the expectations of the genre. To assume that Plath's children's fiction parallels what some have described as a progressive trajectory of her confessional poetry forces readers to discover in it a hidden subversiveness that can only be borrowed from Plath's later work but cannot be substantiated in the children's texts themselves. To read Plath's children's texts as mainstream children's fiction allows for recognizing in them the social constructs of Plath's time and for examining Plath's participation in the discourse surrounding the nature and construction of children's texts.

Plath's interactions with children's literature editors cultivated in her the belief that children's texts should remain uncomplicated. Referencing "The Bed Book" in her letters, she claims: "I rhyme, very simply, 200 two-beat lines about these queer beds" (*L2* 327), whereas elsewhere she states that Hughes's fables were rejected because, according to the accounts of the publisher, they were "too sophisticated" for children (*L2* 111). In her letters and journals, Plath does not discuss subject matter for children's texts, but what is palpable from these sources is her high regard of "The Bed Book" while expressing little confidence in "Mrs. Cherry's Kitchen" and "The It-Doesn't-Matter Suit." Although Plath reworked "The Bed Book" various times, sending it to a total of seven publishers in the span of approximately a year, she did not spend the same energy on the other two works.[7] The "It-Doesn't-Matter Suit" is referenced only twice in her letters and journals, the references being coupled with self-denigration: "Bored at waiting to hear from mail. Two children's books: the Bed Book now seems limited and thin. Max Nix seems rather ordinary. Yet I dream of a transfiguration: a letter of acceptance" (*J* 508–9). When brainstorming about "Mrs. Cherry's Kitchen," Plath speaks fondly about the idea of this book, in the context of her expressed desire for motherhood: "Suddenly, Ted & I looked at things from our unborn children's point of view. Take gadgets: a modern pot & kettle

---

[6]These ideas are widespread in theories on children's literature. In *Children's Literature: A Very Short Introduction*, Reynolds asserts: "Until the late 20th century, there was an unwritten agreement that children's books would not include sex, bad language, or gratuitous violence, on the grounds that writing for children is part of the socializing process and so ought to set good examples and help readers learn approved ways of behaving that are likely to help them lead successful and fulfilling lives" (27).

[7]Plath submitted "The Bed Book" to seven American and British publishers between September 23, 1959, and May 20, 1960. She only sent "The It-Doesn't-Matter Suit" once on September 18, 1959 (Submission Lists, Smith).

story. Shiny modern gadgets are overspecialized—long to do others [sic] tasks" (J 304). She ends the entry with a question: "Complex, perhaps, but possible?" (J 304). When she sends the book to the publisher, she seems overwhelmed with feelings of disappointment. In her journal, she notes: "For some reason, for no reason, it will be rejected: just to make this year of unacceptance complete" (J 320). Fear of failure is also evident when she begins writing "The Bed Book": "I want to begin my Bed Book. Something freezes me from my real spirit: is it fear of failure, fear of being vulnerable? I must melt it. I will get out some more children's book this week. I would rather publish this than a book of poems" (J 476).[8] Although Christodoulides rejects the notion that Plath's fear is attributed to fear of writing, arguing instead that the poet is distressed over journeying back to childhood (16), Plath's statement seems consistent with an overarching fear of rejection that resides in her letters and journals. This type of apprehension is not unique to Plath's writing of children's texts: "What to do with fear of writing?"—she writes unrelated to her children's stories—"Fear of not being a success? Fear of world casually saying we're [writers / she and Hughes] wrong in rejections" (J 520). Her profound longing to become a successful writer cripples her, and every rejection turns into a cosmic sign that defies her aspirations.

Despite Plath's determination, her life as a children's author is short-lived; despite her initial effusiveness on composing "Mrs. Cherry's Kitchen," she does not rework this book, nor does she revise "The It-Doesn't-Matter Suit." Plath's instinct indicates that "The Bed Book" is superior to her other children's texts, hence her eagerness to refashion and resubmit it numerous times. The poem initially had a frame story: in conversation, a brother and sister imagine the existence of magical beds (L2 327). After being prompted by Emilie W. McLeod, the editor of Atlantic Monthly Press, to eliminate the frame, Plath removes the book's conversational aspect and retains its exotic descriptions; this is the version that survives today. As I will demonstrate in the rest of this chapter, "The Bed Book" retains the magic qualities found in "Mrs. Cherry's Kitchen" and "The It-Doesn't-Matter Suit" while dismissing topics that are foregrounded in these two works. Whereas "Mrs. Cherry's Kitchen" and "The It-Doesn't-Matter Suit" would appeal to a child audience via the adults who guard the pillars of children's literature, "The Bed Book" is written for a child audience.

The three Plath children's texts feature domestic settings: kitchens, bedrooms, and households. Nature is not a preferred setting, nor are animals employed as protagonists—despite Plath's fondness for Hughes's animal tales. Plath gravitates toward personification and anthropomorphization of domestic inanimate objects, as domesticity and familial life overlap her interests in child and adult fiction, being suitable settings for both audiences. Beds, gadgets, and transformative suits are also markers of the modern era, the first two for their utility and the latter two evoking the twentieth-century burgeoning consumer. Two of her stories, "Mrs. Cherry's Kitchen" and "The It-Doesn't-Matter Suit," build upon themes of domesticity, familial harmony, and social authority, in which children are deemed inferior and wives and mothers hold the place of mediation between children and the patriarch. The stories also address the relationship between child and society, the child's integration into the community, and the juxtaposition of the child's individuality and society.

---

[8]According to Clark, Plath wrote the book in a single day, after contemplating its plot for six months; finishing it brought her a feeling of intense relief (*Red Comet* 560).

## GENDER ROLES IN "MRS. CHERRY'S KITCHEN" AND "THE IT-DOESN'T-MATTER SUIT"

In "Mrs. Cherry's Kitchen" and "The It-Doesn't-Matter Suit," wives and mothers hold stereotypical women's roles, whereas husbands or fathers appear domineering, owning hierarchically superior positions in the heteronormative family structure. Both stories display the housewife's inherent insularity. The husbands work outside the house without interacting with the featured children, whereas the women are placed indoors, primarily occupied with domesticity and child-rearing. Mama Nix and Mrs. Cherry engage in domestic affairs: cooking, baking, sewing, and above all serving the needs of those around them. Despite Mr. and Mrs. Cherry's childlessness, Mrs. Cherry embodies (grand)motherhood and housewifery, characteristics richly amplified by illustrator David Roberts in his caricature illustrations. The story begins with lists of marvelous concoctions Mrs. Cherry can create with the secret help of magic. While references to smells, tastes, sounds, and colors appeal to young readers by awakening the senses, even alliteration in Mrs. Cherry's name—"Mrs Myrtle May Cherry" (CCS 41)[9]—generates a musical tone to excite the auditory apparatus.[10] To the adult reader familiar with Plath's poetry, these poetic features of narratives for children are reminders that for Plath, "everyday domesticity" becomes "an intriguing aesthetic" (*Women's Poetry* 134).

Mrs. Cherry's secret assistants, "the special kitchen pixies" (CCS 42), contribute to making the kitchen a blissful experience so much so that the housewife finds her work effortlessly undemanding and willfully gratifying. Being surrounded by food, gadgets, and responsibilities, Mrs. Cherry's life is endearing, filled with pure contentment. The story features Plath's influence of magazine advertisements, in which appliances, cleaning products, and tools transfigure domesticity into a surreal space. The references to kitchen technologies parallel the explorations of American consumer culture that Marsha Bryant has noted in such poems as "The Colossus," "Lesbos," and "The Applicant" ("Plath, Domesticity" 22). Similar to "Mrs. Cherry's Kitchen," domestic life in these poems signifies an entrapment in patriarchy while the techno-gadgets conceal a life of drudgery ("Plath, Domesticity" 24–5, 28); contrary to these poems, whose employment of household gadgets harbors subversion and calls into question "maleness" (*Women's Poetry* 136), Mrs. Cherry's domesticity does not empower female agency. Mrs. Cherry's relationship with her husband is characterized by subservience and servility; her life is fulfilling so long as Mr. Cherry's desires are met: "Mrs. Cherry hummed to herself, sitting at the sunny kitchen table and paring carrots for Mr. Cherry's favorite supper of beef stew. She flashed a bright, happy look around her kitchen: at the washing machine, and at the oven baking, and at the icebox rumbling gently as it kept the vanilla ice-cream cold for Mr. Cherry's dessert" (CCS 43). Although the following passage is suffused with irony—"Mrs. Cherry spent the whole Monday morning scouring and scurrying around the kitchen, whisking away invisible dust, polishing silver that gleamed to begin with" (CCS 47)—the overall tone of the story renders Mrs. Cherry the image of a happy housewife, content at pleasing her husband, busy in her modern-day, technologically advanced kitchen.

---

[9]All quotations from the children's stories come from *Collected Children's Stories* (CCS).
[10]The name may have been inspired by one of Plath's favorite children's novels, *Mary Poppins*, in which Cherry Tree Lane is the address that Mary Poppins lands when she meets the Banks family (*L2* 855).

In "The It-Doesn't-Matter Suit," Mama Nix's obsequiousness resembles Mrs. Cherry's traits. Mama Nix is undoubtedly a secondary character, deprived of voice—her lines are limited compared to the rest of the characters—and is equipped with the need to please husband and children. Baking is a quintessentially motherly activity in Plath. Baked goodies delight child readers, who are bound to associate the smells, tastes, and colors with the mothers and grandmothers in their lives. Mama Nix lives in a patriarchal world surrounded by her husband and her seven boys. As Christodoulides points out, Plath draws inspiration from her father's genealogy by selecting names from her paternal lineage and pays tribute to her Austrian-German heritage by setting the story in a central European village (26–7). This attachment to her paternal ancestry further enforces the patriarchy in the story. While everyone in the family is presented with having hobbies and activities outside the house—Papa Nix works at the bank, the sons enjoy skiing, tobogganing, hunting, fishing, and milking the cows—Mama Nix is enveloped in domesticity and child-rearing. The juxtaposition of indoor/outdoor as a binary that distinguishes gender roles is consistent with mainstream portrayals of women in children's literature. Moreover, the suit is a strong marker of patriarchy; hence, Mama Nix herself is not considered one to whom the suit could belong.

Mama Nix plays an important role because of her auxiliary presence; although a secondary character, she helps the men, especially Max, form an identity, while she remains largely unappreciated and unacknowledged. When the family opens the mysterious package, everyone agrees that the suit belongs to Papa, but after trying it, Papa Nix passes it on to his eldest son. Every time the suit is rejected by one of the family members; Mama Nix interjects to tailor it so that it fits the next person in line: "Mama Nix was clever with a needle and a thread. She took a tuck here and a stitch there. When she was through, the suit fitted Paul to a T" (CCS 27). These sentences are repeated with slight variations six times until the suit is made to Max's dimensions. Working silently and accepting her auxiliary role as a servant, Mama Nix, like Mrs. Cherry, gains satisfaction from serving the patriarchs around her. Christodoulides reads the mother figure in "The It-Doesn't-Matter Suit" as the phallic woman, whose sewing needle—a Freudian symbol of the phallus—allows her to dominate the male world and, therefore, renders her superior: "She is the phallic mother, with her needle (her penis) and her power as the provider of nourishment for the family members, that is, someone who can regulate orality, who can impose her own law onto the law of the paternal symbolic order" (28). While without Mama Nix's skillful sewing, the male characters in the story would not have been able to test their desires, and Max wouldn't have discovered himself, Mama Nix's actions do not show domination over the patriarchal order; she is a means that sustains it. She is stoically performing a motherly role, attached to her traditional pattern as wife and mother who assists her children to discover their subjective selves, while she remains largely on the margins, unrecognized, invisible, and voiceless. In this respect, my reading of Mama Nix is more in line with Barai's reading of motherhood in Plath's children's texts. Barai argues that "[the] maternal semiotic that Plath exemplifies in her children's literature ... is not a *break* from the symbolic," but rather illustrates "the mother's experiences of the semiotic from *within* her connection to the symbolic."

While Plath's understanding of the woman's role wavers, as it is demonstrated in her journals and letters, her children's fiction gravitates toward mainstream representations of women. Plath may be eager to contest the traditional female role in her stories and poems, while she deems it felicitous to maintain a rather conventional image of womanhood in her children's stories, a medium that perhaps Plath considers inherently conservative in its genre conventions. It is likely that she does not subvert normative structures for her young audience because she assimilates a stereotypical understanding of the genre. Concurrently, Plath's journals bespeak a proclivity toward more conservative attitudes of womanhood. In her journals, Plath exemplifies delight toward domesticity and speaks fondly of cooking. In a letter to her mother in November 1956, she writes, "I just long to be over in our own house, cooking & keeping it in order for [Ted]" (*L2* 21). The simple pleasures of the household mirror marital harmony; she acknowledges, nonetheless, that her relationship with Hughes transgresses the materiality of marriage to encompass their profound connection to poetry, literature, and writing, areas that set their domestic life apart from other couples' and set Plath apart from other women.

> I didn't have to compromise and accept a sweet balding insurance salesman or an impotent teacher or a dumb conceited doctor like mother said I would. I did what I felt the one thing and married the man I felt the only man I could love, and want to see do what he wanted in this world, and want to cook for and bear children for and write with.
>
> (*J* 435)[11]

Comparing Virginia Woolf's and Plath's feminism, Ferretter argues that for Plath, Woolf's fiction lacks the "physicality, relationship, sex, children, all the materiality of life and family and relationships that she wants to write about" (*Sylvia Plath's Fiction* 22). The image that Plath paints of women and mothers in her children's texts is founded upon mainstream viewpoints of womanhood; it is also an image that reinforces the parent–child bond for the child reader.

Before Plath's later poetry would repudiate the traditional modes of femininity instilled in her by societal norms, Plath demonstrates signs of subjugation as a woman and as a wife and bows to what she views as healthy patriarchy. When writing in her journals about her disappointment in not conceiving a child at the end of 1959, she notes: "Ted should be a patriarch. I a mother" (*J* 500). Her idea of motherhood externalizes her desire to match conventions of femininity while restoring societal structures that yield to male superiority. In 1957, Plath demonstrates the same self-deprecation when she announces in a letter to her mother Hughes's upcoming publication, averring that her husband's success should precede hers: "I am so happy his book is accepted first. It will make it so much easier for me when mine is accepted[.] … I can rejoice then, much more, knowing Ted is ahead of me" (*L2* 72). As Diane Middlebrook states in *Her Husband*, "Plath had always associated wifedom with the obligation to be second-rate" (128); it is this side that Plath chooses to manifest in "Mrs. Cherry's Kitchen" and "The It-Doesn't-Matter Suit."

---

[11]Before her separation from Hughes, Plath denounces a specific type of gender ideology that she associates with mothers and women who promulgate gender-inferiority. Plath delineates her anger against her mother when she asks: "Who am I angry at? Myself. No, not yourself. Who is it? It is my mother and all the mothers I have known who have wanted me to be what I have not felt like really being from my heart and at the society which seems to want us to be what we do not want to be from our hearts: I am angry at these people and images" (*J* 437). She is angry at mothers who perpetuate the idea of compromise and who indoctrinate daughters into "[getting] a nice little, safe little, sweet little loving little imitation man who'll give you babies and bread and a secure roof and a green lawn and money money money every month. Compromise" (*J* 431).

## EXPECTATIONS FOR CHILDREN IN "MRS. CHERRY'S KITCHEN" AND "THE IT-DOESN'T-MATTER SUIT"

As a cultural phenomenon, children's literature reveals the ideology of the culture that shapes it and the ways in which adults—whether unconsciously or not—would like children to internalize prevalent cultural values. When addressing women's agency in her children's fiction, Plath chooses to be complicit with the social institutions that delineate female subjects, either because she does not fully repudiate this vision at the time her children's texts are written or because she deliberately refrains from challenging the normative suppositions of her readership. She employs a similar approach when her stories address the child's relationship to the adult and the integration into the social context.

When exploring the role and impact of ideology in children's texts, Robyn McCallum and John Stephens explain that implicit ideology is featured in texts that reproduce beliefs already accepted by both authors and readers. "Such texts," they stipulate, "render ideology invisible and hence invest implicit ideological positions with legitimacy by naturalizing them. In other words, a book which seems to a reader to be apparently ideology-free will be a book closely aligned to that reader's own unconscious assumptions" (McCallum and Stephens 360). At the same time that children's literature informs children about societal attitudes, it also implicitly delineates figurations of childhood and adulthood: it demonstrates how children should behave with propriety according to or in disobedience of adult rules. As Perry Nodelman declares in *The Pleasures of Children's Literature*, "even the idyllic pleasures of children's literature may represent a desire to teach young people—an attempt to educate children into sharing an adult view of the world and of the nature of childhood" (79). Both "The It-Doesn't-Matter Suit" and "Mrs. Cherry's Kitchen" foreground acceptable attitudes according to normative parental standards. They also covertly indicate the importance of community and socialization as quintessential elements of one's formation of self-knowledge and well-being.

"Mrs. Cherry's Kitchen" exemplifies the children's desire to defy constrictive, authoritative structures, only to remind children that such order cannot be contested. In Mrs. Cherry's sanctuary reside two pixies, whose "job [is] to see that all kitchen folk did their daily work and lived in harmony and content" (CCS 43). In this numinous sub-world, the appliances are under the parental guidance of the pixies, the maternal figures who maintain control. On the day the story takes place, the appliances declare their desire to perform tasks other than the ones they have originally been assigned. The Egg-Beater is certain it "could make lovely white ruffles on Mrs. Cherry's blouses too, if [it] ... were given the chance" to take Iron's place (CCS 44) and all in all, every appliance wishes to switch places with another. The appliances' willingness to perform tasks that they are innately incapable of performing foregrounds a lack of self-knowledge. Self-awareness is imbued at the end of their experience through mediated adult supervision.

The pixies' fear that if they reject the appliances' proposition, the gadgets "may go on strike and stop work altogether" (CCS 45)—a metaphor that further emphasizes the layers of power structure. Therefore, the pixies consent to teach the appliances that the existing order is optimal by letting them acquire this knowledge on their own: "Once the kitchen folk *experience* how impossible it is to do each other's work, they'll be twice as happy tending to their own. But we mustn't let on that we doubt their talent. ... Let them find out for themselves" (CCS 46). Witnessing the chaos generated from their changeabout, the appliances demand to return to their positions: "Oh, let me do my own work once again!" they proclaim (CCS 52). In the end, Plath's anthropomorphic gadgets remain under the control of parental supervision, as their modest endeavor to discover other territories is being thwarted. The implicit ideology here suggests that, although children can test hypotheses, adult reasoning is equipped with foresight that children lack. The appliances' experiment could never have worked; their prescribed roles ultimately define their strengths and weaknesses and, regardless of their strong-will or perseverance, the gadgets are limited in their potential.

Although the role of the parent is to support the child toward self-discovery when the latter so demands, the child will be reminded in the story to trust the word of the parental order. Barai reads the appliances' experience as the child's desire to separate from the mother who is unwilling to let go: "The ostensible transgression of the utensils serves to further establish their enslavement, with subversion feeding into the structure it seeks to subvert." He also interprets the havoc brought about by the appliances as an overturn of the symbolic order—a temporary overturn, nonetheless, which is quickly reinstated and reified (Barai). The appliances were residing in the Imaginary prior to their changeabout, but after an elucidation of the nexus of their identity, they migrate to the symbolic where they obey fixed attitudes as dictated by the Law of the Father. The pixies' authority is underplayed; they are benign without whom the world would be disorderly. The pixies' names are Salt and Pepper, and the references to black and white signify the parent's oscillation between authorial control and provisional release of that control. The juxtaposition of black and white is seen again at the end of the story, when Mrs. Cherry returns from her neighbor's house and her neighbor's children come along, each holding a kitten representing each color. Contrary to the pixies, however, the kitten's colors reflect the mischievous versus orderly side of children, held in the hands of authoritatively superior beings.

"The It-Doesn't-Matter Suit" is preoccupied with similar topics of social authorities since Max Nix is another role model child who judiciously abides by the laws of adults and embodies cultural norms of decorum in order to reach adulthood. However, unlike "Mrs. Cherry's Kitchen," "The It-Doesn't-Matter Suit" underscores that the child's socialization is rendered possible by the child's discovery of individuality. This latter topic marks a shift in Plath's writing of children's fiction as she continues to negotiate ideas of child identity and to discover her place as a children's literature author. Whereas in "Mrs. Cherry's Kitchen," in which the appliances' communal existence undergirds their harmony—community is the basis of the magic that Mr. and Mrs. Cherry relish—for Max, socialization is a result of his gaining a subjective self. To craft a desirable identity, Max Nix depends on the family: first on his older siblings' approval and then on his mother's tending. His identity, however, is complete only with the acknowledgment and endorsement of society.

In the family space, Max is an example of obedience and patience cultivated in children through social conventions. Although he deserves to have the suit—he is the only one out of the seven siblings who does not own a suit despite desiring it for long—Max does not demand it, never stepping up to request it. Rather, he patiently awaits his turn, allowing his father and older siblings to claim it; only after they reject it does the suit become his. For the child reader, Max is an example of decorum, *par excellence* behavior. Concurrently, Max's individuality is not acquired with effort or skill but with forbearance and inactivity. When, early in the story, father and brothers stare at the unopened package, projecting their own desires, each expecting an item that represents his favorite activity, Max is the only one expressing no expectations: "It is too fine, he thought to himself, to be for me"

(CCS 24). Max here belittles himself, believing that whatever the package may hold, it is unlikely to belong to him since he is the youngest, therefore the least possible to claim it. Age marks higher levels of authority, and Max feels too young to raise his voice or express his wishes. Max's implicit submissiveness suggests that authority is granted by age and that propriety demands passivity.

That the suit is a palpable symbol of identity and subjectivity, a form of Max's migrating from childhood to adulthood, is clear when contrasting the beginning and end of the story with respect to Max's name. At the beginning, we read: "Max's whole name was Maximilian, but because he was only seven he did not need such a big name. So everybody called him just Max" (CCS 19). At the end of the story, when Max walks around town with his new suit, the villagers exclaim: "'Look!' they murmured to one another. 'There goes Maximilian in his marvellous suit'" (CCS 37). With his new suit and an elongated name, Max has earned his place in the social sphere. The suit reveals societal conformity, the performative roles individuals acquire when they inhere in cultural and communal existence: "Wherever Max Nix looked in Winkelburg ... he saw people wearing suits. Some people had suits for work[.] ... Some people had suits for weddings ... for skiing" (CCS 21). Suits signify acceptance of societal and cultural norms, as individuals follow expected codes.

What sets Max apart from his siblings and the other villagers is his desire to own a single suit without being limited by the types of activities he can pursue. Whereas Max's siblings are interested in a single task for which they have a matching attire, Max wishes to engage in a plethora of outdoor explorations with a single outfit. Therefore, Max's individuality appears more versatile than either his brothers' or the anthropomorphic appliances' in "Mrs. Cherry's Kitchen." Once integrated into the community, he will retain his individuality, with social conformity not imposing limitations. Furthermore, Max is set apart from his siblings because social criticism does not restrict his choices; the social network does not demarcate him. While every family member realizes the superb quality of the suit, each one of them rejects the outfit because of fear of being ridiculed. It is no longer the activity that confines father and boys to feel compelled to reject the suit; it is the discourse of the community, and it is the perceived image of how the Other might view them that is crippling: "'I shall wear the suit in the toboggan race tomorrow,' [the eldest son] ... said[.] ... What would his team-mates say? Perhaps they would think he was trying to show off in the mustard-yellow suit. He would look like a streak of lightning going down the toboggan track" (CCS 28). To show that the family's perceptions stem from the boys' subconsciousness and not from reality, Plath has the younger siblings reject the suit because, as they claim, animals will react to it and their activities will be ruined.

Mama Nix's sewing ritual marks the threshold that allows her youngest son, Max, to enter the social realm. Max acquires the suit and steps into town, having enacted his own self-image, fully equipped with his own unique identity. Not only does Max engage in all the activities that his brothers feared in the Other criticism, but the voices of the town endorse Max's new self:

Max walked uptown and downtown and round about Winkelburg in his mustard-yellow suit. When he went by, the butcher and the baker, the blacksmith and the goldsmith, the tinker and the tailor, the innkeeper and the schoolteacher, the grocer and the goodwives, the minister and the mayor all leaned out of their doors and windows.

"Look!" they murmured to one another. "There goes Maximilian in his marvelous suit."

And the cats in the alleys and the dogs on the cobbles of Winkelburg followed at his heels, purring and grrring with admiration.

(CCS 37)

It is ambiguous whether the excess admiration Max witnesses is a reflection of his own desires or whether it is a sincere view of the world. Much modernist art exteriorizes the internal world of the child, and in "The It-Doesn't-Matter Suit" both readings hold equal value. In "Identity," Karen Coats declares that modern theoreticians from various disciplines understand the formation of identity as a culmination of identifications or dis-identifications, some of which reside in fantasy. A statement expressing a sense of identity points to discourse that allows the individual to identify with a group, an activity, a performance, to be like or unlike others (Coats 110). Max's self-image is discourse-based, a discourse founded upon the Other's perception; regardless of whether the perception is true or fabricated, it is language that encloses the formation of identity. Coats postulates that in modernist texts, the element of socialization is more marked than in postmodern texts. She explains that modernist books recognize

> the importance of society in the construction of identity, and while many children's books offer an explicit message that their protagonists should embrace their individuality rather than conform to the group, there is almost always an implicit undercurrent of identity management according to group ideals.
>
> (Coats 111)

In Plath's three children's texts, the negotiation between selfhood and group values undergoes various iterations of development. In "Mrs. Cherry's Kitchen," the sense of community is more important than the child's individuality; in "The It-Doesn't-Matter Suit," subjective self and society appear interrelated; finally, in "The Bed Book," the social component is eclipsed, and the child's imagination, subjective self, and inner world are foregrounded.

## "THE BED BOOK": POETRY AS RELEASE FROM SOCIAL AUTHORITY

"The Bed Book" is devoid of the tacit didacticism found in the other two Plath children's texts. Adult authority is omitted and so is the theme of socialization, the child's integration into a community, and his/her relationship to authority figures. Instead, "The Bed Book" celebrates children's consciousness. Its rhythmic and poetic style as well as its poignant imagery contribute to an overall jubilee of children's spirit. The poem compels attention to children's pleasures, displaying to young readers a form of escape from the mundane world. It is a felicitous delineation of versatile beds: a Submarine bed, a Snack bed, a Pocket-size-adjustable bed, a Tank bed, a Jet-Propelled bed and many more. The initial version had a frame, "a kind of dialogue between Wide-Awake Will and Stay-Uppity Sue" (*L2* 317). As evinced by their names, these vibrant characters portray defiance of the basic principles typically associated with beds by imagining an array of whimsical alternatives. Although the narrative frame is no longer part of the book, the characters' names reveal the direction and the tone Plath was aiming for. "The Bed Book" is a book with children speakers, children narratees, and an imagined child audience.

Plath's bedroom is filled with energized characters who cannot conform to the quiet time associated with inactivity. Plath admits writing the poem "[b]ased on the fiction that children's beds, by nature of their age, are dull, merely for sleeping or resting" (*L2* 327). As a symbol of adult rules, the bedroom is subverted and transmogrified into a place of restlessness, a place disenthralled by authorial rule. Many examples of beds are about release and escape. Children aren't traditionally allowed to eat in bed, but Plath's Snack Bed provides dietary options at the most inappropriate time and place. Similarly in the Spottable Bed, messes are welcome: "It never matters / Where jam rambles / And where paint splatters," nor does it matter if cats and dogs "Dance on the covers / With muddyish feet" (*CCS* 6). Both examples flaunt adult rules of discipline and decorum, allowing children to act—or rather, imagine acting—like children. The Bounceable Bed is another example of a bed that provides release while mocking adult order: "From a Bounceable Bed / You bounce into the blue– / Over the hollyhocks / (Toodle-oo!) / Over the owls' / To-whit-to-whoo, / ... You can see if the Big Dipper's / Full of stew, / And you may want to stay / Up a week or two" (*CCS* 14). On the one hand, the bouncy bed provides excitement because it propels the child to a suspended, midair liberation; on the other hand, it incites freedom from commands, such as "do not jump on the bed" or "go to sleep." Illustrators Emily Arnold McCully and David Roberts capture the child being catapulted into the air, their illustrations emitting the type of release the verses are suggesting. Child readers do not derive pleasure merely from the creative description of these beds but also from the chance they are given to innocuously defy adult rules or be absolved of them. With "The Bed Book," Plath discovers the side of children's literature that distances itself from mainstream mottos governed by authorial intervention. As Perry Nodelman notes in "Decoding the Image," some stories promote acceptable behavior as it is defined by adults, whereas others encourage children to indulge "in what we see as natural behaviour" in them, allowing them to be more child-like and less like what adults expect of them (135). "The Bed Book" falls in the second category of stories found in the gamut of children's fiction.

Intertwined with themes of release are arresting images of imaginative exploration and creative freedom in the poem. Many of the beds transport the sleepless narratee away from the quotidian bedroom into exotic and adventurous places. Some beds offer explorations in the ocean, in outer space, in nature, promoting a sense of curiosity through experiencing and discovering. From the Jet-Propelled bed that visits Mars to the Bird-Watching, Elephant, and North-Pole beds, "It's fine if you're / An explorer," the speaker reminds (*CCS* 12). The images in these beds feel riveting to the reader. "In the Elephant Bed / You go where you please. / You pick bananas / Right out of the trees" (*CCS* 11). The ordinary becomes extraordinary. "You can climb up the trunk / And slide down behind. Everyone knows / Elephants don't mind!—" (*CCS* 11). The last verse, featuring the elephant as a means to engage in wild, explorative journeys, consists of an intertextual reference to Dr. Seuss's *Horton Hatches the Egg*, a book that—along with investigating motherhood—underscores perseverance and dedication associated with Horton, the elephant. *Horton Hatches the Egg* was one of Plath's beloved picture books as a child and one for which she wrote a review in 1962 when it first appeared in England (*L2* 856).[12]

---

[12] In her short review of *Horton Hatches the Egg*, Plath keenly recalls her childhood experience with the book: "Horton was hatching it in America when 1 was eight, and 22 years later, on his arrival in Britain, I *still* have by heart the trump couplet" ("Oregonian Original" 660). For Plath, Horton's reward at the end of Dr. Seuss's picture book resembles the reward fathers are granted when they have children.

Though less conspicuous, the theme of unleashing one's creativity is as prominent as that of extreme voyaging. The spilled ink referenced on the Spottable bed illustrates creative expression ["With blankets all splotches / Of black, blue and pink / So nobody'll notice / If you spill ink" (*CCS* 6)], while children will conjure up names for birds on the Bird-Watching bed: "And count all the birds— / Wren, robin and rook— / And write their names / In a Naming Book" (*CCS* 8). Child narratees experience the creative impulse of the book more immediately than the implied readers who are expected to live through these creative junctures vicariously. Significantly, child readers are intuitively encouraged to contribute to Plath's list of imaginative beds and thereby partake in the creative journey of poetry. The poem is an invitation to creative expression and provides mechanisms for child readers to navigate social authority.

The interspersion of nonsense verse marks a distinct difference between "The Bed Book" and "Mrs. Cherry's Kitchen" or "The It-Doesn't-Matter Suit." Autotelic lines such as "[w]ith a pillow bread / To nibble at" (*CCS* 4), "[y]ou can see if the Big Dipper's / Full of stew" (*CCS* 14), "[i]f the tigers jump up / When you happen to sneeze" (*CCS* 11) indicate that jocular wordplay is more important than logical reasoning or an accurate portrayal of the real, all of which promote the reader's release from social and authoritative constraints. The most intriguing example of nonsense in the poem is the Pocket-size bed, which grows when you water it: "You can take out your Bed / Shrunk small as a pea / And water it till / It grows suitably" (*CCS* 10). As Kimberley Reynolds asserts in *Radical Children's Literature*, nonsense literature makes "aesthetic and intellectual demands on readers" (67), "[questions] received wisdom," and "stimulates new ways of thinking" (45). While elements of this type of writing can be spotted in "Mrs. Cherry's Kitchen" and "The It-Doesn't-Matter Suit," "The Bed Book" celebrates them poignantly, suggesting that Plath is experimenting with children's fiction, tilting towards topics more interesting to children than adults. It is this side of "The Bed Book" that Plath recognizes, whether consciously or unconsciously, and therefore continues to send the story to various publishers while at the same time abandoning efforts to publish the other two.

As an emerging children's author, Plath evolves in her choices, initially testing themes that are more appealing to adults, then veering towards themes that tend to children's expectations, offering young readers different identity positions than those anticipated by adult readers. Plath's maturation as a children's literature writer surely feels unfinished. Those familiar with Plath in their childhood may yet grow to relish the idea of encountering her poems and novel as adults, thereby fulfilling one of children's literature's essential contributions: to train children to indulge in adult fiction when they grow up.

# CHAPTER ELEVEN

# Lucent Figs and Suave Veal Chops: Sylvia Plath and Food

LYNDA K. BUNDTZEN

When I tell people that I am a Sylvia Plath scholar, they say, "Oh, she's the poet who killed herself" and "Wasn't she very young?" Or, if they are at all familiar with her poetry in *Ariel* or her novel, *The Bell Jar*, they might say something about her iconic status with feminists and depending on how they feel about feminism, either say something about how man-hating she sounds—"Wasn't she the one who said 'I eat men like air'?"—or express a shared outrage toward her unfaithful husband, Ted Hughes. In either case, I often tell them that they might be surprised by the Sylvia Plath who emerges with startling frequency in her letters and journals. In the A&E biography of Plath, Kate Moses smiles and says, "[s]he out-Martha'd Martha Stewart," remembering the passages where Plath describes in impressive detail the meals she plans, the curtains she sews, the furniture she paints and decorates with hearts and flowers. Plath enjoyed casting herself in the role of domestic goddess, but one who did not see such a big difference between the art of composing a poem and the skill of preparing a good meal. In one of her strange reflections on "battering out a good life," she declares, "I want to be one of the Makaris: with Ted. Books & Babies & Beef stews" (J 269). This line is most likely an allusion to Scottish poet William Dunbar's "Lament for the Makaris, Quhen He Wes Sek" (c. 1505), where only poets are esteemed as "makaris" (makers), as in "the noble Chaucer, of makaris flour." Here Dunbar is not thinking so much of "battering out a good life" but of meditating on last things, because the refrain of the poem is *timor mortis conturbat me* (fear of death confounds me) (Dunbar 49–53). When Plath thinks of being a "maker," she gives priority to her marriage with fellow poet Ted Hughes, and then their partnership in making books, babies, and finally, for her at least, beef stews. And, we know from Hughes, other culinary delights. While on their Cape Cod honeymoon in August 1957, Hughes writes to his brother that though Plath is "the princess of cooks," she has cloyed his appetite with her efforts:

> I have made a pact with Sylvia that when I don't want cream-chiffon pies & all the other fairy palace dishes it's not because she isn't an exquisite cook but because she cooks for relaxation while I eat only by necessity so that there must come occasions when the most Himalayan heaps of pork ... cannot so much as brighten my eye.

He also reveals what will become obvious to a reader of Plath's *Journals*, that cooking was an all-too-tempting diversion: "when she's faced by some tedious or unpleasant piece of work she escapes into cooking" (*LTH* 108–9).

Hughes was probably describing Plath's procrastination from thinking about the forthcoming year of teaching at Smith—her first and last year, it turned out. At the same time, though, she was seeking relief from one of her frequent and painful bouts of writer's block. While Hughes seemed to be having no trouble settling down to write on Cape Cod, Plath was anxious and restless. As Hughes would write years later to Frances McCullough, the first editor of Plath's *Journals*, "[o]ur main programme was her writing. That was absolutely the dominant theme—it was our big invalid" (qtd. in Enniss ix). We know from her journals that she is stricken with a "chill paralysis" because it is almost August, "and no lesson plans, no grammar studied," and she is desperate to "get into novel deep enough so it will go on at the same time." Her hope is that she will be able to both teach and write at the same time—an impossible ambition, as we shall see—and what does she do? The answer:

> After Friday of cooking, whipping yellow oil into yellow egg yolks to make mayonnaise, white sugar into white egg whites to make meringue, yellow butter into yellow custard, and whipped cream folded in to make yellow and white custard, and on and on, I am back to a certain stoic stance: to begin again and write and read in the afternoons and to hell with the beach for a while.
>
> (*J* 292)

In addition to the compulsive whipping of oil, egg yolks, egg whites, and cream that she cites, Plath has been luxuriating in tanning herself on the beach. She scolds herself: "Any idiot can waste the summer getting tan only to lose it" (*J* 292).

Vowing to leave these self-indulgent pursuits, Plath begins to outline a story she proposed to write a couple weeks earlier, titled "THE DAY OF THE TWENTY-FOUR CAKES," about a woman who cannot stop baking cakes:

> Either Kafka litmag serious or SATEVEPOST aim high: woman at end of rope with husband, children: lost sense of order in universe, all meaningless, loss of hopes: quarrel with husband: loose ends, bills, problems, dead end. Wavering between running away or committing suicide: stayed by need to create an order: slowly, methodically begins to bake cakes, one each hour, calls store for eggs, etc. from midnight to midnight. Husband comes home: new understanding. She can go on making order in her limited way: beautiful cakes: can't bear to leave them. Try both styles: do it to your heart's content.
>
> (*J* 288)

A Kafkaesque Martha Stewart run amok? Or simply a desperate housewife? She ultimately decides on the latter version, and even has her protagonist think of leaving "Jock, her strong-willed, taciturn but loving husband [who] is a salesman of office furniture, rising fast" (*J* 292). It is the woman's compulsion, though, "to leave something for [their] children" that stops her flight, and that's when she begins to start baking: "feels the need to keep on, orders four dozen eggs, confectioners sugar, measures out vanilla, baking powder: sense of order, neatness, creativeness. Born homemaker, sense of dignity, richness: knowledge that she's what Jock really needs and wants." When Jock comes home to find her in the kitchen, "she is vital, flushed from baking, at peace with herself" (J 293). Even Norman Rockwell might gag over this.

Before I give you the impression that Plath's fondness for cooking was really a personality disorder, I need to give you a sampling of Plath's hearty appetite and aesthetic appreciation for food. She is quite able to make a reader drool over the simplest menus. Invited to a family dinner by her boyfriend Dick Norton, she waxes rhapsodic over the meal. As she describes the atmosphere in her journal, the table is luminous with

> warm, glowing aqua candles, bright sudden pink-petaled yellow-centered asters. Swordfish and sour cream broiled ... Hollandaise and broccoli. Grape pie and icecream [sic], rich, warm. And port, sharp, sweet, startling gulped with a sudden good sting behind the eyes and a relaxing into easy laughter. Good scalding black coffee. And Dick and I at home an evening, mutually warm, rich, seething with peace.
>
> (J 148)

What an odd mixture of pleasure and pain: "sharp" but "sweet"; "startling gulped" but with a "good sting"; "scalding" coffee; and a mood "seething with peace." Eventually Plath's romantic reverie turns to whether Norton is really the mate she seeks: "The long prosaic loaf of daily bread. But who to eat it with, and when to begin?" (J 148). Norton, as most Plathophiles know, was the model for the all-too-prosaic Buddy Willard of *The Bell Jar*, and no match for Plath's alter ego, Esther Greenwood.

Much later in her journals Plath describes another meal with Ted Hughes that has a totally different aesthetic pitch. After a brisk walk with Hughes in freezing temperatures, they come "home ravenous, to devour seared steak, quenching chef salad, wine, luxurious lucent green figs in thick chilled cream" (J 338). In one of her most enticing descriptions, as if she were insatiable Laura in Christina Rossetti's "Goblin Market" (Greenblatt, et al. 1466–78), she worships a honeydew melon as "wild cold honey-flavored melon-flesh; creamy texture, refreshing, sweet the way sunlight would taste, coming through the clear glassy green bulk of waves" (J 258). One must pause to reflect on why a salad is "quenching," what a "lucent" fig looks like, or what sunlight might taste like, and then on how it might taste if reflected through ocean waves. Finally, celebrating the prize-winning publication of Hughes's first volume of poems, *The Hawk in the Rain*, the couple first "had salad & ham & clear pungent cider at the Eagle pub" for lunch, and later a "gala supper" in a restaurant where she would love to order "[e]scargots? oh yes, madam. And pheasant. & venison," but of frugal necessity and "at the end of resources, settled for ... chicken soup, good & creamy, delicious stuffed tomatoes, turkey with the usual unredeemed chip potatoes & overcooked dried peas, or canned" (J 271). All is not lost though, because for dessert, "[c]hablis & iced lemon mousse transfigured it all. We idled, nibbled, dreamed aloud" (J 271).

For her own culinary endeavors Plath relied heavily on the *Joy of Cooking*, no less a sacred text for her generation than Julia Child's *Mastering the Art of French Cooking* (1961) was for the next. Before the baby boomers, and long before Child made French cuisine *au courant* in America, there was Irma Rombauer's *Joy*, self-published in 1931 to create income after her husband committed suicide. The first edition was illustrated by her daughter Marion Rombauer Becker, with a dramatic cover of St. Martha of Bethany, the patron saint of cooking, wielding a sword over a soon-to-be-slain dragon. It does stir the imagination to wonder what St. Martha of Bethany had in mind for dinner. The subtitle for this first edition promised a "Compilation of Reliable Recipes with a Casual Culinary Chat," and, in the Depression era, many of those reliable recipes were for game like rabbits, squirrel, and opossum. The casual culinary chat offered instructions on canning and preserving fruits and vegetables from the garden. It is doubtful that Sylvia Plath saw this first edition, but she may have been raised on one of the several commercially published editions that followed, and we do know for certain that when she wanted to get serious about cooking in graduate school (as a Fulbright Fellow in Cambridge, England), she suddenly needed to have her 1953 edition. Breathless with the excitement of her new love for Ted Hughes and probably determined to impress him with her cooking skills, she writes her mother: "Ted is teaching me about horoscopes, how to cook herring roes, and we are going to the world's biggest circus tonight. God, such a life! … if you have a chance, could you send over my 'Joy of Cooking'? It's the one book I really miss!" (April 26, 1956, *L1* 1177–8). She reminds her mother again on May 18, 1956, "[C]ould you please possibly send my 'Joy of Cooking'" (*L1* 1195)? Aurelia Plath apparently remembered to bring the *Joy* when she came to England in June.

A year later finds Plath reading her "blessed Rombauer" (*J* 249) as if it were a "rare novel," when she should be "studying Locke" for her Cambridge final exams. She then chastises herself: "Whoa, I said to myself. You will escape into domesticity & stifle yourself by falling headfirst into a bowl of cookie batter." But, she reasons, even the "Big Ones" like Virginia Woolf find comfort "by cleaning out the kitchen. And cooks haddock & sausage. Bless her" (*J* 269). The *Joy* even went with her and Hughes to Spain after their swift marriage in June 1956. On August 17, Hughes's twenty-sixth birthday, she records the contents of "Mr. and Mrs. Ted Hughes' Writing Table," including "[a]n open cookbook … at Ted's right elbow, where I'd left it after finishing reading out recipes of stewed rabbit" for his birthday dinner, and close by on her side of the table, "a ragged brown covered Thesaurus … close to Ted's red covered Shakespeare" (August 17, 1956, *J* 259). Her preparations for this first birthday dinner she will cook for Ted as his wife are lovingly documented. The morning is devoted first to "shopping for rabbit and myriad garnishes for gala stew" (*J* 256-7) in their honeymoon Spanish village, Benidorm. Then, undaunted by the one-burner petrol stove, she creates a feast. She must first "dress" a rabbit, and the 1953 *Joy of Cooking* still has the Depression-era illustration for this delicate operation. But it is late afternoon, and Plath has just awakened from what she describes as a "long deep nap, dropping of end of pier into hypnotized sleep." Now she must pull herself up from the depths and gird her loins for the task:

> Cleared head with washing and cold drink of water; sweaty, reserve of energy growing. Gulped scalding coffee, like surgeon before difficult new operation to be performed for first time. Got out ingredients from larder: Ted lit carbon fire, glowing to red coals in black oven, after much smoking and glowering clouds; scraped carrots naked, cut onion, squushy [*sic*] tomato; cooked down strips of salt pork, floured pink tight rabbit flesh; seared rabbit to savoury brown, chunked in big kettle; made rich dense gravy from drippings, adding flour, salt, boiling water, two packets of condensed soup—vegetable and beef and chicken, glass and a half of wine at Ted's insistence; added sauce to kettle with can of peas, onions, tomato & carrots. Boiled and bubbled, savoury, steaming and delectable.
>
> (August 17, 1956; *J* 258)

The "wine at Ted's insistence" is an ingredient Rombauer says the French like to add. But a reader might pause over some of these details—why should carrots be violently scraped naked? Or, why does Plath portray herself as a surgeon, flaying a bunny's skin to expose "pink tight rabbit flesh"?

After a few years, Plath seems more comfortable in the kitchen than she did assembling this first birthday meal for her husband. Entertaining friends for dinner and playing the part of competent hostess, Plath is swept into a sensual haze while she finishes preparations. She titles the journal entry "a moment, caught, in the stillness of waiting for guests" and attempts to re-create the moment impressionistically (J 329). She revels in her own scent and colors—"[m]y own tigress perfume & the dull-avocado green of my skirt and bright turquoise & gold-lined & white & black paisley patterned jersey warm & snug on me"—while she puts the finishing touches on her cake. A glass of wine gives her the necessary brio: "the white wine drunk during smoothing on thick white marshmellowy [sic] frosting singing thin in my veins—oh the absolute free willingness unleashed which wine brings. The apartment clean-carpeted and empty, bowls of sour cream & onion, pots of tomato & meat sauce, garlic butter, hot water, waiting, waiting" (J 329). The "moment" comes to a crashing halt, however, and we never learn how the dinner party unfolded. From wine singing in her veins and unleashing an exuberant "free willingness," Plath suddenly turns to "after, after, to hell with Sophocles, I shall pick you up & go on with you, to catch up" (J 329–30) and begins a long complaint about never catching up with her teaching preparations. A journal entry that begins with heady excitement descends even further into "[a] nightmare to record," mingling images from paintings of "suffering Christs & corrupt judges & lawyers by Rouault" with images from newspaper clippings about the Holocaust: "three men behind barbwire at a Concentration Camp clipped from the Times from a review which I read about tortures & black trains bearing victims to the furnace" (J 330). The passage is reminiscent of Keats's "Ode to a Nightingale," where he first extols the liberating effects of wine—"That I might drink, and leave the world unseen" with the nightingale's song—and then plummets downward to "Where but to think is to be full of sorrow / And leaden-eyed despairs" (290–3).

Throughout her year of teaching at Smith (1957–8) Plath's happier moments revolve around food, reveries to interrupt classroom anxieties and the familiar drudgery of pedagogy—grading papers, preparing lectures, reading exams. In the middle of a long journal entry wondering, "[w]hat is it teaching kills?" and self-flagellation over her own sense of fraudulence—"[a]nd I: what am I but a glorified automaton hearing myself, through a vast space of weariness, speak from the shell speaking-trumpet that is my mouth the dead words about life, suffering, and deep knowledge and ritual sacrifice"—she will suddenly turn to the calm of preparing dinner, paring "potatoes into cool white ovoids, carrots into long conical spears, onions slippery glossed & bulbous popped & cracked from their rattle-paper skins" (J 346). In answer to her sense of being trapped "between two unachieved shapes: between the original teacher & the original writer: neither," Plath turns to the serenity of those cooking shapes, so easily achieved—ovoids, cones, bulbs. Occasionally she simply pats herself on the back for company-pleasing desserts—a "trusty angel-topped lemon meringue pie" (J 323) or "runny but delicious custard-meringue-raspberry pie" (J 383)—while at other times she seems to revel in hearty meals inspired by her reading. Hence, after "rereading 'Moby Dick' in preparation for the exam deluge tomorrow—am whelmed and wondrous at the swimming Biblical & craggy Shakespearean cadences, the rich & lustrous & fragrant recreation of spermaceti, ambergris—miracle, marvel, the ton-thunderous leviathan"— she "[m]ade a huge fish soup." The next day she interrupts her boredom from sorting exams for a senior professor with "[s]teaming & savory fish soup for lunch, smacking good all onion-essence, chunks of soaked fish & potato steaming, hot, bacon bits, buttery crackers foundering in it" (J 370). Ahab's ship foundered, we know, but crackers?

In contrast to the year of teaching at Smith, marked by many journal entries expressing pleasure over cooking and food, the following year (1958–9) is principally devoted to Plath's "Panic Bird"—her writer's block—and trying to ferret out its neurotic roots in her sessions with psychoanalyst Ruth Beuscher. There are very few lengthy journal entries about cooking from this year—brief mentions by a harried housewife of "chicken & squash ready in the oven for Ted's return from the library, back achey" (J 423) and also complaints by Ted about apparently too-light meals (J 421). Plath's longest entry records a day when she "had been sitting at an abstract poem about mirrors & identity which I hated," followed by "a rejection from The Kenyon sealing hopelessness" (J 404). This gloom over her writing extends to her efforts in the kitchen and, as the following passage shows, nearly threatens Plath with being cut off like her heroine in *The Bell Jar*:

> Where, how, with what & for what to begin? No incident in my life seemed ready to stand up for even a 20 page story. I sat paralyzed, feeling no person in the world to speak to, but off totally from humanity in a self-induced vacuum. I felt sicker & sicker. I couldn't happily be anything but a writer & I couldn't be a writer: I couldn't even set down one sentence: I was paralyzed with fear, with deadly hysteria. I sat in the hot kitchen, unable to blame lack of time, the sultry July weather, anything but myself. The white hardboiled egg, the green head of lettuce, the two suave pink veal chops dared me to do anything with them, to make a meal out of them, to alter their single, leaden identity into a digestible meal. I had been living in an idle dream of being a writer. And here stupid housewives & people with polio were getting their stories into the Satevepost. I went into Ted, utterly shattered, & asked him to tackle the veal chops. And burst into tears. Useless, goodfornothing.
>
> (J 404–5)

What is most curious about this passage is the attribution of "suave" to veal chops as if they were worldly, sophisticated, and debonair young men mocking a young girl of no skill or experience to "Make something of me!" There is also the convergence of composing a poem about identity and the leaden identities of the cooking ingredients, in need of the same kind of magical inspiration from her to turn them into a "digestible meal." Still in a bleak mood months later, Plath says, "I'm not working, only studying to change my ways of writing poems. A disgust for my work. My poems begin on one track, in one dimension and never surprise or shock or even much please" (J 465). To get out of her doldrums, she reads other poets and then blends her taste in poetry—her aesthetic preferences—with the gustatory pleasures of drink: "Read [Richard] Wilbur and [Adrienne] Rich this morning. Wilbur a bland turning of pleasaunces [sic], a fresh speaking and picturing with incalculable grace and all sweet, pure, clear, fabulous, the maestro with the imperceptible marcel. Robert Lowell after this is like good strong shocking brandy after a too lucidly sweet dinner wine, desert [sic] wine" (J 465). Wilbur, like those damnable veal chops, sounds a little too suave for Plath, who was looking for a way to "surprise or shock" that would not come until *Ariel*.[1]

We don't have the two journals Plath kept after she and Hughes moved back to England in 1959 because Hughes—infamously—lost one of them and destroyed the final journal, he says, "because he did not want her children to have to read it (in those days he regarded forgetfulness as an essential part of survival)" ("Plath and Her Journals" 177). The earlier one, with entries covering 1960–2, is presumed stolen, since Hughes left it out for anyone to read in the Devon home he returned to after Plath's suicide. Plath kept a final journal after she moved to London in December 1962, and this is the one Hughes says he destroyed. From her letters to her mother, though, we know that Plath continued to take great pleasure in being a homemaker and mother. When she was pregnant with Frieda and Nicholas, she seemed to give up on her writing altogether and devoted her time to nesting, feeling, she says, "quite cowlike and interested suddenly in soppy women's magazines & cooking & sewing" (*L2* 699). She is ecstatic when she receives

> a big Xmas parcel from you [mother Aurelia] with the two Ladies Home J's which I fell upon with joy and rejoicing—that magazine has so much Americana I love it. Look forward to a good read by the wood fire tonight, & to trying the luscious recipes. Recipes in English women's magazines are for things like Lard & Stale Bread Pie, garnished with Cold Pigs Feet, or Left-Over Pot Roast in Aspic.
>
> (*L2* 698)

Like the *Joy of Cooking*, this magazine represented for Plath an "Americanness which I feel to [sic] need to dip into, now I'm in exile, and especially as I'm writing for women's magazines in a small way now. I shall have fulfilled a very longtime ambition if a story of mine ever makes the LHJ" (*L2* 668). Plath may have seen the feature by fellow American poet Phyllis McGinley, "Cooking to Me Is Poetry," in the January 1960 issue, where she compares the skills of cooking to those of composing poems and supports good "old-fashioned" recipes (66–7), confirming Plath's own aesthetic perceptions about traditional cooking in the American mold, and her antipathy for English cooking. Indeed, for Christmas she spurns the English goose, instead roasting her "1st simply beautiful golden-brown turkey with your [Aurelia's] bread dressing, creamed brussels sprouts & chestnuts, swede (like squash, orange), giblet gravy & apple pies with our last & preciously saved own apples" (*L2* 708). Before the birth of her second child, Nicholas, she tells her mother:

> Each day I bake something to hide away for Ted & Frieda when I'm recovering from the new baby. I have a box of sand tarts cut in shapes with cherries & almonds[,] … a box of tollhouse cookies & a fruitcake. Tomorrow I'll try an apple pie with the very last of our apples.
>
> (*L2* 712)

---

[1] There is another journal entry where Plath compares her various boyfriends to food. Thinking about Richard Sassoon, her greatest love before Ted Hughes, she says, "he can't swim, he is weak in a certain sense, he will never play baseball or teach math: that orange juice and broiled chicken solidity is utterly lacking and it is what Gary has and Gordon has (in the story: Dark Marauder, there will be a great contrast between the delicate snail-and wine taste of Richard and the plain steak-steak and potatoes-with-nothing-done-to-them taste of Gary)" (*J* 566).

What could be more American than Tollhouse cookies and apple pie?

Only nine months after Nicholas's birth, Plath is contemplating divorce from Ted Hughes, who has deserted her and their two children for another woman. She is also "writing like mad—have managed a poem a day before breakfast! All book poems. Terrific stuff, as if domesticity had choked me" (October 12, 1962, *L2* 856). These are, of course, the *Ariel* poems—Plath's October miracle. If we had only the evidence of these poems, then we would probably assume that Plath had never found any joy in cooking. Domesticity in *Ariel* is both dangerous and scary. In "A Birthday Present" the speaker imagines something monstrous hiding just "behind this veil" that "shimmers, it does not stop, and I think it wants me," and "[w]hen I am quiet at my cooking I feel it looking, I feel it thinking" (*CP* 206). In "Cut" a Freudian slip of the knife turns a kitchen accident—"What a thrill— / My thumb instead of an onion" (*CP* 235)—into an epiphany of self-hatred: "Dirty girl, / Thumb stump" (*CP* 235). And then there's the coffee-klatch of two housewives in "Lesbos," the title itself ironic because there is no love lost between these two women. The first line exclaims, "[v]iciousness in the kitchen! / The potatoes hiss" (*CP* 227), while they complain to each other about their lives—tending small children, putting up with boring husbands characterized as "[a]n old pole for the lightning" (*CP* 228) or "hugging his ball and chain" (*CP* 229) as he heads off to work. And "meanwhile there's a stink of fat and baby crap" and "the smog of cooking, the smog of hell" (*CP* 228) hovering over the women. The suffocation of housewifery closes in as one woman leaves and looks back: "I see your cute décor / Close on you like the fist of a baby" (*CP* 229). Even the rabbit Plath dressed and stewed to perfection for Hughes's birthday returns in "Totem," but the "pink tight rabbit flesh" now looks like an "aborted" baby: "Its baby head out of the way, embalmed in spice, // Flayed of fur and humanity" (*CP* 264).

Before *Ariel*, though, and even while Plath was still writing those rosy letters to her mother about domestic bliss with Ted Hughes and singing the praises of *Ladies' Home Journal*, she was writing her novel *The Bell Jar*, much of which is an outright repudiation and satire of 1950s norms for women. Plath did not want her mother to read *The Bell Jar*, characterizing it as a "potboiler" of no artistic merit, and she published it under the *nom de plume* Victoria Lucas. It is as if Plath split herself in two: for her mother, she was the sentimental "Sivvy" of the letters, in love with soppy women's magazines, but in *The Bell Jar* she is the proto-feminist Esther Greenwood, who suspects "maybe it was true that when you were married and had children it was like being brainwashed, and afterward you went about numb as a slave in some private, totalitarian state," an epiphany that Esther arrives at after her boyfriend tells her that she won't want to write poetry anymore after she has children (*B* 85). As for cooking, Esther is purposely hopeless:

> My grandmother and my mother were such good cooks that I left everything to them. They were always trying to teach me one dish or another, but I would just look on and say, "Yes, yes, I see," while the instructions slid through my head like water, and then I'd always spoil what I did so nobody would ask me to do it again.
>
> (*B* 75–6)

One episode of the novel in particular suggests that Plath regarded women's magazines like *Ladies' Home Journal* as poison—figuratively speaking. Plath's heroine, Esther Greenwood, is a college guest editor for a posh women's magazine, just as Plath herself was for *Mademoiselle* in the summer of 1953, before her first breakdown and attempted suicide. On one of their jaunts Esther and the other guest editors in *The Bell Jar* are invited to a banquet by *Ladies' Day* magazine, a portmanteau combining *Ladies' Home Journal* and *Woman's Day*. Esther is thrilled with the food being served by the "staff of the *Ladies' Day* Food Testing Kitchens in hygienic white smocks, neat hairnets and flawless makeup of a uniform peach-pie color" (*B* 25)—a far cry from the kitchen's "stink of fat and baby crap" in "Lesbos" (*CP* 228). Esther tells the reader, "I love food more than just about anything else" and "[n]o matter how much I eat, I never put on weight," so when she sees the "yellow-green avocado pear halves stuffed with crabmeat and mayonnaise, and platters of rare roast beef and cold chicken, and every so often a cut-glass bowl heaped with black caviar" (*B* 24), she pigs out. And I do mean pigs out. She greedily strategizes the placement of one of the caviar bowls, figuring that the girl across from her "couldn't reach it because of the mountainous centerpiece of marzipan fruit," and the girl next to her "would be too nice to ask me to share it with her if I just kept it out of the way at my elbow by my bread-and-butter plate" (*B* 26). While everyone else is behaving decorously, Esther knows that "if you do something incorrect at table with a certain arrogance," not only can you "get away with it," but everyone "will think you are original and very witty" (*B* 27). So Esther dispenses with the cutlery altogether:

> I paved my plate with chicken slices. Then I covered the chicken slices with caviar thickly as if I were spreading peanut butter on a piece of bread. Then I picked up the chicken slices in my fingers one by one, rolled them so the caviar wouldn't ooze off and ate them.
>
> (*B* 27)

Nor, in this porcine depiction, does Esther stop with one plate of chicken and caviar. She polishes off a second and goes on to tackle the avocado and crabmeat salad, announcing, "Avocados are my favorite fruit" (*B* 28). She especially loves them with melted grape jelly in French dressing, "filling the cup of the pear with the garnet sauce" (*B* 28). Only after she has thoroughly gorged herself and is "no longer worried about competition over my caviar," does Esther begin a conversation with her fellow guest editor Betsy (*B* 28).

Later, after a very bad night of continuous waves of nausea and diarrhea, Esther passes out on the bathroom floor. She feels "limp as a wet leaf and shivering all over" (*B* 44). Informed the following morning that the crabmeat "was chock-full of ptomaine," Esther has

> a vision of the celestially white kitchens of *Ladies' Day* stretching into infinity. I saw avocado pear after avocado pear being stuffed with crabmeat and mayonnaise and photographed under brilliant lights. I saw the delicate, pink-mottled claw meat poking seductively through its blanket of mayonnaise and the bland yellow pear cup with its rim of alligator-green cradling the whole mess. Poison.
>
> (*B* 48)

The poison here represents a sickeningly coquettish domesticity. The crab claws poke above the mayonnaise like a coy woman peeping over a blanket, and the avocado holds its poison lovingly like a mother cradling a baby. Plath also suggests that the hygienic purity of the kitchens and the staff—female role models of domestic engineering with their smocks, hairnets, and peach-pie perfect makeup—masks an underlying toxicity for women, and that the American magazine genre typified by *Ladies' Home Journal* is sinister propaganda. Nothing terrible seems to happen to the bright, efficient, stay-at-home-moms in their pages, and if something does, there is always the good advice of the monthly feature, "Can This Marriage Be Saved?" The problem, as Plath explains to her mother (in a letter signed "Sylvia," not "Sivvy"), is that "[i]t is much more help for me, for example, to know that people are divorced & go through hell, that [sic] to hear about happy marriages. Let the Ladies' Home Journal blither about <u>those</u>" (*L2* 875). Yet in the same letter she assures her mother that she is still a super-efficient hostess, preparing a "roast beef potato & corn dinner, with apple cake" for guests (October 21, 1962, *L2* 875). She explodes again, a few days later:

> Stop trying to get me to write about "decent courageous people"—read the Ladies Home Journal for those! ... I believe in going through & facing the worst, not hiding from it. That is why I am going to London this week, partly, to face all the people we know & tell them happily & squarely I am divorcing Ted, so they won't picture me as a poor, deceived country wife.
>
> (October 25, 1962, *L2* 888)

Instead of being a "poor, deceived country wife," she tells her mother she "want[s] to be the most loving & fascinating mother in the world" with a flat in London, where "Frieda & Nick shall have the intelligences of the day as their visitors, and I the Salon that I will deserve" (October 23, 1962, *L2* 884).

Despite Plath's apparent scorn in *The Bell Jar* for the representations of ideal homemakers in American women's magazines and her eventual revelation of this scorn to her mother, she was not immune to its consumer fantasies. In her memoir, "Vessel of Wrath," Dido Merwin takes it as "a warning shot across the bows" when Plath rejects her offer to provide Plath and Hughes with most of what they need to furnish their apartment in London: "But if the Hughes's [sic] elected to go splurging on a posh cooker, refrigerator, and bed, what the hell? Never mind if it made no sense to a couple of flea-marketers like Bill [W. S. Merwin] and me" (*Bitter Fame* 325). Dido goes on to deride Plath's "need for morale-boosting toys" as a sign of her "insecurity" (*Bitter Fame* 325). In December 1962, when Plath was once again equipping a London flat—this time alone—her visiting friend Clarissa Roche reports that "her kitchen was full of American-style gadgets" (*Bitter Fame* 286). Even though "the rooms were tidy, the beds made, and the kitchen" spotless, "Clarissa suspected Sylvia rarely prepared the meals so carefully planned on her weekly menu" (*Bitter Fame* 286).

There is an odd pathos to how often Plath is reported to have eaten heartily in her final days. We have two accounts of Plath's last weekend before she committed suicide: Jillian Becker's testimony in the Anne Stevenson biography *Bitter Fame* and Becker's own memoir *Giving Up: The Last Days of Sylvia Plath*. Despite some discrepancies in tone, both versions portray Plath as deeply depressed, but most composed and sociable when dining. Both, however, depict something incongruous or off-kilter about someone as sick as Plath quite evidently having such a healthy appetite. Plath calls Becker on Thursday, February 7, 1963, and, according to Stevenson, is "hysterical and desperate," "asking for asylum" for herself and her children with Becker (*Bitter Fame* 292). In Becker's own account she simply notes that Plath asked, "May I come round with the children?" (2). When Plath arrives, she immediately withdraws for a nap, ignoring the presence of "one of her erstwhile friends" (Becker 2). After her nap, Jillian Becker invites her to stay the weekend with the children. According to Stevenson, "[a]t dinner Jillian was surprised to see Sylvia eat her steak with enormous relish, commenting on how wonderful it tasted after her diet of mince. Had she forgotten how often the Beckers themselves had taken her out, Jillian wondered" (*Bitter Fame* 292). Becker more generously describes Plath enjoying her menu of "chicken soup, grilled large rump steaks ... mashed potato with plenty of milk and butter, and a salad": "She ate heartily. She always did and it always pleased me; not only because it was a compliment to my cooking but chiefly because eating well was bound to make her feel better. Like most Jewish mothers, I believed in the therapeutic power of good food" (Becker 7). Stevenson notes that "however distraught Sylvia seemed at other times, she always appeared dressed for meals, was calm at table, ate extremely well, and was warmly appreciative of the food Jillian served" (*Bitter Fame* 292). After what is clearly a harrowing night according to both versions, Plath somehow "devoured a good breakfast" (Becker 13) and in Stevenson's version "ate a hearty breakfast, and returned to bed" (*Bitter Fame* 294). Plath was on a cocktail of drugs—both sleeping pills and an antidepressant—and the Becker and Stevenson versions differ on how much medication Plath consumed. Becker claims that she carefully monitored the dosage, making sure that Plath did not take more than the two prescribed sleeping pills, even though she woke at 3:00 a.m. begging for another. Plath's sleep medication, according to Becker, "didn't seem to make her somnolent or even soothe her" (Becker 9). Stevenson, however, reports that Jillian described Plath swallowing "pill after pill—what seemed to her far more than a safe dose—before lying back to rehearse the litany of anguish that was to be repeated day and night throughout the weekend" (*Bitter Fame* 292).

If we believe Stevenson, Jillian Becker regarded Plath as a tiresome house guest, foisting her children's care onto Jillian, alternately eating heartily and sleeping, and subjecting her to a middle-of-the-night "rodomontade, which always trailed round the same course: she hated her mother; she hated Ted for betraying her; 'she' (Sylvia would never speak [Ted's mistress] Assia's name) was hateful; the Hughes family had rejected her," and so on and on. As for her listener, "she might just as well have been 'a mask hanging on the wall,' Jillian says, as Sylvia poured out chaotic memories and obsessions in a feverish delirium" (*Bitter Fame* 293). Because Stevenson makes Jillian Becker sound irritated and unsympathetic, and Plath monstrously self-absorbed, Becker may well have written her memoir as an antidote to *Bitter Fame*'s barely disguised venom. On the Sunday before her suicide, Stevenson says that "although it was a bitterly cold day, Sylvia had not thought to dress [Nicholas] warmly" before sending him off with Jillian's husband to an outing at the zoo, and then "Sunday lunch came and went, with a joint of meat and Sylvia's usual exclamations over its excellence. After eating heartily, Sylvia went up to rest" (*Bitter Fame* 295). This combination of details suggests that Plath was sick enough to be a careless mother but not sick enough to refuse another hearty meal from her gracious hostess, and then, behaving discourteously, to leave the table suddenly to nap. But in Becker's memoir, Plath

> joined us at the table for our usual ample Sunday lunch of soup, roast lamb or beef with all the trimmings, salad, cheese, dessert, wine. I remember that she enjoyed it, saying it was "wonderful" or "marvellous" or something of the sort. She helped Nick with his food, and seemed, I thought, a little more cheerful, a little less tense.
>
> (15)

Becker also says that everyone "lingered at the table ... for an hour or so after the coffee cups had gone cold, talking about something that has left not a trace of memory ... and the wine we had drunk made us sleepy too so we all went to lie down" (16), which sounds far more benign than Stevenson's version.

This is really the last meal we know Plath had. She insisted on returning to her own London flat after she woke up. After putting Frieda and Nicholas in their upstairs bedroom, opening their windows and placing bread and milk next to their "high-sided cots," Plath stuffed towels and cloths under their door and the kitchen door, and turned on the gas in the stove. The following morning she was found "sprawled on the floor, her head on a little folded cloth in the oven" (*Bitter Fame* 296).

PART II

# Affiliations, Influences, and Intertextualities

# CHAPTER TWELVE

# Sylvia Plath's Greek Tragedy

HOLLY RANGER

In a parodic allusion to her history of psychoanalytic treatment, Plath's introductory note for a reading of "Daddy" (*CP* 222–4) describes the poem as "spoken by a girl with an Electra complex" (*CP* 293). Invited, in part, by this statement, the poetic speaker's adoption of an Electra persona in the earlier poems "Electra on Azalea Path" (*CP* 116–17) and "The Colossus" (*CP* 129–30) has been similarly framed by critics with reference to psychoanalysis. When Jung glossed the Electra archetype in *The Theory of Psychoanalysis* as a girl who takes revenge on her mother for murdering her father, he did not cite a source for the narrative but assumed the reader's familiarity with the eponymous mythological figure ("As everyone knows ... ") (Jung 69). One effect of the extensive cultural impact of psychoanalysis in the twentieth century is that for many of Plath's readers today, Electra is more readily recognizable from Jung than from her incarnations in the ancient Greek tragic source texts to which Jung refers: *The Oresteian Trilogy* of Aeschylus and the *Electra* plays of Sophocles and Euripides. Plath herself, however, studied "all [three] Electras" (*J* 224–5) while reading for the English Tripos Tragedy paper at Newnham College, Cambridge.[1] While the presence of Jung's Electra in Plath's poems cannot be dismissed, this essay explores some of the ways in which an understanding of the critical and pedagogical contexts of Plath's literary training in Greek tragedy at the University of Cambridge in the mid-1950s enriches a reading of Plath's allusive poetry beyond the psychobiographical. At the same time, I recognize that Plath's self-mythologization in her poetry is one of the distinctive features and principal innovations of her poetics.[2] This biomythographical conceit is discernible in embryonic form in the juvenilia that engage with characters and tropes from fairy tales, but during and after studying ancient Greco-Roman literature at Cambridge, Plath's poetic speakers metamorphose from Cinderellas into Electras. My argument here is that the tension between Plath's explicitly autobiographical readings of ancient literature in her poetry and her New Critical training in "impersonality" and "objective criticism" focalizes a double movement of complicity and critique that runs

---

[1] Smith holds Plath's inscribed, dated, and annotated copies of Vellacott, *Aeschylus, The Oresteian Trilogy* (1956), and Watling, *Sophocles* Electra *and Other Plays* (1954); it has not been established which edition of Euripides's *Bacchae* Plath read while at Newnham. Plath's reading notes from Cambridge are contained in Plath mss. II, box 13, folders 5–7, Lilly.

[2] Rose has observed that it is a truism of Plath scholarship to comment on the poet's constitution as a myth by critics and to state an intention to bypass that myth (11). My reading, then, is in part a return to the mythological approach to Plath's writing most notably represented by Kroll in *Chapters in a Mythology*, and as described by Gill in *The Cambridge Introduction to Sylvia Plath* (117–19), but one that resists the biographical reductionism and anti-historicist modes of the earlier criticism.

throughout her poetry: a conservative modernist impulse toward classicism coincident with a burgeoning subversive impulse toward subjective poetic expression.

The English Tripos was introduced as a discrete honors degree at Cambridge in 1917 as part of a wider University enterprise in the early twentieth century to expand its bachelor's degree awards from mathematics, theology, and classical philology. The ordinances of the new degree course focused on post-medieval writing in English and held an explicit aim to situate this writing as an inheritance of the Greco-Roman classics via the literatures of the Romance languages French and Italian. This assumption of the existence of an inherited transhistorical canon of works and genres necessitated the creation of comparative examination papers to fulfill the regulations' requirement for a "special subject in the general history of literature, ancient and modern, in connection and comparison with English literature" (qtd. in Collini n.p.). The nineteenth-century Cambridge syllabus had been shaped by elite public school curricula, which supplied Cambridge with a stream of boys trained predominantly in ancient Greek and Latin—a University syllabus which simply required "more of the same" at degree-level ensured success for these students (Stray 41). The persistent influence of the public schools on the Cambridge syllabi of the twentieth century is detected in the first principles of the two compulsory comparative elements of the modern two-part Tripos instituted in 1926, which acclimatized the elite student to English: the Tragedy paper began with the ancient Greek dramatists Aeschylus, Sophocles, and Euripides, and the English Moralists paper began with the ancient Greek philosophers Plato and Aristotle.[3]

The primacy of ancient Greek tragedy in the new English Tripos was reinforced by the prominence of the genre in the aesthetic theory of one of its first teachers, I. A. Richards, famous for his development of "practical criticism" (and whom Plath had met the previous year at Smith College).[4] When Plath arrived in Cambridge in 1955, the Tragedy and practical criticism ("Criticism and Composition") papers were associated with Richards's contemporary and fellow proponent of the New Criticism, F. R. Leavis, whose lectures Plath audited after applying for special permission to do so (*Red Comet* 380).[5] The New Critics, heavily influenced by the essays of T. S. Eliot, had formulated and taught a mode of criticism which attempted to unite aesthetic and moral concerns and to articulate and justify a response to a work of literature on objective grounds. Eliot's criticism employed close readings of literary texts "[t]o divert interest from the poet to the poetry," but its criteria for "classic" literature relied on the acceptance of a shared canon of literature stretching back to ancient Greece against which individual quality could be measured (*Selected Prose* 44). Leavis's version of this "objective criticism" was similarly founded upon the assumption that an accepted tradition or canon of texts existed (Wimsatt 82). His subjective aesthetic value judgments were therefore expressed

---

[3]The comparative Tragedy paper remains a compulsory element of Part II; the Moralists paper has been discontinued from the 2020 matriculation cohort.
[4]Plath attended Richards's lecture, "The Dimensions of Reading Poetry," and an evening reception in his honor on March 3, 1954 (*L1* 702).
[5]According to "Lectures proposed by the Board of the Faculty of English, 1955–56" (611), Leavis presented the lecture series "Appreciation and Analysis" (Wednesdays and Fridays at 10 a.m., Michaelmas Term 1955; Wednesdays at 11 a.m., Lent Term 1956), "Critics and Critical Theory" (Fridays at 12 p.m., Lent Term 1956), and "Critical Approaches to Fiction" (Wednesdays and Fridays at 12 p.m., Easter Term 1956). On the shift in Plath's attitude toward practical criticism, from this early enthusiasm to a later belief that it was "paralyzing" for poetry: see *Annotating Modernism*, 47–8.

as an assessment of a text's placement in this tradition of texts objectively paradigmatic of "the human situation" (Richards 63). While Leavis disagreed with Eliot that poetry should be "Impersonal" ("completely separate in him will be the man who suffers and the mind which creates"), Eliot's disciples in the United States, Cleanth Brooks and Robert Penn Warren (whose works had structured Plath's formal introduction to criticism as an undergraduate at Smith College), followed Eliot in discarding the social context in which literature was generated (*Selected Prose* 40, 41).[6] Notwithstanding the individual modulations among the New Critics, they were united by an acute social conservatism that reinforced the cultural hegemony of "the classics."

Plath's letters home to the United States from Cambridge in her first year as a Fulbright Scholar frequently express an anxiety about finding herself in a cultural and critical environment which assumed a shared knowledge and valuation of the Greco-Roman classical canon. A few weeks into Michaelmas Term, Plath writes, "my enormous ignorances appal [*sic*] me[.] ... Grace here is said solemnly in Latin, and everybody seems to have a classical background" (*L1* 976, 978) or have "already ... picked up' Greek" (*L1* 1093). Plath cringes at having "never read the classics" (*L1* 1004) and "shockingly enough, never touched" the ancient dramatists Aeschylus, Sophocles, or Euripides (*L1* 1085). She expresses an anxiety that this lack of classical Greek literary training makes her appear "uneducated" (*L1* 1004) to her Director of Studies among Newnham's classically educated upper middle-class grammar school "glib girls" (*L1* 1006). Plath's complaints draw our attention because she had read Aeschylus's *Agamemnon* in translation in high school and again at Smith for a paper on "Modern Tragedy in the Classic Tradition" (Lilly). Plath's anxieties may be located in a perceived lack of grounding in the ancient languages, or in having studied ancient texts only in a comparative context and never *per se*, or simply, perhaps, in the passing of time since she had last read a Greek play, but they reveal a complicated nexus of desires—both to learn and to assimilate.

Plath read steadily and widely to "remedy" (*L1* 1005) the disparity between her American education and the knowledge required for the Tragedy paper. She recorded her intention to attend three of the 1955–6 lecture series that fall, in the history of tragic theory (from "Aristotle to Volkelt"), tragedy from Racine to the present, and Elizabethan and Jacobean tragedy, and to focus on ancient tragedy in the new year (*L1* 975).[7] By late January 1956, Plath was immersed in ancient Greek tragedy, reading "all 7 [extant] plays by Aeschylus" (*L1* 1092) and writing a paper on "The Character of Zeus in [Aeschylus's] *Prometheus Bound*" (Lilly) for her tragedy supervision on February 8 (*L1* 1098). In late

---

[6]See also Brooks and Warren, *Understanding Poetry* and Brooks, *The Well Wrought Urn*. Plath's copies of *Understanding Poetry* and *The Well Wrought Urn* are held by Smith. For an account of the classroom contexts in which I. A. Richards and Cleanth Brooks produced their touchstone works of New Criticism, see Buurma and Heffernan, *The Teaching Archive*, chapters 3 and 5; Buurma and Heffernan argue that the curricula of Richards and Brooks were more expansive and collaboratively generated than the canon espoused in their published books.
[7]According to "Lectures proposed by the Board of the Faculty of English, 1955–56," *Cambridge University Reporter* (610–12), Plath is referring to the lecture series "History of Tragic Theory: Aristotle to Volkelt" with Theodore Redpath (Wednesdays and Fridays at 9 a.m., Michaelmas Term 1955), "Tragedy from Racine to the Present Time" with Muriel Bradbrook (Tuesdays and Fridays at 11 a.m., Michaelmas Term, 1955), "Elizabethan and Jacobean Tragedy" with Enid Welsford (Wednesdays at 11 a.m., Michaelmas Term 1955; Wednesdays at 10am, Lent Term 1956), and "Greek Tragedy" with Leonard Potts (Fridays at 10 a.m., Michaelmas Term 1955)—although as Plath planned to concentrate on ancient tragedy "next year" (1956), she may have intended to skip these lectures and self-study in the new year.

February and early March, Plath moved on in her reading from Aeschylus to Sophocles (*J* 210) and Euripides, reading "all Electras" (*J* 224) for a supervision (her copy of Sophocles's *Electra* bears an ink note in Plath's hand, a reminder of a paper assignment, to compare the three ancient Electra plays with Eugene O'Neill's *Mourning Becomes Electra*).[8] Plath also took the opportunity to see two performances of Greek tragedies in February 1956, attending a production of Sophocles's *Philoctetes* in English at the ADC Theatre on the 10th (*L1* 1102), and the Cambridge Greek Play at the Cambridge Arts Theatre on the 21st, a performance of Euripides's *Bacchae* "[i]n Greek (!) … performed here every 3 years (even Oxford gave up plays in Greek in 1932!)," "complete with Cambridge students chanting Greek choruses, [and] modern original music" (*L1* 1122–3).[9] In contrast to these effusive February letters, by late March Plath is coolly alluding to the Greek Play to two American correspondents as a cultural highlight of her time so far in Cambridge (*L1* 1150, 1152). After six months in Cambridge, Plath's anxious epistolary positioning as one lacking a classical background has transformed—via an ingenuous enthusiasm—into a sophisticated self-presentation as "a Cambridge girl now," fully assimilated into its classicizing culture.[10]

Plath's Tripos reading and her immersion in this culture of classicism are reflected in a poem written around this time in the spring of 1956, "Conversation Among the Ruins" (*CP* 21).[11] The poem borrows its title from a 1927 neoclassical painting by Italian artist Giorgio de Chirico (the painting's Italian title is *Colloquio*, "interview"), "a postcard reproduction of which was pinned to the door of the poet's room" at Whitstead (*CP* 275). In de Chirico's painting, a woman wearing a chiton, an ancient Greco-Roman tunic, and who is seated with her back to the viewer, meets the gaze of a man in a modern suit. The man appears to have risen from his seat and now inclines toward the woman and the viewer of the painting from behind a table. Their conversation takes place in a ruined house, the freestanding doorframes and pillars of which now resemble the columns of an ancient temple. Between the columns the viewer glimpses a barren landscape of dusty mountainous terrain. The man's lips are closed, as if listening to the woman, or perhaps both figures have been captured by the painter in a moment of silent stand-off. Plath's sonnet can be read as an ekphrasis in the mode of prosopopeia, spoken in the persona of the woman in de Chirico's painting—and the sestet that comprises the second half of the poem explicitly responds to details from the painting ("Fractured pillars frame prospects

---

[8] Watling, 9 (Smith).
[9] Emphases Plath's own. The 1956 Cambridge Greek Play, produced by Alan Kerr, took place February 20–24 and was the first production with a major female cast, including seven of Plath's peers at Newnham. It was only the second production to have included female cast-members; prior to 1950 only one woman, Janet Case, Virginia Woolf's ancient Greek tutor, had appeared in a Cambridge Greek Play. The actors' text and translation is published as Lucas, *The Bacchae of Euripides. The Greek Text Performed at Cambridge at the Arts Theatre 20–24 February, 1956, by Members of the University, With an English Prose Translation Made for the Cambridge Performance of 1930*. Plath's annotated copy of the performance text is held by Smith.
[10] As she had earlier declared "I'M A SMITH GIRL NOW" (*L1* 180). For an account of the ways in which Plath extended and redefined her modernist and New Critical templates in her pedagogy and poetry, see *Annotating Modernism*.
[11] There are no extant dated manuscripts for "Conversation Among the Ruins" nor a record of its composition date in Plath's journals or calendars. Hargrove dates the poem to spring 1958, placing it among Plath's other "art poems" (66); Steinberg (*Sylvia Plath Archival Documents Hub*) postulates spring 1956. The presence of allusions to Euripides's *Bacchae* in the poem provides evidence, alongside the biographical details, to support Steinberg's proposed composition date.

of rock" *CP* 21).[12] At the same time, the sestet's allusions to the genre of Greek dramatic tragedy and its tragic heroes signal that the poem is drawing on an additional source text, and three specific concordances of character, plot, and image in the opening octave suggest that the first half of the poem responds more clearly to elements of Euripides's *Bacchae*, which Plath had recently seen performed, than to de Chirico's painting.

In the ancient Greek play Dionysus (Bacchus) is the first character to speak, and his opening gesture is a unique act of metatheater, summoning on to the stage his Chorus of singing and dancing bacchae—his maenads, or priestess-followers (Dionysus is the god of wine and altered consciousness, and a god who confounds dichotomies, presiding over the genres of tragedy and comedy).[13] In Euripides, the god enters and overturns the decorous life of Pentheus, king of Thebes, who represents a too-narrow version of civic order and conventional logic. When Pentheus refuses to honor the god or accept him into the Greek pantheon, Dionysus conjures an earthquake which "shatter[s] the house of Pentheus" (Lucas 42) (a recurring image in the Greek text is of breached walls, symbolic of the irrational forces of ecstatic chaos that the god represents entering the ordered city of Thebes).[14] Rereading "Conversation Among the Ruins" with the *Bacchae* in mind, we find Plath's speaker observing a man who is a Dionysiac force, identified in the poem by his divine attributes of intoxicating grapes, music, and an entourage of ecstatic bacchae. His entrance into the speaker's life is a catastrophic event, and she finds, like Pentheus, that her meeting with Dionysus unsettles all sense of order in her life and overturns the familiar conventions of society (and poetry). Finally, just as Pentheus observes the wreckage of his palace, so does Plath's speaker survey the ruins of her house, its walls destroyed by the man's earthshaking entrance—a demolition literalized in the poem by the off-rhymes which shatter the sonnet's rhyme scheme.

Reading "Conversation Among the Ruins" biographically suggests that the poem stages the chaotic shock of Dionysus's entrance into the life of Pentheus as a mythic parallel to the emotional and poetic disturbance of Ted Hughes's entrance into Plath's life in February 1956. Taking its cue from Dionysus's metatheatrical gesture in the *Bacchae*, the poem also metapoetically reflects on Plath's impulse toward classicism and to be "classic" in drawing this mythic parallel. Both the biographical and the metapoetic are in play, for example, in the ambivalent gazes of the poem/painting's two figures ("Rooted to your black look," *CP* 21). The reader wonders whether the speaker sees herself in the classicizing mode as reflected in the male gaze (Hughes entered her life as

---

[12]On "Conversation Among the Ruins," Rose examines the poem's placement by Hughes as the opening poem of *Collected Poems* (89–90), arguing that it is used to signal "the start of a tragic play" (90) and a battle between Apolline [Plathian] and Dionysiac [Hughesian] modes of poetry; Britzolakis, in *Sylvia Plath and the Theatre of Mourning*, argues that Plath's poem transforms de Chirico's mise-en-scène into an excessive mourning ritual (196–7); Sagar suggests that the ruins the poem's speaker finds herself among are "the ruins of her poem ['"Three Caryatids Without A Portico,' by Hugo Robus. A Study in Sculptural Dimensions"] demolished by [Daniel] Huws" in a review published in *Broadsheet* in February 1956 (49–50), and Hedley discusses the poem in relation to the gendered dynamics of the ekphrastic tradition (81–4). Hargrove provides a formal and metrical analysis of the poem (65–8). Although Kroll discusses at length the importance of de Chirico's imagery for the "moon Muses" of Plath's 1958 ekphrastic poems, "The Disquieting Muses" and "On the Decline of Oracles" (23–40), she does not examine "Conversation Among the Ruins," which resists her thesis.

[13]It is the only instance in extant ancient Greek tragedy in which the Chorus are summoned on to the stage by a character in the play.

[14]διατινάξαντος, *diatinaxantos*, "shakes asunder," Euripides, *Bacchae*, 606; the translation provided in the body of the essay above quotes from the play text Plath saw performed.

Plath was immersed in tragedy), or whether she has adopted the dress of a maenad to reveal to the man/Dionysus her intention to become his myth-invoking follower. Yet the poem also seems to be reflecting on the interpellating effect of Plath's modernist, New Critical training at Cambridge, which has written her into the garb of the maenad—a follower of the "classic" tradition, "[c]omposed in Grecian tunic" (*CP* 21). The poet thus observes the speaker/herself in the classicizing mode, concurrently writing herself into a literary tradition and self-consciously scrutinizing the effects on her poetry of this "classical" training at Cambridge, both in ancient Greek and in modes of Eliotian "classic" literature.

Plath's metapoetic self-awareness in "Conversation Among the Ruins" works to some extent to temper the conservative nature of its mythic parallel by adding a complexity to what might otherwise be a facile classicizing gesture. The poem's modernist classicism is also modulated by Plath's explicitly biographical parallel, which evidences a resistance to her training in "classic" impersonal poetry. In his definition of "classicism," Eliot had included personal "living material" ("the emotions and feelings of the writer") as part of "the material at hand" which an artist might draw upon and synthesize, but he had also earlier clarified that a "classic" artistic creation was achieved in an impersonal way ("this Impersonal theory") (*Selected Prose* 177, 40). Eliot argued in "Tradition and the Individual Talent" that the poet must "self-sacrifice," that is, erase any trace of personality in order to gain access to the "historical sense" which informed "classic" literature—a special awareness of the past that perceives the simultaneity of "the pastness of the past" and its "presence" (*Selected Prose* 40, 38). "Conversation Among the Ruins" evidences an attempt to make material Eliot's conception of the simultaneity of the past, the present, and its tradition in the poet's layering of an ancient Greek play, a modernist neoclassical painting, and a contemporary event. At the same time, Plath's foregrounding of the autobiographical "I" as a further textual layer within that palimpsest withstands the subjective effacement and homogenization that cultural hegemony—the legitimizing "tradition"—effects. Paying attention to the allusive practice of "Conversation Among the Ruins" captures an essential tension that runs throughout Plath's poetry between a conservative impulse to write objective, impersonal classicizing poetry (reinforced by the conservative, male gaze of the poetry editors to whom she submitted work) and a burgeoning impulse toward subjective lyric expression.[15] Plath's innovative palimpsestic structure, composed of ancient and modernist cultural texts overlaid by a biographical scene and completed by a metapoetic layer of self-reflection, actively resists the false universalizing of New Criticism's "classic" literature; yet, the poet remains bound by the cultural conservatism to which she had been acculturated through her critical and literary training at Smith and Cambridge in her impulse to be "classic" and align herself with a masculine poetic tradition. Plath recognizes that it is her use of a mythic parallel to place herself in a masculine canonical tradition that distinguishes her as a poet, "certainly not another 'poetess'" ("Foreword" vii).[16]

"Conversation Among the Ruins" stages an ambivalent double movement of complicity in modernist classicizing modes and resistance to New Critical objectivity and

---

[15]On Plath's compositional practices as responsive to her correspondence with editors, see Steinberg, "'Sincerely Yours': Plath and *The New Yorker*."
[16]Parody must invoke and so reinforce the discourse it seeks to subvert, embodying a "mixture of conservative and revolutionary impulses in both aesthetic and social terms" (Hutcheon 115).

impersonality, focalized around the poem's classical Greek allusions. This early poem's blend of myth and autobiography foreshadows in important ways the poetic citation practice Plath employs in her later Electra poems, to which I'll return, and illustrates some of the ways in which she was beginning to transform modernist forms of "classic" and classicizing poetry. A review essay commissioned by the Cambridge literary journal *Gemini* the following spring (1957) reveals Plath writing in a stricter New Critical mode, but it sheds further light on Plath's developing classicizing practice. The poetry collection under review, *The Stones of Troy* by C. A. Trypanis, a scholar of ancient and modern Greek at Exeter College, Oxford, is dense with allusions to Greco-Roman literature, invoking, translating, or refiguring scenes and myths from Homer, Herodas, and Ovid, among many other ancient texts. After allusively noting that the book employs the "mythical method," Plath explicitly introduces the critical framework for her review with a quotation from the final paragraph of Eliot's essay on James Joyce, "*Ulysses*, Order, and Myth": "In using the myth, in manipulating a continuous parallel between contemporaneity and antiquity, Mr. Joyce is pursuing a method which others must pursue after him. ... It is simply a way of controlling, of ordering, of giving a shape and a significance to the immense panorama of futility and anarchy which is contemporary history" (Eliot's argument—that *Ulysses* uses myth to bring order to chaos—and his triple repetition of the "parallel" between the past and the present [*Selected Prose* 177], suggest that Plath already had this essay in mind when she composed "Conversation Among the Ruins"; Plath was familiar with Eliot's essay from Elizabeth Drew's lectures in twentieth-century literature, which she attended at Smith).[17] Although Plath quotes Eliot on Joyce's ethical achievement at the outset, the body of her review is concerned with the aesthetic achievement of Trypanis's "parallel." She does not quote from Eliot directly, but she uses his criteria of success, that is, a "use of appropriate styles and symbols to each division:" an organic use of myth that is not simply a ruse ("an amusing dodge") or "scaffolding erected by the author ... of no interest in the completed structure" (*Selected Prose* 175).

Throughout the review, Plath engages in a practical criticism exercise, demonstrating a close reading of the specific use of language in the poems and consistently drawing attention to the moral relevance of the poems as she sees them. In her analysis, we learn that she disapproves of moments in which the poet's tone is nostalgic or sentimental, lamenting the loss of a heroic past, and she criticizes poems in which the verb or adjective choice is incongruous or unwittingly bathetic, or where the interplay of epic and colloquial diction jars.[18] She finds some metaphors too literal ("[o]ften, meditations on the past are occasioned by the digging up of some ruins"), and she argues that the moral lessons proposed by the poems, while offering novel readings of ancient myth ("For only in giant disasters / True-born and bastards count for the same"), are undercut by their lack of subtlety ("Stones of Troy" 99).[19] The reader learns that Plath prefers the subtleties of Homer himself, and she recommends Richmond Lattimore's 1951 translation of the *Iliad*

---

[17] Plath's class notes from Drew's lectures quote from and paraphrase Eliot's *Ulysses* ("Holograph Notes for English 211"; qtd. in *Annotating Modernism* 61–2). Anthony Cuda dates these notes to 1955, when Plath attended Drew's lectures in her final year at Smith for the Honors Review Unit (cited in *Annotating Modernism*, 86 n152). The poet's copy of Drew, *T. S. Eliot: The Design of His Poetry*, which includes annotations and underlining on the book's introductory discussion of Eliot's use of myth (1), is held by Smith.
[18] Plath, "Review: *The Stones of Troy* by C.A. Trypanis" (1957).
[19] Trypanis, *Stones of Troy*, qtd in Plath, "Stones of Troy," 100.

over that of Trypanis, whose versions are riddled, she argues, with awkward imitations of Homer's epic epithets ("foam-stung sail," "foam-clawed sand," "sky-tall trees").[20]

Plath highlights Trypanis's use of literary and material intertexts to engage with the ancient literary, social, and cultural past (epigraphs from ancient tombs, Byzantine church frescoes, and late antique works of historiography), arguing that such intermediary texts do not necessarily reduce the vividness of feeling expressed by the poem or prevent the poet from meditating on "war, love, death, etc."[21] She also praises the moments where space-time folds and the ancient and the modern are collapsed, such as when a vivid modern speaker observes the ancient myth play out. Plath selects the poem "Icarus" to illustrate the ways in which the finest poems of the collection use ancient myth as a metaphor for a contemporary observation. The poem eschews the narrative method and instead "chooses to view the shadow cast by the winged man and draw a private inference from the myth" ("Stones of Troy" 102):

> I did not hear the cry, nor the splash.
> I did not see the waxen tears. Only the shadow
> Of wings moving across the landscape,
> Hollow footfalls of those we loved,
> Who passed so strangely beyond our life.
>
> (Trypanis, qtd. in "Stones of Troy" [102])

"Every poet has his own Icarus," Plath observes ("Stones of Troy" 102). In moments such as this one, the poet "transforms the material" and provides "fresh insight and impact to history and legend"—an implicit reference to Eliot's argument in "Tradition and the Individual Talent" that "the past should be altered by the present as much as the present is directed by the past" ("Stones of Troy" 100, 103; *Selected Prose* 39). She concludes her review in the Eliotic mode, remarking that the weakest poems are those where the "parallel between old and new is pointed at, rather than realized in the poems' shape and texture"—poems where the mythic scaffolding is conspicuous ("Stones of Troy" 103).

The *Gemini* essay provides an insight into some of the qualities that Plath thought identified an achieved classically allusive poem: a colloquial register, but not one unwittingly bathetic or light; an anti-nostalgic mood, absent of any obvious metaphors or unimaginative classicizing ("marble Ephebes," "marble sleep," "marble stage," "marble steps"); a moral expressive of a private inference implicitly relevant to the grander human experience ("war, love, death, etc."); and while she cautiously appraises the uses of intermediary texts, she celebrates a focus on an element of or an image from the myth, rather than a recontextualization of its narrative entire.[22] Re-reading "Conversation Among the Ruins" in light of this review reveals Plath's earlier experimentation with some of the successful qualities she pinpoints in Trypanis: the use of an intermediary text (de Chirico's painting) that enables her to stage a moment from a myth (the aftermath of Dionysus's earthquake) and the positing of a relation between her ekphrastic meditation and the greater human theme of love and the shock of a personal encounter, although

---

[20]Plath quotes Lattimore, *The* Iliad *of Homer* (296) on the slaughter of Imbrius by Teukros at *Iliad* 13.178–81 ("one turns at random to a modern translation of the *Iliad* ... "); Trypanis, *Stones of Troy*, qtd. in Plath, "Stones of Troy," 101.

[21]Trypanis, *Stones of Troy*, qtd. in Plath, "Stones of Troy," 100.

[22]Trypanis, qtd. in "Stones of Troy" (101); Plath, "Stones of Troy" (100).

the poet had not yet mastered the use of a colloquial diction, nor rid herself of the too-obvious modernist ruins.

Plath reflects in a letter to her mother after filing her review:

> It was a difficult job, as I felt most of the poems were weak, & fought hard to be positive & quote a lot in my 7-page review. But also graphically showed in detail why I felt such worn adjective-noun combinations as "haunted gardens," "golden toys," "jasmine throat," "dusty grey," "ivory chariots," etc. did little to re-awaken the vigor of the greek myths [sic] or transform the greek legends [sic] vitally in the context of modern poems. Honestly, when I pick up <u>The</u> two British monthlies: <u>Encounter</u> & <u>The</u> <u>London</u> <u>Magazine</u>, I shudder & grit my teeth at the cheap, flat "new movement poetry," which never commits itself, but talks about and about: the meanings are dull, often superficial "top-of-the-head" philosophizing, and there is no <u>music</u>, no sense picturing. It is hogwash; not even that good. Both Ted & I are alone, really alone, I feel among young modern poets … to treat the great subjects of life: love, death, war, etc.
>
> (L2 94)[23]

Plath's final comments here ("Honestly … ") broaden from a critique of a single collection of contemporary poetry to an expression of her wider dissatisfaction with the Oxford Movement poets Kingsley Amis, Donald Davie, Thom Gunn, John Holloway, Elizabeth Jennings, Philip Larkin, and John Wain, who commanded the British postwar poetry scene.[24] The distinction that Plath draws between the poetry she and her husband were writing in 1957 and that of the Movement poets centers on their respective uses of myth, and it is a distinction that both poets figured in terms of a duel between Dionysiac (Plath and Hughes) and Apolline (the Movement) modes of poetic expression.[25] While the Movement poets had rejected myth, Hughes and his poetry circle embraced myth, mysticism, and anthropology—Plath's classicizing impulse was now additionally reinforced by a wish to assimilate to a Hughesian mythopoetics.[26] In her own work, Plath was attempting to achieve an organic use of myth that dealt with the subjects of now, "love, death, war" (L2 94; she quotes from her own essay), and she may have hoped to find another ally in the classicizing Trypanis. She ultimately judged that his endeavor had failed. Plath's dissatisfaction can be attributed as much to the criteria with which she judged Trypanis as to the collection's dullness or lack of musicality. For despite her theoretical espousal of a New Critical framework and her employment of Eliot's value-system for classic literature in this review, Plath may have been searching for an unspoken quality, one which tested the boundaries and qualities of the mythical method, and it was this she failed to find in Trypanis, but she lacked the critical framework to express or validate her dissatisfaction. In "Conversation Among the Ruins," Plath's particular

---

[23] Emphases Plath's own.

[24] The Movement poets had recently published two anthologies, *Poets of the 1950s: An Anthology of New English Verse*, edited by Enright, and *New Lines: An Anthology*, edited by Conquest.

[25] On their shared antipathy toward the Movement poets, see Clark, *The Grief of Influence: Sylvia Plath and Ted Hughes* (16–20).

[26] Hughesian mythopoetics are also marked by their anti-Movement language of violence; in a section from Plath's fragmentary unfinished early novel "Falcon Yard," "Venus in the Seventh," the Plath character Jess recites the poem "Conversation Among the Ruins" for the Hughes character, who approves of its violent one syllable words: "Squab, patch, crack" (qtd. in *Red Comet* 435).

strategy to reawaken the vigor and vitality of myth was a striking experimentation with a metapoetic self-reflexive mode and an autobiographical lyric "I"; she had not found this validated in Trypanis. In a series of Electra poems composed two years later in 1959, Plath would return to and extend this experimentation.

"Electra on Azalea Path" and "The Colossus" have both been routinely discussed as narrative works of biomythography in which Plath adopts the persona of the daughter-in-mourning in the family romance of psychoanalysis.[27] While the best of this mode of scholarship recognizes Plath's reflexivity and her conscious placement of the poetic speaker as an analysand in a "theatre of mourning," paying additional attention to Plath's literary training in Greek tragedy and the critical and discursive contexts in which she encountered those texts nuances these psychoanalytic readings in significant ways.[28] Namely, by challenging the assumption that Jung is the primary source text for Plath's allusions to Electra and by adding complexity to the assumed directionality and chain of transmission of the Electra myth from Greek tragedy to Jung to Plath. Important here are the discourses of classical scholarship to which Plath was exposed at Cambridge. In the first half of the twentieth century, anglophone classical scholarship was experiencing a transformation in scholarly voice and mode under the belated influence of nineteenth-century German scholarship, accelerated by the influx of German refugee scholars to Oxford and Cambridge in the late 1930s. One significant and broad change of approach within the discipline was a movement away from purely philological readings of ancient texts toward readings that were socially and historically contextualized, that is, a shift from simply establishing what it was that Euripides said to enquiring what it was that Euripides meant. A second and specific change in discourse revealed the influence of Sigmund Freud's *Interpretation of Dreams* (1899), which had used Sophocles's *Oedipus Tyrannus* to formulate a model for the psycho-sexual development of children. Freud's work had a pronounced impact on the discipline, and classical commentaries and critical editions began to explicitly employ a psychoanalytic framework to elucidate readings of ancient literature. In the early 1930s, for example, Euripides's *Bacchae* had been read as a study in religious (read fascist) fanaticism; by the late 1950s, the play was presented as a study in psychological repression (Oakley 96). One consequence of this psychoanalytic turn in classics was that the translations of Greek tragedy Plath read at Cambridge already had a psychoanalytic lens in place. To illustrate the impact of this psychoanalytic turn on the discipline of classics at Cambridge—that is, its embrace of self-reflexive and biographical modes of scholarship—and its implications for Plath's Electra poems, I have chosen three examples from a text that Plath owned and read, Phillip Vellacott's 1956 Penguin Classics translation of Aeschylus, *The Oresteian Trilogy*.

In the text of *The Choephori* (*The Libation Bearers*)—the central play of *The Oresteian Trilogy* which narrates the murder of Clytemnestra by her children Electra and Orestes—Plath has underlined and marked with a black star in the left-hand margin the lines: "None from outside can help; we must ourselves / Cure our own case" (Vellacott 120).[29]

---

[27]Notably, Butscher, *Sylvia Plath: Method and Madness*; see also, more recently, Bakogianni, "Electra in Sylvia Plath's Poetry."
[28]Rose, *The Haunting of Sylvia Plath*; Britzolakis, *Sylvia Plath and the Theatre of Mourning*.
[29]Plath's copy of Vellacott is inscribed "Sylvia Hughes, 1957," suggesting that the book's annotations date from April or May 1957 when Plath was revising for her Tripos examinations (Smith); Plath completed her review essay on *The Stones of Troy* in late March 1957 as her final task of the term before the revision period began.

Vellacott's words compress and translate *Choephori*, lines 470–3: "Except this way, the house can find no stanching [ἔμμοτον] of its wound [ἄλγος]. Not from without must find its cure [ἄκος], but from itself."[30] In ancient Greek, ἄλγος (*algos*, *Cho.* 470) in the singular, as here, refers primarily to bodily pain, and secondarily—typically in the plural ἄλγεα, *algea*—to grief, and so the metaphor Aeschylus employs "is that of an incurable wound, which breaks out at intervals, like the sore of Philoctetes" (Tucker 111), unable to be staunched (ἰὼ δυσκατάπαυτον ἄλγος, *iō duskatapauton algos*, *Cho.* 478).[31] The use of psychoanalytic language by Vellacott in his translation of these lines—transforming a "wound" to a "case," invoking the "case" studies of Freud's psychoanalytic practice—is therefore a striking interpolation. This shift in emphasis is reinforced by Vellacott's elision within his translation of ἄκος (*akos*, *Cho.* 472), "cure," and the specified form of that cure, the ἔμμοτος (*emmetos*, *Cho.* 471), a type of lint "plug" dressing used for gaping wounds (a word which occurs elsewhere only in medical texts). This elision encourages a reading of "cure" that is suggestive of the "talking cure" employed by Freud, prompted by Vellacott's use of "case." Vellacott's psychoanalytic phrasing may represent an attempt to reflect the linguistic oddity of the medical term ἔμμοτος in translation, but his shift from a suppurating physical wound in the Greek (ἄλγος) to a psychological trauma in English ("case") reveals the influence of the broader psychoanalytic turn of the discipline.[32] Plath's black star in the left-hand margin indicates her attention to this psychoanalytic phrase and marks a moment in the text where her (autobiographical) interest has been piqued ("no one has the power to cure you but yourself," *J* 186).

A second moment of psychoanalytic framing occurs at the beginning of the first play of *The Oresteian Trilogy*, *Agamemnon*, with the return of the eponymous king of Mycenae from the Trojan War. His wife Clytemnestra appeals to the king's vanity to convince him to enter the palace in defiance of a divine taboo by stepping on a carpet of purple-crimson cloth—this moment seals Agamemnon's fate. Clytemnestra argues that Agamemnon should not be concerned by an illogical prohibition (Is the sea not inexhaustibly full of dye? Is he not rich enough to afford its vast stores of purple-crimson?), particularly on a day of celebration (Vellacott 74). The queen declares that Agamemnon's return is like that of Zeus, who brings warmth in spring after winter and coolness in autumn after summer: "[W]hen Zeus / From the unripe grape [ὄμφακος] presses his wine, then through the house / Heat dies, and coolness comes, as through this royal door enters its lord, perfected [τελείου] to receive his own" (*Ag.* 970–4; Vellacott 74).[33] In the introduction to the text, Plath has marked with a vertical line in black ink Vellacott's explication of Clytemnestra's wry metaphors which reveal her murderous intentions to the audience: the sea is her hatred, inexhaustible in its desire for crimson blood to avenge Agamemnon's slaughter of their daughter Iphigenia. Contemporary commentaries on the *Oresteia* were in fact divided on the issue of whether Clytemnestra is talking in metaphors here, with one scholar using his critical edition of the *Agamemnon* to disparage the "unwarranted psychological niceties" (Fraenkel 440) in another scholar's reading of the double

---

[30]Vellacott's translation uses the Greek text of Tucker's critical edition, *The Choephori of Aeschylus*; the translation here is Tucker's (111).
[31]s.v., *A Greek-English Lexicon*, 61 (hereafter *LSJ*).
[32]s.v., *LSJ* 542.
[33]Vellacott used the Greek text of Campbell's *The Agamemnon of Aeschylus*.

entendre of this speech.³⁴ For his translation and critical notes, Vellacott has therefore chosen to employ a psychoanalytic reading that emphasizes the sub-surface discourse of Clytemnestra's words. In Greek, Vellacott continues, an "unripe grape" (ὄμφακος, *omphakos*, 970) euphemistically—invoking its ancient metaphorical usage—refers to a virgin girl "not yet ripe for marriage," and "perfected" (τελείου, *teleiou*) is the word used of an unblemished, ritually cleansed sacrificial victim; Plath has underlined the word "perfected" in Clytemnestra's speech.³⁵ The sexual imagery and the incest narrative suggested by this metaphor—the father has pressed wine (blood) from the unripe grape of the daughter—allude to an earlier moment in the myth, in which Iphigenia was taken from Clytemnestra under the pretext that she would be married to the Greek hero Achilles. When Agamemnon sacrifices his daughter Iphigenia she is dressed as a bride, and Clytemnestra makes a gruesome pun here on the anticipated blood-letting from a broken hymen that was forestalled by Agamemnon's offering of Iphigenia's life blood to the gods in an inverted wedding ceremony. The latent incest imagery uncovered by a psychoanalytic reading of the Greek is signaled to the reader of the translation by Vellacott's framing of this moment in the play in his introduction, but it is also reinforced by the translator's (Freudian) mistranslation of a later moment in the play linked to this one by another metaphorical reference to Iphigenia. In a speech in which Clytemnestra defends her "treacherous" murder of Agamemnon to the Chorus, Vellacott compresses five lines of Greek ("for what he did to my own green shoot [ἔρνος, *ernos*], sprung from him—the much-grieved Iphigenia—in being slain by the sword [ξιφοδηλήτῳ, *xiphodēletoi*] he has paid the price in death for what he started," *Ag.* 1525–9) into two lines in English. He also creates a Freudian sexual subtext by translating the verb "slain by the sword" as a noun ("sword"), switching the object of the sentence from Agamemnon to Iphigenia, and reprising the imagery of the bloodied virgin: Agamemnon was the first party to deceive, Clytemnestra argues, "[w]hen on my virgin daughter / His savage sword descended" (Vellacott 95).³⁶ Plath has marked these two lines in the left-hand margin of her copy of the *Oresteia* with a vertical line in black ink, indicating her alertness to the psychoanalytic themes (in the translation) and incestuous subtext (in the ancient text)—anticipated by her close reading of Vellacott's critical introduction—that circulate around Aeschylus's tragic heroines.

An understanding of the ways in which ancient Greek tragedy was already framed in psychoanalytic terms when Plath read the plays at Cambridge challenges a facile reading of the presence of Electra in Plath's poems as an autobiographical "identification." The lens of the translation and its paratextual apparatus demonstrate that it was as impossible for Plath as it is for her twenty-first-century readers to read the figure of Electra neutrally "after Freud." Moreover, it reveals that Plath's Electra-persona in "Electra" and "The Colossus" is not a transposition of the ancient tragic heroine into a modern setting, but a blend of elements and themes from the tragic narratives and mythic characterizations of Electra, her mother Clytemnestra, and her sister Iphigenia. These allusions are concentrated in the conclusions of both poems. It is Clytemnestra, for example, who

---

³⁴Fraenkel commenting on Thomson's and Headlam's reading of *Ag.* 970–4: "This is another passage couched in language of deliberate obscurity for the sake of double meaning" (101).

³⁵Vellacott, 26, 74; s.v. *LSJ* 1229. Plath has also underlined Clytemnestra's repetition of this ritual formula after Agamemnon's murder: "By Justice, guardian of my child, now perfected" (92).

³⁶ἔρνος, "young sprout, shoot" is also used metaphorically for "offspring," s.v. *LSJ* 691.

is a "hound-bitch" ("Electra," *CP* 117) in *Agamemnon*, and the ambivalence of the phrase at the close of Plath's poem is heightened by the term's twofold employment in the Greek text: while Clytemnestra refers to herself as a loyal "watch-dog" (κύνα, *kyna*, 607), Cassandra returns the term as a "vile [...] as opposed to she-hound" (μισητῆς κυνὸς, *misētēs kynos*, 1228) (Hughes may borrow Plath's phrasing here for his translation of the *Oresteia*: his Cassandra rebukes the "houndbitch" Clytemnestra).[37] And at the close of "The Colossus," the daughter-speaker is "married to shadow"—that is, she is the virgin daughter who has been married to death in an inverted wedding ceremony—and "[n]o longer ... listen[s] for the scrape of a keel / On the blank stones of the landing" (*CP* 130), reversing the extended metaphor Clytemnestra uses to liken the joy of Agamemnon's homecoming to the sight of a long-lost son to a father or the "sight of land to men long at sea" (as Clytemnestra also re-uses the image of a watch-dog (κύνα, *kyna*, 896) in this speech, here, of Agamemnon, Plath may be creating a further allusive link between the loyal speaker of "The Colossus" and the "hound-bitch" of "Electra on Azalea Path" [*CP* 117]).[38] Vellacott's translation of Aeschylus's *The Oresteian Trilogy* also bears upon a reading of Plath's "Full Fathom Five" (*CP* 92–3). Recalling Vellacott's emphasis on the subtext of incest in the Greek play, we find "the old myth" ("archaic") in Plath's poem in an incestuous relation with the father-sea that blurs the subjectivities of Electra and her sister Iphigenia ("Waist down. ... Your shelled bed I remember" [*CP* 93]). This allusion to the imagery of Aeschylus's Greek—via Vellacott—is reinforced by the poem's reference to the breaking of the divine taboo that sealed Agamemnon's downfall at a key moment of action in the play: "you defy other godhood. / ... / Father, this thick air is murderous" (*CP* 93). The double presence of the incest narrative and the extended imagery of the sea-murder of the father-husband from Aeschylus's *Agamemnon* 970–4 suggests that "Full Fathom Five" should be read alongside "Electra on Azalea Path" and "The Colossus" not only as a meditation on "the old father-worship subject" (*J* 518) but also as an Electra poem that engages explicitly with Aeschylus's *Oresteia*. Re-reading "Electra on Azalea Path," "The Colossus," and "Full Fathom Five" after Aeschylus reveals that the poems go beyond the brief plot sketch and characterization provided in Jung's gloss of the Electra archetype, and borrow specific details and vocabulary from the ancient trilogy.

As with the palimpsestic construction of "Conversation Among the Ruins," Plath's Electra poems overlay an ancient text with its adaptation in a psychoanalytic archetypal template which in turn is filtered through a layer of personal biography. One key distinction between the earlier poem and "Electra on Azalea Path" and "The Colossus" is the tone of the final metapoetic layer of self-reflexive analysis, as the speaker observes herself in the act of classical allusion. In these later poems, the voice is explicitly parodic and draws attention to its breaking of the New Critical rules: where Eliot advised that myth should not appear as "scaffolding" in the modern text, Plath's speaker erects "stilts" (*CP* 117) and "little ladders" (*CP* 129), and where Plath criticized Trypanis for his too-obvious use of ruins and marble, her poems foreground the "necropolis" (*CP* 117) of their setting, a ruin like the "Roman Forum" (*CP* 129) filled with "stony actors" (*CP* 117) and shattered

---

[37]Vellacott, *Aeschylus*, 64, 85; Hughes, trans. *The Oresteia*, 59.
[38]"There is no dearer sight than shelter after storm; / No escape sweeter than from siege of circumstance. / Now, after siege and storm endured, my happy heart / Welcomes my husband, faithful watch-dog of his home, / Our ship's firm anchor ... as dear, as to a father's hope / His longed-for son, a spring to thirsty travellers, / Or sight of land unlooked-for to men long at sea" (Vellacott 73) (*Ag.* 895–901).

statuary—"fluted bones and acanthine hair ... littered // [.] ... To the horizon-line" (*CP* 130). This parodic tone may signal Plath's admission of the compromise she has made in her Electra poems. Electra is, after all, in one reading, a myth in which the daughter upholds the law of the father—the phallic order that Clytemnestra attempted to resist—and shepherds the triumph of the patriarchy over the matriarchy. The self-reflexive mode may therefore represent an attempt to resolve the tension between a culturally conservative impulse to write modernist "classic" poems and a nascent subversive impulse toward subjective expression, but the poet's classicizing impulse remains conservative—a wish to assimilate into the cultural hegemony of patriarchal poetic tradition. Where Plath found confidence in her earlier classicizing poetry—a mark of her assimilation into Cambridge life and a Hughesian mythopoetics—she now mocks the earnestness of "Conversation Among the Ruins" as much as she parodies Eliot.

The altered tone of "Electra on Azalea Path" and "The Colossus" foreshadows the bitter burlesque of modernist classicism in Plath's *Ariel* poems. In "Daddy," for example, the symbolic father is the shattered *Colossus of Constantine*, displayed, as Plath would have seen it, in the courtyard of the Capitoline Museum overlooking the Roman Forum ("Marble-heavy ... / Ghastly statue with one gray toe" [*CP* 222]). While in "Edge" (*CP* 272–3), the woman's body is at its most abject when it is most explicitly classical—as Clytemnestra says in *Agamemnon*, "perfected" (τελεῖν, 974; *CP* 272). An understanding of the scholarly framework through which Plath engaged with ancient Greek tragedy does not detract from the innovations of her classicizing poems; it reveals a poet self-reflexively, ambivalently, observing her complicity in an academic poetic tradition founded in social and cultural conservatism.

# CHAPTER THIRTEEN

# "Yeats I like very very much": Sylvia Plath and W. B. Yeats

GILLIAN GROSZEWSKI

In a 1958 recording for the Library of Congress files, Sylvia Plath placed William Butler Yeats first on a list of poets she read for pleasure (*Red Comet* 521).[1] Developing her response, Plath explained: "Yeats I like very very much" (*Red Comet* 522). Ten years earlier, in his essay "Yeats as an Example," W. H. Auden had suggested that

> the young poet naturally looks for and finds the greatest help in the work of those whose poetic problems are similar to his because they have experiences in common. He begins, therefore, with an excessive admiration for one or more of the mature poets of his time. But, as he grows older, he becomes more and more conscious of belonging to a different generation faced with problems that his heroes cannot help him to solve[.]
>
> (384)

In considering Yeats as an example for Plath, Auden's criterion requiring "excessive admiration" is fulfilled in her repeated use of the intensifier when she mentions the Irish poet in her interview. However, by 1958, Plath could already reflect on what she had learned from Yeats, suggesting that she had, with awareness, moved on from that admiration which Auden associated with the youthful stage of influence. She elaborated: "I learned my first changing in sound—assonance and consonance—from Yeats, which actually is technical. I was very excited when I discovered this" (*Red Comet* 522). By Auden's reckoning, the years that followed should have seen Plath encountering difficulties that Yeats could not help her to solve, resulting in her identifying more with her own generation and its issues. However, Plath continued to turn to Yeats in the challenging times ahead. In 1962, weeks before Ted Hughes left Court Green

---

[1] This essay developed from a talk which I was invited to give by Gail Crowther and Peter K. Steinberg in 2020. Thanks are due for this kind invitation, without which the essay would not have emerged.

definitively, Plath visited Yeats's tower at Ballylee (*Red Comet* 769). At the end of that year, just as she was reaching her poetic apotheosis, Plath moved to Yeats's former home at 23 Fitzroy Road in London, where she sought to "have [her] own life too" and attempted to put in place the support she needed in order to fulfill her equally demanding roles as parent and writer (*L1* 875). The poetic support was there—reconnecting with Yeats assisted Plath in overcoming the poetic challenges that arose due to her drive to innovate and experiment with her own work as she developed her artistic self. Auden was right, however, Plath also encountered personal problems at this time, exacerbated by the institutionalized challenges faced by women of her generation "that [her] heroes [could not] help [her] to solve." These problems were themselves embedded in Auden's figuring of the artistic apprentice to Yeats as inherently male. Against these odds, in her poetry, Plath asserted a place of "belonging" to that generation by articulating, and challenging, those problems.

In 1982, Sandra M. Gilbert proposed that a whole community of writers, including Plath, had apprenticed themselves to Yeats. Gilbert went so far as to claim that Plath is "resurrected every day as a crucial member of the visionary company who continue to inhabit the twentieth-century poetic tradition we might call 'Yeats' house'" (220). In her suggestion that Plath is "resurrected" through her affiliation with Yeats, Gilbert echoed the words of Auden, who, more than thirty years earlier, had claimed that: "in poetry as in life, to lead one's own life means to relive the lives of one's parents and, through them, of all one's ancestors; the duty of the present is neither to copy nor to deny the past but to resurrect it" ("Yeats as an Example" 384). The persistence of Yeats's influence on the poets who followed him was also addressed by Seamus Heaney in 1978. In "Yeats as an Example?," a reconsideration of Auden's "appreciative but not ecstatic essay," Heaney asserted that Yeats "is the ideal example for a poet approaching middle age," a proposition which helps to explain Plath's continued engagement with her Irish precursor beyond her initial apprenticeship (107). According to Heaney, it is in middle age that Yeats "bothers you with the suggestion that if you have managed to do one kind of poem in your own way, you should cast off that way and face into another area of your experience until you have learned a new voice to say that area properly" (107). Tracing Plath's engagement with Yeats throughout her poetic career allows us to appreciate the extent to which, at each stage in her adult life, she "learned a new voice" from him, enabling her to present new experiences in poetry (107).

Indeed, at every significant stage in her adult life, Plath turned to Yeats as she worked through "poetic problems" and difficult personal experiences ("Yeats as an Example" 384). As a student at Smith College, in 1953, Plath engaged in an immersive study of Yeats under the tutelage of Elizabeth Drew, which influenced her early experimentation with the villanelle form and the development of her lyrical style. While at Cambridge, Yeats's poetry became significant for Plath in the consolidation of what Hughes referred to as her "supercharged system of inner symbols and images" and her grappling with the influence of her male modernist precursors (*CP* 16). Toward the end of her life, Plath returned to Yeats—the man and the poet—at a challenging time when she sought personal and poetic succor. Although she may not have felt that sense of "belonging" to her own generation, which Auden suggested as the marker of the mature poet breaking free from the influence of their predecessors, Plath's persistent identification with Yeats challenged her to "cast off" the old ways in order to learn "a new voice"—the *Ariel* voice—which articulated the experiences of women of her generation and beyond.

## "LIFE FOR ME CERTAINLY IS A GYRE": YEATS AS AN EARLY EXAMPLE

In *Red Comet*, Clark notes that "Plath had begun assimilating Yeats's influence" as early as 1940 in the poem "Pearls of Dew," written when she was just eight years old (43). In 1952, Aurelia Plath recalled that she and her daughter were reading Yeats together (*LH* 85). However, it was only when she took Elizabeth Drew's class at Smith the following year that Plath first engaged in sustained study of the Irish poet. Plath gave a short paper on Yeats for Drew in early February 1953, and this seems to have initiated an intensive period of study of Yeats's poems, his life, and his critics. Amanda Golden notes that Plath "prepared a presentation on Yeats's poem 'Nineteen Hundred and Nineteen,' and it may have been at this time that she recorded in her journal having read 'critical books about Yeats all day today'" (*Annotating Modernism* 45; quoting *J* 174). After roughly a month of study, on March 1, 1953, Plath wrote in her journals that

> life for me certainly is a gyre, spiraling up, comprehending and including the past, profiting by it, yet transcending it! I am going to make it my job to see that I never get caught revolving in one final repetitive circle of stagnation.
>
> (*J* 177)

Here, Plath engages with the polarity of the Yeatsian concept of the gyre, acknowledging both its positive and negative possibilities, as well as its inevitably cyclical nature. However, she misinterprets the gyre as something which might be mined solely as a positive force resulting in transcendence by suggesting that one might be able to control and avoid the opposite to this buoyant "spiraling up" which, for her, would be a hellish cycle of "stagnation."[2] Perhaps inspired by her engagement with the cyclical concept of the gyre, alongside her reading of Yeats's poetry, in mid-February 1953, Plath began experimenting with the villanelle form—a near-perfect poetic expression of the "repetitive circle of stagnation" that she so feared in her personal life at the time.

On February 20, Plath had been reading books on Yeats and was struck by his line: "The tragedy of sexual intercourse is the perpetual virginity of the soul" (*J* 175).[3] Across the two days, February 20–21, she composed three villanelles, having never attempted the form seriously before. One of the pieces she produced was "Mad Girl's Love Song," which describes the madness of her eponymous speaker who is trapped in a cycle of unfulfilled desire for a lover who may or may not exist. The first refrain of "Mad Girl's Love Song" is doubly constrained not only by the strict, circular rhyme scheme required of the villanelle but also by being in parenthesis:

> I dreamed that you bewitched me into bed
> And sung me moon-struck, kissed me quite insane.
> (I think I made you up inside my head.) ("Mad Girl" 13)

---

[2] In *A Vision*, Yeats suggests that the two states are connected and interdependent: "I see that the gyre of 'Concord' diminishes as that of 'Discord' increases, and can imagine after that the gyre of 'Concord' increasing while that of 'Discord' diminishes, and so on, one gyre within the other always" (68).
[3] Yeats in conversation with John Sparrow in 1931 cited in Jeffares, 267.

The concern with unfulfilled lust belies Plath's engagement with Yeats at the time of composition. Indeed, Clark suggests "The Song of Wandering Aengus" as the "thematic—if not stylistic influence" for the poem (*Red Comet* 228). Certainly, one refrain of Plath's villanelle—"(I think I made you up inside my head.)"— echoes Yeats's opening lines: "I went out to the hazel wood, / Because a fire was in my head" (66). Plath also uses the trope of the aging, longing lover depicted by Yeats as "old with wandering / Through hollow lands and hilly lands" (66). By the end of her poem, however, Plath's speaker echoes the passivity of T. S. Eliot's Prufrock rather than maintaining the chivalry of Yeats's Aengus when she states: "I fancied you'd return the way you said, / But I grow old and I forget your name" ("Mad Girl" 13). The "Love Song" of Plath's title also indicates the competing influence of Eliot within the poem but could equally derive from Yeats's "Girl's Song" from *The Winding Stair*, which opens:

> I went out alone
> To sing a song or two,
> My fancy on a man,
> And you know who.
>
> (296)

In each of their precursor poems, both Yeats and Eliot consider in common the possibility of abandonment to a life defined by the "perpetual virginity of the soul." While Plath's speaker in "Mad Girl's Love Song" is certainly fixated on the fulfillment of her sexual desires, it could also be the case that her realization of the possibility of her own "perpetual virginity of the soul" prompts the insanity which is the "mad girl's" tragedy. Ultimately, Plath leaves the cause of her protagonist's madness uncertain, given that we are told that the object of her fascination may be entirely invented in the first place. While Clark cites Yeats as the predominant thematic inspiration for the poem, the echoes of Eliot suggest him as a further influence. Stylistically, however, the repetition and rhyme of Yeats's early poems, which she had been reading at the time, coupled with her simultaneous study of the gyres in *A Vision*, could have suggested the villanelle to Plath as a fitting form through which to explore the ideas about personal stagnation which were occupying her at the time.

Another villanelle which Plath wrote over these two days, "To Eva Descending the Stair," more obviously bears the influence of her reading Yeats. Although the title of the poem has Eva "descending," she appears to be suspended as she "halt[s] upon the spiral stair" (*CP* 303). The insistence on the circular staircase announces the influence of Yeats's *The Winding Stair* in the first refrain of the villanelle. Throughout the poem, Plath enacts her personal resistance to stagnation and her impulse to ride the up-circling gyre at this time. The repeated, parenthesized refrain—"(Proud you halt upon the spiral stair.)"—emphasizes the stasis of Eva's physical position (*CP* 303). However, the repetition of the phrase, required by the villanelle form, simultaneously associates the line with movement and, formally, works against the literal insistence on Eva's stasis. Clark notes that, in her Cambridge student essays, Plath "appreciated the power of poetic form to imply one meaning while carefully concealing another" and she experimented with this technique in her own work (*Red Comet* 217). In this poem, Eva is told by the unnamed speaker that "stillness is a lie, my dear; / The wheels revolve, the universe keeps running" and, although she might like to stop or descend, she will be swept up and along by the greater force of the universe (*CP* 303). Plath's insistence on movement continues in the lines: "Cryptic stars wind up the atmosphere, / In solar schemes the titled suns go turning," which recall the perpetual motion of the opening line of Yeats's "The Second Coming": "Turning and turning in the widening gyre" (*CP* 303; *Yeats Collected Poems* 210). Writing to her mother, to whom she sent the newly composed villanelles, Plath claimed: "I am getting more proficient with the singing, uncrowded lyric line, instead of the static adjectival smothered thought I am usually guilty of" (*L2* 575). In her letter, Plath acknowledged her desire to escape stasis in her writing, just as she had earlier expressed her determination not to become trapped in a "circle of stagnation" in her life. While Clark reads Plath's focus on villanelle composition over this period as an "orderly restorative exercise" in the face of life's tedium, it can also be viewed as an example of her adult experimentation with Yeatsian rhyme and content (*Red Comet* 228). The restrictions associated with the repeated lines of the villanelle form, which also force syllabic constraint within the line, could have prompted Plath's belief that she was now achieving a "singing, uncrowded lyric line." In her copy of Clement Wood's *The Complete Rhyming Dictionary and Poet's Craft Book*, Plath underlined Wood's definition of the villanelle as a form which "lends itself to seriousness, as well as to frivolity" (87). When she returned to villanelle writing the following year, she continued to tether herself to Yeats but achieved a more lyrical and, at times, frivolous, poem in "Admonitions." In her claim that "[t]he magic golden apples all look good," Plath certainly echoes "The Song of Wandering Aengus" which ends with reference to "[t]he silver apples of the moon, / The golden apples of the sun" (*CP* 319; *Yeats Collected Poems* 67). Still borrowing from Yeats in her invocation of the moon, she modernizes and Americanizes: "From here the moon seems smooth as angel-food" (*CP* 319). The lexis of the fairy tale, anticipating later poems such as "Daddy," almost breaks through here in the references to the "magic golden apples," the "wicked witch," and the moon made of "angel-food," but the image pattern is not fully developed by Plath as an original system in this particular poem.

In spite of these efforts, Plath never included a villanelle in any of her published collections. It might be inferred that she abandoned the form early because she recognized that, poetically, the villanelle itself constituted the "repetitive circle of stagnation" which she had resolved to avoid as a twenty-year-old shortly after composing the poems and reading *A Vision*. Much later, however, in "Daddy," Plath would return to repeated refrains and insistent rhymes reminiscent of the villanelle, adapting the conventions of the form expertly in order to explore the drama of release and freedom from perceived constraint depicted within that poem. Grouping these villanelles among her juvenilia, in his introduction to Plath's *Collected Poems*, Hughes wrote that the "sense of a deep mathematical inevitability in the sound and texture of her lines was well developed quite early on" (*CP* 16). Plath had learned important lessons in lyricism, and in poetic and personal freedom, from Yeats while studying at Smith, but it would be almost another decade before her most famous work drew on the poetic resources she had developed through this early apprenticeship.

## "A TERRIBLE BEAUTY IS BORN": IN "PURSUIT" OF HUGHES

On February 27, 1956, following her passionate first meeting with Hughes the night before, Plath wrote "Pursuit" which she "dedicated" to him (*J* 214). A period of anguish over her instant attraction to Hughes and her ongoing relationship with Richard Sassoon followed. On March 10, she learned that Hughes was back in Cambridge and had been throwing stones at her bedroom window. In her journal, she used a phrase from "Pursuit" to refer to Hughes as her "black marauder" and, in a postscript to her March 10 entry, wrote "[t]he panther wakes and stalks again, and every sound in the house is his tread on the stair; I wrote mad girl's love song once in a mad mood like this" (*J* 233). Referring again to "Pursuit," in which she had written that "[t]he panther's tread is on the stairs, / Coming up and up the stairs," Plath made a clear association between the predatory subject of her poem and Hughes himself (*CP* 23). Plath's claim that she wrote "Mad Girl's Love Song" and "Pursuit" in a similar "mad mood" suggests that she paired the two poems due to their comparable emotional inspiration. However, these poems are also connected due to the fact that they are both inspired, stylistically and thematically, by Yeats. When she sent "Pursuit" to her mother, Plath explained that

> "The Pursuit" is more in my old style, but larger [...]. It is, of course, a symbol of the terrible beauty of death, and the paradox that the more intensely one lives, the more one burns and consumes oneself; death, here, includes the concept of love, and is larger and richer than mere love, which is part of it.
>
> (*L1* 1133)

At this time of emotional upheaval, Plath returned to her "old style" and her old inspiration in order to make sense of her feelings upon meeting Hughes. In her description of the "terrible beauty of death," she alludes to Yeats's "Easter 1916," where the transformative power of the blood sacrifice made by the Irish rebels as they sought to establish independence is recognized: "All changed, changed utterly: / A terrible beauty is born" (202). It is possible that, in composing the poem about Hughes, Plath picked up on the sentiment expressed by Yeats's final lines and applied them to her meeting with her future husband: she seemed, unconsciously, to appreciate that their encounter had changed everything.

Plath acknowledged that "Pursuit" bore clear relation to William Blake's "Tiger, Tiger" and Clark notes that the poem also answers back to Hughes's "The Jaguar" (itself influenced by Rilke's "The Panther") and his "Law in the Country of Cats" (*Red Comet* 426). Although she had prefaced the poem with a quote from Racine, Plath told her mother that "Another epigraph could have been from my beloved Yeats: 'Whatever flames upon the night, Man's own resinous heart has fed.' [*sic*] The painter's brush consumes his dreams, and all that" (*L1* 1134). The poem by Yeats she refers to is "Two Songs from a Play," which became a touchstone for Plath during this period. Its influence on "Pursuit" is clear from the first line—"There is a panther stalks me down"—which follows the same iambic tetrameter of Yeats's precursor poem which opens: "I saw a staring virgin stand" (*CP* 22; *Yeats Collected Poems* 239). The rhyming sound of Yeats's opening line is also echoed in Plath's second stanza: "Insatiate, he ransacks the land" (*CP* 22). Plath takes literally Yeats's suggestion of the heart being used to feed—"Man's own resinous heart has fed"—when she has her speaker proclaim "I hurl my heart to halt his pace" in an attempt to slow the stalking panther (*CP* 23). She also draws inspiration from the sentiment of Yeats's line "[l]ove's pleasure drives his love away" when she describes her speaker's flight: "Appalled by secret want, I rush / From such assault of radiance" (*Yeats Collected Poems* 240; *CP* 23). In spite of her ostensible evasion, however, Plath's speaker is thrilled by the pursuit of the panther. Yeats's line "The painter's brush consumes his dreams," like the closing lines of "Two Songs from a Play" considered by Plath as an alternative epigraph for "Pursuit," suggests artistic creation contingent on self-sacrifice.

This dynamic is played out within "Pursuit" as the description of the chase, in spite of the mortal danger it represents, is the true focus of the speaker throughout the poem—not her escape. Even as she "bolt[s] the door," she is thrilled and complicit in the pursuit (*CP* 23). For the speaker of "Pursuit," the experience is defined by, what Diane Middlebrook describes as "immoderate emotion" but, for the poet, Middlebrook argues, "immoderate emotion paid off" (22).

At the heart of the poem, Plath enacts a similar consideration of the transience of human influence and the significance of the primal spilling of blood which is the subject of the second half of Yeats's poem:

> Odour of blood when Christ was slain
> Made all platonic tolerance vain
> And vain all Doric discipline.
>
> *(Yeats Collected Poems* 240)

Plath's second stanza describes the panther who

> ransacks the land
> Condemned by our ancestral fault,
> Crying: blood, let blood be spilt;
> Meat must glut his mouth's raw wound.
>
> (*CP* 22)

In October 1956, while she was reading St. Paul and the confessions of Augustine, Plath wrote to Hughes about her new appreciation of those lines from Yeats: "I understand more perfectly now, in the midst of this terrifying strong blood-faith" (*L1* 1274). In the consolidation of her understanding of "Two Songs from a Play," Plath made links between symbols that would become central to her own work: the blood sacrifice and the flame of resurrection which is fed by the old self in order to allow a new self to be born. Clark writes of "Pursuit" that the "ungenteel poem was a breakthrough for Plath and heralded the beginning of a new creative direction" (*Red Comet* 426). Certainly, Plath herself believed this to be the case. In a letter to Hughes, she later reflected on the moment, claiming that she was experiencing "the consecration of my new writing, which properly began with you and 'Pursuit'" (*L1* 1257). Plath's reinterpretation of Yeats's lines, after gaining a greater appreciation of their religious context, chimes with her use of "consecration" in order to describe her creative "rebirth." She would experience this spiritual feeling of artistic transformation once more in her career and, again, it would be at a time of heightened emotional stimulation. As she had done at Smith in 1953 and at Cambridge in 1956, when she faced emotional upheaval in 1962–3, Plath would turn to Yeats for personal and poetic inspiration while she worked to convert those experiences into poetry.

## "BECAUSE I HAVE COME INTO MY STRENGTH, / AND WORDS OBEY MY CALL": YEATS AS A LATE EXAMPLE

In the 1980s, Gilbert considered Plath's late residence in Yeats's former home in London as indicative of her seeking out "Yeats's implicit approval" and finding "a poetic father—a liberating male muse rather than an inhibiting male master—to match the poetic mother she had discovered in Virginia Woolf" ("In Yeats' House" 219). For Gilbert, Plath gravitated toward Yeats because "among all the male modernists, [he] had the most reverence for female power" (219). At the time that Plath was reaching poetic maturity, Gilbert describes a literary landscape which was divided into "highly cultured intellectual men (Pound, Eliot, Joyce, Lawrence) and their female counterparts, literary ladies" who included "Teasdale, Millay, Olive Higgins Prouty" (207). Gilbert also includes Yeats in her list of the "highly cultured intellectual men" (208). However, there existed a further subdivision within the male modernist literary patriarchy, which Gilbert elides but which Hughes and Plath did not: that between the modernist schools of Eliot and Pound, and that of Yeats. Plath, for many of the reasons Gilbert outlines, gravitated toward Yeats whereas Hughes, initially due to his association with Faber and Faber, became a disciple of Eliot. Early in their relationship, Plath characterized her husband as a second Yeats, telling her brother that he "bangs and smashes through speech to go better than Yeats" (*L1* 1173). Less than a week later, however, she reclaimed the position of Yeats's inheritor for herself, telling her mother that "I am younger than Yeats in my saying" (*L1* 1179). In her interview with Lee Anderson for the Library of Congress in 1958, Plath explained her preference for Yeats, describing him as "an anti-type of Eliot" (*Red Comet* 522). As their relationship evolved, Plath moved closer in her identification with Yeats while Hughes became more aligned with Eliot. On the same day that she wrote "Wintering," October 9th, 1962, Plath wrote to Ruth Beuscher that "Ted is everywhere in the literary world, like T. S. Eliot" (*L2* 852). Just as Gilbert suggests Yeats as a "poetic father" for Plath, Eliot became a poetic father-figure for Hughes from the moment he overruled Charles Monteith and decided to have Hughes's *The Hawk in the Rain* (1957) added to the Faber and Faber poetry list (Harding 79). Hughes's positioning of himself in relation to Eliot later in his career, however, was complicated by Plath's identification with Yeats to the extent that Hughes's commentary on the Irish poet following Plath's death can be read as a coded consideration of her artistic self and work.

In the address which he gave at the unveiling of Eliot's blue plaque in London, in 1986, Hughes asserted that Eliot shared "his supremacy in modern English with one other poet [...] W. B. Yeats" (*A Dancer to God* 5). According to Hughes, the poets were equal in stature but different in sentiment: Yeats "drew his artistic principles and his visionary strength out of the roots of [the] old, insular world," whereas Eliot, "was the prophet of a new world" (*A Dancer to God* 5). While Gilbert figured Plath's alignment with Yeats as an exploration of "the relationship between male authority and female identity," in his identification of a difference between the mastery of Eliot and Yeats, Hughes gestured toward an acknowledgment of a split in the inheritance of differing modernist sensibilities which was at play in Plath's interest in Yeats ("In Yeats' House" 206). Both Gilbert and Hughes show signs of Yeats's powerful, almost mystical, influence when they use the same word—"visionary"—to describe him and his disciples. Plath's "system of inner symbols and images" aligned with Yeats's repeated exploration of the theme of resurrection through self-sacrifice, and his interest in reconciling the self and the anti-self in forging an artistic identity. In her late poems, Plath, like Yeats, drew strength from exploring, what Hughes called, the "roots of the old, insular world." In a letter to the priest, Michael Carey, dated February 4, 1963, just one week before her death, Plath claimed: "I write, at present, in blood, or at least with it. Any difficulty arises from compression or the jaggedness of images thrusting up from one psychic ground root" (*L2* 966). In crafting his distinction between Yeats and Eliot, Hughes's words describing Yeats drawing his "visionary strength out of the roots of [the] old, insular world" echo those of Plath. Indeed, it is this echoing of words that is the subject of one of her final poems, which shares its title with a poem by Yeats, "Words."

In the *Birthday Letters* poem, "A Dream," Hughes refers to Plath's "Words," which ends: "[f]rom the bottom of the pool, fixed stars / Govern a life" (*CP* 270). One of the last pieces she wrote, on February 1, 1963, the poem concluded the edition of *Ariel* as it was published by Faber and Faber in 1965. In isolation, the final line suggests a fated inevitability in the face of life's vicissitudes. Hughes's reference to the line in "A Dream" implies an evolving genesis for Plath's phrase: "Not dreams, I had said, but fixed stars / Govern a life" (*TH:CP* 1119). Hughes's words suggest a correction to a misquotation or misinterpretation of a phrase on Plath's part at a much earlier date while on their honeymoon in France in 1956. However, neither poet accurately renders the phrase from its source, which is likely to be Yeats's morality play *The Hour-Glass*, in which the Wise Man is told by the Fool that: "when one gets quiet, then something wakes up inside one, something happy and quiet like the stars—not like the seven that move, but like the fixed stars" (*Collected Works* 98).[4] The link between dreaming, sleeping, and waking, which forms part of the misconception corrected by Hughes in his poem, is embedded within the phrase "something wakes up inside one," but Yeats's reference to the "fixed stars" suggests a positive, "happy" acknowledgment of one's destiny.

From the early moments of Yeats's play, the Wise Man knows that he is working against time—the hour-glass of the play's title—in an effort to preserve his immortal soul. He has been visited by an angel who assures him that he will die within the hour but grants him time to inspire faith in others. When, at the last moment, he receives an assurance from the Fool that he is a believer, the Wise Man embraces his fate rapturously, exclaiming: "I am going to the country of the fixed stars! ... I understand it all now. One sinks in on God; we do not see the truth; God sees the truth in us" (*Collected Works* 107). For Yeats, the "fixed stars" that govern symbolize the patient guidance of a forgiving God and lead the lost toward the salvation of truth. Writing in Yeats's house at a profoundly difficult time, Plath drew on his play and poem in "Words" which contemplates the act of recalling or re-experiencing words: "Years later I / Encounter them on the road— / Words dry and riderless, / The indefatigable hoof-taps" (*CP* 270). Her poem shares its title with a piece by Yeats from *The Green Helmet and Other Poems* which Plath had underlined heavily. The acknowledgment of impending death contained in *The Hour-Glass* is also explored in Yeats's "Words" in the line "I grew weary of the sun" which itself echoes Macbeth's late words: "I 'gin to grow aweary of the sun / And wish th'estate o' th' world were now undone" (*Yeats Collected Poems* 100). However, the overwhelming theme of the poem is love that is articulated but not returned:

[E]very year I have cried, "At length
My darling understands it all,
Because I have come into my strength,
And words obey my call";

---

[4] Steven Gould Axelrod has suggested works by William Shakespeare, John Milton, Robert Lowell, and Theodore Roethke as possible sources for the phrase. With the exception of Lowell, none of these sources use the precise words "fixed stars" and Lowell was a self-confessed disciple of Yeats's which suggests Yeats as the originator for his use of the phrase. See *The Wound and the Cure of Words* 65, 75. The phrase also occurs in *A Vision* in which Yeats writes of the "eighth sphere, the sphere of the fixed stars" (252).

> That had she done so who can say
> What would have shaken from the sieve?
> I might have thrown poor words away
> And been content to live.
>
> (*Yeats Collected Poems* 100)

Whereas, in her poem, Plath views her animalistic words as disobedient, "dry and riderless," in his poem, Yeats's more biddable words "obey my call." For Yeats, some indication of understanding from his love object, whom Plath, in her annotations, identified as Maud Gonne, would have enabled him to stop living out his romance in writing and begin living his life more fully (*Yeats Collected Poems* 88). Plath, however, holds out no such hope and, in her invocation of the line from *The Hour-Glass* to conclude her poem, embraces the cold comfort of truth and, perhaps, God. To the priest, Michael Carey, with whom she had been corresponding toward the end of her life, she wrote on February 4, three days after she had completed this poem, "How about Yeats for the lyrical?" (*L2* 967). It is possible that, for Hughes, the inspiration that Plath drew from Yeats's play about the salvation of the immortal soul and his poem about unrequited love suggested "Words" as an appropriate one with which to conclude *Ariel*, as it was first published, in 1965.

## "I STARTED MY COLONY LATE": YEATS AND THE BEE SEQUENCE

In his reconsideration of "Yeats as an Example?," Heaney dwelled particularly on "The Stare's Nest by My Window" which he believed considered "the purpose of art in the midst of life" (109). The poem opens:

> The bees build in the crevices
> Of loosening masonry, and there
> The mother birds bring grubs and flies.
> My wall is loosening; honey-bees,
> Come build in the empty house of the stare.
>
> (*Yeats Collected Poems* 230)

In the prologue to *Red Comet*, Clark cites the poem and claims that "Plath would have understood Yeats's famous entreaty to reconstruct in the halls of ruin" (xxviii–xxix). Clark's assertion that "[Plath] had built" in completing *Ariel* suggests a product that was worth the sacrifice reminding us of Plath's fascination with Yeats's "Two Songs from a Play" in which "[t]he painter's brush consumes his dreams" (*Red Comet* 240). However, such a sentiment does not account for the change in attitude to "the purpose of art" which Yeats articulated later in his career. Having initially admired the "terrible beauty" of the blood sacrifice of the rebels in "Easter 1916," in "The Man and the Echo," Yeats agonized over the influence of his play *Cathleen Ní Houlihan* on the Irish rebels wondering, "Did that play of mine send out / Certain men the English shot?" (393). As Heaney recognized, in his later work, Yeats no longer advocated for the simplistic exchange of art for life that he had considered fundamental in "Two Songs from a Play."

Audre Lorde warned that "the master's tools will never dismantle the master's house," noting that "it is only in the patriarchal model of nurturance that women 'who attempt to emancipate themselves pay perhaps too high a price for the results'" (110–11). In spite of her exploration of female influences on Plath's writing, even the title of Gilbert's consideration of Plath's residence at Fitzroy Road—"In Yeats' House"—places her within a patriarchal model, as does this essay. Using Lorde's analysis, we might conclude that Plath's situation within this model cost her too dearly. However, in placing herself amongst these men, in Yeats's house, Plath created a space for women coming after her to inhabit and incubate. This act was Yeatsian in its imperative. For Heaney, "The Stare's Nest by My Window" presents "a deeply instinctive yet intellectually assented-to idea of nature in her benign and nurturing aspect as the proper first principle of life and living. The maternal is apprehended, imitated and warmly cherished" ("Yeats as an Example?" 110). Within his poem, Yeats encourages the bees to build in the starling's empty nest, which itself sits in the crevices of the man-made walls. In his reading, Heaney sees Yeats advocating for the (female) bee to build upon the (female) nest as a way to ensure life and growth amidst the crumbling (male) masonry. It was this entreaty that Plath understood. In her bee sequence, we see her creating space for others to inhabit—not (re)building the edifice.

In October 1962, Plath began her bee sequence following a trip to Ireland. To her mother, she described the connection she made with Yeats while there:

I went to Yeats' tower in Ireland in August, near dead from flu & the prospect of bringing the children up alone on next to nothing, & felt that although I was dead in body, my soul began to wake. It was very weird, feeling this timelessness of the untouched place, its beauty, the immanence of Yeats.

(*L1* 914)

In the face of returning to Devon, to live alone, Plath was sustained by personal and poetic associations with Yeats. It is perhaps unsurprising that, in her copy of Yeats's poems, it is the image of a solitary life, amongst the bees in "The Lake Isle of Innisfree," that Plath chose to underline: "And live alone in the bee-loud glade" (39). After she returned to Court Green, from October 3 to 7, she worked on the bee sequence, writing to Richard Murphy on the same day that she completed "The Swarm" that Ireland was "the first pure clear place I have been for some time" (*L2* 846).

Of her bee poems, it is "The Bee Meeting," which bears the clearest marks of her engagement with "The Lake Isle of Innisfree." Plath describes a ritualistic pagan initiation ceremony during which her speaker characterizes herself as extremely vulnerable: "In my sleeveless summery dress I have no protection, / And they are all gloved and covered, why did nobody tell me?" (*CP* 211). However, eventually, she is subsumed into the group:

I am led through a beanfield.

Strips of tinfoil winking like people,
Feather dusters fanning their hands in a sea of bean flowers,
Creamy bean flowers with black eyes and leaves like bored hearts.

(*CP* 211)

The combination of the beehives and the beans recalls Yeats's "Lake Isle of Innisfree" but without any of the associated peace. Instead, Plath's speaker describes a constant, menacing buzz amidst the "bee-loud glade," and this threatening atmosphere returns in "The Arrival of the Bee Box" and "Stings." By the time she wrote "Wintering" on October 9, Plath's speaker was far more assertive than the frightened speaker of "The Bee Meeting." Rather than seeking peace from her surroundings, the speaker finds peace in herself, which she articulates when she says, "I have my honey," and in her female community when she claims "[t]hey have got rid of the men" (*CP* 217, 218). Heaney wrote of Yeats's final poems that "if the maternal instincts are the first, perhaps they call us back at the very end also" ("Yeats as an Example?" 110) and a similar, simultaneous preoccupation with both maternity and posterity is evident in Plath's "Wintering." Indeed, she seems to be speaking to Yeats's "The Stare's Nest by My Window," even extending his vision, when she asks "will the hive survive"? (*CP* 219).

In "In Memory of W. B. Yeats," Auden claimed that Yeats "became his admirers" (245). Yeats was not reborn in Plath but he helped her to develop her poetic style and system of symbols each time she returned to his example throughout her life. Heaney's definition of Yeats's influence best describes his example for Plath:

> He proves deliberation can be so intensified that it becomes synonymous with inspiration. Above all, he reminds you that art is intended, that it is part of the creative push of civilisation itself.
>
> ("Yeats as an Example" 107–8)

In writing her *Ariel* poems, Plath rose to the poetic challenges which Yeats had laid down for her. Although her hero could not help her to solve her personal problems, the example he set ensured that the poetry she had written all of her life secured a place for her—and a space for other women after her—in the creative crevices of civilization.

CHAPTER FOURTEEN

# The Law of Similarity and the Law of Contact: Sylvia Plath, Ted Hughes, and Sympathetic Magic

KATHERINE ROBINSON

In *Chapters in a Mythology* (1976), Judith Kroll argues that "[t]he logic of sympathetic magic, which appears widely in Plath's late poetry might well be called one of the physical laws of the world of her poetry" (125), but it was also one of the laws governing Plath's and Hughes's shared poetic world. In *The Grief of Influence* (2011), Heather Clark establishes the importance of tracing the "shared aesthetic ideals" (16) that shaped Plath's and Hughes's poetic sensibilities before their famous first meeting at the *Saint Botolph's Review* launch party in Cambridge; these shared ideals formed the basis for their literary relationship. This chapter documents one occult aspect of those shared ideals: the separate yet remarkably similar early discoveries of sympathetic magic that preceded their first meeting. This mutual fascination both fueled their creative partnership and shaped the posthumous relationship between *Birthday Letters* and Plath's poetry.

Both Plath and Hughes first discovered sympathetic magic in James George Frazer's *The Golden Bough* (first published in 1890) in which Frazer defines two branches of sympathetic magic:

> If we analyse the principles of thought on which magic is based, they will probably be found to resolve themselves into two: first, that like produces like, or that an effect resembles its cause; and, second, that things which have once been in contact with each other continue to act on each other at a distance after the physical contact has been severed. The former principle may be called the Law of Similarity, the latter the Law of Contact or Contagion.
>
> (Frazer 11)

Frazer calls magic in which "like produces like" "homeopathic magic." He calls magic in which objects once in contact continue to influence each other at a distance "contagious magic" (Frazer 11). Contagious magic frequently, however, includes elements of imitation, relying, for example, on images of the person or animal the magician wishes to affect. He terms this branch of sympathetic magic, ruled by the Law of Similarity, "imitative magic" or "homeopathic magic." Because contagious magic often relies on imitative magic, Frazer writes that "[i]n practice the two branches are often combined" (Frazer 12). I will discuss both "contagious" and "imitative" magic in this chapter, but I will use the term "sympathetic magic," as Frazer does, to refer more generally to forms of magic reliant on both principles.

*The Golden Bough* is a study of magic, not an endorsement of it. Frazer's descriptions of sympathetic magic unfold within the context of his scholarly attempt to "discern the spurious science behind the bastard art" (Frazer 12) of sympathetic magic, but those tenets of sympathetic magic—spurious as they may be in the natural world—prove more tenable in the making of poetry and in the shaping of poetic legacies. The Law of Similarity and the Law of Contact articulated by Frazer could describe, too, Plath's and Hughes's own poetic relationship as it unfolded in the matrix of their absorption in the literature and lore of sympathetic magic.

## "PATHS COINCIDENT:" THE LAW OF SIMILARITY

In "St Botolph's" (*Birthday Letters*), Hughes describes that first meeting at a launch party for *Saint Botolph's Review:*

> Falcon Yard:
> Girl-friend like a loaded crossbow[ … .]
>                    The hall
> Like the tilting deck of the *Titanic:*
> A silent film, with that blare over it. Suddenly—
> Lucas engineered it—suddenly you.
>
> (TH:CP 1051)

Hughes evokes the scene using fragments of sentences, juxtaposed like so many snapshots. But for all its plainness, the diction is densely allusive. That anachronistic crossbow recalls W. B. Yeats's "No Second Troy" in which the lover is endowed with "beauty like a tightened bow" (*Yeats Collected Poems* 101). The Falcon Yard hall is "like the tilting deck of the *Titanic*." If the simile is logically extended, then what approaches the *Titanic* is an iceberg, and Plath's entrance evokes Thomas Hardy's "The Convergence of the Twain":

> IX
>      Alien they seemed to be;
>      No mortal eye could see
> The intimate welding of their later history,
> X
>      Or sign that they were bent
>      By paths coincident
> On being anon twin halves of one august event,
> XI
>      Till the Spinner of the Years
>      Said "Now!" And each one hears,
> And consummation comes, and jars two hemispheres.
>
> (289)

Culminating in that "consummation," Hardy's poem describes its own kind of marriage. Plath and Hughes were, likewise, alien to each other, from two different continents, and

Hughes's first impression emphasizes her Americanness: "It seemed your long, perfect, American legs / Simply went on up" (*TH:CP* 1052). But the early folkloric and occult discoveries these two poets had already made were paths coincident; their intellectual foundations were doubles, doubles that came into extraordinary metamorphic contact in Cambridge. As in the Law of Similarity, like attracted like.

## *"PORTRAIT AS SOUL": PEOPLE AND IMAGES*

Plath's mother gave her a 1922 abridged edition of *The Golden Bough* as a Christmas gift in 1953 when she was an undergraduate at Smith College (*L1* 822). It became an invaluable resource for her senior honors thesis, "The Magic Mirror: A Study of the Double in Two of Dostoevsky's Novels." Writing to her mother, Plath lamented that "right now it seems as it is impossible that I ever have a thoughtful, well-written thesis done, because now all reading is apparently unrelated (except that it is all about doubles)" (*L1* 822). Plath elaborates that she is reading "stories all about doubles, twins, mirror images and shadow reflections. And your book gift 'The Golden Bough', comes in handy, as it has an excellent chapter on 'the soul as shadow and reflection'" (*L1* 822).

Many chapters in Plath's edition of *The Golden Bough*, now in Smith College Special Collections, remain uncut. She did not read the book in its entirety; rather, her annotations reflect her focused use of the book, and those annotations confirm her assertion that her interest in the book was an extension of her desire to learn about folkloric images of the double. But all the chapters Plath annotated share an even more interesting theme: they describe ways the soul can separate from the body and come to harm, or how the soul, even securely contained in the body, can be harmed through magical words, magical images, or magical rituals. But what heals that rupture is also often a form of sympathetic magic: images of the soul draw it back to its body.

In many cultures, Frazer argues, an image of a person is considered to be magically connected to that person. "Perils of the Soul" (chapter XVIII) includes a description of a Chinese funeral, and Plath underlined the explanation for why attendants at the funeral stepped back a few paces when the coffin lid was closed: "for a person's health is believed to be endangered by allowing his shadow to be enclosed in a coffin" (190). In the same chapter, she also underlined Frazer's explanation that the "savage" frequently "regards his shadow or reflection as his soul, or at all events as a vital part of himself" (189). She underlined, too, the logical and perilous extension of that belief about shadows: "For if it is trampled upon or struck ... he will feel the injury as if it were done to his person" (Frazer 189). If it is severed, he will die. On the next page, she underlined an iteration of the same idea: "injury done to the shadow is felt by the person or animal as if it were done to his body" (Frazer 190). In the margin of that page, Plath wrote, "equation of mirror or water image to soul." She wrote the note "portrait as soul" next to Frazer's explanation of why people in some cultures are reluctant to have their portraits painted: they believe that the portrait can represent the soul (193). This disquietingly powerful relationship between people and images of them springs both from the Law of Similarity and from the Law of Contagion—something once associated with a person, his shadow, will always be so associated with him, and whatever happens to it will befall his own body.[1]

---

[1] For discussions of Plath's thesis research about the image of the double, see Axelrod, "The Mirror and the Shadow," and Hammer, "Plath's Lives."

As a teenager living in Mexborough, Hughes was recording his own interest in the powerful occult relationship between images and people. The British Library holds a folklore notebook he kept as a teenager, and he recorded an example of the terrifying immediacy of that relationship. In it, he noted that burning an image of someone could be the burning of a person's soul (British Library Add MS 88918/9/12). This note is in the notebook's early pages, pages written in the tidy, sloping handwriting associated with Hughes's teenaged years. That handwriting allows us to date these pages to his time in Mexborough Grammar School. In Mexborough, Hughes first discovered folklore in a serialized encyclopedia sold in his father's newsagents shop. Mark Wormald has identified it as Arthur Mee's *The Children's Encyclopedia*, and a 1992 letter to Anne-Lorraine Bujon describes the "jolt" of first discovering folklore in it (Wormald 59). He describes the "mania" that ensued as he began to collect folktales. That mania, he wrote, has "continued ever since ... in cyclic waves of renewed realisation that these things are the great treasures of the world" (*LTH* 624).

He gathered those "treasures" in this notebook, and it contains no sources, but the other notes surrounding it have allowed me to trace this particular note to *The Golden Bough*. Hughes's library, now housed at Emory, contains a thirteen-volume Macmillan & Co. unabridged edition of *The Golden Bough* (published 1911–15) and a 1935 abridged Macmillan edition, but we have not before been able to identify when he read *The Golden Bough*. Tracing these notes to Frazer allows us to understand that Hughes first read *The Golden Bough* very early and, more importantly, allows us to understand the nature of his initial engagement with *The Golden Bough*. The nature of his interest was remarkably similar to Plath's; his only notes about *The Golden Bough* pertain to the Law of Similarity and the Law of Contagion. Like Plath, he was interested in magical duplication.

That note about burning someone's image is Hughes's summation of Frazer's description of one instance of the Law of Similarity: "The Peruvian Indians moulded images of fat mixed with grain to imitate the persons whom they disliked or feared and then burned the effigy on the road where the intended victim was to pass. This they called burning his soul" (Frazer 30). But Hughes's adjacent notes allow us to know with more certainty that this note refers to *The Golden Bough*. Hughes notes that seal skins move in the ebbing tide, and he notes that eating nightingales produces insomnia. The first note summarizes Frazer's statement that "some of the ancients" believed that "the skins of seals even after they had been parted from their bodies, remained in secret sympathy with the sea, and were observed to ruffle when the tide was on the ebb" (Frazer 52). (Hughes's word choice recalls Frazer's in that note.) This image of an enduring, secret connective tissue between remnants of the animal body and its aquatic home expresses the law of contagion: two things once in contact remain so. The second note is Hughes's condensation of Frazer's statement that "[t]he ancient Greeks thought that to eat the flesh of a nightingale would prevent a man from sleeping" (Frazer 52). In this instance, like creates like: a wakeful bird that sings all night, when ingested, creates wakefulness.

## *MAGICAL WORDS*

The folklore notebook, too, contains our earliest documented glimpse of Hughes's interest in using words to guard against magical dangers and to undo curses. In his early, tidy handwriting he recorded a chant that could be used to protect against threats ranging from evil wishes to grass mice (BL Add MS 88918/9/12). But in the folklore Hughes was collecting, words were not always so benevolent. Hughes describes a man stolen away from his wedding by trolls. The man escapes, but a troll shouts that a red rooster will crow above his house. When the man arrives home, his house is on fire. A spoken metaphor becomes the most frightening kind of speech act: a verbal image produces real flames. Like attracts like.

Researching her senior honors thesis, Plath, too, gathered ideas about the magical potency of words. In *The Golden Bough*, she underlined passages in "Tabooed Words" (chapter XXII) illustrative of the occult tie that binds words to what they represent. She marked Frazer's description of the "Ojebway" (Ojibwa) belief that a man should never say his own name because his name is "a living piece of himself" (Frazer 246). Saying his name would, thus, dissipate his "energy and constitution." She marked, too, Frazer's explanation of "[t]he custom of abstaining from saying the names of the dead" observed by the "Albanians of Caucasus" (Frazer 251) because they feared those names would conjure ghosts. Above the chapter heading, she wrote, "names can never hurt me," a fragment of the familiar children's rhyme: "[S]ticks and stones / will break my bones, / but names will never hurt me." But that rhyme itself is a protective chant, a versified defense against words, which, as children know, can cause a great deal of harm.

## DOUBLES: PSYCHIC SPLITS

Names, reflections, portraits: these are all kinds of doubles. Thanking her mother for the gift of *The Golden Bough*, Plath wrote that her thesis would focus on the types of "doubles" Dostoevsky depicts and on his "literary methods of presenting them" (*L1* 824). The final draft of her thesis begins by distilling her reading of *The Golden Bough* into a compact explanation of the folkloric origins of doubles: "The theme of the Double has its origins in the earliest tribal traditions and superstitions which regard the shadow, the reflection, and the portrait as equivalent to the human soul" ("Magic Mirror" 1).

In Mexborough, Hughes, too, was gathering folkloric stories about doubles. *Gaudete* (1977) tells the story of Reverend Lumb, who is kidnapped by the spirits and replaced with a double made from an oak log. Hughes's teenaged folklore notebook includes the blueprint for Lumb: in it, Hughes notes that when a man is carried off by fairies, his shadow is placed into a log.

Twentieth-century psychologists, however, were more interested in the doubles that reside in the mind than in doubles encased in folkloric logs, and Plath was also reading about psychology for her thesis. As Kroll notes, Plath's reading of Otto Rank's essay "The Double as Immortal Self" shaped her own conception of the psychological and spiritual valences of the double (205–6). Plath's interest in folkloric representations of the double unfolded in the context of this interest in psychology. Kroll demonstrates that a psychic split—a form of psychic doubling—characterizes Plath's later *Ariel* poems. Kroll argues, for example, that "[t]he woman in 'Edge' *is* dead, but the perspective with which the speaker ... identifies herself—and thus the dead woman's perspective on herself is eternal or transcendent" (205). Kroll traces Plath's poetic interest in this splitting of the self to her early use of Rank's "The Double as Immortal Self" in her thesis, and Kroll quotes Plath's summary of Rank's argument: "Otto Rank ... analyses the gradual shift from the conception of the Double as the immortal soul to that of the Double as the symbol of death" (Kroll 206). But Kroll also argues that, whether the double symbolizes the soul or heralds the arrival of death, it represents "the mortal and immortal (and separable) self" (206).

As an undergraduate at Pembroke College, Cambridge, Hughes was also learning about psychic doubles. I have traced Hughes's Pembroke College Library borrowing records, and in May 1952 he borrowed *The Meaning of Dreams* (1924) by Robert Graves.

In a chapter titled "Theory of the Double Self," Graves summarizes the work of the Cambridge academic, W. H. R. Rivers, an anthropologist who worked with shell-shocked First World War veterans at Craiglockhart War Hospital. Graves met Rivers when he himself was a patient in that hospital. Graves writes that "Dr. Rivers, in an argument based on a long acquaintance with cases of 'abnormal' psychology, traces the part played in dreams by what is called Dissociation, that is the breaking up of the human individual into two or more rival 'selves' under the stress of difficult circumstances" (Graves 20). That idea that the self could separate and divide was to become central to both Plath's and Hughes's poetry and to their own literary relationship.

## "HERE IS THE POEM LEADING ITS DOUBLE LIFE": THE LAW OF CONTACT

The dubious foundation of contagious magic—"things which have once been in contact with each other are always in contact" (Frazer 11)—proves rather more certain in describing the literary doublings in Plath's and Hughes's poetry. *Birthday Letters* (1998), published thirty-five years after Plath's death, brims with poetic doubles for the poems in Plath's *Collected Poems* (1981), edited by Hughes. Accepting the Forward Prize for *Birthday Letters*, Hughes described those poems, written over the course of two decades, as "occasions ... in which I tried to open a direct, private, inner contact with my first wife" (*Ariel's* Gift 22). That word "contact" evokes, too, the painful attempt to make good the promise of contagious magic: contact, once made, persists. Hughes turned poetry into the realm where that contact persisted. His poems summon a woman through small acts of verbal imitative magic, but *Birthday Letters* also acknowledges both the impossibility of contact and the persistence of an absence so palpable it manifests as images of perpetual almost-contact. Many of *Birthday Letters* poems enact the psychic split Kroll identifies in "Edge." Hughes's "The Blue Flannel Suit" ends with the lines "I am stilled / Permanently now, permanently / Bending so briefly at your open coffin" (*TH:CP* 1086). The speaker's experience of perception has been doubled: he is both at the coffin and observing himself there.

To call these poems "doubles" is not, however, to argue that they are identical. In the introduction to her Smith College thesis, "The Magic Mirror" (1955), Plath writes that the "device of the double ... often reveals hitherto concealed character traits in a radical manner" (Plath 3). Hughes's poems serve as just this sort of double for the Plath poems to which they respond; they reveal concealed traits in those poems.

In his essay "Sylvia Plath: The Evolution of 'Sheep in Fog'" (1988), Hughes articulates connections between Plath's diction in that poem and the Phaeton and Icarus myths that had fascinated her. Using his own knowledge of Plath's mythic interests, he excavates the poem's submerged but vital mythic substructure. In *Birthday Letters,* his poetic responses to Plath's poems serve a similar editorial function: they make explicit the learned but implicit occult and mythical frameworks of Plath's poems. They showcase concealed or unnamed aspects of her poetry.

In her edition of *The Golden Bough,* Plath annotated passages detailing the occult risks of naming a person or thing directly, and writing about Plath's work, Hughes is alert to the heightened poetic power to be found in refraining from stating a name directly. Describing Plath's use of the Phaeton and Icarus myths in "Sheep in Fog," he acknowledges that "one can see how any mention of either would have killed the suggestive power of the mythic ideas" ("Evolution" 206). More overt imagistic traces of those myths do, however, remain in Plath's drafts, and describing a facsimile of an edited draft of "Sheep in Fog," he remarks, "Here is the poem leading its double life" ("Evolution" 196); the poem's own double is made of those aspects that, in the final draft, became concealed. The role Hughes assumed as editor involved giving his own perception of those doubles—a perception facilitated by the occult interests he shared with his first wife—articulate life.

That editorial role changed him, too: Hughes became his own double. That essay was originally delivered as a lecture to the Wordsworth Trust, and Hughes states in it that the *Ariel* poems "document Plath's struggle to deal with a double situation—when her sudden separation from her husband coincided with a crisis in her traumatic feelings about her father's death" ("Evolution" 191). That formal separation arrives with blunt force. Hughes is two men: the lecturer speaking and also that distant figure of "her husband." Diane Middlebrook's book about their literary marriage, *Her Husband: Hughes and Plath—A Marriage* (2003), takes its title from that distanced and distancing phrase. By contrast, Hughes's poetic responses to Plath's poems bridge that rift: in these poems, he is speaking, as that husband and his excavation of occult structures in Plath's poems unfolds within the matrix of his imagined reconstruction of their marriage.

## "THE LADY AND THE EARTHENWARE HEAD" AND "EARTHENWARE HEAD"

"I had a vision in the dark art lecture room today of *the* title of my book of poems. It came to me suddenly with great clarity that *The Earthenware Head* was the right title, the only title" (*J* 332), Plath wrote in her journal in winter 1958. In that same entry, she lamented her recent lack of writing and asked, "What thoughts few as they are, revolve in my head? The Double: The Earthenware Head … how all photograph-portraits do catch our souls—part of a past world, a window onto the air and furniture of our own sunken worlds" (*J* 333). That winter, Plath had returned to Northampton, Massachusetts, to teach at Smith College, where—reading *The Golden Bough* as an undergraduate—she had first learned stories about the live circuit connecting portrait and soul.

Her poem "The Lady and the Earthenware Head" explores the boundaries between what is and is not part of the self and what is and is not animate, suggesting those boundaries are unnervingly thin. The poem eschews the word "double," but Plath's erudite knowledge about doubles and sympathetic magic infuses the poem's imagery. The bust that inspired the poem was an art project completed by Plath's Smith classmate, Mary Derr (Hammer 71); perhaps that is why Plath thought "suddenly" of the title *Earthenware Head* when she found herself in that dark Smith College art lecture room. Even the carefully noted location of her insight suggests that things remain in contagious contact with the places they originated.

Plath's speaker no longer wants that clay head, but she "felt loath to junk it" (*CP* 69). She worries that whatever fate it meets will magically ensnare her as well. The head is "[f]ired in sanguine clay": already the distinction between animate and inanimate flickers out of focus. "Sanguine" describes a ruddy color, derived from French *sang*, meaning blood and thus already indicating biological life, but "sanguine" also describes a cheerful disposition. Clay becomes imbued with cheerfulness, but if this head has a disposition, it is not a sanguine one: its look is "spite-set," and it "fit nowhere" (*CP* 69).

If the speaker throws it into an "ash heap," however, "rough boys" might find it and might

> Maltreat the hostage head in shocking wise
> And waken the sly nerve up
>
> That knits to each original its coarse copy.

(CP 69)

Plath's language animates the head again: "molest" can mean "annoy," but it more frequently refers to human sexual crimes. That "sly nerve" seems, at first, lodged in this animate and animated clay head. Only as the sentence completes itself across the distance of the stanza break does that nerve become the tie that binds "coarse copy" to original woman. That word "sly" is notable, too. Like a sly fox stealing through the margins of a field or city, this nerve, clever and furtive, steals across psychic margins and enacts a sleight of hand: it makes what should not be possible seem to be possible. The word "lady" is formal, respectable, even stilted. By contrast, "[c]oarse copy" suggests that, in the tradition of Dr. Jekyll and Mr. Hyde, that copy embodies the unacknowledged, repressed, yet ever-present psychological impulses which co-exist with that careful respectability yet "fit nowhere."

As if naming her fear might summon its fulfillment, the speaker never names the harm she fears. But the poem, as it continues, conjures rather than dispels the magic of contagion. She considers dropping the head into a "tarn," but "her courage wavered: / She blenched, as one who drowns" (CP 69). "Wavered" again erodes that boundary between animate and inanimate: beneath the tarn's swaying water, the head would seem to waver, like Narcissus's swaying reflection. "Wavered" also describes, however, the living woman's hesitation. In so doing, the word becomes its own verbal embodiment of that nerve: in the realm of speculative imagination, what befalls the head befalls the woman and vice versa.

Finally, the speaker decides to leave the head in a "crotched willow," where it will slowly degrade and become "simple sod" (CP 70). That word "crotched" is another persistent mark of molestation—a law of contagion the speaker cannot escape. But she never leaves the head in that willow. At the end of the poem, the head still rests on her shelf. Perhaps the thought of molded earthenware becoming shapeless earth disquiets her—that trajectory embodies the Christian liturgical summary of human life and death: "from dust were ye made and dust shall ye be." Shape is all that differentiates individuals from anonymous dust, and a return to simple sod signifies death as surely as drowning does, although it is a different kind of fate—more organic, more inevitable, and arguably less traumatic.

> [O]n her shelf, the grisly visage endured,
> ...
> It ogled through rock-fault, wind-flaw and fisted wave—
> An antique hag-head, too tough for knife to finish,
> Refusing to diminish
> By one jot its basilisk-look of love.

(CP 70)

Again, that voyeuristic word "ogled" recalls the "rough boys" who might have "molested" the head. The magic of contagion, again, swarms around it, although this time the head is the one who ogles. Its presence on that bookshelf suggests, too, that those repressed but ever-present impulses embodied by the lady's "coarse copy" are an inextricable part of her own poetry and poetry making—that coarse copy lodges on the bookshelf in the same place books of poems dwell. There, its contagious magic summons the wild, rough natural world out of which that earthenware head was made. Rocks, wind, and waves fill the room, which has become subject to wind, weather, geological time. The head, ogling through geologic change, is, finally, much older than the lady it represents. But even that elemental world is animate: waves are "fisted," and "wind-flaw" evokes "windflaws," wild gusts, but also human flaws, aspects of character concealed. Verbal registers, too, clash in that phrase "antique hag-head." "Antique" evokes something more genteel than a "hag," but these opposing registers, welded together, linguistically enact the relationship between person and double which, as typified by Dr. Jekyll and Mr. Hyde, is often one of opposites. The paradox of the divided self is that although one part may seek to repress the other, that repressed part endures.

In *The Haunting of Sylvia Plath* (1991), Jacqueline Rose suggests that the relationship between lady and head embodies the relationship between an author and her literary afterlife and, in so doing, inverts the direction of time itself: "the effigy haunts the original" (2). Similarly, posthumous literary interpretations pervade Plath's own work: "the effigy, like the earthenware head of her poem, haunts her" (*Haunting* 3).

While the title of Hughes's poem "The Earthenware Head" (*Birthday Letters*) is a rough effigy of Plath's title, Hughes's poem also excavates her poem's occult context.[2] Hughes describes carrying that head out onto Grantchester meadows where they lodge it in a willow tree: "[a] twiggy crotch, nearly an owl's porch, / Made a mythic shrine for your double" (*TH:CP* 1079). Hughes's title already showcases absence: the lady has disappeared, a disappearance that marks the elegiac turn of Hughes's poem. What remains is the earthenware head, although even that has gone missing: the ending of the poem reveals that they could no longer find it when they returned to look: "[w]e could not seem to hit on the tree" (*TH:CP* 1079). Now only a poem, a representation of a representation, remains.

In *Ariel's Gift* (2000), Erica Wagner writes that this image "of the head separated off from Plath recalls the dual nature of her personality, and casts her as a female Orpheus, her head still singing though severed from her body" (86). Hughes's descriptions of this head are rougher than Plath's; they evoke a bloody death. The lips are "raw-edged / With crusty tooling." That word "crusty" evokes dried blood. He and an imagined version of his wife are carrying this severed head, but it is the dead version of his wife, and they are both carrying that version. The "whorls" of the river in Hughes's poem are "ferrying slender willow yellows" (*TH:CP* 1079); the Cam itself becomes a portal to the underworld.

Hughes retains Plath's image of a "crotched willow" but inverts it to a "healed bole-wound / a twiggy crotch." Turning that adjective into a noun makes the implication of biological rebirth explicit, and the earthenware head is crowning out of the body of a tree. While the head has gone missing, the tree remains as an animate, sexual, life-giving body. In that moment of rebirth, the head is where an owl should be: that twiggy crotch is "nearly an owl's porch." That mythic double evokes Athena, and Blodeuedd, a woman in *The Mabinogi* who becomes an owl; those medieval Welsh stories were

---

[2]For a comparison of how "Lady and the Earthenware Head" and "The Earthenware Head" preserve and diverge from Plath's own prose accounts of what happened to the clay effigy, see Hammer, 69–70.

another important shared context for Plath and Hughes. This double, the owl, can see in darkness that renders other birds powerless. The willow tree is a real one: venerable willow trees line the Cam as it winds from Grantchester to Cambridge, but Hughes's notes about Robert Graves's *The White Goddess*, recorded during his first term at Pembroke College (1951), include an extensive description of the symbolic meaning of the willow. He notes that Helicon, where the nine muses reside, is named for the willow (British Library Add MS 88918.9.12). Here, the head lodges in the source of poetry itself, tree of the muses. Dispossessed qualities that "fit nowhere" may not be the subject of poetry, but they lodge in the same place poetry does.

Plath's poem eschews the word "double," but Hughes's poem does not. It makes explicit, too, the fears fueling Plath's poem. "You ransacked thesaurus in your poem about it, / Veiling its mirror, rhyming yourself into safety" (*TH:CP* 1079), Hughes writes. That mirror evokes Plath's knowledge of *The Golden Bough,* and its mirrors veiled after a funeral. Plath's diction displays the fruits of that ransacked thesaurus; she imagines dropping the head into a "tarn." That Cumbrian and Yorkshire word is hardly ever used in New England, but a thesaurus offers synonyms: verbal doubles. Such borrowed diction allows the poem to avoid simple names. To name something directly is to conjure it, and synonyms veil names.

## MAN IN BLACK

Plath's most famous evocation of sympathetic magic is "Daddy" (1962), written after she and Hughes had separated. Guinevara Nance and Judith Jones argue in "Doing Away with Daddy: Exorcism and Sympathetic Magic in Plath's Poetry" that Plath "employs what Frazer in *The Golden Bough* refers to as 'sympathetic magic' in 'Daddy" (127). A closer examination of Plath's annotations in *The Golden Bough* reveals how precisely Plath's undergraduate reading of Frazer informed this poem. Plath also annotated a chapter in *The Golden Bough* called "Public Scapegoats" (chapter LVII), which includes descriptions of rituals for banishing evil spirits. Frazer describes a festival celebrated by the "Mandan Indians" whose goal was "the expulsion of the devil" (Frazer 562). Frazer writes that "[a] man, painted black to represent the devil, entered the village from the prairie" (562). This devil-representing man was chased out of the village in a ritual that affected rather than symbolized that expulsion. Plath underlined the phrase "a man, painted black to represent the devil," and this phrase foreshadows "Daddy," in which the speaker describes her father as a "devil" and declares that she made a "model" of him, "a man in black" (*CP* 221).

That poem's origin in their powerful shared fascination with sympathetic magic launched "Daddy" into enduring contact with Hughes's subsequent poems. In "Picture of Otto" (*Birthday Letters*), Hughes describes himself in a tomb with Otto Plath: "I never dreamed, however occult our guilt, / Your ghost inseparable from my shadow / As long as your daughter's words can stir a candle" (*TH:CP* 1167).

Like occult practices, poetic metaphor often welds together tangible objects and abstract concepts. In "Daddy," the dizzying collision of metaphor and reality creates a sense of disorientation—of a world whose boundaries have barely coalesced. The poem opens with the repetitive, incantatory language of spells. The first line is a syntactical double:

You do not do, you do not do
Any more, black shoe
In which I have lived like a foot.

(*CP* 222)

Repetition, taut rhymes, and occult allusions cordon Plath's poem off from ordinary speech acts. In Plath's undergraduate thesis, one chapter section about *The Brothers Karamazov* is titled "Ivan's Devil." It includes a description of Ivan's nightmare about a devil, a devil who only vanishes when the sound of knocking begins. Plath compares this passage's "force" to that described in Thomas DeQuincey's essay "On the Knocking at the Gate in Macbeth" ("Magic Mirror" 49). "Like Ivan," Plath argues, "we have been bewitched by the apparition of the Devil," and she borrows DeQuincey's description of the knocking in *Macbeth*, "awful parenthesis," to describe Ivan's nightmare ("Magic Mirror" 49). "Daddy," too, is an "awful parenthesis," a moment of hallucinatory intensity set apart from ordinary reality, bewitching its reader into sharing that intensity and introducing its own devil.

Plath's speaker states that she has tried to die, herself, in order to get back to the father, but she survived:

And then I knew what to do.
I made a model of you,
A man in black with a Meinkampf look
And a love of the rack and the screw.
And I said I do, I do.

(*CP* 224)

"[D]addy, I'm finally through," Plath writes, an exorcism Kroll traces to Frazer (*CP* 224). Kroll writes that "the notion that 'as the image suffers, so does the man'—affecting the real subject through a proxy—nicely describes the marriage to a model of Daddy, and explains why, 'If I've killed one man, I've killed two'" (124–5). Plath's model is such an effigy, but the next lines suggest that model is life-sized and alive: "I do, I do." That phrase evokes marriage vows, another linguistic double. The poem never explicitly states that this "model" is the speaker's husband, but it surrounds that model with things associated with Plath's husband, which, through contagious magic, would forever be in contact with him. The poem invokes the number of years Plath and Hughes were married: seven. Finally, it invokes Hughes's sartorial habits: the model is a "man in black," and Daniel Huws, one of Hughes's closest Cambridge friends, wrote that Hughes invariably wore a black corduroy jacket in Cambridge (21). Jonathan Bate writes that, in Cambridge, Hughes "dressed in black, dying his own corduroy from the Sutcliffe Farrar factory" (69). (The Farrars were his mother's family.)

Plath's poem "Man in Black" (1959) describes Hughes walking out toward the Massachusetts ocean: "And you, across those white / Stones, strode out in your dead / Black coat, black shoes" (*CP* 119–20). Hughes's own response to this poem, its poetic double, is titled "Black Coat," and it describes his memory of that day on the Massachusetts coast. That day was "[m]y sole memory / Of my black overcoat" (*TH:CP* 1109), and that claim evokes an act of psychic superposition. Plath's description of that black coat, culminating in that evocation of a "man in black" in "Daddy," was so total and so powerful that it replaced all his own memories.

Indeed, Hughes's poem traces the origins of the contagious magic that conjoined him and Otto Plath to that moment when he stood, in his black coat, by the American ocean. He writes that he had "[n]o idea / How that double image" of "the body of the ghost and me" suddenly "[c]ame into single focus" (*TH:CP* 1109). He describes the cold ocean, out of which "your father" had just climbed and writes that

> I did not feel
> How, as your lenses tightened,
> He slid into me.
>
> (*TH:CP* 1109)

In a ghostly sense, the father lives through Hughes's body and possesses it. Writing about Frazer, Kroll notes, too, that "[t]he location of devils to be cast out is sometimes a place, but usually it is a person who is possessed" (125). But in a physical sense, that final line powerfully and uncomfortably evokes a sexual violation, the feared and postponed violation that haunts "The Lady and the Earthenware Head." Black clothes are the agents through which the spell of contagious magic melds him to Otto Plath.

*The Golden Bough* vividly illustrates the possibility that the soul can be manipulated from afar or lost entirely. For both Plath and Hughes, poetry became the medium through which that possibility could be confronted. That confrontation became its own form of sympathetic magic, summoning rather than neutralizing the magic of contagion. In "After Plath: The Legacy of Influence," Fiona Sampson has convincingly demonstrated that Plath's "poetic legacy" begins with her influence on Hughes (393). That legacy is a powerful one, and it is, too, the literary embodiment of Frazer's Law of Contact. The laws that fired Plath's poetry came to describe its legacy as well. Sampson argues, finally, that "Plath's influence has passed into the vocabulary of the poetically possible" (357), and Sampson's diction evokes the fundamental changes sympathetic magic provokes. Plath's poetry grappled with the occult permanence of contact. That poetry itself enduringly changed the poetic tradition with which it came into contact.

# CHAPTER FIFTEEN

# "I am a miner": Long Poems and Literary Succession in *Ariel* and *Crow*

JENNIFER RYAN-BRYANT

Sylvia Plath's *Ariel* and Ted Hughes's multi-volume *Crow* sequence emerged during an interlude between literary modernism and postmodernism that Brian McHale and Lynn Keller define as a transitional moment in modern American poetics. While McHale describes the long poem as a "modernist invention" (2), he also identifies several distinctive postmodernist traits in long poems after 1960. Modernist long poems almost uniformly reject chronological approaches to narrative, for instance, whereas postmodernist poets create sustained stories (McHale 3). Keller suggests, in addition, that modernist long poems rely upon collage techniques, while mid-twentieth-century works engage with contemporary social issues and return to narrative ("Twentieth-Century" 536–7). In keeping with these concerns, the narrative voice of *Ariel* illuminates several issues that are central to Plath's poetics: ambivalence toward motherhood's duties, anxiety about artistic creation, personal betrayal, and evolving views of the material world. Plath also sustains a thematic continuity throughout her sequence by alternately addressing and posing challenges to the lyric object. While her work's voice does not attain the narrative continuity of a named character like Crow, it holds its own advantages: it draws our attention to tropes that recur across poetic situations, and it imagines the diverse fates of the poems' subjects. Crow, on the other hand, emerges from the fallout of humanity's worst decisions in order to comment on the moral ambivalence that defines us. The images that accompany his birth seem to signal that destiny has set him apart, and he is able to communicate directly with his chosen deity, but no matter how much knowledge he takes in, he is unable to resist his basest impulses toward ruin. He examines the settings into which he has emerged and evaluates the problems that exist therein, yet often forestalls any sort of ethical position in favor of hedonistic abandon.

Both Plath and Hughes were familiar with several examples of Western long poems, such as the ancient Greek epic tales of *The Iliad* and *The Odyssey* (eighth century BCE) and historical sagas like *Beowulf* (c. 975). These pieces are intended to record and celebrate periods of particular national significance, in part through epic catalogues. Early modern long poems extend these conventions through political allegory, as in Dante Alighieri's *The Divine Comedy* (1320) and Edmund Spenser's *The Faerie Queen* (1596); religious contemplation, as in John Milton's *Paradise Lost* (1674); and symbolic fiction, as in Sir

Philip Sidney's *Astrophil and Stella* (*c.* 1580), among other narrative devices. Such devices persist through the nineteenth century in long poems as diverse as William Wordsworth's *The Prelude* (1850), Henry Wadsworth Longfellow's *The Song of Hiawatha* (1855), Elizabeth Barrett Browning's *Aurora Leigh* (1856), and Walt Whitman's *Song of Myself* (1892). Keller and McHale understand the period to which Plath's and Hughes's work belongs as reflecting some major shifts in the long poem's provenance. Though modernist poets like T. S. Eliot, Ezra Pound, Hart Crane, H. D., and William Carlos Williams attempted to establish lasting literary reputations by writing epic poems that diverged from their classical precedents through, for instance, achronological and fragmented narration, references to earlier histories as metaphors for current social conditions, revisions of ancient stories, and collages of cultural allusions, the genre remains fluid throughout the late twentieth and twenty-first centuries.

Plath and Hughes contributed to the more recent phases of this complex history by experimenting with loose narrative organizations and exploiting the symbolic resonance of recurring images and rhetorics in their work from the 1960s. Each of them produced, as a result, a sequence of narratively and formally related pieces that rewards interpretation as a single long work. Both sequences were published in the mid-twentieth century, during the period that Keller identifies as centered on autobiography, aesthetic periodization, and resistance to social norms ("Twentieth-Century" 537). Plath left behind a final arrangement of *Ariel* when she died in 1963, and Hughes published his *Crow* sequence in several volumes between 1967 and 1971. The close chronological appearance of these two collections and their engagement with several common themes suggest that clear points of contact exist between them.

## A STAGE IN THE CAREER: COMPOSING THE SEQUENCE

The factors that motivated first *Ariel* and then the *Crow* poems differ significantly. Plath sought to create a collection that would showcase her mature compositional skills and her poetic persona's triumph over a series of interrelated social and ideological problems. *Ariel* explores the challenges of motherhood, public presentations of femininity and womanhood, the role that personal histories play in shaping poetic metaphor, ambivalent attitudes toward romantic partnership, and the formation of an autonomous creative self. Critics have singled out several of the collection's individual poems as particularly evocative of these concerns, including "Morning Song," "The Rabbit Catcher," "Lady Lazarus," "Daddy," and the four concluding bee poems. Both Lynda K. Bundtzen and Erica Wagner devote considerable space to assessing these pieces' significance within the overall scope of *Ariel*, while Heather Clark, Judith Kroll, Diane Middlebrook, Marjorie Perloff, Jacqueline Rose, and Sue Vice identify the insights that individual poems provide into Plath's emotions, experiences, or professional goals.[1] The themes that these poems trace recur throughout several of the volume's other poems as well. "Morning Song" describes a mix of uncertainty about early parenthood and wonder at its strange beauty that is echoed in "Nick and the Candlestick" and "You're"; the almost satirical rage and

---

[1] See Clark, *The Grief of Influence*; Kroll, *Chapters in a Mythology*; Middlebrook, *Her Husband*; Perloff, "The Two *Ariels*: The (Re)Making of the Sylvia Plath Canon"; Rose, *The Haunting of Sylvia Plath*; and Vice, "Sylvia Plath: *Ariel*."

condemnation that color "The Rabbit Catcher," "Lady Lazarus," and "Daddy" recur in "A Secret," "The Other," "The Courage of Shutting-Up," and "The Rival." "The Bee Meeting," "The Arrival of the Bee Box," "Stings," and "Wintering" position the bees' various metaphorical connotations in relation to significant poetic landscapes. Like the settings of "Ariel," "Stopped Dead," "Berck-Plage," and "The Moon and the Yew Tree," the bees' homes contain identifiable landmarks and illuminate some of the inspirations for Plath's poetics. These oft-cited poems point readers toward some of the major tropes, themes, and even individual word choices that recur throughout Plath's work. The book's sequential nature emerges not just through these familiar elements, however, but also in its repeated resistance to the strictures of midcentury American domestic life and in its experiments with poetic form. Here she carefully defines several strategies for achieving narrative cohesion in concert with arguments on behalf of social transformation.

Hughes formulates a looser narrative coherence in the Crow sequence, in part because it includes previously unpublished pieces that appear only in his *Collected Poems* (2005) as well as poems from five different collections: *Four Crow Poems* (1970), *A Few Crows* (1970), *Crow: From the Life and Songs of the Crow* (1970), *Crow Wakes* (1971), and *Poems: Ruth Fainlight, Ted Hughes, Alan Sillitoe* (1971). He achieves a sense of character evolution and overall argument across the poems through Crow's psychological traits and his commentary on various social issues. American artist Leonard Baskin had contacted Hughes just a few weeks after Plath's death to commission a poem that would accompany one of Baskin's crow sketches. Hughes refused initially but began serious work on the collection by the mid-1960s, at roughly the same time that his edition of *Ariel* was published in London. He first described Crow's origin as the intention "just to write his songs, the songs that a Crow would sing. In other words, songs with no music whatsoever, in a super-simple and a super-ugly language which would in a way shed everything except just what he wanted to say without any other consideration" (Faas 208). In the poems that resulted, Crow gives voice to the writer's potential failures and his inspirations.

Hughes's career lasted for thirty-five years after Plath's death; he published twenty-five more collections of poetry in addition to numerous other writings. His interest in the natural attributes of the English countryside, which he had first explored in *The Hawk in the Rain* (1957) and *Lupercal* (1960), culminated in the commitment to ecocriticism and activism that unites the poems of *River* (1983). Terry Gifford notes that "[i]n the same year as the publication of *River* Hughes contributed to a book titled *West Country Fly Fishing* (1983), an overview of the history of the fishery on two Devon rivers, the Taw and the Torridge" (84). His attention to this particular region reflects his boyhood experiences and points to his increasing concern for the rivers' water quality (Gifford 85). Hughes worked throughout his career to commemorate and improve his beloved English landscapes, in both literary and real-world forums. The two periods after 1963 in which Hughes digresses significantly from this trajectory are the late 1990s, when he was revising and compiling *Birthday Letters* (1998) and *Howls and Whispers* (1998), and the second half of the 1960s, when he was composing the Crow sequence. The Crow poems are an interruption of sorts, not a culmination or an endpoint but a pause for ontological reflection.

Plath's formal techniques and thematic concerns would have continued to evolve beyond the strategies she uses in *Ariel*; yet, the poems' complex structures and subtle condemnations of ordinary domesticity already align the collection with other writers' later works. Reading it as a long poem reveals Plath's key contribution to this genre in particular. Lynn Keller labels the long poem "a generic hybrid" that encompasses diverse methodologies (*Forms of Expansion* 2–3). Plath's work, for instance, contains elements of both the lyric sequence and twentieth-century experimentalism. Keller defines the lyric sequence as a group of poems that "treat narrower portions of a culture, more confined history, or more inward perspectives" than do traditional epics. Experimental long poems, on the other hand, attempt to "deliberately disrupt conventions of ordinary and poetic language" (*Forms of Expansion* 5–6). While Plath's *Ariel* poems do not rely upon the mechanically generative techniques of Oulipo writers or experiment with the rift between sound and meaning, as in some Language poetry, she does employ techniques that help her poems to resist narrative continuity and conventional denotation. At the same time, she expands the collection's social relevance by fragmenting its familiar domestic narratives and by curating a poetic vocabulary whose terms gain new significance through iconoclastic usage. A consistent narrative voice—by turns joyful, sarcastic, analytical, reflective, and outraged—ties the *Ariel* poems together. As in Hughes's Crow poems, the individual pieces' intent varies, but they illustrate experiences, emotions, and desires that emerge from the same psyche.

## "IF THE MOON SMILED": THE VOICES OF *ARIEL*

Several expressive modes shape the narrative of the *Ariel* poems, three of which best articulate the speaker's varying motivations and concerns. In "Nick and the Candlestick" and "You're," the narrative examines anxiety about the responsibilities of family life alongside the satisfying fact of creation. Poems like "A Secret," "The Other," "The Courage of Shutting-Up," and "The Rival" convey anger at personal betrayal but also celebrate the accomplishment of laying painful truths open to public view. Finally, "Ariel," "Stopped Dead," "Berck-Plage," and "The Moon and the Yew Tree" illustrate some of the natural landscapes in which Plath's narrative is situated; their disjunctive images, repeated lines and words, and uncommon vocabulary function as metonyms for her radical refashioning of the everyday world. These narrative threads work together to provide *Ariel* with thematic continuity and an experimental approach to the lyric sequence. As Susan Stanford Friedman suggests, Plath refuses the largely masculinist tradition of the long poem by participating in "an oppositional writing and reading process" (18); the new compositional strategies she develops in *Ariel* enable her to redefine the long poem on her own terms.

Plath centers one of *Ariel*'s narratives on the close analogies between motherhood and writerly creation. The opening and closing lines of "Nick and the Candlestick" recall the beginning of "Morning Song" by connecting the positive sentiments generated by the child's presence to the objects that populate the speaker's rooms. Like the "fat gold watch" that opens the first *Ariel* poem (*AR* 5), the "waxy stalacmites" of "Nick" evoke the tactile elements of the mother-child relationship (*AR* 47). The neologism here represents a melding of "stalagmite" and "stalactite," a creative choice that Plath consciously made (*The Other Sylvia Plath* 25–6), which suggests that the parent's constant fatigue clouds the outlines of ordinary language while the trappings of family life wall her in. Plath describes the child's surroundings as an enclosure made up of natural stone and earth, its properties sharp to the touch but also protective; the contexts that inspired the poem may include "the effects of environmental poisoning" ("*Ariel* and Other Poems" 117) and "impending atomic catastrophe" (*Cambridge Introduction* 55). The poem's speaker expresses pain over the isolation she shares with her child, perhaps even a "maternal ambivalence" about their situation (Vice 507), but she also cherishes the space they have created. While the beginning of the poem emphasizes the work she must do to keep her child safe, the final stanza offers a succinct assessment of Nick's importance: "You are the baby in the barn," she concludes, linking his presence to much older mythologies of birth and salvation (*AR* 48).

Plath extends this assessment of the child's qualities in "You're," the earliest *Ariel* poem she composed (*A Critical Study* 67), whose title serves as the assumed subject of the poem's twelve individual sentences. This piece focuses on the baby's physical traits, often likened to those of an animal, rather than on his surroundings, and celebrates the feelings of anticipation that signal his arrival. As in much of her earlier work, Plath creates surrealist adjective-noun pairs as a means of capturing the baby's unique attributes. He is a "traveled prawn" who is as fidgety as a "creel of eels"; these physical qualities seem almost inhuman as the speaker waits for a being whose appearance she cannot control or predict. Yet the baby's existence is finally confirmed as completely positive: he is a new beginning with every possibility for joy, a "clean slate, with your own face on" (*AR* 77). Both "Nick and the Candlestick" and "You're" suggest an analogy between motherhood and artistic creativity—the relationship between these two types of creation points to the poems' function as a kind of ars poetica within Plath's oeuvre. At the same time the startling associations that the speaker imagines and her uncertainty reiterate the anxiety that filters through "Morning Song."

In contrast to the visions of creation that "Nick and the Candlestick" and "You're" advance, "The Rabbit Catcher," "Lady Lazarus," and "Daddy" rank among the most widely discussed *Ariel* poems because of their clear autobiographical roots. Plath wrote all three poems in 1962, the first just after she learned of Hughes's affair with Assia Wevill in May and the latter two during October's interlude of frenzied activity.[2] Many readers are familiar with the story of Plath's separation from Hughes, her difficulties in coping with two small children alone at Court Green, and the illnesses that all three suffered during the fall of 1962. The poems' narrative voice is motivated not by biographical details, however, but by the speaker's desire to resist conventional domesticity, which results in antagonism toward her subjects and a literal fragmentation of the narrated lines. Plath frequently repeats words, adds exclamation points and question marks for emphasis, interrupts narrative arcs with catalogues, employs apostrophe to address living persons rather than absent ones, and locates images that recur in earlier poems within new, unfamiliar contexts. In "The Rival," for instance, she compares the title subject to the moon, suggesting that this body does not represent peaceful serenity or blank indifference, as in "Barren Woman" or "The Moon and the Yew Tree," but rather deadly power: "beautiful, but annihilating" (*AR* 73). That same image echoes through "The Other," in "[o] moon-glow, o sick one" (*AR* 41), but this piece's sparser lines and regular questions underline the speaker's intention to recount misdeeds dispassionately, even if the subject of her anger remains ambiguous (*A Critical Study* 92–3). The poem's conclusion—"[y]ou smile. / No, it is not fatal" (*AR* 42)—suggests that she has achieved a distance from these painful events.

Both "A Secret" and "The Courage of Shutting-Up" also rely upon recontextualized images from Plath's oeuvre, truncated narrative arcs, and varying expressive modes. To achieve an analytical voice, she incorporates repetition and catalogue as well. In addition to the "intense" rhyming words that recur in each stanza (*Cambridge Introduction* 64), "A Secret" includes a dialogue about a metaphorical entity locked in a drawer that is breathing and giving off a rank scent; its escape produces "[a] stampede, a stampede" (*AR* 22).

---

[2]The volume also contains several other pieces that flesh out this compositional period, including "A Secret," "The Other," "The Courage of Shutting-Up," and "The Rival."

These repetitions allow Plath to recreate the impact that the story's emotions have on its participants and to describe its material elements. Similarly, in "The Courage of Shutting-Up," she repeats color words—pink, black, silver, blue, purple, white—and body parts to indicate the real cost of suppressing the truth; for Plath, that cost echoes Philomel's story, in which she avenges the physical violations she has suffered by speaking in "the language of the body" (*Cambridge Introduction* 68). Simple repetitions like "the eyes, the eyes, the eyes?" (*AR* 45) draw the reader's attention to the horror and fear that accompany secrets. The narrative that Plath conveys in these four poems centers on betrayal and revelation, just as in her other 1962 poems. The voice that she cultivates here, however, pares down the story. The narrator's betrayals fuel not just rage but also a drive to separate herself from her problems and to focus, instead, on new acts of invention.

The third narrative strand that draws together the *Ariel* poems manifests in the poetic landscapes that serve as metonyms for Plath's writing goals and inspirations. "Berck-Plage," which links a French beach that once housed a veterans' hospital to the slow death of Plath's and Hughes's neighbor in Devon (Hughes "Notes," *CP* 293), is set at the seaside, in a neighbor's living room, and in a graveyard. Sandra M. Gilbert describes the beach itself as "flat and vast in all directions," with a "damper, the concrete bunkers, the hospitals, and the tubular steel wheelchairs glittering in the sun," as well as "the rickety wooden *cabines* in a rainbow of pastels that serve as private bathhouses," much as they did in Plath's time ("On the Beach with Sylvia Plath" 122). These familiar spaces echo through Plath's earlier work as well, in references to her childhood home and her father's premature death. The dead man in "Berck-Plage" evokes both distaste and sadness in the speaker, while the priest's confident voice, steady step, and "black boot," the "hearse of a dead foot" (*AR* 50), recall images of her father from "Daddy" and "Electra on Azalea Path." These settings represent familiar domesticity even as the overlaid narrative of Percy Key's death evokes the speaker's struggle to resist the roles she has often played. The volume's title poem, inspired by a horse Plath rode in Devonshire (Hughes "Notes," *CP* 294), again trims the setting's narrative and description to a few concentrated details. The reader catches glimpses of the horse's running body, the wind moving through the speaker's hair, and the purposeful energy that the ride creates. The poem's opening "substanceless blue / Pour of tor and distances" (*AR* 33) gains focus and momentum by the end, as the speaker imagines herself, after a breathless ride, an arrow hurtling into "the cauldron of morning" (*AR* 34); the ride suggests both the joy of bodily energy and the possibility of "self-immolation" ("*Ariel* and *Other Poems*" 115). A similarly ambiguous energy animates the setting of "Stopped Dead," though this piece is driven by antipathy toward the speaker's companions rather than by the solitary experience that inspired the "active version of feminine creation" found in "Ariel" (*The Grief of Influence* 153). Inspired by Plath's memories of Hughes's uncle Walter Farrar (F. Hughes "Forward," *AR* xvi), "Stopped Dead" portrays a vague European landscape. The speaker characterizes the land around her suddenly stopped car only as "violent," with "a goddam baby screaming off somewhere." Plath suggests that this irritation arises from the predictable callousness of the country's citizens and expresses bemusement over the uncle's dull everyday existence, a microcosm for society's general indifference toward art. The poetic narrator's strategy for escaping her own entrapment in the situation recalls the fantastical ending of "Lady Lazarus"; she will walk away from this ordinary life "[a]nd live in Gibraltar on air, on air" (*AR* 43). Like the earlier piece's narrator, too, she locates her life's motivation in her ability to create independently.

Plath also employs several compositional techniques that help to fragment the poetic narrative in "The Moon and the Yew Tree." This portrait of the moon, first written as an exercise set by Hughes (Stevenson 229; *A Critical Study* 46), expands the terms of its earlier appearances to include an opaque yet faithful entity that watches over the speaker, showing her love but not mercy. Associated with the color blue, coldness, and baldness—all familiar traits within Plath's oeuvre—the moon "drags the sea after it like a dark crime" and always sits directly above the yew tree. The yew, in turn, points the viewer's gaze upward toward the moon, but "the message of the yew tree is blackness—blackness and silence" (*AR* 65), rather than a gesture of hope or solidarity. In this twenty-eight-line poem, the words "cold," "blue," "black," "moon," and "tree" repeat several times to indicate the obsessive nature of the narrative voice. Plath intensifies this compulsive tone by compiling the poem from several short sentences, often two per line, rather than fewer long ones. The caesuras that result lend the poem a sense of urgency without relief.

The landscapes that these poems depict—the French seaside, a living room, a moor at sunrise, an anonymous European roadside, and a church graveyard—reveal some key preoccupations of Plath's poetics. These sites for self-reflection allow her to showcase distinctive compositional strategies; the poems' repeated lines, interjections, recurring words, and moments of self-referentiality disrupt the narratives she had initially established and compel the reader to enter into new scenes. Similar efforts to re-envision the old and familiar unite Plath's narratives of motherhood and betrayal as well. Forced into uncomfortable or even hostile situations, her poetic speaker responds by reimagining the purpose that her surroundings serve and by looking ahead to new possibilities for self-expression.

## CROW AT BIRTH, IN THE WORLD, AT REST

The initial installment in Hughes's own lyric sequence appeared just a few years after the first UK edition of *Ariel*. He wrote more than a hundred Crow poems between the mid-1960s and the early 1970s; many of them appear in his *Collected Poems*, but several more unpublished and uncollected pieces can be found in the Hughes Papers at Emory University (Brandes 513). He also prepared the ground for Crow's appearance in a few poems that he wrote before compiling the five dedicated collections. These early forays into Crow's world include "Three Legends," which marks the first moment when "Crow blinked at the world" (*TH:CP* 191); "Crowquill," in which the titular object draws a connection between the act of writing and the cycles of the natural world: "The feather is still falling" (*TH:CP* 198); and "Crow's Feast," which recounts Crow's brazen scavenging and concludes, in his voice, that "'[e]verything God does not want is mine'" (*TH:CP* 200). Hughes focused on the Crow series almost exclusively once he had established these themes: origins, creation, and looting. In conversation with Ekbert Faas, he notes that the poems developed so quickly that they were "a shock to write" (207).

Critics have formulated several hypotheses about Crow's nature. Rand Brandes describes him as "what has been written out of the Bible," a "poetic poltergeist, a supernatural 'character' in a cosmic psycho-drama," a "fusion of shamanistic and mythic figures from around the globe," an "epic hero," and an "everyman" (514). Jonathan Bate points out that Hughes drew upon trickster figures from several different world mythologies in compiling the character; Crow "has a kind of tragic joy, is 'repetitive and indestructible,' a 'demon of phallic energy'" who "makes fatal mistakes, indulges tragic flaws," but always "'rattles along on biological glee'" (289–90). Neil Roberts characterizes the series simply as "an epic folk-tale" (79). The poems reflect and react to the unimaginable pain Hughes endured during this period, after not only Plath's death but also the deaths of Wevill and their daughter Shura in 1969; yet, the mythologies they evoke recur throughout Hughes's oeuvre. The character of Crow was inspired in part by the Irish mythological figure of Morrigna, the Celtic goddess of war and destruction who comprises three related figures: Macha, the Crow; Morrigan, the battle goddess; and Badbh, the battle Crow (Brandes 515). These mythological precedents position Crow as a critic of both Christian and masculinist traditions (Brandes 520–1). Because crows are scavengers by nature, the poems depict Crow picking his subjects out of the detritus of modern Western society, chewing up and digesting some topics while discarding or defiling others. The voice that he employs throughout this process includes elements of satire, reflection, condemnation, celebration, and anger, but Hughes sustains it through Crow's consistent focus on the world's hypocrisy and his attempts to learn something from the trash he finds. The lyric sequence that Crow inhabits traces his lifespan, from creation through dissolution, by following his evolving perspective on the purpose that humankind might serve.

Hughes's Crow poems fall into four rough categories that follow the trajectory of the character's life: origin poems, poems that depict his scavenging efforts, poems in which he gains new knowledge about the human world, and poems about his own—or the world's—end. In several of the origin poems, for instance, Hughes links Crow's physical birth to the world's fundamental nature but underscores the fact that his protagonist's sacred beginnings do not preclude repeated acts of defiance or blasphemy. In "Crow's First Lesson," Crow responds to God's attempts to teach him speech with physical gasps and vomiting, but no words. However, his expectorations produce several animals that populate the earth and finally "Man's bodiless prodigious head," which immediately grapples with woman as if anticipating the full propagation of the human race (*TH:CP* 211). "Crow Tyrannosaurus" depicts the moment when "Creation quaked voices" (*TH:CP* 214); Crow responds by focusing on signs of predation and death rather than on new beginnings. Even his efforts to move away from his own instincts in this poem result in more violence: "Weeping he walked and stabbed" (*TH:CP* 215). Only in "The Door" does Hughes suggest a gentler origin for Crow. Describing the "earth's plants" and animals as body parts metonymic of the body politic, he notes that Crow comes flying through "a doorway in the wall," an "eye's pupil," in order to find a permanent home (*TH:CP* 220). Thus Hughes intimates that Crow witnessed the beginnings of human creation; yet, he would rather obfuscate the world's problems or feed on it than witness its beauty. His voice provides commentary in these poems but does not contribute to his new home's value or artistry.

The majority of the Crow poems center on his life's work, which alternates between scavenging for scraps and learning about potential life philosophies. The voice that Hughes creates for Crow in these poems combines objective assessments of his environment with a celebratory, self-indulgent glee. In some instances, he stands apart from the reader, his actions couched in third-person narration, while in others he recounts his adventures directly, often in an anaphoric style. In one example of the third-person perspective, Hughes describes Crow as the ruler of a city made of bones; the title "King of Carrion," earned because of his tendency to hoard offal, leaves him with an "empty world" in which he is left to "reign over silence" (*TH:CP* 209). Crow's insatiable desire for rotting flesh recurs in several other scavenging poems. It eclipses even the world's creator, who sleeps through his many questions about the purpose of existence in "Crow Communes"; here he sees God's presence as "a great carcase," from which he "tore off a mouthful and swallowed" (*TH:CP* 224). This interaction, which Keith Sagar describes as "an unholy parody" of religious communion (117), improves Crow's strength and powers of cognition, yet also leaves him feeling dismayed at his own behavior. When he narrates his observations, Crow employs distinctive poetic devices, as in "Crow's Undersong," which describes his female subject in alternately positive and negative terms. Hughes uses anaphora to relate her actions, which reflect both Crow's desire for her and his disgust with humanity: the poem starts by noting that "she cannot come all the way" but finally concludes, after sixteen anaphoric statements, that "If there had been no hope she would not have come" (*TH:CP* 237). Similarly, in "Crow and the Birds," Hughes describes Crow's poetic situation through a series of sentence fragments that begin with "When" or "And." These partial statements, which juxtapose various birds' movements through the natural world to the detritus that humans leave behind, conclude with a final image of Crow's dissolution, as he "spraddled head-down in the beach-garbage, guzzling a dropped ice-cream" (*TH:CP* 210). Though several of these moments of scavenging also hint at Crow's interest in worldly qualities that surpass the merely physical, he takes pleasure here in self-indulgence and immorality.

Hughes identifies a second stage in Crow's maturation in several poems that portray genuine learning. These pieces also lay the groundwork for Hughes's observations about a potential theory of poetic creation, or *ars poetica*, later in the sequence. In both "Crow's Theology" and "Crow's Vanity," for example, Crow comes to understand the effects of his actions. "Crow's Vanity" highlights the contrast between the "civilizations towers gardens" around Crow and the fog that obscures his view simply because "he was breathing too heavy" (*TH:CP* 230). This insight into the relationship between his decisions and the state of the world exists in "Crow's Theology" as well. Here he contemplates God's love for him, wondering at the same time "what / Loved the stones and spoke stone?" (*TH:CP* 227). Crow's recognition that God and other creatures exist apart from him signals a key stage in his evolution toward moral culpability, one reflected in his questions and repeated phrases. Two key examples of this type of education, "Carnival" and "Examination at the Womb-Door," describe in third person narration the relationships that Crow sees between his actions and the changing shape of human society. While he continues to act out violently in "Carnival," he also sees that his bodily fluids have decorated both "Schopenhauer's spectacle case" and "Beethoven's score" (*TH:CP* 216): his choices contribute to the artifacts that humans value. When interrogated in "Examination at the Womb-Door" about his physical attributes and the sources of his disregard for human existence, he answers "*Death*" to every question but is rebuked at the end when, responding to a question about "who is stronger than death," he answers, "[*m*]*e, evidently*" (*TH:CP* 218–19; italics in original). Crow offers no answer to the reproach he receives; rather, he allows the poem to conclude, his silence suggesting that he has taken the correction to heart.

The voice that narrates the poems about the end of Crow's life relies upon simple statements, repetitions, and expanded spacing to suggest that he self-destructs slowly but inevitably. Through these devices Hughes indicates, perhaps, that the responsibility for Creation—rather than the desire merely to participate in acts of creation—is more than Crow can ultimately bear. "Crow Blacker than Ever" describes a falling-out between man and God that Crow tries to mend, resulting not in harmony but in Crow "[c]rying: 'This is my Creation'" and "Flying the black flag of himself" (*TH:CP* 244). Hughes suggests in this piece and in "Crow's Song of Himself" that even Crow's most laudable efforts do not change his essential nature. God punishes Crow in eight different ways in the latter poem, producing something unique and valuable each time, but when God gives up on trying to reform him, Hughes relates, "Crow stropped his beak and started in on the two thieves" (*TH:CP* 247). In each case, he takes over his supposed deity's role but attempts destruction rather than any real creation. Crow's resistance to reformation molds him into an immovable being around whom societies rise and fall, one who is, as in "The Contender," "[g]rinning into the black / Into the ringing nothing" (*TH:CP* 268). The final collected Crow poem, "Crow the Just," suggests that, rather than functioning as a trickster figure who acts on behalf of the world, Crow makes decisions primarily for himself. "This is how he kept his conscience so pure," Hughes notes, "[h]e was black" (*TH:CP* 272). The matter-of-fact voice of the Crow poems thus ties his existence to the origins of the world. Yet the sequence concludes without identifying any kind of consistent drive toward redemption in him. In suggesting that Crow cannot or will not change, Hughes also makes a broader commentary on human nature. Like Plath's narrator, Crow attempts to reimagine or remake his physical surroundings, but the result is almost always chaos. The sequence reflects Hughes's despair during this nadir in his life, but it also constitutes an experimental approach to composition that enriches his later work. Crow's repeated attempts to assume control over his world, and his consistent failure to surmount his own shortcomings, serve as a metaphor for the artist's struggle to achieve innovative forms of expression. Read as a continuous long poem, the Crow pieces represent a necessary stage in Hughes's poetics; their blunt critiques and caustic imagery prepare the ground for his later environmental work and for the personal revelations of *Birthday Letters*. The sequence also introduces his readers to the ideas about the purpose of poetic composition that Hughes continued to develop across his career.

## UNANTICIPATED CONVERSATIONS

*Ariel*'s poems assess Plath's contemporary contexts as writer, mother, public intellectual, and estranged spouse, while the Crow poems sometimes dismiss the new experiences that its title character undertakes as evidence only of the world's corruption. This occasional thematic disjunction is echoed in the two sequences' narrative voices. Plath's varying speakers, concerned at different times with the demands of motherhood, personal betrayals, and the metaphorical potential of the world itself, offer her readers immediate social engagement; Hughes's Crow makes an argument that evolves over the course of the sequence about his often cataclysmic mistakes, which function as metonyms of the general failings that define Western civilization. Yet both of these perspectives incorporate the poetic innovations of the mid-twentieth century through the experimental rhetoric in which their speakers' ideas are couched, including Plath's repetitions and surrealistic juxtapositions, and the scatological imagery and frequent use of dialogue that define Crow's character. At the same time, though Crow's story seems to gesture toward the fate of the human world as a whole, and his despair often reflects the failings that he witnesses around him, he too exists within a relatively circumscribed environment, just as *Ariel*'s narrator does. Their narratives also explore the ways in which not only personal obstacles but also broad social concerns serve as metaphors for the complexities of artistic creation. Plath and Hughes shared this interest throughout their careers; as Heather Clark points out, they "could not help borrowing images, cadences, and even words" from one another's work (*The Grief of Influence* 110). In the poems' limited narrative focus and departure from conventional poetic techniques, coupled with the thematic coincidences that filter through Hughes's and Plath's work from this period, the two sequences make a significant contribution to the history of the modern long poem.

# CHAPTER SIXTEEN

# "Not Mrs. Hughes and Mrs. Sillitoe": Sylvia Plath and Ruth Fainlight in the 1960s

HEATHER CLARK

Sylvia Plath has often been twinned with Anne Sexton, whom she met in Robert Lowell's 1959 creative writing seminar in Boston, and whose work elicited Plath's admiration and jealousy. Sexton's poetry, as many critics have observed, was a major influence on Plath.[1] The poets' triple martini afternoons at the Boston Ritz are now legend, but according to Sexton herself, she and Plath never became close. The poem "Sylvia's Death," Sexton wrote in 1966, "makes everyone think I knew her well, when I only knew her death well" ("The Barfly Ought to Sing" 92). Less storied but equally important is Plath's literary friendship with Ruth Fainlight. Like Plath, Fainlight was an American of Eastern European heritage married to a famous writer from the North of England; a devotee of Robert Graves; and a poet who hoped to combine writing and motherhood. This friendship was, for both women, a source of creative and emotional support, and had consequences for Plath's art. Yet it has received little scholarly attention.

Plath had already published a volume of poetry and achieved recognition within the British literary establishment when she met Fainlight in the spring of 1961. Though Fainlight had published in prestigious magazines, she would not publish her first collection, *Cages*, until 1963. This fact, perhaps combined with her Jewishness, meant that Plath did not see Fainlight as a doppelgänger and potential rival as she did American Cambridge contemporaries like Jane Baltzell and Janet Burroway. Fainlight earned Plath's trust and admiration in a way few other literary women had; she was the only woman poet to whom Plath ever grew close.

Plath came to know Fainlight at a time in her life when she turned increasingly to the theme of motherhood in her poetry. Plath was one of the first poets in English to write about childbirth, miscarriage, abortion, postpartum anxiety, and maternal ambivalence. Her poetry of motherhood laid the groundwork for future women poets to approach a subject whose terrors and joys were not adequately—let alone authentically— reflected in postwar poetry. The lived experience and artistic ramifications of motherhood and

---

[1] See, for example, Cam.

miscarriage were things Plath discussed with just one literary friend: Ruth Fainlight. Fainlight offered Plath support and a sounding board; Fainlight's poem, "Sapphic Moon," influenced Plath's "Elm" and "Three Women"—a debt that, until now, has remained unacknowledged. Although Fainlight's name is not usually invoked as an influence on *Ariel*, her role in Plath's life and work during the early 1960s deserves deeper critical consideration.

During the first week of February 1961, Sylvia Plath suffered a miscarriage. Normally Plath turned to her writing as a way of restoring order, but miscarriage was a taboo subject in the 1960s—or at least, as Fainlight remembered, "unseemly" (Fainlight Interview). Even the word "pregnant" was considered too indelicate for American network television in the 1950s. There was no female elegiac tradition mourning the unborn—an astonishing omission from the literary canon given that around a quarter of all pregnancies end in miscarriage.

When Plath began writing her elegy for her lost baby, "Parliament Hill Fields," completed on February 11, 1961, she was writing in uncharted territory, giving voice to an experience shared secretly by millions of women. In June 1961, she would read "Parliament Hill Fields" on the BBC. She began with a short introduction that did not obscure the poem's devastating subject: the speaker is caught, Plath says,

> between the grief caused by the loss of a child and the joy aroused by the knowledge of an only child safe at home. Gradually the first images of blankness and absence give way to images of convalescence and healing as the woman turns, a bit stiffly, and with difficulty, from her sense of bereavement to the vital and demanding part of her world which still survives.
>
> (*Spoken Word* audio recording)

Rarely was miscarriage given such a public forum. "Your absence is inconspicuous; / Nobody can tell what I lack," Plath read. "I suppose it's pointless to think of you at all. / Already your doll grip lets go" (*CP* 152).

This was not the first poem in which Plath had bravely flouted the taboos of maternity. Right from the start, Plath's poems of pregnancy and motherhood reflected as much anxiety and ambivalence as they did happiness. Her freewheeling 1959 poem, "Metaphors," about pregnancy ("I'm a riddle in nine syllables" [*CP* 116]), is deceptively lighthearted. The pregnant woman, Plath writes, is "a means, a stage, a cow in calf" (*CP* 116). These metaphors, which come near the poem's end, suggest a loss of selfhood; the woman has become breeding stock. The last line depicts a speaker who has ruefully "[b]oarded the train there's no getting off" (*CP* 116). During the autumn of 1959, when Plath was pregnant with her daughter Frieda, she wrote "The Manor Garden" at Yaddo. The poem is a dark twist on Yeats's beneficent "A Prayer for my Daughter" (211–14). Plath hopes to bestow a blessing but she cannot deny the forces that threaten her baby:

> The fountains are dry and the roses over.
> Incense of death. Your day approaches.
> [...]
> You inherit white heather, a bee's wing,
> Two suicides, the family wolves,
> Hours of blankness.
>
> (*CP* 125)

Though the poem is set in Yaddo's garden, here it is the lifeless garden of Plath's late poem "Edge," inhabited by "blue mist" "dragging the lake," crows, worms, and "broken flutings" (*CP* 125). "The Manor Garden" is the antithesis of the sentimental feminine homily, offering neither comfort nor blessing to the unborn child. Another pregnancy poem, "You're" (1960), is giddy at times—the baby is like "[a] creel of eels, all ripples. / Jumpy as a Mexican bean" (*CP* 141). Yet the baby is also "moon-skulled," "[m]ute," "[v]ague as fog" (*CP* 141). The speaker grasps at buoyancy but cannot elide the undercurrent of fear that presses at her from another angle.

After Frieda was born in April 1960, Plath wrote frequently to others about her delirious love for her daughter. But the poems she wrote during the summer of 1960 were filled with images of deformity, numbness, sterility, and terror. Gone were the playful invocations of "You're"—"[o] high-riser, my little loaf" (*CP* 141). Instead, there is "Stillborn." The grim title refers not to a baby, but to poems that refused to come to life:

O I cannot understand what happened to them!
They are proper in shape and number and every part.
They sit so nicely in the pickling fluid!
They smile and smile and smile and smile at me.
And still the lungs won't fill and the heart won't start. (*CP* 142)

Plath continues, in the final stanza, "they are dead, and their mother near dead with distraction, / And they stupidly stare, and do not speak of her." (*CP* 142)

"Morning Song," which Plath wrote in February 1961 about a week after "Parliament Hill Fields," celebrates her living child. The poem, with its memorable first line, "[l]ove set you going like a fat gold watch," is joyful in places: the living baby's "clear vowels rise like balloons" (*CP* 156, 157). Yet the poem is not sentimental. Plath treats the pious culture of motherhood ironically when she writes, "[o]ne cry, and I stumble from bed, cow-heavy and floral / In my Victorian nightgown" (*CP* 157). As in Plath's other poems of motherhood, the speaker registers unease with her massive new responsibility:

I'm no more your mother
Than the cloud that distills a mirror to reflect its own slow
Effacement at the wind's hand.

(*CP* 157)

The stars outside are "dull" (*CP* 157). By courageously giving voice to maternal ambivalence and miscarriage in her art, Plath rejected the limits imposed upon women's dialogue about the difficulties of pregnancy, childbirth, and motherhood. In doing so, she suggested that such anxieties and ambivalences were not pathological. It was a view her new friend Ruth Fainlight would confirm at a crucial time in Plath's artistic, and maternal, development.

On May 31, 1961, Sylvia Plath and Ted Hughes attended the Hawthornden Prize ceremony, presided over by Cecil Day Lewis, in London. Hughes had won that year's prize, which was presented to him by the previous year's winner, Alan Sillitoe. Sillitoe was married to Ruth Fainlight, and the two literary couples took to each other immediately. Fainlight, who described herself as "a New Yorker and a Jew who had 'married out,'" was the daughter of a Ukrainian-American mother and British-Polish father who had moved to Britain at fifteen and married her first husband at eighteen ("Jane and Sylvia" 9).

She "ran away" with Sillitoe at twenty and lived with him in France and Spain for several years. In Mallorca, she became close to Graves, whom she considered her mentor. ("That was my education," Fainlight Interview.) She had been "thrilled" by the connection to Laura Riding as well. Like Plath and Hughes, she was enormously impressed by *The White Goddess*, which she called "the poet's handbook" (Fainlight Interview). Fainlight, like Plath, was an aspiring poet married to a more successful writer, who also happened to be a working-class Northerner. Sillitoe's *The Loneliness of the Long-Distance Runner* was an international bestseller that had established him, in Fainlight's word, as "a media 'star'" (Bush Interview). Fainlight thought she and Plath "were both very lucky because we had very lovely, obliging husbands": they simply assumed Hughes and Sillitoe would share the housework and childcare, and give them time to write. "What other people were doing was neither here nor there. We were young, we were artists and we thought we were different than anyone else." Although Fainlight came to believe her own career "suffered" as a result of Sillitoe's fame, she thought Plath and Hughes's poetic relationship was "exemplary" (Fainlight Interview).

Fainlight's first impression of Plath was "of a burningly ambitious and intelligent young woman trying to look like a conventional, devoted wife but not quite succeeding. There was something almost excessive about that disguise" ("Jane and Sylvia" 12).

> I empathized with her immensely because we were both in such similar situations, and it was so bizarre. We were both Americans, both married to these charismatic men from the North who were very much in the public eye, and we were nobodies. I was more of a nobody than her because she at least had a book and a child. I didn't have either[.] ... We had an enormous amount in common. And we were both suffering under the "Oh you write as well do you Mrs. Sillitoe?" She less of course. She was more assertive than me. She was very good at holding her own.
>
> (Fainlight Interview)

Fainlight recognized Plath as someone who, like her, abided by "then-current ideas of femininity" picked up in postwar America, but who also "shared profounder self-destructive traits" ("Jane and Sylvia" 9). "Sylvia tormented herself with impossible goals of domestic achievement," Fainlight said. But she herself had the same impulse: "'Whether the artist can be a young woman / is the first question'—not, please note, whether a young woman can be an artist—was the theme of much of my early poetry" ("Jane and Sylvia" 9). Fainlight recalled how she and Plath "struggled with the dichotomy of being writers' wives as well as writers, and were maimed in our separate ways" ("Jane and Sylvia" 9).

The two couples dined together at Chalcot Square or at the Sillitoes' flat in Notting Hill that summer. Fainlight remembered "heaps of books and papers" around the Hugheses' flat, Plath's bright chatter as she cleared the table, and Hughes's loving attention toward Frieda. Both seemed to her "equally, and touchingly, youthful. It was galling to have met such a congenial pair just before they left London" ("Jane and Sylvia" 12). Plath, too, would miss her new friend when she moved to Devon in September 1961, five months pregnant with her son Nicholas. She wrote to Fainlight about the lack of educated women in North Tawton: "I am very happy with Court Green, my study, the babies, but mad for someone to talk to & woefully self-pitying about our just discovering you & Alan & then moving off. The women here are much worse than the men, who at least have their work. It's like a cattery. I never knew what 'provincial' meant before" (*L2* 737). She had joked to Fainlight earlier in September that she had one study, while "Ted has 3 or 4 in case he wants a change," and asked Fainlight to visit her "in the late, grim heart of autumn" (L2 647).

When Fainlight wrote to Plath of a threatened miscarriage in the early autumn of 1961, Plath offered her support and sympathy in one of the most generous letters she wrote:

> It's difficult & in a way impertinent to tell you how very much I am wishing things to go well for you, because noone can ever really identify deeply enough with someone else's special predicament to make the words "I know how you feel" carry their full weight. But our sad & confusing experience of losing a baby last winter has made me feel much closer to the difficulties & apprehensions of childbearing & much more profoundly involved with them.
>
> (L2 658–9)

Fainlight had already suffered three previous miscarriages. Plath's support, and her willingness to recognize and acknowledge the profundity of Fainlight's loss in a culture that refused to do so, likely brought the women closer. Miscarriage was as alienating an experience as it was appalling, but Plath and Fainlight's correspondence shows they did not suffer in silence. Plath spent two nights with Fainlight in London soon after she sent this letter, in early November 1961. By then, both women were pregnant—another shared maternal experience that would have strengthened their bond.

It was around this time that Plath began a long poetic sequence about childbirth, which she wrote from December 1961 to late January or early February 1962. The sequence had different sections with variant titles: "Woman as Landscape" / "The Ninth Month" / "Waking in Winter"; "Fever in Winter" / "Fever"; and "New Year on Dartmoor." These verses, with their images of annihilation, atrocity, and shrieks, look forward to "Elm" and other *Ariel* poems.

This sequence laid the groundwork for "Three Women" that March, Plath's proto-feminist verse play eventually produced by Douglas Cleverdon and broadcast on the BBC's Third Programme on August 19 and September 13, 1962. "Three Women" was inspired by Ingmar Bergman's 1958 award-winning film, *So Close to Life*, which Plath probably saw in London in early March 1961.[2] The film is set in a maternity ward and focuses upon the experiences of three women: one who has a miscarriage early in her pregnancy; another whose full-term baby dies shortly after delivery; and an unmarried mother who considers giving up her baby. Plath probably saw Bergman's film after her own miscarriage and appendectomy-related hospital stay. But she had set off on a different direction in the spring of 1961, choosing to write *The Bell Jar*. Now, in March 1962, with her second child a little over two months old, Plath was drawn back to maternity and childbirth, subjects she could mine for dramatic potential.

Anne Stevenson has called "Three Women" "the first great poem about childbirth in the language" (240). There are no speaking roles for men, who function primarily as oppressors. "Three Women" was a turning point for Plath, who harnessed and honed the freer, more intimate voice of "The Moon and the Yew Tree" to explode female

---

[2]Plath mentioned attending a twelve-week series of Ingmar Bergman films in a February 26, 1961 letter to Aurelia (L2 582). She later told Aurelia in a June 7, 1962, letter that "Three Women" was "inspired by a Bergman film" (L2 777).

taboos surrounding miscarriage, postpartum depression, and abortion. Plath was, as Stevenson noted, inventing a new tradition. Her previous poems, with the exceptions of "The Colossus" and "Parliament Hill Fields," could not have been called feminist. But that winter Plath was preparing *The Bell Jar* for publication, with its condescending boyfriends, unsympathetic male doctors, vicious workplaces, mental hospitals, electric shocks, and sexual assaults. Prose was a better vehicle for her scathing, cynical indictment of Eisenhower's America than poetry, with its courtly requirements of rhyme and meter. Poetry's formalist grace notes had largely checked Plath's anger and resentments—until "Three Women." The play's focus on the darker aspects of maternity was nothing short of radical. (Sexton would publish "The Abortion" in 1962's *All My Pretty Ones*, yet that poem is full of self-blame.) "Three Women" opened up new poetic pathways for Plath, setting her on a course toward "Daddy" and "Lady Lazarus," where superhuman female heroines wrest control of their destinies from the patriarchy. The play stands as a bracing antidote to a subject that is still routinely sanitized and sentimentalized.

In mid-April of 1962, Plath wrote to Fainlight, congratulating her on her new son David. "Baby boys are wonderful beings & he and Nicholas should be able to coo & gurgle at each other companionably when you come down" (*L2* 761). Plath invited the family to stay at her home, Court Green, in Devon, and told Alan Sillitoe that she had an extra study where he could work. (She did not extend the same invitation to Fainlight.)

The Sillitoes arrived with baby David on May second after an eight-hour drive. Both seemed fatigued when they appeared at Court Green, but it was Fainlight's birthday, and they had brought a bottle of champagne to celebrate. During the visit, Plath and Fainlight spent hours gathering daffodils, and laid them carefully in cardboard boxes for the grocer. There were hundreds, thousands, it seemed. Fainlight became dizzy from the effort. The flowers began to appear almost menacing, with their "eye-like" black dots and "sulphur" yellows. "Too many sexual organs. Looking down the trumpets of the daffodils again and again and again, it absolutely freaked me after a while," Fainlight recalled (Fainlight Interview). "Sylvia laughed, but I hurried back into the house" ("Jane and Sylvia" 14).

During this visit, Fainlight felt "a palpable tension" between Plath and Hughes ("Jane and Sylvia" 14). The couple avoided looking at each other, or even speaking to each other; Fainlight noticed that the air between them seemed much more strained than it had during their companionable meals in London. "It wasn't good. But we didn't discuss it at all. I wouldn't have initiated a discussion about it. And she didn't. … We wanted just to talk about poetry and be poets. The difficulties of everyday life we were glad to put to one side. We didn't have complaining coffee klatch conversations" (Fainlight Interview). Away from the men, the two women nursed their babies together in Plath's study while Plath read "Elm," which she had dedicated to Fainlight, out loud. Fainlight thought the poem "extraordinary" (Fainlight Interview).

Plath had begun "Elm" three weeks before Fainlight's visit, during a restless early dawn. The first draft dates from April 12, and the poem went through at least fifteen drafts before it was finally finished on April 19. Written in declarative, unrhyming tercets, "Elm" is an elaboration upon the final "message" from the last line of Plath's "The Moon and the Yew Tree"—"blackness and silence" (*CP* 173).

> I know the bottom, she says. I know it with my great tap root:
> It is what you fear.
> I do not fear it: I have been there.
>
> (*CP* 192)

Familiar Plathian images appear—the sea, galloping horses, hooves, echoes, poisons, hooks, clouds, shrieks, the moon, "malignity." The speaker initially mimes the voice of the Elm, who mocks and taunts: "Love is a shadow. / How you lie and cry after it" (CP 192). Plath's reference to electroshock therapy suggests that the Elm symbolizes depression: "I have suffered the atrocity of sunsets. / Scorched to the root / My red filaments burn and stand, a hand of wires" (CP 192). The eleventh stanza confirms this identification. "I am terrified by this dark thing / That sleeps in me; / All day I feel its soft, feathery turnings, its malignity" (CP 193). The poem ends with a startling image of a "murderous" face in the branches of the tree that "petrifies the will" (CP 193). This image was originally a reflection of the speaker's own face in the windowpane in several earlier drafts.

There are also veiled references to miscarriage. Plath eventually dedicated "Elm" to Fainlight, who, as noted above, had suffered three previous miscarriages before David's birth in 1962. Peter K. Steinberg suggests that Plath's sympathetic letter to Fainlight in the wake of her threatened miscarriage suggests a new reading of the first tercet of "Elm": "I know the bottom, she says. I know it with my great tap root: / It is what you fear. / I do not fear it: I have been there" (CP 192). But the poem is connected to Fainlight, and miscarriage, in another way.

"Elm" was influenced by Fainlight's own poem about miscarriage, "Sapphic Moon," which Plath read in the February 18, 1962, issue of *Encounter*. In Fainlight's poem, a woman tries in vain to protect herself from the moon's "cold malignancy." The moon

> Passes like X-ray through lovers' caresses and arms,
> Enters the womb like an instrument [...]
> Then sows bright mercury seeds of death [...]

In an April 16 letter to Fainlight, written while she was working on "Elm," Plath expressed her deep admiration for this poem: "It is a real White Goddess poem, and a voice on its weird fearsome own. I think it is a rare thing" (L2 762). Plath likely recognized the poem's "weirdness" as her own. Phrases such as "cold malignancy" and "bright mercury seeds of death" alongside references to X-rays, searings, scarrings, and Hiroshima sound as if they came from Plath's own pen. The word "malignity" in "Elm" echoes Fainlight's "malignancy," while the third draft of "Elm" contains the excised line, "a lunar Xray of barrenness," not unlike Fainlight's moon, which "[p]asses like X-ray through lovers' caresses."

"Elm" can be read, like "The Moon and the Yew Tree," as a poem about depression and alienation. But the references to Fainlight's "Sapphic Moon" also suggest miscarriage. In "Elm," the speaker wonders, "[a]re those the faces of love, those pale irretrievables? / Is it for such I agitate my heart?" (CP 193). These "loves" are the "shadow" the speaker cries after. There is a hint of an elegy, in "Elm," for Plath's lost baby. Indeed, a line from the second draft of "Elm," about a childless, grieving mother, confirms the original connection to miscarriage.[3]

Fainlight's moon, resonant of fertility and the menstrual cycle, also influenced "Three Women." In Fainlight's poem, the moon, visible through a window, "enters the womb like an instrument" to sow the "seeds of death." Plath practically lifts Fainlight's lines for

---

[3] The phrase "as a woman with no children" has been excised in the draft, and replaced with "like a childless woman" ("Elm" drafts, Smith).

the Second Voice of the miscarrying secretary in "Three Women": "There is the moon in the high window," she begins, midway through the poem:

> I feel it enter me, cold, alien, like an instrument.
> And that mad, hard face at the end of it, that O-mouth
> Open in its gape of perpetual grieving.
> It is she that drags the blood-black sea around
> Month after month, with its voices of failure.
> I am helpless as the sea at the end of her string.
> I am restless. Restless and useless. I, too, create corpses.

(CP 182)

Plath's letters from this time are full of complaints about the cold and the rain, endless housework, and baby care. These burdens, the weather, plus a predisposition to postpartum depression, suggest that Plath was suffering both physically and psychologically during that "cold mean spring" of 1962 (J 668). With no psychiatrist for miles, she may have been seeking psychological explanations for her depression in her art, just as she had at Smith College in her Dostoyevsky thesis. In late August 1962, Plath would tell Howard Moss at *The New Yorker* that "Elm" explored "various moods, I think, of anguish" (L2 815).[4]

On May 12, Plath wrote to Fainlight about the dedication of "Elm." "Could I dedicate my elm tree poem to Ruth Fainlight? (Or would you prefer your maternal & wifely self, Ruth Sillitoe? I had thought of the poet-self first)" (L2 772). Fainlight was "slightly disconcerted" by the question, whose answer seemed obvious: "[W]e were two poets, Sylvia Plath and Ruth Fainlight, not Mrs. Hughes and Mrs. Sillitoe, and our friendship was centred on this crucial reality" ("Jane and Sylvia" 14).

Fainlight later admitted that she felt oppressed by Plath's "impression of great confidence as a mother, though perhaps I was deceived by a fierce need to assure herself, even more than to convince me, that she could play this particular role as well as everything else she set out to do" ("Jane and Sylvia" 10). Plath had begun painting hearts and flowers on the backs of chairs and cupboards, and the impulse and the symbolism troubled Fainlight. "Sylvia painting those little Germanic hearts and flowers all over Court Green ... Trying to be the perfect everything. I know, I've gone through it, of wanting to be the best at it, and it's a total waste of time and energy" (Fainlight Interview). But the pressure to embrace domesticity was "absolutely" a force in mothers' lives, she said (Fainlight Interview). "I was quite certain about my own discomfort with the part. Alone, or at home with Alan, I could just about manage to function in this novel and demanding situation, but I shrank from comparisons" ("Jane and Sylvia" 10).

The Sillitoes and their three-month-old son would leave England to join Jane and Paul Bowles in Tangier during the spring of 1962. "It now seems plausible that one of my strongest motives in agreeing to leave England just then was to escape the company of other mothers and babies," Fainlight said ("Jane and Sylvia" 10). "What I remember best is a tremendous sense of relief as we crossed the Channel" ("Jane and Sylvia" 10). Fainlight felt her load lighten in Tangier, where she could afford a maid who cooked, cleaned, and watched the baby while she wrote—a setup Plath herself longed for.

---

[4] *The New Yorker* would initially reject "Elm" in late June 1962 but accept in September 1962 (L2 815; 847).

Fainlight's domestic and literary freedom was probably on Plath's mind as her marriage broke down during the summer of 1962. She began to consider moving to Spain with her children. Hughes, she wrote Fainlight on September eighth, "will set us up for 3 months in Spain this winter," near Málaga, where his friend Ben Sonnenberg lived (*L2* 822). She asked Fainlight, in Morocco, for her practical advice about traveling by car with children: "What route did you take, where stay, did you reserve ahead, etc. etc. Ted never will make a plan till the day ahead, but I would like to know what I can expect. Are there Paddipads [diapers] in Spain. Strained babyfoods? Is there a God? Where is Franco?" She fantasized about meeting Fainlight in Spain and arranging play dates for their little boys. Nicholas, she wrote, "is gorgeous now. ... I adore him" (*L2* 822). She hoped it would be easier to find a nanny there as it was "almost impossible" in Devon. "Have a 2nd novel I'm dying to write and no time. Which I suppose is better than lots of time & no novel." She signed off, "please write," and enclosed a copy of "Elm" (*L2* 822). Plath did not mention her looming separation in her light, chummy letter. She may have hoped she and Hughes could return to each other in the place they had honeymooned, far from Devon's gray skies. But the reconciliation did not happen.

By the autumn of 1962, the marriage was over, and Plath was living alone in Devon with her infant and toddler. She was furious at Hughes for leaving her in a small village with no nanny amongst the "cow people" (*L2* 873). She loved her children passionately, yet admitted to her mother, "I have so much writing in me, the children are a kind of torture when on my neck all day" (*L2* 875). The villagers were friendly, "but they are no life. ... I am well-liked here, in spite of my weirdness, I think, though of course everybody eventually comes round to 'Where is Mr. Hughes.' I hate Ted with a passion" (*L2* 875). She was "appalled" by the situation in which she now found herself after scaling such heights of ambition and domestic happiness: "Years of my life wasted" (*L2* 875).

And yet she was almost cheerful in a letter she wrote to Fainlight on October 22. She had begun writing some of the best poems of her life during this period, she confided—nearly a poem a day in the month of October, a Keatsian deluge. She knew the poems would make her name. Hughes's leavetaking had unleashed a creative torrent:

> I am getting a divorce from Ted. I write you in confidence, and as a sister-mother-muse-friend. I know you & Alan must have all sorts of wonderful and famous friends, but to me you are the dearest couple I knew in England. You can imagine, Ruth, after our talk about less-famous, or even infamous wives of famous husbands, how I automatically assume that all "our" friends will now of course be just Ted's friends. I hope that with us it is not so.
>
> Well, so much for this mother in me. The writer is delighted. ... Psychologically, Ruth, I am fascinated by the polarities of muse-poet and mother-housewife. When I was "happy" domestically I felt a gag down my throat. Now that my domestic life, until I get a permanent live-in girl, is chaos, I am living like a spartan, writing through huge fevers & producing free stuff I had locked in me for years. I feel astounded & very lucky. I kept telling myself I was the sort that could only write when peaceful at heart, but that is not so, the muse has come to live, now Ted is gone, and my God! what a sweeter companion. (*L2* 880–2)

By November 1962, Plath had abandoned her plans to move to Spain and Ireland, partly because she had begun to form a tentative romantic relationship with the London critic Al Alvarez. She also began to realize that her career would be better served by moving to

London, where au pairs were plentiful, than by isolating herself in Connemara. While flat hunting, she found that the house where W. B. Yeats had once lived as a child—around the corner from her old flat on Fitzroy Road—was for rent. If only she could spend her winters in Yeats's London house and her summers in Devon, she wrote to Fainlight. Plath had nearly wept on her London trip at the sight of museums and cafes. She invited Fainlight and baby David to Devon or London in April while Sillitoe was visiting the Soviet Union. Fainlight agreed and set about making arrangements that included a visa for her Moroccan nanny and a driver's license for herself.

Plath moved to London in mid-December of 1962, but the high soon gave way to despair and loneliness. In mid-January she became uncharacteristically gloomy about her future, and let her guard down in a letter to her mother: "I just haven't felt to have any <u>identity</u> under the steamroller of decisions & responsibilities of this last half year, with the babies a constant demand. ... How I would <u>like</u> to be self-supporting on my writing! But I need <u>time</u>. I guess I just need somebody to cheer me up by saying I've done all right so far" (*L2* 958). Fainlight understood Plath's predicament, writing from Tangier that January that she knew no one there and sometimes longed for London. "And yet, thinking about the people whom I call my friends there, the people I used to see, I remember meetings that left me despondent and unsatisfied" ("Jane and Sylvia" 17–18). Something about London, Fainlight wrote, "seemed to be destructive." Fainlight felt she had not had time to settle down in Morocco: "And when I momentarily do sense what being settled down will be like, I usually panic" ("Jane and Sylvia" 17–18). What was the optimal situation for working, she wondered to Plath, solitude or multitude? Fainlight had described Plath's own complicated feelings about writing, home, and exile. Yet Fainlight reassured Plath she looked forward to her upcoming April trip to Devon, and plays and movies in London—"and talking and talking and talking." She asked Plath to send her the "secret novel" she had been working on ("Jane and Sylvia" 17–18).

Fainlight wrote Plath again on February 3rd to say that she would be back in London at their old Pembridge Crescent flat by early March, and that she would spend April with Plath in Devon. "Everything was packed up," Fainlight remembered, "and we'd gone to an awful lot of trouble to get our maid out of Morocco, to come to England" (Fainlight Interview). Fainlight had learned to drive and made arrangements for her car to be shipped over to England. She had no idea that Plath, who had fired her au pair and was now on her own, was ill and slipping into a depression.

Fainlight would learn of Plath's death in the *Observer*, in an article written by Alvarez, a week before she was to return to England from Morocco.

> I could not understand why there was a photograph of Sylvia and some accompanying text surrounded by a heavy black line at the top of the book's page. It was hard to take in what I read, I had to go back to the beginning two or three times until the fact that this was an announcement of Sylvia's death began to penetrate, and even more time was needed before I had absorbed the details of Al Alvarez's carefully worded piece. I burst into tears and flung myself onto Fatima's [Fainlight's nanny] comforting bosom. Alan hurried in, alarmed by the sound of noisy weeping.
>
> ("Jane and Sylvia" 16)

"I was absolutely devastated," she said. "I always feel about Sylvia that we never had enough time together" (Fainlight Interview). She later acknowledged that when she had decided to move to Morocco, she had chosen Jane Bowles over Plath. And yet, she *had* been on the verge of reuniting with Plath, with a nanny she had "brought to England for the specific purpose of looking after the three children while Sylvia and I went for walks or drove around the lanes of Devon, talking about poetry." She would wonder darkly about the consequences of her choice, "whether, if I had been there when Sylvia moved back to London, everything might have been different" ("Jane and Sylvia" 16). Had Plath survived another month, she would have had her closest literary friend back in London, as well as shared a nanny. "Could I have saved Sylvia?" Fainlight asked herself. "Perhaps—at least for that particular moment of crisis. But how long until the next?" ("Jane and Sylvia" 16). In a later poem, she wrote, "That poetic meeting never happened, yet / I dream about it. What more to say? Everyone / knows the story's ending" (2012).

# CHAPTER SEVENTEEN

# Beelines: Reading Plath through Edith Sitwell and Carol Ann Duffy

MARSHA BRYANT

In 1985 Sylvia Plath became British in *The Bloodaxe Book of Contemporary Women Poets: Eleven British Writers*.[1] Scottish poet and future British laureate Carol Ann Duffy published her debut volume that year, *Standing Female Nude*. Four years prior, Victoria Glendinning and Geoffrey Elborn published the first biographies of English poet Edith Sitwell. The proximity of these seemingly disconnected events in literary history has remained unremarked. After all, recent discussions linking Plath to earlier British women poets have focused on Stevie Smith, to whom Plath wrote a fan letter in 1962 (*L2* 907–8).[2] Moreover, most critics consider Plath as a turning point rather than a point of continuity for the British canon, plotting her entry through Ted Hughes and Devon. Such discussions focus especially on Plath's connections to the next generations of women poets. For example, Fiona Sampson declares that Plath "stands both as a kind of gatekeeper and as a permission giver, particularly for women writing poetry in Britain today" (355). Duffy acknowledged this enabling influence in her Faber edition of Plath's poems, published the same year as her first laureate volume *The Bees* (2012). Although Duffy and her reviewers did not consider Sitwell's literary influence, we can find it in her bee poems along with Plath's. Sitwell was a formative figure in Plath's early career, the subject of two college papers and a visible presence in several early poems.

Plotting lines of affiliation in British women's poetry has never been an easy undertaking. But it would prove less difficult if these lines were not under constant threat of erasure. As I have argued elsewhere,[3] Sitwell's place in the women's poetry canon has been obscured because her work does not fit standard experiential models that built the brand. It was not until 2005 that Sitwell, Plath, and Duffy would appear in the same women's poetry anthology. My essay offers beelines for connecting these three poets. I discuss Plath's writing *about* and *through* Sitwell, featuring her largely ignored essays on Sitwell's poetry

---

[1] I am grateful to Cassandra Laity and to *Feminist Modernist Studies*, where some portions of this essay first appeared. I am also grateful to Amanda Golden for sharing gleanings from her archival research on Plath's teaching.
[2] See, for example, Masud, "Plath in the Context of Stevie Smith."
[3] See my "Queen Bees" essay.

and connecting her bee sequence to Sitwell's "The Bee Oracles." I also assess Duffy's writing *about* and *through* Plath's poems. Finally, I consider the configuration of Sitwell, Plath, and Duffy in anthologies of British women's poetry, including Anglo-American collections and British-focused anthologies. My beelines widen our sense of Plath's place in the British canon.

## PLATH READING SITWELL

Modernism's *grande dame*, Sitwell had a formidable presence in the midcentury years that fostered Plath's early career. New Directions heralded her inaugural American lecture tour with the tribute volume *A Celebration for Edith Sitwell* (1948). By 1950, she had published over thirty-five books, which established the poet, critic, and biographer as a cross-Atlantic woman of letters. Sitwell became a Dame Commander of the British Empire in 1954 (as Duffy would in 2015). Plath submitted papers on Sitwell during her freshman and junior years at Smith (in 1951 and 1953), citing from her own copy of *The Canticle of the Rose: Poems 1917–1949*, *A Celebration for Edith Sitwell*, and other sources. "I guess I don't quite measure up to Edith yet, dear me!" Plath wrote her mother during her sophomore year (*L1* 386). While teaching at Smith, Plath measured herself against her contemporary rivals and poetry's "ageing giantesses & poetic godmothers," Sitwell and Marianne Moore (*J* 360). She assigned both poets in the first-year English course she taught at Smith during the 1957–8 academic year ("Sylvia Plath's Teaching and the Shaping of Her Work" 256).

Plath wrote her most extended responses to Sitwell in the early 1950s, when her own poems began to appear in American magazines. Her 1951 paper, "A New Idiom," focuses on the poetics of Sitwell's early style. Here Plath praises Sitwell's technical capacities for patterning sound devices and distilling images to maximize sensation, viewing this experimental style as a highly complex crafting of language. Rather than a *voice* expressing the poet's personal experience and feelings, Sitwell's *new idiom* manifests her heightened capacity to apprehend the world and open it for attuned readers. The paper also recounts how Plath found *The Canticle of the Rose* in The Hampshire Bookshop in Northampton. Noticing the book and sitting down with it, the emergent poet became so immersed in its pages that another customer's child remarked on the duration of her reading. Plath returned to purchase Sitwell's book, and she "heavily underlined" her copy of *Canticle* (now housed at Smith College), Amanda Golden observes.[4]

Sitwell's poetic language infused poetry with sensation while avoiding sentimentality—an artful balance that appealed to Plath. Her freshman paper quotes extensively from "Some Notes on My Own Poetry," the standard preface to Sitwell's volumes of selected and collected poems. She cites Sitwell's self-explication of "Dark Song," which begins:

> The fire was furry as a bear
> And the flames purr...
> The brown bear rambles in his chain
> Captive to cruel men.
>
> (59)

---

[4] I am grateful to Golden for sharing research notes on Plath's personal library.

Sitwell plots the poem's assonances and dissonances across a grid of interlocking meanings hinging on vowels, consonants, and micro-rhythms. For example: "The long, harsh, animal-purring 'r's and the occasional double vowels, as in 'bear' and 'fire,' though these last are divided by a muted 'r,' are intended to convey the uncombatable animal instinct" (xxv). A critical hyperacusis is at work in such explanations, which can elude traditional definitions of poetic rhyme and meter. Plath underlined Sitwell's unique terms "*dropping* dissonances" and "sinking or dulled dissonances" in this commentary on "Dark Song" (xxv). "A New Idiom" applies Sitwell's sonics to poems from *Bucolic Comedies*, parts of *The Sleeping Beauty*, and the "Five Songs" section of *Canticle*. Plath also recommends Sitwell's poetics as a regimen for training readers to let go of passive reading practices that respond only to expected patterns. Noting Sitwell's impact on Plath, Karen V. Kukil points out that "her own near rhymes become more original and nuanced" after writing this first essay on her English predecessor ("Beyond *Letters Home*" 286).

The rest of Plath's 1951 paper functions as user test and endorsement of Sitwell's technique, asserting that its intricate variations and unified sensory effects compel strong emotional responses. For example, Plath applauds the freshness she finds in these lines from "King Cophetua and the Beggar Maid": "The five-pointed crude pink tinsel star / Laughed loudly" (11). Fusing natural and artificial imagery, Sitwell's language renders a sonic celestial body. From *The Sleeping Beauty* Plath chooses the image of "the pink schoolgirlish fruits" hanging from trees (85), praising Sitwell for moving beyond the worn-out figures in hackneyed love poems. Plath finds a heightened beauty in this jarring synthesis of images in "Spring":

"… a maiden fair as an almond-tree,
With hair like the waterfalls' goat-locks; she

Has lips like that jangling harsh pink rain,
The flower-bells that spirt on the trees again."

(4)

Linking the tree's graceful form and the waterfall's leaping foam to the maiden's youthful beauty, Plath asserts that the culminating "flower-bells" encapsulate Sitwell's lines as a linguistic-sensory network. Think of it as a panoramic objective correlative. For the emergent poet, Sitwell's amalgam of feminine, fluid, and animal bodies was fitting, not fantastical; nothing was extraneous in its extreme rendering of reality. In her copy of *Canticle*, Plath underlined Sitwell's defense of her alleged overreliance on "strange" images and synesthesia, which aimed "to pierce down to the essence of the thing seen, by discovering in it attributes which at first sight appear alien but which are acutely related—by producing its quintessential color (sharper, brighter, than that seen by an eye grown stale) and by stripping it of all unessential details" (xvi). Plath would employ parallel techniques in "Poppies in July," fusing her poem's flaming flowers with women's mouths and clothing in a riotous pastoral image (*CP* 203).

During her junior year, Plath wrote the more ambitious paper, "Edith Sitwell and the Development of Her Poetry" (Lilly). It cites thirty-two poems from across the poet's career, situating their distinctive style within the British canon. Plath saw her famous predecessor as a poet of dazzling range and wide scope, relishing Sitwell's "bucolic eden, her rocketing jazz fantasies, her nightmare cannibal land, her wartorn hell of the cold, and her metaphysical sun-permeated universe" (qtd. in *Red Comet* 217). Curiously, Plath's critics and biographers have spent considerably more time on the James Joyce thesis she *did not* write than on the twenty-nine-page Sitwell paper she *did*. This 1953 essay reveals Sitwell's importance to enlivening Plath's poetic language, to positioning her own relationship to modernism, and to plotting a British canon that includes women poets.

As in her 1951 paper, Plath begins her analysis by defending Dame Sitwell's theory and practice of poetic *texture*: the interrelation of consonants and vowels that augments the soundscape of rhyme. Plath finds that in Sitwell's lines, even a mere syllable can come alive in the poet's hands. She argues that these intricately woven sound effects constitute a precise system that undergirds the bucolic and circus worlds of Sitwell's early poetry. For Plath, Sitwell's sonic excess and shocking sensations present a different level of density than the usual modernist toolkit of fragmented images and paradoxical phrases. To emphasize this point, Plath points to her New Critical training as a reader of W. B. Yeats's visionary poems, T. S. Eliot's *The Waste Land*, and W. H. Auden's *The Age of Anxiety*. She assures her instructor, Elizabeth Drew, that she is indeed up to the task of tackling Sitwell.

Plath's 1953 analysis of Sitwell's early poems pays particular attention to their stock characters: circus performers and especially country maidens and kitchen maids. Extending her freshman paper's engagement with the dull "goose-girl" Anne from "On the Vanity of Human Aspirations," Plath compares her to Jane, the kitchen maid from "Aubade." Both bird-like characters are stunted by their environments. Confined to kitchen and barnyard, Jane will never question her position or imagine a world beyond her domestic role:

> Jane, Jane,
> Tall as a crane,
> The morning light creaks down again;
>
> Comb your cockscomb-ragged hair,
> Jane, Jane, come down the stair.

(6)

Plath links Jane's unperceptive mind to her bird-like attributes: her awkward height and ruffled hair. Pointing to the poem's rendering of Jane's kitchen fire as carrots and turnips, Plath shows how Sitwell limits the maid's transcendence to "eternities of the kitchen garden" (6)—a contrast Plath also summarizes in the teaching notes she used as a Smith instructor. These notes highlight the poem's cockscomb motif and striking synesthesia (creaking and whining light). As Amanda Golden points out, Plath included "Aubade" in her students' readings for the last day of class (*Annotating Modernism* 201). "Aubade" likely influenced the duck-like woman Plath fashioned in her 1956 poem, "Miss Drake Proceeds to Supper" (*CP* 41). A similar character appears in *The Bell Jar* as Miss Norris, whose Caplan room is next to Esther Greenwood's (190).

In addition to engaging more of Sitwell's female figures, Plath compares her luxurious language and sensuous descriptions to Christina Rossetti's in "Goblin Market." By including Rossetti in her paper's modern poetry canon, Plath plots a female line she might join; all three poets would appear in *Without Adam: The Femina Anthology of Poetry* (1968). Plath's 1953 paper also situates Sitwell within modernism's standard male line, comparing "Gold Coast Customs" (1929) to Yeats's "Nineteen Hundred and Nineteen" (232–7) and Eliot's poems "The Hollow Men" and "Burnt Norton."

The second half of Plath's 1953 paper focuses on the postwar poetry that made Sitwell a laureate contender. These poems often depict a mechanized and animalistic world where sacred symbols have lost their meaning. Plath is especially drawn to Sitwell's "Three Poems of the Atomic Age" which culminate *Canticle of the Rose*. Timely and visionary at once, their depictions of nuclear winter and Absolute Zero reveal a poet of deep humanity and peerless technique, Plath argues. Invoking Eliot's *The Waste Land* and Auden's Yeats elegy, Plath spends considerable time on "The Song of the Cold," which she considers one of Sitwell's crowning achievements. It opens with a "polar sun" and a planet on the brink of oblivion:

> Huge is the sun of amethysts and rubies,
> And in the purple perfumes of the polar sun
> And homeless cold they wander.
> But winter is the time for comfort and for friendship,
> For warmth and food—
> And a talk beside a fire like the Midnight Sun—
> A glowing heart of amber and of musk. Time to forget
> The falling night of the world and heart, the polar chaos
> That separates us each from each. It is no time to roam
> Along the pavements wide and cold as Hell's huge polar street,
> Drifting along the city like the wind
> Blowing aimlessly, and with no home
> To rest in, only famine for a heart—
>
> (187)

Plath comments on the aimless denizens' isolation from one another in their living death, noting how Sitwell's shortened lines also appear to constrict from the cold. The human heart lies frozen beyond repair in this "Cainozoic period" of atomic gods: "Even the beat of the heart and the pulse is changed to this: / The counting of small deaths, the repetition / Of nothing, endless positing and suppression of / Nothing" (*Canticle* 188–9). Man's inhumanity has murdered the old restorative sun, a theme Plath notes in several of Sitwell's later poems.

Plath ventured into atomic poetics with her English sonnet "Second Winter," which appeared in the December 1958 issue of the *Ladies' Home Journal*. Overlaying a late freeze with blighted romance and nuclear winter, Plath warps her description of a flower into images of munitions and pyrotechnics. The dormant seed prepares to "launch / Bright fireworks of flowers" that will "kindle" the atmosphere and burst into flames. In this "traitor climate" of the Cold War, regeneration and love are doomed to fail. The sonnet's culminating quatrain imbues the natural sun with Christian symbolism, rendering an atomic sun that is "frozen in a crown of thorns" like Sitwell's in "Dirge for the New Sunrise" (143).

The conclusion to Plath's 1953 paper turned to Sitwell's recurring figure of a life-affirming Sun that warms the chilled heart as it renews the world. She affiliates with Sitwell as a different kind of sun-worshipper, extolling the revelatory impact of her predecessor's late poems. Indeed, Plath expresses a desire to read Sitwell's poems aloud before an audience—even to sing them or perform interpretive dances by Paradise Pond to mark the coming of Spring. Given Plath's sustained and enthusiastic engagement with Sitwell's work, the erasure of this beeline in many accounts of her career has been extraordinary.

## DUFFY READING PLATH

Plath was nineteen years old when she was pulled into Sitwell's *Canticle of the Rose* in The Hampshire Bookshop. Duffy was twenty-five when she received Plath's *Collected Poems* for her birthday. In the preface to her Faber edition of Plath's poems, Duffy recounts this "first true—and electrifying—encounter" with her predecessor, whom she saw less as a foremother than "a superior contemporary" (xiii). Duffy plots her own emergence through this literary relationship, deeming as "Plath-enabled" her breakthrough poem that won the National Poetry Competition, "Whoever She Was" (xiii). Duffy's edition of Plath includes the entire four-poem bee sequence, omitting Hughes's addition of "The Swarm" to *Ariel* (1965).

As Plath found in Sitwell, Duffy found in Plath a generative force for renewing poetic diction and voice. Indeed, Duffy considers Plath a highly *stylized* poet. The laureate's characterizations of Plath's "glittering language" uncannily resemble critical responses to Sitwell's early style. Duffy finds in Plath's poems "a comic playfulness, a great appetite for sensuous experience, a delight in the slant rhymes and music of her verse, bravado, brio, a tangible joy in the unflowering of her genius." While Duffy also takes into account the range of emotions and women's experience reflected in Plath's poems, her emphasis is on Plath as a "vocational poet" rather than a confessional one (Preface xv). Duffy's preface positions Plath as a British poet by linking her to the English landscape (Devon, the moors) and to canonical modern poets (Oscar Wilde, Yeats, and Auden). Yet Plath's ultimate importance for Duffy is her role as presiding poet of the English, Scottish, Irish, and New Zealander women whose careers preceded *and* came after *Ariel*. These figures include Fleur Adcock (who anthologized Plath), Elaine Feinstein (who wrote a biography of Hughes), U. A. Fanthorpe, Liz Lochhead, Vicki Feaver, and Eavan Boland. Significantly, Duffy's first official laureate volume laid claim to a British literary tradition that includes Plath. Although Duffy did not lay claim to Sitwell in her bee poems, their bardic sensibility and planetary scope parallel her predecessor's in "The Bee Oracles." Sitwell's late poems responded to a world under threat of nuclear war, and Duffy's *The Bees* reckons with catastrophes of climate change.

## BEE ORACLES, BEE MEETINGS, AND BEE RECKONINGS

Because Plath fashioned her bee sequence to end *Ariel*, her signature volume, we tend to consider it as a solo act: a non-affiliated rendering of her autobiographical voice. Yet as Christina Britzolakis reminds us, Plath's "unifying metaphor" of beekeeping "insists on the materiality of writing as a social practice" ("*Ariel* and Other Poems" 121). This would include the material circulation of her British literary forebears as well as the bee poems' first appearance in print. Bees were a staple image in Sitwell's symbolic order, most famously in her two-part poem, "The Bee Oracles." Invoking Greek myths that link bees with the oracle of Delphi, Sitwell overlays an arid modern world with ancient powers of prophecy and regeneration. Lynda K. Bundtzen sees these myths as an "ancient analogue" for Plath's bee sequence. She reminds us that Pindar's Pythian odes refer to the oracle's high priestess as the Delphic Bee, and the Homeric Hymn to Hermes refers to three bee maidens (*The Other* Ariel 152). Sitwell's bee poems embrace this mythology more fully than Plath's, connecting her "Priestesses of the Gold Comb" to "the Thriae"—a trinity of winged nymphs on Mount Parnassus who taught Apollo divination (240).[5]

Significantly, beekeeping is female in Sitwell's poem. "I: The Bee-Keeper" envisions a mythic old woman attending to her hives; she is a world mother who claims sisterhood with "the Bee-Priestesses." Nurtured in "the holy Dark," Sitwell's bees rise in their "gold

---

[5] See the Theoi *Greek* Mythology website: https://www.theoi.com/

bodies bright as the Lion," singing "the great Hymn of Being" that renews a depleted world. "The Beekeeper" was an early title for Plath's bee sequence, Karen Jackson Ford points out (143). Sitwell's priestess bees resound their song in "II: A Sleepy Tune," poised for flight from the world's wintering:

> "And now only the cold
> Wind from the honey-hive can know
> If still from strength comes sweetness—if from the lion-heart
> The winged swarms rise!"
>
> (237–41)

We can see parallel images in Plath's bee poems; her queen bee rises in a "lion-red body" in "Stings" (*CP* 215), while "Wintering" foretells her future flight alongside female attendants. Plath knew "The Bee Oracles" from *Canticle of the Rose*. And because she enjoyed listening to Sitwell's recordings in college, Plath likely heard the English poet's elegant reading of "The Bee-Keeper" on her 1955 Caedmon album. Since "The Bee Oracles" became emblematic of Sitwell herself, Plath's title for her 1959 poem "The Beekeeper's Daughter" can signal a living poetic influence as well as a lost father (*CP* 118). Plath's bee sequence first entered culture in the April 1963 issue of *The Atlantic*, which contained an advertisement for Sitwell's bestseller *The Queens and the Hive*. Titled "Bees," Plath's two-part poem consisted of "The Arrival of the Bee Box" and "Wintering." Plath and Sitwell were the only women poets who appeared in this issue of the magazine.

Since Sandra M. Gilbert and Bundtzen published their early discussions of Plath's bee sequence,[6] critics have compellingly pointed out how it foregrounds anxieties about gender and reproduction—focusing especially on the poems' fraught images of femininity, sexuality, and death. In "The Bee Meeting," for example, "scarlet flowers" on plant tendrils appear to be "blood clots," and the hive's "new virgins" lie in wait to kill off their "murderess" queen (*CP* 211, 2). "The Bee Meeting" also reads as a perilous pastoral, a mode Plath brought to her 1956 poem, "Bucolics" (*CP* 23–4). Pastiching English ballads, this earlier poem punished its trysting woman with "cruel nettles," leaving her abandoned and alone in the landscape. More immersive, "The Bee Meeting" hinges on the initiate speaker's crisis of legibility as she regards rural neighbors she finds inscrutable. Even gender is rendered ambiguous; the villagers in their protective clothing appear as "knights in visors" with "[b]reastplates of cheesecloth" (*CP* 211). As the villagers lead the speaker "to the shorn grove, the circle of hives," the poem's Audenesque series of questions takes on sinister intonations: "Whose is that long white box ... why am I cold" (*CP* 211, 212). Although she stays on the perimeter, the speaker stands her ground as Plath stakes her bee sequence in British bucolics.

In "The Arrival of the Bee Box," the speaker's hive of her own first signifies a primal chaos. Yet it also ushers in a deep cultural past parallel to the elemental plant kingdom and early civilizations in Sitwell's "The Bee Oracles." Drawn to the "din" of her confined bees, Plath's speaker finds their excess sound "dangerous" and "unintelligible" (*CP* 213). Yet as she bends closer, she hears the origins of Western language: from "African"

---

[6]See Gilbert, "A Fine, White Flying Myth: Confessions of a Plath Addict" (1978) and Bundtzen, *Plath's Incarnations: Woman and the Creative Process* (1983).

intonations to the "furious Latin" of "a Roman mob" (*CP* 213). Because Plath aims to break through to Britishness in *Ariel,* the Latinate underpinnings of English poetry constitute a literary commodity as precious as the pastoral landscape. Ian Twiddy finds a self-reflexive hesitation before the bee box, which he reads as Plath negotiating "the size of this poetic inheritance" (110); the speaker's pause parallels the uneasy entry to the foreboding grove in "The Bee Meeting." More confident in "Stings," the speaker handles her honeycombs "bare-handed," donning "cheesecloth gauntlets" like the local bee agent (*CP* 214). One month after Plath completed her sequence, her letter to Smith spoke of being "rooted" in her beekeeping (*L2* 907). Plath's beekeeper identity helped her establish a literary place within Britishness.

Duffy's bee poems are less centered on women's experience than Plath's and less elevated in tone than Sitwell's. Yet they form beelines with both poets. In her first laureate volume, Duffy disperses her bee motif across nine poems that interweave literary, personal, national, and environmental themes. These poems do not form a sequence but serve as a unifying device across *The Bees*. Even though Duffy genders as female the volume's primary beekeeper and poet figures, reviewers focused mostly on its allusions to the traditional line of male British poets. Yet Plath's influence is equally palpable. For example, Duffy's "Ariel" quotes from a song in *The Tempest* ("Where the bee sucks, there suck I"), but her title alludes to Plath's *Ariel* as well as to Shakespeare. Duffy also alludes to Plath's title poem through her own poem's "dual register" that Angelica Michelis terms "bucolic / sexual pleasure" counterpoised with "fear of annihilation" (348). Duffy brings a Sitwellesque timelessness and elemental dimension to "Virgil's Bees" even as she invokes his *Georgics*, blessing "air's gift of sweetness" and sounding its lilting light with a pastoral list of vibrant flowers (23). Jane Dowson points out that Duffy's frequent shifts between singular and plural personal pronouns reflect her "sense of being both original and bound to her peers" (15). The volume's beelines to Sitwell and Plath are part of this networked dynamic.

"Bees" and "A Rare Bee" bookend Duffy's volume by figuring bees as literary language, intersecting with the poetics of Plath's bee sequence. Echoing "Wintering"—which sets its black mass of bees against white snow like letters on a page—Duffy's bees are "blurs on paper," literally *buzzwords*. In their *besotted* and *brazen* state, these bees create an alliterative din animating poet and page alike. "Bees" departs from the appalling and alienating noise in Plath's bee box. In "Hive," Duffy smooths Plath's *furious Latin* into "Latin murmurs," sounding within "time's hum," a communal "blurry sound" of "the hive, alive, us" (3, 31). "A Rare Bee" furthers the volume's connections to Plath as it alludes to ancient Greek associations of bees with prophecy and poetry. Plath's "Stings" links bees to truthfulness as they swarm to attack a lying man's lips, unleashing through their deaths their queen's writerly red marks in the sky. Moreover, as Ford argues, Plath's poem "fulfills" the speaker's foretelling of freeing the bees in "The Arrival of the Bee Box" (149). The female poet-quester of Duffy's poem ventures into a mythic forest to gain the true tongue of a poet through the rare bee's purest honey. Saddling her steed, the "girl, poet, knight" straddles gender boundaries like the visored honey seekers in "The Bee Meeting." But when she asks the bee to "*bless my tongue with rhyme, poetry, song,*" it stings her mouth and dies into living legend. In both poems, the bees' sacrificial act begets writing.

Like Sitwell, Duffy brings religious elements to her bee imagery, marking their dual role in spiritual and planetary health. In Sitwell's "The Bee Oracles," the "Bee in the

Spirit" tells of "gold combs" hidden within the world's "cold rock" (239). In "The Bee Carol," Duffy's grounded cluster of winter bees shields their Queen from the cold, a "silent hive" and a Christmas blessing (59). "Telling the Bees" invokes British folk customs to expand ritualistic meanings. In her analysis of Plath's bee sequence, Bundtzen invokes the practice of "telling the bees" news of their keeper's death or other family events; these poems provide a fitting end to *Ariel* because they mark the death of Plath's marriage (*The Other* Ariel 152). In Duffy's poem, the hallowed bee circle is ruptured, forming "a scattered bracelet" alongside their "burgled hive." Like a broken rosary that once encircled the land, Duffy's disrupted bee colony has lost its capacity for *telling;* it is no longer a ritual communicant (52). As Dowson asserts, "Telling the Bees" translates a traditional "iconography of prayer" to her volume's "global concerns about endangered species" (78). We see this widening scope in the poem's Plathesque image of "black blood in the sea," which merges dead honeybees with environmental consequences of colony collapse disorder. Duffy also sounds this alarm in "Ariel," where the bees ingest "neonicotinoid insecticides" in lethal fields. Shakespeare's words "merrily, / merrily" sound ironically here, broken into single-word lines that rupture the poem's pastoral landscape of cowslips and lavender, which will yield to "land monotonous with cereals and grain" (52, 11). Michelis sees Duffy yoking pastoralism with "a postmodern language of apocalypse" here (349), a foreboding fusion we also find in Plath's "Second Winter" and Sitwell's atomic poems. In "The Bee Oracles," Sitwell's mythic beekeeper inhabits "the plain of the world's dust," bending to her hives as she awaits her bees' rising (237). In "Virgil's Bees," Duffy invokes us to "bless the beekeeper" who wisely places her hives in gardens and orchards "where beelines end" (23).

## BEELINES IN BRITISH WOMEN'S POETRY

My beelines prompt new ways of thinking about Plath and canonicity, returning us to the women's poetry anthologies that brought her into the British canon while widening our perspective beyond women's experience. We can retrace my Plath-Sitwell beeline by returning to their presence in Joan Murray Simpson's 1968 anthology, *Without Adam*. Published by Femina Press in London, it did not aim to anthologize poems "specifically feminine in outlook" (18), but rather to highlight thematically arranged poets from Anne Bradstreet and Aphra Behn to Plath and Adcock. While the brief biography of Plath labels her American, "The Moon and the Yew Tree" marks her presence in the English landscape. Sitwell also had two poems included, but no biography. Plath fared better than Sitwell in the wave of Anglo-American collections of women's poetry published in the 1970s and 1980s. Louise Bernikow's *The World Split Open* (1974) was a notable exception, pronouncing Sitwell "a grande dame of English letters" and praising her poems about the Second World War (159). Published in New York, this anthology omitted Plath; its historical range stopped at 1950. Cora Kaplan omitted Sitwell from her anthology *Salt and Bitter and Good* (1975), published in London and New York. It placed Plath in proximity to twelve British poets, including Rossetti, Smith, and Vita Sackville-West. As the anthology's sole contemporary poet, Plath extends an Anglo-American line of women reaching back three centuries. She also becomes a conduit to those "senior women poets" in the UK that Duffy invokes in her Plath edition (xiv). Yet such canonical plotting renders Plath without a clear British foremother, as she did not engage Smith's work until her final years.

The 1980s marked a tipping point in Plath's relation to the British poetry canon. She anchored Adcock's *The Faber Book of 20th Century Women's Poetry* (1987), represented by twenty poems and occupying more space than any other poet. Grudgingly, Adcock included one Sitwell poem, discounting as mere "surface tricks" the early stylistic innovations Plath so admired. Adcock also aims to shift readers' sense of Plath, foregrounding the late poems' superior "technical ability" and deeming them the work of "a rigorously trained mind" (8, 5). Strikingly, this anthology includes "The Arrival of the Bee Box," marking the bee sequence's importance and furthering Plath's ties to the English landscape. Jeni Couzyn dubbed Plath British in her 1985 *Bloodaxe Book of Contemporary Women Poets: Eleven British Writers*, importing her with other "born elsewhere" poets who built their reputations in the UK—including Adcock and Anne Stevenson. Smith fronts this anthology, which reflects an American emphasis on women's experience. Sitwell appears in the book's introduction as one of the "great women poets" like Smith who rejected marriage, a key figure for modern and contemporary women's poetry (28, 17). Yet Sitwell and Plath are antithetical poets for Couzyn. Her introduction to Plath's section portrays a poet beset by babies and doomed by domesticity, reinforced with the selections "Event" and "The Applicant." This anthology breaks the two poets' beeline as it breaks Plath into Britishness.

Sitwell frames Deryn Rees-Jones's overview of the women's canon in her 2005 *Modern Women Poets*, which also includes Plath and Duffy. This anthology foregrounds "the British and Irish poetic traditions," including American poets who shaped it (22). In her Plath headnote, Rees-Jones cites the journal entry naming Sitwell and Moore as modernist godmothers. Sitwell is clearly the major figure here, appearing prominently in the anthology's introduction and fronting the companion critical study, *Consorting with Angels: Essays on Modern Women Poets*. Sitwell's career proves fundamental to Rees-Jones's historical sense of women's poetry, especially to the occupational hazards of breaking through gendered stereotypes. The anthology headnote for Sitwell positions her "at the centre of London literary life for over 40 years," reinforcing Rees-Jones's pointed reminder that she was "one of the most visible of twentieth century women poets" (56, 17). *Modern Women Poets* includes two Sitwell poems that Plath discussed in her 1953 paper, "Waltz" and "Still Falls the Rain." Sitwell strengthens the anthology's thematic approach; her images of motherhood and revisions of fairy tales anticipate the later poets' engagement with domesticity and myth (including Plath's "Cut," "Daddy," and "Lady Lazarus," plus Duffy's "Little Red-Cap"). Duffy reflects the anthology's contemporary feminist "mainstream," reinforced with several poems featuring women characters (20). Rees-Jones also acknowledges Duffy's status as a literary celebrity but does not connect her popularity with Sitwell's; both poets considerably widened the audience for women's poetry.

Sitwell was a generative figure for Plath's development as a poet, as Plath was for Duffy's. What do we gain by situating Plath between two British Dame Commanders: the first female laureate contender and the first female laureate? Several things, I think. My beelines highlight poems that do not quite conform to the contours we often expect from women's poetry anthologies and feminist literary criticism: poems that stress bodily or psychological dimensions of women's experience, poems that stress women's household relationships. While some of these components do shape my trio's bee poems, the poems I have discussed here also emphasize different kinds of relationships—including each poet's sense of place within the British canon, her place within the environment, and her place within a shifting literary and planetary climate. Put another way, a public voice sounds in these poems that augments the more personal voices (authentic or performed). Beelines widen the soundscape of women's poetry. Beelines also open new routes through what I've termed the WP Network: the dynamic affiliations of poets, critics, and anthology editors through whom the phenomenon *women's poetry* coalesces and disseminates. Direct and multidirectional, beelines can reveal the outliers whose forays marked the lines we find to restore the hive.

# CHAPTER EIGHTEEN

# Medusa's Metadata: Aurelia Plath's Gregg Shorthand Annotations

CATHERINE RANKOVIC

Nearly 700 letters from Sylvia Plath to her mother, Aurelia Schober Plath, can be found in Sylvia Plath mss. II files in the Lilly Library at Indiana University. Aurelia, a professional instructor of Gregg shorthand, inscribed on these letters and their envelopes scores of comments and notes to herself and to posterity. One hundred and fifty-nine of these annotations are in Gregg shorthand. The Lilly Library also has 158 books from Plath's personal library. Shorthand appears in six of those books, for a total, in the books, of twenty-seven shorthand annotations. Never before cataloged or transcribed, these annotations provide new metadata about Plath and her relationship with her only surviving parent and provider. The notes include Aurelia's most urgent and personal responses to her daughter's needs, marriage, suicide, and posthumous fame. This essay argues that Aurelia's annotations in her daughter's letters and books, given further study, can alter the ways readers view Aurelia and the Plaths' mother–daughter synergy. In the absence of Aurelia's half of their remarkably intense correspondence, the annotations begin to make visible Aurelia's contributions to Plath's development and legacy.[1]

I first saw Aurelia's shorthand written on an aerogramme she received from Ted Hughes. This aerogramme, dated March 15, 1963, is the first letter Hughes sent Aurelia after her daughter's suicide on February 11 of that year. This letter was pinned up in a glass case along with other Plath memorabilia in an exhibition titled "Sylvia Plath: Transitions," for the Sylvia Plath Symposium at Indiana University in 2012.[2] Handwritten in the March 15, 1963, letter's lower left margin were three Gregg shorthand characters plus a standard exclamation point. The exhibit card called these "unreadable shorthand." I inquired and was invited to see the letters and books in the library's Plath archive. They

---

[1] I am grateful to the Estate of Aurelia S. Plath for permission to use her annotations for scholarly purposes. Correspondence, Plath mss. II, boxes 1–6a, Lilly.
[2] The Lilly holds 1,934 letters, postcards, and aerogrammes Plath sent to her mother and to others, and letters sent by others to Aurelia S. Plath (ASP) during Plath's lifetime and afterward.
 Plath mss. II, Lilly, boxes 1–6, http://webapp1.dlib.indiana.edu/findingaids/view?brand=general&docId=InU-Li-VAC4841&doc.view=entire_text

were laden with shorthand marginalia that no one had yet transcribed, that is, translated into English.

I had learned Gregg shorthand in high school in the 1970s, just as portable office recording technologies were, in the United States, rendering Gregg and other forms of rapid writing obsolete. My training in Gregg spanned two years: one year to learn the symbols and how to deploy them, and one year to train with recorded and live dictation to build speed to a benchmark 120 words per minute and then transcribe the shorthand back into English with 95 percent accuracy. I was one of the thousands, if not millions, of women who learned to write some form of shorthand in US high schools and business colleges during the entirety of the twentieth century, which demonstrates the pervasiveness of Gregg shorthand. This was vocational training for clerical employment, the largest category of work then open to female high-school and college graduates. John Robert Gregg brought the invention he called "Light-Line Phonography" (1888) from Ireland to the United States in 1893.[3] He published its first viable textbook, *Gregg Shorthand*, in 1898. With a phonetic alphabet made of symbols, which Esther Greenwood in *The Bell Jar* calls "curlicues," it is solely a written language. Also called stenography, shorthand gave women an advantage in the job market over candidates who had typewriting skills only. The length of time required to master the supremely efficient writing system called Gregg is the only inefficient thing about it.

Gregg's system vanquished its dozens of competitors. Its arch-rival Pitman shorthand, favored in Britain, made especial use of fountain pens, and the very popular "Speedwriting," invented in the 1920s by shorthand instructor Emma Dearborn (1874–1937), best served note-takers rather than professionals. Speedwriting allows its writer to take dictation at a speed of about forty to sixty words per minute, while eighty words per minute was the speed ordinarily required of entry-level Gregg stenographers.[4] In the United States, the generic term "shorthand" when used today most likely means Gregg. Aurelia taught Gregg shorthand professionally, for years, at her own alma mater, Boston University's College of Practical Arts and Letters. Sylvia Plath asked Aurelia to give her Gregg shorthand lessons in the summer of 1953. According to Aurelia, after four lessons they agreed to quit (*LH* 124).

The earliest Gregg shorthand annotation in the Plath correspondence at the Lilly is penned sidewise on page four of a letter dated July 8, 1948, sent by Plath from summer camp to her mother. Plath's letter mentions a sore throat and aching back. Aurelia wrote in shorthand on the letter: "camp ask Sylvia 1. How is your back? 2. Do you drink your tea?" The latest annotations are dated 1974, on letters between Aurelia Plath and Ted and Carol Hughes (Boxes 1–6a, Lilly). In Plath's personal library, the earliest shorthand annotations are fourteen annotations in Sara Teasdale's poetry book *Dark of the Moon* (1926), which has "Aurelia F. Schober" and the date "December 29, 1926" written in longhand on its flyleaf. Plath's bookplate on the same flyleaf includes her name in her distinctive rounded longhand and thick black ink she had adopted in youth as her trademark ink. Aurelia Plath's lithe and elegant longhand differs unmistakably from her daughter's. The latest dated shorthand annotation in Plath's personal library is in Plath's paperback copy of E. M. Forster's novel *Howards End*, and the date written is "3/24/68."

---

[3]Northway, "The History of Modern Stenography."
[4]See Fidler, "Shorthand and Speedwriting – What's the Difference?" and "The History of Gregg Shorthand."

Because Plath died in 1963, a shorthand annotation in Olive Higgins Prouty's novel *Home Port* (1947) saying, "Sylvia's stone took six years to be erected!" might have been written in 1969 or later, but that annotation is undated.

Plath's *Journals*, letters, and novel *The Bell Jar* all mention her ambivalence about learning Gregg shorthand to compete for the office jobs then open to educated women, mostly clerical. Although knowing Gregg gave job applicants an advantage over other applicants for secretarial work, Plath did not perceive shorthand as advantageous or aspirational, but as a way the job market coerced women to work as servants to bosses who were almost always men. Given Plath's many mentions of shorthand, is there a chance that Plath herself made some of the shorthand annotations in the Lilly Library? No, for these reasons:

- The instances of shorthand in the Lilly Library span the years 1926–74, outside of the range of Plath's lifetime.
- According to the Gregg shorthand textbook current in 1953, the first four lessons teach the symbolic, phonetic Gregg alphabet and diphthongs. After four lessons, students cannot yet write their own names or words of more than one syllable, nor have they learned any "brief forms," an advanced high-speed Gregg feature Aurelia often used.
- Shorthand appears only on materials sent to Aurelia or that passed through her hands. In 1983 Aurelia donated to the Plath Collection at Smith College materials annotated with Gregg shorthand. These include two letters from Olwyn Hughes, one magazine cover, and various imprinted books and pages dated 1949, 1968, 1972, and 1979. Drafts and typescripts that Smith purchased directly from Sylvia Plath's estate, such as the drafts of the *Ariel* poems, have no shorthand annotations.
- The Gregg shorthand in the Plath collections at the Lilly Library and Smith is consistently of textbook quality, befitting a professional instructor.
- The content, when transcribed, rules out Plath's authorship.
- Plath herself stated that she did not know shorthand. On August 1, 1958, Plath asks her mother whether she could possibly be hired as a court reporter "over people with shorthand." On November 19, 1960, Plath states, "I never will need shorthand" (*L2* 542).
- But Plath did need some form of rapid writing skill when she wanted a clerical job at Harvard University in spring 1959; the job required it. Plath then borrowed a Speedwriting book and taught herself Speedwriting in a few weeks. Instead of a set of symbols, Speedwriting uses the familiar cursive Roman alphabet.[5]

The Lilly had purchased Plath's letters and other materials from Aurelia in March of 1977. No scholar had ever mentioned in print having an interest in what the shorthand might say. I saw that no one else might shoulder this task unless I did. I returned to the

---

[5]SP to ASP, November 19, 1960. Plath first asked her mother to mail her the Speedwriting textbook she had left in Wellesley in her letter of September 23, 1960. See also Rankovic, "I Never Will Need Shorthand."

Lilly in 2013 to begin cataloging and transcribing. In 2017, I received permission from the Estate of Aurelia S. Plath to publish and discuss my findings.

So, what did my first glimpse of shorthand say? On the March 15, 1963, letter, Aurelia drew an arrow in black ink pointing to Hughes's statement: "I don't want ever to be forgiven." She wrote in shorthand in the letter's left margin: "You won't be!"

As evidenced in her comments toward Hughes, Aurelia's shorthand includes some plainspoken personal opinions. In some cases, her shorthand was probably intended as a form of encryption. For example, when Aurelia purchased Teasdale's *Dark of the Moon* in 1926 ("to make a black day brighter ... and it did," she wrote, in shorthand, on the flyleaf) she was a twenty-year-old college junior, and the shorthand annotations conceal private romantic musings from prying eyes. Yet anyone schooled in Gregg can read them. Taking into account all materials with Gregg shorthand at both the Lilly and those I have cataloged and transcribed at Smith, there is arguably a pattern of encryption in Aurelia's shorthand remarks on correspondence to, from, and about Ted and Olwyn Hughes.[6] However, shorthand does not equal "secret code." I can imagine, though, that Aurelia's remarks regarding the Hugheses, which start in 1956, are garbed in shorthand as a token gesture toward discretion. Aurelia also expressed in shorthand things she forbade herself openly to say. For example, on Sylvia's letter of October 23, 1956, reporting that she and Ted Hughes, newlyweds, are finally about to move in together, Aurelia's shorthand reads: "No children please! Say this indirectly!"

It is important to note that Aurelia's longhand annotations far outnumber those in shorthand, and begin on Sylvia's earliest surviving letters to her mother, dated 1938, ten years before any shorthand appears. Tracy Brain, one of the few scholars to mention Aurelia's annotations, wrote that they deserved a study of their own, but I did not catalog the longhand annotations unless the longhand was mixed with shorthand (*The Other Sylvia Plath* 33). From 1943 onward, Aurelia marked and annotated her daughter's letters with an array of instruments and inks, in margins and on envelopes, clearly taking care not to interfere with or deface the text.[7] While reading Sylvia's books, Aurelia paid special attention to passages Sylvia had marked, choosing for her own annotations a writing instrument or ink very clearly different from Sylvia's. Aurelia's longhand and shorthand annotations in the Plath mss. II and Plath's personal library form a superscript or descant to what became the Plath biographical narrative whereby what Sylvia wrote—often in private form—was taken as infallibly true. The shorthand material offers metadata about her artist daughter's youth as it unfolded into ambitious and sometimes agonizing young adulthood. Some of the shorthand was written in retrospect as Aurelia grieved her dead daughter and suffered collateral damage as Plath's work and biography became sensationalized. Is this Medusa in the margins, committing micro-aggressions against her daughter's texts, which eventually belittled her mother and engulfed her? "I write comments on letters to use in my replies," Aurelia wrote in longhand on a letter from Sylvia dated September 24, 1962, but the transcriptions show that is not always the case.

Before Plath became a public figure, her mother wrote notes, mostly to herself, on the letters she received from her daughter or on their envelopes: "file in safe in my bedroom" (envelope, April 25, 1951); "share with Gordon if the time is right" (envelope, August 30,

---

[6]For example, Olwyn Hughes to ASP, May 28, 1968. Plath Collection, Smith.
[7]ASP redacted only two of Plath's letters, dated September 23, 1962, and November 22, 1962.

1954) or "wonderful letter!" (envelope, March 13, 1962). It appears that Aurelia annotated most of the letters soon after they arrived, but she also added some annotations later. For instance, the notes on an envelope postmarked November 19, 1952, read:

[In Aurelia's longhand] First dread note:

[In shorthand] Sylvia cheered up on thanksgiving vacation. Myron helped. But I believe this was the beginning of our trouble in the summer of 1953.

Throughout the correspondence, Aurelia lightly and consistently penciled in longhand any missing dates on letters from her daughter, including the day of the week and a best guess, with a question mark, if the date seemed uncertain.

After Plath's suicide, we see that Aurelia reread and annotated her daughter's letters, often in longhand and affixing the date of the annotation. At a point yet to be determined, Aurelia understood that strangers might be reading these letters. After that, it seems that what she wished to say to posterity she then chose to write in longhand, often dating her annotations, as if to help future scholars. It is good to remember that Aurelia collected and preserved these primary materials and might have censored them far more radically or destroyed them, but instead made them public. In no case were any of the few redactions, erasures, or strikeouts punitive or unreasonable—and, while cataloging, I discovered that half the time the erasures were still legible. In Plath's copy of *Howards End*, adjacent to Forster's unflattering description of people "bored by psychology and shocked by physiology" (289), Aurelia wrote in shorthand, "like my sister." Aurelia then scratched out "sister" but failed to obliterate it.

Some of Aurelia's annotations combine longhand and shorthand. Doing so might have been a matter of convenience, as if she had been swiftly taking notes during a telephone call. Other times, only shorthand would fit in the narrow margins of Plath's postcards, letters, and aerogrammes. Aurelia used a blank half-page on her daughter's letter of October 23, 1950,[8] to take down verbatim, in pencil, a portion of what seems to have been a panel discussion about the brotherhood of man. Earlier that month, Plath had left home for her first year at Smith, and her brother Warren was away at prep school, so Aurelia was having her first taste of freedom from parenthood. We now know one of the things Aurelia did with her free time. That Gregg shorthand annotation is the longest in the findings, at 250 words. Even the sometimes fragmentary evidence the shorthand provides can be enough to support the impression, entirely new, that Aurelia was actively interested in politics: on the envelope enclosing Sylvia's letter of January 9, 1953, Aurelia listed in shorthand eleven "subjects questions for a pol discussion group." Among the topics, which are geared to students, are communism, religion, and race. It is not wrong to begin to think that Aurelia had political views which might have been a model or whetstone for her daughter's.

Reviewers of Aurelia's edition of Sylvia's letters, titled *Letters Home* (1975), typically wrote that Plath's letters were often cheery performances tailor-made to please her mother, whose editing foregrounded a happy, affectionate, sexless Sylvia that critics did not recognize. "Sivvy's life as Mrs. Plath would have us see it," said Maureen Howard

---

[8]SP to ASP, *c.* October 23, 1950, misdated October 9, 1950. *Letters* editors Steinberg and Kukil determined the October 23 date and that this was the first of two letters SP sent that day to ASP.

in *The New York Times Book Review* (1). The jacket copy on *Letters Home* says, "There is much to be read between the lines." Yet the two volumes of *The Letters of Sylvia Plath*, published in 2017 and 2018, show that Plath's letters to all correspondents, except psychiatrist Dr. Ruth Beuscher and Aurelia, were chirpy and brimful of her successes, in part because Plath had so many. From girlhood, Sylvia wrote her mother constantly and in detail about her illnesses, fears, defeats, shocks, economies, politics, and shortcomings more frankly than to other correspondents. Anyone asserting that Aurelia purged *Letters Home* of "all" these "negative" things has not carefully read the book. For her editing, subjected by legal agreement to extensive and anonymous editing by Hughes—editing so severe that Aurelia's editor at Harper & Row, Frances McCullough, forced Hughes to make concessions—Aurelia received innumerable raspberries from readers who felt sure they knew Plath much better than her mother did.

As if the dozens of openly readable postcards Plath sent home were not evidence enough, the shorthand transcriptions prove that Plath's letters home were not for her mother's eyes and gratification alone. Aurelia typically shared Sylvia's letters with her entire family, and Sylvia was aware of that. Aurelia respected her daughter's requests to keep certain letters confidential, seven times writing on envelopes, in shorthand, phrases such as "do not share." These notes sometimes specify family members: "Do not let Dot and Frank see this" (January 16, 1960). We find in the transcriptions that Aurelia acted as a curator for Sylvia's letters, possibly also sharing them outside the family, such as with Plath's boyfriend Gordon Lameyer.[9] Aurelia's shorthand says she planned to store in her safe Plath's letter of April 25, 1951. This short, ecstatic letter, not in *Letters Home*, says Plath will be hosting boyfriend-to-be Dick Norton and then another date on the upcoming Saturday, and she is excited about being Norton's guest at Yale University on the weekend of May 11. The letter closes, "Love to the world—even Stalin—Love, your own Sivvy" (*L1* 310). As far as we know, Aurelia preserved all of Sylvia's letters. We are left to guess why Aurelia wanted to isolate this particular one.

In the summer of 2013, I began cataloging Aurelia's shorthand annotations in boxes 1–6a and in the books in Plath's personal library. When doubting a transcription, I consulted three generations of Gregg shorthand textbooks and dictionaries. This is because Gregg shorthand evolved along with the business world's requirements and vocabulary. Periodic revisions also made it leaner and easier to learn. Aurelia, who graduated from college in 1928, was probably schooled in what is now called "Pre-Anniversary" Gregg, likely that edition's fifth and final iteration (1916–28).[10] In 1929 the "Anniversary" edition replaced it. Aurelia would have taught that edition at Boston University's College of Practical Arts and Letters from 1942, when she began teaching there, until the "Simplified" edition of Gregg came out in 1949. That edition was superseded by the "Diamond Jubilee" edition (1963–78), the edition I learned. No iteration of Gregg is a radical departure, but each can be different enough so that, for example, a single shorthand character formerly transcribed as "love" is now the brief form for "will have." Gregg's efficiency is such that the stroke representing "d" can be read as "would," "did," "dear," "date," "dollars," or the suffixes "-ward" and "-hood." When written as a downstroke, the same symbol is the letter "j." How does one know that same symbol is a downstroke? Context is everything.

---

[9]Shorthand annotation on the envelope of a letter from SP to ASP, August 30, 1954.
[10]"About the Pre-Anniversary Gregg Shorthands," https://gregg.angelfishy.net/abpreann.shtml, retrieved March 17, 2021.

I returned to the Lilly repeatedly to page again through the correspondence and the books Plath had owned to fill in any blanks and revisit the few shorthand characters that resisted transcription. I separated the transcription data from the Lilly into two Microsoft Excel spreadsheet data sets: the correspondence and the books. I treated letters and their envelopes as separate physical artifacts and cataloged them by the date written or stamped (such as a postmark) on the artifact itself.[11] The book spreadsheet includes standard bibliographical information. The correspondence spreadsheet includes the year, month, and date affixed to the artifact; the name of the letter's author and its addressee; the shorthand characters' location (for example, the page number, top or bottom, left or right margin, on the envelope's verso, and so on); the medium used (pencil or pen); and the color of the penciling or ink. I noted strikeouts, erasures, and any special features, such as whether the characters were circled or unusually large. Annotations with longhand and shorthand mixed are indicated, and both the longhand and shorthand are included in the transcription spreadsheet. There are columns for further references, and acknowledgments for the assistance and corrections I received regarding the context, the transcriptions, or a letter's date.[12] In two cases, the shorthand author transcribed it; in one of those cases, the shorthand was not Gregg.[13] When stray marks on the artifacts could be mistaken for shorthand but are not, I noted them.[14]

Aurelia Plath composed her annotations under varied circumstances over a span of nearly fifty years. It is hoped that the transcriptions will remove any hesitation scholars felt about exploring Aurelia's annotations and, through them, the facts of Aurelia's life and character, these in their turn illuminating Plath's. Other currently available resources for the inevitable reframing of the Plaths' mother–daughter relationship include the two volumes of *The Letters of Sylvia Plath*, observations from Sylvia's peers and friends in interviews kept in the Rosenstein papers at Emory University, the first and successive edits of *Letters Home*, and, because Sylvia destroyed Aurelia's half of the mother–daughter correspondence, the intensely personal letters Aurelia wrote to others, preserved in others' archives.

Commonly, scholars interpret the Plaths' mother–daughter relationship through the few most embittered or critical of her daughter's writings. None of these scholars had alongside them, or could now present, a list of enough facts about Aurelia so as to constitute a reliable biographical timeline. Aurelia's editor at Harper & Row deleted from Aurelia's introduction to *Letters Home* several scenes of mother–daughter conflict ending with Aurelia morally triumphant, diminishing the impression that Aurelia had opinions, a job, and autonomy.[15] By contrast, Plath's father Otto's life and character, outside of what his daughter wrote about him, is well researched and accounted for. The shorthand transcriptions open to critique the one-dimensional portrayals of Aurelia as either the monstrous "Medusa" or a pitiable empty shell who somehow brought up two remarkably successful children.

---

[11] These data sets are freely available for download at the website https://epublications.marquette.edu/aureliaplath/.
[12] Dates of the letters correspond to those in *The Letters of Sylvia Plath*.
[13] See "Dick Norton Knew Shorthand," aureliaplath.blogspot.com, posted by Author, September 5, 2016.
[14] I welcome corrections or alternative transcriptions of shorthand annotations, or findings of shorthand I have not yet cataloged.
[15] For example, in a deleted passage, college student Plath criticizes her mother's hairdo and second-hand clothes. Aurelia reports that, amused, she refrained from replying, "I dress this way the better to provide for *you*, my dear" (box 30, folder 67, Smith).

In *Letters Home*, Aurelia Plath's voice—consistent with the voice in her surviving letters—asked the world to believe she and Sylvia loved each other, that Aurelia knew her daughter well, that Aurelia was not like *The Bell Jar*'s pious "Mrs. Greenwood," and that artists betray people.[16] At the moment that Plath scholars felt free to toss "Medusa's" monument *Letters Home* into the dustbin, the complete *Letters* and the shorthand annotations shed new light on Aurelia's role in supporting and developing a great artist and hint that some of our perceived conclusions about Aurelia were premature.

---

[16]ASP also wrote Gregg shorthand annotations on her manuscript of *Letters Home*, which is also at the Lilly. Cataloging the shorthand on that manuscript was outside of the scope of this project.

# CHAPTER NINETEEN

# "I may hate her, but that's not all": Mother–Daughter Intimacy in the Plath Archive

JANET BADIA

Sylvia Plath's writings often deal, rather infamously, with her family, including husband Ted Hughes, children Frieda and Nicholas, and parents Otto and Aurelia Plath. Plath's poems about her parents in particular—including "Daddy" and "Medusa"—are among some of her most well-known pieces of writing. Given the attention her parents receive in her writings, as well as the general biographical interest in Plath's life and art, it is not surprising that both Otto and Aurelia Plath feature importantly in Plath scholarship. Otto Plath, in particular, has received considerable attention, a reflection no doubt of the outsized impact his death had on the eight-year-old Sylvia but also the ways in which his death took center stage in the very poems that would bring her fame following her suicide in 1963. As it turns out, though, it may well be Aurelia Plath who hovers over Plath's writing and career (both lived and posthumous) most dominantly. My use of the word "hover" here is intentional, evoking as it does the idea of the helicopter parent so prevalent in today's discourse around parenthood but suited, some have argued, to Aurelia as well. Plath herself, as Heather Clark notes in her groundbreaking biography of Plath, raged at her mother for "hovering too close," an indication of just how "close, complicated, and often difficult" their relationship could be (*Red Comet* 3, 20). The word "hover" also suggests how Aurelia appears to haunt, specter-like, the edges of the Sylvia Plath archive, shaping publication decisions regarding Plath's work and making her presence felt throughout the archived materials.

Of course, I am not the first scholar to recognize Aurelia Plath's influence on her daughter's life and work. Previous scholarship has grappled with everything from Aurelia's representation within Sylvia Plath's writings themselves, to her editing and publication of *Letters Home*, to her displeasure over publication decisions made by the Plath estate over the years.[1] Despite such scholarly attention, "there seems to be," in Clark's words, "only

---

[1] See, for example, Bundtzen's *Plath's Incarnations: Woman and the Creative Process*, especially chapter two; Brain's "Sylvia Plath's Letters and Journals," especially pages 146–51; and Malcolm's *The Silent Woman*, especially pages 39–40.

one version of Aurelia in the popular imagination" (*Red Comet* 22). In *The Haunting of Sylvia Plath*, Jacqueline Rose presents one of the more provocative considerations of the mother–daughter relationship in her examination of the saga over the publication of *Letters Home*. While Rose focuses on the significance of what was omitted from the final collection of letters when it debuted in 1975, her discussion of the particular points of tension between Aurelia Plath and Ted Hughes over the editing of the unpublished letters serves as a helpful entry point for thinking about the broader issue of Aurelia's role in the Plath archive. For Rose, Aurelia's investment in controlling the narrative of the letters reflects a desire to "assert the exclusive, inviolable intimacy of the mother-daughter relationship," even as the publication of the letters themselves, she argues, would come to undermine that intimacy (81). As Catherine Rankovic points out, Rose's conclusion overlooks the degree to which many of the items in *Letters Home* that appear on the surface to be written by Plath to her mother are actually letters intended to be shared with the immediate and even extended family, an observation that complicates Rose's conclusion and invites deeper consideration of the nature of intimacy in the context of Plath and Aurelia's relationship as it is constructed through archival material.[2]

Whether one agrees with Rose's conclusion about Aurelia's controlling intentions or not, her examination helpfully calls our attention to the multifaceted role Aurelia Plath has played as the editor of *Letters Home* in the construction of the narrative about Plath's life and work. Writing nearly ten years after Rose, Tracy Brain sheds additional light on this role in her discussion of Aurelia's annotations to Plath's original letters in her critical study, *The Other Sylvia Plath*, and then later in *The Cambridge Companion to Sylvia Plath*. As a result, those unable to visit the archives get a much clearer picture of Aurelia's role, not simply as editor of *Letters Home*, but as an archivist of Plath's life and work.

In this essay, I hope to contribute to the conversation about Aurelia's role in Plath's life and work by examining her presence in the Plath archives at both the Lilly Library at Indiana University and the Mortimer Rare Book Collection at Smith College. In particular, I want to focus on her own personal annotations to Plath's writing within the larger context of how both reading and writing figure as acts of embraced and resisted intimacy between mother and daughter, as evidenced in Plath's letters and journals, and the challenges scholars face in their explorations of this intertextual terrain. In many ways, this work is now easier to do given the publication of *The Letters of Sylvia Plath* in two volumes "complete and unabridged" (*L1* xix). As Peter K. Steinberg and Karen V. Kukil note in their introduction to the volumes, only 383 of the 856 letters written by Plath to her mother and family were published in *Letters Home*, and those were often only excerpted (*L1* xx). Because of the relative completeness of the current volumes of letters, readers not only have a much richer sense of who Plath was as a correspondent, a creative and professional writer, a friend, a wife, and a mother, but they also have a fuller picture of the relationship between her and her mother, a picture revealed not only in the letters Plath wrote to her mother but in her correspondence with others in

---

[2]Catherine Rankovic notes that this assumption that the letters Plath sent home would be shared is evident in how Plath herself would write "do not share this one" on some letters, which Aurelia Plath would often underscore by writing, in Gregg shorthand, "do not share" on the envelope of the letter. For this observation, among many others, I am indebted to Rankovic. Our conversations about Aurelia began in 2017 when I had the pleasure of presenting on a panel alongside her at the Belfast conference, Sylvia Plath: Letters, Words, and Fragments. More recently, she has shaped this project by generously reading and offering feedback on a draft of this essay.

which Aurelia is the topic. Those with access to the archives have had access to this fuller picture for some time, but general readers have had to depend on scholarly summaries of the omitted letters until now. In some ways, the publication of *The Letters of Sylvia Plath* may make research about the letters in the archive itself appear superfluous. However, in my discussion of the letters throughout this essay, I wish to maintain the idea of the archive, first, and most obviously, because I want to discuss Aurelia's annotations on the letters, which go largely, though understandably, unaddressed in *The Letters of Sylvia Plath*, and second because the letters have been for over four decades now an important part of the archive, shaping our collective understanding of the author from the edges, so to speak, of Plath studies. At the same time as we celebrate the work both volumes of *The Letters of Sylvia Plath* make possible, it is important to recognize the still one-sided view we have of this particular mother–daughter relationship. Indeed, Rankovic's efforts to expand our knowledge about Aurelia's life and to recover her voice in the narratives we construct about Plath and Aurelia's relationship, which is evident not only in her contribution to this essay collection but in her blog "Studying Aurelia Plath," are revealing to us just how one-sided our views have been. Rankovic's research, combined with the publication of *The Letters of Sylvia Plath* and Clark's *Red Comet: The Short Life and Blazing Art of Sylvia Plath*, invites us to turn our attention back to Aurelia, while also enabling us to do so in important new ways.

As Gail Crowther and Steinberg point out in *These Ghostly Archives*, Aurelia Plath's contributions to the archive at Indiana University in 1977 expanded the initial collection Sylvia Plath had established there when she sold a selection of typescripts, worksheets, and prose to Indiana in 1961 (22). Given that the archive's focus is largely on materials and artifacts that pre-date Plath's marriage to Hughes, one goes into the Lilly Library already with specific frameworks in mind. Certainly, as Crowther, Steinberg, and Brain all argue, Plath's identity as beloved daughter comes to the forefront of the story, as does Aurelia's grief as a mother. The nature of the archive as a repository of Aurelia's grief is perhaps most obvious in those annotations on Plath's letters that show Aurelia reading backwards with an eye toward the telling signs of the tragedy to come, such as when she writes on the envelope to one letter from November 1952 the words "first dread note," before continuing on in shorthand with a note explaining that, while Plath had cheered up over the Thanksgiving vacation, the visit had nonetheless marked "the beginning of our trouble in the summer of 1953" when Plath attempted suicide at the age of twenty (Letter, Sylvia Plath to Aurelia, November 19, 1952).[3]

However, this discursive materialization of grief is not the only layer of what we might call the "Aurelia annotative archive." Indeed, this archive is both broader and more intriguing than previous scholarship suggests. In general, the annotative artifacts tend to fall into four broad, though not comprehensive, categories: there are Aurelia's notes in the margins of Plath's correspondence to her mother, which includes but is not limited to the letters Aurelia would include in *Letters Home* (including, in some cases, extensive comments made on the envelopes of the letters themselves); there are notes in

---

[3]Material from the Lilly Library and Smith are used with permission from the Aurelia Plath Estate. I am indebted to Barbara Blauvelt for the initial transcription of Aurelia Plath's shorthand notations that first enabled my interest in this project to develop and for Rankovic's exhaustive work transcribing and, importantly, sharing her transcriptions of all of Aurelia Plath's annotations, which allowed me to verify the content and in some cases correct it. All definitive transcriptions of Aurelia's shorthand are provided with Catherine Rankovic's permission.

the margins of letters Aurelia received from Plath readers in the decades following the publication of *Letters Home* that were often heavily annotated by Aurelia before being archived; there are notes in the margins and on versos of other letters, including ones Aurelia received from Olwyn Hughes, as well as her responses to them, and as Rankovic has discussed, there are notes Aurelia made to books saved from Plath's personal library. Beyond this large archive at the Lilly Library, Aurelia's presence in the Plath archive extends to artifacts held at Smith as well, where one encounters Aurelia, among other places, through notes she added to the cover pages and in the margins of magazines that featured Plath's posthumous publications.

Many of Aurelia's annotations are made in Gregg shorthand, a fact one has to consider within the context of the tension between Plath and her mother over shorthand. Although Plath would write to her mother in 1952 expressing the wish that her mother would teach her shorthand—a scheme she believes will help her land a job in the publishing house business—and does so again in an April 1953 letter, by 1955 her attitude toward shorthand had soured (*L1* 423, 596). "I will not sacrifice my time to learn shorthand," she writes to her mother,

> because I do not want any of the jobs which shorthand would open up[.] ... I do not want the rigid hours of a magazine or publishing job. I do not want to type other people's letters and read their manuscripts. I want to type my own and write my own. So secretarial training is out for me. That I know.
>
> (*L1* 596)

Plath's rejection of learning shorthand, despite her mother's insistence on the practicality of the skill, had clearly become a source of tension at this point, a tension, moreover, that appears to be tied to her building frustration over the circumscribed life she imagines Aurelia wants for her. Whatever one makes of the significance of the presence of Gregg shorthand on Plath's letters in light of this tension, Aurelia's use of shorthand complicates the question of audience significantly and may well have hindered previous appreciation of the annotations since they could prove difficult to transcribe. Fortunately, we now have Rankovic's groundbreaking transcriptions of the Gregg shorthand, which are available online and discussed elsewhere in this collection, finally enabling examinations of the large body of annotations by those not trained in Gregg shorthand ("Aurelia Plath's Shorthand Transcriptions").

In Brain's discussion of Aurelia's annotative practices, she focuses her attention on the marginalia composed in standard English and identifies the potential range of audiences for it (including Aurelia herself as editor, the deceased Plath, and the researcher in the archive), as well as the various functions served by Aurelia's annotations, including their editorial nature as notes clearly meant to assist in the filing/ordering of information, their redactive function as in the case of those sections that have been scored out with a black marker, and their manipulative function as opportunities to direct researchers' attention in ways not possible in the published manuscript itself ("Sylvia Plath's Letters and Journals" 146–51). In short, Brain concludes that Aurelia's annotations are her way of "build[ing] her own narrative upon" the letters, of controlling the reader's interpretation, of justifying and defending herself, and, more poignantly, of "having an argument with a correspondent who cannot reply" (150).

Brain's treatment of these annotations has played an important role in drawing attention to the myriad layers of Plath's archive. I revisit her work here because it provides a launching point for my own sense of the importance of the annotations and because it demonstrates the challenge of formulating an approach to Aurelia's role. In *Marginalia: Readers Writing in Books*, H. J. Jackson argues that readers' annotations "are a familiar but unexamined phenomenon. We do not understand it well." Moreover, "what difference does the presence of notes make to the reader who follows? Under what circumstances could such notes be considered value added to the book, and for what audience?" (4). Amanda Golden's *Annotating Modernism: Marginalia and Pedagogy from Virginia Woolf to the Confessional Poets* has already demonstrated for us the value added of Plath's own annotations to books in her personal library. In the case of Aurelia's marginalia, I would like to argue that the annotations make a great deal of difference. At the same time, it is important to recognize that the annotations do not exist in a vacuum; they have important contexts of their own, not all of them connected to the texts they mark. For the purposes of my own examination, I want to focus on annotations that cluster into two general categories: those that demonstrate the particular challenges Aurelia faced as both the grieving mother and the aggrieved mother, and those that demonstrate the intimacy of reading, shared writing, and shared experience between Aurelia and Plath.

Despite Plath's often harsh treatment of her mother in her private and public writings—as seen, for example, in "The Disquieting Muses," "Medusa," and *The Bell Jar*—Aurelia occupied a rather privileged position as a reader of Plath's work. In fact, Aurelia was often the first reader of Plath's works, a pattern that started while Plath was a child and that continued throughout her career. As early as 1943, when Plath was just ten years old, she was enclosing original lines of poetry in letters to her mother, often as gifts. A March 20, 1943, letter written to Aurelia, includes five short verses that appear to be inspired in part by "the nicest book I have ever read," which a young Sylvia recounts in detail over the course of the letter (*L1* 7). Establishing a pattern that would hold throughout her six years of summer camps (1943–8), Plath often uses her letters to her mother from camp to report on her poetry production and submissions to newspaper editors. A July 1946 letter includes a poem titled "Mornings of Mist," for example, and suggests Sylvia regarded poetry as an important point of exchange in the mother and daughter's letter writing (*L1* 70–1). As if she were a mother cheering on her own daughter, Sylvia even notes how Aurelia's latest letter "sounded like a lovely poem in blank verse" (*L1* 71). Such encouragements targeted at persuading Aurelia to turn to professional writing of one kind or another would become a pattern that runs throughout Plath's letters to her mother.

As Steinberg and Kukil explain in their introduction to *Volume I* of *The Letters of Sylvia Plath*, letter writing played an important role in the daily lives of the Plath family; Plath wrote more than 700 letters to her mother, which were frequently shared with her family (*L1* xxiii). While at camp as a young girl, Sylvia wrote almost daily to her mother, detailing the activities of her days from meals eaten to physical exercise to the creative arts she enjoyed and spent money on. The letters represented to Sylvia a form of connection "second best to talking" (*L1* 108). They also underscored the importance of her mother as empathetic listener: "I know you're hearing and understanding what I'm doing. I must have someone understanding to talk to" (*L1* 108). This feeling continues into Plath's early adulthood and beyond. In a letter written to her mother in March 1951, Plath, then in her first year at Smith, acknowledges that writing letters to her mother is the least she can do after receiving "the fat yellow-stamped crowd of morale boosting letters you sent all week" (*L1* 294). As this letter suggests, the benefit of exchanged letters appears, for Plath, to be mutual, so much so that when failing to live up to the expected routine of correspondence while serving as an exhausted nanny for the Mayo family in

1951 she experiences regret for what she has deprived Aurelia of in the process: "I feel very sorry I don't write more often, mummy, because your letters are great sustenance to me" (*L1* 354).

When the subject is writing more specifically, a young Plath appears to have regarded her mother as a test audience, a role not particular to Aurelia but distinct in its relative continuity across Plath's writerly life. In a rather long letter sent in October 1951 and characteristic of the detailed, play-by-play accounts she often sent Aurelia regarding her social affairs at Smith (a letter, Plath instructs, "To be read at leisure, sitting down … in a good light … slowly"), Plath abruptly turns from ruminations over a date with Constantine Sidamon-Eristoff to a "very rough" and "fragmentary bit of free verse" she seeks her mother's opinion on (*L1* 381, 380). Enclosing a newly composed sonnet in a letter to Aurelia the following month, Plath requests that her mother, "See what [she] can derive from this chaos" (*L1* 393). When she sends another sonnet less than two weeks later, Plath's discussion of it constructs Aurelia not only as an interested audience but as a reader in-tune with the nuances of Plath's developing skills as a writer. "Note," writes Plath, "the new rhymes" representing her "attempts to get away from being continually hackneyed" (*L1* 396). The following summer Plath would write to Aurelia, excited about the arrival of a telegram from the fiction editor at *Mademoiselle* informing her she had won first prize in their college fiction contest and would be publishing her submission, "Sunday at the Mintons'." She notes that "although I only told Perry [Norton] & Paul Dalton about the story, I get great pleasure out of sharing it with you who really understand how terribly much it means as a tangible testimony that I have got a germ of writing ability" (*L1* 449–50). On the one hand, examples such as this one lend evidence to the perspective widely held by scholars—and indeed by Plath herself—that Plath offered her publishing successes to Aurelia as gifts of one kind or another. On the other hand, one can acknowledge that Plath also benefited from the exchange in ways that worked well for her, at least for a time, suggesting a gift exchange more complicated than scholars have understood it to be. Aurelia certainly appears to have understood it as a mutually beneficial one, in any case. In fact, Aurelia intended one day to return to Plath the letters she had written home, extending this idea of texts as gifts within a complete, though deferred, cycle of exchange. As Aurelia writes in the introduction to *Letters Home*,

> [t]hroughout these years I had the dream of one day handing Sylvia the huge packet of letters. I felt she could make use of them in stories, in a novel, and through them meet herself at the varied stages in her own development and taste again the moments of joy and triumph and more clearly evaluate those of sorrow and fear.
>
> (3)

When analyzing the full collection of letters Plath wrote to her mother, in fact, the degree to which Plath shared her writing life with her mother stands out starkly. Letter after letter is consumed with details about poems, stories, essays, publication acceptances and rejections, papers written for her college courses, and more that are rivaled only by details from her dating life and later her marriage and separation from Hughes. Through it all, Plath appears to regard her mother not only as a first reader of her creative endeavors, but as a sounding board for all things related to the writing and publishing process. Plath also suggests that she values her in those roles. Especially on matters related to publishing in women's magazines, Plath seeks and follows Aurelia's advice on a number of occasions, writing, for example, in a 1954 letter that "I acted immediately upon your suggestion and sent the story off to WOMAN'S DAY. You were right about it being too short for most magazines" (*L1* 844). Even when she doesn't appear to be seeking her mother's advice, Plath's attention to details about what poem or story she is sending where and why suggests Aurelia played an important role in Plath's processing and decision-making, even if only the role of a passive listener. As Plath put it in the letter about "Sunday at the Mintons'" cited above: "God, I'm glad I can talk about it with you—probably you're the only outlet that I'll have that won't get tired of my talking about writing" (*L1* 450).

To return to my discussion of Aurelia's role as reader of Plath's poems in particular, one of the most unexpected examples of a text shared with Aurelia is the poem "Pursuit," which Plath sent, along with another poem ("Channel Crossing"), to Aurelia in March 1956. In the letter containing the poems, Plath writes, "I'll be so eager to hear what you think of these" (*L1* 1133), before going on in some detail to explain the growth and shifts in scope she herself sees in them, as well as the influences on the poems. About "Pursuit," in particular, Plath gives her mother instruction for how to read it (noting, as she often does, that it is meant to be read aloud), and wondering if her mother will see "the simple seductive beauty of the words," if she would just read it "slowly and deliberately" enough (*L1* 1133, 1134). That Plath should send her mother—and wish to have approvingly read—a poem we know she wrote immediately after her first, now rather notorious, encounter with Hughes underscores the complexities of Plath's relationship with her mother. For Rose, these complexities arise from "a process of exchange" that "troubles the available identifications—the distinctions, for example, between mother and lover, between Aurelia Plath and Ted Hughes" (*Haunting* 80). But in reaching for such an interpretation, Rose risks overlooking a simpler one: namely, that the sharing of "Pursuit" represents the degree to which Aurelia and Plath construct intimacy, above all, through shared texts and the mother and daughter's often intertwined and intertextual reading lives, of which the exchange of poems was a crucial part. Certainly, it is true that central to their relationship was a mutual love of reading, shared reading experiences, and conversations about texts—particularly, to quote Aurelia—conversations about how specific texts "made us *feel*" (*LH* 31, emphasis mine).

One of the earliest glimpses of this affectively charged relationship comes in Aurelia's introduction to *Letters Home*. In it, she notes that Sylvia "read almost all the books I collected while I was in college, used them as her own, underlining passages that held particular significance to her" (*LH* 32). For Aurelia, this marked a continuation of practices from Plath's childhood, which she illustrates in her introduction with the example of reading a poem by Edna St. Vincent Millay together, an experience that especially moved both of them and that, Aurelia suggests, represented a "sort of psychic osmosis" between them that would come to define their relationship at large, from her perspective (*LH* 32). In her biography of Plath, Clark documents another specific instance of a shared reading experience, this one in 1948 when both Aurelia and Plath read and annotated a single copy of *Emerson: The Basic Writings of America's Sage* (103). In her own writing, Plath would express a similar sentiment about the importance of their shared reading lives. She observes in one letter, for example, that her courtship with Hughes felt like she was living amidst the world of "all the poets we love together" (*L1* 1166). Even as Plath struggled through the winter of 1962 following her separation from Hughes, Aurelia wrote to her daughter about books, as evidenced in the few surviving examples of Aurelia's letters to her daughter we have. In two December letters, she goes into considerable detail about works she had recently completed and includes long excerpts from them in some cases.

She also informs Plath in a December letter that she has renewed her subscription to the *Ladies' Home Journal* (Letters, Aurelia Plath to Sylvia, December 4, 1962, and December 8, 1962).[4] That Aurelia would devote such attention to the experience of reading during Plath's most difficult time likely underscores the degree to which Aurelia believed that written texts could be salves of sorts, as well as tethers linking mother and daughter to one another.

This belief in the restorative effects of shared texts is perhaps most clear in the case of *Ladies' Home Journal*, an example of textual sharing that comes to take on significant meaning over the course of Plath and her mother's relationship. While Plath tells Dr. Ruth Beuscher that she is the one who turned her onto *Ladies' Home Journal*,[5] it is Aurelia who made possible Plath's enjoyment of the magazine once she and Hughes moved back to England. As she tells Aurelia in an October 1961 letter in which she asks her to "pack me off a *Ladies' Home Journal* or two," she is homesick for the magazine, particularly its "special Americanness" (*L2* 668). Aurelia obliges, as we know from Plath's response a few weeks later: "Today came a big Xmas parcel from you with the two Ladies Home J's which I fell upon with joy and rejoicing—that magazine has so much Americana I love it. Look forward to a good read by the fire tonight" (*L2* 698). That Plath would soon after write to Aurelia expressing "how awfully homesick" for her mother she has been since the birth of her second child suggests interesting connections between mother-love, motherland, and written texts as mutually binding forces that can tie two people to one another. Marsha Bryant's examination of Plath's engagement with *Ladies' Home Journal* sheds additional light on these connections. As Bryant explains, unlike its rivals, *Ladies' Home Journal* "included a poetry department on its contents page" throughout the 1950s, and "poetry figured into the *Journal*'s discourse of domesticity" in ways that shaped Plath's own poetry, perhaps explaining why this particular magazine mattered so much in the mother–daughter gift exchange (*Women's Poetry* 218, 219).

In totality, this shared intimacy around reading, letter writing, and written texts is important for what it can teach us about Plath's intellectual life and the thoughts and feelings that might have been shaping her own writing, even as we recognize that Plath's letters should not be taken as direct reflections of her "true" self, as other scholars have rightfully cautioned. At the same time, we should not discount or explain away Plath's self-representational project in the letters as one somehow less authentic than her other self-representational projects, such as her journals and poems. While deserving of more attention than I can give it here, a lack of resolution on the issue of Plath's multiple self-representations does not negate the usefulness of an examination of the letters that focuses on the ways both mother and daughter construct mother–daughter intimacy in their writings. Shared intimacy is also a useful framework for understanding Aurelia's role as archivist of Plath's work. As Aurelia makes clear in the introduction to *Letters Home*, textuality allows her to establish a narrative of "intimacy"—to use her own word

---

[4] I am grateful to Peter K. Steinberg for generously sharing his knowledge of these letters with me.
[5] In a January 1961 letter to Beuscher, Plath writes, "my first American ladies' magazine story will be dedicated to you: it was you started me reading the LHJ" (*L2* 566). In her biography of Plath, however, Clark notes that Plath first began reading *Ladies' Home Journal* in 1944 (64). Perhaps her acknowledgement to Beuscher merely signals her rediscovery of the magazine in adulthood, but it also seems possible that the acknowledgment is part of the narrative Plath is building about the magazine in her imagination as she works to articulate its significance in her life and work.

from the opening paragraph of the introduction (3)—between mother and daughter. The degree to which Aurelia is invested in and tested this narrative is evident both in the notes she wrote on the letters at the time of their receipt and in those notes she made while preparing *Letters Home*.[6]

On the May 1952 letter she numbers 219, for example, Aurelia writes on the front of the envelope in black ink "get Thomas Wolfe 'You Can't Go Home Again.'" In blue ink characteristic of the later annotations she made in the process of editing the letters, Aurelia notes that in the letter Plath referred to Auden. The back of the envelope contains, in black ink, an extensive note on Auden's techniques, a list of his poems that she ostensibly plans to read, and additional notes on W. B. Yeats, Stephen Spender, and Wilfred Owen—notes researched and written, it would seem, in response to Plath's mentioning in the letter that Auden was to be a guest instructor at Smith the following year (Letter, Plath to Aurelia, April 30, 1952; *L1* 438–9). Similarly, on the letter she marks #50, Aurelia writes the word "use" and includes the following note: "mentions my reading of 'The Lady's Not for Burning.'" Aurelia's note highlights Plath's reference in the letter to the play by Christopher Fry, which she happens to have in her possession having been lent it by a friend. Plath's mention of the play appears to be a reaction to Aurelia's own enjoyment of the book. As she exclaims in the letter, "I'll have to read it, now, you make it sound so delightful!" (Letter, Plath to Aurelia, November 4, 1950; *L1* 215). A third, rather poignant example underscores how these shared experiences of literature transcended Plath's death. In an April 1960 letter marked #24, Plath mentions that she plans to see Eugène Ionesco's play *Rhinocéros*; Aurelia adds an annotation about her own plan to see the same play the following Monday, in 1974 (Letter, Plath to Aurelia, April 29–30, 1960; *L2* 465).

Beyond the manuscript to *Letters Home*, the importance of Aurelia as reader is on display in the magazine issues preserved in the Plath Collection at Smith. Particularly relevant to my argument here is the October 1972 issue of *McCall's* that contains not only Plath's story, "The Mother's Union," but also, as Aurelia notes on the cover to the issue, another essay that has both nothing and everything to do with Plath. The essay by a young Joyce Maynard (who in 1972 had just begun living with J. D. Salinger) is entitled "My Parents Are My Friends" and subtitled "A self-portrait of a vanishing species—a loving daughter—by an extraordinary 18 year-old writer." Maynard's essay is literally intertwined with Plath's story throughout the issue of the magazine because of the use of layout jumps: one turns from the first page of Maynard's essay on page 79 to the first page of Plath's story on page 80. Interestingly, Aurelia annotates Maynard's essay more heavily than Plath's own story, suggesting perhaps that Aurelia sees Maynard as a stand-in for Plath, and the very first annotation in Gregg shorthand to the opening page of "My Parents Are My Friends" perhaps explains why: "excellent and was my aim in life for my mother was my best friend!"

---

[6] It is worth noting that the letters and tributes Aurelia received from fans following the publication of *Letters Home* would likely have reinforced for her that this investment in intimacy paid off. Among those letters Aurelia saved is ample evidence that readers felt more deeply connected to both Plath and Aurelia through their experience of reading *Letters Home* and that they gained some deeper insight into their interconnected private lives through the public sharing of their correspondence. One particular correspondence stands out especially, as the letter writer refers in his salutation to Aurelia as mother and expresses being moved by Aurelia's salutation of him as son.

Further into the essay, Aurelia highlights, both through marginal notes and underlining, several passages that are important to my examination here, including one that calls attention to Maynard's description of how she and her mother would work over story scripts together working paragraph by paragraph over how a story might be improved and another about how her "parents' greatest compliment to us was their high expectations" (146). She underscores Maynard's mention of how her family never ate in silence and instead her mother would always tell a story, about which Aurelia writes in the margin: "Sylvia's first hour home from college had us all sitting around her enthralled by her accounts not only of events but of new ideas—door opening!"

That so many threads should become intertwined in this one archived artifact is fascinating, especially for those grappling to better understand the peculiarities of this particular mother and daughter relationship. A story about a community of mothers, an essay by a grateful daughter that highlights the symbiosis of the lives of parents and their children, and the image of Aurelia as enthralled reader of Plath's texts, both in life and after death, encapsulates the mother–daughter intimacy that preoccupies Aurelia's public constructions of their relationship. That all of this comes through via the inscription of Plath's text by Aurelia—in this case, on her printed publication but in other cases on her original letters—invites us to think about what all is at play here. Just whose story is being told? Just whose archive is being preserved here? It seems especially important to ask such questions in light of Plath's private writings about her mother, writings in which Plath situates her own texts at the heart of a struggle for self-possession.

That is to say, while the act of mutual reading figures in Plath's writing as a relatively unproblematic shared experience between mother and daughter, Plath's early and continued practice of sharing her writing and publishing successes with her mother signifies something different. I am thinking here most obviously of Plath's long, intense, and at times uncomfortably mean explorations of her emotions toward her mother that we become witness to in the full notebooks included in *The Unabridged Journals of Sylvia Plath*—emotions centered on Plath's anxieties that her mother's appropriation of her writings had blocked her creative productivity. Most notable perhaps is Plath's December 1958 entry in "Notes on Interview with RB" that begins with Plath's dramatic admission that finally having permission to hate her mother has hit her "like a sniff of cocaine"—"better than shock treatment" (*J* 429)—and that culminates, for my purposes here, with several paragraphs detailing Plath's realization that, as she puts it, "[t]o spite your mother, you don't write because you feel you have to give the stories to her, or that she will appropriate them" (*J* 448). Underscoring this sentiment, this time making use of shouting capital letters, Plath continues: "My work is to have fun in my work and to FEEL THAT MY WORKS ARE MINE. She may use them, put them about her room when published, but I did them and she had nothing to do with them." And as though needing the words to reverberate in her head and on her page, she repeats: "MY WRITING IS MY WRITING IS MY WRITING. Whatever elements there were in it of getting her approval I must no longer use it for that, I must not expect her love for it. She will use it as she has always used it, but this must not upset me. I must change, not she" (*J* 449).

As these passages suggest, the entanglement of shared textuality, shared subjectivity, and shared love coalesces at the site of Plath's own writing, just as they do at the site of Aurelia's writings, including in the introduction to *Letters Home* and her annotations. In an annotation to a 1952 letter in which Plath tells Aurelia that "[c]heery, morale boosting missives will be much appreciated" (*L1* 409), Aurelia adds: "Why I wrote so much!" Whether the explanation is meant for her deceased daughter, the researcher in the archive, or just herself, it expresses a sentiment not unlike Plath's own understanding of the purpose of letter writing. "I love and live for letters," she tells her mother in an October 1962 letter (*L2* 866).

Although much more could be said about Plath and Aurelia's psychic entanglements, I want to turn back to the matter of shared texts in order to tie together some important loose threads in my examination. First, while they are most stark in the private writings, Plath did not withhold her feelings of resentment and hatefulness entirely from her mother, and it appears she may have weaponized the withholding of texts—and even their destruction—in her fight for self-possession. Assuming word had not yet leaked out to Aurelia, one can imagine her shock upon learning from Plath in an October 1962 letter that she is about to have a "secret" novel published (*L2* 861). When Plath does share the news of her novel with her mother, all traces of her past practice of sharing texts as an act of love and intimacy are gone, replaced with aggression. "I have, if you want to know, already had my 1st novel finished and accepted," she announces to her mother in this (literally) feverishly written letter (*L2* 861). It is a letter, moreover, that asserts Plath's desire to "make a new life," that brashly rejects Aurelia's wish to visit her in England ("it would be psychologically the worst thing to see you now or to go home"), and shoves in Aurelia's face her creative productivity: "I am a writer ... I am a genius of a writer, I have it in me. I am up at five writing the best poems of my life, they will make my name," all while simultaneously diminishing Aurelia's mutual claim to Plath's newest publication (*L2* 861). Furthermore, that "the best poems of her life" include "Medusa," written on the same day as this particular letter, captures, in a remarkable way, the degree to which Plath was waging a war on all fronts. Ejecting Aurelia from her role as privileged reader, Plath presents none of her new poems to her mother. Nor will Plath countenance Aurelia's textual encroachment. In another letter written just a few days later, one by now well-known to many readers, Plath unleashes on her mother:

> Don't talk to me about the world needing cheerful stuff! What the person out of Belsen—physical or psychological—wants is nobody saying the birdies still go tweet-tweet but the full knowledge that somebody else has been there & knows the <u>worst</u>, just what it is like. It is much more help for me, for example, to know that people are divorced & go through hell, that [*sic*] to hear about happy marriages. Let the Ladies' Home Journal blither about <u>those</u>.
>
> (*L2* 874–5)

While Plath goes on to apologize to her mother two days later, asking for forgiveness for "my grumpy sick letters," she doubles down on her rejection in a letter written four days after the initial rant: "Now stop trying to get me to write about 'decent courageous people'—read the Ladies Home Journal for those! It's too bad my poems frighten you—but you've always been afraid of reading or seeing the world's hardest things—like Hiroshima, the Inquisition or Belsen" (888).

That on both occasions Plath frames her rejection of her mother as a rejection of the *Ladies' Home Journal* is significant. In Plath's imagination, the magazine, as we have already seen, is tied up with mother-love. If it is her trusted "mother-person" (*J* 435), Dr. Ruth Beuscher, who led her to start reading the magazine, it is her mother Aurelia that keeps her supplied with it. Furthermore, it is the magazine that most connects Plath to the "Americana" of her motherland. While it seems clear that what Plath is rejecting is the ideology represented by the *Ladies' Home Journal*, to leave the matter there risks overlooking the ways in which the mother–daughter relationship has been fused at the very place where both women's subjectivities meet: at the site of shared texts, powerfully manifest in the example of this particular women's magazine with its blend of poetry and domesticity, a magazine that Plath alternately loved and hated, coveted and rejected. "I may hate her, but that's not all," Plath writes in her journals." "I pity and love her too. After all, as the *story* goes, she's my mother" (*J* 445, emphasis mine).

# PART III
# Media and Pedagogy

# CHAPTER TWENTY

# Plath and Media Culture

NICOLA PRESLEY

Sylvia Plath's relationship to media culture was marked by the rapid development of technology and the new media artifacts and products that were created as a result. Media both constructs and is constructed through societal and cultural forces, and although media cannot be seen to represent a clear sense of lived experience, it does elucidate contemporaneous values and expectations. Moreover, by exploring media culture alongside literary texts, it is possible to assess the intersection of social and textual traces. While Plath's relationship with *popular* culture has been explored by a number of critics, such as Marsha Bryant, Jacqueline Rose, Robin Peel, and Christina Britzolakis, this chapter seeks to explore the textual traces of media culture in Plath's writing through close reading and a wider consideration of media discourses. I am using the term "media culture," following André Jansson, who argues that the term demonstrates how *"media products* become cultural (via their incorporation within webs of significance) and, conversely, how these products enter into and become influential for the formation of webs of significance" (10). Media culture, therefore, encompasses both *products* of media, such as television and radio programming, and the media technologies themselves. I am concerned here with Plath's relationship to media as both product and object—the way in which readers, listeners, and viewers interact with the media object itself, in addition to their consumption of the media output.

Two of Plath's short stories, "Superman and Paula Brown's New Snowsuit" and "The Shadow," demonstrate the ways in which she incorporates media culture into her work. These stories have received a great deal of critical attention; Robin Peel, for example, writes that "Plath had described the formative influence of radio drama on the imagination of the child" (134). Luke Ferretter provides an excellent reading of the two stories alongside their cultural contexts in *Sylvia Plath's Fiction*. Jacqueline Rose argues that the stories are "linked by the central place they give popular culture" (*Haunting* 199). My reading here builds on this earlier work by focusing on the stories' intertextual relationship with specific radio programming and comic books, paying particular attention to Plath's incorporation of popular cultural figures such as Superman and The Shadow. An acknowledgment of this connection expands the textual borders of Plath's prose and positions her work in a critical dialogue with the messages of media culture.

Susan Bassnett writes that "political affairs during Plath's lifetime meant something very different than they had meant to previous generations[.] ... The generation that came to maturity in the 1950s suffered from the shadow cast by the past and the shadow cast by the future menace of nuclear conflict" (22). This tension between past and future can be seen in both of the stories; they both take place just after America entered the war and were written by Plath in the 1950s at the height of Cold War atomic fears. The unfolding of war in Europe in 1939 was broadcast to millions of American families as was Roosevelt's decision for America to join after the Japanese attacked Pearl Harbor. J. Fred MacDonald argues that "American children fought World War II in front of their radio sets[.] ... At home, America was protected from spies and saboteurs by the central characters of Superman [and his fellow superheroes]" (68). Indeed, the comic book of Superman urged its readers—"ALL RED-BLOODED YOUNG AMERICANS"—to adhere to the Superman "code" and to "aid the cause of justice" (Morrison 16). Superman was created by Jerry Siegel and Joseph Shuster and the hero first appeared in *Action Comics* in 1938. Due to the character's popularity, the radio show began in 1940 (Sterling and O'Dell 715). By the 1950s, Superman had become a global cultural icon representing good, humility, super strength, and the desire to rid the world of evil and injustice. He is characterized by his appearance: the blue suit with the gold and red "S" emblem and his red cape and red boots, which Grant Morrison argues "added a patriotic touch of Stars and Stripes Americana to the character" (27).

In Plath's 1955 story "Superman and Paula Brown's New Snowsuit," the narrator describes Superman's blue suit as "shining," as he appears to her in her "technicolor dreams" (*JP* 282, 281). Superman teaches her to fly, and she, along with her friend David, worships him. The superhero becomes a mythic, God-like figure; he is omnipotent and has the freedom to fly anywhere, perhaps the ultimate emblem of freedom. Superman defeats his evil enemies who continually plot against him, which adds to his attraction to the listeners in a period when America was fighting numerous enemies. In "Superman," the narrator is haunted by her own enemies when she is accused of ruining Paula's snowsuit by pushing her into an oil slick despite Paula slipping of her own accord. Paula blames her, and the other children join in, chorusing, "[y]ou did it" (*JP* 285). The narrator's mother and Uncle Frank are told about the incident and sit at the table "solemn and sorrowful in the candlelight" (*JP* 286) while she protests her innocence. Uncle Frank explains to her that "you have never had to hide anything from me, you know that. Only tell me how it really happened" (*JP* 287). It is at this moment that her relationship with Uncle Frank is irreversibly altered. The fact that Uncle Frank is of such importance is noteworthy because of the story's intertextual dialogue with radio programming. Macdonald argues that "the air was filled with dozens of network and local 'uncles'—like *Uncle Don* on WOR, *Uncle Olie and His Gang* on CBS, and *Uncle Elmer's Children's Hour* on WJAS—who related stories and songs and introduced regular characters" (44). These "Uncles" could be relied upon by children as trusted figures and, in fact, may have operated *in loco parentis* by reading stories to children. As Eskenazi explicates in his memoir of radio: "I see now that these characters actually were part of an extended family—mine. They filled in the empty spaces in my life: the father (or fatherly types), a sister, a brother" (2). In "Superman," Uncle Frank fills the symbolic space left by the death of the narrator's father.

The characters of Uncle Frank and Superman are intermingled in the mind of the narrator. She says, "I was sure that he [Uncle Frank] bore an extraordinary resemblance to Superman incognito" (*JP* 282). Superman, of course, has his own alter ego of Clark Kent that allows him to live unnoticed in the human world. By fantasizing that Frank is Superman in disguise, she is clinging to the hope that Superman lives among us to help in times of trouble. The ending of the story, after the false accusation of ruining Paula's snowsuit and her growing awareness of the horrors of the Second World War, destroys the ideal of both the fictive Superman and his disguised self on earth as Frank. When Frank talks to her in the bedroom, he appears featureless, losing his resemblance to Superman and becoming a shadowy stranger. She concludes: "[T]he silver airplanes and the blue capes all dissolved and vanished, wiped away like the crude drawings of a child in colored chalk from the colossal blackboard of the dark. That was the year the war began, and the real world, and the difference" (*JP* 287).

Superman also appears in Plath's story "The Shadow" (1959), where fellow superhero The Shadow has a more central role. The character of The Shadow was first featured on radio in 1930 as the narrator of *The Detective Story Hour*, and due to his popularity, the radio program *The Shadow* was launched in 1937 on the Mutual Network (Sterling and O'Dell 689). The Shadow was a master of disguise, able to assume multiple identities in the comic book adaptation, although in the radio show, he only had one alter ego—that of Lamont Cranston. He also fought crime and evil but was a far more mysterious figure than Superman. The Shadow had the ability to disappear and could only be placed by his disembodied voice. Each episode of *The Shadow* began with the famous introductory line: "Who knows what evil lurks in the hearts of men? The Shadow knows." This line was spoken by the character in an eerie and echoing voice, punctuated by ominous laughter. It is actually a rather frightening sound, but children knew that The Shadow was only interested in fighting "the bad guys" and were comforted by his "enlightening" statement, as Sadie puts it in Plath's story (*JP* 151). Sadie also recalls the regular ending of the program, again spoken by the superhero with the same sardonic laughter—"The weed of crimes bears *bitter* fruit. Crime does *not* pay" (*JP* 151–2). Sadie says, "[W]e had no cause to wonder: *Will* the good people win? Only: *How?*" (*JP* 152). "The Shadow" ends on a similar note to "Superman and Paula Brown's New Snowsuit" with Sadie saying to her mother, "I don't think there is any God, then. ... Not if such things happen" (*JP* 155). Both narratives represent the loss of childhood and innocence; the worshipped figures that represent justice to the child—Frank, Superman, The Shadow, and God—all simultaneously, as one, fail to live up to expectations when situated in the real world.

In both stories, the ending of innocence is accompanied by the draining of color from the world. Plath's references to color relate back to the comic books, as shown in "The Shadow" when Sadie sees the "gaudily covered comic books" in the store (*JP* 150). This shadow and the absence of color thus have the effect of erasing the pages, obliterating the comfort of childhood stories. At the end of "Superman and Paula Brown's New Snowsuit," the narrator can feel a "black shadow creeping up the underside of the world like a flood tide" (*JP* 287). Similarly, the day of the snowsuit incident is "bitterly cold, and the skies were gray and blurred with the threat of snow" (*JP* 284). When Paula falls, "[t]he dull, green light of late afternoon came closing down on us, cold and final as a window blind" (*JP* 285). In "The Shadow," after Sadie's nightmare about the Japanese film, she compares the shock of a dream without a happy ending to the disappearance of color: "If a familiar color—the blue of Winthrop Bay, and the sky over it, or the green of grass, trees—suddenly vanished from the world and left a pitch-black gap in its place. I could not have been more bewildered or appalled" (*JP* 152). Sadie's use of "appalled" prefigures the appearance of the word in a number of Plath's late poems, which also contain an ominous darkness. For instance, in "Thalidomide" (1962), the speaker states that "[y]our dark / Amputations crawl and appall" (*CP* 252). Similarly, in "The Arrival of the Bee Box" (1962), the persona is afraid of the "dark, dark" of the bee box, although "it is the noise that appalls me most of all" (*CP* 213).

The title of "The Shadow" itself, on the one hand, refers to the radio character, but on the other, denotes the shadow in Sadie's mind that lengthens until "the whole globe seemed sunk in darkness" (*JP* 155). Sadie and the unnamed narrator have a childhood filled with "elementary colors" (*JP* 151) and "colors ... clear and definite as patterns seen through a kaleidoscope" (*JP* 281). The expiration of childhood blurs those colors into dangerous and unknown shadows. In a 1950 letter to her German pen-pal, Hans-Joachim Neupert, Plath wrote: "I would much rather read a book and have the pictures and images made in my own mind than to have someone else think for me. I believe that everyone must think for himself—and imagine for himself. Why live if we are just an echo and a reflection?" (*L1* 160).

Although Plath is writing about reading books here, this argument about the importance of the imagination is also relevant to reading comic books and listening to the radio. But at the conclusion of these stories, the narrators are failed by their imaginary, colorful heroes, and they are disappointed by the fiction of the cultural texts. Finally, then, the narrators' journeys in both stories into adolescence, awareness, and enforced maturity come to symbolize the opening lines of each episode of *The Shadow*: "Who knows what evil lurks in the hearts of men? The Shadow Knows." As of course, by the end, the narrators also know. For Plath at this time, media culture is responsible for the muting of the colorful imagination.

In the same letter to Neupert, Plath writes:

> And television! It has become the goal of the poorest family to own a television set … to sit around a screen and watch crude vaudeville shows and baseball and football which are a national craze. It is so easy to shut off thought … to be lulled into a dreamy, self-conscious state to these entertainments which numb our creative intelligence.
>
> (*L1* 160)

This letter is crucial for dating one of her unpublished manuscripts in the Lilly Library. The poem is entitled "Virus TV," and is not included in Ted Hughes's selection of Juvenilia in the 1981 *Collected Poems*. It is undated, but clues within can help to situate it. Plath's speaker in "Virus TV" mentions Milton Berle in the opening stanza, and Berle was the presenter of the *Texaco Star Theater* (later, *The Milton Berle Show*), which moved from radio to television in 1948. The second stanza alludes to *Hopalong Cassidy*, which was first broadcast on television in 1949, and then syndicated by NBC in 1950 (Kackman 80). Although the television series of *Hopalong Cassidy* did not begin its initial run until 1952, studios edited previous *Hopalong Cassidy* feature films into smaller segments, thus creating a networked series. This places "Virus TV," at its earliest, as written in 1949, although, as Kackman has shown, *Hopalong Cassidy*'s huge popularity came after NBC's syndication in 1950 (80). Therefore, it is likely that the poem was written in, or after, 1950. The letter dated January 2, 1950, contains views which are consistent with the poem, and also contains images that appear within it. "Virus TV" includes references to baseball and vaudeville shows and is an attack on the ubiquity and quality of television. More specifically, the virus metaphor implies that television is a cultural contagion, which multiplies and infects the masses. In her exploration of Plath's relationship with popular culture, Christina Britzolakis argues that "during the 1950s, liberal fears about the decline of true individuality and the menace of conformity were commonplace" (*Sylvia Plath and the Theatre of Mourning* 14). "Virus TV" and the letter to Neupert are both expressions of these fears of cultural standardization. Through a series of rhyming couplets, the speaker expresses concern here about the content of television programming, which seems quite different from the light-hearted entertainment shows of Berle, and *Hopalong Cassidy*, although Plath's speaker also expresses concern about children's viewing habits in general.

The style of "Virus TV" is something of an anomaly in Plath's early manuscripts. It is full of errors and mistakes, such as the misspelling of Milton Berle. By using the word "boil" instead of his actual surname, Plath associates his name with a symptom of infection, the "Virus TV" of the title. In misspelling words at the end of each line, like "fatigue," "heard of," "acidy," and others, Plath utilizes rhyming couplets but also creates visual eye rhymes. The reason for this is twofold. One, the visual rhymes refer to the visual imagery of the television set, and two, in its simplicity and errors, the poem links watching television with a lower standard of literacy. Britzolakis notes the typographical and spelling errors in Plath's "[t]ypescript on writing a true confession," published as an appendix in her *Journals* and argues that the mistakes "seem to ventriloquise the sloppy, dissolute identity of 'sylvia' the trash writer, who is denied the dignity of a capital letter" (*Sylvia Plath and the Theatre of Mourning* 149). Thus, when Plath writes about popular culture in "Virus TV," she uses a similar technique of deliberate misspellings and poor grammar to make a wider point about the educational limitations of the television audience, and the readers of "trash" fiction.

Plath's views on television developed throughout her lifetime; she understood its appeal to mass audiences even as she critiqued the limitations of this new visual medium. The production of television programs was a source of fascination for Plath. For instance, at *Mademoiselle* in June of 1953, she and the other student editors were invited to watch the recording of *Two for the Money*, a quiz show hosted by Herb Shriner. In a letter to her mother describing this experience she wrote:

> To see the TV cameras roll down the ramps and focus on 3 stage sets, and then to see the picture simultaneously on the TV sets ahead, was really intriguing. TV is a rising thing ... I wonder what it would be like to write for it[.]
>
> (*L1* 638)

On the same day, Plath wrote to Myron Lotz to tell him about the show and described it as an "experience I'll never forget" (*L1* 639).

Ted Hughes was invited to take part in *Wednesday Magazine*, a British television program, in April of 1961. Plath writes to Aurelia about watching the "fascinating" program being filmed: "I watched the TV monitor screen at the same time as the real studio. First they did a run through, then criticized it, then broadcast 'live'" (*L2* 609). After the experience of viewing Hughes on television, Plath's next completed poem was "Insomniac" (1961), which deals with themes of doubling, and copying, recalling the "live" program, and seeing it simultaneously on the screen. The character in the poem is male, although the speaker is not gendered, which suggests that the narrator is spectating the character. The opening line, "[t]he night sky is only a sort of carbon paper" (*CP* 163), is an assertion that immediately brings to mind duplication. Memories are presented as being like filmed images: "Over and over, the old, granular movie / Exposes embarrassments" (*CP* 163). The "granular" nature of the movie suggests the television screen rather than that of cinema, and it is a constant presence for the character. In the fourth stanza:

> His head is a little interior of gray mirrors.
> Each gesture flees immediately down an alley
> Of diminishing perspectives, and its significance
> Drains like water out the hole at the far end.
>
> (*CP* 163)

The reflective gestures seem to recall the experience of watching Hughes in the studio while at the same time observing him on the screen. The size of the man on the screen is certainly a diminished figure, and the mirrored interior of his mind demonstrates multiple perspectives and an inability to escape from scrutiny. As the self is repeatedly duplicated, it begins to lose its shape and definition before becoming a waste product: drain water. Thus, "Insomniac" features the image of the double that so often fascinated Plath, and Steven Gould Axelrod writes that Plath's mirrors "expose a self already on the margins of disintegration" ("The Mirror and the Shadow" 292). In this poem, the experience of watching Hughes and his televisual reflection enhanced this idea of the disintegrating self, refracted through multiple screens. Plath told Aurelia that "this is [Ted's] first & last TV program" (*L2* 609), and the end of the poem refers to "trivial repetitions" (*CP* 163), an allusion to Hughes's dismissive attitude toward any further television appearances.

Despite Plath's views on television throughout most of the 1950s, she uses a television set in her 1956 story "The Wishing Box," first published in *Granta* in 1957. Although I have argued elsewhere ("Plath and Television") for the significance of television in this story, I wish to extend this with a comparison to a 1955 episode of the sitcom *The Honeymooners*, since both the story and the sitcom illustrate the same false promise television offered to women. In the episode, entitled "TV or not TV," housewife Alice insists that her husband buy her a television set. "I want a television set Ralph ... I am sick and tired of this ... you're out all day long." "The Wishing Box" tells the story of a suburban couple, Agnes and Harold. Harold goes out to work while Agnes stays at home, depressed and jealous of Harold's vivid dreams and professional lifestyle from which she feels "exiled" (*JP* 214). "[B]y dint of much cajolery, Agnes persuaded Harold to buy a television set on the installment plan" (*JP* 219), mirroring *The Honeymooners* since the "worry" of debt from a credit agreement is the excuse Ralph uses for not buying a television. Alice gets her television, but the episode's conclusion shows that the television merely extends her isolation. Ralph purchases one with his neighbor, which is positioned in Alice and Ralph's house in the main living space. As the two men watch the television, "Alice retreats to her bedroom, a prisoner in a house taken over by television" (Spigel 50). The purchase of the television actually adds to Agnes's isolation and depression in "The Wishing Box" as she watches it all afternoon while drinking sherry. The alcohol and television numb her to such an extent that Harold's face becomes a blur when he returns home. Although I am not suggesting that Plath saw this particular episode of *The Honeymooners* (and indeed, it is unlikely that she did so), the similarity between the program and the story demonstrates Plath's cultural critique of ideas about television and its particular and gendered role in the suburban household. The title of the story comes from a dream Agnes recalls having as a seven-year-old, where she imagined a "wishing-box land" (*JP* 215). The wishing boxes looked somewhat mechanical, like "coffee grinders," and the user had to speak their wish into the box while turning the handle (*JP* 215). Sandra M. Gilbert notes that the title is also inspired by "the 'wishing box' full of sleeping pills" that Agnes uses to cause her death ("In Yeats' House" 213). However, the "wishing box" also surely refers to the television set and the promise it made to cure the loneliness of the suburban housewife.

In Erving Goffman's 1961 study of asylums and their inmates, he compares the situation of patients using "removal activities" such as "solitary TV watching" to "the bored and weary housewife who takes a few minutes for herself" out of her day (68). During the 1950s, there was an increase in the number of people suffering from mental illnesses, or perhaps more accurately, an increase in the number of people who sought help from doctors and psychiatrists for their condition. As the cultural historian Allison McCracken points out, "in 1954 and 1955, the number one identified health problem in the US was 'emotional disease'" (52). She notes that over half of all the patients were women, most of whom were married, and one of the reasons for the high number of admissions may be as a consequence of the pressure on women to fulfill their role as perfect suburban housewives. This increase in reported "emotional diseases" occurred at the same time as the meteoric rise of television. While it would be absurd to claim that television created these diseases, it is interesting to note that in some of Plath's writing, representations of television featured in relation to these mental illnesses and how, and some patients' cases included some reference to television.

Plath worked as an administrator in 1958 at Massachusetts General Hospital's psychiatric clinic. She documented this experience, published as "Hospital Notes" in an appendix in the unabridged *Journals of Sylvia Plath*. The notes detail some case histories from the hospital, and many of the patients' stories indicate television's involvement in their illnesses. One patient, Ferrara, is too afraid to leave the house because "something might happen," so he stays home watching TV shows (J 626). Another, Edward Cutter, has a "sense of unreality," and "[w]hen he watches TV he feels he is the one who is creating everything" (J 627). Finally, Minnie Lassonde stated that "people on TV talked crazy talk" and "she dreamed about things she'd seen on the TV during [the] day" (J 628). Plath collected these case histories to "expand" her writing and her view of herself (J 424), but she also provides the reader with a fascinating look at case histories that would surely be inaccessible due to confidentiality. The three case histories above are remarkable in that they show three people experiencing mental illness, all citing representations of television as a part of that illness, but in each case, the television aspect is different. For Ferrara, television represents stability, a place of safety away from the potential danger of the outside world. By observing people on television within the confines of the home, he feels far safer than venturing outside. On the other hand, Minnie Lassonde *is* threatened by the television's presence in the home, and she cannot even escape in sleep as the television pursues her in dreams. Cutter's mental state is heightened by the simulation of the real on the television, and he imagines himself as "Big Brother" controlling what he (and presumably others) sees.

In the short story "Johnny Panic and the Bible of Dreams," written at the same time as the "Hospital Notes," the protagonist details the case of Harry Bilbo, who developed a fear of "the filth in this world" (JP 165). The condition became so bad that Bilbo's mother had to turn "the TV knobs" for him, and Bilbo eventually becomes a recluse. He is cured thanks to the "white-coated tinkerers" who persuade him to turn "on the TV himself" (JP 166). Later, when the protagonist is led to electric shock therapy, she describes the box as "covered with dials and gauges" (JP 170), which serves to remind us of Bilbo's reluctance to turn the knobs on the television, and the fear of the "other" box in the living room.

Furthering the comparisons between the discourses of the treatment of mental illnesses and television, televisions and television rooms increasingly became a feature in hospitals in the 1950s. Eugene Glynn argues that they had a particular function in asylums and were not merely for entertainment purposes:

> [television] is used, certainly, in every hospital and in every institution as an extremely effective non-chemical sedative. It is well known that fixing on a moving visual stimulus inhibits motor activity. The prime example of this is the situation of hypnosis,

and the concentration and stillness of television watchers certainly is reminiscent of the hypnotized.

(180)

In Alex Beam's history of McLean Hospital, he details contemporaneous criticism of the treatment patients received. McLean was criticized for failing to provide stimulation for patients, with many finding little to occupy their time, other than, of course, the TV room (Beam 183). This was evident during Plath's stay at McLean, when her benefactor, Olive Higgins Prouty, wrote to director Franklin Wood to complain: "I usually find Sylvia wandering listlessly up and down the corridor and when I leave she says she will do the same, as there is nothing else to do" (Beam 154). In one of the few letters that survive from when Plath was at McLean, she wrote to Edward Cohen on Monday, December 28, 1953:

Our ward of ten people is very attractive, having a diningroom, two bathrooms, a large livingroom overlooking the golf course and the lights of the town below, and containing several bridge tables, a lovely piano, and a TV set to amuse away the evenings.

(*L1* 657)

It is possible that Plath was putting "a brave face" on things in this letter to Cohen, as in the same year she wrote to Myron Lotz, insisting that she "never watch[ed] TV" (*L1* 639). However, the letter to Lotz was written more than two months before her stay at McLean, and with such a paucity of evidence, it is difficult to know whether or not Plath did find the television set entertaining. However, this letter does demonstrate Plath's awareness of media audiences, and it is clear that she understood the function of the television to provide entertainment to the patients. The installation of a television set in hospitals is a way to normalize the experience for patients, of providing a reflection of home. As Anna McCarthy suggests, "[t]he very fact that [television] is a medium of transmission, of communication across distance, means that televisual representation—often charged with an aura of temporal immediacy—is seen as linking disparate places" (14). A patient can be watching the same programming as she would at home, perhaps the same program that her family is currently enjoying at the same time. There is a comforting familiarity in the broadcast images in whatever environment they appear. This gives the viewer a sense of stability and creates an impression of a shared experience, even when the audience is not watching together.

More generally, Plath's observations elucidate an understanding of diverse audiences, marked by different modes of consumption for each medium. Karen Ross and Virginia Nightingale explore the evolution of media audiences and the development of the relationship between consumers and media texts. They note how "media technologies also impose interaction regimes on their audiences that physically limit what people can do while in the process of engaging with media technologies" (13). In "The Wishing Box," Agnes initially attends the cinema to cope with her loneliness but decides that watching television is "much better than the movies," as she could drink sherry at the same time (*JP* 219). Agnes would not be able to drink sherry in the cinema due to societal limitations and therefore opts to hide from public space. She continues to engage with media culture, but she chooses television for its location in the domestic sphere, thus allowing her to enact her private activities. John Fiske writes: "In going out to cinema we tend to submit to its terms, to become subject to its discourse, but television comes to us, enters our cultural space, and becomes subject to our discourses" (74). Conversely, in "Virus TV," the speaker declares that she would rather see a movie, and this actually forms part of the cure for the "virus" of television.

Elsewhere, films can be dangerous viewing. In "Superman" and "The Shadow," the protagonists go to the cinema to watch a movie for a birthday party, which in "Superman" is named as Disney's *Snow White and the Seven Dwarfs*. The narrator of "Superman" is allowed by her mother to go to the cinema, but her mother does not know that it is a double feature presentation and that the other film is about a Japanese prisoner of war camp containing graphic scenes of violence and torture. The narrator is deeply horrified by what she sees: "Our war games and the radio programs were all made up, but this was real, this really happened" (*JP* 284). Seeing these atrocities being committed, so close up, on the big screen makes them authentic and abhorrent, and they are a world away from the fictitious radio programs. And in *The Bell Jar*, cinema becomes a cause for illness. Esther Greenwood goes to see a "very poor" movie in New York with the other magazine interns (*B* 41). As the film unfolds, Esther begins to feel unwell, and she describes the audience as looking "like nothing more or less than a lot of stupid moonbrains" (*B* 42). She takes pleasure in treading on the audience members' feet as she leaves the cinema, and she wonders "whether it was the awful movie giving me a stomachache" (*B* 42). Of course, Esther is suffering from food poisoning, but both the film and the audience contribute to her discomfort. She dislikes the uniformity of the people in the cinema, and to return to Fiske's argument, Esther has to submit to the "terms" of the cinema. She rebels against this by leaving and disturbing the other viewers who are enraptured by the power of the media text.

The examples discussed in this chapter demonstrate Plath's awareness of media forms and the myriad ways that audiences can—and do—engage with each medium. In her professional life, Plath herself engaged with the medium of television, from her early rejection of it in "Virus TV" to her ambition to write for television. In a letter to Aurelia in 1955, Plath mentions a story she has written for the Christopher Awards, "Tomorrow Begins Today," and confirms her research for a television version: "I've read up on TV requirements and limitations and been realistic in my sets, main characters, and immediate interest angle" (*L1* 879). Plath here shows a commercial awareness of television; she might not be a viewer, but she can exploit its popularity to further her career. And, of course, the importance of radio in the development of Plath's career—especially with the BBC—has been well documented, particularly by Robin Peel. Media culture converges in the poetry and prose to create new connections between media and literature, as well as a new lens through which to read Plath's work.

## CHAPTER TWENTY-ONE

# "I imagine that a man might not praise it as much": Reception of "Three Women" and Plath's BBC-Recorded Poetry

CARRIE SMITH

Kate Atkinson's 2018 novel *Transcription* draws on the similarities between the British Broadcasting Corporation in the 1950s and MI5 during the Second World War. This comparison would have seemed particularly pertinent to a young writer trying to establish herself with the BBC in the 1950s and 1960s. Letters with proposals for programs winged their way into the imposing broadcast house, where an occluded process of decision-making often resulted in rejection. With access to archival records from the BBC Written Archive, we can now follow and reconstruct that paper trail showing the decision-making process to reveal the crosscurrents of politics, literary taste, and tastemakers. This chapter will elucidate those pathways to illustrate the barriers that Plath's poetry had to overcome. I will go on to argue, however, that once on the air, radio's history as complex gendered, institutional, professional space, both for those making radio and those listening to it, makes it the ideal vehicle for Plath's radiogenic piece "Three Women" and her later poetry which skillfully blended world events and domestic settings. Rather than analyzing Plath's recordings and re-treading ground adeptly laid out by Kate Moses in the chapter, "Sylvia Plath's Voice, Annotated," I wish to extract Plath's work with the BBC from her other spoken word recordings (for the Woodberry Poetry Room, for example) and recontextualize these spoken word events within the institutional and national settings in which they were embedded and, crucially, in their audience reception.

The BBC Written Archive in Reading, UK, contains records of the day-to-day life of the BBC in paper form—minutes from meetings, memos, contracts, internal notes concerning commissioning of programs, expense receipts, scripts, audition notes, and so on. The archive also contains individual contributor files; under "Sylvia Plath" we find two files, each containing letters from Plath proposing programs to various producers along with their replies, internal discussions of the merits of the poems she sent, financial agreements, and contracts. One can also find references to Plath in other places in the archive—it contains a vast array of microfiche scripts of programs in their original form, which can differ from the edited versions that reach the air; for example, the lengthier interview transcript of Plath and Hughes's "Two of a Kind." Plath appears unexpectedly in other files—in Jill Balcon's contributor file, for example. Balcon was an actress who read "Three Women" in 1962 and 1968 for the BBC.[1] Plath material related to the BBC can also be found in Douglas Cleverdon's archive held by Lilly Library, Indiana University. Cleverdon, who produced Plath's "Three Women," was a Features Producer for the Third Programme and was responsible for bringing some important pieces to radio such as Dylan Thomas's *Under Milk Wood* and David Jones's *In Parenthesis*. His archive contains individual folders dedicated to Plath's work including marked-up scripts, letters, and audience response reports, as well as notes cross-referencing the content with the BBC Written Archive. Plath's draft manuscripts for "Three Women" are held by Smith College. Taken together, these archives reinsert the composition of her extended poem into the institutional contexts of its creation, but also the creation of her professional authoritative voice. They remind us of the people woven into that process, as well as helping us to think about the life of "Three Women" after broadcast as it was received by the radio audience in their homes.

Plath's letters show her engagement with radio throughout her life. A letter from the young Plath to Margot Loungway Drekmeier in 1946 gives a blow-by-blow account of what she was listening to on Massachusetts radio stations WBZ and WEEI, which included radio theatre, a story and various pieces of music, finishing with the bathetic intrusion of an advert for Raleigh cigarettes, to which she exclaimed: "What a let down!" (*L1* 82). Advertising was one of the ways that the BBC would differ from the American radio Plath grew up with; the BBC's revenue came from license fees and, in contrast with the diversity of radio stations available in other countries, it held a domestic radio broadcasting monopoly until 1973.[2] At the point that Plath was trying to bring her work to air (her contributor files at the BBC Written Archive run from 1957 to 1962) the BBC had three main programs in the UK—the Light Service, the Home Service, and the Third Programme. This three-tier system had been in place since 1946. John Reith, who was the first Director General of the BBC, had originally enshrined the principles of information, education, and entertainment at its center.[3] He felt that the new set of programs established after he had left, in which the Third contained the "highbrow" content, was a betrayal of the democratic principles of British radio. As Kate Whitehead notes, the Third was:

> an important patron of creative writers, especially during the post-war paper shortage, and it had a strong influence on literary tastes and developments of the time. … Virtually every creative writer working in Britain during that period had come into contact with the Third Programme, whether as a contributor of material or as part of the audience influenced by its frequently avant-garde broadcasts.
>
> (1)

---

[1] Jill Balcon was a film, television and theatre actress. She was particularly famous as a reader of verse. At twenty-one she was part of the Apollo Society founded by Peggy Ashcroft, Stephen and Natasha Spender in the 1940s to perform poetry and music around the country. Letters in the BBC Written Archive show that audiences singled out her reading in poetry programs for praise.

[2] See Hilmes.

[3] See Briggs's multi-volume history of the BBC.

Plath's "Three Women" and most of the poetry programs she was involved in found their home on the highbrow Third.

Although in the early period of the BBC, women occupied key managerial and creative positions—Hilda Matheson was the BBC's first Director of Talks, for example—as well as the corporation holding more relaxed views concerning married women working and forward-thinking ideas about the gender pay gap, their literary programming and decision-making remained uneven in regard to women's involvement in radio at all levels.[4] In the BBC radio poetry archives from the 1950s, we find documents with titles such as "Elder Poets: Twenties and Thirties"; the document lists thirty-two names only two of which were women (Edith Sitwell and Laura Riding). In the next document in the series, "Younger Poets: Thirties to Fifties," out of forty-seven names, four are women (Kathleen Raine, Elizabeth Jennings, Ruth Pitter, and Kathleen Nott). A list of "American Poets" written in the same year yields twenty names, only one of whom is a woman (Marianne Moore). Although these women poets were certainly not the only women whose work was broadcast on the BBC at this time, they are the BBC's chosen exemplars demonstrating the close ranks into which any emerging female poet was attempting to break. This is mirrored in print; for example, the anthology of contemporary American poetry edited by Donald Hall that Plath reviewed on the BBC in 1962 contained two women poets—Denise Levertov and Adrienne Rich. The volume was revised and expanded in 1972; the only women poets added were Anne Sexton and Plath herself.[5]

So, how would a young, ambitious, female poet in the 1950s get her work onto the radio? The answer is—with great difficulty and, often, through male contacts within the BBC, who provided mentorship, opportunities for networking and championed certain writers to make programs. Many of the author contributor files at the BBC Written Archive are made up of writers' letters asking the BBC to feature their work. In the late 1950s to early 1960s when Plath was working with the BBC, writers and academics would propose programs independently to a producer or producers would suggest programs that would then go before the Poetry Committee, which would recommend whether an idea or a script was suitable for broadcast on the Third Programme. This was the path of Plath's "Three Women" proposed by influential producer Douglas Cleverdon. In 1950, however, Cleverdon noted in a report that the Third Programme tended to reject unestablished writers who might require input from the BBC to develop their writing for radio, highlighting the power of BBC's gatekeeping function:

> Discouragement is by far the easier course; it saves infinite time and trouble, it clears the desk, it induced a gratifying magisterial glow, and it is safer (for the high standards of the Third can always be cited in self-defense). Encouragement on the other hand, leads frequently to interminable correspondence and interviews, delays and recrimination, and perhaps final rejection.
>
> (Third Programme Memos, R19/1295/7)

---

[4]See Murphy, *Behind the Wireless: A History of Early Women at the BBC* and Andrews, *Domesticating the Airwaves: Broadcasting, Domesticity and Femininity.*
[5]On the construction of anthologies and canon see Golding. *From Outlaw to Classic: Canons in American Poetry.* For a consideration of the gendered aspect of taste-making see González, "Gender Politics and the Making of Anthologies: Towards a Theory of Women's Poetry."

The rejection rate for work sent in was high; in a 1953 letter Val Gielgud, Head of Drama, notes that out of 250–300 unsolicited plays received each month, "it is rare for the acceptance rate to be higher than two percent" and another BBC employee worried that "a large proportion of unsolicited scripts were rejected outright on a single opinion" (Drama Policy File, 5b R19/280/7). Youth was also counted against writers. Harman Grisewood, who was the Controller of the Third, was not in favor of broadcasting young poets; in a memo from 1951, he writes: "I don't believe we should have our withers wrung by Youth in this matter of Poetry [...] very few of these [young poets] have a grown-up critical view of it; and very few indeed are any good at all" concluding "I don't believe we miss much of any quality" (R19/933/3, June 28, 1951).

Not only unsolicited writers, but also female writers were at a disadvantage. The BBC was, to an extent, a boys' club rewarding those with connections; a letter from the Controller of the Third Programme to the Director of Sound Broadcasting notes that the BBC had been "laying itself open to charges of favoritism and downright irresponsibility. It has appeared to be unfairly neglectful of much fine contemporary writing, and unduly partial to work of such poets as have taken the trouble to peddle and advertise their wares in BBC programme circles" (qtd. in Whitehead 157). As Linda Russo puts it of Joanne Kryger's inclusion in a mostly male *avant-garde* group, she "enjoyed the advantages of 'having been "taken up" by male writers who "made" the places where poetry was made'" (qtd. in González 183). Male editors also continued to dominate the publication of "little magazines" in the 1950s and 1960s, such as David Ross's *Saint Botolph's Review* (1956), Rodney Banister and Peter Redgrove's *Delta* (1953–81), which published Hughes and Plath (*Delta* was then taken over by Philip Hobsbaum).[6] Throughout the BBC archives, it is possible to catch glimpses of the practical difficulties of women's working lives as broadcasters; in letters, they briefly reference fitting in rehearsals around breastfeeding schedules and ask if their children would be welcome in the studios. The BBC contributor files of Jill Balcon give brief insights into the gendered difficulties of working at the BBC, which she carefully codes as inconvenient, unchangeable but surmountable. Balcon writes in 1953, for example, "now that I'm several stone lighter again and not likely to give birth on transmission may I—please—come and work for you again?" (Balcon, File 2). A proportion of BBC meetings were held in nearby pubs, and while these meetings did not exclude women, it did make it more difficult for writers like Plath with young children, particularly when residing outside of London, to break into those circles of "favouritism."[7]

Plath's association with her husband, Ted Hughes, was both a help and a hindrance in the process of getting her poetry to the air; a help because he gave her an "in" with

---

[6]In the 1960s, "[m]agazines that devoted special issues to women's literature, as a self-conscious movement or tendency, also began to appear, including Valerie Sinason's *Gallery* and the Caribbean-orientated *Savacou*; *Women's Liberation Review* devoted all its pages to feminism and feminist literature" (Miller and Price 124). See Miller and Price. *British Poetry Magazines 1914–2000: History and Bibliography of "Little Magazines."*

[7]Although there was some regional little magazine poetry publishing in the 1950s and 1960s, 24 percent of new titles came from London in 1950s and 23 percent in the 1960s (125 new titles in the 1960s from London, the largest figure outside of London was twenty-five titles from Oxford), the majority of these publications came from University towns. That said, a number of cottage industry mimeograph magazines with only a few issues from small towns and villages showed desire for a "radically decentred" form of publishing (Miller and Price 123). This was also reflected in tensions between regional BBC broadcasting and programs coming out of London. See Hajkowski, *The BBC and National Identity in Britain, 1922–1953*.

the BBC boys' club through producers such as George MacBeth and Douglas Cleverdon (the latter Plath described as "Ted's Producer" [*L2* 785]), and a hindrance because trying to establish herself independently after their separation was difficult. Association with Hughes meant a connection to a certain type of British poetry, when in the late 1950s and early 1960s she was keenly exploring a different kind of American poetry. One memo from a BBC employee describes her poems as "like her husband on an ordinary day" (BBC Plath, File 1). "Three Women," a radiogenic work for Cleverdon, was composed as a piece to be broadcast. Even the internal BBC memo requesting the contract be drawn up states, almost as a kind of qualification, that Plath was married to Hughes (box 21, Lilly). Cleverdon's introduction to the 1968 publication of "Three Women" highlights the link between his production of *The Wound* by Hughes and his commission of Plath's piece.[8] He connects Hughes's short story with the memory of meeting Plath for lunch to discuss instigating the project with her. Even after Plath and Hughes had separated, Hughes continued to recommend her poetry to Cleverdon for broadcast. Cleverdon wrote to Plath in 1962 explaining that Hughes had told him that she had been writing some excellent new poems and asking her if they would work as a broadcast with her commentary.

Plath worried that another potential barrier to broadcasting was the sound of her voice and her accent. She wrote to Dorothy Benotti in 1962, "I am delighted you think I have an English accent, Dotty. Everybody over here thinks I come from the Deep South, they think my American accent is so broad!" (*L2* 930). As Heather Clark explains when considering Plath's complex feelings about being an American in Cambridge, "[h]er adoption of an English accent was likely a response to her 'colonial' insecurities—her growing awareness of her 'gauche' American mannerisms" (*The Grief of Influence* 89). As linguist Lynda Mugglestone writes, in British society, "proper and elegant language was in turn to be fairly unambiguously located in those non-regional norms of a 'standard' and in the marked associations with social status" (141). She further argues that the desirability of a non-regional standard accent was linked to notions of "purity" as a "cardinal virtue for the female sex" (141) in all areas. Accent and gender were also fundamentally intertwined with class. A study carried out by John Edwards in 1979 asked adults to listen to a set of recordings of children's voices who were "of an age before the onset of distinctive pitch differences" (qtd. in Mugglestone 171). For the most part the voices of girls and boys were still identified without difficulty, but "systematic patterns of misidentification" were found when the listeners identified class. In general, listeners misidentified working-class girls as boys and middle-class boys as girls: "[g]irls, in other words, are apparently expected to sound 'middle class', whilst these allocations of male identity confirmed the masculine associations of working-class language." The listeners "rated working-class voices as rougher, lower, and more masculine" (qtd. in Mugglestone 171). The reception and critique of women's voices on air were often concerned with their higher pitch not transmitting effectively. The deeper register of Plath's voice meant it would, in fact, transmit better on the radio. A 1937 opinion piece in a local newspaper printed a variety of views of women's voices. One male listener noted: "some female voices are exceedingly good, but it is undoubtedly necessary that their voices should

---

[8]For more on the artistic influence of Hughes's play on Plath's work, see Walker, "Plath and the Radio Drama."

be rather low, and deep," whilst "Miss Phyllis Bentley, of Halifax, the novelist" stated, "[i]f the microphone is unkind to the female voice, the engineers should do something about it. It is absurd to leave out their voices because the engineers cannot tackle the problem" (March 15, 1937).

In fact, Plath's American background and accent lent itself to some of the programs she made for the BBC. She wrote to Aurelia and Warren Plath in 1960, "I hope I can persuade the BBC to accept a program about young American women poets which I am drawing up, now that they seem willing enough to record my odd accent" (*L2* 555). Tracy Brain describes Plath's "speaking voices" in plural as "trespass[ing] against all forms of borders" and settles on the term "midatlanticism" to locate her (*The Other Sylvia Plath* 45, 46). She made programs connected to America, such as a program exploring what it was like to be a US immigrant in Britain ("What Made You Stay?" on the BBC Home Service). In the surviving recorded extracts of "What Made You Stay?" (1962), Plath speaks very quickly to begin with, slowing down as the program progresses and she seems to relax a little. She manages to laugh, for example, when she says in error, "the weather infects me, affects me [laughs] I say infects me it really does infect me, the weather affects me intensely" (BBC Sound Archives 27571). The British weather represents an invasive, unhealthy force that oscillates between "infecting" her body and "affecting" her mind and emotions paralleling many of her early letters home in which she expressed unhappiness with Britain's weather, food, health service in unfavorable comparison with America (a sentiment that no doubt pleased her mother). Her poems included in "The Weird Ones" (BBC Third Programme) were read in the context of a "selection of poems from books published in the United States in 1961" (*Radio Times* issue 2043) and a piece that would have been read by Plath but was recorded after her death, "Ocean 1212-W" was originally to be recorded under the title "Landscape of Childhood," as it explores the environment of her American childhood. These programs were part of Plath's reflection on her status as an alien in Britain—a sense of "perpetual displacement" (*The Other Sylvia Plath* 46). As Al Alvarez explained in the BBC broadcast after her death, "she could only write poems out loud when she discovered her own speaking voice, that is, her identity" (qtd. in "Sylvia Plath's Voice, Annotated" 93). Her work for and behind the microphone at the BBC, particularly programs reflecting on America from the distance of Britain, strengthened her well-documented shift toward speaking her poetry aloud in her "odd accent" (*L2* 555) that "hover[ed] at different points over the Atlantic" (*The Other Sylvia Plath* 45). In this way her BBC work became part of the environment of the composition of *Ariel*.

Although an inexperienced broadcaster, Plath was influenced by listening to the broadcasts and recordings of other women poets; after hearing one of Riding's broadcasts, she subtitled a poem "On Listening to Laura Riding," and listening to one of Stevie Smith's recordings she was moved to write to her to ask if they could meet. Alice Entwistle notes, "broadcasting helped to embed Plath's developing sense of poetic identity, partly for financial reasons; it also affected her idiom" (909). As with Plath's discussion in her letters home of the large potential financial income Hughes could earn from readings and recordings, it was financially worthwhile for Plath to make her work radiogenic. Whilst the handful of critics who discuss Plath's radio work focus on the effect radio has on her poetic voice in this period, fewer remember to acknowledge that this change can also be attributed to financial motives. For example, she writes to poet and producer George MacBeth: "I sort of had you in mind when I wrote it and I hoped you might like it" (867). To an extent, she was tailoring her poetic writing to suit the palates of BBC producers in order to supplement her income. In doing so, it caused her to think about not only the aural form of poetry, but also importantly about the person who would be consuming the broadcast, both the producer and the listener at home.

"Three Women" was Plath's only poetic work written specifically for the radio.[9] Poetry programs could be proposed to the Controller of the Third Programme from three departments: Talks, Features, Drama. As Hugh Chignell explains:

> The late 1940s and early 1950s witnessed the production of some extraordinary and ambitious dramas mainly by Features Department including *The Dark Tower* as well as *In Parenthesis* and *The Ascent of F6* [.] ... The 1950s themselves could easily be called a "golden age" of radio drama as Beckett, Pinter and, the prolific, Giles Cooper among others were writing for the medium.
>
> (2)

Although the 1960s remained a "productive time" for radio drama, in 1963, Val Gielgud retired and, as Chignell argued, "[w]hat followed was, arguably, the decline of radio drama as television drama became increasingly confident and successful" (2). As with the work of many poets producing literature for the radio in this period (1940s–1960s), Plath's piece blurred the line between lyrical radio play and extended narrative poem. As Whitehead explains, poets were:

> commissioned to write works under a variety of headings, "verse plays," "dramatic monologues," "radio phonic poems" (making as much use of *musique concrète* as of the spoken word), "ballad operas," and so on. These categories took them well out of the format of the poetry "magazine" or "anthology[.]"
>
> (163)

"Three Women" is a poem for voices detailing the thoughts of a "wife," a "secretary," and a "girl." Copies of the script of "Three Women" can be read in multiple locations, including the British Library and Lilly Library.[10] The scripts and the special edition printed by Turret Books (1968) use "Wife," "Secretary," and "Girl" to differentiate the parts rather than Voice One, Two, and Three as in Plath's *Winter Trees* (1971) and *Collected Poems* (1981). The few extant manuscripts for the piece show that Plath originally named the voices Amy, Moll, and Myra before changing them to Voice One, Two, and Three. Whilst it is not clear from surviving archival evidence where "wife," "secretary," and "girl" came from, they are part of the broadcast text in script and performance form, which differentiate it from the printed page by clearly defining the life-stage of each woman before the voices begin to speak. The opening announcement from the broadcast states that "[t]he wife gives birth to a son: the secretary suffers a miscarriage: the girl has an illegitimate daughter, who will be adopted" (box 21, Lilly). In her letters, Plath writes that the poem is based on a film *Brink of Life* (1958) also known as *So Close to Life* by Swedish director Ingmar Bergman in which three women talk in a maternity ward

---

[9] Plath wrote short reflective pieces for radio, on life as an American in the UK, for example, and broadcast poetry written for the page, but "Three Women" was her only verse piece written specifically for the radio medium.

[10] "Three Women," Vol. cviii, Add MS 88589, Alvarez Papers, British Library; Cleverdon II, box 21, Lilly. Copies can also be read at BBC Written Archives Centre, Emory, and Smith.

(*L2* 777).[11] As Entwistle explains, "Three Women" "hovers between dialogue and a sequence of short lyric monologues" (910). It was recorded twice for the BBC Third Programme, in 1962 and 1968. Only the 1968 broadcast has survived and can be listened to onsite at the British Library, London.

Due to its publication as a print poem, in-depth study of "Three Women" in its media context is only just emerging. It is often divorced from its context as written for radio and therefore made to be heard in one sitting. The ephemerality of broadcasts has always been part of the debate over poetry on the radio by poets and producers alike. In the mid-1940s, George Barnes (Controller of the Third Programme) started hosting dinners with authors to discuss literature on the radio and what "the place of poetry was in the Third" (Whitehead 79). Kathleen Raine was the only female writer in attendance. Her arguments on this topic were particularly concerned with the impermanence of broadcasts; she claimed that the attempt to reach flawlessness in verse required the durability of the print medium (R19/933/2 November 20, 1947). One commentator in the Audience Research Report for "Three Women" noted that the "poem needed to be seen in print and pondered upon" (box 21, Lilly). However, if one examines the poem, one finds that words are consistently repeated, building a cumulative effect of the course of the 378 lines. One word used to particular effect is "flatness." It is employed in different ways, both as a perceived judgment from the outside world on the woman who has not managed to bring her child to term and *by* that woman as a judgment against men—their flatness and inability to carry children are described by her: "They are so jealous of anything that is not flat! / They are jealous gods / That would have the whole world flat because they are" (*CP* 179).

I suggest that the poem's radiogenic qualities lie in what Entwistle calls "a powerful lyric economy" (910). This economy is compounded by the use of repetition. Repetition of vocabulary is part of the poem's and radio's main arsenal in the face of the form's ephemerality. Plath uses it to great effect in "Three Women" to facilitate the comprehension of the listener engaging with her long, multipart poem. This repetition is also exploited by the readers of the broadcast, particularly Jill Balcon. Balcon read the part of the secretary for both the 1962 and 1968 recordings of Plath's "Three Women"; she was the only recurring reader from the first production. In the surviving 1968 recording Barbara Jefford reads the part of "The Wife," opening the piece, Balcon's part as "The Secretary" follows. Balcon speeds up, slows down, and modulates her tone with more light and shade than Jefford. She articulates the consonants of each word very clearly, reading not just with clarity but also with intelligibility. Her reading allows the many repetitions of the piece to stand in equal importance to each other; she does not lose the second voicing of the same phrase because the listener has heard it once, but instead sounds it with the same clarity and intensity as the first. Her part carries the piece's discussion of pregnancy loss and what it means to move in the world having lost multiple children. She reads the lines: "I can love my husband, who will understand. / Who will love me through the blur of my deformity / As if I had lost an eye, a leg, a tongue" (BBC typescript, box 21, Lilly); her sophisticated and precise reading making the silence surrounding pregnancy loss, her loss of tongue, and therefore of voice, all

---

[11]For more on the poem's connection to the film see Fraser, "Technologies of Reproduction: The Maternity Ward in Sylvia Plath's *Three Women* and Ingmar Bergman's *Brink of Life*."

the more poignant. Balcon's final monologue as the secretary's includes the line "I am a wife," which, unlike Plath's typescript and the published poem, is placed in the middle of a line on its own in the script (box 21, Lilly). An earlier script shows a producer mark-up after rehearsal indicating it should be on its own line (box 21, Lilly). Balcon pauses before and after the line, giving it the space it asks for marooned in the center of the line. The unsounded, but expected, accompanying second half of the sentence "and mother" haunts the line in the pauses.

The audience research reports responding to the broadcast of "Three Women" are particularly important as they allow us a glimpse of how the text was received by listeners and because they were used by the BBC as a measure of the success of a broadcast. There are two reports, one August 19, 1962, and the other June 9, 1968. The earlier report notes that the piece "was greeted with 'mixed feelings by a fairly large number of listeners in the small sample audience'" (box 21, Lilly). The subject matter of the piece was deemed inappropriate for treatment in a poetic broadcast. One commentator found it "too intimate for so public a reading." A "Civil servant (male)" in the 1968 audience report made the case with overt sexism and classism that women's experiences were not the stuff of serious poetry, he remarked:

> that it was a woman's poem, an "obstetric" poem; "Miss Plath put it more poetically, more intensely but I think it's really only tarted up street-corner gossip—the head scarves, the gently moving prams, the packets of Tide."

The commentator attempts to quell the poem by using scientific, masculine language (obstetric) before relegating such experiences to conversations that should only be had between women, and not women he deems serious or important. Plath's piece is certainly not "gossipy" in tone, making the civil servant's comment an exercise in mental gymnastics. Although he acknowledges that the piece is "poetic" and "intense," because it details women's particular experiences of birth and loss, it cannot help but be relegated to the status of private conversation/gossip between women. The irony of his statement lies in the fact that he has put his finger upon what makes the piece exciting and interesting, and, as I argue, what lies at the center of Plath's radiogenic engagement with broadcasting. The thoughts of three women in a maternity ward were not the usual material for broadcasts. "Three Women" allows us to hear such intimate thoughts and, in doing so, foregrounds marginalized, female experiences making those voices and experiences public broadcast on the national institution of the BBC.

Radio's gendered technological history, which influences its unique properties, shapes both the institutional history of the medium and the reception of its audience. In Britain, early radio was characterized by its reputation as a complex, technological "toy" to be played with and administered by male members of the household. The earliest radios were kits put together at home and required headphones to listen to the broadcasts; this often meant that men listened whilst women sat in "an imposed silence" watching them in thrall to the "ugly box" (Moores 120). As radio technology developed and premade sets became both commercially readily available and financially in-reach, the ritual of listening altered; sets no longer required headphones and instead became an activity for the whole family. In the choice words of one advertising slogan in the 1930s: "Goodbye to knob twiddling" (Andrews 3). In addition, radio programming was planned with a gendered audience in mind. During the day, it evolved to cater to housewives and was structured around "the imagined daily routine of the mother" (Moores 123). Stephen Barnard explains that the housewife is "particularly central to BBC radio mythology" in which programs like *Housewives Choice* (1946–67) were "designed as a kind of recognition of or even reward to the female populace for giving up their wartime occupations in the munitions factories and service industries and returning to an almost wholly domestic role" (126).

Although the BBC mainly pitched programs about housewifery and children to women during the day, the radio set sat in the domestic space of the home imbued with the radical potential to bring the sound of the wider world into that space.[12] Radio's challenge to isolation helped to merge or layer the domestic and the public spheres. Plath, sitting in her home in isolated, rural north Devon could switch on the radio and be connected to discussions of politics, arts, places, and so on, beyond that small pocket of England. This mixing of subjects echoes early broadcasting pioneer Olive Shapley's description of how women consumed early radio:

> *Women's Hour* was at that time unique amongst radio shows. Though it certainly tried to lighten the household chores and give listeners a new interest, albeit an appropriately feminine one, it also tried to open a window on the world outside, in a way which listeners themselves may not have had time or opportunity to do.
>
> (125)

Plath conceived of radio in these terms; she and Hughes bought a radio for their house so that Plath could continue learning German and Italian, thus bringing access to Europe and learning into the small Devon village that they had made their home (*L2* xxxix). She noted in a letter that radio "keeps us in contact with the world" (159). As a "housewife" in 1929 noted in *The Radio Times*, "the task of cleaning the kitchen went down a little better while listening to the intelligent observations of an intelligent woman" (Issue 279).

The access to the wider world that radio provided to female listeners at home affected both the home space and a sense of other listeners in similar homes. As Maggie Andrews explains:

> In the 1920s and 1930s the entry of "the wireless" into the domestic space of the home dramatically changed men and women's experience of domesticity, offering education and reducing isolation through a shared listening experience and a sense of belonging to wider imagined communities.
>
> (xi)

This also speaks to radio's history as a communicative medium, as David Trotter explains, "[r]adio began as a connective medium enabling instantaneous, real-time, interactive, one-to-one, telegraphic communication" (8). Andrews draws on Benedict Anderson's concept of "imagined communities," in which "the members of even the smallest nation will never know most of their fellow members, meet them, or even hear them, yet in the minds of each lives the image of their communion" (6). This idea of radio listeners as an imagined

---

[12]See: Lacey, *Feminine Frequencies: Gender, German Radio, and the Public Sphere, 1923–1945*; Hilmes, *Radio Voices: American Broadcasting, 1922–1952*.

community is explored in terms of BBC radio and nationality by Thomas Hajkowski, but also it has interesting connotations for women as an imagined community.[13] Discussing the radio daytime serial soaps in America, which were aimed at women, Hilmes touches on ideas related to this topic of imagined communities:

> female writers and producers ... opened up a space on the public airwaves for a feminine subaltern counterpublic to emerge, who responded to the serials' attempts to open up the restricted sphere of private discussion to topics usually dismissed as "women's issues"—private, personal and therefore unsuited to public discourse.
> (160)

"Three Women" seems aware of the potential "feminine subaltern counterpublic" and the chance to draw on "private" discourse; Plath's choice of three women's separate thoughts, which form a kind of telepathic dialogue with each other, implies a dialogue with the mind of a fourth, the female listener. The 1962 Audience Research Report on "Three Women" gives us the response of a woman commenter who was aware of her own particular status as a female, maternal listener and also the presence of male audience members listening in or perhaps, more accurately, "overhearing": "I have given this poem a high rating because I found it so very moving ... though I imagine that a man might not praise it as much, but to a woman who is a mother it really 'lived'. The language was extremely beautiful" (box 21, Lilly). Another commentator described it as "authentic and unsentimental" and noted that "it is rather surprising that such a fundamental experience as birth has so little literature of its own" (box 21, Lilly). In "Three Women," Plath was writing "A Literature of Its Own." Although not all of the female listeners agreed that she had captured the experience of birth and pregnancy accurately, they were in no doubt to whom the broadcast was addressed and felt moved to apply the piece to their own experiences.

Plath's radiogenic poem finds a home in this multilayered domestic/public space, but so, in a different way, does the poetry of *Ariel*. Using poetic language, "Three Women," puts the spotlight on the private thoughts of three women going through intensely personal experiences. On the other hand, Plath's *Ariel* poems draw on the other side of this public/private divide bringing the public into the private.[14] In Plath's earlier 1960 correspondence with Owen Leeming at the BBC concerning airing her short stories, she shows awareness of the potential for her work to cross the BBC's "subject taboos" (*L2* 529), but with "Three Women" and the *Ariel* poems she has turned this tightrope walk between the acceptable and the taboo into part of their strengths. These poems both speak in this dual mode to and about the woman living in a rural community from which she feels utterly isolated. As Plath notes in an interview with Peter Orr:

---

[13]To suggest "women" here as one homogenous group would be a fallacy, particularly in 1950s/1960s Britain where fissures of race and class ran deep. In this case, Plath's imagined community would likely mirror herself—white, educated, and middle class. Criticism of racial tensions in Plath's work is developing field, for an early intervention see: Pereira, "Be(e)ing and 'Truth': Tar Baby's Signifying on Sylvia Plath's Bee Poems," and for a general discussion of race and the radio minstrel show in the United States see: Hilmes, *Radio Voices* (75–96).
[14]For an exploration of confessional poetry in connection with this interaction between public and private see Nelson, *Pursuing Privacy in Cold War America*.

> I think that personal experience is very important, but certainly it shouldn't be a kind of shut-box and mirror looking, narcissistic experience. I believe it should be *relevant*, and relevant to the larger things, the bigger things such as Hiroshima and Dachau and so on.
>
> (169–70)

Just as "Three Women" takes on the subjects of working women's lives, of premature transition from girlhood to womanhood, of women's relations with the medical profession, alongside its main theme of motherhood, the *Ariel* poems also mix themes connected to domesticity and the home with broader subjects. The status of "Three Women" as a piece for broadcast, to speak to listeners in their homes contributes to the *Ariel* poems' awareness of the play between public/private, taboo, performance, and listening.

Plath found that, despite the barriers in the way of a young, female, American poet crossing an institutional and gender-marked threshold onto the BBC, her American background and voice became a useful unique selling point that took her beyond the initial access that her husband's contacts had given her to help her develop a place on British radio that was uniquely hers. This reflects her exploration of American poetry as a new and exciting jumping-off point for writing the poetry that would become *Ariel*. That said, her most important work for radio, "Three Women," was based on imagining what connected her to the community of British women who had experienced pregnancy and motherhood in all its forms and giving their stories and voices poetic treatment on the highbrow Third Programme. These considerations, both her difference from those around her and their shared bonds, map onto the public/private dichotomy that radio challenges. In turn, the struggle to shape a radiogenic poetry laid the groundwork for poetic strategies in *Ariel*, which draws, in part, on isolated Devon life and shows how the wider world can both be drawn into that life and found in miniature there.

## CHAPTER TWENTY-TWO

# Sylvia Plath's "Three Women": Producing a Poetics of Listening at the BBC

NERYS WILLIAMS

Writing to Olwyn Hughes on June 18, 1962, Sylvia Plath mentions that she has completed the final draft of her radio script, "Three Women: A Poem for Three Voices," to be broadcast on the BBC's Third Programme.[1] Plath expresses her joy at accomplishing this commission while caring for her two children, Frieda barely two, and Nicholas a newborn:

> I just feel to be lifting a nose & a finger from the last 3 years cow-push of carrying, bearing, nursing & nappy-squeezing. My study is my poultice, my balm, my absinthe. I've just done a very long dramatic poem for 3 voices (3 women in a maternity ward, miscarriages, illegitimacies & such, after Bergman) which Douglas Cleverdon, Ted's producer, will produce. Very excited about the chance to do longer stuff.
> 
> (*L2* 785)

By this point, Plath was an experienced performer of her poetry on the radio. Plath first approached the BBC in 1957 when she sent the poems "Spinster" and "Black Rook in Rainy Weather" to D. S. Carne Ross for consideration for broadcast in the series *The Poet's Voice*. The poems were rejected. However, between 1958 and 1959, she was recorded reading her own work three times in America. A breakthrough moment was reached in 1960 when Plath's two poems "Candles" and "Leaving Early" were accepted for *The Poet's Voice*. Between 1962 and 1963, Plath was in demand at the BBC's Third Programme as a contributor, interviewee, and reviewer. Collaborating with producers George MacBeth, Douglas Cleverdon, and Owen Leeming, Plath's voice was heard

---

[1] I have read copies of four BBC broadcast scripts held at: BBC Written Archives Centre, the British Library, Emory University, and Plath's Archive at Smith. However, there is only one word variation between them and the *CP*. Consequently, this chapter uses the *CP* as its source, due to issues of general accessibility. The title given for the original Emory typescript is "Three Women: A Monologue for Three Voices."

regularly.[2] We know that she contributed to at least seventeen BBC radio broadcasts between November 20, 1960, and January 10, 1963, of which seven survive.

"Three Women" was commissioned by the Features Department, produced by Cleverdon and first broadcast on August 19, 1962. Set on a maternity ward, "Three Women," an extended blank verse poem, examines the experiences of birth, miscarriage, and adoption. Critics have approached Plath's script through readings of the Plath archive, feminist theory, and studies in the medical humanities.[3] Regarded as one of Plath's important social poems, "Three Women" has been read as a reflection on "women's biological and cultural being" and as a "revolutionary text" (*The Wound and the Cure of Words* 166). Surprisingly, scant attention has been given to contextualizing the work as a poem *written* for broadcast; that is, as work to be listened to and performed as a *sonic* text. This chapter recognizes the difficulty of fully analyzing or "reconstructing" the making of "Three Women," given that the original archive recording has disappeared from the BBC's Sound Archive.[4] My discussion briefly contextualizes Plath's work in relation to a lineage of poetic experimentation in radio drama at the BBC. Historically, the BBC's Literary Output Committee (1943) was crucial in encouraging a culture of recruiting new writing for radio broadcast. Combining material from the BBC Written Archives at Caversham, as well as Cleverdon's papers at the Lilly Library and elements of sound theory, I examine how Plath's "Three Women" enacts a responsiveness to the collaborative and sonic demands of radio production. In a late interview, Plath insists that "I feel that this development of recording poems, of speaking poems at readings, of having records of poets" offer a return to "the old role of the poet, which was to speak to a group of people" (Orr 170). I argue that Plath's work displays an acute understanding of the technical requirements of radio writing required by her producer. Moreover, "Three Women" strategically uses the intimacy of radio listening as an opportunity to perform a powerful social and public comment on the experiences of childbirth, abortion, and disability to a listening public.

## THE ARCHIVE: COLLABORATION WITH DOUGLAS CLEVERDON AT THE BBC

How might one construct the collaboration between Plath and the BBC, given that the original recording is now lost? Hugh Chignell warns that often the scarcity of archived recordings means that the history of the genre is "skewed" (2). One initial solution might be to consult the original radio scripts, which are sometimes available in the BBC's Written Archive Centre; however Chignell warns that this approach, if used in isolation, "fundamentally denies the sonic quality of sound drama" (2). Ian Whittington offers an approach to reconstructing what he calls "the acoustic past" by "focusing on the archival traces" left by the writer (46). He warns that for the literary scholar,

---

[2]The British Library issued a CD collection *The Spoken Word: Sylvia Plath* which includes the following BBC Programs and series: *The Poet's Voice, The Living Poet; Two of a Kind*—a joint interview with Ted Hughes broadcast under the title of "Poets in Partnership," *The Poet's Voice, What Made You Stay?*, and *New Comment*.
[3]See, for example, Kuczynski, Fraser, and Souffrant's studies.
[4]On January 8, 2000, a new production of the poem, titled "Three Women" was aired on the BBC Radio 3's *Between the Ears* produced by Susan Roberts, and is archived at *The British Library*. A radio production by Pacifica Radio (Berkeley) was broadcast on KPFA, April 27, 1972, and is accessible via openculture.

there is always a danger of "fetishizing" the archive. Whittington insists that "[a]rchival reconstructions must always position themselves as contingent and partial achievements; their conclusions are not so much absolute certainties as productive interpretation" (46). Explicating elements of the institutional framework that Plath was working with, as well as the working practices of producer Douglas Cleverdon, offers a way of recreating, however incompletely, the dynamic of producing "Three Women" as a radio broadcast. Cleverdon's archived, papers as well as his unpublished manuscript "The Art of Radio" offer us key insights into how the producer approached the sonic text, or what he termed as "sound radio" ("Writing for Radio," box 5, Lilly).

Cleverdon joined BBC radio in 1939 following a career in book publishing. He was recruited by Laurence Gilliam as a features producer for the newly formed BBC Third Programme in 1946. The Third established an ambitious role in cultural programming in broadcasting history. In the words of the BBC Director General William Haley, its content was to "be directed to an audience that is not of one class, but that is perceptive and intelligent" (i). Three years prior, the BBC had set up the Literary Output Committee in response to a letter from Harold Nicolson critically evaluating literary broadcasting on the Home Service. Nicolson's criticism was robust: "our literary output is too small, too ill-timed, too unintellectual and too second rate" (Graves, January 6, 1943). Since its inception in 1943, the Committee had attempted to address how poetry should be better adapted to the radio. Regarding future poetry input, the Committee proposed that radio should serve "as a platform" for new verse not only from Great Britain "but from the Dominions and the Empire and a platform for which poets would willingly write poetry designed for broadcast and to be spoken aloud" (Grigson and Potter, May 31, 1943). The Third Programme offered an experimental premise that promoted new writing for radio; it attempted to place into practice the suggestions made by the Literary Output Committee, particularly in relation to the broadcasting of poetry. Following the creation of the Third Programme, there was a further concerted campaign to recruit new writers to the BBC.

In 1962 Plath's "Three Women" was commissioned via Cleverdon and the Features Department, not by the radio drama department. This distinction is an important one. The Features Department was recognized as having a strong history of advocating writing for radio that experimented with the medium itself, as opposed to relying on adaptations from literary texts. From the late 1930s, the BBC offered staff contracts in Feature producing to several poets as writers, broadcasters, and producers, which included Louis MacNeice, Rayner Heppenstall, D. G. Bridson, and Geoffrey Grigson. For Cleverdon, feature programs had key radiogenic characteristics: "The feature is the only form of radio programme which does not derive from some external source such as the theatre, the concert hall, the pulpit, the lecture-room, or the music-hall" ("On the Scope of Feature Programmes" box 5, Lilly). Cleverdon adds that for many production departments, "radio is a medium in which a pre-existing work is presented to a much larger audience, rather than an art form in itself" ("On the Scope of Feature Programmes"). The inception of the Third Programme supported feature producers' advocacy of writing that experimented with radio as a medium. The 1947 *BBC Yearbook* insisted that the credo of the Features department was that "no programme service can live a healthy life on an exclusive diet of classics. Radio must initiate or die, publish new work or be damned" (48). Cleverdon asserted that radio was also conducive to poetic exploration: "Radio is *par excellence* the medium for the poet—not merely in its simplest form of enabling him to read his own poems aloud to his listeners. There is in radio no limit to the evocative power of words;

it is the medium of the ear alone" ("The Art of Radio" 7–8). As the late historian of the BBC Asa Briggs notes, there was an "intimate connection between feature writing and poetry" (Vol. IV, 641) with the development of this genre being furthered by the close relationship established between poets and producers with an interest in experimenting with its broadcast form.

## A QUESTION OF GENRE: THE "PLAY OF IDEAS"

In his account of the production, Cleverdon emphasizes that "Three Women" "is the first and only poetic work that Sylvia Plath wrote specifically for broadcasting." He credits Plath with creating "an admirably straightforward piece of radio writing, a simple but dramatically effective sequence of monologues by three women" ("On *Three Women*" 229). Plath was familiar with Cleverdon's work as a radio producer; in 1962 he produced Ted Hughes's first radio drama *The Wound*.[5] Cleverdon emphasizes that after his collaboration with Hughes, it was "natural" that "the idea should emerge of a radio piece by Sylvia Plath also" (227). A BBC memo on the May 16, 1962, states that Cleverdon is happy with the commission and a contract for a script of fifty-four seven-lined stanzas is requested by the producer. In a letter from Cleverdon to Plath that same day, the producer confirms that the Third Programme has now accepted "Three Women." He proposes that he "should very much like to discuss some minor points with you," adding that he is "delighted to have the opportunity of producing the script" (Plath Correspondence, Box 2, Lilly). A contract was issued on May 13, 1962, and the broadcast itself was scheduled for August 19, 1962. "Three Women" was later repeated on September 13 of that year.[6] Plath would also have been familiar with Cleverdon's collaboration with Dylan Thomas. Cleverdon's radio production of *Under Milk Wood* won a Prix Italia in 1954. The producer was instrumental not only in advocating the commission, but also in encouraging the writing and finalizing of the script. Linda Wagner-Martin asserts that Thomas's radio play for voices was "one of [Plath's] ... earliest models of truthful, comic—sometimes bawdy—drama" (*Sylvia Plath: A Biography* 199). According to Donald E. Morse, Plath would also have listened to the Argo recordings of Thomas's poetry played by her high-school class teacher Mr. Crockett. Morse proposes that listening to Thomas's voice had an important impact: "that hearing penetrated deeply into Plath's poetic consciousness" (88–9). Heather Clark's biography of Plath states with certainty that early in 1954 as a student Plath played at home "over and over" a recording of Thomas's "Do Not Go Gentle into That Good Night" (*Red Comet* 307). One can speculate that these early encounters with Thomas's performances informed Plath's understanding of the auditory text and writing for broadcast. There is no indication in further BBC memos that Cleverdon requested any major changes to Plath's script, which is remarkable for a first-time commissioned radio work. Cleverdon's reflections on the radio drama emphasize that the producer's role is to encourage his commissioned authors: "Treat writers with respect—don't alter the scripts except for cogent reasons—they can write better than you can though; you know the

---

[5] First Broadcast February 1, 1962, on the Third Programme.

[6] "Three Women" was originally performed by Penelope Lee in the role of the wife, Jill Balcon as the Secretary, and Janette Richer as the student. A later transmission occurred on June 9, 1968, to coincide with the first publication of the text in a limited edition copy for Turret books. On January 8, 2000, a new production of *Three Women* was aired on the BBC Radio 3's *Between the Ears*.

technical frills" ("The Radio Play," box 5, Lilly). Modestly, he abbreviates the producer's role as being there to "interpret, not to impose his own ideas" ("The Radio Play").

Cleverdon's unpublished manuscript "The Art of Radio" reflects in more detail upon the collaborative dynamic between producer and poet. In contrast to radio drama department producers, he indicates that feature producers could "encourage individual writers by close personal contact and collaboration, particularly as most of them were themselves poets or writers and moved in literary rather than theatrical circles" ("The Art of Radio" 65–6). Key to the practice of the BBC Radio Features Department was the role of developing new work from emerging writers. Cleverdon states that rather than relying on adapting literary works for the radio, one "admirable function" of Features was "to encourage poets to create works for the medium of radio, which, by its concentration on the spoken word, offer opportunities for dramatic or poetic evocation that none of the other mass media can rival" ("On *Three Women*" 227). This sense of a text being written *exclusively* for radio is crucial to understanding Plath's "Three Women," with its dependence on the soliloquy as a compelling form for engaging the listener.

Cleverdon's "A Note on Radio Drama" offers a way into thinking about the structure of Plath's "Three Women" and its performance as a social text (box 5, Lilly). "Three Women" uses the format of three separate soliloquies broken across a thirty-minute script, addressing the audience with overheard meditations, which creates an impression of intense intimacy. Cleverdon points to the possibility of the radiogenic text, creating what he terms "the play of ideas." Reflecting on the technical process of performing and recording, he comments on the intersubjective dynamic that is created between the speaking voice and listener. For Cleverdon, the microphone offers "an extraordinary sympathetic means of expression to the dramatist who has something to say or something to discuss which he convinces could be made interesting to an audience a millions" ("A Note on Radio Drama"). The time constraints of a radio play create an intensity of listening, which allows issues to be "presented vividly and with some individual meaning to each member of the audience" ("A Note on Radio Drama"). He adds that the play of ideas cannot perform as an *agitprop*; the concept driving the production needs to offer nuance:

> It is not enough to take a theory and exploit it in long speeches delivered by dummies. The characters involved in the discussion must have personalities, and the discussion must follow some dramatic formula of a recognisable kind.
> ("A Note on Radio Drama")

Crucially, Cleverdon had prior experience of using a three-voice structure in his radio adaptation of David Jones's First World War poem, *In Parenthesis*.[7] Alexander Laurie proposes Cleverdon's use of three intervening voices, separate from the soldiers' dialogues in this literary allusive text, enables the closer engagement of a public listening audience. Plath's subject material in "Three Women" is equally as complex as the traumatic representations of warfare in *In Parenthesis*. However, in Cleverdon's production, the use of three voices is iterated in a minimal scaled-down rendition.

---

[7]Broadcast on the Third Programme, November 19, 1946.

## PLATH'S "THREE WOMEN"

In "Three Women," Plath balances a relationship between a "play of ideas" and establishing a lyric intensity with her audience; this radio drama is often evaluated as offering a stylistic bridge between *The Colossus* and *Ariel*. "Three Women" was billed in the *Radio Times* as the "Soliloquies of three women in a maternity ward" (*Radio Times* 19). Plath's three female speakers remain consciously unnamed. The first woman's marital status and occupation are unspecified; she gives birth to a son. The second speaker, often referred to by critics as a married secretary, enters the ward miscarrying her child. The third, a student, is carrying a child but chooses to have her daughter adopted. In a letter to her mother, Plath specifies that the three monologues began as a working through of Ingmar Bergman's film *Brink of Life* (L2 456). Bergman's film focuses on three female patients' experiences on a maternity ward: Cecilia, who is struggling to overcome a miscarriage; Hjordis, who has attempted to abort her unborn child; and Stina, who enthusiastically awaits the birth of her baby only to lose her child through a traumatic birthing scene. Plath's radio play is tailored toward three different voices, and in the production, this was to be emphasized through the choice of reading voices. However, two of the three readers engaged for the production were, at the last moment, unable to take part. Cleverdon comments that, as a consequence, "the voices were not as differentiated as they should have been," an issue which is echoed in the feedback from BBC Listeners' Reports ("On Three Women" 229). Plath's "Three Women" draws inspiration from Bergman's intimate consideration of the traumas of medical experience for women; his filmic technique of often painful close-ups is mirrored in Plath's choice of the soliloquy as a framing device for her own portraits.[8] However, one distinguishing feature between them is that there is no interaction between the women on Plath's ward. The discovery and sharing of personal narratives form a key factor of the women's healing in Bergman's film. Plath's use of the soliloquy form as a framework enables us to experience moments of intense subjectivity and the shifts in lyric time associated with physical and mental trauma. This way, "Three Women" enables taboo material to find enunciation in a public realm.

The experience of listening to a radio drama is framed by an experience of transience; words on the page quickly become sounds broadcast, vanishing into the ether. Cleverdon recognizes that the critical and cultural dominance of the published work made it difficult to attract writers and poets to the radio studio. However, the prospect of a mass audience was a compelling element for new writers: "the difficulty is to get the poets to write for what appears at first such an ephemeral medium ... some of them are beginning to realise that there is an immense reservoir of appreciation for them to draw upon" (8).[9] Sound theorist Salomé Voegelin admits that "[s]ound's ephemeral invisibility obstructs critical engagement, while the apparent stability of the image invites criticism" (*Listening to Noise and Silence* xi). She argues that the act of listening is key to the process of producing meaning; Voegelin proposes that "[s]ound narrates, outlines and fills but it is always ephemeral and doubtful. Between my heard and the sonic object / phenomenon I will never know its truth but can only invent it, producing a knowing for me" (*Listening to Noise and Silence* 5). Plath's "Three Women" is attuned to the need for characterization

---

[8] Bergman's film is also known by the title *So Close to Life* (1958).
[9] First Editions of Broadcast Poets and some others. Presidential address to the Private Libraries Association, April 11, 1978, 8.

and identity to emerge through the performance of her script. She uses the form of the soliloquy as a way of engaging her listeners in the interpretation of an intensely private experience.

"Three Women" offers different linguistic textures to distinguish the roles, identities, and experiences of the three voices. The first voice evokes an empathy with nature; her fertility is related to diurnal processes of sun, stars, and moon. A synchronicity exists between her perception, birthing, and world. Initially, Plath frames the first voice as a spectacle, "a great event," whose actions are premeditated and entertains a knowingness about her condition (CP 176). This sense of an emergent, but secure selfhood is reiterated by the words "I know" and "I am ready" (CP 176). By contrast, the second voice communicates the urgency and anxiety of a miscarriage. The women's body is seen as an extension of the machinery which surrounds her and creates a sequence of crashing sounds. Her pregnant body is an automaton fastened to the typewriter that she works upon; simulating movement, her feet become "mechanical echoes" or "steel pegs" (CP 177). Lyric time is suspended, and there is an extreme disconnect between the speaker's environment and her perception. The female body becomes a textual body amidst the sea of blankness and flatness. In her opening soliloquy, the second voice proposes that she finds it impossible to convene the distinguishing features of a human expression "to conceive a face, a mouth" (CP 177). Plath draws on the auditory imagination to recreate the sensation of panic as the miscarriage advances. A cityscape is dramatized as becoming consciousness itself; trains enter her mind roaring their "departures, departures" (CP 177). Compared to the first voice's claim to knowledge and security, the second is a container to a body that is to be dispersed, whose pulse "wanes"; a being who is now a "disease I carry home" (CP 177).

The third and final speaker is associated with critical observation and offers a political voice. Her analysis begins with her unwanted pregnancy and extends to the institutionalization of childbirth. It can be argued that the third voice is the most literary or allusive characterization. Her description of conception offers studied echoes of Yeats's "Leda and the Swan" as well as Hilda Doolittle's "Leda." This citational texture is evoked in remnants of lines such as "a great swan with its terrible look" (241). The startling evocation of color in a pallid landscape is reminiscent of Doolittle's rendering of Leda's rape (120–1). In direct opposition to the first voice's maternity as being in harmony with cosmic forces, the third voice presents conception and pregnancy in distinctly unnatural terms. The third voice is not ready for birth. She protests at the evolving life in her body with the rhetorical theatricality of Lady Macbeth: "I should have murdered this, that murdered me" (180).

John Drakakis, in his overview of radio drama, emphasizes how sound and rhythm are necessary to create "the systematic association of poetically conceived image and effects." He adds that the inflection of this momentum is gradual; the subtle aggregation and repetition of images create a structure that "enable the listener to hold in mind related sequences of sound for which there be no objective visual validation" (Drakakis 5). Importantly for radio drama, this act of visualization creates another reality held in "the imagination of the listener" (Drakakis 6). For this reason, radio drama has been referred to as a "theatre of the mind"; Neil Verma states that this phrase serves "as a synonym for the genre, if not the entire medium, and it has become … one of the most prolific forms of narrative fiction for two decades of the twentieth century" (2). Bartosz Lutostański proposes that radio narratives are unlike other artistic forms such as theater and film since they are "sound-driven" (119). He adds, "[t]his is to say, in radio 'all the signs are auditory' and can be divided into speech, music, sounds and silence" (Lutostański 119). In "Three Women," Plath carefully builds up associative and sonic patterning to create crucial interpretative associations and intersections between the three soliloquies. The reiteration of what Michel Riffaterre terms "kernel" words sutures interpretative images across the broadcast.[10] The following words resound throughout the performance: *flat* and *flatness, white, red, blank, wound, mouth, blackness,* and *face*. Cleverdon's retrospective account of the script draws attention to the evocative archetypes that are created by the repetition of these key words, creating crucial associations for the listener with birth, loss, anxiety, and performance:

> Against the whiteness of the hospital, the white sheets, the white cold wing of the great swan, the white clouds rearing a world of snow, there is projected a garden of black and red agonies. ... The evocation of vivid colour is matched in intensity by the startling directness of the imagery; and the emotional experience is shaped by poetic discipline into the most austere and monosyllabic forms. In radio, nothing can equal a poet's visualizing imagination, dramatically expressed in clear and speakable language.
> ("On *Three Women*" 229)

Plath recontextualizes the key words for different nuance and effect in the three soliloquies. For the first voice, whiteness relates to the impending birth; it offers a spot of reflective time where time stands still: "The sheets, the faces are white and stopped, like clocks" (*CP* 179). By comparison, for the second voice, the whiteness of the hospital sheets evokes the erasure of potential life itself "like the faces of my children" (*CP* 178). For the third voice, whiteness is associated with actions that appear beyond her control, attributed to the "white, cold wing" of conception (*CP* 178). Whiteness is also associated with the operating theatre as a white horror chamber filled with surgical instruments and sounds of pain. The color red serves to mark moments of crucial narrative development in the broadcast. Red is associated with the first voice's postnatal body and placenta, "a red lotus opens in its bowl of blood" (*CP* 181). For the second, red is associated with the evidence of a miscarriage, and at the close, a return to a performative identity, the lipstick on "the old mouth" (*CP* 183). Red for the third voice symbolizes the impossibility of being a mother to the "red terrible girl" with a head carved in "red, hard wood" (*CP* 182).

"Three Women" offers a challenge to the narrative arc in more conventional forms of radio dramas. Plath refutes neat narrative which leads to a moment of "epiphanic" understanding. Undoubtedly, there are instances of climax in the text, which coincide with the first voice's pain at birth, the second voice's loss, and the third's preparation for adoption. But there are other crosscurrents in the text that resist a definitive representation of maternal experience; the script defies a plot-based narrative propelled by cause and effect. As Leah Souffrant observes, for poets representing motherhood, narrative and lyric forms frequently "bleed into each other intense surges of love and frustration, for example, expose a blurring of emotion" (25), Souffrant adds that motherhood presents a complex temporal relationship between "rituals of daily life and the explosive quality of experience, even in its most mundane" (26). Some listeners appreciated "Three Women"

---

[10]See Riffaterre. In Rifaterre's analysis kernel words in combination create multiple interpretative matrices: "Descriptive systems become codes by permutation of kernel words" (66).

for exposing taboo subject matter on the airwaves. The BBC's Audience Research Report for "Three Women" states that a third of their sample was "greatly impressed by the poem." Crucial to their appreciation was the fact that "it was an unusual subject, but one worthy of the poet's attention, has been tackled with sympathy, perception and authenticity" (*Three Women* An Audience Research Report). Overall the program's appreciation was below the average response, rating at 60 percent (poetry and features programs on The Third Programme averaged at 61 percent and 64 percent, respectively).

Audience feedback offers an insight into how groundbreaking Plath's subject matter was to its radio listeners. One listener comments that "it is authentic and unsentimental" and adding that "it is rather surprising that such a fundamental experience as birth has so little literature of its own." (*Three Women* An Audience Research Report). In the UK at this time, there was a growing awareness of the dangers of Thalidomide.[11] A haunting of Thalidomide babies enters and retreats at various points. These images often present a conflict between personal loss and attempts to heal; there are references by the first voice to "terrible children / Who injure my sleep with their white eyes, their fingerless hands" (185). By meditating on ideas of miraculous healing, this voice narrates how deformities can be overcome: "the body of a starfish can grow back its arms" (184). Written some five months before abortion was legalized in the UK and a year following the breaking of the Thalidomide scandal, "Three Women" places women's gynecological rights to the center stage for a listening public. Motherhood for Rachel Blau DuPlessis "leads to, demands, provokes, and excites innovations in poetry and inventions in poetics" (ix). Significantly Plath adapts the literary soliloquy to perform radiogenically, in order to convene a commentary on maternity rights.

## "I TALK TO MYSELF / MYSELF ONLY": PRODUCING A POETICS OF LISTENING

Feedback from the BBC's Listeners' report offers an insight into the tensions created by "Three Women." Listeners critical of the broadcast thought that while the radio program's excursion into "morbid psychology" was "perceptive," the overwhelming result was "too intimate for so public a reading" (*Three Women* An Audience Research Report). Examining the intersubjective exchange created by "Three Women" is key to understanding the collaborative poetics of listening that Plath and Cleverdon produced. A perception of intimacy is crucial to the delivery of the soliloquy and is also a key characteristic of radio drama's "theater of mind." A sense of articulation and listening as an intimate and private act is encapsulated by the first voice's statement, "I talk to myself, myself only" (179). We are reminded that "Three Women" was broadcast to a mass audience of public listeners. At this time, it is estimated that the average audience for the Third Programme was a million-and-a-half listeners.[12] As George Orwell notes in "Poetry and the Microphone,"

---

[11] Barbara Brookes: "Distillers withdrew the drug on December 3, 1961. In May 1962 the Ministry of Health sent a memorandum to medical officers of health stating that 'every possible effort should be taken' to prevent the birth of deformed babies. Doctors were advised to identify from their records any patient for whom thalidomide had been prescribed" (152). See also Plath's poem "Thalidomide" (*CP* 252).

[12] See Newby, "The Third Programme," *BBC Lunchtime Lecture*. He comments that the listening audience for the Third had "remained steady for years."

there is a paradox inherent to radio broadcasting: "Millions may be listening, but each is listening alone" (167). I will briefly consider what radio listening entails and how Plath's script prepares the listener for an experience of an "intimate" encounter in her broadcast.

Jean-Luc Nancy's *Listening* asks a fundamental question: "What does it mean for a being to be immersed entirely in listening, formed by listening or in listening, listening with all his being?" Nancy considers the intersubjective exchange that is produced by the listening audience. His discussion moves us beyond lazily reflecting on the sonic "musicality" of any work. Instead, he places a focus on the exchange inherent within it:

> Speaking—speaking and listening ... for speaking is already its own listening—is the echo of the text in which the text is made and written, opens up to its own sense as to the plurality of its own possible senses. It is not, and in any case not only, what one can call in a superficial way the musicality of a text.
>
> (35)

The complexity of this interaction between speaking and listening as a relationship between sound and subjectivity is framed by Voegelin as an experience of doubt: "Sound provides an incomplete picture and brings signifiers into doubt" (*Political Possibility of Sound* 120). Voegelin insists that sound does not provide rigid structures of meaning "it does not offer us a certain form, but it is the moment of production of what the thing and the listener are" (*Political Possibility of Sound* 120). Above all, Voegelin stresses that this moment of making meaning, the encounter between sound and listener, has no premeditated interpretation. Listening for her is an action that combines intensity and incompletion: "the invisible process of production where things have no *a priori* and distinct meaning or definition" (*Political Possibility of Sound* 120). Radio listening inscribes within it an encounter between an intimate voice and the listening ear. For Kate Lacey, listening offers a sense of "radical openness," a listening public is made of listeners "inhabiting a condition of plurality and intersubjectivity" (8). Crucially, Lacey proposes that listening offers a "powerful conceptual corrective to nostalgic political models based on idealized notions of the face-to-face dialogic encounter" (8–9). She argues that too often we have culturally overprivileged listening in the language of a "visual logic" (9). Lacey is clear that this formulation overemphasizes individual and dyadic relations: "It is a construct that implicitly privileges interpersonal, private conversation over impersonal, public communication" (9).

There are constant references to faces by all three voices throughout Plath's "Three Women," be they unformed, erased, or only eventually coming into a sustained focus. A desire for a recognition of something that exceeds the self reminds us of an ideal of an intersubjective ethics, that at its most basic offers a sense of responsibility to another. One might think of Emmanuel Levinas's *Otherwise Than Being*, where the idea of an "encounter" is not the epic wandering of an imperial self that seeks to appropriate the other to a form of knowledge (3–20). This meeting or summoning of responsibility in the philosopher's work is prompted dramatically (and visually as Lacey reminds us) as a dialogic "face to face encounter." The insistence on the immediacy of this encounter privileges not only spontaneity but also the necessity of a performative response to the other. Plath makes full use of this visualization of faces through the medium of radio.

The evocation of faces during all three soliloquies enables a sense of a shared overarching experience, even though the three women do not engage directly with one another. For the first voice, faces are largely spectatorial, separate, and related to hospital staff aiding her birth. Images of faces are also used to represent a natural world that is in harmony with a maternal vulnerability and openness: "the narcissi open white faces in the orchard" (185). For Plath's second voice, this craving for an encounter with an expressive face is linked to ideas of growth and development. However, the faces of her multiple unborn children are left blank. They become affiliated with the threatening and featureless faces of masculine power and public life: "Governments, parliaments, societies, / The faceless faces of important men" (179). The figure of the face forms an essential moment of encounter and recognition for the third voice, this time linked to ideas of conception. On viewing a reflection, the speaker reveals, "[t]he face in the pool was beautiful, but not mine" (177). Plath extends this moment of conception to the birth of writing and an ambiguous creativity. In the midst of images of disembodiment, there is the patient presence of the figure of a face developing as witness to events "the face / Went on shaping itself with love, as If I was ready" (178).

Cleverdon comments how central visualization is for Plath's receptive listening audience: "The evocation of vivid colour is matched in intensity by the startling directness of the imagery[.] … In radio, nothing can equal a poet's visualizing imagination" ("On *Three Women*" 229). Lacey proposes that from radio's early years, producers were attuned to a paradox of using visualizing language as a prompt for an auditory imagination: "Radio was not a visual medium, but producers were very aware listeners would conjure up images in their mind's eye in response to acoustic cues, while at the same time being liberated from the tyranny of the image" (98–9). In producing a poetics of listening in "Three Women," Cleverdon affirms the complex balancing act between intimate and public life, as well as the relationship between visual image and auditory imagination inscribed in Plath's language.

Milton A. Kaplan, an early commentator on the relationship between poetry and radio, asserted that the popularity of radio offered the possibility of a public listenership for poetry: "The opportunity to write for a huge audience and the compulsion to concentrate that expression will almost surely turn us to poetry for maximum compression and force" (259). Through her sensitivity to the process of radio listening, Plath's collaboration with Cleverdon at the BBC ensures that the sonic envelope in which the gender politics of surrounding maternity, birth, and motherhood are embedded is given an intimate yet paradoxically public platform.

# CHAPTER TWENTY-THREE

# Sylvia Plath's "The Jailor" as Radical Feminist Text

BETHANY HICOK

A few months after radical feminists staged a coup and took over publication of the New York-based, radical left newspaper *RAT Subterranean News* in 1970, the editors published Sylvia Plath's 1962 poem "The Jailor" in their June issue (11).[1] That same year, Robin Morgan included the poem in her anthology *Sisterhood Is Powerful* (510–11). This radical feminist context stands in stark contrast to the poem's first posthumous appearance in 1963 when Ted Hughes selected it, along with nine other poems from the same period, for the British literary magazine *Encounter*.[2] *Encounter* was one of the most important literary magazines of the anti-Communist liberal left and funded by the United States Congress for Cultural Freedom, a Cold War cultural vehicle that writers would learn much later was backed by the CIA.[3] It would be hard to find two more different publications: one of the male-dominated, liberal left-leaning, anti-communist, state-sanctioned *Encounter*; the other, the feminist Marxist radical *RAT*, with its show of solidarity for the Black Panthers and its critique of US imperialism abroad, particularly in Vietnam (the United States had just invaded Cambodia). Plath, it should be noted, did not choose either of these venues for her work. But since Plath had already published two poems in *Encounter* during her lifetime,[4] it is likely she would have approved of the publication of a significant grouping of poems in such a prestigious literary publication.

It is doubtful Plath would have approved of *RAT*, but since she died before the beginning of the Women's Liberation Movement (WLM), it is impossible to know what Plath would have said or done by 1970. Still, the publication of this particular poem in

---

[1] The June 1970 issue of *RAT* and Plath's poem as it appeared there can be accessed free through the Roz Payne Sixties Archive at the Center for Digital Research in the Humanities at the University of Nebraska-Lincoln: https://rozsixties.unl.edu/items/show/717
[2] Hughes selected ten of Plath's poems for the October 1963 issue of *Encounter*, which were published in the following order: "Death & Co.," The Swarm, "The Other," "Getting There," "Lady Lazarus," "Little Fugue," "Childless Woman," "The Jailor," "Thalidomide," and "Daddy." See "Ten Poems by Sylvia Plath," October 1963. Available online, *Unz Review: An Alternative Media Selection*, http://www.unz.com/print/Encounter/Contents/?Period=1963
[3] For a thorough discussion of *Encounter*, which ran from 1953 to 1990, and the central role it played in the Congress for Cultural Freedom, see Chapter 12, "Magazine 'X,'" of Saunders, *The Cultural Cold War: The CIA and the World of Arts and Letters*, 165–89.
[4] Plath published two poems in *Encounter* during her lifetime, "A Winter Ship," February 1961, and "The Colossus," April 1962 (cited in *L2*, 660n).

two such different periodicals provides an instructive contrast for thinking about poetry production during this period. *Encounter* was prestigious, an acceptable literary outlet for one's work and one recognized by those who gave out poetry prizes and fellowships. *RAT* was neither prestigious nor socially sanctioned; it was not likely to yield any monetary gain or recognition outside the movement. And that difference is precisely the point. *RAT* provides a new context for reading Plath's work. "The Jailor" documents the terror, shame, violence, and intimacy of domestic abuse and rape—issues that gained significant traction in the 1970s among feminist political activists and poets. New York radical feminists held their first "Speak-Out" on rape in 1971, the first battered women's shelters opened in the United States in 1973, and feminists had a significant impact on rape law reform (Schulhofer 336–8). In the larger context of the politics of feminist *RAT*, "The Jailor" can be seen as a contribution to the work of the newspaper's radical feminism, proceeding from the same radical feminist premises: (1) that in patriarchy women constitute "a sex-class" and that women's subordination within the family is directly related to larger social structures of oppression in the public sphere (Echols 3); and (2) that a consciousness of one's own oppression leads to an understanding of the oppression of peoples worldwide. Alice Echols dates the beginning of the radical feminist movement to the fall of 1967 when radical women began to meet in the United States in small groups in order "to discuss the problem of male supremacy" (3). She argues that "within two years radical feminism had established itself as the most vital and imaginative force within the women's liberation movement" (3).

Moreover, feminist periodicals, such as *RAT*, and the poetry published in them, drove the movement. As Nancy Berke has argued, "In the feminist movement of the late 1960s and 1970s, poets, and the poetry they wrote, were integral to the movement's organizing and theorizing" (162). Poetry was not only an individual means of expression for the poet, but a "'tool' for movement building and resistance" (Berke 162). Much of this activism is visible in the many periodicals and anthologies of the period. Polly Joan and Andrea Chessman's 1978 *Guide to Women's Publishing* documents some seventy-three feminist periodicals and sixty-six presses operating between the late 1960s and mid-1970s. But Joan and Chessman's guide is selective. Joyce Latham estimates that by 1970, there were more than 500 feminist periodicals, newsletters, and magazines being published in the United States (222). Stephen Voyce has noted the importance of these periodicals, anthologies, and small press publications in establishing and expanding the political activism of the Women's Liberation Movement and its feminist networks:

> Magazines like *R[AT], Speakout, The Second Wave, Moving Out, Aphra, Women: A Journal of Liberation, Sinister Wisdom,* along with presses such as Daughters, Diana Press, Kelsey Street Press, Shameless Hussy, and the Women's Press Collective disseminated a considerable body of work throughout the United States and Canada. By 1978 feminist small presses had collectively sold over one million books and pamphlets. Anthologies like *No More Masks!: An Anthology of Poems by Women* (1973), *Rising Tides: Twentieth-Century American Women Poets* (1973), and *The World Split Open: Four Centuries of Women Poets in England and America, 1550–1950* (1974) established a counter-tradition of writing that helped readers to redress literary history by challenging its legacies of gender exclusion.
>
> (163–4)

Anthologies, such as Morgan's 1970 *Sisterhood Is Powerful*, which includes a section called "poetry as protest," Voyce argues, were integral to "the WLM's political work" (164). Morgan published "The Jailor" as the last poem in the "poetry as protest" section, and since she was also a member of the *RAT* collective, she undoubtedly had a hand in publishing the poem in *RAT*, as well, further underscoring Voyce's point. Voyce's focus on the WLM consists of only one chapter of a larger project that examines poetic communities, avant-garde activism, and Cold War culture, so he does not concentrate specifically on feminist periodicals as "unique texts," as Barbara Green has argued, which are

> compelling in their juxtapositions of diverse and eye-catching materials ... [which] embed the literary in the rich mixed medium of economic writings, political journalism, interviews, personal journalism, information regarding the business of political meetings, marches, and meeting minutes, book and theater reviews.
> (Green, "Feminist" 192, 200)

While Green focuses on the feminist periodicals of an earlier feminist activism between 1905 and 1938, her point is equally applicable to the feminism of the 1960s, 1970s, and early 1980s.

While Plath has long been claimed by feminists as an avatar of feminism,[5] her poem's placement in *RAT*, the primary focus of this chapter, broadens the scope of that feminist discussion. Its appearance in a feminist periodical immediately shifts the context of Plath's poem from the private, domestic sphere, to the "feminist public sphere," embedding it "in the rich cultural spaces and activities of feminism" (Green 198). Moreover, the context is radical and intersectional. The feminists who took over *RAT* called themselves a radical feminist collective that, like several other radical feminist groups at the time, such as the Third World Women's Alliance (TWWA), took an intersectional approach to feminism that saw sexism, racism, and imperialism as interlocking systems of oppression. The *RAT* editors also devoted quite a bit of space to counterrevolutionary movements, such as the Black Panthers and the Weather Underground (at this time known as the Weatherman). A focus on freeing political prisoners associated with these groups in the June 1970 issue globalizes the prisoner theme of Plath's poem. The June issue reflects this intersectional approach, including several articles that focus specifically on American imperialism abroad; an article by Connie Morales critiquing the Puerto Rican cultural practice of *cortejas* (married men having a woman on the side), which ends with a call to arms: "FORWARD SISTERS IN THE STRUGGLE! / MACHISMO IS FASCISM! / SELF-DETERMINIATION FOR ALL PUERTO RICANS!" (5); and the guidelines of the radical feminist group "The Feminists," who called marriage domestic slavery and worked to abolish it as an institution (8–9). The content, in short, demands revolutionary change—sometimes, in the case of Weatherman fugitive Bernardine Dohrn's "Declaration of a State of War," calling for the violent overthrow of "Amerikan" institutions (4–5).[6] Plath's poem in this context, then, becomes part of the collective voice, rather than merely an expression of the individual, private pain

---

[5] Gilbert writes of discovering the power of Plath's work early on when she was still in high school and reading *Seventeen* magazine where Plath's 1951 story "Den of Lions" was published ("A Fine, White Flying Myth" 585).
[6] Note that Dohrn uses the radical Left's derogatory spelling of American with a k, a practice used throughout the newspaper, symbolizing the view that America is a racist, fascist and oppressive society, like Nazi Germany. Sometimes used, as with the Black Panthers, with three k's for the Ku Klux Klan: Amerikkka.

of a failed marriage, as "The Jailor" has often been read. As Laurel Brake has argued "periodical culture in general imagines authorship as a collective rather than a singular enterprise" (qtd. in Green, "Feminist" 202). At this moment, when we are reconsidering Plath in the light of new publications based on material issuing from the Plath archive (most recently the massive two-volume publication of *The Letters of Sylvia Plath*), it is more crucial than ever to consider Plath's archive in broader terms, exploring the ways that a recontextualizing of her work might lead to fresh insight on the role Plath's poetry has played in second-wave radical feminist discourse.

*RAT* began publication in New York in March 1968. The editors (Jeff Shero, Alice Embree, and Gary Thiher) came from Austin, Texas, where they had worked on another underground newspaper and belonged to a Texas anarchist group (Antliff 155). As the activist artist Susan Simensky Bietila describes it: "*R[AT]* covered the political and countercultural movements vividly," but it quickly devolved into sensationalism (Antliff 155). It takes only a quick tour through *RAT*'s pages in the archives at Williams College to see this de-evolution firsthand. Morgan, one of the key members of the *RAT* collective, a leading feminist figure, and, at the time of the takeover, a member of W.I.T.C.H. (Women's International Terrorist Conspiracy from Hell), exposed the sexism and misogyny of the male-dominated New Left in a satiric essay "Goodbye to All That" (6–7).[7] Published in the first all-women's issue of *RAT*, the essay became one of the iconic statements of the movement. At the beginning of the piece, Morgan describes what prompted the women's takeover:

> So *R[AT]* has been liberated, for this week, at least. Next week? If the men return to reinstate the porny photos, the sexist comic strips, the "nude-chickie" covers (along with their patronizing rhetoric about being in favor of Women's Liberation)—if this happens, our alternatives are clear. *R[AT]* must be taken over permanently by women—or *R[AT]* must be destroyed.
>
> (6)

In her interview with Allan Antliff, Simensky Bietila describes what happened: "The women who had been working at the *R[AT]* all along had been in SDS (Students for a Democratic Society) and other student groups. They were amazingly intelligent and articulate radicals who had been doing all these menial jobs" (Antliff 157). Before the takeover of *RAT*, the women got together and put out a women's issue, which was so successful, according to Simensky Bietila, they decided to seize the newspaper:

> The takeover was kind of interrelated with the street theater going on at the time: people involved in the *R[AT]* had been involved in the feminist demonstration at the Miss America Pageant in Atlantic City [September 7, 1968]. ... The *R[AT]* women attended meetings held by a range of feminist radical "consciousness raising," activist-oriented groups, as well as others—it was all one interlocking network.
>
> (157–8)

---

[7]For a thorough analysis of Morgan's essay as feminist satire, see Hedrick.

The kind of "performative activism," to borrow Green's phrase, described in these accounts was central to the radical feminist movement, and there is evidence that feminism drew Plath's work into this circle. For instance, Honor Moore chose "The Applicant" as the first poem in her 2009 Library of America anthology *Poems from the Women's Movement*, further emphasizing Plath's role as avatar. "The Applicant" performs gender by using the language of advertising to expose the rigid sex roles of the marriage market, staging a mock interview between the speaker and the male applicant for a wife, who by the end of the poem has been reduced to an automaton, an "it": "A living doll, everywhere you look. / It can sew, it can cook, / It can talk, talk, talk. // … Will you marry it, marry it, marry it" (*AR* 12). Moore notes in her introduction to the anthology that the formation of feminist consciousness-raising groups in the early 1970s changed the way they read the writers who had preceded them: "In this new context," she writes, "Sylvia Plath was no longer an isolated victim, but the avatar of a new female literary consciousness" (xx). Many of Plath's *Ariel* poems ("Lady Lazarus," "Lesbos," "Medusa," "Daddy") treat gender as a performance, calling into question, in Judith Butler's words, "those naturalized and reified notions of gender that support masculine hegemony and heterosexist power" (33–4). Moreover, "Daddy," as Voyce has argued, moves from the personal to the political, as it "unfolds [in] a series of private references to a father / husband figure that are filtered through the cultural signs (god, Nazi, devil, vampire, teacher)" (194). Thus,

> Plath, more capably than nearly anyone in post-war verse, demonstrates the meaning of the "personal *is* political," not by opposing private to public spheres of life, but rather *by exposing an identical patriarchal logic governing them both*. The domestic sphere joins the school, the prison, the media, the church, and the court as one more state apparatus socializing Western subjects.
>
> (Voyce 194)

While such a movement might be apparent in "Daddy" and "The Applicant," Plath's "The Jailor" is more likely to be read as a "private" poem that hews closely to the breakup of Plath's own marriage. Its placement as part of the "poetry of protest" in Morgan's anthology and in *RAT*, however, tells a different story.

By the time Plath's "The Jailor" ran in the June 1970 issue of the newspaper, *RAT's* contents thoroughly reflect an intersectional, radical feminist framework. Two broadsheet pages at the beginning are devoted to a pair of articles under the heading "Back from Hanoi," a personal brief memoir and an interview with a journalist/activist (2–3, 27). In the personal memoir, the anonymous writer focuses on her own experience of consciousness-raising. In a classic radical feminist move, she outlines how her understanding of her own oppression as a woman helped her to understand what was happening to the Vietnamese people during the war with Vietnam:

> Now, because I am beginning to understand my own oppression, I can fight for the Vietnamese—men and women both—their suffering is more real to me. … Indochina is not A war. It is OUR war. The more we understand our oppression as women, the more we will identify with the Vietnamese. And the stronger we will become, as women, as revolutionaries.
>
> (2)

A transcribed tape from Weatherman fugitive Bernardine Dohrn, "A Declaration of a State of War," follows. Dohrn, James Mellen, and Mark Rudd were leaders of the original Weatherman, later called The Weather Underground, a militant group of young white Americans formed in 1969, emerging from a faction of SDS called Third World Marxists (Lambert 1). Dohrn was on the run, having been indicted along with eleven other Weatherman members "on federal charges of riot and conspiracy" after staging a direct action that led to riots in Chicago in October 1969 (Lambert 4). Dohrn's declaration (a manifesto of sorts) articulates Weatherman's positions:

> All over the world, people fighting Amerikan imperialism look to Amerika's youth to use our strategic position behind enemy lines to join forces in the destruction of the empire.
>
> Black people have been fighting almost alone for years. We've known that our job is to lead white kids to armed revolution. We never intended to spend the next five or twenty-five years in jail. Ever since SDS became revolutionary, we've been trying to show how it is possible to overcome the frustration and impotence that comes from trying to reform this system.
>
> (Dohrn 4)

The editors' choice to run Dohrn's statement (even though they had issues with the sexism of the Weatherman group) is a testament to the newspaper's interest in creating a lively forum for the exchange of ideas. Instead of censoring Dohrn, they published a "Weather Report" to air their "disagreements with the politics of Weatherman which become decisive around the issues of sexism and class" (5). Although the editors ultimately agree with Weatherman's support of "the international revolution of oppressed peoples and the struggle here at home," they cannot abide the group's sexism, which is at odds with women's liberation (5):

> There is no question that any group that does not deal relentlessly with its sexism is not revolutionary. Sexism is as destructive and annihilating to the potential of human life as racism is. The exercise of male privilege is as damaging and oppressive to women as the exercise of white skin privilege is to non-whites.
>
> (5)

The recognition that one's own oppression is shared by others, and that the sex-class system is wide-ranging and damaging to human flourishing is a clear message throughout the publication. Other essays show solidarity for political prisoners and for Native American activists who were "seizing" the offices of the Bureau of Indian Affairs across the country in protest against the US Government's failure to "fulfill its treaty promises of education, medical services ... and economic aid to the 315 US tribes," a story the mainstream media had failed to cover ("Seize the Land" 21). This issue of *RAT* also celebrates world leaders who were taking back their countries from imperialist powers, such as Sirimavo Bandaranaike, elected for a second term in 1970 as prime minister of Ceylon (later Sri Lanka), and her "radical program" to make the country independent from Great Britain and free from United States influence—all reflecting the newspaper's consistent focus on anti-imperialism at home and abroad ("Up ... in Ceylon" 10).

But perhaps the group represented in this issue of *RAT* most relevant to Plath's poem in terms of its figuring of marriage as domestic slavery is The Feminists, a radical group active from 1968 to 1973. Ti-Grace Atkinson founded the group after her split with the National Organization for Women (NOW), because it was not radical enough (Echols 167–8). In their *RAT* piece, The Feminists outline their organizational principles and structure, but their other writings and political actions underscore some of the themes of Plath's poem. On September 23, 1969, for instance, the group initiated and staged one of a number of actions to disrupt local government and make their point about marriage. In this case, "five members stormed into New York City's Marriage License Bureau to charge its officials with fraud. They distributed a leaflet at the action which asked women: 'Do you know that rape is legal in marriage? ... Do you know that you are your husband's prisoner?'" (qtd. in Echols 170). This language speaks directly to the language of Plath's poem. In that sense Plath's poem fits comfortably into *RAT*'s radical content, its performative language, and its intersectional goals around the issues of women's status in marriage, anti-imperialism, and imprisonment and freedom.

"The Jailor" is printed on its own broadsheet page, fully integrated into artwork that was clearly designed for and inspired by the poem.[8] The background of the image looks like a black ink wash, forming the wall of what looks to be a prison cell. Because of the 11 x 17-inch broadsheet format, the blackness of the cell looms especially large over a huddled figure that can be found at the bottom right of the image. The poem, reprinted in black typeface against a white rectangular background, takes up a full two-thirds of the vertical space in the left half of the image. "By Sylvia Plath" appears etched in the wall in white, handwritten, large letters beneath the poem. The title, "The Jailor," in the same lettering, takes up the top third of the image. The crouching female figure (the slight build, body shape, and hair suggest that she is a woman) is mostly in darkness, except for light falling on her right side, the tops of her legs from her knees down, and the top of her head. Light shows in cracks beyond and to the left of her. Given that the poem is printed against a white background, it almost seems as if Plath's poem itself provides the major source of light in the cell, framing a window onto the outside world.

Given the layout, graphics, context, and political journalism surrounding it, *RAT*'s readers may have brought fresh associations to Plath's poem, which describes in violent, graphic detail, the intimate, sexual, and frightening relationship between the victim and her jailer. In this scenario, she is clearly his sex slave: *Her* "night sweats grease *his* breakfast plate" (emphasis mine) from the first line. He is the "rattler of keys." She has been "drugged and raped," "[s]even hours knocked out of [her] right mind, / Into a black

---

[8]All quotations from "The Jailor" are taken from the poem as published on p. 11 of *RAT*, the same version of which had appeared in *Encounter*. "The Jailor" was spelled with an o in both of these publications. Hughes left the poem out of both the British (1965) and American (1966) editions of *Ariel* and then changed the spelling to "The Jailer" in the 1981 *Collected Poems*, and so critics who discuss the poem often use the spelling from this edition. However, Plath's drafts, housed at Smith, indicate that she spelled it with an "e" in early drafts but switched to the "o" spelling in later drafts and then consistently used that spelling. *Ariel: The Restored Edition* (2004) uses the spelling with an "o," which archival evidence shows was clearly Plath's preferred spelling. In *RAT*, the editors provide a very short bio in a small box at the bottom right corner of the preceding page with an arrow leading to the poem on the next page. It would be easy to miss this box, in fact. And given the import of this issue of *RAT* and the concerns of radical feminism, it is odd that the editors chose to focus on Plath's marital status and children instead of her professional life as the author of *The Colossus*, *Ariel*, and *The Bell Jar*. The bio reads: "Sylvia Plath was born in 1932. She was married to Ted Hughes in 1956. In 1960 she gave birth to a daughter, and, in 1962, to a son. In 1963, she committed suicide."

sack"; he has been "burning [her] with cigarettes." She is a "[l]ever of his wet dreams." The poem calls attention to this relationship as part of a sex-class system: sex, slavery, and violence become one through a series of images. The third stanza describes how the speaker has been dropped "from a terrible altitude" by the sleeping pill ("my red and blue zeppelin") she has taken, her "[c]arapace smashed / ... spread to the beaks of birds." Beaks become "little gimlets" in the fourth stanza, boring holes. The proximity of the beaks to the speaker's body ("carapace" reduces the body to that of an insect) elaborates on the rape of the previous stanza, deflected by the strange line that follows: "What holes this papery day is already full of!" As the speaker says later, "I die with variety," but unlike "Lady Lazarus," she does not rise from her deaths "and eat men like air." More explicitly, as it turns out, The Jailor has been making holes in her: "He has been burning me with cigarettes, / Pretending I am a Negress with pink paws." Again, Plath uses imagery here that emphasizes the speaker's status as his sex slave, deepening the point by establishing a connection with the African slave trade with the gendered word "Negress." For the purposes of Plath's poem, the "pink paws" emphasize softness, vulnerability, and femaleness, but also qualities that underscore the animal, non-human, and cat-like (also a feminine signifier). This image follows an earlier one, as well, that applies to the speaker herself described as "relax[ing]" into the "black sack" she has been thrown into like a "foetus or cat;" the speaker had also equated herself with an insect earlier, whose "carapace" has been smashed. So, in this poem's formulation, both women are reduced to helpless and vulnerable creatures.

On the subject of the Africanist imagery, the criticism is mostly mute with the exception of Steven Gould Axelrod's reading. Axelrod places this reference alongside other literary uses of the "Negro" by white American writers, such as Herman Melville's *Benito Cereno*, representing, for Axelrod, "'the uncanny return of the repressed'" (*Wound and the Cure of Words* 216). But who, or what, is being repressed? The terrible history of slavery? Plath's own fear or desire projected onto the black woman as a figure for that repression? The Jailor's? If we were to return to Plath's oeuvre and its use of race, as Renée R. Curry has done, it would be difficult to overlook the potential racism of such an image. In her book *White Women Writing White*, Curry finds that "racism ... becomes repeatedly enlivened through Plath's insistence on the black / white binary" upon which much of her poetry relies (126). Curry notes that,

> Of the 224 poems printed in Plath's *The Collected Poems*, a remarkable fifty percent of them (117 poems) use the words "white" and/or "black" as intricate signifiers of power, (im)purity, fear, and thought. Eleven poems address skin color, twelve poems discuss the significance of whiteness, and fourteen poems refer to peoples other than whites such as Africans, Indians, Latinos, Chinese, and Negroes.
> (*White Women Writing White* 125)

It is hard to argue with these numbers; Plath's use of light and dark, as well as the appearance of the "Negress" in this poem, operates in the larger cultural system upon which Plath draws.

As published in *RAT*, however, surrounded by statements of solidarity for the oppression of others, particularly women of color in the United States and throughout the world, it might be possible to partially reclaim this figure from Plath's poem as the symbol of someone else's racism (The Jailor's) or other male authority figures, themselves called "pigs" (the favored term of the time) elsewhere in this issue of *RAT*—women forced to seek help from male gynecologists, police, jailers.[9] The stanza ends with two sentences that could speak for all those who find themselves persecuted or tortured: "I am myself. That is not enough."

As with much of the work of this issue of *RAT*, Plath's poem focuses on crime and punishment. "How did I get here?" the speaker asks in stanza seven, and then she names herself an "Indeterminate criminal." Indeterminate is the key word and takes us into the center of the speaker's horror. The criminal (and by extension her crime) has not been determined by motives, it is not settled or decided, not fixed or established; it is uncertain (to cite a few of the definitions in the OED). To not know what one has been locked up for—that is the ultimate defeat. It is possible that Plath, who was living in Britain in 1962, was also aware of the widely discussed debate over British prison reform that focused on determinate and indeterminate prison sentences, which eventually led to the 1967 Criminal Justice Act. This Act established a system of review for prisoners of both types of prison sentences and opened up the possibility of parole for those who had been "rehabilitated." At the center of the debate in 1962, when the poem was written, was the issue of "indeterminate prison sentences," discussed by Dr. Rupert Cross, Lecturer in Law at Oxford University, on BBC radio and then published in *The Listener* in February 1962. Cross had argued that "indeterminate sentences" were better for prisoners because, rather than put their fate in the hands of a judge at the time of sentencing, a group of prison executives, who had responsibility of the prisoner during his incarceration, would have a better sense of the prisoner's "progress and prospects on release" (Guiney 15). For Cross, an "indeterminate sentence" was preferable and possibly more just. For Plath, "indeterminate criminal" marks the wife's status in an abusive marriage. Her crime, her sentence, and why she is being abused, are indeterminate.

As the artwork illustrates, this woman lives in the shadow of that "indeterminate crime": the shadows of the prison cell, the shadow of the jailer and his art, the shadow of his larger stature, greater fame. It is in his "shadow" that she has "eaten [her] ghost ration." As Axelrod has argued: "Shadow existence in Plath's poetry implies the political failure to extricate oneself from illegitimate and destructive authority, and more specifically the inability to function freely as a woman artist" (*Wound and the Cure of Words* 215). She can "imagine him / Impotent as distant thunder"; she cannot "wish him dead or away"; the imagination fails her: "That, it seems is the impossibility. // That being free." Plath ends the poem with a series of crucial questions that take us deep into the psychic terrain of the mutual dependency of this jailer and his prisoner:

... What would the dark
Do without fevers to eat?
What would the light
Do without eyes to knife, what would he
Do, do, do without me?

Clearly this poem is closely related to Plath's poem "Daddy" and its repetition and variations on the verb "do." The two poems are both meditations on authoritarian power

---

[9]In an article on the FBI informant George Demmerle, *RAT*'s editors printed an enormous pig's head at the top of the second page of the article. See "george," *RAT*, June 5–19, 6–7. The title of an article on gynecologists asks, "Are Our Doctors Pigs?" *RAT*, June 5–19, 12.

and the sadomasochism that keeps the machinery of abuse operating. As Laura Frost argues, fascism—explicitly addressed in "Daddy"—"signifies a series of opposites for Plath: subjugation and oppression, control and freedom, sadism and masochism, and hate and love" (47). With these lines from "The Jailor" and throughout, Plath's poem establishes the deep psychic connections, the intimacy that keeps this violent duo locked in their prison: Hegel's master/slave dialectic depends on the binary that keeps the relationship in place. You cannot have one without the other.

Just two years after Plath's poem appeared in *RAT*, Webster Schott's 1972 review, "The Cult of Plath," appeared in *Washington Post Book World*, dismissing both Plath's art and her readers: "Sylvia Plath was a sick woman who made art of her sickness. ... Some young people, having limited experience, need literature to help them feel bad, and they will celebrate Plath for a while" (qtd. in "The 'Priestess'" 170). Such representations of Plath (and her readers), Janet Badia argues, often end up denigrating both and, ultimately, can be seen as part of deeply paternalistic cultural moments, which, as Badia points out, continue into the twenty-first century: "the reception and critical history of Plath's work genders the Plath reader, diagnoses her as depressed and sick, and assesses her as an uncritical consumer of 'bad' literature" ("The 'Priestess'" 164). These were criticisms of Plath and her readers that, as Badia notes, have their roots in the initial reception of Plath by male critics in the 1960s and 1970s. At nearly the same time, then, that Schott was denigrating the Plath reader (not an accident, I'm sure), feminists, such as those in the *RAT* collective, were drawing Plath into the countercultural fold as an icon of the feminist revolution. It was NOT Plath who was sick; it was the patriarchy. Plath's "The Jailor," in this context, becomes part of the all-important work of consciousness-raising that was so necessary to driving the movement forward.

As I have been arguing, the appearance of "The Jailor" in *RAT* provides a countercultural reading of Plath that places her poetry as contributing to the important work of radical feminism in 1970. Plath's poem in this context joins the creation of a new aesthetic that combines artistic practice with public and political engagement, an aesthetic that Simensky Bietila defines in describing the work she did for *RAT*: "Art should inspire critical thinking and operate in the public sphere—be seen, understood, and embraced by a much wider audience—by people who agree and are inspired as well as those who disagree" (Antliff 172). In the context of *RAT*, Plath's "The Jailor" operates not only as a scene of "private abjection," as Lynda K. Bundtzen has called it, but as part of a public discourse on enslavement and liberation (*The Other* Ariel 69). Because Plath died before she became a famous poet, an icon, an avatar, a myth, or a cult figure, her reputation, her career, and her biography were seized by others, including the editors of *RAT*. But until now, the standard account of Plath's posthumous treatment by others, whether positive or negative, has belonged mostly to family members and to Hughes. After publishing the poem in *Encounter*, Hughes left "The Jailor" out of both the British (1965) and American (1966) editions of *Ariel*, along with other poems, such as "The Rabbit Catcher." He would go on to publish these poems in Plath's 1981 *Collected Poems*, which won the Pulitzer Prize. In the introduction to that volume, Hughes obliquely explains his decision to excise these poems from the *Ariel* editions: "It [*Ariel*] omitted some of the more personally aggressive poems from 1962" (*CP* 15). In this sentence, Hughes whitewashes himself as both the agent of this decision and the object of the poems' so-called aggressivity. Radical feminism had a brief moment in this history when Robin Morgan, in Bundtzen's words, "identifie[d] the jailer as Ted Hughes and charge[d] him in [her poem] 'Arraignment (I)' with torture and murder," in a way that echoed "The Jailor" (*The Other* Ariel 69).

I suspect that Morgan herself, a prominent member of the *RAT* collective, had a hand in seizing Plath's poem for *RAT*'s radical purposes.

In a final note on this counter history of "The Jailor," Morgan clearly had to seek copyright permission to include Plath's poem in the anthology, which was published by Random House: "Copyright © 1964 by Ted Hughes" appears prominently at the bottom of the first page of the poem. But in *RAT*, the poem was published in full without copyright acknowledgment (and presumably without permission). Copyright has been fraught territory for scholars working in and around Plath's archive. *RAT*'s editors, true to radical feminist ideology, simply seized the poem and printed it without so much as a nod towards the Estate. Their flaunting of property rights captures the radical spirit of a moment and a movement when poets such as Judy Grahn were mimeographing their latest poems and handing them out at poetry readings.[10] In the same spirit, Plath's poem joined others of the movement that were passed along to Sisters who quoted and sometimes misquoted them—until they, too, became part of the Wave.[11]

---

[10] Grahn's memoir, *A Simple Revolution: The Making of an Activist Poet*, is one of the best accounts of this period and its on-the-ground activism. Grahn was at the epicenter of West Coast activism, poetry-making, and community building during the 1960s, 1970s, and 1980s.

[11] I am very grateful to my Williams College student Ruth Kramer who discovered Plath's poem while working in Williams College Special Collections on an archival fellowship. I would also like to thank Lisa Conathan, Head of Special Collections, and Anne Peale, Special Collections Librarian, Williams Libraries, for building an incredible collection of primary documents on poetry and Feminism for my course at Williams on the Feminist Poetry Movement.

CHAPTER TWENTY-FOUR

# Archival Pedagogy: Curating Edna O'Brien's Sylvia Plath Television Play

AMANDA GOLDEN

Following the success of *Virginia: A Play* in 1980, the Irish writer Edna O'Brien set her sights on another twentieth-century women writer, Sylvia Plath.[1] During an interview with *The Paris Review*, published in the summer of 1984, O'Brien linked both writers, noting the ways that their lives ended: "Many wonderful writers write one or two books and then kill themselves. Sylvia Plath for instance. She was much younger than Virginia Woolf when she committed suicide, but if she had survived that terrible crisis, I feel she would have written better books" (*The Paris Review*). There is a sense here of the unfinished, of what Plath could have gone on to accomplish, had she lived. It was Plath's life and work, however, that became the focus of the television play O'Brien came to develop. Decades later, her project inspired an instance of archival pedagogy as my students worked critically to piece together connections between O'Brien's scripts and what they learned about Plath, formulating their own impressions of literary history.[2]

On April 18, 1985, O'Brien received a Commissioning Brief from the British Broadcasting Corporation for a Sylvia Plath project, due by the end of December of the same year.[3] A second document, dated June 3, 1985, clarified that it was to be a new work, a "tv play" that would be fifty minutes long.[4] Preparing for this task, O'Brien filled notebooks with information about Plath's life and writing. On a loose page, O'Brien

---

[1] I thank my students Rebekah Geevarghese and Uzma Patel; Maeve O'Brien, as her discussions of Edna O'Brien and Plath led to my students' project; Anita Helle for her careful editing; and Elizabeth J. Donaldson, Amy E. Elkins, and Margaret Konkol for commenting on drafts of this chapter. This paper began as a presentation with Geevarghese and Patel for Fordham University's Transnational Print Culture Conference in 2017 and was revised for a presentation at the American Conference for Irish Studies in 2019. I am grateful to Cathal Pratt and Keri Walsh at Fordham for hosting.
[2] Writing to O'Brien on February 3, 1986, Plath's friend Elizabeth Sigmund asked whether O'Brien had prepared a play about Plath for the BBC (box 8, folder 40, Rose). O'Brien responded that it was put aside as the BBC was not able to receive permissions (box 1, folder 26, Smith).
[3] Brenda Reid, Producer for BBC2 Plays, "Commissioning Brief," April 18, 1985, BBC Written Archives Centre.
[4] From Senior Assistant Contracts, Copyright Department, June 3, 1985, BBC Written Archives Centre.

added the date of May 21, 1985. She then moved on to full sheets of paper, sketching out the dialogue by hand before typing, editing, and retyping her drafts.[5]

O'Brien's notebooks, manuscripts, and typescripts—now housed in Emory University's Stuart A. Rose Manuscript, Archives, and Rare Book Library—became the subject of "Revealing the Roots of Sylvia Plath," a digital project by my New York Institute of Technology students, Rebekah Geevarghese and Uzma Patel, in the summer of 2017.[6] Working from scans of the items in O'Brien's archive, the students became curators, designing a digital project displaying and interpreting selections from this collection. Throughout the stages of this process—from the students' reading of texts by and about Plath to their creation of the project—Geevarghese and Patel gained experience interpreting primary sources and developing a digital resource. As a platform for the project, Scalar, an open-source publishing service created for digital scholarship, enabled a certain legibility, giving students the ability to present the materials they encountered in a fashion that would make sense to others.[7] The Scalar display also removes the archival research process from the reading room to shape a communicable project, rather than enshrining the object to admire for its own sake. While we have not made the project public, the process and the product have nonetheless been an experiment in digital scholarship. The resulting project speaks to an image of Plath that O'Brien depicted, in a fashion that makes new meaning. As Margaret Konkol puts it, "students can and do create new knowledge." In the case of "Revealing the Roots of Sylvia Plath," this knowledge comes in the form of interpreting materials and creating a resource that will teach others about them.

O'Brien's materials are unusual because they record an effort that in some ways did not come to fruition. Even as her television play may never have aired, however, O'Brien's placement of her notes and drafts in an archive makes them materials for scholarly and pedagogical use. As Logan Esdale points out in a parallel case regarding Gertrude Stein's *Ida*:

> We can re-create Stein's workshop experience because concurrent with the start of *Ida* she began constructing her archive at the Yale University Library. Having a public archive motivated her to systematically keep the novel's draft materials, something she

---

[5]"*Sylvia Plath*, Notebook," box 76, folder 4 and "*Sylvia Plath*, MS and TS," box 76, folder 5, Rose. These materials have not, to my knowledge, been published. O'Brien's early novels were adapted as movies and she later composed screenplays (*Conversations* xv, 15; *Country Girl* 211). Regarding O'Brien's writing for the screen, see also O'Brien to Rachel MacKenzie, August 25, 1962, NYPL. The introduction to O'Brien's interview with *The Paris Review* mentions three screenplays (*The Paris Review*). O'Brien also notes in *Country Girl* that when they visited her, Jane Fonda and friend suggested O'Brien write a screenplay for Peter Fonda. In a letter from 1985, Louis Malle complimented one of O'Brien's scripts (Letter, Louis Malle to Norma, June 16, 1985, Rose).

[6]This project was generously funded by a Student and Faculty Collaboration Grant from the College of Arts and Sciences at New York Institute of Technology. See "A Study in Archives." The method and concept of this project were inspired by Konkol's course in which her students created a digital archive of John Ringling's ("Public Archives"). Konkol's students compiled a "Delights of the Archive" portion of their project that "presents singular 'finds' that created affective resonances for us. This section is as important as the catalogs … as it captures the curiosity that drives research and the pleasure of deciphering marginalia, inscriptions, and the handling of old books." In the discussion following the roundtable, "Scholarly Editing Now" at the Modern Language Association Convention in 2020, Karen V. Kukil and Heather Cass White also noted the importance of asking students editorial questions.

[7]Tara McPherson, in *Feminist in a Software Lab*, sees the relationship among materials as central to feminist digital scholarship and design. Making materials accessible and depicting relationships, whether between texts or of writers' responses to each other, are relational.

had never done before. The decision to save the drafts, as well her correspondence and related, unpublished texts, was Stein's invitation to us to study her creative process.

(xi)[8]

This invitation, for readers of O'Brien's Plath scripts, means the possibility for further consideration of how women writers respond to each other's work and depths of such exchanges. Considering such artifacts, students and scholars attempt to understand the fragments that remain.

This chapter engages three elements of archival pedagogy: teaching students to design a digital archival project, the O'Brien materials with which the students worked, and the project the students designed. In this instance, students approached for the first time what Linda Anderson, Mark Byers, and Ahren Warner describe as "the manner in which a literary work invents or reinvents itself over time and across material contexts (from rough notebook drafts, for instance, to fair copies and annotated proofs)" (8). Building a digital project meant interpreting this corpus, selecting artifacts, and creating a context in which to display them.

For students, digital curation presents the opportunity to reflect on the making of literary history and to participate in shaping future interpretations of archives. As Jean-Christophe Cloutier puts it, "[t]he word *archival* bespeaks an underlying notion that documents have an afterlife, that they can be put to new, unpredictable uses and form the basis for new interpretive and narrative acts" (2). Technology adds to these possibilities and students can have a role in constructing archival knowledge through their research. Konkol underscores that "[t]he benefit of involving students in the planning ... of a digital archival project ... is that it is a necessary and fruitful exercise to articulate our assumptions about who interprets the archive and who controls historical narratives." Students can not only become better readers of the inevitably fragmentary texts that belong in archives, but they can also become interpreters of them, altering the ways we will understand the past.

## "I SHALL NEVER GET YOU PUT TOGETHER ENTIRELY"

In Plath's case, guiding students in the construction of archival knowledge builds on a foundation of archival themes in Plath's poems. In the opening line of her poem, "The Colossus," the speaker concedes, addressing the statue she is working to restore: "I shall never get you put together entirely" (*CP* 129). The poem itself has archival import, dealing as it does with the problem of working with remnants. Plath's choice of "shall" in the poem's first line signals a sense of decorum. Its formality recalls Shakespeare's "Shall I compare thee to a summer's day?" But its determination is reminiscent of Edna St. Vincent Millay's "I shall forget you." For Millay and Plath, the choice of "shall" makes a concession to the polite, feminine, and humble, attributes traditionally associated with women's writing, and which women writers often resist. Plath's syntax in the second half of the line reflects the ways that these aspects inform the speaker's work in constructing archival memory.

---

[8]Thank you to Emily Setina for bringing this edition to my attention.

The narrator of "The Colossus" is caretaker and curator; her "hours are married to shadow" (*CP* 130). Plath's metaphor speaks to what Cloutier calls the "shadow archive," the materials that remain to be brought to light. Such artifacts rest behind and illuminate both past and present. Interpreting such fragments means engaging in what Marlo Starr calls "the slow labor of archival research" (197). In the archive, Starr argues, scholars can "reveal the particular human details that slip through big-data representations" (198). "Human details" include the impressions of lived life—the three decades that Plath's speaker has spent "[s]caling little ladders with gluepots and pails of Lysol" (*CP* 129)—that one can glean from primary sources. As she drafted her television play, O'Brien could not get Plath put together any more than Plath's speaker in "The Colossus" could capture the memory of a voice she can no longer hear. The fact that O'Brien placed her notebooks and drafts in the archive at Emory means that there is a corpus to attend to, a "cornucopia" "[o]f [an] ... ear" for shelter, as the sculpture provides in Plath's poem (*CP* 130).

In his reflection on the beginning of Plath's poem, "The Colossus," Peter Davison noted, "[t]his fragmentation of the body yearned for reassemblage" (181). Such an interpretation suggests that the father is calling to his daughter, the curator of his memory.[9] He sees the daughter as subject to the father's demands beyond the grave. Viewing the protagonist as a curator stresses what she does with this call and brings her skill to bear on it. She interprets the archive's shadows instead of being subject to them. An archive like O'Brien's is itself a reshuffling of Plath's life and work. Digital interfaces seek to make materials accessible and logical, in this case by the scope of a life and the span of an oeuvre. Bringing archival materials to students, however, means teaching them to interpret artifacts that are fragmentary and unclear.

For "Revealing the Roots of Sylvia Plath," constructing an archival project using digital tools meant that the students needed to learn how to work with archival materials and a digital platform, ultimately designing a resource that would teach others about Plath and her writing.

## WORKING WITH THE MATERIALS

O'Brien's notes chart the textual terrain she navigated and the ideas to which she attended. In her notebooks, she collected materials from primary and secondary sources, including Plath's *Letters Home* (1975) and Edward Butscher's biography, *Sylvia Plath: Method and Madness* (1976). In 2021, these sources are outdated. Students and scholars have reconsidered Plath's life and work, attending to the wealth of materials in her archives, and the two volumes of Plath's letters (published in 2017 and 2018) have replaced the edited, abridged collection *Letters Home*. O'Brien may have developed some sense of discrimination as she sifted through early Plath biographies. Following the publication of Anne Stevenson's biography *Bitter Fame*, Al Alvarez sent O'Brien a copy of the review he published, noting that he felt the need to express to others that he felt it lacked quality (October 31, 1989, Rose). Included with the review is a page of published responses from Stevenson and Olwyn Hughes, and Alvarez's answer to them. In his piece, Alvarez

---

[9] For considerations of the archive as body, see Chen, Bundtzen, *The Other* Ariel, and Sekula.

proposes: "A properly rounded biography of Sylvia Plath, taking account of her personal failings as well as her strengths, would indeed be welcome" ("Plath: An Exchange").

O'Brien may have sought to present Plath realistically, accounting for her strong points and her weaknesses. In 1984, just before O'Brien likely started her work on Plath, Philip Roth proposed during an interview: "At the center of virtually all your stories is a woman, generally a woman on her own, battling isolation and loneliness, or seeking love, or recoiling from the surprises of adventuring among men" (45). In her response to Roth, O'Brien concedes that as a writer she has not been drawn to women whose lives have had happy endings: "I have depicted women ... almost always searching for an emotional catharsis that does not come" (*Conversations* 46). The idea of searching is akin to that of writing. It recalls Plath's account of writing a poem during her interview with Peter Orr of the British Council in 1962: "Having written one, then you fall away very rapidly from having been a poet to becoming a sort of poet in rest, which isn't the same thing at all" (172). Such exploration is also that of working through materials. The challenge for students and scholars of curating O'Brien's archive is giving life to the process of seeking and the results of the search, both for O'Brien as a writer and for those who approach her papers.

Readers of both Plath's and O'Brien's archives encounter what Starr called the "human details" that emerge in the archive. O'Brien, for instance, edited her drafts using multiple colors of ink, even with metallic silver pens. While O'Brien was probably not aware of it, her ink is reminiscent of the pink Smith Memorandum Paper that Plath brought home from the history department supply closet while teaching at Smith College in the spring of 1958(*J* 344). These pages were to encourage Plath to finish the novel she aspired to write and became the paper on which she typed *The Bell Jar* when she returned to England and then turned over to compose her late poems, including those she included in her "Ariel and other poems" typescript.[10] On the pink pages, as Gail Crowther has put it, "Plath's writing swirls and spikes as though the pages are alive and jumping. They almost breathe" (*Three-Martini Afternoons* 205). O'Brien's text breathes at a different pace. In her memoir *Country Girl* (2012), O'Brien recalls meeting Plath and later gaining a sense of admiration for her poetry, her "words, so perfectly placed, so perfectly honed, the beautiful imagery, the gravity" (301). In her notebooks and drafts, O'Brien is drawing connections and bringing words to her emerging sense of Plath's life.

Both Plath's and O'Brien's archives depict practices of "experimentation, revision and recreation," aspects that Anderson, Byers, and Warner have noted in their consideration of poets' archives are often eclipsed by technology (9). As they see it, "the contemporary archive emphasises the material and technologically mediated nature of these activities. What kinds of (re)writing, for instance, are specific to the small, hardbound notebook or the Microsoft Word document?" (Anderson, Byers, and Warner 9). O'Brien's response to this question is her list in a small early notebook; she lists a series of jars, the phrases taking up the small size of its back cover. She inserts a later version of this list on the first page of a typed draft of her script, following an overview of the events to follow. On the typed page, its lines are shorter, resembling that of a poem. Its former presence in the notebook is of elongated letters, collecting and stretching thoughts to fill the space.

Moving from handwritten notes to typescript drafts, O'Brien builds toward lines and stage directions. In one instance, she repeats a phrase in her small notebook,

---

[10]These materials are in the Sylvia Plath Collection at Smith.

documenting her ideas as she works toward finding the right one. After handwritten drafts and edited typescripts, O'Brien begins again on page one of a typescript. The television play begins early in the day with Plath's memories, set against a chorus of ocean waves, both threatening and peaceful (1). O'Brien specifies that Plath's voice will also fluctuate throughout the initial segment; she will appear at times aggressive, shy, and embarrassed (1). The figures whom Plath knew and admired are not literally present, but have a presence, while Plath is solitary (1). As such, we see aspects of the struggle for catharsis, or connection in this case, that O'Brien identified in her conversation with Roth. She then includes an updated list of glass items, some displaying items of significance in *The Bell Jar* and Plath's life. These objects include "a bell jar," a ship in a bottle, and three separate "laboratory jar[s]" displaying the faces of a baby, President Eisenhower, and Otto Plath (1). Readers of *The Bell Jar* and those familiar with Plath's biography know these subjects; they haunt Esther Greenwood and endure in Plath's imagination. Rather than experience the enclosure of a bell jar as the speaker or the reader of the novel might, the room itself presents such a space, with jars of evidence on display.

As the scene opens in "Sylvia's Room," the contents are white and include a baby stroller, a piano, and a gas stove. Recalling the cold London weather Plath encountered in 1963, it is snowing (2). Plath delivers her first line, "[t]he snow has no voice," the last line of her late poem, "The Munich Mannequins" (*CP* 263). Throughout her script, O'Brien weaves in lines from Plath's poetry and fiction. In this case, O'Brien did not include quotation marks or any other indication that it is from Plath's poem, though some viewers might recognize it.

Plath for O'Brien was a Colossus whom she attempted to understand, and her screenplay was a resemblance constructed and created for a for a mid-eighties television audience.

## CREATING DIGITAL ROOTS

For my students, developing "Revealing the Roots of Sylvia Plath" was a process that introduced them to O'Brien's project from its beginnings to its more complete form. Geevarghese and Patel approached O'Brien's materials by asking how best to make them accessible to a scholarly audience. The students questioned the shape the project should take, the themes to emphasize, and using Scalar, they were able to give the project a structure. They learned how to arrange pages both in a linear table of contents and as a nonlinear map, the image of which helped to inspire their choice of a title for the project. As Geevarghese and Patel created this digital artifact, they made visible on one screen what O'Brien envisioned for another.

To better understand O'Brien's vision of Plath, whom they had not studied before, the students read widely, becoming familiar with Plath's novel *The Bell Jar*, her *Unabridged Journals*, and her *Collected Poems*. Once we turned to the scans of O'Brien's notebooks and typescripts, Geevarghese and Patel noted reflections in a shared Google Doc, following the example of Karen V. Kukil's "Editing the Poetry of Sylvia Plath" interterm courses at Smith College.[11] Geevarghese and Patel collected themes, quotations, and intersections

---

[11] Regarding teaching with archival materials, see Kukil, "Teaching the Material Archive."

between Plath's work and O'Brien's drafts, considering what passages to display and how they communicate O'Brien's writing process. I was impressed with the thoroughness they brought to this task, encountering Plath's life for the first time through O'Brien's early gaze. I would ask questions in response to their observations, building in a critical component to their work as they made their way through the materials and decided upon a design for their digital project.[12] The students' task had added meaning because they were making sense out of materials with which even renowned scholars were not familiar.

As the students read O'Brien's manuscripts and typescripts, the goal was partly to understand the project that O'Brien pursued. The detective work that this task invited provided motivation, as did the understanding that the results could be of use to future scholars. Naomi J. Stubbs at LaGuardia Community College involved her students in her research, and they helped to create print and digital editions of a nineteenth-century diary (48). Stubbs argues that students "were especially drawn to the fact that what they were doing was new work" (54). In the O'Brien project, the digital dimension meant building a new artifact with a purpose, organization, and selection of materials chosen by the students. Such a project is one that, as Diane Jakacki and Katherine Faull put it, presents "the rare chance for undergraduate students to also engage in the research process typical for a humanities scholar: namely, the discovery of artifacts, [and] the formulation of research questions, followed by the analysis and synthesis of findings culminating in the publication of initial findings in a digital medium" (361). Interpreting archival materials, students not only examine such fragments but also reassemble them, pairing passages and analyzing threads.

Once Geevarghese and Patel gained a foothold in the material, I asked them to begin thinking about what form the digital project should take. I shared examples of Scalar and Omeka projects, and they decided to use Scalar. They were particularly taken with Amardeep Singh's students' edition of Claude McKay's *Harlem Shadows*. In this project, each poem is tagged thematically. Using Scalar's visualization tools, readers can access the collection of poems using a range of keywords, seeing poems arranged in clusters connected by lines. The table of contents is displaced as a means of navigation. Rather than move from one poem to the next in order of pagination, readers find poems by subject and draw new associations among them.[13]

As Geevarghese and Patel learned from examples like *Harlem Shadows* and watched instructional videos, they approached the pages of their Scalar "book," determining what content to add and what paths to create. The students decided to use the sea as a theme for the project and selected a background image for the home page from my

---

[12] Geevarghese and Patel had previously taken writing courses with me that adopted multimodal frameworks, FCWR 101: Foundations of College Composition and FCWR 151: Foundations of Research Writing at New York Tech. These courses were based on those at the Georgia Institute of Technology, where Marion L. Brittain Postdoctoral Fellows teach multimodal composition with a WOVEN (Written, Oral, Visual, Electronic, and Nonverbal) framework. Regarding WOVEN, see Burnett and Cooper, "Multimodal Synergy."

[13] Scalar's innovative format presents new possibilities for scholarship. McPherson notes that the journal "*Vectors* engaged intersectional, political, and feminist work at the level of content but also integrated form and content so that the theoretical implications of the work were manifest in the aesthetic and information design. Scalar is now seeking to integrate these methodologies at the level of software design" ("Designing for Difference" 185).

own photographs from a 2010 visit to Winthrop, Massachusetts, where Plath spent her childhood (Figure 4). The students were also playful in their use of O'Brien's handwriting, placing the word "Sylvia" in O'Brien's hand as a thumbnail for the project on Scalar. They created a table of contents that moves chronologically through Plath's life. The home page for "Revealing the Roots of Sylvia Plath" contains the linear table of contents and a nonlinear map of pages, a feature of Scalar. This facet contributes to the students' metaphor of Plath's "roots." The pages include: "Overview: Past of Plath," "Childhood," "Winthrop, Massachusetts," "The Sea of Inspiration," "Daddy: Otto Plath," "Ariel," "Aurelia," "Sylvia on Ted Hughes," "Sea and Emotion in O'Brien's Play," and "Ted Hughes and Sylvia Plath" (Figure 4).

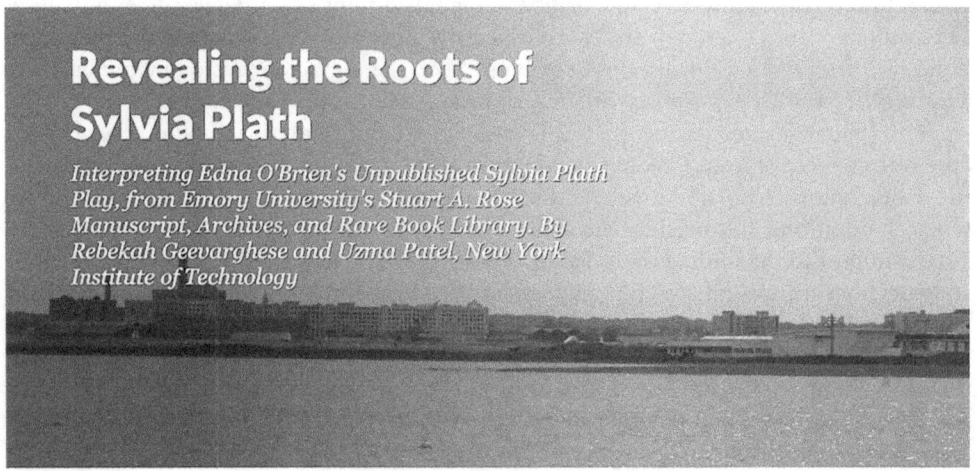

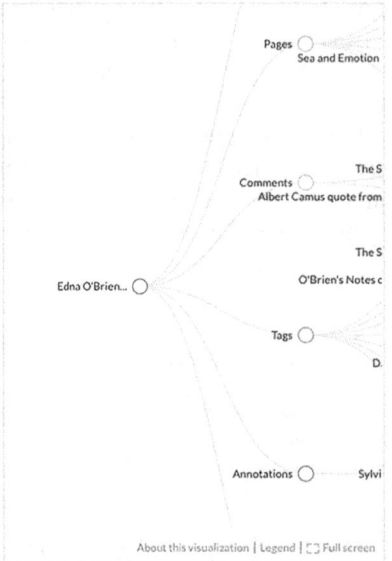

FIGURE 4 "Revealing the Roots of Sylvia Plath" by Rebekah Geevarghese and Uzma Patel. Image of Digital Project Homepage.

The contents of the pages differ, introducing connections among Plath's life and work. One page displays a photograph of Plath and Hughes when they returned to New York on the boat from England in 1957. The pages titled, "Aurelia," "Ariel," and "Sea and Emotion in O'Brien's Play," contain short excerpts from O'Brien's typescript drafts. The page devoted to "Aurelia" presents a passage from one of O'Brien's typescript drafts envisioning a moment when Plath states that she has no sense of what it means to experience joy. Her mother then counters by pulling out and reading from her daughter's letters. In doing so, O'Brien's Aurelia mirrors that of Aurelia's publication of *Letters Home*. O'Brien's Plath responds by covering her ears, imagining Plath's rejection of the efforts Aurelia pursued posthumously.

In *Shadow Archives*, Cloutier concludes that "[i]f the archival is a pastness to come, then an archival sensibility thirsts for the timeless rather than the timely" (148). In the case of Plath's "Colossus," the speaker's "hours are married to shadow," but her efforts are for the future. The "[m]ule-bray" and "pig-grunt" are utterances she has worked to interpret (*CP* 129). At the poem's close, she "[n]o longer ... listen[s]" for "the scrape of a keel / On the blank stones of the landing" (*CP* 130). The past remains in fragments. But the work of understanding its incompleteness, or attempting to understand its presence in lived reality, is ongoing.

The resignation of Plath's speaker is also one that is inherent in digital curation. Archival digital pedagogy reveals gaps. One cannot entirely reconstitute a past work in a new medium. Rather, the digital landscape enables new possibilities and connections. Designing a project also becomes a process of selection. A single project cannot address all the stories that archives contain. Introducing readers to these fragments, connecting them in a legible order, and making them accessible mean approaching a work that itself would have remained in the shadows. O'Brien and my students pursued different kinds of restorative and creative work, each engaging the technology of their time. Both efforts continue the work of Plath's speaker in "The Colossus," seeking to interpret a prior world.

# CHAPTER TWENTY-FIVE

# Feminist Recovery, Service Learning, and Community Engagement in a Sylvia Plath Studies Undergraduate Seminar

JULIE GOODSPEED-CHADWICK

This chapter presents both conceptual elements and concrete outcomes of a Sylvia Plath Studies seminar, which incorporated service learning and community engagement initiatives. The course treats feminist recovery and explores the possibilities of service learning and community engagement within literary studies and gender studies. Through study of poetry, biography, and life writing, students created artifacts that demonstrate that the learning outcomes—integration and application of knowledge—can be met in exemplary fashion, in a manner that fosters student engagement. The course itself was designed to work in tandem with my own scholarship in feminist recovery efforts, and so this aspect in connection with a focus on the representation of female bodies and feminist values[1] in Plath studies constituted the theme of the course.[2] We studied the work and lives of Sylvia Plath, Assia Wevill,[3] and Ted Hughes and produced two projects that demonstrate the ways in which service learning and community engagement encourage student investment, enhance learning experiences inside and outside the classroom, and prompt our communities to share in and support our pursuit of knowledge. Bringing literary projects to a larger public is important in a time when the humanities are embattled, and what we do in literary studies and women's studies is vital to understanding and

---

[1]Feminism, as I define it for my students, encompasses values associated with equality and equity; analyses of power; empowerment, choice, and advocacy; and the disruption of the status quo, especially when it means supporting underrepresented or marginal people who need representation.
[2]Please see *Reclaiming Assia Wevill: Sylvia Plath, Ted Hughes, and the Literary Imagination* for the content covered in the course.
[3]Assia Gutmann-Steele-Lipsey-Wevill tends to be referred to by her first name in scholarship rather than by one of the more ephemeral last names she used. She is most well known as Assia Wevill, and in this chapter, variations of this name are used in accordance with what makes the most sense stylistically.

transforming discursive formations and cultural norms. This practice also invites the public to appreciate and value our scholarly efforts and work done in the humanities more broadly, once they see and experience the exciting and important work we do in academia. To this end, we might be mindful of the significance of each class session and fold into our lectures, discussions, assignments, and community engagement-service learning activities the articulation of the same, namely, the significance of our work as teachers or students.

An important concept underpinning the course I will outline here is *feminist recovery* in one sense of the term: as Adrienne Rich explains, "Re-vision—the act of looking back, of seeing with fresh eyes, of entering an old text from a new critical direction—is for women more than a chapter in cultural history: it is an act of survival." She continues: "A radical critique of literature, feminist in its impulse, would take the work first of all as a clue to how we live, how we have been living, how we have been led to imagine ourselves, how our language has trapped as well as liberated us" (167). In other words, we can approach poems and, if literature is broadly construed, letters, too, and consider how we are reading them in the twenty-first century. What aspects of the given work resonate with students: what appears relevant and significant to them and their own interests, lives, and world? The answers to that can determine the direction and shape traditional assignments, such as synthesis papers or seminar papers, and community engagement and service learning projects can take.

What we teach and how we teach it—what we choose to highlight and what we expect from our students and our rationale for doing so—will inform every aspect of a course and students' experience of it. A feminist framework established the trajectory of study in this Plath studies course because it served undergraduates as both a special topics literature seminar and a women's studies one.[4] The service learning and community engagement components allowed the students to engage in public scholarship through two projects: (a.) an exhibition, and (b.) an all-communities (everyone is welcome) presentation and discussion. The course material and the projects enabled us to consider and reflect upon what, from the instructor's and students' perspectives, is important to teach and learn in Plath studies, literary studies, and women's studies. For instance, we had to consider what it is about Plath's, Hughes's, and Wevill's texts that teach us about ourselves and/or gives us insight into our world; why sexist and misogynistic rhetoric is dangerous and damaging; and why we need explorations of literature to revisit, recover, and reform our ideas, ideologies, and expectations of women and of gender and gendered dynamics in interpersonal relationships.[5] The projects I will discuss below could certainly be reconfigured and reshaped to suit the content of other seminars.

In thinking about promoting the humanities, community engagement, and public scholarship, we have the opportunity to think about what it means to be public

---

[4] According to Nelson, "[f]eminist critics, too, regarded Plath's rage and madness as a protest against inauthenticity, in this case masks of femininity that stifled female creativity and self-expression. With the central insight of second-wave feminism—the personal is the political—Plath seemed to take on a more active, critical role, producing a damning critique of patriarchal institutions" ("Plath, History and Politics" 32).

[5] Axelrod addresses the impetus undergirding such efforts. Plath's poems, he argues, "provide an image of a woman's immense creative drive at war with forces that would impede, paralyse and silence her voice. Paradoxically, those negative forces become integral to her project. Plath's ferocious attempt to inscribe her texts against the odds, to complete her signature, becomes one of the great stories in the history of English-language poetry" ("The Poetry of Sylvia Plath" 74).

humanists. Evan Carton defines the "public humanities" as that which "is about finding both practical and conceptual locations, spaces, and translations between various kinds of humanities work that people are doing" (qtd. in Ellison 289). Julie Ellison considers a third space for public humanities work that braids together academic and public approaches to the humanities, and she calls this "a space for the practice of public scholarship" (289). This third space is in alignment with the trajectory of community engagement efforts in the humanities, which Gregory Jay identifies as a "move *from* public humanities *to* public scholarship and engagement" (qtd. in Ellison 290). One way to enact this move is to transpose the undergraduate classroom to the public sphere, wherein students are actors on the public humanities stage—literally, as on a platform at a public community library—who work with their scholarship and the scholarship of their professor to produce scholarly products that engage community members on campus and away from it. Specifically, my students and I partnered with two entities: our university library for an exhibition and the downtown community public library, which serves as a hub of civic discourse and academic learning, as the site of a community-wide presentation and discussion, led by the students and moderated by their professor. The presentation and discussion of selected texts by Plath, Hughes, and Wevill were architected by the students, informed by the feminist approaches and women's studies concerns that infused the Plath Studies course. These community engagement and public scholarship efforts further muddy the seemingly reified "academic-public binary in the humanities" that Ellison references (291). Furthermore, these projects were designed to be service learning opportunities, allowing students to learn about and reflect on what is most meaningful and relevant—what resonates to them, making the work something in which they were personally invested—within Plath studies and women's studies in twenty-first-century public spheres and diverse communities, all in service to those very communities.

The students assumed ownership of products designed for community outreach in the spirit of taking what they were learning and giving back to the university and wider community via library science and literary-literacy service. In our course and in our attendant projects, students packaged and presented what we found to be vital in our understanding of how gender is construed as an organizing principle in our literature and in society at large. Through assessment of students' abilities in traditional ways (grading papers) and non-so-conventional ways in literary studies (blueprints, exhibition, a community-engaged presentation, and back-and-forth discussion of literary texts), it was evident to me that undergraduate students could demonstrate their abilities to (1.) recover and recuperate women from a feminist perspective; (2.) develop discerning readings of various types of texts (e.g., poetry, letters, journal entries, biography, and film); (3.) participate in sophisticated discussions of highly stylized texts; and (4.) produce insightful and convincing writing about lives, literature, and issues that matter in academe and outside of it. Upon successful completion of the course, the students could demonstrate and showcase learning by understanding and articulating interpretations of sophisticated texts, analyzing and synthesizing diverse banks of information, and creating impressive feminist projects invested in course content.

A course treating Plath, Hughes, and Wevill could offer a survey of the ways in which these three figures and their published literary output intersect, as our course did. For example, we began with Yehuda Koren and Eilat Negev's biography of Wevill, which is a biography of Plath and Hughes, too, to some extent, *Lover of Unreason: Assia Wevill, Sylvia Plath's Rival and Ted Hughes's Doomed Love* (2006). Koren and Negev's book provides an introduction to the principal figures of the course, offering arguments that reframe how we might view Wevill, Plath, and Hughes, and delivers published excerpts from archival materials that are valuable in and of themselves. We also considered Assia's Sea Witch commercial and briefly reviewed an article concerning it, which, again, reinforced our mission to recover Assia from a feminist standpoint. In his article, "Cinema Advertising and the Sea Witch 'Lost Island' Film (1965)," Richard Farmer posits, "The film was scripted by a JWT [J. Walter Thompson] copywriter, Assia Wevill, who is now perhaps better known for having an affair with Ted Hughes, a relationship which may have driven Sylvia Plath to suicide" (6). That interpretation—and others like it online and in published literary and biographical scholarship—motivated us to center Assia in our research, the course, and its service learning projects. At one point, Assia was one of the most successful copywriters in England, and yet her legacy is tarnished and diminished. More often than not, the responsibility for Plath's suicide is assigned to her, and Assia's impressive accomplishments, such as the Sea Witch commercial and her once-celebrated literary translations of Yehuda Amichai's *Poems* (1969), are minimized or dismissed. To restore Assia to a more proper place in literary history, we studied the poems she selected for her translations of Amichai's poems. As one of the most acclaimed Israeli poets, Amichai's poems are worthy of study in their own right, but as P. J. Kavanagh, *The Guardian*'s 1968 book reviewer of Assia's translations—which were published in a smaller book in 1968 that foreshadowed the bigger collection that would include those poems and new ones in 1969—remarks, "[t]he translations of [Amichai's] *Selected Poems* by Assia Gutmann [Wevill] are so stunning, such good poems in English, that it seems absurd to treat them as translations at all" (6).

Plath's poems about Assia, published in Plath's *Collected Poems* (1981), add additional motivation to recuperate the figure of Assia Wevill. As masterful as Plath's 1962–3 poems about Assia are, they constitute, finally, exercises in discursive formations that perpetuate the castigation of Assia and that reify sexist stereotypes of the beautiful but dangerous and destructive woman without pity: the fabled la belle dame sans merci. Both Plath and Hughes participate in the negative (i.e., circumscribing and hurtful) portrayals of a femme fatale who destroys everyone in her life, including herself. Assia's positive attributes or admirable accomplishments are neither spotlighted nor acknowledged in Plath studies or Hughes studies with the exception of recovery work: she becomes a one-dimensional archetype instead of a complex person. The students needed to become familiar with the gendered dynamics of Plath's poems about Assia (notable departures from the feminist content and feminist aesthetics of the *Ariel* poems) and with Hughes's poems about Assia in *Capriccio* (1990) and *Birthday Letters* (1998), both featured in his *Collected Poems* (2003). To further contextualize Hughes's poetic accounts of Assia, we read his published letters to and about her in *Letters of Ted Hughes* (2007). Other (re)sources incorporate and synthesize Plath's and Hughes's perspectives about Assia: for example, the film *Sylvia* (2004) reinforces rather than complicates the poetic storylines found in Plath's and Hughes's poetry, while the documentary *Ted Hughes: Stronger Than Death* (2015) complicates and adds nuance to conventional stories. The students were tasked with interrogating narratives to understand how they were put together, identifying values upheld or championed in any given text; and discerning takeaway messages from each poem, letter, journal entry, and film or documentary.

Following our examination and discussion of these texts as a group, the students were ready to finalize the design of the first service learning-community engagement-public scholarship project: the library exhibition, installed at our university's library in a heavy traffic area.⁶ This exhibit was installed on October 27, Plath's birthday. The second service learning-community engagement-public scholarship project was an extension of the first: the students presented and discussed poems by Plath, Hughes, and Wevill, as well as presenting the argument that we need to rethink this sensational love triangle, to the community outside our university at the downtown library in the city where our university is located.⁷ The second project took place on the last day of regular class for the semester; because the reading for the course had been completed by this point, the students were best able to field questions posed by the audience and showcase what they had learned. Due to the fact that we had multiple groups involved (our class and its supporters and friends; our university as a whole; the public county library; and the local media, in addition to social media), we were able to present in front of a robust audience and discuss significant feminist issues within literature. Specifically, students chose to focus on Plath and Assia, examining how they have been portrayed in the past (often in sexist ways) and how we might move forward in envisioning feminist futures that hinge on multiple and diverse representations that consider contexts that celebrate women's lives and accomplishments in the humanities as meaningful contributions to literature and art, and that suggest or provide feminist perspectives on their lives and work. This multifaceted rationale dovetails with Anita Helle's observation that the Pulitzer Prize-winning Plath is frequently positioned "behind" her British poet laureate husband "in the politics of the literary gaze" ("Reading Plath Photographs" 186).

The power of an exhibition is its ability to manifest a "narrative arc around the room" ("Reading Plath Photographs" 188), one that is not unlearned after the exhibition is

---

⁶Here is the assignment description of the first service learning-community engagement project, the *Library Exhibition (with Blueprint) and Justification*: You will work with your professor, your classmates, and our designated librarian. After creating a mockup (a blueprint of the exhibition with brief rationales for the items included therein that you will submit to the designated librarian and your professor after your group has reached consensus), you will display books and text (or install other media, such as a Powerpoint slideshow) that highlight what you wish to show you are learning and what you deem to be important for others to learn from the course. Three governing principles in designing the exhibition and in writing your justification (a written text that you will submit to your professor) might include the following considerations: What is important to include? Why is it important, or why should others know about this text or artifact? How do all the items relate or fit together? Each of you will submit an individual justification, from your perspective. In your one-page (minimum), single-spaced justification, you will elaborate on your role and your thoughts about the Sylvia Plath Studies exhibition as a process and a completed service learning product. You are encouraged to address the governing principles suggested above.

⁷What follows is the assignment description of the second service learning-community engagement-public scholarship project, the *Service Learning Literature Project (with Blueprint) and Reflection*: This project allows you to capitalize on what you have learned in the course and to give back to our community. You will design, implement, present, and lead an open-to-the-community discussion about selected (by you!) readings from our course at the downtown public library. You will work with the designated librarians and your professor for this service-learning project. You will select readings that you think are important and will construct and orchestrate a one-hour session in which you lead the community through the selected texts. Much like the library exhibition, you will want to consider these governing principles: What is important to include in the on-site readings? Why are these texts important, and what should members of the community know about these texts or artifacts? What discussion questions and mini lectures/explanations should you create, construct, and include in the all-community invited discussion about works related to Sylvia Plath Studies? How can you market the event to reach (and invite) as many people as possible? You will submit both a blueprint and a reflection in connection with this project to your professor. In your one-page (minimum), single-spaced reflection, you will describe your role and your thoughts about the Sylvia Plath Studies community literature presentation and discussion as a process and as a service learning-community engagement-public scholarship product. You are encouraged to address the governing principles suggested above.

dismantled. The library exhibition and the community literature presentation and discussion shared the title "Breaking the Rules of the Game: Changing the Narrative of Sylvia Plath and Assia Wevill." The title refers to Hughes's poem about Plath and Assia titled "Rules of the Game" in *Capriccio* and retitled "The Other" in his *Collected Poems*, the poem in which Hughes creates a scenario involving female rivalry and competition, wherein a winner and a loser will emerge. He accuses Assia of stealing what rightfully belongs to Plath, going so far as to claim she steals Plath's life. Assia represents the loser of the metaphorical game on multiple levels. By the end of the poem, we are given to understand that Assia will forfeit her ill-gotten gains to the ghostly Plath, who endeavors to take back what is hers. In the library exhibit, next to Hughes's poem "Last Letter," the students installed triangular rods to connect the three writers visually and to emphasize the love triangle that all three experienced in life and that all three recorded in their literary and personal writings, most famously in literature authored by Plath and Hughes. Among the items displayed were Plath's published poems, novel, and journals, as well as accompanying explanations and commentary that served to open up her life and work to a general audience. Texts that span genres formed a necessary part of the exhibit, my students discovered, because they point beyond reductive understandings of Plath's life, work, and the people in it, and they suggest that, while Truth may be elusive, many truths may emerge. As Tracy Brain remarks, "[a]nybody who is interested in Plath's own story will find her letters and journals a fascinating source of information, though not necessarily more 'true' or reliable than the multitude of literary biographies about her" ("Sylvia Plath's Letters and Journals" 140).

Also featured were materials related to Assia, who, instead of being portrayed as the notorious "other woman" in the Plath-Hughes romance as she typically is, was presented as someone impressive through her own accomplishments and as someone who deserves recognition. For example, her Sea Witch commercial played on a loop as part of the exhibit,[8] and examples of her work in print advertising were displayed, in addition to her 1969 book of Amichai poems. Other texts about Plath and Wevill were featured, as were books by Hughes. Also included (and of note) was a poetry-art book by Plath and Hughes's daughter, Frieda Hughes, who, in turn, wrote a poem about Assia and Assia and Ted's daughter, Shura (*Alternative Values* 108–9). Photographs of Shura, Assia, Plath, and Hughes adorned the exhibit, bringing faces to the stories offered in compact form. Displaying and situating photographs became a teachable moment for us and for our audience because, in the case of Plath, the "framed and photographed body exists outside Plath's writing as a cultural image and inside her writing as a metaphor of vision and an emblem of cultural reproduction" ("Reading Plath Photographs" 187). We interpret and draw attendant conclusions about such images, and my students opted to provide captions for some photographs, guiding analyses, while leaving some uncaptioned and thus positioned in an open-ended circuit of interpretation and meaning within the exhibition.

Designed in bright colors, the palette of the exhibition balanced the serious subject matter, and the bright colors emphasized Plath's own decorating preferences and the expressed need for color in one's life that is documented in her unpublished novel "Falcon Yard," of which the students read fragments in class after we received permission from the

---

[8]The History of Advertising Trust has archived the video on its website: https://www.hatads.org.uk/catalogue/record/f42d2656–397d-4c2a-a698-a989d795a15c.

Sylvia Plath Estate to do so. Artificial snow gathered on the shelves of the exhibit, too, as a gesture to the snow imagery found in poems about Plath and Assia by Hughes and to the actual snow of the season. The artificial snow served as a reminder that Plath, Wevill, and Hughes were real people working and living in the real world; in many respects, the same world in which we live. I offer this extended example of what my students produced with the aim that it might generate ideas of how classes might structure and design an exhibition or modify and enhance what my students brought to life.

During the last week of classes, the students led the all-community presentation and discussion session that focused on Plath, Hughes, and Wevill in a room called the Red Room at the public library. (To fit the occasion, a reading of an excerpt from Hughes's poem "Red," about Plath, opened the event.) As a whole, the presentation outlined the narrative set up by the exhibition on campus, and that was on display at the time. Three poems were distributed to the audience on-site for discussion: Plath's "Wintering," Amichai and Assia's "Eye Examination," and Hughes's "The Other." The poem that garnered the most attention was "Wintering," due to its gendered declaration: "The bees are all women, / Maids and the long royal lady. / They have got rid of the men" (CP 218). During the discussion of these lines, we countered the interpretation that feminists are separatists and that feminist poetry always takes a hostile view of men. Expectations that Plath must be "manhating," and her poetry will reveal this characteristic lead those who have not had the opportunity to closely study her work to come to a misreading of it. Instead, we highlighted the centering of women and the domestic in the imagery of "Wintering," as well as the privileging of feminine spaces and the feminist qualities of choice and agency, which suggest empowerment, within the poem. We also foregrounded the theme of rebirth or liberation, underscoring our reading of the poem as one that closes on an optimistic note. To be forthcoming, we featured "Wintering" in the public presentation and discussion to show Plath's ability to express hope. Although her suicide cannot be ignored, the students believed it should not define her work or who she might have been. Consequently, they designed and donned T-shirts, to wear for their second service learning-community engagement-public scholarship project, that were emblazoned with a sketch of Plath and sported a quotation from her unabridged *Journals*: "let me live, love, and say it well in good sentences" (184). My students were drawn to the moments in which we see Plath's vibrancy and enthusiasm for life: for example, Plath declares in her journal, "God, I overflow with the vitality and ecstasy of being alive!" (J 160). Ultimately, the students and I wished to show that while there can be misreadings, there are countless convincing interpretations, grounded in the text, of the same poem, such as "Wintering," that emphasize Luke Ferretter's argument about her prose: "Many of Plath's women," explains Ferretter, "are postmodern characters, whose identity endlessly recedes in layer after layer of image and identification, without a clearly distinguishable original over which these images are laid" (*Sylvia Plath's Fiction* 166). Plath's work encompasses more than death wishing and is not predisposed to misandry, the students argued. Instead, imagining feminist futures might be a theme that a class could embrace and treat in their projects, as my class did.

Service learning, community engagement, and public scholarship in literature courses are relatively rare, particularly when compared to the service learning or community engagement opportunities in the social sciences. And yet, there are many possibilities for service learning and community engagement in the humanities, especially if literature professors and students partner with librarians and libraries. To date, the Modern Language Association has published one book dedicated to service learning and literary studies (2015). And only one entry focuses on literature in *Quick Hits for Service-Learning: Successful Strategies by Award-Winning Teachers* (2010). The author of that piece queries, "Can an American literature course … be reworked to viably integrate service-learning without loss of valuable content?" (Bontempo 51). She concludes, "although social sciences and education may seem to provide a more 'natural' fit for service-learning, it is the Arts & Humanities that offers students a reflective context for examining the full range of community life" (Bontempo 52). My experience indicates that service learning and community engagement, transformed into public scholarship, foster student learning and activate what students already know and maximize their learning and the opportunities for more of it in order to give back to communities inside and outside the university.

Because we sought to underscore the relevance of literature to the world outside of the university and to "inspire individuals in local communities to read classic works of literature" (VanDette 55), especially works by Plath and Hughes, we were interested in partnering with our university library and the community library to serve these purposes. As Emily VanDette notes, "[w]ith their shared value for reading, literature classrooms and libraries are natural partners. Libraries have a long history of building literary collections and hosting book discussions, literature exhibits, and readings" (54). Also, libraries strive to "restore the role of the library as a civic and cultural center" (VanDette 54), making a partnership between libraries and the university literature-women's studies classroom all the more suitable. And for literature-women's studies students, the opportunities to design, stage, and deliver such projects allow them to claim new lines on their résumés, as well as giving them interesting and useful products to discuss in their graduate school applications or job interviews.

The Plath Studies undergraduate seminar, with its service learning-community engagement-public scholarship components, allowed us to consider and reflect upon what is important for us to teach and learn in literary studies and women's studies. For instance, we had to consider what it is about Plath's, Hughes's, and Wevill's texts that resonates with us and teaches us about ourselves and gives us insight into our world; why sexist and misogynistic rhetoric is dangerous and damaging; and why we need explorations of literature to revisit, recover, and reform our ideas, ideologies, and expectations of women and of gender and gendered dynamics in interpersonal relationships. As one of the students explains in the anonymous course evaluations, "Plath's life and mine bear so few similarities outside of our gender and love of writing. But she writes on such a deep and honest level that connection is inevitable. That is why she is still commonly read over 50 years after her death. She speaks to the experience of being a woman in a way that has not changed." For another, the projects allowed us "to display Plath and Assia as we now see them: courageous, beautifully talented, and inspiring." Perhaps what we need more of in the world is this very impetus and its manifestation: the feminist act of supporting, valuing, and celebrating the lives and significant literary and creative accomplishments of courageous, talented, and inspiring women. We remain cognizant of the fact that the writers we study are engaged in the project of, as Plath phrases it, "word-making, world-making" (*J* 332).[9]

---

[9]The two service learning-community engagement-public scholarship projects comprised one of three finalists for the Indiana University Faculty Academy on Excellence in Teaching's 2017 Innovate Award in Community Engagement. As for the student course evaluations, the students rated the course 5.0/5.0 with a 100 percent response rate.

PART IV

# Editing the Archives

# CHAPTER TWENTY-SIX

# Sylvia Plath in the Round

KAREN V. KUKIL

Early in my career as a rare book librarian and literary archivist at Yale University, I learned from Wilmarth S. Lewis, editor of British eighteenth-century writer Horace Walpole, the benefit of studying a writer in the round and the principles of editing their manuscripts. For over fifty years, Mr. Lewis collected Walpole's manuscripts, library, private press publications, paintings, and furniture from Strawberry Hill, insisting "objects are documents." Indeed, the pink paper selected to write a novel can give a rose cast to an author's plot, the elm wood of a writer's desk may inspire a poem, and an early self-portrait can predict a woman's future. As I have realized, it takes a lifetime to absorb all the available information about Sylvia Plath, to read and teach all her poetry and prose, to carefully edit her manuscripts, to locate and process new collections of Plath material, to curate exhibitions that document her life in the round, and to walk with grace in the footsteps of Sylvia Plath.

For the past thirty years, it has been my great honor to curate the Virginia Woolf and Sylvia Plath Collections at Smith College and teach classes with their manuscripts. Since I was an undergraduate English major at Trinity College in the mid-1970s, I have engaged in close readings of Woolf and Plath, studied their creative process from drafts to publication, noted their influences, and visited their landscapes. After I arrived at Smith in November 1990, my priority became processing and posting online catalog records and finding aids for both the Woolf and Plath Collections. President Jill Ker Conway and rare book curator Ruth Mortimer had acquired the Sylvia Plath Collection from Ted Hughes in 1981. The collection contains artwork, correspondence, manuscripts of poetry and prose, personal papers, photographs, furniture, and over 180 annotated volumes from the library of Sylvia Plath. In 1983 Plath's mother, Aurelia Plath, donated additional manuscripts, photographs, family papers, correspondence, Plath's typewriter, and some clothing. Once Plath's college friends added their letters from Plath to the collection, I began teaching editing courses for the Archives and Book Studies Concentration programs and offering select presentations to English courses. These courses were enhanced by a collection of first editions of the work of Sylvia Plath and Ted Hughes donated by Ann Safford Mandel. There was also helpful background information available to students in the collections of two early biographers—the Edward Butscher Collection of Papers on Sylvia Plath (MRBC-MS-00002) and the Houghton Mifflin Company Collection on Anne Stevenson's biography of Plath, *Bitter Fame* (MRBC-MS-00003)—which I also processed before Janet Malcolm and a slew of other Plath scholars visited the Mortimer Rare Book Room to conduct their research.

This teaching and research experience with seasoned scholars helped prepare me when out of the blue one day in 1998, Frieda Hughes, who inherited Plath's copyrights from her father, asked me to edit her mother's unabridged adult journals, and later, Plath's collected letters. As an editor of Plath's *Journals* and *Letters*, I have always been careful to present Plath in the round—relying on her own words and not editing her into my version of Sylvia Plath. Working out the editing protocols for the unabridged journals, Frieda Hughes and I decided to publish an exact transcription of over 1,000 pages of journal in Smith's collection with strictly factual endnotes based upon primary source information. An exhaustive index incorporating established forms of proper names and Library of Congress subject headings completes the publication. The unabridged *Journals of Sylvia Plath, 1950–1962* were published in 2000 by Faber and Faber in London and Anchor Books in New York to the great relief of scholars who wanted full access to all of Plath's extant words instead of the heavily redacted American edition of her journals previously published by Ted Hughes and Frances McCullough at the Dial Press in 1982. "Reviving the Journals of Sylvia Plath," my talk in 2000 at the International Writers' Day program of British PEN at the Café Royal in London, which was later published on the British Library website, stressed Plath's zest for life instead of death—she savored it all: "children, sonnets, love and dirty dishes" (*J* 225).

Editing Plath's complete letters was a mammoth undertaking that benefited from the extraordinary talents of my co-editor, Peter K. Steinberg. With extensive research, we located, transcribed, annotated, and indexed over 1,400 letters written between 1940 and 1963 to more than 140 correspondents, which we found in various repositories and private collections. In 2017, Faber & Faber in London and Harper in New York published *Volume I* of *The Letters of Sylvia Plath*, followed by *Volume II* in 2018. *Volume II*, which includes letters written by Plath after her twenty-fourth birthday in October 1956 until her death in February 1963, was enhanced at the last moment by a new cache of heartbreaking missives to Plath's psychiatrist, Dr. Ruth Beuscher, outlining the breakdown in her marriage to Ted Hughes. Reviewers, including John Carey of *The Sunday Times*, found the letters in *Volume II* "terrible in their intensity" and "unmatched in literature."

Plath's journals and letters have yielded fresh archival and pedagogical projects. Beginning in 2009 and continuing after the publication of the letters, I shared my editing practices with students in the Archives Concentration program as we transcribed and proofed the 170 original Plath letters at Smith. All of the Smith students who transcribed letters in my courses are fully acknowledged in the published *Letters*. The students and I modeled our headers and footnotes on W. S. Lewis's *Yale Edition of Horace Walpole's Correspondence*. I even invited the living recipients of Plath's letters, who were mostly alumnae, to visit the last class each year so that students could ask questions and complete their factual footnotes. In the process, Plath's college roommate Marcia Brown (later Marcia B. Stern) found an incomplete typescript of "marcia" by Plath that was unknown to scholars and is now part of the Plath Collection. In the middle of my archives course, the poetry editor at Faber and Faber contacted me to see if I would edit a selected edition of Plath's letters, but I felt it was important to give scholars full access to every letter Plath wrote, not just my favorites. In 1975 Aurelia Plath had published *Letters Home*, a selected edition of her daughter's letters in reaction to the American publication of *The Bell Jar*. As she told Frances McCullough in an April 14, 1971, letter, Aurelia resented being identified with the "sanctimonious utterances and insipid personality" of the mother in *The Bell Jar* (box 29, folder 29, Smith). She was determined to present a more wholesome relationship with her daughter in *Letters Home* through carefully selected and edited letters.

Editing Plath's letters and journals has allowed me to better understand her literary influences. For example, when the British Library asked me and three other scholars (Heather Clark, Mark Ford, and Peter K. Steinberg) to select examples to share from the *Letters of Sylvia Plath* for a program in London on October 23, 2018, I focused on Plath's December 15, 1956, letter to Marcia B. Stern in which she announced her marriage to Ted Hughes and predicted that he "will be the best poet since Yeats & Dylan Thomas" (*L2* 38). Hughes went on to become the Poet Laureate of England in 1984. The second letter I read was written on September 29, 1962, to Dr. Beuscher when Plath discovered a stash of love poems that Hughes had written about his mistress, Assia Wevill, and realized her marriage to Hughes was over. In her postscript, Plath thanked Dr. Beuscher for her advice to divorce Hughes: "The divorce like a clean knife. I am ripe for it now" (*L2* 845). The next morning Plath sat down at her elm plank desk (rough cut for a coffin lid and hand sanded by Hughes) and wrote the first draft of her poem "A Birthday Present," in which she wanted the truth and a fresh start for her upcoming thirtieth birthday present.[1] The poem ends:

And the knife not carve, but enter

Pure and clean as the cry of a baby,
And the universe slide from my side.

(*CP* 208)

It is now possible to trace the genesis of many poems like this one through Plath's published letters, which are fully indexed. In Plath's October 19, 1962, letter to Clarissa Roche, for example, she includes news about the breakdown in her marriage to Hughes and her own poor health: "I am at present totally without access to friend or relative and have been stupidly ill, lost a lot of weight & am running a flickery 103° fever, getting up each morning at 4 a.m. to write, my one quiet time." (*L2* 873). The next morning, Plath sat down and wrote the first draft of "Fever 103°." The six drafts of "Fever 103°," now preserved in the Plath Collection at Smith, are all dated October 20, 1962, even though some of them bear edits after her interview with Peter Orr of the British Council on October 30, 1962.

We can see earlier inspiration for Plath's short stories in the first volume of Plath's letters when she discusses her student years at Smith. This time period is relevant when considering her recently published story "Mary Ventura and the Ninth Kingdom." It depicts a college-aged protagonist, on a train ride that does not come to an end, with a mysterious woman as her guide. Plath composed this story in 1952 but did not publish it in her lifetime. I was invited to write an introduction to the story for the spring 2019 issue of the *Hudson Review*. The process I used to research this introduction is instructive. I was able to trace through Plath's letters and journals her activities during the fall 1952 semester when she wrote this short story. I learned that her academic courses on Dante and Chaucer and pleasure reading of Kafka, including her marginalia on the pages of her copies of these authors, informed the plot. Descriptive letters and journal entries

---

[1] Plath's holograph and typescripts of "A Birthday Present" September 30, 1962, are in the Plath Collection, Smith (box 7, folder 31).

about train travel to Princeton and her supportive relationships with mentors, including Professor Mary Ellen Chase, contributed realistic passages and believable character development (*L1* 514–5, *J* 153).[2]

In addition to seeing the landscapes that inspired Plath, it has been equally informative to meet family members, like Frieda Hughes, and hear firsthand stories. Friends who knew Plath have shared stories over the years, bringing to life the feeling of being in her presence. At the Sylvia Plath Literary Symposium held at Oxford University's Rothermere American Institute in 2007, Marcia Stern attended, telling of Plath's exuberance as she became excited over a song or story when they were roommates at Smith. Such voices underscore the importance of listening to firsthand accounts, hearing the tone of friends' recollections and the sound of a writer's voice as she reads a poem aloud. I often play recordings of Woolf and Plath for students so they can hear these writers' voices. We watch BBC documentaries and other programs. I also encourage students to experience the landscapes of their authors whenever they can. In this way, the publication of Plath's *Letters* underscores the importance of delving into the sources of those letters and listening to firsthand accounts.

Plath's *Letters* cover her time abroad as a Fulbright Scholar, studying in England at Newnham College, Cambridge University and offer a wealth of ways to experience the landscapes through which she moved. During this time, Plath visited Paris and Rome, seeing Europe for the first time.[3] In my role as an instructor, I recently helped a French graduate student from the Sorbonne who was studying Plath and *The Bell Jar*. She wanted to get a sense of American culture in the fifties. Living at Smith for a year as part of Smith's Interdisciplinary Studies Diploma Program and researching multiple facets of Plath's life in the archives was a start. Inès could trace Plath's creative process from an outline of the novel through various drafts in the Plath Collection. She was able to read Plath's quarterly reports for the officials of the Eugene F. Saxton grant, learning what Plath hoped to convey in *The Bell Jar*. Reading Plath's correspondence with her editor at Heinemann in London who was concerned about potentially libelous passages and examining subsequent editions of *The Bell Jar* with scholarly introductions was another step. This allowed Inès to contextualize passages in *The Bell Jar* with private journal entries and entertaining letters to family and friends. For example, the beginning of *The Bell Jar* was practically lifted from Plath's journal passage about the execution of the Rosenbergs when Plath was a guest editor at *Mademoiselle* in the summer of 1953. Similarly, Plath's 1959 journal entry about visiting her father's grave in Winthrop, Massachusetts, to deal with the loss and sense of abandonment following his death when she was eight years old was included almost in its entirety in *The Bell Jar*. But the novel came alive for both of us when we were invited by a Smith alumna to visit the 9 Willow Street apartment on Beacon Hill where Plath lived with her husband, Ted Hughes, when they decided to give up teaching and become full-time writers and start a family. Before arriving in Boston, Inès and I also visited Plath's family home in Wellesley, Massachusetts, and McLean Hospital in Belmont, Massachusetts. Throughout both volumes of *Letters*, Plath returns to her home in Wellesley, Massachusetts. After moving from Winthrop to Wellesley at age ten, Plath

---

[2] While at Smith, the classrooms in Seelye Hall, where the English Department is housed, were steps away. I have been inspired to write about visiting the sites that informed the work of writers whose papers I have studied and curated in pieces like "In the Footsteps of Sylvia Plath."
[3] A photograph from Plath's time in Rome is on the cover of *The Bloomsbury Handbook*.

lived at 26 Elmwood Road with her brother, mother, and grandparents. Besides reading descriptions in letters, scholars can examine photographs from this period at Smith in the Helle Collection of Plath Family Photographs (MRBC-MS-00273); it is instructive to see Plath's modest family house in person on the outskirts of a wealthy suburb of Boston. It was in the cellar of this house that Plath unsuccessfully tried to escape the confines of her narrowly defined future by taking an overdose of sleeping pills in 1953. This desperate act eventually landed Plath at McLean Hospital where she slowly recovered with the help of her psychiatrist, Dr. Ruth Beuscher. It was at McLean that Plath began to understand her complicated psyche and later at Smith where she brilliantly completed her undergraduate education, going on to win a Fulbright fellowship.

Dr. Ruth Beuscher, whose papers are preserved at Smith under her maiden name, Ruth Tiffany Barnhouse (SSC-MS-00202), include fourteen letters from Plath ending with her heartbreaking last known letter written on February 4, 1963 (box 3, folder 14). Ruth was a self-made woman who defied conventions, divorced her first husband, put herself through medical school, divorced her second husband, Dr. William Beuscher, in 1962, and returned to her maiden name after she joined the ministry. She also had six children. Unsurprisingly, Ruth cautioned Sylvia when her marriage began to unravel: "Just don't get out of the driver's seat in your own life" (September 17, 1962, box 17, folder 24). On a practical level, when I met Ruth Tiffany Barnhouse to assess her papers for the Sophia Smith Collection of Women's History, Ruth mentioned that when she was Plath's psychiatrist at McLean Hospital in 1953, she wrote a prescription for birth control so that Plath could safely experiment on equal terms with her male lovers ("Conversation with Ruth Tiffany Barnhouse").[4] Unmarried women could not get birth control without a doctor's prescription in the 1950s. Plath wanted it all—a good education, international travel, exciting experiences, marriage, home, children, and a successful career as a writer. Dr. Beuscher gave her the confidence to defy conventions and her family's expectations and vigorously pursue her own dreams.

Just as the *Letters* flesh out critical personal relationships, such as Plath's relationship with her therapist, they chart critical stages in her poetic career. To this end, the *Letters* also include Plath's auditing of Robert Lowell's poetry seminar with Anne Sexton and George Starbuck at Boston University in the spring of 1959. Plath admired Lowell "immensely as a poet" once he turned to mining the personal mode in his writing, as well as the honesty and lack of "inhibitions" of Anne Sexton's poetry (*L2* 303).[5] Plath and Hughes lived on Beacon Hill and were thrilled to read and socially interact with the poets surrounding Lowell and his wife, Elizabeth Hardwick, in the late 1950s, including Richard Wilbur, W. S. Merwin, Philip Booth, Adrienne Rich, and Stanley Kunitz.[6] As soon as Plath moved to London with Hughes, she signed a contract on February 10, 1960, with Heinemann for *The Colossus*. England was receptive to her more brazen poetic style after her influential year with Robert Lowell and a ten-week stay with Hughes at Yaddo, an artists' community in Saratoga Springs, New York.

In addition to behind-the-scenes archival work of gathering and documenting Plath papers, over the years, I have curated Plath exhibitions that attempted to document Plath's life in the round. The *One Life: Sylvia Plath* exhibition on display from June 30, 2017,

---

[4]Kukil, "Conversation with Ruth Tiffany Barnhouse," Nantucket, MA, October 5–6, 1998.
[5]See *Three-Martini Afternoons*.
[6]See *The Fading Smile* regarding this period in Plath's life.

through May 20, 2018, at the National Portrait Gallery included Plath's February 20, 1940, letter to her mother decorated with her first self-portrait followed by a *Triple-Face Portrait*, painted a decade later that predicted the "triple-threat woman" she eventually hoped to be: "wife, writer, & teacher (to be swapped later for motherhood)" (*L2* 110). Her second draft of *The Bell Jar* typed on pink Smith College memorandum paper was on display near a February 4, 1954, letter to Wellesley neighbor Philip McCurdy, typed on yellow memorandum sheets from *Mademoiselle*, in which Plath suggested they return to a more "platonic relationship" following their recent sexual encounter during which Plath used the diaphragm prescribed by Dr. Beuscher (*L1* 675–6). A series of photographs chronicled the evolving stages of Plath's life including one taken by Rollie McKenna in 1959 at Plath's 9 Willow Street apartment in Boston. The exhibition ended with drafts written on pink paper of Plath's Ariel poems, including "Elm," which was on display below the top of Plath's elm plank desk and a color photograph taken by Swedish photographer Siv Arb of Plath with Frieda and Nicholas at their Court Green property in Devonshire beneath a giant elm. Once Plath and Hughes separated, Plath moved back to London with her children and began a new book of poems, written on white bond paper. One of the poems from this final stash concluded the Smithsonian exhibition along with a February 4, 1963, letter to Marcia Stern. "Kindness" contains one of Plath's most powerful lines and is a perfect articulation of her relationship to her craft: "The blood jet is poetry, / There is no stopping it" (*CP* 270).

Locating every letter written by Sylvia Plath for the *Letters* project also attracted new collections to Smith. Jane Anderson, Plath's classmate from Wellesley who also had a mental breakdown and was hospitalized at the same time as Plath at McLean Hospital, received Plath's first letter written on February 25, 1954, when she returned to Smith after her breakdown (*L1* 693–8). The Jane V. Anderson Papers (MRBC-MS-00342) were received as a bequest in 2010. Anderson sued Ted Hughes and AVCO Embassy Pictures when the 1979 film version of *The Bell Jar* was released because she felt the movie defamed and humiliated her. Plath used Anderson as the basis for her character Joan Gilling in the novel, and these court proceedings are part of the Anderson Papers at Smith along with other letters. Smith's most recent donation from William Sigmund in 2019—the Elizabeth Sigmund Collection of Photographs and Correspondence Related to Sylvia Plath ((MRBC-MS-00443)—includes documents from Elizabeth Compton (later Sigmund), who was Plath's closest friend in Devonshire. Elizabeth and her first husband, David Compton, even lived at Court Green with their children after Plath's death. Family, friends, and all the early biographers of Plath corresponded with Elizabeth. After Faber and Faber dropped Plath's dedication to Elizabeth and David Compton in their edition of *The Bell Jar*, Elizabeth engaged in a heated correspondence with Charles Monteith at Faber and with Olwyn Hughes, who handled permissions for the Plath Estate until this mistake was rectified in later editions. The Judith G. Raymo Collection of Sylvia Plath Papers and Books is a potential new donation to Smith and includes a few drafts of Plath's poetry and prose, such as "Mary Ventura and the Ninth Kingdom," along with early English and translated editions of *The Bell Jar* and other works by Plath in Catalan, Chinese, Danish, Dutch, French, German, Hebrew, Hungarian, Italian, Norwegian, Polish, Portuguese, Spanish, and Turkish. Plath's contributions to popular culture are also documented in artist's books, broadcasts, and dramatic and musical adaptations in the Raymo Collection.

For thirty years, I have answered over 15,000 reference questions about Plath from around the world. I have also guided a wide array of international Plath scholars in our

Special Collections Reading Room at Smith and have been impressed by their diversity, including all ages, genders, and backgrounds. I believe it is Plath's fearlessness and honesty in vividly describing her life experiences in her journals and letters, often recrafted into more universal messages in her poems and prose, that resonate with this wide spectrum of readers. We read Plath's private thoughts in her journals and overhear entertaining conversations with family and friends in her letters. But it is in Plath's poetry and prose that we meet one of the most erudite and dazzling creative writers of the twentieth century. By studying every aspect of Plath's life and creative work in the round, we truly begin to appreciate her genius.

CHAPTER TWENTY-SEVEN

# "They will come asking for our letters": Editing *The Letters of Sylvia Plath*

PETER K. STEINBERG

This chapter addresses my role in co-editing the two-volume edition of *The Letters of Sylvia Plath* by locating, transcribing, proofing, and annotating the letters and developing a system for managing the project.[1] The dispersal of Plath's papers and the scores of people to whom she wrote meant that organizing and keeping track of all of the project's facets were of the utmost importance. First, though, one might wonder why such an edition was needed. Sylvia Plath's letters to her family, and a select few others, were published in *Letters Home* in 1975. The volume was edited by Plath's mother, Aurelia Schober Plath. For the book, Ted Hughes—who inherited the copyright to his late wife's estate—gave Aurelia Plath copyright of the letters in the book but retained "the right to final approval" ("Book Ends" BR37). He sought certain information not be made public; his "deletions had to do with the couple's two children, removing private domestic details and excising some tart references by Miss Plath to contemporaries; he also removed some glowing descriptions of himself in early love letters" ("Book Ends" BR37).[2] When published seven years later, *The Journals of Sylvia Plath* (1982) sustained significant editorial intervention as well, and criticism was sharp. Reviewing the *Journals* in *The New York Times Book Review*, Nancy Milford proposed, "[t]he question about these Journals is always the same: who is doing the cutting? And why? There is almost no rage

---

This paper has been adapted and enlarged from my keynote talk at the Sylvia Plath: Letters, Words and Fragments conference held at Ulster University, November 10–11, 2017.

[1] Over five Januarys from 2009 to 2013, Karen V. Kukil taught an annual, week-long course to students at Smith College entitled "Editing the Correspondence of Sylvia Plath." The stimulus for this course grew out of a comment made in conversation with Plath biographer Linda Wagner-Martin in October 2007 that a complete volume of Plath's letters was overdue. In January 2012, I both took this course and helped to teach the students about footnotes and primary sources. Sitting in on the classroom instruction was helpful in establishing some ground rules to consider for exact, documentary transcription. Later that year, I was asked to be the lead transcriber of *The Letters of Sylvia Plath*. After several years of almost singular work on the books, my role was elevated first to that of co-editor and ultimately to lead editor because of my completing "the lion's share of work on this edition with superior erudition and dedication" (*L1* xi).

[2] "Book Ends" concludes tantalizingly: "So more unpublished letters remain—including a packet found among her possession labeled 'For Mother'" (BR37).

expressed in these Journals, no sex described, but everywhere suggested" (BR31).³ In her 1975 review of *Letters Home*, Maureen Howard had similarly disapproved of the excessive deletions that "reduce some of the letters to bits and pieces" (BR2). With a full, complete edition of Plath's letters, we aimed to restore the narrative of her life as she saw fit to relate it as well as reveal the range of her epistolary voices.

Plath wrote between one and four letters a day in her earliest correspondences to her family, most frequently on pre-stamped US postal cards. While *Letters Home* prints twenty-four letters from Plath's first semester at college in the autumn of 1950, *The Letters of Sylvia Plath* includes eighty-seven. All but three of these are to her mother.⁴ As a result, *The Letters* introduce readers to what it was like for Plath living away from home, developing study and social habits, dating, and worrying over grades and papers, to name a few subjects. While preparing her 1989 biography of Plath, *Bitter Fame*, Anne Stevenson felt that in her encounter with the original letters, the Plath that she met lived in an "as-yet-unfictionalized, still happening present" (qtd. in Malcolm 77). It is an ironic sentiment for a biographer—whose business it is, in part, to fictionalize, cut, and splice events—to admit. But such a sentiment speaks to the everyday details that *The Letters* bring to light. In certain instances, Plath wrote home in the morning after a class, at midday after a quiz or paper was submitted, and then also at the end of the day, just before bed, summarizing what occurred in the intervening hours. The particular details Plath recorded, which could be repetitive, were one reason so few letters from this autumn were included in *Letters Home*. These aspects, however, give Plath's letters their urgency and introduce readers to a fuller portrait of her life at the time.

Another reason to compile a fuller version of Plath's letters was to correct the dating and transcription inaccuracies in *Letters Home*. For example, the first letter in that book is dated September 27, 1950. Plath, however, wrote it three days earlier on the 24th. The second letter in *Letters Home* was dated September 28. It is, in reality, a collage of two different letters: the first two paragraphs originated in a letter Plath wrote on the 27th, and the third paragraph was taken from the fourth letter Plath sent home on the 26th.⁵ Aurelia Plath's decision to merge the contents of letters was intentional, but she did not provide an explanation for it in *Letters Home*. Many dates printed in the book derive from the date on the postmark, not the date on—or dates over which—a letter actually was written. Plath often used ellipses in her letters to change subjects. When she added ellipses at the ends of letters, she may have been indicating that the correspondence would continue. In *Letters Home*, Plath's ellipses were not differentiated from their standard application to show editorial omissions.⁶ Many of Plath's words or grammatical idiosyncrasies were revised without any editorial indication of the changes made. Thus *Letters Home* was inaccurate, and it failed to present Plath fully as a daughter, sister,

---

³The 1982 *Journals* was published in the United States only. Plath's unabridged *Journals* were published in 2000 by Faber (UK) and Anchor Books (US).
⁴Eighty-four letters were sent to Aurelia Schober Plath in ninety-two days. It is worth pointing out that *The Letters of Sylvia Plath, Volume I* publishes 154 letters from 1940 to the point where Plath starts college. Plath likely wrote dozens of other letters to family and friends but they were not located.
⁵Another example is Plath's June 21, 1952, letter to her mother. In *Letters Home* it is listed as two separate letters on the same day; however, it is just a single correspondence. Plath sometimes misdated her letters, too. Instances of this are footnoted throughout the volumes.
⁶In Plath's abridged *Journals* the editors used undifferentiated ellipses as well as "[Omission]" to denote textual cuts.

niece, and wife, presenting a singularity of voice. *The Letters of Sylvia Plath* displays a full chorus of recipients to family, friends, fans, strangers, and business contacts.

Having read the letters Plath received from the BBC, which are held by Smith College, I was curious to read her letters to various contacts held by the BBC Written Archives Centre in Reading, England.[7] Plath's business correspondence showed how she interacted with professional contacts, an area that has received neither general nor critical attention. (Plath famously said in an October 1962 interview that after her first publication at the age of eight-and-a-half, she considered herself "a bit of a professional" [Orr 167].)

Plath's letters are dispersed among more than forty-five libraries and archives from Jerusalem, Israel, to Seattle, Washington. Most of the original letters—more than 940— are held by the Lilly Library. In addition to these publicly available holdings, many letters are still in private collections.[8] I located letters by regularly scouring WorldCat, library and archive websites, and auctions. We also sent requests to people to whom we knew (or suspected that) Plath wrote to in the attempt to see if they still owned them and would share. Before too long, the count of letters exceeded 1,000 and continued to grow to more than 1,400 letters.[9] Developing an Excel spreadsheet enabled me to list all the letters and add new material as it was sourced and procured.[10] The column headers were: Author (sometimes Plath co-authored a letter), Recipient, Date, Day of the Week (for the header information), Transcribed by, Transcription checked, Library/Archive, Collection, and Notes. The Notes field tracked, for example, which letters were misdated in *Letters Home*, the order in which letters should be printed when more than one was composed in a given day, and if the letter included creative writing. Towards the end of the project, a column was added to indicate the volume in which the letter appeared.

The spreadsheet was flexible in that it could be sorted in any number of ways. Each column served an important purpose, the least of which was a fast way to get a total number for any of the data being tracked. Eventually, I created additional sheets: the first sheet was my master copy; a second sheet became the one used to sort information; a third sheet tracked individual recipients and archives; and a fourth sheet recorded letters Plath mentioned writing in a variety of sources (letters, journals, and wall/pocket calendars, to name a few). The number of letters Plath mentioned writing exceeded 700; however, it cannot be deemed definitive or complete.[11] According to the spreadsheet, Smith students

---

[7]In 2008, I asked Gail Crowther if she would travel to the BBC archives and transcribe the letters they held. Later, Crowther located Marian Foster, a neighbor of Plath's in North Tawton, who had saved letters from both Plath and Hughes. Crowther provided further support in helping to identify people for the footnotes, as well as offering additional contextual information to many of Plath's letters, particularly in the Devon period from September 1961 to December 1962. I must express my gratitude to Crowther for her invaluable contribution to *The Letters of Sylvia Plath*.
[8]In addition to collectors who have obtained letters from auctions or the rare book and manuscript market, some letters are owned by the original recipients and/or their descendants. For example, Andrew Wilson sourced the letters to Constantine Sidamon-Eristoff to his family and provided copies that were printed *Volume I*.
[9]At the time of writing this essay the current count of known letters is 1,444.
[10]Poet and Plath scholar David Trinidad was instrumental in helping to build an initial list of letters as he had worked extensively with the 1960–1 letters from when Plath was in London held by the Lilly. The support and advice that Trinidad provided throughout the *Letters* project are simply unquantifiable.
[11]The information recorded is interesting to consider. For example, it would be possible to create an imaginary list of letters Plath wrote using these referenced letters as well as working with the hundreds of letters she saved from correspondents such as Richard Norton, Richard Sassoon, and Eddie Cohen. That is, a list could be drawn up based on the fair assessment that for each letter she received, Plath either initiated the exchange or sent a reply back.

made preliminary transcriptions of approximately 102 letters. While working on the books, I transcribed many other letters held by that institution, including two caches of letters that I located—to her childhood friend's mother, Marion Freeman, and to Yale student J. Melvin Woody—that the college now holds. In addition, I decided to include the many letter excerpts that Plath copied into her journals. While these were published in 2000, it felt significant to me to place them in the run of compiled letters because they provided otherwise lost content for her epistolary relationships with her recipients. This is particularly the case for the eight letters to Richard Sassoon from November 22, 1955, to April 18, 1956.[12] In the process, I re-annotated them when necessary taking advantage of the fact that more information was available now than in the late 1990s when the *Journals* were being prepared. I transcribed the letters not held by Smith—in excess of 1,300—and sought to let the documents—Plath's own words—dictate how I presented them, respecting her deletions, additions, and spelling mistakes. Fortunately, there were few challenges when it came to transcription; even though Plath made mistakes, she was a largely efficient typist and her handwriting was rarely illegible.

In October 2013, Frieda Hughes provided an authorization note requesting that all holders of Plath's letters supply us with copies of their materials and to allow access to photograph or photocopy documents relevant to the project. The liberty to acquire the papers that work in congruence with the letters greatly facilitated my ability to research and write the footnotes. It was only when I began to receive photocopies of the letters that I fully understood the magnitude of the work in front of me. Every couple of weeks a stack of photocopies was delivered to my house. My general procedure was to assign a date to the letter (many of Plath's first letters from college were dated simply with the day of the week, and some were undated altogether), scan the letter to PDF, and then work on transcribing it. There was a lot to coordinate, so while I made, reviewed, and proofed transcriptions, I also searched for new letters, coordinated permissions and fees for photographs and illustrations, wrote captions, and composed the majority of the nearly 4,400 contextual footnotes, which is where I felt I could put my own particular stamp on the book. As *Letters Home* lacked a traditional index, we felt this part of the book needed to be especially robust.[13] Building the index, which in manuscript exceeded 200 pages, at this early stage made a swifter task of adding page numbers in the proofing stage, discussed below.

In working with the vast majority of the letters, I observed that Plath's writing style was nuanced: at turns casual (informal), business-like (formal), and often quirky with regard to spelling, punctuation, and corrections. My conclusion was that she had her own unique way of communicating with people; that her letters were representations of her self, like the components of DNA. Plath sometimes corrected her letters when a mistake was made. She also left many errors as they were. Often the same letter had instances of both a corrected and an uncorrected typo, and I felt it was important to honor and respect the original—to ensure that each letter's "translation" to the printed page was as authentic as possible. There is no experience like working with the primary document, so my intention was therefore to make the surrogate as close to the original as possible.

---

[12]For more on Sassoon's letters from Plath, see Wilson, *Mad Girl's Love Song*.
[13]*Letters Home* listed only the poems it reproduced by title and first line.

The file names of the PDFs and Word documents I made—each letter was a single document—had to be ordered to sort in a meaningful way, so I came up with a file-naming schema to keep everything chronological and to provide, at the merest glance, the most important metadata about each letter in an effort to maintain intellectual control.[14] I gave supporting documentation the same file name as the letter and included a keyword, such as a person's name or a film title, to help recall its purpose. For example, Plath mentioned seeing a performance of Tennessee Williams's *The Glass Menagerie* in her November 21, 1955, letter to her mother. At all possible instances, I sought multiple levels of data corroboration. Plath saw the play on Friday, November 18, 1955, recording her attendance not just in the letter but also in her two simultaneously kept pocket and desk calendars. I found Andor Gomme's review of the performance, published on November 19, 1955, in *The Cambridge Review*, and photographed it. I named the file: "1955_11_21_Sylvia_Plath_to_Aurelia_Plath_Supporting_Glass_Menagerie.jpg." While the footnotes may not always present all the information I acquired, in this instance, I recorded simply: "Performed at the ADC Theatre, Park Street, Cambridge, on Friday November 18, 1955"—I was careful to keep all of the documentation should more details ever be needed (*L1* 1014).

I proofed each letter transcription and its annotations, if any were present, at least three times before assembling the first draft of the full manuscript. The editing of the complete drafts of the manuscript received more balanced participation. For example, my co-editor Karen V. Kukil marked up instances in letters she wanted me to check and sent copies to me via the post or, later, email. I then reviewed her comments and suggestions against the copies of original letters.

Frieda Hughes's letter asking that archives provide copies and allow access to materials related to Plath's letters was a gift in order to create the footnotes. Researchers interested in the Plath holdings at the Lilly Library are limited in what they can do (photograph or request photocopies/scans).[15] In 2014, I hired a research proxy to photograph all of Plath's pocket calendars. Then, visiting the Lilly in person in March 2015, I photographed her early diaries, the majority of her poems and prose, her scrapbooks, and selected school papers. Having access to thousands of images—which I also largely transcribed—enabled the building of the detailed, contextual footnotes.[16] These, often minute, details allow readers to appreciate and understand Plath's life story.[17] For example, Plath's April 6, 1954, letter to Gordon Lameyer is seven densely typed pages long. In print, it takes up ten full pages in *Volume I*. Plath recounts her long spring vacation excursion to New York City, along with time spent socializing in and around Boston while Lameyer was at sea for the Navy. Because this letter is so long and invited more footnotes than any letter in either

---

[14]Information included was date, sender, recipient, and holding repository. Formatting the date YYYY-MM-DD allowed for true chronological sorting. An example is: 1958_12_24_Sylvia_Plath_to_John_Lehmann_University_of_Texas_Ransom.

[15]The restrictions—which were put in place by the Plath Estate in the 1970s when the Indiana University acquired the archive from Aurelia Schober Plath—stipulated that only works written for publication could be copied.

[16]The act of transcribing these documents served as a basis to aid me in becoming familiar with them to the point where they sprang to mind when Plath mentioned them in letters. In addition, it enabled full-text search capability on my computer which helped in keeping information organized as well as at my fingertips.

[17]With so many historical periodicals now digitized, the window into the past—and Plath's life—has never been more accessible. Researchers can see what Plath read in those publications and consider how what she read influenced her life and writing.

volume—thirty-two—it took more than three weeks to transcribe, proof, and annotate it. The footnotes identify fourteen people and describe her experiences (she saw two plays, five movies, and two exhibits and ate at five restaurants).

The footnotes in both volumes of *Letters* also serve as a bibliography of the poems, stories, articles, and school papers that Plath composed, indicating when she wrote them and when they appeared in print.[18] Reviewing these periodicals for bibliographic information led to finding a previously unknown letter to the editor that she sent to *Mademoiselle* in early 1955. Her commentary on and praise of the February issue that year were published in the March issue. Later, from 1961 to 1962, Plath reviewed books for the *New Statesman*. She sent clippings to her mother and Olive Higgins Prouty, her college scholarship benefactress. Her reviews appeared as blurbs in newspaper advertisements and on book jackets. *Volume II* of *The Letters* includes the citations for these review excerpts for the first time. As a result, the volume demonstrates how, in Plath's words, "[m]y children's reviews are starting to 'take'" (*L2* 912). Alongside her success as a poet and novelist, she was becoming a professional critic.[19]

There were some instances where Plath included clippings with her letters and finding the issues of the publications in which she published can shed light on scope of her reading. Two inserts of note were cartoons. The first is from the March 15, 1953, issue of *The New York Times Book Review*, which she included with a letter to Gordon Lameyer on June 12, 1954. This cartoon was easy to trace, as the name of the periodical was visible on the verso, as was the copyright year. The second clipping was by the artist L. H. Siggs and printed in the March 3, 1955, issue of *Punch*, the British humor and satirical magazine. Plath sent it to her mother on April 25, 1955, with a caption about "Peter," the Plath family parakeet. She did so a few weeks after learning of her acceptance to the University of Cambridge, and this shows that she was reading up on current events in her future country of residence. It took several years to identify this clipping. I compiled a list of the periodicals Plath mentioned reading along with a list of those to which she may have had access and searched for the places where Siggs published his works.

There were times when the project seemed to be complete, and then more material would surface. In early December 2015, Frieda Hughes sent me photocopies of thirty-four letters (sixteen to Ted Hughes written in October 1956 when the couple was living apart temporarily, and eighteen to his parents). Plath's letters to Hughes are filled with references to then recent issues of *The New Yorker*, contemporary American and British poets and poetry, Plath's reading and courses, and Plath's and Hughes's own poems—some of which no longer survive. A tantalizing thing this is, as can be seen in Plath's last letter to Hughes from October 22: "I wrote two very very slight poems this morning … 'evergreens' is particularly written to send to the new yorker" (*L1* 1325). Hughes comments briefly on "Evergreens" and "Sheen & Speck"—the other poem—in his reply the following day. For "Evergreens," Hughes questioned some of Plath's phrasing: "womb how green is fled," "Each year," "Rich, dark, green," and "grieve," which, though severely fragmented, gives readers *something* of the poem. For "Sheen & Speck," Hughes

---

[18] Not just for Plath, but also, eventually, for Hughes's writings, too.
[19] Plath edited a poetry supplement for *Critical Quarterly* in 1961. She was an adjudicator for poetry competitions such as the Guinness Poetry Competition and Cheltenham Festival of Literature. Plath was also invited to be on the BBC program *The Critics* in May 1963 and to host an American Poetry Night at a London poetry festival in July 1963. Of course, her death prevented fulfillment of these opportunities.

quoted back the word "verdant," which he claims is a bit too eighteenth century, and the phrases "watery radiance" and "like any rage-struck man," neither of which he cared for. Many of Hughes's letters to Plath were included in the *Letters of Ted Hughes* (2007); however, this portion of his letter was excised.[20]

Now that *The Letters of Sylvia Plath* are available, one can more fully appreciate the letters Plath and Hughes exchanged. Plath herself foresaw this possibility. On October 6, 1956, she wrote: "Darling, be scrupulous and date your letters. When we are old and spent, they will come asking for our letters; and we will have them dove-tail-able" (*L1* 1281). Hughes did not heed Plath's request. Thus, working with his undated letters is like walking into a labyrinth without a flashlight. Had Hughes dated his letters, their arrangement in his *Letters* might be different. Where possible, I provide adjusted dates to his letters to Plath in the footnotes. Shortly after work on these letters to Hughes and his parents was complete in early 2016, we learned of the Harriet Rosenstein archive, which held fourteen letters to Ruth Beuscher.[21] Due to the nature of the letters and the archive, we were requested not to discuss its existence for a period of time. I made attempts throughout the spring to obtain copies, but all requests either were denied or ignored.

Faber received the manuscript of *The Letters of Sylvia Plath* on May 31, 2016. While waiting for the proofs, scheduled for review in May 2017, the letters from Plath to Melvin Woody were made available and I underwent an intense flurry of last-minute work to squeeze them into *Volume I*. From start to finish, the proofing of *Volume I* took about six weeks, in part because I added several hundred last-minute footnotes. Seeing the letters in their final page format made them look, feel, and read totally new, and, as a result, it was clear that extra information was needed. Adding page numbers to the pre-constructed index took about one month. Reading the letters in order to fill out the index was a different way to interact with the text, and, like seeing the page proofs, it allowed for a fresh way to engage with Plath's words. As *Volume I* was published in September 2017, I was reviewing the manuscript of *Volume II*: both re-proofing the letters and adding hundreds of new footnotes. My aim was to build upon what I learned from bringing the first volume to fruition to make completing the second volume more efficient. It did not, in the end, save any time, as history was set to repeat itself: as I reviewed successive proofs of the second volume between January and April 2018, there were more instances where Plath's letters seemed to me to need additional information.

It was during this first round of proofing *Volume II* that Smith received the Beuscher letters after a legal settlement. Kukil transcribed the fourteen letters for Frieda Hughes and then with Frieda's permission sent the transcriptions to me to be annotated. Including these letters required, in some instances, moving footnotes around, revising other glosses, and even deleting some because the subject of the letters made the need for a footnote obsolete. We were aware that we could come under criticism for including them because they were letters written to her former therapist. However, since Plath's

---

[20]Immediately after discussing the poems in this October 23, 1956, letter, Hughes related his dream of catching an "enormous fish"—the source of his later poem "Pike" (*LTH* 84).

[21]The archive came to light in the days immediately following the passing of Olwyn Hughes on January 3, 2016. A stipulation in Rosenstein's possession of the letters from Plath to Dr. Beuscher was that they not be made public until all named people were deceased. At the time of their resurfacing, the only remaining living person discussed in the letters was Frieda Hughes. Before this, in 2013, I wrote to Rosenstein asking if she had any materials that could contribute to the book and was told that no, she did not. However, her archive contains more than a dozen additional letters to other recipients.

therapy "Notebooks" were included in her unabridged *Journals*, there was a precedent for publishing material of such a sensitive, private nature. Four letters were generally social and often signed "Love," which indicated that the patient-doctor relationship was murky. Ten letters told the story of Hughes's affair with Assia Wevill and its effect on Plath from her point of view, in her own words.[22]

As proofing *Volume II* continued, more new letters were located: two early missives to a cousin, June Johnson Helle; a *circa* December 1962 Christmas card to an aunt, Frieda Plath Heinrichs; and photocopies of three letters to Perry Norton.[23] We squeezed the card to her aunt into its chronological place in *Volume II*, but the rest, plus a few still newer epistles totaling nine in all, were added as Appendices to their respective volumes when the paperback editions were published in 2019.[24] Every letter acquired was printed.[25] Publishing all the letters avoided the tricky decisions that would ultimately lead to a collection that reflected an editor's—or even a publisher's—interpretation of their subject. In *Letters Home*, Aurelia Plath made evaluations by "sifting important from unimportant" information, but it was our preference to enable the reader to have access to everything and to make decisions for themselves about the quality of the content of the letters ("Book Ends" BR37). The result is less interference with Plath's voice and her story. Publications such as *The Journals of Sylvia Plath* (2000), *Ariel: The Restored Edition* (2004), and now *The Letters of Sylvia Plath* show that the Plath Estate, as well as her publishers, recognize the desire of Plath's readers is for completeness and transparency.

Editing *The Letters of Sylvia Plath* was a privilege. The trust placed in me by all parties was extraordinary. As editors, readers, and admirers of Plath's work, we owe it to her to let her voice stand—errors and all—and not repeat the same mistakes and alterations made by former editors and literary custodians. In some instances, such as when Frieda Hughes sent me copies of her mother's letters to her father and grandparents, I felt more powerfully than ever the honor of working on this project, that I may have been one of the first "outsiders" to read them.[26] The labor that went into the two volumes of *The Letters of Sylvia Plath* was my life's priority, but I also maintained a full-time job. I had to fit in this "extracurricular" work somehow and made every possible sacrifice to the effort. I transcribed and/or proofed for an hour or so in the early morning, often on the train to and from work, at lunch, and for up to two hours a day in the evenings. On weekends I spent up to twelve hours per day on *The Letters*. Lucky for me that while I was keeping this schedule, my wife was very patient. I would be remiss if I neglected to encourage all

---

[22] It is interesting, perhaps, that Plath never mentioned the name "Assia Wevill" in any letters to her friends and family members to whom she wrote about Hughes's adultery.

[23] Because of her proximity to the Lilly Library, I asked Julie Goodspeed-Chadwick to look through the Wagner-Martin mss. where, several years earlier, Trinidad had sourced three letters to Daniel and Helga Huws. I must acknowledge my gratefulness to Goodspeed-Chadwick for locating the letters to Perry Norton.

[24] The paperback editions, with added content and minor corrections, were published in the UK only.

[25] The Rosenstein archive, now held by Emory, opened for research in January 2020. It contains letters to David Freeman, Anthony Thwaite, Helder and Suzette Macedo, and Elizabeth Sigmund, which we were not able to include having received no response from Rosenstein after several inquiries.

[26] One letter from Plath to Hughes, written October 7–8, 1956, was printed in *Sylvia Plath: Drawings* (2013), but I do not remember any sensation at all around its inclusion. At least, embarrassingly enough, I did not draw any conclusions from it: such as that there might be more. *Sylvia Plath: Drawings* developed from the exhibition and sale of Plath's ink sketches at the Mayor Gallery, London, from November 2 to December 17, 2011, was a more commercial publication than the Mayor Gallery's catalogue, *Sylvia Plath: Her Drawings*, printed in a limited edition of 1,000 copies to accompany the exhibit.

to read the books' Acknowledgements because whatever our individual efforts, this was a product built by a community of Plath (and Hughes) scholars. My motivation throughout the project was inspired by a line in Plath's poem "The Rabbit Catcher": "There was only one place to get to" (CP 193).

# BIBLIOGRAPHY

Adcock, Fleur. *The Faber Book of 20th Century Women's Poetry*. Faber and Faber, 1987.
Aeschylus. *Aeschylus:* Agamemnon, *Vol. II: Commentary on 1–1055*. Edited by E. Fraenkel, Oxford UP, 1950.
Aeschylus. *The Oresteia of Aeschylus*. Edited and translated by G. Thomson and W. Headlam. Cambridge UP, 1938.
Alexander, Paul. *Rough Magic: A Biography of Sylvia Plath*. Viking, 1991.
Alvarez, Al. Letter to Edna O'Brien, October 31, 1989, Box 1, Folder 23, Edna O'Brien Papers, MSS 855, Rose.
Alvarez, Al. "A Poet and Her Myths." *The New York Review of Books*, September 28, 1989, pp. 34–6.
Amichai, Yehuda. *Poems*. Translated by Assia Gutmann [Wevill], Harper & Row, 1969.
Amichai, Yehuda. *Selected Poems*. Translated by Assia Gutmann [Wevill], Cape Goliard, 1968.
Anderson, Benedict. *Imagined Communities: Reflections on the Origin and Spread of Nationalism*. Verso, 2006.
Anderson, Jane V. Papers, Mortimer Rare Book Collection, MRBC-MS-00342, Smith.
Anderson, Linda, Mark Byers, and Ahren Warner. "Introduction: Poetry, Theory, Archives." *The Contemporary Poetry Archive: Essays and Interventions*. Edinburgh UP, 2019, pp. 1–24.
Andrews, Maggie. *Domesticating the Airwaves: Broadcasting, Domesticity and Femininity*. Continuum, 2012.
"Angels Gilded Here—Vanity Fair." Silverwoods Advertisement. *Los Angeles Times*, September 13, 1953, p. C8.
*Annie Hall*. [Film] Directed by Woody Allen. Performers Woody Allen and Diane Keaton. Jack Rollins and Charles H. Joffe, 1977.
Antliff, Allan. *Anarchy and Art: From the Paris Commune to the Fall of the Berlin Wall*. Arsenal Pulp Press, 2007.
"The Archaeology of Reading." *Archaeology of Reading*, archaeologyofreading.org/further-reading/. Accessed June 30, 2021.
"Are Our Doctors Pigs?" *RAT*, June 5–19, 1970, p. 12.
"Ariel Satellite Is Still Working." *The Times (London)*, September 10, 1962, p. 5.
Aswell, Mary Louise, editor. "Foreword: 'The Wing of Madness'." *The World Within: Fiction Illuminating Neuroses of Our Time*, introduction and analyses by Frederic Wertham, McGraw-Hill, 1947, pp. vii–ix.
Auden, W. H. *Collected Poems*. Edited by Edward Mendelson, Faber and Faber, 2007.
Auden, W. H. "Yeats as an Example" (1948), *The Complete Works of W.H. Auden: Prose Volume II 1939–1948*. Edited by Edward Mendelson, Faber and Faber, 2002.
Axelrod, Steven Gould. "The Mirror and the Shadow: Plath's Poetics of Self-Doubt." *Contemporary Literature*, vol. 26, no. 3, 1985, pp. 286–301.
Axelrod, Steven Gould. "The Poetry of Sylvia Plath." *The Cambridge Companion to Sylvia Plath*, edited by Jo Gill, Cambridge UP, 2006, pp. 73–89.

Axelrod, Steven Gould. *Sylvia Plath: The Wound and the Cure of Words*. Johns Hopkins UP, 1990.

Bachelard, Gaston. *The Poetics of Space*. Beacon Press, 1994.

"Back from Hanoi." *RAT*, June 5–19, 1970, pp. 2–3, 27.

Badia, Janet. "The 'Priestess' and Her 'Cult': Plath's Confessional Poetics and the Mythology of Women Readers." *The Unraveling Archive: Essays on Sylvia Plath*, edited by Anita Helle, U of Michigan P, 2007, pp. 159–81.

Badia, Janet. *Sylvia Plath and the Mythology of Readers*. U of Massachusetts P, 2011.

Bakogianni, Anastasia. "Electra in Sylvia Plath's Poetry: A Case of Identification." *Living Classics: Greece and Rome in Contemporary Poetry in English*, edited by Stephen Harrison, Oxford UP, 2009, pp. 194–217.

Balcon, Jill. Letter 1953, File 2, 1952–56, BBC Written Archives Centre, Reading, UK.

Banner, Gillian. "Sylvia Plath and Holocaust Poetry." *Immigrants & Minorities*, vol. 21, no. 1–2, 2002, pp. 231–48.

Barai, Aneesh. "Speaking the Space between Mother and Child: Sylvia Plath, Julia Kristeva, and the Place of Children's Literature." *Space and Place in Children's Literature, 1789 to the Present*, edited by Maria Sachiko Cecire, Hannah Field, Kavita Mudan Finn, and Malini Roy. EBook ProQuest Research Library. Ashgate, 2015, pp. 39–56.

Barnard, Stephen. "Mother's Little Helper: Programmes, Personalities and the Working Day." *Women and Radio: Airing Differences*, edited by Caroline Mitchell, Routledge, 2000.

Barnhouse, Ruth Tiffany Papers. Sophia Smith Collection, SSC-MS-00202, Smith.

Bassnett, Susan, *Sylvia Plath: An Introduction to the Poetry*. Palgrave, 2004.

Bate, Jonathan. *Ted Hughes: The Unauthorised Life*. Harper, 2015.

*Batman: The Animated Series*. [Television Show]. DC Comics, Warner Bros. Animation, Warner Bros. Television, September 5, 1992 to September 15, 1995.

Bayley, Sally. "Sylvia Plath and the Costume of Femininity." *Eye Rhymes: Sylvia Plath's Art of the Visual*, edited by Kathleen Connors and Sally Bayley, Oxford UP, 2007, pp. 183–204.

*BBC Yearbook 1947*. BBC, 1947, pp. 47–9.

Beam, Alex. *Gracefully Insane: The Life and Death of America's Premier Mental Hospital*. Perseus Books, 2001.

Becker, Jillian. *Giving Up: The Last Days of Sylvia Plath*. Ferrington, Bookseller and Publisher, 2002.

*Before Midnight*. [Film] Directed by Richard Linklater, performers Julie Delpy and Ethan Hawke, Castle Rock Entertainment, 2013.

Bell, Michael Mayerfeld. "The Ghosts of Place." *Theory and Society*, vol. 26, no. 6, 1997, pp. 813–36.

Berke, Nancy. "The World Split Open: Feminism, Poetry, and Social Critique." *A History of Twentieth-Century American Women's Poetry*, edited by Linda A. Kinnahan. Cambridge UP, 2016, pp. 155–69.

Berman, Jeffrey. *Surviving Literary Suicide*. U of Massachusetts P, 1999.

Bernikow, Louise. *The World Split Open: Four Centuries of Women Poets in England and America, 1552–1950*. Vintage, 1974.

Beuscher, Ruth. Letter to Sylvia Plath. September 17, 1962, Box 17, Folder 24, Smith.

Bishop, Elizabeth. *Poems*. Farrar, Straus and Giroux, 2011.

Bloom, Emily C. *The Wireless Past: Anglo-Irish Writers and the BBC, 1931–1968*. Oxford UP, 2017.

Bloom, Harold. *Bloom's Major Poets: Sylvia Plath*. Chelsea House Publishers, 2000.

Bontempo, Barbara T. "Enriching Arts & Humanities through Service-Learning." *Quick Hits for Service-Learning: Successful Strategies by Award-Winning Teachers*, edited by M. A. Cooksey and Kimberly T. Olivares, Indiana UP, 2010, pp. 51–2.

"Book Ends." *The New York Times Book Review*. December 14, 1975, p. BR37.

Borges, Jorge Luis. *Labyrinths*. New Directions, 1962.

Borges, Jorge Luis. *The Library of Babel*. David R. Godine, 2000.

Boswell, Matthew. "'Black Phones': Postmodern Poetics in the Holocaust Poetry of Sylvia Plath." *Critical Survey*, vol. 20, no. 2, 2008, pp. 53–64.

Brain, Tracy. *The Other Sylvia Plath*. Longman, 2001.

Brain, Tracy. "Sylvia Plath and You." *Sylvia Plath in Context*, edited by Tracy Brain, Cambridge UP, 2019, pp. 84–93.

Brain, Tracy, editor. *Sylvia Plath in Context*. Cambridge UP, 2019.

Brain, Tracy. "Sylvia Plath's Letters and Journals." *The Cambridge Companion to Sylvia Plath*, edited by Jo Gill, Cambridge UP, 2006, pp. 139–55.

Brandes, Rand. "Ted Hughes: *Crow*." *A Companion to Twentieth-Century Poetry*, edited by Neil Roberts, Blackwell Publishing, 2003, pp. 513–23.

Briggs, Asa. *The History of Broadcasting in the United Kingdom*, 5 vols, Oxford UP, 1961–95.

Briggs, Asa. *The History of Broadcasting in the United Kingdom*, 5 vols, Oxford UP, 1961–95, IV 1979.

British Broadcasting Corporation. Internal BBC Memo to George Macbeth, File 1, Plath, Written Archives Centre, Reading, UK.

British Broadcasting Corporation. "Sylvia Plath Commissioning Documents." June 3, 1985. BBC WAC_T48_451. BBC Written Archives Centre, Reading, UK.

Britzolakis, Christina. "*Ariel* and Other Poems." *The Cambridge Companion to Sylvia Plath*, edited by Jo Gill, Cambridge UP, 2006, pp. 107–23.

Britzolakis, Christina. "Dreamwork: Sylvia Plath's Cold War Modernism." *Women: A Cultural Review*, vol. 24, no. 4, 2013, pp. 263–73.

Britzolakis, Christina. "On Daddy," MAPS: Modern American Poetry. https://www.modernamericanpoetry.org/criticism/christina-britzolakis-daddy. Accessed July 3, 2021.

Britzolakis, Christina. *Sylvia Plath and the Theatre of Mourning*. Oxford UP, 1999.

Brookes, Barbara Lesley. *Abortion in England 1900–1967*. Routledge, 2014.

Brooks, Cleanth. *The Well Wrought Urn: Studies in the Structure of Poetry*. Harcourt, Brace & World, 1947.

Brooks, Cleanth and Robert Penn Warren. *Understanding Poetry*. Holt, Rinehart and Winston, 1938.

Bryant, Marsha. "Ariel's Kitchen: Plath, *Ladies' Home Journal*, and the Domestic Surreal." *The Unraveling Archive: Essays on Sylvia Plath*, edited by Anita Helle, U of Michigan P, 2007, pp. 211–35.

Bryant, Marsha. "Plath, Domesticity, and the Art of Advertising." *College Literature*, vol. 29, no. 3, 2002, pp. 17–34.

Bryant, Marsha. "Queen Bees: Edith Sitwell, Sylvia Plath, and Cross-*Atlantic* Affiliations." *Feminist Modernist Studies*, vol. 2, no. 2, 2019, pp. 194–211, doi: 10.1080/24692921.2019.1621690.

Bryant, Marsha. *Women's Poetry and Popular Culture*. Palgrave, 2011.

Bryant, Marsha. "The WP Network: Anthologies & Affiliations in Contemporary American Women's Poetry." *A History of Twentieth-Century American Women's Poetry*, edited by Linda A. Kinnahan, Cambridge UP, 2016, pp. 186–201.

Bundtzen, Lynda K. "Lucent Figs and Suave Veal Chops: Sylvia Plath and Food." *Gastronomica*, vol. 10, no. 1, Winter 2010, pp. 79–90.
Bundtzen, Lynda K. *The Other* Ariel. U of Massachusetts P, 2001.
Bundtzen, Lynda K. *Plath's Incarnations: Woman and the Creative Process*. Ann Arbor: U of Michigan P, 1978.
Burnett, Rebecca E. and L. Andrew Cooper. "Multimodal Synergy: The Synergy of Modes and Media in Academic and Professional Communication." *Georgia Tech WOVENText Supplement*, pp. 26–56. https://canvas.instructure.com/courses/866713/files/29541465/download?wrap=1. Accessed July 26, 2021.
Bush, Katy Evans. "The Poet Realized: An Interview with Ruth Fainlight." *Contemporary Poetry Review*, September 2008. http://www.cprw.com/Bush/fainlight.htm. Accessed June 30, 2021.
Butler, Judith. *Gender Trouble: Feminism and the Subversion of Identity*. Routledge, 1990.
Butscher, Edward. *Sylvia Plath: Method and Madness*. 1976. Schaffner Press, 2003.
Buurma, Rachel Sagner and Laura Heffernan. *The Teaching Archive: A New History for Literary Study*. U of Chicago P, 2020.
Cam, Heather. "'Daddy': Sylvia Plath's Debt to Anne Sexton." *American Literature*, vol. 59, no. 3, 1987, pp. 429–32.
Campbell, A. Y., translator. *The* Agamemnon *of Aeschylus*. Liverpool UP, 1936.
Carey, John. "Review: The Letters of Sylvia Plath Volume II." *The Sunday Times*. September 9, 2018. https://www.thetimes.co.uk/article/review-the-letters-of-sylvia-plath-volume-ii-1956–1963-edited-by-peter-k-steinberg-and-karen-v-kukil-dispatches-from-a-heart-in-agony-mgw37px9d. Accessed June 9, 2021.
Carroll, Alice. "Look Your Bedroom Best." *Good Housekeeping*, July 1954, pp. 194–6.
Casson, Lionel. *Libraries in the Ancient World*. Yale UP, 2001.
Chadwick, Tom and Pieter Vermeulen. "Literature in the New Archival Landscape." *Literature Interpretation Theory*, vol. 31, no. 1, 2020, pp. 1–7.
Charles, Elizabeth. "Decolonizing the Curriculum." *Insights*, vol. 32, no. 1, 2019, p. 24. DOI: http://doi.org/10.1629/uksg.475. Accessed July 23, 2021.
Chaudhary, Atika and Gary L. Lemons. "Finding Our Voices: Connecting across Time, Space, Age, Race and Profession." *Underserved Women of Color, Voice, and Resistance: Claiming a Seat at the Table*, edited by Sonja M. Brown Givens and Keisha Edwards Tassie, Lexington Books, 2014, pp. 1–22.
Chen, Amy Hildreth. "Archival Bodies: Twentieth Century Literary Collections." Ph.D. Diss., Emory University, 2013.
Chignell, Hugh. *British Radio Drama, 1945–63*. Bloomsbury Academic, 2019.
Christodoulides, Nephie. *Out of the Cradle Endlessly Rocking: Motherhood in Sylvia Plath's Work*. Rodopi Press, 2005.
Chrzanowksi, Gerhard. "Contrasting Responses to Electric Shock Therapy in Clinically Similar Catatonics: Psychological Indications in Therapy and Prognosis." *Psychiatric Quarterly*, vol. 17, 1943, pp. 282–93.
Clark, Heather. *The Grief of Influence: Sylvia Plath and Ted Hughes*. Oxford UP, 2011.
Clark, Heather. Interview with Ruth Fainlight. May 2016, London.
Clark, Heather. *Red Comet: The Short Life and Blazing Art of Sylvia Plath*. Knopf, 2020.
"Classic Ads: Sea Witch." *YouTube*, uploaded by ukclassictelly, September 27, 2012. https://www.youtube.com/watch?v=F1Zs7ag9VaM.
Cleverdon, Douglas. "The Art of Radio in Britain 1922–1966," Cleverdon MS, BBC Written Archives Centre, Caversham, UK.

Cleverdon, Douglas. BBC Memo Contracting "Three Women," Cleverdon mss. II, Box 21, Lilly.
Cleverdon, Douglas. "Correspondence with Plath," Cleverdon mss. II, Box 2, Lilly.
Cleverdon, Douglas. "First Editions of Broadcast Poets and Some Others." Presidential address to the Private Libraries Association, April 11, 1978.
Cleverdon, Douglas. "The Growth of Milk Wood: With the Textual Variants of under Milk Wood by Dylan Thomas." *The Growth of Milk Wood: With the Textual Variants of under Milk Wood by Dylan Thomas*. Dent, 1969, pp. 7–8.
Cleverdon, Douglas. *The Growth of Under Milk Wood*. New Directions, 1969.
Cleverdon, Douglas. "A Note on Radio Drama," Cleverdon mss. II, Box 5, Lilly.
Cleverdon, Douglas. "On the Scope of Feature Programmes: Producing for the Third." Cleverdon mss. II, Box 5, Lilly.
Cleverdon, Douglas. "The Radio Play," Cleverdon mss. II, Box 5, Lilly.
Cleverdon, Douglas. "Third Programme Requirements" for the first quarter of 1951, report, R19/1295/7, Third Programme Memos, BBC Written Archives Centre, Reading, UK.
Cleverdon, Douglas. "On *Three Women*." *The Art of Sylvia Plath: A Symposium*, edited by Charles Newman, Faber and Faber, 1970, pp. 227–9.
Cleverdon, Douglas. "Writing for Radio," Cleverdon mss. II, Box 5, Lilly.
Cloutier, Jean-Christophe. *Shadow Archives: The Lifecycles of African American Literature*. Columbia UP, 2019.
Coats, Karen. "Identity." *Keywords for Children's Literature*, edited by Philip Nel and Lissa Paul, New York UP, 2021, pp. 109–12.
Cohen, Debra Rae, Michael Coyle, and Jane Lewty, editors. *Broadcasting Modernism*. UPF, 2009.
Cohen, Octavus Roy. "Where There's Smoke." *Redbook*, October 1949, pp. 26–7.
Collini, Stefan. "The 'Tragedy' Paper at Cambridge." *Cambridge Authors RSS*, 2009. www.english.cam.ac.uk/cambridgeauthors/the-tragedy-paper-continuity-and-change/. Accessed June 30, 2021.
Connors, Kathleen and Sally Bayley, editors. *Eye Rhymes: Sylvia Plath's Art of the Visual*, Oxford UP, 2007.
Conquest, Robert, editor. *New Lines: An Anthology*. Macmillan, 1956.
Cousteau, Jacques. *The Silent World*. Harper & Brothers, 1953.
Couzyn, Jeni, editor. *The Bloodaxe Book of Contemporary Women Poets: Eleven British Writers*. Bloodaxe Books, 1985.
Cramer, Judith. "Radio: The More Things Change … The More They Stay the Same." *Women in Mass Communication*, 3rd edn, edited by Pamela J. Creedom and Judith Cramer, Sage, 2006.
"Critics Award Honors 1950s Design." *Women's Wear Daily*, October 13, 1950, p. 5.
Crowther, Gail. "The Comforts of Whiteness," May 31, 2020. https://gailcrowther.com/2020/05/31/the-comforts-of-whiteness/. Accessed June 30, 2021.
Crowther, Gail. *The Haunted Reader and Sylvia Plath*. Fonthill Media, 2017.
Crowther, Gail. *Three-Martini Afternoons at the Ritz: The Rebellion of Sylvia Plath & Anne Sexton*. Simon and Schuster, 2021.
Crowther, Gail and Peter K. Steinberg. *These Ghostly Archives: The Unearthing of Sylvia Plath*. Fonthill Media, 2017.
Cuda, Anthony. "Dangerous Moments: Eliot and Plath." Presentation. T. S. Eliot Society Annual Meeting, St. Louis, MO, September 22, 2017.

Curry, Renée R. "Daughters of the Dust, the White Woman Viewer, and the Unborn Child." *Teaching What You're Not: Identity Politics in Higher Education*, edited by Katherine J. Mayberry, NYU Press, 1996, 335–56.

Curry, Renée R. *White Women Writing White: H.D., Elizabeth Bishop, Sylvia Plath, and Whiteness*. Greenwood Press, 2000.

Dahl, Roald. *Charlie and the Great Glass Elevator*. Knopf, 1972.

Davidson, Cathy. "Humanities 2.0 Promise, Perils, Predictions." *PMLA*, vol. 23, no. 1, 2013, pp. 707–17.

Davison, Peter. *The Fading Smile: Poets in Boston from Robert Lowell to Sylvia Plath*. 1994. Norton, 1996.

Degen, Monica and Kevin Hetherington. "Hauntings." *Space and Culture*, vol. 1, no. 11–12, December 2001, pp. 1–6.

Derrida, Jacques. *Archive Fever*. 1995. Translated by Eric Prenowitz. U of Chicago P, 1996.

Derrida, Jacques. *Of Grammatology*. Translated by Gaytri Chakravorty Spivak. Johns Hopkins UP, 1981.

Dienstfrey, Patricia et al. "Foreword." *The Grand Permission: New Writings on Poetics and Motherhood*. Wesleyan UP, 2003, pp. vii–ix.

Dohrn, Bernardine. "War: Weather Report." *RAT*, June 5–19, 1970, pp. 4–5.

Donaldson, Elizabeth J. "The Corpus of the Madwoman: Toward a Feminist Disability Studies Theory of Embodiment and Mental Illness." *NWSA Journal*, vol. 14, no 3, 2002, pp. 99–119.

Donaldson, Elizabeth J. "*The Snake Pit*: Mary Jane Ward's Asylum Fiction and Mental Health Advocacy." *Literatures of Madness: Disability Studies and Mental Health*, edited by Elizabeth J. Donaldson, Palgrave Macmillan, 2018, pp. 109–26.

Doolittle, Hilda. *Collected Poems*. New Directions, 1986.

Dowson, Jane. *Carol Ann Duffy: Poet for Our Times*. Palgrave Macmillan, 2016.

Drakakis, John. *British Radio Drama*. Cambridge UP, 1981.

"Drama Policy File." 5b, R19/280/7, BBC Written Archive, Reading, UK.

Drew, Elizabeth. *T. S. Eliot: The Design of His Poetry*. C. Scribner's Sons, 1949. Former Owner Plath, Smith.

Duffy, Carol Ann. *The Bees*. Faber and Faber, 2011.

Duffy, Carol Ann. "Preface." *Sylvia Plath Poems Chosen by Carol Ann Duffy*. Faber and Faber, 2012, pp. xi–xv.

Duffy, Carol Ann. *Standing Female Nude*. Anvil Press Poetry, 1985.

Dunbar, William. *The Poems of William Dunbar*, edited by David Laing, vol. 1, Laing and Forbes, 1834.

DuPlessis, Rachel Blau. "Foreword." *The Grand Permission: New Writings on Poetics and Motherhood*, edited by Patricia Diensfrey and Brenda Hillman, Wesleyan UP, 2003, pp. vii–xi.

Eberly, Rosa A. *Citizen Critics: Literary Public Spheres*. U of Illinois P, 2000.

Echols, Alice. *Daring to Be Bad: Radical Feminism in America, 1967–1975*. U of Minnesota P, 1989.

Eco, Umberto. *The Role of the Reader: Explorations in the Semiotics of Texts*. Indiana UP, 1984.

Edel, Leon and Adeline R. Tintner. *The Library of Henry James*. U of Michigan P, 1987.

Edward Butscher Collection of Papers on Sylvia Plath. Mortimer Rare Book Collection, MRBC-MS-00002, Smith.

Elborn, Geoffrey. *Edith Sitwell: A Biography*. Sheldon, 1981.

Eliot, T. S. *The Complete Poems and Plays*. Harcourt, Brace & World, Inc., 1952. Former Owner Plath, Smith.
Eliot, T. S. *Selected Prose of T. S. Eliot*. Edited by Frank Kermode, Faber and Faber, 1975.
Eliot, T. S. *The Use of Poetry and the Use of Criticism*. Faber, 1933.
Elizabeth Sigmund Collection of Photographs and Correspondence Related to Sylvia Plath, MRBC-MS-00441, Mortimer Rare Book Collection, Smith.
Ellis, Jonathan. "Mailed into Space: On Sylvia Plath's Letters." *Representing Sylvia Plath*, edited by Sally Bayley and Tracy Brain. Cambridge UP, 2011, pp. 13–31.
Ellison, Julie. "The New Public Humanists." *PMLA*, vol. 128, no. 2, March 2013, pp. 289–98.
Empson, William. "Donne the Space Man." *The Kenyon Review*, vol. 19, no. 3, 1957, pp. 337–99.
Engel, Laura and Ruth Rutter, editors. "Women and Archives," *Tulsa Studies in Women's Literature*, vol. 40, no. 1, Spring 2021 special double issue.
Enniss, Stephen C. "Introduction," *"No Other Appetite": Sylvia Plath, Ted Hughes, and the Blood Jet of Poetry*, edited by Stephen C. Enniss and Karen V. Kukil, The Grolier Club, 2005, pp. vii–xi.
Enniss, Stephen C. and Karen V. Kukil, editors. *"No Other Appetite": Sylvia Plath, Ted Hughes, and the Blood Jet of Poetry*. The Grolier Club, 2005.
Enright, D. J., editor. *Poets of the 1950s: An Anthology of New English Verse*. Kenkyusha, 1955.
Entwistle, Alice. "Three Twentieth-Century Women Poets: Riding, Smith, Plath." *The Cambridge History of English Poetry*, edited by Michael O'Neill, Cambridge UP, 2010, pp. 897–917.
Esdale, Logan. "Introduction to Gertrude Stein." *Ida: A Novel*, edited by Logan Esdale, Yale UP, 2012.
Eskenazi, Gerald. *I Hid It under the Sheets: Growing Up with Radio*. U of Missouri P, 2005.
Euripides and James E. Thorold Rogers. *The Bacchae*. Parker, 1872.
Faas, Ekbert. *Ted Hughes: The Unaccommodated Universe*. Black Sparrow Press, 1980.
Fainlight, Ruth. "Jane and Sylvia." *Crossroads*, vol. 61, Spring 2004, pp. 8–19.
Fainlight, Ruth. Letter to Sylvia Plath, January 12, 1963. Box 17, Folder 28, Sylvia Plath Collection, Smith. Published in full in "Jane and Sylvia," *Crossroads*, pp. 17–8.
Fainlight, Ruth. "1963—World Events." *Jubilee Lines*, edited by Carol Ann Duffy, Faber and Faber, 2012.
Fainlight, Ruth. "Sapphic Moon." *Encounter*, vol. 18, no. 2, February 18, 1962, p. 77.
Fajkovic, Muhamed and Lennart Björneborn. "Marginalia as Message: Affordances for Reader-to-Reader Communication." *Journal of Documentation*, vol. 70, no. 5, 2014, pp. 902–26.
Farge, Arlette. *The Allure of the Archives*. Translated by Thomas Scott-Railton. Yale UP, 2013.
Farland, Maria. "Sylvia Plath's Anti-Psychiatry." *The Minnesota Review: A Journal of Creative and Critical Writing*, vols. 55–7, 2002, pp. 245–56.
Farmer, Richard. "Cinema Advertising and the Sea Witch 'Lost Island' Film (1965)." *Historical Journal of Film, Radio and Television*, 2016, pp. 1–19, doi:10.1080/01439685.2015.1129709. Accessed June 30, 2021.
"Fashion Confidential: Lingerie News." *Vogue*, vol. 1, April 1954, pp. 146–51.
"Fashions for the Nicest Hours of the Day." *Good Housekeeping*, November 1955, pp. 95–106.
"Feminists, The." *RAT*, June 5–19, 1970, pp. 8–9.
Ferretter, Luke. "'Just Like the Sort of Drug a Man Would Invent': *The Bell Jar* and the Feminist Critique of Women's Health Care." *Plath Profiles*, vol. 1, pp. 136–58.
Ferretter, Luke. *Sylvia Plath's Fiction: A Critical Study*. Edinburgh UP, 2010.
Fidler, Adam. "Shorthand and Speedwriting – What's the Difference?" July 25, 2011. ExecutiveSecretary.com. Accessed July 26, 2021.

Fields, Jill. *An Intimate Affair: Women, Lingerie and Sexuality*. U of California P, 2007.
"First Broadcast." Season 1, episode 1, Third Programme, February 1, 1962.
"First Editions of Broadcast Poets and some others. Presidential address to the Private Libraries Association, April 11, 1978." Cleverdon mss. II, Lilly.
Fiske, John. *Television Culture*. Routledge, 1987.
Fogarty, Anne. *The Art of Being a Well Dressed Wife*. V&A Publishing, 2011.
Ford, Karen Jackson. *Gender and the Poetics of Excess: Moments of Brocade*. UP of Mississippi, 1997.
Forster, E. M. *Howards End*. Vintage Books. Former Owner Plath, Lilly, 1955.
Foucault, Michel. "What is an Author?." *The Death and Resurrection of the Author?*, edited by William Irwin, Greenwood Press, 2002, pp. 9–22.
Fraenkel, Eduard. *Aeschylus, Agamemnon*. II, Oxford UP, 1950.
Fraser, Linda Lussy. "Technologies of Reproduction: The Maternity Ward in Sylvia Plath's *Three Women* and Ingmar Bergman's *Brink of Life*." *Women's Studies*, vol. 28, no. 5, 1999, pp. 547–74, doi:10.1080/00497878.1999.9979277.
Frazer, James George. *The Golden Bough: A Study in Magic and Religion* [abridged]. The Macmillan Company, 1922. Former Owner Plath, Smith
Frazer, James George. *The Golden Bough: A Study in Magic and Religion Part I. The Magic Art and the Evolution of Kings*, 3rd edn, Macmillan and Co., 1911–1915.
Frazer, James George. *The Golden Bough*, Enhanced Media Published, 2015.
Freud, Sigmund. *The Interpretation of Dreams*. 1899. Translated by A. A. Brill, Macmillan, 1913.
Friedan, Betty. *The Feminine Mystique*. Norton, [1963] 2001.
Friedman, Susan Stanford. "When a 'Long' Poem Is a 'Big' Poem: Self-Authorizing Strategies in Women's Twentieth-Century 'Long Poems.'" *Dwelling in Possibility: Women Poets and Critics on Poetry*, edited by Yopie Prins and Maeera Shreiber, Cornell UP, 1997, pp. 13–37.
Froehlich, Annette, editor. *Outer Space and Popular Culture: Influences and Interrelations*. Springer Verlag, 2020.
Frost, Laura. "'Every Woman Adores a Fascist': Feminist Visions of Fascism from *Three Guineas* to *Fear of Flying*." *Women's Studies*, vol. 29, 2000, pp. 37–69.
Fuss, Diane. "Corpse Poem." *Critical Inquiry*, vol. 30, Autumn 2003, pp. 1–30.
"george," *RAT*, June 5–19, 1970, pp. 6–7.
Gerovitch, Slava. "The Human inside a Propaganda Machine." *Into the Cosmos: Space Exploration and Soviet Culture*, edited by James T. Andrews and Asif A. Siddiqi, U of Pittsburgh P, 2011, pp. 77–106.
Gielgud, Val. Letter, 1953, R19/280/7, Drama Policy File 5b, BBC Written Archives Centre, Reading, UK.
Gifford, Terry. "Hughes's Social Ecology." *The Cambridge Companion to Ted Hughes*, edited by Terry Gifford, Cambridge UP, 2011, pp. 81–93.
Gilbert, Sandra M. "A Fine, White Flying Myth: Confessions of a Plath Addict." *The Massachusetts Review*, vol. 19, no. 3, Autumn 1978, pp. 585–603.
Gilbert, Sandra M. "On the Beach with Sylvia Plath." *The Unraveling Archive: Essays on Sylvia Plath*, edited by Anita Helle, U of Michigan P, 2007, pp. 121–38.
Gilbert, Sandra M. "In Yeats' House: The Death and Resurrection of Sylvia Plath." *Critical Essays on Sylvia Plath*, edited by Linda Welshimer Wagner-Martin, G.K. Hall & Co, 1984, pp. 204–22.
Gilbert, Sandra M. and Susan Gubar. *The Madwoman in the Attic: The Woman Writer and the Nineteenth-Century Literary Imagination*. Yale UP, 1984.

Gilbert, Sandra M. and Susan Gubar. *Still Mad: American Women Writers and the Feminist Imagination, 1950–2020*. Norton, 2021.
Gill, Jo. *The Cambridge Introduction to Sylvia Plath*. Cambridge UP, 2008.
Gill, Jo, editor. *Modern Confessional Writing: New Critical Essays*. Routledge, 2005.
Ginsberg, Allen. *Howl*. 1956. City Lights Books, 1988.
Ginzburg, Carlo. "Microhistory: Two or Three Things That I Know about It." *Critical History*, vol. 20, no. 1, 1993, pp. 10–35.
Glendinning, Victoria. *Edith Sitwell: A Unicorn Among Lions*. Knopf, 1981.
Glynn, Eugene David. "Television and the American Character—A Psychiatrist Looks at Television." *Television's Impact on American Culture*, edited by William Yandell Elliott, Michigan State UP, 1956, pp. 175–82.
Goffman, Erving. *Asylums Essays on the Social Situation of Mental Patients and Other Inmates*. Penguin, 1961.
Goffman, Erving. *Stigma: Notes on the Management of a Spoiled Identity*. Prentice Hall, 1963.
Golden, Amanda. *Annotating Modernism: Marginalia and Pedagogy from Virginia* Woolf *to the Confessional Poets*. Routledge, 2020.
Golden, Amanda. "Sylvia Plath's Library: The Marginal Archive." *The Contemporary Poetry Archive*, edited by Linda Anderson, Mark Byers, and Ahren Warner, Edinburgh UP, 2019, pp. 111–23.
Golden, Amanda. "Sylvia Plath's Teaching and the Shaping of Her Work." *Sylvia Plath in Context*, edited by Tracy Brain, Cambridge UP, 2019, pp. 255–63.
Golden, Amanda. "Sylvia Plath's Teaching Syllabus: A Chronology." *Plath Profiles*, vol. 2, Summer 2009, pp. 209–20. https://scholarworks.iu.edu/journals/index.php/plath/article/view/4746. Accessed June 30, 2021.
Golding, Alan. *From Outlaw to Classic: Canons in American Poetry*. U of Wisconsin P, 1995.
González, Matilde Martín. "Gender Politics and the Making of Anthologies: Towards a Theory of Women's Poetry." *SPELL: Swiss Papers in English Language and Literature*, vol. 18, 2006, pp. 175–91.
"*Good Housekeeping*'s Simplicity Patterns: Make Sweet Sleep-Timers." *Good Housekeeping*, November 1955, pp. 277–80.
"*Good Housekeeping* Simplicity Patterns: Nighttime Nostalgia." *Good Housekeeping*, November 1958, pp. 239–41.
Goodspeed-Chadwick, Julie. *Reclaiming Assia Wevill: Sylvia Plath, Ted Hughes, and the Literary Imagination*. Louisiana State UP, 2019.
Gordon, Avery. *Ghostly Matters: Haunting and the Sociological Imagination*. U of Minnesota P, 1997.
Gordon Bramer, Julia. *Fixed Stars Govern a Life: Decoding Sylvia Plath*. Stephen F. Austin State UP, 2014.
Grahn, Judy. *A Simple Revolution: The Making of an Activist Poet*. Aunt Lute Books, 2012.
Graves, Cecil. Letter to Director General Sir Cecil Graves, Literary Output Committee, January 6, 1943, BBC Written Archives Centre, Caversham, UK.
Graves, Robert. *The Meaning of Dreams*. London, 1924.
Green, Barbara. "The Feminist Periodical Press: Women, Periodical Studies, and Modernity." *Literature Compass*, vol. 6, no. 1, 2009, pp. 191–205.
Green, Barbara. *Spectacular Confessions: Autobiography, Performative Activism, and the Sites of Suffrage, 1905–1938*. St. Martin's Press, 1993.
Green, Betty and Beryl Tucker. "Your Children Are Looking at You!" *Parents' Magazine*, April 1947, p. 111.

Gregg, John R. *Gregg's Shorthand: A Light Line Phonography for the Millions*. "Published by the Author," 1898.

Gregg, John R. et al. *Gregg Shorthand Manual Simplified*. McGraw-Hill, 1949.

Grigson, Geoffrey and Stephen Potter. Literary Output Committee, memo, May 31, 1943, BBC Written Archives Centre, Caversham, UK.

Grisewood, Harman. Internal BBC memo, June 28, 1951, R19/933/3 BBC Written Archive, Reading, UK.

Grobe, Christopher. *The Art of Confession: The Performance of Self from Robert Lowell to Reality TV*. NYU Press, 2017.

Gubar, Susan. "Prosopopoeia and Holocaust Poetry in English: Sylvia Plath and Her Contemporaries." *The Yale Journal of Criticism*, vol. 14, no. 1, Spring 2001, pp. 191–215.

Guiney, Thomas. "An Idea Whose Time Had Come?: The Creation of a Modern System of Parole in England and Wales, 1960–1968." *Prison Service Journal*, 2018, pp. 14–17.

Hajkowski, Thomas. *The BBC and National Identity in Britain, 1922–1953*. Manchester UP, 2010.

Haley, William. "Breaking Ground in Radio." Supplement to *The Listener*, September 26, 1946.

Hammer, Langdon. "Plath's Lives: Poetry, Professionalism, and the Culture of the School." *Representations*, vol. 75, no. 1, 2001, pp. 61–88.

Harding, Jason, editor. *T. S. Eliot in Context*. Cambridge UP, 2011.

Hardy, Thomas. *Collected Poems*. Macmillan and Co., 1919.

Hargrove, Nancy D. *The Journey toward Ariel: Sylvia Plath's Poems of 1956–1959*. Lund UP, 1994.

Harmon, Jim. *The Great Radio Heroes*. Ace, 1967.

Healy, Dan Cambridge Poets. Oleander Press, 2013.

Heaney, Seamus. "The Indefatigable Hoof-taps: Sylvia Plath." *Finders Keepers: Selected Prose 1971–2001*. Faber and Faber, 2002, pp. 218–31.

Heaney, Seamus. "Yeats as an Example?" *Finders Keepers: Selected Prose 1971–2001*. Faber and Faber, 2002.

"Hear Sylvia Plath's Barely-Known Radio Play, Three Women." *Open Culture*, October 5, 2016. www.openculture.com/2016/10/hear-sylvia-plaths-barely-known-radio-play-three-women.html.

Hedley, Jane. "Sylvia Plath's Ekphrastic Impulse." *I Made You to Find Me: The Coming of Age of the Woman Poet and the Politics of Poetic Address*. Ohio State UP, 2009, pp. 81–4.

Hedrick, Elizabeth. "Robin Morgan, Jane Alpert, and Feminist Satire." *Tulsa Studies in Women's Literature*, vol. 33, no. 2, 2014, pp. 123–50.

Helle Collection of Plath Family Photographs. Mortimer Rare Book Collection, MRBC-MS-00273, Smith.

Helle, Anita. "Electroshock Therapy and Plath's Convulsive Poetics." *Sylvia Plath in Context*, edited by Tracy Brain, Cambridge UP, 2019, pp. 264–74.

Helle, Anita. "Reading Plath Photographs: In and Out of the Museum." *The Unraveling Archive: Essays on Sylvia Plath*, edited by Anita Helle, U of Michigan P, 2010, pp. 182–210.

Hetherington, Kevin. "Phantasmogoria/ Phantasm Agora: Materialities, Spatialities and Ghosts." *Space and Culture*, vol. 1, no. 11–12, December 2001, pp. 24–41.

Hicklin, Liz. "Memories of Love, Poetry and Dancing with Ted Hughes." *AGE* newspaper, Sharon Grey Column, "Correspondence and Papers from Ted Hughes to Liz Hicklin," Add MS 89198, British Library.

Hicok, Bethany. "Introduction." *Elizabeth Bishop and Literary Archive*, edited by Bethany Hicok, Lever Press, 2020, e-book. https://doi.org/10.3998/mpub.11649332. Accessed February 1, 2021.

Higgins, Charlotte. *This New Noise: The Birth and Troubled Life of the BBC*. Guardian Faber Publishing, 2015.

Hilmes, Michele. *Radio Voices: American Broadcasting, 1922–1952*. U of Minnesota P, 1997.

"The History of Gregg Shorthand." CookandWiley.com. Accessed March 10, 2021.
Homer. *The Iliad of Homer*. Translated by Richmond Lattimore, Cambridge, 1966.
hooks, bell. *aint I a woman*. Routledge, 2015.
Houghton Mifflin Company Collection on *Bitter Fame*. Mortimer Rare Book Collection, MRBC-MS-00003, Smith.
Howard, Maureen. "The Girl Who Tried to Be Good." *The New York Times Book Review*, December 14, 1975, Section 7, pp. 1–2.
Hughes, Frieda. *Alternative Values: Poems & Paintings*. Bloodaxe Books, 2015.
Hughes, Frieda. Foreword to *Ariel: The Restored Edition*, by Sylvia Plath, Harper Perennial, 2004, pp. xi–xxi.
Hughes, Olwyn and Anne Stevenson, reply by Al Alvarez. "Sylvia Plath: An Exchange." *The New York Review of Books*, October 26, 1989. https://www.nybooks.com/articles/1989/10/26/sylvia-plath-an-exchange/. Accessed January 28, 2020.
Hughes, Ted. *Birthday Letters*. Faber and Faber, 2009.
Hughes, Ted. *Collected Poems*. Edited by Paul Keegan. 2003. Farrar, Straus and Giroux, 2005.
Hughes, Ted. *A Dancer to God: Tributes to T. S. Eliot*. Farrar, Straus and Giroux, 1993.
Hughes, Ted. Folklore Notebook. BL Add MS 88918/9/12. British Library.
Hughes, Ted. Forward, *The Journals of Sylvia Plath*. Edited by Ted Hughes, Consulting Editor and Frances McCullough. Random House, 1982, pp. xi–xiii.
Hughes, Ted. "Last Letter." *New Statesman*, edited by Melvyn Bragg, October 11, 2010, pp. 42–4.
Hughes, Ted. *Letters of Ted Hughes*. Edited by Christopher Reid, Faber and Faber, 2007.
Hughes, Ted. "Notes on Poems 1956–1963." *Collected Poems*, edited by Sylvia Plath. Harper Perennial, 2008, pp. 275–96.
Hughes, Ted, translator. *The Oresteia by Aeschylus in a New Version by Ted Hughes*. Faber and Faber, 1999.
Hughes, Ted. "Sylvia Plath and Her Journals." *Winter Pollen: Occasional Prose*, edited by William Scammell, Picador, 1994.
Hunter, Dianne. "Sylvia Plath's Man in Black." *European Journal of Women's Studies*, vol. 12, no. 1, February 2005, pp. 45–60, doi:10.1177/1350506805048855. Accessed June 30, 2021.
Hutcheon, Linda. *A Theory of Parody: The Teachings of Twentieth-Century Art Forms*. U of Illinois P, 2000.
Huws, Daniel. *Memories of Ted Hughes: 1952–1963*. Richard Hollis, 2010.
"I dreamed I was a toreador … " Maidenform Advertisement, *Ladies' Home Journal*, April 1951, p. 4.
"I dreamed I went shopping … " Maidenform Advertisement, *Seventeen*, November 1949, p. 13.
"I dreamed I won the election … " Maidenform Advertisement, *Ladies' Home Journal*, October 1952, p. 31.
Jackson, H. J. *Marginalia: Readers Writing in Books*. Yale UP, 2001.
Jakacki, Diane and Katherine Faull. "Doing DH in the Classroom: Transforming the Humanities Curriculum through Digital Engagement." *Doing Digital Humanities*, edited by Constance Crompton et al., Routledge, 2016.
Jansson, André. "The Mediatization of Consumption." *Journal of Consumer Culture*, vol. 2, no. 1, 2002, pp. 4–31, doi:10.1177/146954050200200101.
Jeffares, A. Norman. *W. B. Yeats: Man and Poet*. Routledge and Kegan Paul Ltd., 1949.
Joan, Polly and Andrea Chesman. Guide to Women's Publishing, Dustbooks, 1978.
Jung, Carl G. *The Theory of Psychoanalysis*. The Journal of Nervous and Mental Disease Publishing Company, 1915.

Kackman, Michael. "Nothing on but Hoppy Badges: *Hopalong Cassidy*, William Boyd Enterprises, and Emergent Media Globalization." *Cinema Journal*, vol. 47, no. 4, 2008, pp. 76–101.

Kaplan, Cora, editor. *Salt and Bitter and Good: Three Centuries of English and American Women Poets*. Paddington Press Ltd., 1975.

Kaplan, Milton Allen. *Radio and Poetry*. Columbia UP, 1949.

Kavanagh, P. J. "An Awkward Shyness." *The Guardian*, July 12, 1968, p. 6.

Kaysen, Susanna. *Girl, Interrupted*. Virago, 2000.

Keats, John. *The Complete Poetry and Selected Prose of Keats*. Edited by Harold Edgar Briggs, Modern Library, 1967.

Kelly, Erin. "Red Ruling in Early Printed Books." Presentation. Treasures and Tea. University of Victoria Libraries, Victoria, BC, September 20, 2017.

Keller, Lynn. *Forms of Expansion: Recent Long Poems by Women*. U of Chicago P, 1997.

Keller, Lynn. "The Twentieth-Century Long Poem." *The Columbia History of American Poetry*, edited by Jay Parini, Columbia UP, 1993, pp. 534–63.

Kendall, Tim. "From the Bottom of the Pool: Sylvia Plath's Last Poems." *Sylvia Plath*, edited by Harold Bloom, Infobase Publishing, 2007, pp. 146–64.

Kendall, Tim. *Sylvia Plath: A Critical Study*. Faber and Faber, 2001.

Kennedy, John F. "Radio and Television Address to the American People on the Soviet Arms Build-up in Cuba, October 22, 1962." *JFK Presidential Library and Museum*. www.jfklibrary.org/learn/about-jfk/historic-speeches/address-during-the-cuban-missile-crisis. Accessed September 16, 2020.

Kennedy, Maev. "Gnawed Roman Skeleton that Inspired Sylvia Plath Poem Goes on Display." *The Guardian*, May 23, 2012. https://www.theguardian.com/books/2012/may/23/roman-skeleton-sylvia-plath-cambridge. Accessed 24 May 2023.

Kerouac, Jack. *Pic*. Penguin, 2019.

Kersnowski, Alice Hughes, editor. *Conversations with Edna O'Brien*, U of Mississippi P, 2014.

Konkol, Margaret. "Public Archives, New Knowledge, and Moving beyond the Digital Humanities/Digital Pedagogy Distinction." *Hybrid Pedagogy*, September 8, 2015. http://hybridpedagogy.org/public-archives-and-new-knowledge/. Accessed February 2, 2020.

Koren, Yehuda and Eilat Negev. *Lover of Unreason: Assia Wevill, Sylvia Plath's Rival and Ted Hughes's Doomed Love*. Da Capo, 2007.

Krebs, Gunter. "Chronology of Space Launches." *Gunter's Space Page*. space.skyrocket.de/directories/chronology. Accessed September 17, 2020.

Kroll, Judith. *Chapters in a Mythology: The Poetry of Sylvia Plath*. 1976. Harper & Row, 2007.

Krulwich, Robert. "A Very Scary Light Show: Exploding H-Bombs in Space." *National Public Radio*. www.npr.org/sections/krulwich/2010/07/01/128170775/a-very-scary-light-show-exploding-h-bombs-in-space?t=1601650519385. Accessed October 2, 2020.

Kuczynski, Sarah A. "'There Is No Miracle More Cruel Than This': Readian Relaxation and Maternal Agency in Plath's *Three Women*." *Literature and Medicine*, vol. 36, no. 1, 2018, pp. 146–63.

Kukil, Karen V. "Beyond *Letters Home*: Plath's Unabridged Correspondence." *Sylvia Plath in Context*, edited by Tracy Brain, Cambridge UP, 2019, pp. 284–94.

Kukil, Karen V. "Conversation with Ruth Tiffany Barnhouse." Nantucket, MA, October 5–6, 1998.

Kukil, Karen V. "The Fires of Heaven and Hell: Sylvia Plath's 'Fever 103°.'" *Faber & Faber*, September 6, 2018. www.faber.co.uk/blog/sylvia-plath-fever-103/. Accessed June 30, 2021.

Kukil, Karen V. "The Genesis of 'Mary Ventura and the Ninth Kingdom.'" *The Hudson Review*, Spring 2019. https://hudsonreview.com/2019/05/the-genesis-of-mary-ventura-and-the-ninth-kingdom/#.YP-APFNKjt0. Accessed July 26, 2021.

Kukil, Karen V. "In the Footsteps of Sylvia Plath." *Smith College Library*, Smith College, June 3, 2016. libraries.smith.edu/sites/libraries/files/docs/in_the_footsteps_of_sylvia_plath.pdf. Accessed June 30, 2021.

Kukil, Karen V. "Reviving the Journals of Sylvia Plath." *The British Library*, December 11, 2015. www.bl.uk/20th-century-literature/articles/reviving-the-journals-of-sylvia-plath. Accessed June 30, 2021.

Kukil, Karen V. "Scholarly Editing Now." Presentation. Modern Language Association Convention. Seattle, WA. January 11, 2020.

Kukil, Karen V. **"Teaching the Material Archive at Smith College."** *The Boundaries of the Literary Archive*, edited by Carrie Smith and Lisa Stead. Ashgate, 2013, pp. 171–88.

Lacey, Kate. *Feminine Frequencies: Gender, German Radio, and the Public Sphere, 1923–1945*. U of Michigan P, 1996.

Lacey, Kate. *Listening Publics: The Politics and Experience of Listening in the Media Age*. Polity Press, 2013.

Lambert, Laura. "Weather Underground." *Britannica Academic*, Encyclopaedia Britannica, August 2017. academic.eb.com/levels/collegiate/article/Weather-Underground/603854#. Accessed August 27, 2019.

Laozi. *Tao Te Ching: A New English Version*. Edited by Stephen Mitchell. Harper & Row, 1988.

Latham, Joyce M. "Off/On Our Backs: The Feminist Press in the 'Sex Wars' of the 1980s." *Protest on the Page: Essays on Print and the Culture of Dissent since 1865*, edited by James L. Baughman et al., U of Wisconsin P, pp. 221–40.

Lattimore, Richmond. *The* Iliad *of Homer*. U of Chicago P, 1951.

Lawrie, Alexandra. "Who's Listening to Modernism? BBC Features and Audience Response." *Media History*, vol. 24, no. 2, 2018, pp. 239–51.

"Lectures Proposed by the Board of the Faculty of English, 1955–56." *Cambridge University Reporter*, p. 611.

Lee, Clarissa Ai Ling, "Voices of Feminism and Schizophrenia in Plath's Poetry." *Applied Semiotics*, vol. 14, 2004. http://french.chass.utoronto.ca/as-sa/ASSANo14/index.html. Accessed June 20, 2020.

Lemert, Charles. "The Dead, the Living and Those Yet to Come." *Contexts*, vol. 10, no. 4, 2011, pp. 16–21.

Lennon, John. "Woman Is the Nigger of the World." *Some Time in New York City*. Apple Records, 1972 track 1. Vinyl LP.

Leonard, Garry M. "'The Woman Is Perfected. Her Dead Body Wears the Smile of Accomplishment': Sylvia Plath and 'Mademoiselle' Magazine." *College Literature*, vol. 19, no. 2, 1992, pp. 60–82.

"Leopard Print Lingerie by Vanity Fair." *Chicago Daily Tribune*, December 16, 1953, p. B3.

"Leopard—Running Wild." *Chicago Daily Tribune*, October 30, 1953, p. 13.

Lerner, Ben. *The Hatred of Poetry*. Fitzcarraldo Editions, 2016.

Leshan, Eda J. "A Program on Family Rituals for Your Discussion Group." *Parents' Magazine & Better Homemaking*, September 1961, pp. 126–7.

Levinas, Emmanuel. *Otherwise Than Being; or, Beyond Essence*. Translated by Alphonso Lingis, Kluwer Academic Publishers, 1991.

Lewis, Cara L. *Dynamic Form: How Intermediality Made Modernism*. Cornell Online Scholarship, Cornell UP, 2020.

Liddell, Henry, Robert Scott, Henry Jones, Roderick McKenzie, Peter Glare, and Anne Thompson. *A Greek-English Lexicon*. 1940, 9th edn, Oxford UP, 1996.

"The Living Poet." BBC, Third Programme, London, July 8, 1961.
Lorde, Audre. *Sister Outsider: Essays and Speeches*. Crossing Press, pp. 110–13.
Love, Ann Burnside. "The Legend of Plath, the Scent of Roses." *Washington Post*, April 29, 1979.
Lowell, Robert. "Foreword." Sylvia Plath, *Ariel*. Harper and Row, 1966. pp. vii–ix.
Lowell, Robert. *Life Studies and for the Union Dead*. Farrar, Straus and Giroux, 2007.
Loy, Mina. *The Lost Lunar Baedeker*. Carcanet, 1997.
Lucas, D. W. *The Bacchae of Euripides. The Greek Text Performed at Cambridge at the Arts Theatre 20–24 February, 1956, by Members of the University, with an English Prose Translation Made for the Cambridge Performance of 1930*. Bowes & Bowes, 1955.
Lutostański, Bartosz. "A Narratology of Radio Drama: Voice, Perspective, Space." *Audionarratology: Interfaces of Sound and Narrative*, edited by Jarmila Mildorf and Till Kinzel, Gruyter, 2016, pp. 117–32.
MacDonald, J. Fred. *Don't Touch That Dial!: Radio Programming in American Life, 1920–1960*. Nelson-Hall, 1979.
"Major Gagarin retires." *The Guardian*, July 14, 1961, pp. 1–2.
Malcolm, Janet. *The Silent Woman: Sylvia Plath and Ted Hughes*. 1994. Random House, 1995.
Malle, Louis. Letter to Norma, June 16, 1985, Box 8, Folder 30, Edna O'Brien Papers, Rose.
Mandel Brothers Advertisement. "Nylon Tricot Lingerie in Leopard Design & 'Little Princess' Cotton Quilt Robe." *Chicago Daily Tribune*, December 13, 1953, p. 45.
Martin, Willa. "She Was Going Crazy—and She Knew It." *The Des Moines Register*, April 28, 1946, p. 8G.
Mary, Jane Ward Collection. Howard Gotlieb Archival Research Center. Boston University, Boston, MA.
Masud, Noreen. "Plath in the Context of Stevie Smith." *Sylvia Plath in Context*, edited by Tracy Brain, Cambridge UP, 2019, pp. 65–74.
Maynard, Joyce. "My Parents Are My Friends." *McCall's*, October 1972, pp. 79,146,148,150, and 152.
Mazzaro, Jerome. "Sylvia Plath and the Cycles of History." *Sylvia Plath: New Views on the Poetry*, edited by Gary Lane, Johns Hopkins UP, 1979, pp. 218–40.
McCallum, Robyn and John Stephens. "Ideology in Children's Books." *Handbook of Research on Children's and Young Adult Literature*, edited by Shelby A. Wolf, Karen Coats, Patricia Enciso, and Christine A. Jenkins. Routledge, 2011, pp. 359–71.
McCarthy, Anna. *Ambient Television: Visual Culture and Public Space*. Duke UP, 2003.
McCracken, Allison. "Study of a Mad Housewife." *Small Screens, Big Ideas Television in the 1950s*, edited by Janet Thumim, I.B. Tauris, 2002.
McGinley, Phyllis. "Cooking to Me Is Poetry." *Ladies' Home Journal*, vol. 86, January 1960, pp. 66–7.
McHale, Brian. *The Obligation toward the Difficult Whole: Postmodernist Long Poems*. U of Alabama P, 2004.
McPherson, Tara. "Designing for Difference." *differences*, vol. 25, no. 1, 2014, pp. 177–88.
McPherson, Tara. *Feminist in a Software Lab: Difference + Design*. Harvard UP, 2018.
Meyerowitz, Joanne, editor. *Not June Cleaver: Women and Gender in Postwar America 1945–1960*. Temple UP, 1994.
Michelis, Angelica. "'Where Bees Pray on Their Knees': Spiritual and Religious Symbolism in Carol Ann Duffy's *The Bees*." *Symbolism: An International Annual of Critical Aesthetics*, vol. 12, no. 13, 2013, pp. 336–51.

Micir, Melanie. *The Passion Projects: Modernist Women, Intimate Archives, Unfinished Lives.* Princeton UP, 2019.
Middlebrook, Diane. *Her Husband: Hughes and Plath—A Marriage.* Penguin, 2003.
Mikulka, Katie. "Sylvia Plath on War." *National Portrait Gallery.* npg.si.edu/blog/sylvia-plath-on-war. Accessed October 5, 2020.
Mildorf, Jarmila and Till Kinzel, editors. *Audionarratology: Interfaces of Sound and Narrative.* De Gruyter, 2016.
Milford, Nancy. "From Gladness to Madness." *The New York Times Book Review*, May 2, 1982, pp. 30–2.
Millay, Edna St. Vincent. "I Shall Forget You Presently, My Dear (Sonnet IV)." Poets.org. Academy of American Poets. https://poets.org/poem/i-shall-forget-you-presently-my-dear-sonnet-iv. Accessed January 29, 2020.
Miller, David and Richard Price, compilers. *British Poetry Magazines 1914–2000: History and Bibliography of "Little Magazines."* The British Library, 2006.
Miller, Ellen. "Sylvia Plath and White Ignorance: Race and Gender in 'The Arrival of the Bee Box.'" *Janus Head*, vol. 10, no. 1, 2007, pp. 137–55.
Mitchell, Margaret. *Gone with the Wind.* 1936. Penguin, 2019.
Mitchell, Paul. *Sylvia Plath: The Poetry of Negativity.* Universitat De València, 2011.
Miyatsu, Rose. "'Hundreds of People Like Me': A Search for a Mad Community in *The Bell Jar.*" *Literatures of Madness: Disability Studies and Mental Health*, edited by Elizabeth J. Donaldson, Palgrave Macmillan, 2018, pp. 51–69.
Montefiore, Jan. *Feminism and Poetry: Language, Experience, Identity in Women's Writing.* Pandora, 1987.
Moore, Honor. "Introduction." *Poems from the Women's Movement*, edited by Honor Moore, Library of America, 2009.
Moore, Honor. *Poems from the Women's Movement*, Library of America, 2009.
Moores, Shaun. "From 'Unruly Guest' to 'Good Companion': The Gendered Meanings of Early Radio in the Home." *Women and Radio: Airing Differences*, edited by Caroline Mitchell, Routledge, 2000.
Morales, Connie. "Women's Oppression: Cortejas." *RAT*, June 5–19, 1970, p. 5.
Morgan, Robin. "Goodbye to All That." *RAT*, February, 9–23, 1970, pp. 6–7.
Morgan, Robin, editor. *Sisterhood Is Powerful: An Anthology of Writings from the Women's Liberation Movement.* Random House, 1970.
Morse, Donald E. "Sylvia Plath and the Trope of Vulnerability." *Hungarian Journal of English and American Studies (HJEAS)*, vol. 6, no. 2, 2000, pp. 77–90.
Morrison, Toni. *The Origin of Others.* Harvard UP, 2017.
Morrison, Toni. *Playing in the Dark: Whiteness and the Literary Imagination.* Random House, 2007.
Moses, Kate. "Appendix: The Oral Archive." *The Unraveling Archive: Essays on Sylvia Plath*, edited by Anita Helle, U of Michigan P, 2007, pp. 269–74.
Moses, Kate. "Sylvia Plath's Voice, Annotated." *The Unraveling Archive: Essays on Sylvia Plath*, edited by Anita Helle, U of Michigan P, 2007, pp. 89–120.
Mugglestone, Lynda. *Talking Proper: The Rise and Fall of the English Accent as a Social Symbol.* Oxford UP, 2007.
Murphy, Jerome Ellison. "God's Lioness and God's Negress: The Feminine and the Figure of the African-American in Plath." *Plath Profiles*, vol. 5, Summer 2012, pp. 169–78. https://scholarworks.iu.edu/journals/index.php/plath/article/view/4380/4001. Accessed June 30, 2021.

Murphy, Kate. *Behind the Wireless: A History of Early Women at the BBC*, Palgrave Macmillan, 2016, pp. 83–114.
Nance, Guinevara and Judith Jones. "Doing Away with Daddy: Exorcism and Sympathetic Magic in Plath's Poetry." *Critical Essays on Sylvia Plath*, edited by Linda Wagner, G. K. Hall and Company, 1984, pp. 124–9.
Nancy, Jean-Luc. *Listening*. Translated by Charlotte Mandell, Fordham UP, 2009.
Narbeshuber, Lisa. "The Poetics of Torture: The Spectacle of Sylvia Plath's Poetry." *Canadian Review of American Studies*, vol. 34, no. 2, 2004, pp. 185–203.
Nelson, Deborah. "Plath, History and Politics." *The Cambridge Companion to Sylvia Plath*, edited by Jo Gill, Cambridge UP, 2006, pp. 21–35.
Nelson, Deborah. *Pursuing Privacy in Cold War America*. Columbia UP, 2002.
Newby, P. H. "The Third Programme." *BBC Lunchtime Lectures*. BBC Publications, 1965.
"The Next Coat Shapes in Fashion–In Fur." *Vogue*, August 1, 1953, pp. 146–7.
Nikolajeva, Maria. *Children's Literature Comes of Age: Toward a New Aesthetic*. Garland, 1996.
"Nine Nice Reasons for Staying Home." *Good Housekeeping*, November 1957, pp. 86–93.
Nodelman, Perry. "Decoding the Images: How Picture Books Work." *Understanding Children's Literature*, edited by Peter Hunt. Taylor and Francis, 2014, pp. 128–39.
Nodelman, Perry. *The Pleasures of Children's Literature*. Longman, 1992.
Norman, Dawn Crowell. "Beauty Prescriptions with a Man in Mind." *Ladies' Home Journal*, November 1954, p. 187.
Northway, Lorraine. "The History of Modern Stenography." https://www.stenoworks.com/pages/History-Of-Steno.html. Accessed July 22, 2020.
"Nylon Tricot Lingerie in Leopard Design & 'Little Princess' Cotton Quilt Robe." Mandel Brothers Advertisement. *Chicago Daily Tribune*, December 13, 1953, p. 45.
Oakley, S. P. "Dodds' Bacchae." *Classical Commentaries: Explorations in a Scholarly Genre*, edited by Christopher Stray and Christina Shuttleworth Kraus, Oxford UP, 2016.
O'Brien, Edna. "The Art of Fiction." Interview with Shusha Guppy, *The Paris Review*, issue 92, Summer 1984. https://www.theparisreview.org/interviews/2978/the-art-of-fiction-no-82-edna-obrien. Accessed June 30, 2021.
O'Brien, Edna. *Country Girl: A Memoir*. Little, Brown and Company, 2013.
O'Brien, Edna. Letter to Elizabeth Sigmund. February 17, 1986, Box 1, Folder 26, Elizabeth Sigmund collection of photographs and correspondence related to Sylvia Plath (MRBC-MS-00447), Smith.
O'Brien, Edna. Letter to Rachel MacKenzie. August 25, 1962, NYPL.
O'Brien, Edna. "*Sylvia Plath*, MS and TS." Box 76, Folder 5, Edna O'Brien Papers, MSS 855, Rose.
O'Brien, Edna. "*Sylvia Plath* Notebook." Box 76, Folder 4, Edna O'Brien Papers, MSS 855, Rose.
O'Brien, Edna. *Virginia: A Play*. Harcourt Brace Jovanovich, 1981.
O'Leary, Nora. "Bright Ideas ... for Mother and Daughter." *Ladies' Home Journal*, February 1958, p. 80.
O'Rourke, Meghan. "Subject Sylvia." *Poetry*, vol. 183, no. 6, March 2004, pp. 335–44.
Orwell, George. "Poetry and the Microphone." *Radiotext(e)*, edited by Neil Strauss. (Semiotext(e), 1993), pp. 165–71 (166–9). Originally published as *New Saxon Pamphlet* March 3, 1945.
Peel, Robin. "Body, Word and Photograph: Sylvia Plath's Cold War Collage and the Thalidomide Scandal." *Journal of American Studies*, vol. 40, no. 1, 2006, pp. 71–95.
Peel, Robin. *Writing Back: Sylvia Plath and Cold War Politics*. Fairleigh Dickinson UP, 2002.

Pelt, April. "Esther's Sartorial Selves: Fashioning a Feminine Identity in *The Bell Jar*." *Plath Profiles*, vol. 8, 2015, pp. 13–24.
Pereira, Malin Walther. "Be(e)ing and 'Truth': Tar Baby's Signifying on Sylvia Plath's Bee Poems." *Twentieth Century Literature*, vol. 42, no. 4, 1996: 526–34. doi: 10.2307/441881. Accessed June 30, 2021.
Perloff, Marjorie. "The Two *Ariel*s: The (Re)Making of the Sylvia Plath Canon.'" *American Poetry Review*, vol. 13, no. 6, November/December 1984, pp. 10–18.
Plath, Aurelia. Annotation. Letter from Sylvia Plath, January 4, 1952, Lilly.
Plath, Aurelia. Annotation. Letter from Sylvia Plath, May 11, 1952, Lilly.
Plath, Aurelia. Annotation. Letter from Sylvia Plath, April 29–30, 1960, Lilly.
Plath, Aurelia. Annotation. *McCall's*, October 1972, Smith.
Plath, Aurelia. "Letter to Frances McCullough." April 14, 1971, Box 29, Folder 29, Smith.
Perry, Laura. "Plath and the Culture of Hygiene." *Plath in Context*, edited by Tracy Brain. Cambridge UP, 2019, 191–200.
"Plath." File 1. BBC Written Archive, Reading. Plath, Aurelia Schober. Annotation. Letter from Sylvia Plath, November 4, 1950, Lilly.
Plath, Sylvia. *Ariel*. Harper & Row, 1966.
Plath, Sylvia. *Ariel: The Restored Edition*. Harper Perennial, 2004.
Plath, Sylvia. *The Bed Book*. Illustrated by Emily Arnold McCully. Harper and Row, 1976.
Plath, Sylvia. *The Bed Book*. Illustrated by Quentin Blake. Faber and Faber, 1990.
Plath, Sylvia. "Bees." *The Atlantic*, April 1963, pp. 70–1.
Plath, Sylvia. *The Bell Jar*. Harper Perennial, 1999.
Plath, Sylvia. "A Birthday Present." Holograph and Typescript Drafts, September 30, 1962, Box 7, Folder 31, Smith.
Plath, Sylvia. "The Character of Zeus in *Prometheus Bound*," Plath mss. II, Box 13, Folder 4, Lilly.
Plath, Sylvia. *Collected Children's Stories: Sylvia Plath*. Illustrated by David Roberts. Faber and Faber, 2001.
Plath, Sylvia. *The Collected Poems*. Edited by Ted Hughes. Harper & Row, 1981.
Plath, Sylvia. "Edith Sitwell and the Development of Her Poetry." (English paper submitted March 25, 1953). Plath mss. II, Box 10, Folder 7, Lilly. Transcription by Stephanie Luke.
Plath, Sylvia. "Elm" drafts. Box 9, Folder 81, Sylvia Plath Collection, Smith.
Plath, Sylvia. "Falcon Yard" [Notes and Fragments, "Hill of Leopards," and "Venus in the Seventh"]. Boxes 139 and 140, Folders 19, 24, and 11, MSS 644, Ted Hughes Papers, Rose.
Plath, Sylvia. "Fever" drafts. Box 9, Folder 96, Smith.
Plath, Sylvia. "Holograph Notes for English 211: 20th Century, Miss Drew," Box 20, Folder 17, Smith.
Plath, Sylvia. *The It-Doesn't-Matter Suit*. Illustrated by Rotraut S. Berner. Faber and Faber, 1996.
Plath, Sylvia. "The Jailor." *RAT*, vol. 5, no. 9, 1970, p. 11.
Plath, Sylvia. "The Jailor." *Sisterhood Is Powerful: An Anthology of Writings from the Women's Liberation Movement*, edited by Robin Morgan, Random House, 1970, pp. 510–11.
Plath, Sylvia. *Johnny Panic and the Bible of Dreams*. Harper Perennial, 2000.
Plath, Sylvia. *The Journals of Sylvia Plath, 1950–1962*. Edited by Karen V. Kukil, Faber and Faber, 2000.
Plath, Sylvia. "Leaves from a Cambridge Notebook." *Christian Science Monitor*, March 5, 1956, p. 17 and March 6, p. 15.

Plath, Sylvia. Letter to Ruth Beuscher. February 4, 1963, Box 3, Folder 14, Ruth Tiffany Barnhouse Papers, Sophia Smith Collection, SSC-MS-00202, Smith.

Plath, Sylvia. *Letters Home: Correspondence, 1950–1963*. Edited by Aurelia Schober Plath. Harper& Row, 1975.

Plath, Sylvia. *The Letters of Sylvia Plath Volume I: 1940–1956*. Edited by Peter K. Steinberg and Karen V. Kukil, Faber & Faber, 2017.

Plath, Sylvia. *The Letters of Sylvia Plath, Volume II: 1956–1963*. Edited by Peter K. Steinberg and Karen V. Kukil, Faber & Faber, 2018.

Plath, Sylvia. "Mad Girl's Love Song." *Smith Review*, Spring 1953, p. 13.

Plath, Sylvia. "The Magic Mirror: A Study of the Double in Two of Dostoevsky's Novels." 1955. Smith College, English Special Honors Thesis.

Plath, Sylvia. "Modern Tragedy in the Classic Tradition." Plath mss. II, Box 10, Folder 8, Lilly.

Plath, Sylvia. *Mrs. Cherry's Kitchen*. Faber and Faber, 2002.

Plath, Sylvia. "A New Idiom." (English paper submitted May 9, 1951). Box 10, Folder 8, Lilly, Transcription by Amanda Golden.

Plath, Sylvia. "New Poems." Box 6, Folder 16, Smith.

Plath, Sylvia. "Oregonian Original." *New Statesman*, July 6, 1962, p. 660.

Plath, Sylvia. *Poems*. Selected by Carol Ann Duffy. Faber and Faber, 2012.

Plath, Sylvia. "Review: *The Stones of Troy* by C. A. Trypanis." *Gemini*, vol. 2, 1957, p. 102.

Plath, Sylvia. "Second Winter." *Ladies' Home Journal*, December 1958, p. 143.

Plath, Sylvia. *The Spoken Word: Sylvia Plath*. Audio CD, British Library Sound Archive, 2010.

Plath, Sylvia. Submission Lists. Box 14.2, Folder 307, Smith.

Plath, Sylvia. *Sylvia Plath: Drawings*. HarperCollins, 2013.

Plath, Sylvia. "Sylvia Plath." *The Poet Speaks: Interviews with Contemporary Poets Conducted by Hilary Morrish, John Press and Ian Scott-Kilvert*, edited by Peter Orr. Routledge & Kegan Paul, 1966.

Plath, Sylvia. Teaching notes for Edith Sitwell's "Aubade," Box 13, Folder 10, Plath mss. II, Lilly.

Plath, Sylvia. "Ten Poems by Sylvia Plath," *Encounter*, October 1963, pp. 45–52. Available: *Unz Review: An Alternative Media Selection*. http://www.unz.com/print/Encounter/Contents/?Period=1963. Accessed June 30, 2021.

Plath, Sylvia. "Three Women." Cleverdon mss. II, Box 21, Lilly.

Plath, Sylvia. "Three Women." Vol. cviii, Add MS 88589, Alvarez Papers, British Library,

Plath, Sylvia. "Three Women." [radio] 1968, BBC Sound Archives, NP1217R C1, British Library.

Plath, Sylvia. "Two Poems." *Critical Quarterly*, vol. 3, no. 2, June 1961, pp. 140–1, doi:10.1111/j.1467-8705.1961.tb01154.x.

Plath, Sylvia. *The Unabridged Journals of Sylvia Plath 1950–1962: Transcribed from the Original Manuscripts at Smith College*. Edited by Karen V. Kukil. Random House, 2000.

Plath, Sylvia. "Untitled collage, probably 1960." Box 21, Folder 2, Smith.

Plath, Sylvia. "A Walk to Withens." *Christian Science Monitor*, June 6, 1959, p. 12.

Plath, Sylvia. *Winter Trees*. Faber and Faber, 1971.

Poe, Edgar Allan. "The System of Dr. Tarr and Prof. Fether." *Graham's Magazine*, vol. 28, no. 5, 1845, pp. 193–200.

Pollock, Vivian R. "Moore, Plath, Hughes, and 'The Literary Life.'" *American Literary History*, vol. 17, no. 1, 2005, pp. 95–117.

Popova, Maria. "Archives." *Brain Pickings Icon*. www.brainpickings.org/?s=The+it-doesn%27t+matter+suit. Accessed June 30, 2021.

Prendergast, Catherine. "On the Rhetorics of Mental Disability." *Embodied Rhetorics: Disability in Language and Culture*, edited by James C. Wilson and Cynthia Lewiecki-Wilson, Southern Illinois UP, 2001, pp. 45–60.

Presley, Nicola. "Plath and Television." *Sylvia Plath in Context*, edited by Tracy Brain, Cambridge UP, 2019, pp. 147–56, doi:10.1017/9781108556200.015.

Prouty, Olive Higgins. *Home Port*. Houghton Mifflin, 1947.

Radford, Gary P., Marie L. Radford, and Jessica Lingel. "The Library as Heterotopia: Michel Foucault and the Experience of Library Space." *Journal of Documentation*, vol. 71, no. 4, 2015, pp. 733–51.

*Radio Times*. Issue 279, February 1, 1929.

*Radio Times*. Issue 2023, August 16, 1962.

*Radio Times*. "The Weird Ones." Issue 2043, November 1, 1962.

Raine, Kathleen. R19/933/2. November 20, 1947, BBC Written Archive, Reading, UK.

Ranganathan, S. R. *The Five Laws of Library Science*. Madras Library Association, 1931.

Rankine, Claudia. *Citizen: An American Lyric*. Penguin, 2014.

Rankovic, Catherine. "Aurelia Plath Shorthand Transcriptions," 2019. https://epublications.marquette.edu/aureliaplath. Accessed July 1, 2021.

Rankovic, Catherine. "Aurelia S. Plath Shorthand Transcription Table from Correspondence in the Lilly Library Plath Archive Plath mss. II," 2019. *Aurelia Plath Shorthand Transcriptions*. 2. https://epublications.marquette.edu/aureliaplath/2. Accessed July 1, 2021.

Rankovic, Catherine. "Aurelia S. Plath Shorthand Transcription Table from Smith College Mortimer Rare Book Collection." 2019. *Aurelia Plath Shorthand Transcriptions*. 5. https://epublications.marquette.edu/aureliaplath/5/. Accessed July 1, 2021.

Rankovic, Catherine. "I Never Will Need Shorthand: Sylvia Plath and Speedwriting." *Plath Profiles*, vol. 11, 2019.

Reader, Ian and Tony Walter. *Pilgrimage in Popular Culture*. Palgrave Macmillan, 1993.

Rees-Jones, Deryn. *Consorting with Angels: Essays on Modern Women Poets*. Bloodaxe Books, 2005.

Rees-Jones, Deryn, editor. *Modern Women Poets*. Highgreen: Bloodaxe Books, 2005.

Reid, Brenda. "Commissioning Brief." April 18, 1985. BBC WAC_T48_451. BBC Written Archives Centre, Reading, UK.

Reynolds, Kimberley. *Children's Literature: A Very Short Introduction*. Oxford UP, 2011.

Reynolds, Kimberley. *Radical Children's Literature: Future Visions and Aesthetic Transformations in Juvenile Fiction*. Palgrave, 2006.

Rich, Adrienne. "When We Dead Awaken: Writing as Re-Vision." *Adrienne Rich's Poetry and Prose*, edited by Barbara Charlesworth Gelpi and Albert Gelpi, Norton, 1975, pp. 166–77.

Richards, I. A. *Principles of Literary Criticism*, 1924. Edited by John Constable, Routledge, 2001.

Riffaterre, Michael. *Semiotics of Poetry*. Indiana UP, 1984.

Riley, Denise. "Does Sex Have a History? 'Women' and Feminism." *New Formations*, vol. 1, Spring 1987, pp. 35–46.

Roberts, Neil. *Ted Hughes: A Literary Life*. Palgrave Macmillan, 2006.

Rodell, Mary F. "My Name Is Mary!" *Ladies' Home Journal*, January 1950, pp. 42–3.

Rodengen, Jeffrey L. *The Legend of VF Corporation*. Write Stuff Enterprises, 1998.

Rodriguez, Lara Rossana. "The Strains of Confessional Poetry: The Burdens, Blunders, and Blights of Self-Disclosure." CUNY Academic Works, 2016.

Rombauer, Irma S. and Marion Rombauer Becker. *Joy of Cooking*. Bobbs-Merrill, 1953.

Rose, Jacqueline. *The Haunting of Sylvia Plath*. 1991, Harvard UP, 1992.

Rosenstein, Harriet. "Harriet Rosenstein Research Files on Sylvia Plath, 1910–2018." MSS 1489, Rose.
Ross, Karen E. and Virginia Nightingale. *Media and Audiences: New Perspectives*. Open UP, 2003.
Ross, Shawna. "Toward a Feminist Modernist Digital Humanities." *Feminist Modernist Studies*, vol. 1, no. 3, 2018, pp. 211–29.
Rossetti, Christina. "Goblin Market." *The Norton Anthology of English Literature*, edited by Stephen Greenblatt, Carol T. Christ, Catherine Robson, and M. H. Abrams, 8th ed., E, Norton, 2006, pp. 1466–78.
Roth, Philip. "A Conversation with Edna O'Brien." 1984. *Conversations with Edna O'Brien*, edited by Alice Hughes Kersnowski, U of Mississippi P, 2014, pp. 40–8.
Rovito, Maria. "Toward a New Madwoman Theory: Reckoning the Pathologization of Sylvia Plath." *Journal of Literary & Cultural Disability Studies*, vol. 14, no. 3, 2020, pp. 317–32.
Sagar, Keith. *The Laughter of Foxes: A Study of Ted Hughes*. Liverpool UP, 2006.
Saldívar, Toni. *Sylvia Plath: Confessing the Fictive Self*. Peter Lang Publishing, 1992.
Sampson, Fiona. "After Plath: The Legacy of Influence." *Sylvia Plath in Context*, edited by Tracy Brain, Cambridge UP, 2019, pp. 350–9.
Saunders, Frances Stonor. *The Cultural Cold War: The CIA and the World of Arts and Letters*. New Press, 2000.
Schappell, Elissa. "The Mysterious, Anonymous Author Elena Ferrante on the Conclusion of Her Neapolitan Novels." *Vanity Fair*, August 27, 2015. http://www.vanityfair.com/culture/2015/08/elena-ferrante-interview-the-story-of-the-lost-child. Accessed July 3, 2021.
Schulhofer, Stephen. "Reforming the Law of Rape." *Law & Inequality*, vol. 35, no. 2, 2017, pp. 335–52.
"Second Thoughts on the Paris Collections—Fath's Fur-Printed Fleece Coat." *Vogue*, September 15, 1953, pp. 126–7.
"Seize the Land." *RAT*, June 5–19, 1970, p. 21.
Sekula, Allan. "The Body and the Archive." *October*, vol. 39, Winter 1986, pp. 3–64.
Seuss, Dr. *Horton Hatches the Egg*. 1940. HarperCollins Children's Books, 2019.
Sexton, Anne. *All My Pretty Ones*. Houghton Mifflin, 1962.
Sexton, Anne. "The Barfly Ought to Sing." *TriQuarterly*, vol. 7, Fall 1966, p. 92.
Shapley, Olive. *Broadcasting a Life*. Scarlet Press, 1996.
Shakespeare, William. "Shall I Compare Thee to a Summer's Day (Sonnet 18)." Poets.org. Academy of American Poets. https://poets.org/poem/shall-i-compare-thee-summers-day-sonnet-18. Accessed January 29, 2020.
Showalter, Elaine. "Women and the Literary Curriculum." *College English*, vol. 32, no. 8, May 1971, pp. 855–62.
Siddiqi, Asif A. *Challenge to Apollo: The Soviet Union and the Space Race, 1945–1974*. NASA, 2000.
Sigmund, Elizabeth. Letter to Edna O'Brien, February 3, 1986. Box 8, Folder 40, MSS 855, Edna O'Brien Papers, Rose.
*The Silence of the Lambs* [Film]. Dir. Jonathan Demme. Orion Pictures, 1991.
Simpson, Joan Murray, editor. *Without Adam: The Femina Anthology of Poetry*. Femina Books, Ltd., 1968.
Singh, Amardeep. "'Harlem Shadows' (1922) Title Page," https://scalar.lehigh.edu/mckay/media/harlem-shadows-1922-title-page. Accessed July 1, 2021.

Sitwell, Edith. *The Canticle of the Rose, Poems: 1917–1949*. Vanguard, 1949. Former Owner Plath, Smith.
Smart, Billy. "The BBC Television Audience Research Reports, 1957–1979: Recorded Opinions and Invisible Expectations." *Historical Journal of Film, Radio and Television*, vol. 34, no. 3, 2014, pp. 452–62, doi:10.1080/01439685.2014.937187. Accessed July 1, 2021.
Smith, Caroline J. "'The Feeding of Young Women': Sylvia Plath's *The Bell Jar*, *Mademoiselle* Magazine, and the Domestic Ideal." *College Literature*, vol. 37 no. 4, 2010, pp. 1–22. doi:10.1353/lit.2010.0002.
*The Snake Pit*. [Film] Directed by Anatole Litvak. 20th Century Fox, 1948.
*So Close to Life*. [Film] Directed by Ingmar Bergman. Nordisk Tonefilm, 1958.
"Some Suggestions." *Yorkshire Post and Leeds Intelligencer*, March 15, 1937.
Sophocles, *Sophocles* Electra *and Other Plays*. Translated by E. F. Watling. Penguin, 1954. Former Owner Plath, Smith.
Souffrant, Leah. "Mother Delivers Experiment: Poetry of Motherhood: Plath, Derricotte, Zucker, and Holbrook." *WSQ: Women's Studies Quarterly*, vol. 37, no. 2, 2010, pp. 25–41, doi:10.1353/wsq.0.0198. Accessed July 1, 2021.
"SPARQL." *Wikipedia*, Wikimedia Foundation, November 19, 2020, en.wikipedia.org/wiki/SPARQL. Accessed July 1, 2021.
Spender, Dale. *Man Made Language*. Routledge and Kegan Paul Ltd, 1980.
Spigel, Lynn. *Welcome to the Dreamhouse: Popular Media and Postwar Suburbs*. Duke UP, 2001.
Spitz, Marc. *Twee: The Gentle Revolution in Music, Books, Television, Fashion, and Film*. HarperCollins, 2014.
Spivak, Gayatri Chakravorty. "Can the Subaltern Speak?" *Colonial Discourse and Post-Colonial Theory: A Reader*, edited by Patrick Willams and Laura Chrisman, Columbia UP, 1993, pp. 66–111.
"Sputnik 3." *Encyclopedia Astronautica*. www.astronautix.com/s/sputnik3.html. Accessed October 5, 2020.
Stade, George. "Introduction. Nancy Hunter Steiner." *A Closer Look at Ariel*. Harper's Magazine Press, 1973.
"Starfish Prime." *Wikipedia, Wikimedia Foundation*. en.wikipedia.org/wiki/Starfish_Prime. Accessed September 30, 2020.
Starr, Marlo. "Slow Writing: Archival Research in the Digital Age." *PMLA*, vol. 133, no. 1, 2018, pp. 197–8.
Stead, Lisa and Carrie Smith, editors. *The Boundaries of the Literary Archive: Reclamation and Representation*. Routledge, 2017.
Steedman, Carolyn. *Dust*. Manchester UP, 2001.
Steinberg, Peter K. *A Celebration, This Is: A Website for Sylvia Plath*. https://sylviaplathinfo.com. Accessed May 13, 2021.
Steinberg, Peter K. "Putting Sylvia Plath's 'Context' in Context." July 15, 2012. *Sylvia Plath Info*. https://sylviaplathinfo.blogspot.com/2012/07/putting-sylvia-plaths-context-in.html. Accessed July 23, 2021.
Steinberg, Peter K. "'Sincerely Yours': Plath and *The New Yorker*." *Sylvia Plath in Context*, edited by Tracy Brain, Cambridge UP, 2019, pp. 52–62.
Steinberg, Peter K. *Sylvia Plath*. Chelsea House Publishers, 2004.
Steinberg, Peter K. *Sylvia Plath Archival Documents Hub*. www.sylviaplath.info/collections.html. Accessed July 1, 2021.

Sterling, Christopher H. and Cary O'Dell. *The Concise Encyclopedia of American Radio*. Routledge, 2010.
Stevenson, Anne. *Bitter Fame: A Life of Sylvia Plath*. Houghton Mifflin, 1989.
Strangeways, Al. *Sylvia Plath: The Shaping of Shadows*. Associated UP, 1998.
Stray, Christopher. "A Parochial Anomaly: The Classical Tripos 1822–1900." *Teaching and Learning in Nineteenth-Century Cambridge*, edited by Jonathan Smith and Christopher Stray, Boydell Press, 2001.
Stubbs, Naomi J. "What's in It for Me? Student-Faculty Collaboration and Critical Editing." *Teaching Undergraduates with Archives*, edited by Nancy Bartlett et al. Maize Books, 2019, pp. 48–58.
"Success Story: Pleated In." *Vogue*, April 15, 1953, p. 105.
Sullivan, Shannon. "Critical Philosophy of Race." *Critical Philosophy of Race*, vol. 5, no. 2, Special Issue: Race after Obama and Non Racialism, Colour Blindness and Post-Racialism, 2017, pp. 171–82.
*Sylvia*. [Film] Directed by Christine Jeffs. Produced by Alison Owex. Executive Produced by David M. Thompson, Tracey Scoffield, and Robert Jones. Focus Features, 2004.
Szasz, Thomas. "Literature and Medicine." *Literature and Medicine*, vol. 1, no. 1, 1982, pp. 146–63, doi:10.1353/lm.2011.0203. Accessed July 1, 2021.
Teasdale, Sara. *Dark of the Moon*. Macmillan, 1926. Former Owner Plath, Lilly.
*Ted Hughes: Stronger Than Death*. [Documentary] Directed and Produced by Richard Curson Smith. Produced by Lucy Evans. Executive Produced by Ross Wilson and Liz Hartford. BBC, 2015.
Teicher, Craig Morgan. *We Begin in Gladness: How Poets Progress*. Graywolf Press, 2018.
"*Three Women* An Audience Research Report LR/62/1392." BBC Audience Research. R9–6-128, BBC Written Archives Centre, Caversham, UK.
"*Three Women*" Audience Research Reports 1962 and 1968, Cleverdon mss. II, Box 21, Lilly.
"Third Programme Memos." R19/1295/7, BBC Written Archive, Reading, UK.
Travers, P. L. and Mary Shepard. *Mary Poppins*. Houghton Mifflin Harcourt, 2015.
Trotter, David. *Literature in the First Media Age: Britain between the Wars*. Harvard UP, 2013.
Tucker, T. G., translator. *The Choephori of Aeschylus*. Cambridge UP, 1901.
Tuite, Rebecca C. "Plath and Fashion." *Sylvia Plath in Context*, edited by Tracy Brain, Cambridge UP, 2019, pp. 125–36.
Tuite, Rebecca C. "Sleepwear in Hollywood Film and Television, and the US Sleepwear Industry, 1945–c.1977." PhD diss., Bard Graduate Center, New York City, forthcoming 2021.
Tuite, Rebecca C. Telephone Conversation with Janet Rafferty, September 18, 2017.
Tunstall, Lucy. "Plath and the Lyric." *Sylvia Plath in Context*, edited by Tracy Brain, Cambridge UP, 2019, pp. 94–104.
"TV or Not TV." [TV program] *The Honeymooners*, season 1, episode 1, CBS, October 1, 1955.
Twiddy, Ian. "Plath and the Pastoral." *Sylvia Plath in Context*, edited by Tracy Brain, Cambridge UP, 2019, pp. 104–14.
"Up ... in Ceylon." *RAT*, June 5–19, 1970, p. 10.
VanDette, Emily. "The Literature Classroom, College Library, and Reading Publics: Building Collaborative Critical Reading Networks." *Service Learning and Literary Studies English*, edited by Laurie Grobman and Roberta Rosenberg, MLA, 2015, pp. 54–67.
Van Dyne, Susan R. *Revising Life: Sylvia Plath's Ariel Poems*. U of North Carolina P, 1994.

Vellacott, Philip, translator. *Aeschylus, The Oresteian Trilogy*. Penguin, 1956. Former Owner Plath, Smith.
Verma, Neil. *Theater of the Mind: Imagination, Aesthetics, and American Radio Drama*. U of Chicago P, 2012.
Vice, Sue. "Sylvia Plath: *Ariel*." *A Companion to Twentieth-Century Poetry*, edited by Neil Roberts, Blackwell Publishing, 2003, pp. 500–12.
Voegelin Salomé. *Listening to Noise and Silence: Towards a Philosophy of Sound Art*. Bloomsbury, 2013.
Voegelin Salomé. *The Political Possibility of Sound: Fragments of Listening*. Bloomsbury Academic, 2019.
Voyce, Stephen. "The Women's Liberation Movement: A Poetic for a Common World," *Poetic Community: Avant-Garde Activism and Cold War Culture*, U of Toronto P, 2013, pp. 162–201.
Vuong, Ocean. *On Earth We're Briefly Gorgeous: A Novel*. Penguin Press, 2019.
Wagner, Erica. *Ariel's Gift: Ted Hughes, Sylvia Plath and the Story of* Birthday Letters. Faber and Faber, 2000.
Wagner-Martin, Linda W. *Sylvia Plath: A Literary Life*. 2nd edn. Palgrave Macmillan, 2003.
Wagner-Martin, Linda W. *Sylvia Plath: A Biography*. St. Martin's Press, 1987.
Walker, Andrew. "Plath and the Radio Drama." *Sylvia Plath in Context*, edited by Tracy Brain, Cambridge UP, 2019, pp. 42–50.
Ward, Mary Jane. *Counterclockwise*. Henry Regnery, 1969.
Ward, Mary Jane. *The Snake Pit*. Random House, 1946.
Watling, Edward. *Sophocles* Electra *and Other Plays*. Penguin, 1954.
"Weather Retort." *RAT*, June 5–19, 1970, p. 5.
Wellington, L. Internal BBC Memo, R19/280/7, Drama Policy File 5b, BBC Written Archives Centre, Reading, UK.
"What Made You Stay?" [radio] 1962. BBC Sound Archives 27571. British Library.
"What Transatlantic Visitors Buy in the USA." *Vogue*, February 1, 1959, p. 172.
White, Gillian. *Lyric Shame: The "Lyric" Subject of Contemporary American Poetry*. Harvard UP, 2014.
White, Heather Cass. "Scholarly Editing Now." Presentation. Modern Language Association Convention. Seattle, WA. January 11, 2020.
Whitehead, Kate. The Third Programme: A Literary History. Oxford UP, 1989.
Whittington, Ian. "Archaeologies of Sound: Reconstructing Louis MacNeice's Wartime Radio Publics." *Modernist Cultures*, vol. 10, no. 1, 2015, pp. 44–61, doi:10.3366/mod.2015.0097. Accessed July 1, 2021.
Wiese, Otis Lee. "Live the Life of McCall's." *McCall's*, May 1954, p. 27.
Wilbur, Richard. *New and Collected Poems*. Harcourt Brace Jovanovich, 1988.
Willoughby, Vanessa. "Black Girls Don't Read Sylvia Plath." *The Hairpin*, November 2014. https://medium.com/the-hairpin/black-girls-dont-read-sylvia-plath-1a8034c986b6. Accessed June 15, 2021.
Wilson, Andrew. *Mad Girl's Love Song: Sylvia Plath and Life before Ted*. 2013. Scribner, 2015.
Wilson, Andrew. "Searching for Sylvia." *The Sunday Times*, February 17, 2013.
Wimsatt, William K. "The Concrete Universal." *The Verbal Icon: Studies in the Meaning of Poetry*, 1947, William K. Wimsatt and Monroe C. Beardsley, U of Kentucky P, 1954.
Winder, Elizabeth. *Pain, Parties, Work: Sylvia Plath in New York, Summer 1953*. HarperCollins, 2013.

Witchell, Alex. "After 'The Bell Jar,' Life Went On: A Reunion of *Mademoiselle*'s Class of '53." *The New York Times*, June 22, 2003, p. ST1.
Wood, Clement, editor. *The Complete Rhyming Dictionary and Poet's Craft Book*. Garden City Books, 1936. Former owner Plath, Smith.
Wood, Summer. "Freedom of 'Choice': Parsing the Word That Defined a Generation." *The Women's Movement Today: An Encyclopaedia of Third-Wave Feminism*, edited by Leslie L. Heywood, Greenwood Press, 2006, pp. 422–5.
Woods, Marjorie Binford. "Mary Jane Ward Declares Her Book Not Autobiography." *The Indianapolis Star*, July 14, 1946, p. 65.
Wormald, Mark. "Irishwards: Ted Hughes, Freedom and Flow." *The Ted Hughes Society Journal*, vol. 6, issue 2, 2017, pp. 58–77.
Yeats, W. B. *Collected Poems of W. B. Yeats*. Macmillan and Co., Limited, 1952. Former Owner Plath, Smith.
Yeats, W. B. *The Collected Works of W. B. Yeats Volume II: The Plays*. Edited by David R. Clark and Rosalind E. Clark. Scribner, 2001.
Yeats, W. B. *A Vision*. Macmillan, 1962.
Young, Louise B. *Earth's Aura*. Knopf, 1977.
"You're the Prettiest Mommy on Earth." *Good Housekeeping*, October 1941, p. 56.
Zajdel, Melody. "Apprenticed in a Bible of Dreams: Sylvia Plath's Short Stories." *Sylvia Plath: Modern Critical Views*, edited by Harold Bloom, Chelsea House, 1989, pp. 149–61.
"Zero-Gravity Plane on Final Flight." *Nasa*. www.nasa.gov/vision/space/preparingtravel/kc135onfinal.html. Accessed September 18, 2020.
Zhang, Jenny. "They Pretend to Be Us while Pretending We Don't Exist," *Buzzfeed.com*. https://www.buzzfeed.com/jennybagel/they-pretend-to-be-us-while-pretending-we-dont-exist. Accessed February 19, 2016.
Zuba, Jesse. "'Poets of the First Book, Writers of Promise': Beginning in the Era of the First Book Prize." *American Literature*, vol. 82, no. 4, December 2010, pp. 753–78.

# INDEX

"9 Willow Street" (Hughes, T.) 80n11
"55 Eltisley" (Hughes, T.) 80n11

"The Abortion" (Sexton, A.) 192
Abrams, M. H.
   (ed.) *The Norton Anthology of English*
      *Literature* 127
*Action Comics* 234
Adcock, Fleur 204, 207–8
   *The Faber Book of 20th Century Women's*
      *Poetry* 208
"Admonitions" (Plath, S.) 66, 157
"Aerialist" (Plath, S.) 60n25
Aeschylus 9, 139–42, 149–51
   *Agamemnon* 141, 149, 151–2
   *The Choephori* 148–9
   *Oresteia* 149–51
   *The Oresteian Trilogy* 139, 148–9, 151
*Aeschylus, Agamemnon* (Fraenkel, E.) 149
*Aeschylus, The Oresteian Trilogy*
   (tr. Vellacott, P.) 139n1, 148–50,
      151n38
African American 11–12, 95, 103–4, 107
"After Plath: The Legacy of Influence"
   (Sampson, F.) 176
*Agamemnon* (Aeschylus) 141, 149, 151–2
*The Age of Anxiety* (Auden, W. H.) 202
Alighieri, Dante 177, 301
   *The Divine Comedy* 177
"All the Dead Dears" (Plath, S.) 56–8
*All My Pretty Ones* (Sexton, A.) 192
Allen, Woody 26
   *Annie Hall* 26
*Alternative Values: Poems & Paintings*
   (Hughes, F.) 294
Alvarez, Al 53, 60, 60n25, 195–6, 248, 282
   "Sylvia Plath: An Exchange" 283
Amichai, Yehuda 292, 294–5
   *Eye Examination* 295
   *Poems* 292
   *Selected Poems* 292
Amis, Kingsley 147
"Among the Bumblebees" (Plath, S.) 107

"Among the Narcissi" (Plath, S.) 81, 82n13
*Anarchy and Art: From the Paris Commune to*
   *the Fall of the Berlin Wall* (Antliff, A.)
      270, 276
Anderson, Benedict 252
Anderson, Jane V. 45, 304
Anderson, Lee 98n3, 160
Anderson, Linda 281, 283
   "Introduction: Poetry, Theory, Archives"
      283
Anderson, Sherwood 105
Andrews, Maggie 245n4, 252
   *Domesticating the Airwaves: Broadcasting,*
      *Domesticity and Femininity* 245n4, 251
Anglo-American 20, 65, 200, 207
*Anne Sexton's Confessional Poetics* (Gill, J.) 8
*Annie Hall* (Allen, W.) 26
*Annotating Modernism: Marginalia and*
   *Pedagogy from Virginia Woolf to the*
   *Confessional Poets* (Golden, A.) 9, 86,
      140n5, 142n10, 145n17, 155, 202, 223
Antliff, Allan 270, 276
   *Anarchy and Art: From the Paris Commune*
      *to the Fall of the Berlin Wall* 270, 276
*Aphra* 268
"Appendix: The Oral Archive" (Moses, K.) 8n14
"The Applicant" (Plath, S.) 98, 116, 208, 271
*Ariel* (Plath, S.) 1, 7, 9, 11, 19, 21, 26–7, 81,
   83–4, 90, 94, 96, 98, 101, 125, 131–2,
   152, 154, 161–2, 164, 169, 171,
   178–83, 186, 188, 191, 204, 206–7,
   213, 248, 253–4, 260, 271, 276, 292
"Ariel" (Plath, S.) 28, 55, 65–6, 71, 93, 96–8,
   100, 108, 179–80, 182, 206–7, 286–7
"*Ariel* and Other Poems" (Britzolakis, C.) 180,
   182, 204, 283
*Ariel: The Restored Edition* (Plath, S.) 1–2,
   180–3, 271, 314
"Ariel Satellite Is Still Working" (Article in
   *The Times*) 66
*Ariel's Gift: Ted Hughes, Sylvia Plath and the*
   *Story of* Birthday Letters (Wagner, E.)
      170, 173

# INDEX

Aristotle 140–1
Arnold, Matthew 105
   "The Forsaken Merman" 105
"The Arrival of the Bee Box" (Plath, S.) 25, 28, 91, 94, 96, 98, 109, 164, 179, 205–6, 208, 235
*The Art of Confession: The Performance of Self from Robert Lowell to Reality* (Grobe, C.) 8
"The Art of Radio in Britain 1922–1966" (Cleverdon, D.) 9, 257–9
*Astrophil and Stella* (Sidney, P.) 178
Athanasiou-Krikelis, Lissi 5
Atkinson, Kate 243
   *Transcription* 243
Atkinson, Ti-Grace 273
*The Atlantic* 205
"Aubade" (Sitwell, E.) 202
Auden, W. H. 6, 153–4, 164, 202–5, 227
   *The Age of Anxiety* 202
   "In Memory of W. B. Yeats" 164
   "Yeats as an Example" 153–4
"Aurelia Plath's Shorthand Transcriptions" (Rankovic, C.) 222
*Aurora Leigh* (Browning, E.) 178
Axelrod, Steven Gould 2, 95, 101, 161n4, 167n1, 238, 274–5, 290n5
   "The Mirror and the Shadow: Plath's Poetics of Self-Doubt" 167n1, 238
   *Sylvia Plath: The Wound and the Cure of Words* 2, 95, 101, 161n4, 256, 274–5

*Bacchae* (Euripides) 139n1, 142–3, 142n11, 143n14, 148
*The Bacchae of Euripides. The Greek Text Performed at Cambridge at the Arts Theatre 20–24 February, 1956, by Members of the University, with an English Prose Translation Made for the Cambridge Performance of 1930* (Lucas, D. W.) 142n9, 143
Bachelard, Gaston 5, 79
   *The Poetics of Space* 79
"Back from Hanoi" (article in *RAT*) 271
Badia, Janet 7, 18, 276
   "The 'Priestess' and Her 'Cult': Plath's Confessional Poetics and the Mythology of Women Readers" 276
   *Sylvia Plath and the Mythology of Readers* 18
Balcon, Jill 244, 244n1, 246, 250–1, 258n5
"Balloons" (Plath, S.) 21, 99

Baltzell, Jane 187
Banister, Rodney 246
Barai, Aneesh 111, 117, 120
   "Speaking the Space between Mother and Child: Sylvia Plath, Julia Kristeva, and the Place of Children's Literature" 111
Barba, Sharon
   (ed.) *Rising Tides: Twentieth-Century American Women Poets* 268
Barbizon Hotel 31–2, 35–6
"The Barfly Ought to Sing" (Sexton, A.) 187
Bark, Anne Voss
   *West Country Fly Fishing* 179
Barnard, Stephen 251
Barnes, George 250
"Barren Woman" (Plath, S.) 181
Baskin, Leonard 179
Bassnett, Susan 233
Bate, Jonathan 175, 183
Bayley, Sally 1n3, 34
   (ed.) *Eye Rhymes: Sylvia Plath's Art of the Visual* 1, 18, 37
   (ed.) *Representing Sylvia Plath* 1n3
   "Sylvia Plath and the Costume of Femininity" 34–5, 34n10
BBC archives 246, 309n7
*The BBC and National Identity in Britain, 1922–1953* (Hajkowski, T.) 246n7
BBC Written Archive 8, 243–5, 244n1, 249n10, 255n1, 256, 279n3–4, 309
*BBC Yearbook 1947* 257
"On the Beach with Sylvia Plath" (Gilbert, S.) 182
Beam, Alex 240
   *Gracefully Insane: The Life and Death of America's Premier Mental Hospital* 240
"Beauty Prescriptions with a Man in Mind" (Norman, D.) 38
Becker, Jillian 134–5
   *Giving Up: The Last Days of Sylvia Plath* 134–5
Becker, Marion Rombauer 127
   *Joy of Cooking* 4, 127–8, 131
"The Bed Book" (Plath, S.) 5, 111–15, 112n4, 114n7, 122–4
Beddow, Di 5
"The Bee Carol" (Duffy, C.) 207
"The Bee God" (Hughes, T.) 98
"The Bee Meeting" (Plath, S.) 163–4, 179, 205–6
"The Bee Oracles" (Sitwell, E.) 10, 200, 204–7
"Bee in the Spirit" (Sitwell, E.) 206

"Be(e)ing and 'Truth': Tar Baby's Signifying on Sylvia Plath's Bee Poems" (Pereira, M.) 253n13
"The Bee-Keeper" (Sitwell, E.) 204–5
"The Beekeeper's Daughter" (Plath, S.) 28, 98, 205
*The Bees* (Duffy, C.) 199, 204, 206
"Bees" (Duffy, C.) 206
*Before Midnight* (Linklater, R.) 26
*Behind the Wireless: A History of Early Women at the BBC* (Murphy, K.) 245n4
Behn, Aphra 207
*The Bell Jar* (Plath, S.) 1, 4, 11, 31, 34, 41, 43, 46–9, 51, 70, 78, 84, 109, 111, 125, 127, 130, 132–4, 191–2, 202, 212–13, 218, 223, 241, 283–4, 300, 302, 304
Bell, Michael Mayerfeld 77, 80–1
"The Ghosts of Place" 77, 81
*Benito Cereno* (Melville, H.) 274
Benotti, Dorothy 247
*Beowulf* 177
"Berck-Plage" (Plath, S.) 81, 82n13, 179–80, 182
Bergman, Ingmar 191, 191n2, 249, 255, 260, 260n8
*Brink of Life* 249, 260
*So Close to Life* 191, 249, 260n8
Berke, Nancy 268
"The World Split Open: Feminism, Poetry, and Social Critique" 268
Berle, Milton 236–7
Berman, Jeffrey 17
*Surviving Literary Suicide* 17
Berner, Rotraut S. 112
Bernikow, Louise 207
*The World Split Open: Four Centuries of Women Poets in England and America, 1552–1950* 207
Beuscher, Ruth 65, 130, 160, 216, 226, 226n5, 229, 300–1, 303–4, 313, 313n21
"Beyond *Letters Home*: Plath's Unabridged Correspondence" (Kukil, K.) 201
*Birthday Letters* (Hughes, T.) 54–6, 58n18, 61n29, 80–1, 80n11, 93, 161, 165–6, 170, 173–4, 179, 186, 292
"A Birthday Present" (Plath, S.) 21, 132, 301, 301n1
Bishop, Elizabeth 2, 23, 104
*Bitter Fame: A Life of Sylvia Plath* (Stevenson, A.) 134–6, 183, 282, 299, 308
Björneborn, Lennart 86–7

"Marginalia as Message: Affordances for Reader-to-Reader Communication" 86–7, 89
"Black Coat" (Hughes, T.) 175
Black Panthers 267, 269, 269n6
"Black Rook in Rainy Weather" (Plath, S.) 58, 60, 255
"Blackberrying" (Plath, S.) 97
Blake, Quentin 112
Blake, William 158
"Tiger, Tiger" 158
*The Bloodaxe Book of Contemporary Women Poets: Eleven British Writers* (ed. Couzyn, J.) 10, 199, 208
Bloom, Emily C. 8
*The Wireless Past: Anglo-Irish Writers and the BBC, 1931–1968* 8
Bloom, Harold 101
*Bloom's Major Poets: Sylvia Plath* 101
*Bloom's Major Poets: Sylvia Plath* (Bloom, H.) 101
"The Blue Flannel Suit" (Hughes, T.) 170
"Body, Word, and Photograph" (Plath, S.) 64
Boland, Eavan 60, 61n28, 204
Bontempo, Barbara T. 296
"Enriching Arts & Humanities through Service-Learning" 296
"Book Ends" (article in *The New York Times Book Review*) 307, 307n2, 314
Booth, Philip 303
"From the Bottom of the Pool: Sylvia Plath's Last Poems" (Kendall, T.) 73
Borges, Jorge Luis 83, 89n13
"The Library of Babel" 83, 89n13
Bowen, Elizabeth 8
Bowles, Jane 194, 197
Bradstreet, Anne 207
Brain, Tracy 6–7, 18, 21, 37, 40, 58, 61, 64, 214, 220–2, 248, 294
*The Other Sylvia Plath* 18, 37, 37n18, 40, 48n6, 55n8, 58, 61, 64, 180, 214, 220, 248
(ed.) *Representing Sylvia Plath* 1n3
"Sylvia Plath and You" 21
"Sylvia Plath's Letters and Journals" 219n1, 222, 294
Brake, Laurel 270
Brandes, Rand 183–4
"Ted Hughes: *Crow*" 183–4
"Breaking the Rules of the Game: Changing the Narrative of Sylvia Plath and Assia Wevill" (Exhibition) 294

Bridson, D. G. 257
Briggs, Asa 258
  *The History of Broadcasting in the United Kingdom* 244n3
Brill, A. A.
  (tr.) *The Interpretation of Dreams* 148
*Brink of Life* (Bergman, I.) 249, 260; See also So Close to Life
British Broadcasting Corporation 3, 8, 26–7, 188, 191, 241, 243–8, 250–60, 263, 265, 275, 279, 302, 309
*British Poetry Magazines 1914–2000: History and Bibliography of "Little Magazines."* (Miller, D.; Price, R.) 246n6–7
*British Radio Drama* (Drakakis, J.) 261
Britzolakis, Christina 11, 143n12, 148n28, 204, 233, 236–7
  "*Ariel* and Other Poems" 180, 182, 204
  *Sylvia Plath and the Theatre of Mourning* 143n12, 148n28, 236–7
*Broadcasting Modernism* (eds Cohen, D.; Coyle, M.; Lewty, J.) 8
Brontë, Emily 80
  *Wuthering Heights* 57, 80
Brooke, Rupert 59, 59n23
Brookes, Barbara Lesley 263n11
Brooks, Cleanth 141
Brothers Grimm
  *Snow White and the Seven Dwarfs* 241
*The Brothers Karamazov* (Dostoevsky, F.) 175
Brown, Marcia 35, 300; See also Marcia B. Stern
Browning, Elizabeth Barrett 178
  *Aurora Leigh* 178
Bryant, Marsha 10, 116, 226, 233
  "Plath, Domesticity, and the Art of Advertising" 36, 116
  *Women's Poetry and Popular Culture* 116, 226
*Bucolic Comedies* (Sitwell, E.) 201
"Bucolics" (Plath, S.) 205
Bujon, Anne-Lorraine 168
Bundtzen, Lynda K. 4, 178, 204–5, 205n6, 207, 219n1, 276, 282n9
  *The Other Ariel* 204, 207, 276, 282n9
  *Plath's Incarnations: Woman and the Creative Process* 205n6, 219n1
"Burnt Norton" (Eliot, T. S.) 202
"The Burnt-out Spa" (Plath, S.) 28
Burroway, Janet 187
Bush, Katy Evans

"The Poet Realized: An Interview with Ruth Fainlight" 190
Butler, Judith 271
Butscher, Edward 148n27, 282, 299
  *Sylvia Plath: Method and Madness* 148n27, 282
Buurma, Rachel Sagner 9
  *The Teaching Archive: A New History for Literary Study* 9n15, 141n6
Byers, Mark 281, 283
  "Introduction: Poetry, Theory, Archives" 283

*Cages* (Fainlight, R.) 187
Cambridge 5–6, 8–9, 53–6, 58–62, 103, 105, 128, 139–42, 144–5, 148, 150, 152, 154, 156–7, 159, 165, 167, 169–70, 174–5, 187, 247, 302, 311–12
"Cambridge Collection" (Plath, S.) 53, 53n2, 55n10, 60
*The Cambridge Companion to Sylvia Plath* (ed. Gill, J.) 1n3, 220
*The Cambridge Introduction to Sylvia Plath* (Gill, J.) 33, 105–6, 139n2, 180–2
"Cambridge Manuscript" See "Cambridge Collection"
*The Cambridge Review* 60n25, 311
"Cambridge was our courtship" (Hughes, T.) 54
"Candles" (Plath, S.) 255
*The Canticle of the Rose: Poems 1917–1949* (Sitwell, E.) 10, 200–3, 205
*Capriccio* (Hughes, T.) 292, 294
Carey, John 300
Carey, Michael 160, 162
"Carnival" (Hughes, T.) 185
Carton, Evan 291
*Cathleen Ní Houlihan* (Yeats, W. B.) 162
*A Celebration for Edith Sitwell* (ed. Villa, J.) 200
Chalcot Square 78–9, 190
*Challenge to Apollo: The Soviet Union and the Space Race, 1945–1974* (Siddiqi, A.) 63n2
"Channel Crossing" (Plath, S.) 225
*Chapters in a Mythology: The Poetry of Sylvia Plath* (Kroll, J.) 139n2, 165, 169, 178n1
"The Character of Zeus in *Prometheus Bound*" (Plath, S.) 141
*Charlie and the Great Glass Elevator* (Dahl, R.) 67
Chase, Mary Ellen 302

Chaucer, Geoffrey 58–9, 58n18, 59n20, 125, 301
　"The Wife of Bath's Tale" 58
Chessman, Andrea 268
　*Guide to Women's Publishing* 268
Chester, Laura
　(ed.) *Rising Tides: Twentieth-Century American Women Poets* 268
Chignell, Hugh 249, 256
Child, Julia 127
　*Mastering the Art of French Cooking* 127
childbirth 49, 187, 189, 191, 256, 261
"Childless Woman" (Plath, S.) 100, 267n2
*Children's Literature Comes of Age: Toward a New Aesthetic* (Nikolajeva, M.) 113
*Children's Literature: A Very Short Introduction* (Reynolds, K.) 114n6
de Chirico, Giorgio 142–3, 143n12, 146
　*Colloquio* 142
*The Choephori* (Aeschylus) 148–9
*The Choephori of Aeschylus* (tr. Tucker, T. G) 149, 149n30
Christ, Carol T.
　(ed.) *The Norton Anthology of English Literature* 127
*The Christian Science Monitor* 55, 80n10
Christodoulides, Nephie 111, 115, 117
　*Out of the Cradle Endlessly Rocking: Motherhood in Sylvia Plath's Work* 111
"Chronology of Space Launches" (Krebs, G.) 71
"Cinema Advertising and the Sea Witch 'Lost Island' Film (1965)" (Farmer, R.) 292
*Citizen: An American Lyric* (Rankine, C.) 22
Civil Rights Movement 21, 103
Cixous, Hélène 111
Clark, David R.
　(ed.) *The Collected Works of W. B. Yeats Volume II: The Plays* 161
Clark, Heather 6–7, 56, 155–9, 162, 165, 178, 186, 219, 221, 225, 247, 258, 301
　*The Grief of Influence: Sylvia Plath and Ted Hughes* 7, 56, 147n25, 165, 178n1, 182, 186, 247
　*Red Comet: The Short Life and Blazing Art of Sylvia Plath* 1n3, 48n6, 61n28, 98, 115n8, 140, 147n26, 153–60, 162, 201, 219–21, 258
Clark, Rosalind E.
　(ed.) *The Collected Works of W. B. Yeats Volume II: The Plays* 161
Cleverdon, Douglas 9, 191, 244–5, 247, 255–60, 262–3, 265
　"The Art of Radio in Britain 1922–1966" 9, 257–9
　"A Note on Radio Drama" 259
　"The Radio Play" 259
　"On the Scope of Feature Programmes: Producing for the Third" 257
　"On *Three Women*" 258–60, 262, 265
　"Writing for Radio" 257
*So Close to Life* (Bergman, I.) 191, 249, 260n8; *See also* Brink of Life
clothing 32–4, 37–8, 40, 201, 205, 299
Cloutier, Jean-Christophe 12, 281–2, 287
　*Shadow Archives: The Lifecycles of African American Literature* 3n8, 12, 287
Coats, Karen 122
　"Identity" 122
Cohen, Debra Rae 8
　(ed.) *Broadcasting Modernism* 8
Cohen, Edward 45, 240
Cold War 6, 33, 64–5, 68, 203, 233, 267, 269
*Collected Children's Stories: Sylvia Plath* (Plath, S.) 112, 112n2–3, 116–17, 116n9, 119–24
*The Collected Poems* (Hughes, T., ed. Keegan, P.) 40, 56, 61, 80–1, 93, 98–9, 107, 161, 166–7, 170, 173–6, 179, 183–6, 292, 294
*The Collected Poems* (Plath, S., ed. Hughes, T.) 5, 9–10, 18, 20–2, 24–8, 41, 54–61, 63, 66–72, 75, 78, 80–1, 84, 91, 93–100, 107–9, 132–3, 139, 142–4, 151–2, 154, 156–9, 161, 163–4, 170–2, 174–5, 182, 188–9, 192–4, 201–3, 205–6, 235–8, 249–50, 261–2, 274, 276, 281–2, 284, 287, 292, 295, 301, 304, 315
*The Collected Works of W. B. Yeats Volume II: The Plays* (eds Clark, D.; Clark, R.) 161
Collini, Stefan 140
　"The 'Tragedy' Paper at Cambridge" 140
*Colloquio* (de Chirico, G.) 142
*The Colossus* (Plath, S.) 27, 55, 260, 273n8, 303
"The Colossus" (Plath, S.) 10, 107, 116, 139, 148, 150–2, 192, 267n4, 281–2, 287
"A Comparison" (Plath, S.) 26, 40
*The Complete Poems and Plays* (Eliot, T. S.) 59, 59n21
*The Complete Rhyming Dictionary and Poet's Craft Book* (Wood, C.) 106, 157
Compton, David 304
Compton, Elizabeth 304

*The Concise Encyclopedia of American Radio* (Sterling, C.; O'Dell, C.) 234–5
"The Concrete Universal" (Wimsatt, W.) 140
Connors, Kathleen
   (ed.) *Eye Rhymes: Sylvia Plath's Art of the Visual* 1, 18, 37
Conquest, Robert 147n24
*Consorting with Angels: Essays on Modern Women Poets* (Rees-Jones, D.) 208
"The Contender" (Hughes, T.) 185
"Context" (Plath, S.) 103–4
"The Convergence of the Twain" (Hardy, T.) 166
"Conversation Among the Ruins" (Plath, S.) 142–7, 142n11, 143n12, 147n26, 151–2
"Conversation with Ruth Tiffany Barnhouse" (Kukil, K.) 303, 303n4
*Conversations with Edna O'Brien* (ed. Kersnowski, A.) 280n5, 283
Conway, Jill Ker 299
cooking 34, 116, 118, 126–32, 135
"Cooking to Me Is Poetry" (McGinley, P.) 131
Cooksey, M. A.
   (ed.) *Quick Hits for Service-Learning: Successful Strategies by Award-Winning Teachers* 296
Cooper, Giles 249
"The Corpus of the Madwoman: Toward a Feminist Disability Studies Theory of Embodiment and Mental Illness" (Donaldson, E.) 4n11
*Country Girl: A Memoir* (O'Brien, E.) 280n5, 283
"The Courage of Shutting-Up" (Plath, S.) 179–82, 181n2
"The Couriers" (Plath, S.) 28
Court Green 75, 80n10, 81, 153, 163, 181, 190, 192, 194, 304
Cousteau, Jacques 72
   *The Silent World* 72
Couzyn, Jeni 208
   (ed.) *The Bloodaxe Book of Contemporary Women Poets: Eleven British Writers* 10, 199, 208
Coyle, Michael 8
   (ed.) *Broadcasting Modernism* 8
Crane, Hart 178
Crockett, Wilbury 105, 258
Cross, Rupert (Dr.) 275
*Crow* (Hughes, T.) 7, 178
"Crow and the Birds" (Hughes, T.) 185

"Crow Blacker than Ever" (Hughes, T.) 185
"Crow the Just" (Hughes, T.) 186
*Crow: From the Life and Songs of the Crow* (Hughes, T.) 179
"Crow Tyrannosaurus" (Hughes, T.) 184
*Crow Wakes* (Hughes, T.) 179
"Crowquill" (Hughes, T.) 183
"Crow's Feast" (Hughes, T.) 183
"Crow's First Lesson" (Hughes, T.) 184
"Crow's Song of Himself" (Hughes, T.) 185
"Crow's Theology" (Hughes, T.) 185
"Crow's Undersong" (Hughes, T.) 184
"Crow's Vanity" (Hughes, T.) 185
Crowther, Gail 5, 75n1, 153n1, 221, 283, 309n7
   *These Ghostly Archives: The Unearthing of Sylvia Plath* 5, 61n30, 75n1, 79, 221
   *Three-Martini Afternoons at the Ritz: The Rebellion of Sylvia Plath & Anne Sexton* 283, 303n5
Cuban Missile Crisis 65
"The Cult of Plath" (Schott, W.) 276
Curry, Renée R. 10, 21, 101, 110, 274
   "Daughters of the Dust, the White Woman Viewer, and the Unborn Child" 110
   *White Women Writing White: H. D., Elizabeth Bishop, Sylvia Plath, and Whiteness* 11, 21, 101, 274
"Cut" (Plath, S.) 65n5, 97, 132, 208

"Daddy" (Plath, S.) 87, 95–6, 99–100, 108, 113, 139, 152, 157, 174–5, 178–9, 181–2, 192, 208, 219, 271, 275–6, 286
"Daffodils" (Hughes, T.) 80n11
Dahl, Roald 67
   *Charlie and the Great Glass Elevator* 67
Daiches, David 6
*A Dancer to God: Tributes to T. S. Eliot* (Hughes, T.) 160
*Daring to Be Bad: Radical Feminism in America, 1967–1975* (Echols, A.) 268, 273
*Dark of the Moon* (Teasdale, S.) 212, 214
"Dark Song" (Sitwell, E.) 200–1
"Daughters of the Dust, the White Woman Viewer, and the Unborn Child" (Curry, R.) 110
Davidow, Ann 34
Davie, Donald 147
Davis, Robert Gorham 105
Davison, Peter 282
"Day of Success" (Plath, S.) 39n20, 78, 79n8

"THE DAY OF THE TWENTY-FOUR
    CAKES" (Plath, S.) 126
Dearborn, Emma 212
"Death & Co" (Plath, S.) 28, 267n2
"On Deck" (Plath, S.) 68
"A Declaration of a State of War" (Dohrn, B.)
    272
"On the Decline of Oracles" (Plath, S.)
    143n12
"Decoding the Images: How Picture Books
    Work" (Nodelman, P.) 123
Degen, Monica 77
*Delta* 246
Demme, Jonathan
    *The Silence of the Lambs* 49
"Den of Lions" (Plath, S.) 269n5
DeQuincey, Thomas 175
    "On the Knocking at the Gate in Macbeth"
    175
Derr, Mary 171
Derrida, Jacques 90n14
"The Detective" (Plath, S.) 75, 100
*The Detective Story Hour* (Radio Show) 235
di Prima, Diane 4
"Dialogue En Route" (Plath, S.) 67
"Dick Norton Knew Shorthand" (Rankovic, C.)
    217n13
Dickinson, Emily 23, 105
Didion, Joan 4
"Dirge for the New Sunrise" (Sitwell, E.) 203
"The Disquieting Muses" (Plath, S.) 143n12,
    223
*The Divine Comedy* (Alighieri, D.) 177
"Do Not Go Gentle into that Good Night"
    (Thomas, D.) 258
"Dodds' Bacchae" (Oakley, S. P.) 148
Dohrn, Bernardine 269, 269n6, 272
    "A Declaration of a State of War" 272
    "War: Weather Report" 272
"Doing Away with Daddy: Exorcism and
    Sympathetic Magic in Plath's Poetry"
    (Nance, G.; Jones, J.) 174
*Domesticating the Airwaves: Broadcasting,
    Domesticity and Femininity*
    (Andrews, M.) 245n4, 251
Donaldson, Elizabeth J. 4n11
    "The Corpus of the Madwoman: Toward
    a Feminist Disability Studies Theory of
    Embodiment and Mental Illness" 4n11
Donne, John 67, 68n9
"Donne the Space Man" (Empson, W.) 67
Doolittle, Hilda 261; *See also* H. D.
    "Leda" 261

"The Door" (Hughes, T.) 184
Dostoevsky, Fyodor 105, 169, 194
    *The Brothers Karamazov* 175
"The Double as Immortal Self" (Rank, O.) 169
Dowson, Jane 206–7
*Dr. Jekyll and Mr. Hyde* (Stevenson, R.) 172–3
Dr. Seuss 123, 123n12
Drakakis, John 261
    *British Radio Drama* 261
"A Dream" (Hughes, T.) 161
Dreiser, Theodore 105
Drekmeier, Margot Loungway 244
Drew, Elizabeth 6, 145, 145n17, 154–5, 202
Duffy, Carol Ann 10, 199–200, 203–4, 206–8
    "The Bee Carol" 207
    *The Bees* 199, 204, 206
    "Bees" 206
    "Hive" 206
    "Little Red-Cap" 208
    "A Rare Bee" 206
    *Standing Female Nude* 199
    "Virgil's Bees" 206–7
    "Whoever She Was" 204
Dunbar, William 125
    "Lament for the Makaris, Quhen He Wes
    Sek" 125
    *The Poems of William Dunbar* 125
DuPlessis, Rachel Blau 263
"dying to talk" (Plath, S.) 22
*Dynamic Form: How Intermediality Made
    Modernism* (Lewis, C.) 8

*On Earth We're Briefly Gorgeous* (Vuong, O.) 22
"The Earthenware Head" (Hughes, T.) 56,
    171, 173, 173n2
*Earth's Aura* (Young, L.) 70
"Easter 1916" (Yeats, W. B.) 158, 162
Eberly, Rosa 85, 85n4
Echols, Alice 268, 273
    *Daring to Be Bad: Radical Feminism in
    America, 1967–1975* 268, 273
"Edge" (Plath, S.) 72, 96, 99–100, 152, 170,
    189
"Edith Sitwell and the Development of Her
    Poetry" (Plath, S.) 201
"Editing the Poetry of Sylvia Plath" (Kukil, K.)
    284
Edwards, John 247
"Eisenhower collage" (Plath, S.) 65
Elborn, Geoffrey 199
Electra (archetype) 9, 139, 142, 145, 148,
    150–2
"Electra" (Plath, S.) 150–1

*Electra* (Sophocles) 139, 142
"Electra on Azalea Path" (Plath, S.) 9, 139, 148, 151–2, 182
Eliot, T. S. 6, 59, 59n20, 86, 105, 140–1, 144–7, 145n17, 151–2, 156, 160, 178, 202–3
   "Burnt Norton" 202
   *The Complete Poems and Plays* 59, 59n21
   "The Hollow Men" 202
   *The Love Song of J. Alfred Prufrock* 156
   *Selected Prose of T. S. Eliot* 140–1, 144–6
   "*Ulysses*, Order, and Myth" 145, 145n17
   *The Use of Poetry and the Use of Criticism* 59
   *The Waste Land* 59, 59n20–1, 86, 202–3
Ellis, Jonathan 3, 11
Ellison, Julie 108, 291
   "The New Public Humanists" 291
"Elm" (Plath, S.) 6, 70, 73, 100, 188, 191–5, 193n3, 194n4, 304
Embree, Alice 270
*Emerson: The Basic Writings of America's Sage* (Emerson, R., ed. Lindeman, E. C.) 225
Emerson, Ralph Waldo
   *Emerson: The Basic Writings of America's Sage* 225
Empson, William 67, 68n9
   "Donne the Space Man" 67
*The Encounter* 5, 147, 193, 267–8, 267n2–4, 273n8, 276
Enniss, Stephen C. 7, 126
   (ed.) *"No Other Appetite": Sylvia Plath, Ted Hughes, and the Blood Jet of Poetry* 7, 126
"Enriching Arts & Humanities through Service-Learning" (Bontempo, B.) 296
Enright, D. J. 147n24
Entrikin, Nicholas 77
Entwistle, Alice 248, 250
Esdale, Logan 280
   (ed.) *Ida: A Novel* 280
Eskenazi, Gerald 234
Euripides 139–43, 139n1, 142n11, 143n14, 148
   *Bacchae* 139n1, 142–3, 142n11, 143n14, 148
"To Eva Descending the Stair" (Plath, S.) 156
"Event" (Plath, S.) 28, 208
"Evergreens" (Plath, S.) 312
"Evolution" (Plath, S.) 171
"Examination at the Womb-Door" (Hughes, T.) 185

*Eye Examination* (Amichai, Y., ed. Gutmann, A.) 295
*Eye Rhymes: Sylvia Plath's Art of the Visual* (eds Connors, K.; Bayley, S.) 1, 18, 37
Faas, Ekbert 183
   *Ted Hughes: The Unaccommodated Universe* 179
*The Faber Book of 20th Century Women's Poetry* (Adcock, F.) 208
*The Faerie Queen* (Spenser, E.) 177
Fainlight Interview 188, 190, 192, 194, 196
Fainlight, Ruth (m. Sillitoe) 6, 187–97
   *Cages* 187
   "Jane and Sylvia" 189–90, 192, 194, 196–7
   *Poems: Ruth Fainlight, Ted Hughes, Alan Sillitoe* 179
   "Sapphic Moon" 6, 188, 193
Fajkovic, Muhamed 86
   "Marginalia as Message: Affordances for Reader-to-Reader Communication" 86–7, 89
"Falcon Yard" (Plath, S.) 147n26, 294
Fanthorpe, U. A. 204
Farland, Maria 43
   "Sylvia Plath's Anti-Psychiatry" 43
Farmer, Richard 292
   "Cinema Advertising and the Sea Witch 'Lost Island' Film (1965)" 292
"Fashions for the Nicest Hours of the Day" (article in *Good Housekeeping*) 33n7, 37n18
Faulkner, William 105
Faull, Katherine 285
"Faun" (Plath, S.) 60n24, 61n29
Feaver, Vicki 204
Feinstein, Elaine 204
"Female Author" (Plath, S.) 20, 109
*Feminine Frequencies: Gender, German Radio, and the Public Sphere, 1923–1945* (Lacey, K.) 252n12
*The Feminine Mystique* (Friedan, B.) 102
feminism 4–5, 17, 26, 32, 34, 36, 38, 43, 95, 98–9, 102–3, 108, 111–13, 118, 125, 132, 178, 190–2, 205, 208, 256, 267–73, 276–7, 289–93, 295–6
"The Feminist Periodical Press: Women, Periodical Studies, and Modernity" (Green, B.) 269–70
Ferretter, Luke 43, 48n7, 49, 105, 113, 118, 233, 295
   *Sylvia Plath's Fiction: A Critical Study* 43, 48n7, 113, 118, 233, 295

"Fever 103°" (Plath, S.) 20, 71, 95, 99, 301
*A Few Crows* (Hughes, T.) 179
Fields, Jill
   *An Intimate Affair: Women, Lingerie and Sexuality* 36
"A Fine, White Flying Myth: Confessions of a Plath Addict" (Gilbert, S.) 205n6, 269n5
"Finisterre" (Plath, S.) 96
First World War 170, 259
Fisher, Alfred Young 105
Fiske, John 240–1
*Fixed Stars Govern a Life: Decoding Sylvia Plath* (Gordon-Bramer, J.) 66
Fogarty, Anne 38
   *Wife Dressing* 38
*Forbidden Planet* (Film) (Wilcox, F.) 67
Ford, Karen Jackson 205–6
Ford, Mark 301
*Forms of Expansion: Recent Long Poems by Women* (Keller, L.) 180
"The Forsaken Merman" (Arnold, M.) 105
Forster, E. M. 212, 215
   *Howards End* 212, 215
Foss, Diana 23
Foucault, Michel 89–91
   "What Is an Author?" 90
*Four Crow Poems* (Hughes, T.) 179
Fraenkel, Eduard 149, 150n34
   Aeschylus, *Agamemnon* 149
Fraser, Linda Lussy 250n11, 256n3
   "Technologies of Reproduction: The Maternity Ward in Sylvia Plath's *Three Women* and Ingmar Bergman's *Brink of Life*" 250n11
Frazer, James George 8, 165–9, 174–6
   *The Golden Bough* 8, 165–71, 174, 176
Freeman, Marion 310
Freud, Sigmund 117, 132, 148–50
   *The Interpretation of Dreams* 148
Friedan, Betty 38, 101–2
   *The Feminine Mystique* 102
Friedman, Susan Stanford 180
Fromm, Erich 105
Frost, Laura 105, 276
Fry, Christopher 227
   *The Lady's Not for Burning* 227
Fulbright Scholar 141, 302
"Full Fathom Five" (Plath, S.) 72, 151

Gagarin, Yuri 68–70, 72
Geevarghese, Rebekah 279n1, 280, 284–6, 285n12
   "Revealing the Roots of Sylvia Plath" 280, 282, 284, 286
*Gemini* 145–6
"Gender Politics and the Making of Anthologies: Towards a Theory of Women's Poetry" (González, M.) 245n5, 246
"Getting There" (Plath, S.) 108, 267n2
"The Ghost's Leavetaking" (Plath, S.) 67
"The Ghosts of Place" (Bell, M.) 77, 81
Gielgud, Val 246, 249
Gifford, Terry 179
   "Hughes's Social Ecology" 179
Gilbert, Sandra M. 4, 6, 106, 154, 159–60, 163, 182, 205, 205n6, 238, 269n5
   "On the Beach with Sylvia Plath" 182
   "A Fine, White Flying Myth: Confessions of a Plath Addict" 205n6, 269n5
   *The Madwoman in the Attic: The Woman Writer and the Nineteenth-Century Literary Imagination* 106
   *Still Mad: American Women Writers and the Feminist Imagination, 1950–2020* 4
   "In Yeats' House: The Death and Resurrection of Sylvia Plath" 6, 160, 163, 238
Gill, Jo 1n3, 8, 105–6, 139n2
   *Anne Sexton's Confessional Poetics* 8
   (ed.) *The Cambridge Companion to Sylvia Plath* 1n3, 220
   *The Cambridge Introduction to Sylvia Plath* 33, 105–6, 139n2, 180–2
   (ed.) *Modern Confessional Writing: New Critical Essays* 8
Gilliam, Laurence 257
"Girl's Song" (Yeats, W. B.) 156
*Giving Up: The Last Days of Sylvia Plath* (Becker, J.) 134–5
*The Glass Menagerie* (Williams, T.) 311
Glendinning, Victoria 199
Glynn, Eugene David 239
"Goblin Market" (Rossetti, C.) 127, 202
Goffman, Erving 43–4, 238
   *Stigma: Notes on the Management of a Spoiled Identity* 43
"Gold Coast Customs" (Sitwell, E.) 202
Golden, Amanda 9–10, 19, 86, 105, 155, 199n1, 200, 200n4, 202, 223
   *Annotating Modernism: Marginalia and Pedagogy from Virginia Woolf to the Confessional Poets* 9, 86, 140n5, 142n10, 145n17, 155, 202, 223
   "Sylvia Plath's Teaching and the Shaping of Her Work" 19, 200

*The Golden Bough* (Frazer, J.) 8, 165–71, 174, 176
Gomme, Andor 311
*Gone with the Wind* (Mitchell, M.) 109
Gonne, Maud 162
González, Matilde Martín 245n5, 246
    "Gender Politics and the Making of Anthologies: Towards a Theory of Women's Poetry" 245n5, 246
*Good Housekeeping* 37n18, 38
"Goodbye to All That" (Morgan, R.) 270
Goodspeed-Chadwick, Julie 10, 314n23
Gordon, Avery 76n3, 77–8, 77n5, 81, 81n12
Gordon-Bramer, Julia 66
    *Fixed Stars Govern a Life: Decoding Sylvia Plath* 66
*Gracefully Insane: The Life and Death of America's Premier Mental Hospital* (Beam, A.) 240
Grahn, Judy 277, 277n10
*Granta* 238
Grantchester Meadows 54, 56, 59n23, 173–4
Graves, Cecil 257
    "Letter to Director General Sir Cecil Graves, Literary Output Committee" 257
Graves, Robert 169–70, 174, 187, 190, 257
    *The Meaning of Dreams* 169–70, 257
    *The White Goddess* 174, 190
Green, Barbara 5, 269–71
    "The Feminist Periodical Press: Women, Periodical Studies, and Modernity" 269–70
    *Spectacular Confessions: Autobiography, Performative Activism, and the Sites of Suffrage, 1905–1938* 5, 269–70
Green, Betty 38
    "Your Children Are Looking at You!" 38
*The Green Helmet and Other Poems* (Yeats, W. B.) 161
Greenblatt, Stephen 127
    (ed.) *The Norton Anthology of English Literature* 127
Gregg, John Robert 212
    *Gregg's Shorthand: A Light Line Phonography for the Millions* 212
Gregg shorthand 7, 211–17, 216n10, 218n16, 220n2, 222, 227
*Gregg's Shorthand: A Light Line Phonography for the Millions* (Gregg, J.) 212
*The Grief of Influence: Sylvia Plath and Ted Hughes* (Clark, H.) 7, 56, 147n25, 165, 178n1, 182, 186, 247

Grigson, Geoffrey 257
Grisewood, Harman 246
Grobe, Christopher 8, 103n2
    *The Art of Confession: The Performance of Self from Robert Lowell to Reality* 8
Groszewski, Gillian 6
*The Guardian* 292
Gubar, Susan 4, 21n1, 106
    *The Madwoman in the Attic: The Woman Writer and the Nineteenth-Century Literary Imagination* 106
    *Still Mad: American Women Writers and the Feminist Imagination 1950–2020* 4
*Guide to Women's Publishing* (Joan, P.; Chessman, A.) 268
Guiney, Thomas 275
    "An Idea Whose Time Had Come?: The Creation of a Modern System of Parole in England and Wales, 1960–1968" 275
Gunn, Thom 147
Gutmann, Assia 289n3, 292; See also Assia Wevill
    (ed.) *Eye Examination* 295
    (tr.) *Poems* 292
    (tr.) *Selected Poems* 292

H. D. 178; See also Hilda Doolittle
Habermas, Jurgen 90, 90n15
Hajkowski, Thomas 246n7, 253
    *The BBC and National Identity in Britain, 1922–1953* 246n7
Haley, William 257
Hall, Donald 245
Hammer, Langdon 9, 167n1, 171, 173n2
    "Plath's Lives" 9, 167n1, 171, 173n2
Harding, Jason
    *T. S. Eliot in Context* 160
Hardy, Thomas 105, 166
    "The Convergence of the Twain" 166
Hargrove, Nancy D. 56n14, 57n15–16, 60n26, 142n11, 143n12
*Harlem Shadows* (McKay, C.) 285
*The Hatred of Poetry* (Lerner, B.) 25
*The Haunting of Sylvia Plath* (Rose, J.) 2, 2n6, 63–4, 66, 90, 106, 113, 148n28, 173, 178n1, 220, 225, 233
de Havilland, Olivia 45, 50
*The Hawk in the Rain* (Hughes, T.) 56n13, 61n30, 127, 160, 179
Haworth 75, 80
Hawthorne, Nathaniel 105
Heaney, Seamus 19–20, 26, 154, 162–4

"The Indefatigable Hoof-taps: Sylvia Plath" 19
"Yeats as an Example?" 162–4
Heffernan, Laura 9, 141n6
  *The Teaching Archive: A New History for Literary Study* 9n15, 141n6
Hegel, Georg Wilhelm Friedrich 276
Heinrichs, Frieda Plath 314
Helle, Anita 50n10, 87n10, 279n1, 293
  "Reading Plath Photographs: In and Out of the Museum" 293–4
  (ed.) *The Unraveling Archive: Essays on Sylvia Plath* 2
Helle, June Johnson 314
Hemingway, Ernest 105
Heppenstall, Rayner 257
*Her Husband: Hughes and Plath—A Marriage* (Middlebrook, D.) 7, 118, 171, 178n1
"The Hermit at Outermost House" (Plath, S.) 28
Herodas 145
Hetherington, Kevin 77
Hicklin, Liz 61, 61n29
Hicok, Bethany 5, 11
Hilmes, Michele 252n12, 253, 253n13
  *Radio Voices: American Broadcasting, 1922–1952* 244n2, 252n12, 253n13
*The History of Broadcasting in the United Kingdom* (Briggs, A.) 244n3
"Hive" (Duffy, C.) 206
Hobsbaum, Philip 246
"The Hollow Men" (Eliot, T. S.) 202
Holloway, John 147
The Holocaust 17, 21, 21n1, 129
*Home Port* (Prouty, O.) 213
homemaking 5, 38, 126, 131, 134
Homer 145–6, 204
  *The Iliad of Homer* 145, 146n20, 177
  *The Odyssey* 177
*The Honeymooners* (TV Program) 238
hooks, bell 102–3, 106–7
*Hopalong Cassidy* (TV Series) 236
*Horton Hatches the Egg* (Seuss, Dr.) 123, 123n12
"Hospital Notes" (Plath, S.) 239
*The Hour-Glass* (Yeats, W. B.) 161–2
*Housewives Choice* (Radio Show) 252
Howard, Maureen 215, 308
*Howards End* (Forster, E. M.) 212, 215
Howe, Florence
  (ed.) *No More Masks!: An Anthology of Poems by Women* 268
*Howls and Whispers* (Hughes, T.) 179

*The Hudson Review* 301
Hughes, Carol 212
Hughes, Frieda 2, 39, 78, 131, 134, 136, 182, 188–90, 219, 255, 294, 299–300, 302, 304, 310–14
  *Alternative Values: Poems & Paintings* 294
Hughes, Nicholas 131–2, 134–6, 181, 190, 192, 195, 219, 255, 304
Hughes, Olwyn 27, 213–14, 222, 255, 282, 304
  "Sylvia Plath: An Exchange" 283
Hughes, Ted 5, 7–8, 10, 20, 27, 38–40, 42, 54–6, 58, 60–1, 72, 78, 80–1, 93–4, 98–9, 107, 113–15, 118, 125–32, 134–5, 143, 147, 151, 153–4, 157–62, 165–71, 173–86, 189–90, 192, 195, 199, 204, 211–14, 216, 219–21, 224–6, 236–8, 244, 246–8, 252, 255, 258, 267, 276–7, 286–7, 289–96, 299–304, 307, 312–15
  "9 Willow Street" 80n11
  "55 Eltisley" 80n11
  "The Bee God" 98
  *Birthday Letters* 54–6, 58n18, 61n29, 80–1, 80n11, 93, 161, 165–6, 170, 173–4, 179, 186, 292
  "Black Coat" 175
  "The Blue Flannel Suit" 170
  "Cambridge was our courtship" 54
  *Capriccio* 292, 294
  "Carnival" 185
  (ed.) *The Collected Poems* 5, 9–10, 18, 20–2, 24–8, 41, 54–61, 63, 66–72, 75, 78, 80–1, 84, 91, 93–100, 107–9, 132–3, 139, 142–4, 151–2, 154, 156–9, 161, 163–4, 170–2, 174–5, 182, 188–9, 192–4, 201–3, 205–6, 235–8, 249–50, 261–2, 274, 276, 281–2, 284, 287, 292, 295, 301, 304, 315
  *Collected Poems* 40, 56, 61, 80–1, 93, 98–9, 107, 161, 166–7, 170, 173–6, 179, 183–6, 292, 294
  "The Contender" 185
  *Crow* 7, 178
  "Crow and the Birds" 185
  "Crow Blacker than Ever" 185
  *Crow: From the Life and Songs of the Crow* 179
  "Crow the Just" 186
  "Crow Tyrannosaurus" 184
  *Crow Wakes* 179
  "Crowquill" 183

"Crow's Feast" 183
"Crow's First Lesson" 184
"Crow's Song of Himself" 185
"Crow's Theology" 185
"Crow's Undersong" 184
"Crow's Vanity" 185
"Daffodils" 80n11
*A Dancer to God: Tributes to T. S. Eliot* 160
"The Door" 184
"A Dream" 161
"The Earthenware Head" 56, 171, 173, 173n2
"Examination at the Womb-Door" 185
*A Few Crows* 179
*Four Crow Poems* 179
*The Hawk in the Rain* 56n13, 61n30, 127, 160, 179
*Howls and Whispers* 179
"The Jaguar" 158
(ed.) *The Journals of Sylvia Plath* 126, 307, 308n20
"King of Carrion" 184
"Last Letter" 294
"Law in the Country of Cats" 158
*Lupercal* 179
"Notes on Poems 1956–1963" 182
(tr.) *The Oresteia by Aeschylus in a New Version by Ted Hughes* 151n37
"The Other" 179–81, 181n2, 267n2, 294–5
"The Owl" 61, 61n29
"Perfect Light" 80n11
"A Picture of Otto" 107, 174
"Pike" 313n20
*Poems: Ruth Fainlight, Ted Hughes, Alan Sillitoe* 179
"Red" 80n11, 295
*River* 179
"Robbing Myself" 80n11
"Rules of the Game" 294
"St Botolph's" 58n18, 166
"Sam" 55n11
"The Shot" 40
"Swans" 56n12
"Sylvia Plath: The Evolution of 'Sheep in Fog'" 170
"Sylvia Plath and Her Journals" 131
"Three Legends" 183
*The Wound* 247, 258
"Wuthering Heights" 70, 80, 96
"X" 54, 54n4
"You Hated Spain" 94, 99

Hughes, Walter 182
"Hughes's Social Ecology" (Gifford, T.) 179
"'Hundreds of People Like Me': A Search for a Mad Community in *The Bell Jar*" (Miyatsu, R.) 43
Hunter, Dianne 21
Huws, Daniel 143n12, 175, 314n23

"I Shall Forget You Presently, My Dear (Sonnet IV)" (Millay, E.) 281
*Ida: A Novel* (Stein, G., ed. Esdale, L.) 280
"An Idea Whose Time Had Come?: The Creation of a Modern System of Parole in England and Wales, 1960–1968" (Guiney, T.) 275
"Identity" (Coats, K.) 122
"Ideology in Children's Books" (McCallum, R.; Stephens, J.) 119
*The Iliad of Homer* (Homer, tr. Lattimore, R.) 145, 146n20, 177
"The Indefatigable Hoof-taps: Sylvia Plath" (Heaney, S.) 19
"Insomniac" (Plath, S.) 69, 96, 237–8
*The Interpretation of Dreams* (Freud, S., tr. Brill, A. A.) 148
*An Intimate Affair: Women, Lingerie and Sexuality* (Fields, J.) 36
"Introduction: Poetry, Theory, Archives" (Anderson, L.; Byers, M.; Warner, A.) 283
Ionesco, Eugène 227
  *Rhinocéros* 227
"The It-Doesn't-Matter Suit" (Plath, S.) 111–20, 112n3–4, 114n7, 122, 124

Jackson, H. J. 85, 223
  *Marginalia: Readers Writing in Books* 85, 223
"The Jaguar" (Hughes, T.) 158
"The Jailer" (Jailor) (Plath, S.) 5, 98–9, 267–71, 267n2, 273–4, 273n8, 276–7
Jakacki, Diane 285
James, Henry 105
"Jane and Sylvia" (Fainlight, R.) 189–90, 192, 194, 196–7
Jansson, André 233
Jarrell, Randall 2
Jay, Gregory 291
Jefford, Barbara 250
Jeffs, Christine
  *Sylvia* (Film) 292
Jennings, Elizabeth 147, 245

Jewishness 11, 93, 95–6, 99, 108, 135, 187, 189
Joan, Polly 268
  *Guide to Women's Publishing* 268
"Johnny Panic and the Bible of Dreams" (Plath, S.) 4, 43, 49–51, 65, 239
*Johnny Panic and the Bible of Dreams* (Plath, S.) 26, 40–1, 51, 58, 64–6, 72, 79, 84, 103, 107, 234–6, 238–41
Jones, David 244, 259
  *In Parenthesis* 244, 249, 259
Jones, Judith 174
  "Doing Away with Daddy: Exorcism and Sympathetic Magic in Plath's Poetry" 174
*The Journals of Sylvia Plath* (eds Hughes, T.; McCullough, F.) 126, 307, 308n20
*The Joy of Cooking* (Rombauer, I.; Becker, M.) 4, 127–8, 131
Joyce, James 6, 105, 145, 160, 201
Jung, Karl 105, 139, 148, 151
  *The Theory of Psychoanalysis* 139
Juniper Hill 45–6, 48, 48n4

Kackman, Michael 236
  "Nothing on but Hoppy Badges: 'Hopalong Cassidy'" 236
Kafka, Franz 126, 301
Kaplan, Cora 207
  *Salt and Bitter and Good: Three Centuries of English and American Women Poets* 207
Kaplan, Milton A. 265
Kavanagh, P. J. 292
Kazin, Alfred 105
Keats, John 23, 129, 195
  "Ode to a Nightingale" 129
  "This living hand" 23
Keegan, Paul
  (ed.) *Collected Poems* 40, 56, 61, 80–1, 93, 98–9, 107, 161, 166–7, 170, 173–6, 179, 183–6, 292, 294
Keller, Lynn 177–80
  *Forms of Expansion: Recent Long Poems by Women* 180
  "The Twentieth-Century Long Poem" 177–8
Kendall, Tim 5, 17–19, 23, 26, 73
  "From the Bottom of the Pool: Sylvia Plath's Last Poems" 73
  *Sylvia Plath: A Critical Study* 5, 17, 181, 183
Kennedy, John F. 65

"Radio and Television Address to the American People on the Soviet Arms Build-up in Cuba, October 22, 1962" 57, 65
Kennedy, Maev 57
Kermode, Frank
  (ed.) *Selected Prose of T. S. Eliot* 140–1, 144–6
Kerouac, Jack 109
  *Pic* 109
Kersnowski, Alice Hughes
  (ed.) *Conversations with Edna O'Brien* 280n5, 283
"Kindness" (Plath, S.) 96, 304
"King Cophetua and the Beggar Maid" (Sitwell, E.) 201
"King of Carrion" (Hughes, T.) 184
"On the Knocking at the Gate in Macbeth" (DeQuincey, T.) 175
Konkol, Margaret 279n1, 280–1, 280n6
  "Public Archives, New Knowledge, and Moving beyond the Digital Humanities/Digital Pedagogy Distinction" 280n6
Koren, Yehuda 291
  *Lover of Unreason: Assia Wevill, Sylvia Plath's Rival and Ted Hughes's Doomed Love* 291
Krebs, Gunter 71
  "Chronology of Space Launches" 71
Kristeva, Julia 89n12, 111
Kroll, Judith 139n2, 143n12, 165, 169–70, 175–6, 178, 178n1
  *Chapters in a Mythology: The Poetry of Sylvia Plath* 139n2, 165, 169, 178n1
Krook, Dorothea 105
Krulwich, Robert 71
  "A Very Scary Light Show: Exploding H-Bombs in Space" 71
Kryger, Joanne 246
Ku Klux Klan 97, 269n6
Kukil, Karen V. 1, 7, 12, 18, 201, 220, 223, 284, 311, 313
  "Beyond *Letters Home*: Plath's Unabridged Correspondence" 201
  "Conversation with Ruth Tiffany Barnhouse" 303, 303n4
  "Editing the Poetry of Sylvia Plath" 284
  (ed.) *The Letters of Sylvia Plath* 1–2, 4, 7, 12, 18, 56, 216–18, 220–3, 270, 300–4, 307–9, 312–14

(ed.) *"No Other Appetite": Sylvia Plath, Ted Hughes, and the Blood Jet of Poetry* 7, 126
"Reviving the Journals of Sylvia Plath" 300
(ed.) *The Unabridged Journals of Sylvia Plath 1950–1962: Transcribed from the Original Manuscripts at Smith College* 1–2, 4, 6, 12, 18, 35, 38–40, 42, 45, 54–5, 61, 63–4, 66, 68, 75, 94, 98–9, 105, 114–15, 118, 125–30, 139, 142, 151, 155, 157–8, 171, 194, 200, 216, 228–30, 237, 239, 283–4, 295–6, 300, 310, 314

Lacey, Kate 252n12, 264–5
  *Feminine Frequencies: Gender, German Radio, and the Public Sphere, 1923–1945* 252n12
*Ladies' Home Journal* 37n18, 38, 131–4, 203, 226, 226n5, 229
"The Lady and the Earthenware Head" (Plath, S.) 56, 58, 171, 173n2, 176
"Lady Lazarus" (Plath, S.) 21n1, 23, 65n5, 84, 87, 95, 113, 178–9, 181–2, 192, 208, 267n2, 271, 274
*The Lady's Not for Burning* (Fry, C.) 227
Laing, David
  (ed.) *The Poems of William Dunbar* 125
"The Lake Isle of Innisfree" (Yeats, W. B.) 163
Lambert, Laura 272
  "Weather Underground" 272
"Lament for the Makaris, Quhen He Wes Sek" (Dunbar, W.) 125
Lameyer, Gordon 34, 36, 54n3, 216, 311–12
"Landscape of Childhood" (Plath, S.) 248
Laozi 68
  *Tao Te Ching: A New English Version* 68
Larkin, Philip 147
"Last Letter" (Hughes, T.) 294
Latham, Joyce M. 268
Lattimore, Richmond 145, 146n20
  (tr.) *The Iliad of Homer* 145, 146n20, 177
Laurie, Alexander 259
"Law in the Country of Cats" (Hughes, T.) 158
Lawrence, D. H. 6, 105, 160
"Leaves from a Cambridge Notebook" (Plath, S.) 55, 55n7
"Leaving Early" (Plath, S.) 78, 255
Leavis, F. R. 140–1, 140n5
"Leda" (Doolittle, H.) 261
"Leda and the Swan" (Yeats, W. B.) 261

Lee, Clarissa Ai Ling 113
Leeming, Owen 253, 255
Lemert, Charles 80–1
Lennon, John 95, 97
Leonard, Garry M. 36, 40n21
"Leopard Print Lingerie by Vanity Fair" (Article in *Chicago Daily Tribune*) 36n15–16
"Leopard—Running Wild" (Article in *Chicago Daily Tribune*) 36n15
Lerner, Ben 25
  *The Hatred of Poetry* 25
"Lesbos" (Plath, S.) 28, 63, 116, 132–3, 271
"Letter in November" (Plath, S.) 79n9, 82n13
"Letter to Director General Sir Cecil Graves, Literary Output Committee" (Graves, C.) 257
*Letters Home: Correspondence, 1950–1963* (Plath, S., ed. Plath, A.) 18, 155, 212, 215–22, 224–8, 282, 287, 300, 307–10, 314
*The Letters of Sylvia Plath* (Plath, S., eds Steinberg, P.; Kukil, K.) 1–2, 4, 7, 12, 18, 56, 216–18, 220–3, 270, 300–4, 307–9, 312–14
  *Volume I: 1940–1956* 1, 5–6, 33–6, 45, 53–4, 59, 61, 73, 103, 128, 141–2, 154, 158–60, 163, 167, 169, 200, 216, 220, 222–5, 227–8, 236–7, 240–1, 244, 300, 302, 304, 311–13
  *Volume II: 1956–1963* 4, 22, 27, 39, 48, 58, 65, 78, 104, 114–15, 118, 122–3, 131–2, 134, 147, 157, 162–3, 190–6, 199, 206, 213, 226–7, 229, 237–8, 247–8, 250, 252–3, 255, 260, 300–1, 303–4, 312–14
*Letters of Ted Hughes* (ed. Reid, C.) 56, 126, 168, 292, 313, 313n20
Levenson, Christopher 57n17
  (ed.) *Poetry from Cambridge 1958* 57
Levertov, Denise 245
Levinas, Emmanuel 264
  *Otherwise than Being; or, Beyond Essence* 264
Lewis, Cara 8
  *Dynamic Form: How Intermediality Made Modernism* 8
Lewis, Cecil Day 189
Lewis, Wilmarth S. 299–300
  *Yale Edition of Horace Walpole's Correspondence* 300
Lewty, Jane 8
  (ed.) *Broadcasting Modernism* 8

"The Library of Babel" (Borges, J.) 83, 89n13
"The Library as Heterotopia: Michel Foucault and the Experience of Library Space" (Radford, G.; Radford, M.; Lingel, J.) 89–90
Lindeman, Eduard C.
  (ed.) *Emerson: The Basic Writings of America's Sage* 225
Lingel, Jessica
  "The Library as Heterotopia: Michel Foucault and the Experience of Library Space" 89–90
Lingis, Alphonso
  (tr.) *Otherwise than Being; or, Beyond Essence* 264
Linklater, Richard 26
  *Before Midnight* 26
*The Listener* 275
*Listening* (Nancy, J., tr. Mandell, C.) 264
"On Listening to Laura Riding" (Plath, S.) 248
*Listening to Noise and Silence: Towards a Philosophy of Sound Art* (Voegelin, S.) 260
"The Literature Classroom, College Library, and Reading Publics: Building Collaborative Critical Reading Networks" (VanDette, E.) 296
*Literature in the First Media Age: Britain between the Wars* (Trotter, D.) 8
"Little Fugue" (Plath, S.) 79n9, 267n2
"Little Red-Cap" (Duffy, C.) 208
Litvak, Anatole 4, 45, 47
"Live the Life of McCall's" (Wiese, O.) 33
"The Living Poet" (Plath, S.) 64, 256n2
Lochhead, Liz 204
*The London Magazine* 103, 147
*The Loneliness of the Long-Distance Runner* (Sillitoe, A.) 6, 190
Longfellow, Henry Wadsworth 178
  *The Song of Hiawatha* 178
Lorde, Audre 4, 162–3
"Lorelei" (Plath, S.) 72
*The Lost Lunar Baedecker* (Loy, M.) 68
Lotman, Yuri 113–14
Lotz, Myron 237, 240
"Love Is a Parallax" (Plath, S.) 66
*The Love Song of J. Alfred Prufrock* (Eliot, T. S.) 156
*Lover of Unreason: Assia Wevill, Sylvia Plath's Rival and Ted Hughes's Doomed Love* (Koren, Y.; Negev, E.) 291

Lowell, Robert 2, 6, 19, 104, 130, 161n4, 187, 303
Loy, Mina 68
  *The Lost Lunar Baedecker* 68
  "Songs to Joannes" 68
Lucas, D. W. 142n9, 143, 166
  *The Bacchae of Euripides. The Greek Text Performed at Cambridge at the Arts Theatre 20–24 February, 1956, by Members of the University, with an English Prose Translation Made for the Cambridge Performance of 1930* 142n9, 143
Lucas, Victoria (pseudonym of Sylvia Plath) 47–8, 132
*Lupercal* (Hughes, T.) 179
Lutostański, Bartosz 261–2
  "A Narratology of Radio Drama: Voice, Perspective, Space" 262
*Lyric Shame: The "Lyric" Subject of Contemporary American Poetry* (White, G.) 3n9, 19

*The Mabinogi* 173
*Macbeth* (Shakespeare, W.) 54, 55n7, 175
MacBeth, George 247–8, 255
*McCall's* 33, 227
McCallum, Robyn 119
  "Ideology in Children's Books" 119
McCarthy, Anna 240
McCracken, Allison 239
McCullough, Frances 126, 216, 300
  (ed.) *The Journals of Sylvia Plath* 126, 307, 308n20
McCully, Emily Arnold 112, 123
McCurdy, Philip 304
MacDonald, J. Fred 234
McGinley, Phyllis 131
  "Cooking to Me Is Poetry" 131
McHale, Brian 177–8
  *The Obligation toward the Difficult Whole: Postmodernist Long Poems* 177
McKay, Claude 285
  *Harlem Shadows* 285
McLean Hospital 4, 45–6, 240, 302–4
McLeod, Emilie W. 115
MacNeice, Louis 8, 257
"Mad Girl's Love Song" (Plath, S.) 155–6, 158
*Mad Girl's Love Song: Sylvia Plath and Life before Ted* (Wilson, A.) 32n3, 35, 310n12
*Mademoiselle* 31–2, 32n2, 34–6, 36n14, 41, 132, 224, 237, 302, 304, 312

*The Madwoman in the Attic: The Woman Writer and the Nineteenth-Century Literary Imagination* (Gilbert, S.; Gubar, S.) 106
"The Magic Mirror: A Study of the Double in Two of Dostoevsky's Novels" (Plath, S.) 167, 169–70, 175
"Major Gagarin retires" (Article in *The Guardian*) 69
Malcolm, Janet 64, 67, 219n1, 299, 308
  *The Silent Woman: Sylvia Plath and Ted Hughes* 64, 219n1, 308
"Man in Black" (Plath, S.) 175
"The Man and the Echo" (Yeats, W. B.) 162
Mandel, Ann Safford 299
Mandell, Charlotte
  (tr.) *Listening* 264
"The Manor Garden" (Plath, S.) 188–9
"Marginalia as Message: Affordances for Reader-to-Reader Communication" (Fajkovic, M.; Björneborn, L.) 86–7, 89
*Marginalia: Readers Writing in Books* (Jackson, H. J.) 85, 223
Martin, Willa 48
  "She Was Going Crazy—and She Knew It" 48
Marx, Karl 105, 267, 272
"Mary Jane Ward Declares Her Book Not Autobiography" (Woods, M.) 48
*Mary Ventura and the Ninth Kingdom* (Plath, S.) 1
"Mary Ventura and the Ninth Kingdom" (Plath, S.) 301, 304
*Mastering the Art of French Cooking* (Child, J.) 127
Masud, Noreen 199n2
maternity 8, 42, 164, 188, 191–2, 249, 251, 255–6, 260–1, 263, 265
Matheson, Hilda 245
Maynard, Joyce 227–8
  "My Parents Are My Friends" 227
*The Meaning of Dreams* (Graves, R.) 169–70, 257
*Media and Audiences: New Perspectives* (Ross, K.; Nightingale, V.) 240
"Medusa" (Plath, S.) 28, 87, 217–19, 223, 229, 271
"Megrims" (Plath, S.) 61, 61n30
Mellen, James 272
Melville, Herman 274
  *Benito Cereno* 274

"In Memory of W. B. Yeats" (Auden, W. H.) 164
Merwin, Dido 134
  "Vessel of Wrath" 134
Merwin, W. S. 134, 303
"Metamorphoses of the Moon" (Plath, S.) 66, 68n8
"Metaphors" (Plath, S.) 188
Mexborough 168–9
Michelis, Angelica 206–7
Middlebrook, Diane 7, 118, 159, 171, 178, 178n1
  *Her Husband: Hughes and Plath—A Marriage* 7, 118, 171, 178n1
Milford, Nancy 307
Millay, Edna St. Vincent 160, 225, 281
  "I Shall Forget You Presently, My Dear (Sonnet IV)" 281
Miller, David
  *British Poetry Magazines 1914–2000: History and Bibliography of "Little Magazines."* 246n6–7
Miller, Ellen 21, 24–5
Milton, John 161n4, 177
  *Paradise Lost* 177
"The Mirror and the Shadow: Plath's Poetics of Self-Doubt" (Axelrod, S.) 167n1, 238
miscarriage 6, 187–9, 191–3, 249, 255–6, 260–2
misogynist 290, 296
"Miss Drake Proceeds to Supper" (Plath, S.) 202
Mitchell, Margaret 109
  *Gone with the Wind* 109
Mitchell, Stephen
  (ed.) *Tao Te Ching: A New English Version* 68
Miyatsu, Rose 43, 46
  "'Hundreds of People Like Me': A Search for a Mad Community in *The Bell Jar*" 43
*Modern Confessional Writing: New Critical Essays* (ed. Gill, J.) 8
"Modern Tragedy in the Classic Tradition" (Plath, S.) 141
*Modern Women Poets* (Rees-Jones, D.) 208
modernism 3, 6–9, 27, 68, 122, 140, 142n10, 144–5, 147, 152, 154, 160, 177–8, 200, 202, 208
Montefiore, Jan 106
Monteith, Charles 160, 304

"The Moon and the Yew Tree" (Plath, S.) 70, 73, 79n9, 82, 82n13, 96, 179–82, 191–3, 207
Moore, Honor 271
  (ed.) *Poems from the Women's Movement* 271
Moore, Marianne 6, 10, 25–6, 200, 208, 245
  "Poetry" 25
Moores, Shaun 251
  "From 'Unruly Guest' to 'Good Companion': The Gendered Meanings of Early Radio in the Home" 251
Morales, Connie 269
Morgan, Robin 267–71, 270n7, 276–7
  "Goodbye to All That" 270
  *Sisterhood Is Powerful: An Anthology of Writings from the Women's Liberation Movement* 267–8
"Morning Song" (Plath, S.) 41, 78, 87–8, 178, 180–1, 189
Morrison, Grant 234
Morrison, Toni 11, 24, 104, 109, 234
  *The Origin of Others* 24, 234
  *Playing in the Dark: Whiteness and the Literary Imagination* 11
Morse, Donald E. 258
Mortimer, Ruth 299
Morton, Mary 78, 79n8
Moses, Kate 8n14, 125, 243
  "Appendix: The Oral Archive" 8n14
  "Sylvia Plath's Voice, Annotated" 243, 248
Moss, Howard 194
motherhood 6, 26, 37, 39, 114, 116–18, 123, 177–8, 180–1, 183, 186–9, 208, 254, 262–3, 265, 304
"The Mother's Union" (Plath, S.) 227
*Mourning Becomes Electra* (O'Neill, E.) 142
*Moving Out* 268
"Mrs. Cherry's Kitchen" (Plath, S.) 111–16, 112n2, n4, 118–22, 124
Mugglestone, Lynda 247
  *Talking Proper: The Rise and Fall of the English Accent as a Social Symbol* 247
"The Munich Mannequins" (Plath, S.) 28, 100, 284
Murphy, Jerome Ellison 11–12, 109
Murphy, Kate 245n4
  *Behind the Wireless: A History of Early Women at the BBC* 245n4
Murphy, Richard 163
"Mushrooms" (Plath, S.) 21, 60

"My Parents Are My Friends" (Maynard, J.) 227
"Mystic" (Plath, S.) 28

Nance, Guinevara 174
  "Doing Away with Daddy: Exorcism and Sympathetic Magic in Plath's Poetry" 174
Nancy, Jean-Luc 264
  *Listening* 264
"A Narratology of Radio Drama: Voice, Perspective, Space" (Lutostański, B.) 262
"Natural History" (Plath, S.) 60n25
Nazism 90, 95, 100, 108, 269n6, 271
Negev, Eilat 291
  *Lover of Unreason: Assia Wevill, Sylvia Plath's Rival and Ted Hughes's Doomed Love* 291
Nelson, Deborah 33, 38–9, 64, 253n13, 290n4
  "Plath, History and Politics" 33, 38–9, 290n4
  *Pursuing Privacy in Cold War America* 64, 253n14
Neupert, Hans-Joachim 236
"A New Idiom" (Plath, S.) 200–1
"The New Public Humanists" (Ellison, J.) 291
*The New Statesman* 312
*The New York Times Book Review* 216, 307, 312
*The New Yorker* 194, 194n4, 312
Newby, P. H. 263n12
  "The Third Programme" 257, 263, 263n12
Newnham College 53–4, 61, 139, 139n1, 141, 142n9, 302
"Nick and the Candlestick" (Plath, S.) 65n5, 178, 180–1
Nicolson, Harold 257
Nietzsche, Friedrich 105
"The Night Dances" (Plath, S.) 25, 71
Nightingale, Virginia 240
  *Media and Audiences: New Perspectives* 240
Nikolajeva, Maria 113–14
  *Children's Literature Comes of Age: Toward a New Aesthetic* 113
"Nineteen Hundred and Nineteen" (Yeats, W. B.) 155, 202
*No More Masks!: An Anthology of Poems by Women* (ed. Howe, F.) 268
"*No Other Appetite*": *Sylvia Plath, Ted Hughes, and the Blood Jet of Poetry* (eds Enniss, S.; Kukil, K.) 7, 126

"No Second Troy" (Yeats, W. B.) 166
Nodelman, Perry 119, 123
   "Decoding the Images: How Picture Books Work" 123
   *The Pleasures of Children's Literature* 119
Norman, Dawn Crowell
   "Beauty Prescriptions with a Man in Mind" 38
*The Norton Anthology of English Literature* (eds Christ, C.; Robson, C.; Greenblatt, S.; Abrams, M. H.) 127
Norton, Dick 127, 216
Norton, Perry 224, 314, 314n23
"A Note on Radio Drama" (Cleverdon, D.) 259
"Notes on Poems 1956–1963" (Hughes, T.) 182
"Nothing on but Hoppy Badges: 'Hopalong Cassidy'" (Kackman, M.) 236
Nott, Kathleen 245
"November Graveyard" (Plath, S.) 80

Oakley, S. P. 148
   "Dodds' Bacchae" 148
O'Brien, Edna 10–11, 279–87
   *Country Girl: A Memoir* 280n5, 283
   *Virginia: A Play* 279
O'Brien, Maeve 11
*The Obligation toward the Difficult Whole: Postmodernist Long Poems* (McHale, B.) 177
*The Observer* 196
occult 7, 99, 112, 115–16, 120, 130, 157, 165–76
"Ocean 1212-W" (Plath, S.) 72, 248
O'Dell, Cary 234–5
   *The Concise Encyclopedia of American Radio* 234–5
"Ode to a Nightingale" (Keats, J.) 129
*The Odyssey* (Homer) 177
*Oedipus Tyrannus* (Sophocles) 148
Olivares, Kimberly T.
   (ed.) *Quick Hits for Service-Learning: Successful Strategies by Award-Winning Teachers* 296
O'Neill, Eugene 142
   *Mourning Becomes Electra* 142
Ono, Yoko 95, 97
"Oregonian Original" (Plath, S.) 123n12
*Oresteia* (Aeschylus) 149–51
*The Oresteia by Aeschylus in a New Version by Ted Hughes* (tr. Hughes, T.) 151n37

*The Oresteian Trilogy* (Aeschylus, tr. Vellacott, P.) 139, 148–9, 151
*The Origin of Others* (Morrison, T.) 24, 234
O'Rourke, Meghan 103
Orr, Peter 253, 256, 283, 301, 309
   (ed.) *The Poet Speaks: Interviews with Contemporary Poets Conducted by Hilary Morrish, John Press and Ian Scott-Kilvert* 256, 309
Orwell, George 263
   "Poetry and the Microphone" 263
"The Other" (Hughes, T.) 179–81, 181n2, 267n2, 294–5
*The Other Ariel* (Bundtzen, L.) 204, 207, 276, 282n9
*The Other Sylvia Plath* (Brain, T.) 18, 37, 37n18, 40, 48n6, 55n8, 58, 61, 64, 180, 214, 220, 248
*Otherwise than Being; or, beyond Essence* (Levinas, E., tr. Lingis, A.) 264
*Out of the Cradle Endlessly Rocking: Motherhood in Sylvia Plath's Work* (Christodoulides, N.) 111
Ovid 145
Owen, Wilfred 227
"Owl" (Plath, S.) 61
"The Owl" (Hughes, T.) 61, 61n29

*Pain, Parties, Work: Sylvia Plath in New York, Summer 1953* (Winder, E.) 32n2, 35–6
"The Panther" (Rilke, R.) 158
*Paradise Lost* (Milton, J.) 177
*In Parenthesis* (Jones, D.) 244, 249, 259
*Parents' Magazine & Better Homemaking* 38
*The Paris Review* 279, 280n5
"Parliament Hill Fields" (Plath, S.) 188–9, 192
"A Parochial Anomaly: The Classical Tripos 1822–1900" (Stray, C.) 140
Patel, Uzma 279n1, 280, 284–6, 285n12
   "Revealing the Roots of Sylvia Plath" 280, 282, 284, 286
"Pearls of Dew" (Plath, S.) 155
Peel, Robin 6, 64–6, 71, 233, 241
   *Writing Back: Sylvia Plath and Cold War Politics* 64–5, 65n5, 71, 95
Pereira, Malin Walther 101, 253n13
   "Be(e)ing and 'Truth': Tar Baby's Signifying on Sylvia Plath's Bee Poems" 253n13
"Perfect Light" (Hughes, T.) 80n11
Perloff, Marjorie 101, 178, 178n1

"The Two *Ariels*: The (Re)Making of the
      Sylvia Plath Canon" 101, 178n1
Perrault, Charles
   *The Sleeping Beauty* 201
Perry, Laura 11, 11n17
   "Plath and the Culture of Hygiene" 11n17
*Philoctetes* (Sophocles) 142, 149
*Pic* (Kerouac, J.) 109
"A Picture of Otto" (Hughes, T.) 107, 174
"Pike" (Hughes, T.) 313n20
Pitter, Ruth 245
"In Plaster" (Plath, S.) 19, 22–3, 96, 109
Plath, Aurelia Schober 7, 18, 128, 131,
      155, 211–29, 237–8, 241, 248, 287,
      299–300, 307–8, 314
   (ed.) *Letters Home: Correspondence,
      1950–1963* 18, 155, 212, 215–22,
      224–8, 282, 287, 300, 307–10, 314
"Plath and the Culture of Hygiene" (Perry, L.)
      11n17
"Plath, Domesticity, and the Art of
      Advertising" (Bryant, M.) 36, 116
Plath Estate 219, 221n3, 304, 311n15, 314
"Plath, History and Politics" (Nelson, D.) 33,
      38–9, 290n4
Plath, Otto 57, 107–8, 174–6, 217, 219, 284
Plath, Sylvia
   "Admonitions" 66, 157
   "Aerialist" 60n25
   "All the Dead Dears" 56–8
   "Among the Bumblebees" 107
   "Among the Narcissi" 81, 82n13
   "The Applicant" 98, 116, 208, 271
   *Ariel* 1, 7, 9, 11, 19, 21, 26–7, 81, 83–4,
      90, 94, 96, 98, 101, 125, 131–2, 152,
      154, 161–2, 164, 169, 171, 178–83,
      186, 188, 191, 204, 206–7, 213, 248,
      253–4, 260, 271, 276, 292
   "Ariel" 28, 55, 65–6, 71, 93, 96–8, 100,
      108, 179–80, 182, 206–7, 286–7
   *Ariel: The Restored Edition* 1–2, 180–3,
      271, 314
   "The Arrival of the Bee Box" 25, 28, 91,
      94, 96, 98, 109, 164, 179, 205–6, 208,
      235
   "Balloons" 21, 99
   "Barren Woman" 181
   "The Bed Book" 5, 111–15, 112n4, 114n7,
      122–4
   "The Bee Meeting" 163–4, 179, 205–6
   "The Beekeeper's Daughter" 28, 98, 205

*The Bell Jar* 1, 4, 11, 31, 34, 41, 43, 46–9,
      51, 70, 78, 84, 109, 111, 125, 127,
      130, 132–4, 191–2, 202, 212–13, 218,
      223, 241, 283–4, 300, 302, 304
"Berck-Plage" 81, 82n13, 179–80, 182
"A Birthday Present" 21, 132, 301, 301n1
"Black Rook in Rainy Weather" 58, 60,
      255
"Blackberrying" 97
"Body, Word, and Photograph" 64
"Bucolics" 205
"The Burnt-out Spa" 28
"Cambridge Collection" 53, 53n2, 55n10,
      60
"Candles" 255
"Channel Crossing" 225
"The Character of Zeus in *Prometheus
      Bound*" 141
"Childless Woman" 100, 267n2
*Collected Children's Stories: Sylvia
      Plath* 112, 112n2–3, 116–17, 116n9,
      119–24
*The Collected Poems* 5, 9–10, 18, 20–2,
      24–8, 41, 54–61, 63, 66–72, 75, 78,
      80–1, 84, 91, 93–100, 107–9, 132–3,
      139, 142–4, 151–2, 154, 156–9, 161,
      163–4, 170–2, 174–5, 182, 188–9,
      192–4, 201–3, 205–6, 235–8, 249–50,
      261–2, 274, 276, 281–2, 284, 287,
      292, 295, 301, 304, 315
*The Colossus* 27, 55, 260, 273n8, 303
"The Colossus" 10, 107, 116, 139, 148,
      150–2, 192, 267n4, 281–2, 287
"A Comparison" 26, 40
"Context" 103–4
"Conversation among the Ruins" 142–7,
      142n11, 143n12, 147n26, 151–2
"The Courage of Shutting-Up" 179–82,
      181n2
"The Couriers" 28
"Cut" 65n5, 97, 132, 208
"Daddy" 87, 95–6, 99–100, 108, 113, 139,
      152, 157, 174–5, 178–9, 181–2, 192,
      208, 219, 271, 275–6, 286
"Day of Success" 39n20, 78, 79n8
"THE DAY OF THE TWENTY-FOUR
      CAKES" 126
"Death & Co" 28, 267n2
"On Deck" 68
"On the Decline of Oracles" 143n12
"Den of Lions" 269n5

"The Detective" 75, 100
"Dialogue En Route" 67
"The Disquieting Muses" 143n12, 223
"Edge" 72, 96, 99–100, 152, 170, 189
"Edith Sitwell and the Development of Her Poetry" 201
"Eisenhower collage" 65
"Electra" 150–1
"Electra on Azalea Path" 9, 139, 148, 151–2, 182
"Elm" 6, 70, 73, 100, 188, 191–5, 193n3, 194n4, 304
"To Eva Descending the Stair" 156
"Event" 28, 208
"Evergreens" 312
"Evolution" 171
"Falcon Yard" 147n26, 294
"Faun" 60n24, 61n29
"Female Author" 20, 109
"Fever 103°" 20, 71, 95, 99, 301
"Finisterre" 96
"Full Fathom Five" 72, 151
"Getting There" 108, 267n2
"The Ghost's Leavetaking" 67
"The Hermit at Outermost House" 28
"Hospital Notes" 239
"Insomniac" 69, 96, 237–8
"The It-Doesn't-Matter Suit" 111–20, 112n3–4, 114n7, 122, 124
"The Jailer" (Jailor) 5, 98–9, 267–71, 267n2, 273–4, 273n8, 276–7
*Johnny Panic and the Bible of Dreams* 26, 40–1, 51, 58, 64–6, 72, 79, 84, 103, 107, 234–6, 238–41
"Johnny Panic and the Bible of Dreams" 4, 43, 49–51, 65, 239
"Kindness" 96, 304
"The Lady and the Earthenware Head" 56, 58, 171, 173n2, 176
"Lady Lazarus" 21n1, 23, 65n5, 84, 87, 95, 113, 178–9, 181–2, 192, 208, 267n2, 271, 274
"Landscape of Childhood" 248
"Leaves from a Cambridge Notebook" 55, 55n7
"Leaving Early" 78, 255
"Lesbos" 28, 63, 116, 132–3, 271
"Letter in November" 79n9, 82n13
*Letters Home: Correspondence, 1950–1963* 18, 155, 212, 215–22, 224–8, 282, 287, 300, 307–10, 314

*The Letters of Sylvia Plath* 1–2, 4, 7, 12, 18, 56, 216–18, 220–3, 270, 300–4, 307–9, 312–14
"On Listening to Laura Riding" 248
"Little Fugue" 79n9, 267n2
"The Living Poet" 64, 256n2
"Lorelei" 72
"Love Is a Parallax" 66
"Mad Girl's Love Song" 155–6, 158
"The Magic Mirror: A Study of the Double in Two of Dostoevsky's Novels" 167, 169–70, 175
"Man in Black" 175
"The Manor Garden" 188–9
*Mary Ventura and the Ninth Kingdom* 1
"Mary Ventura and the Ninth Kingdom" 301, 304
"Medusa" 28, 87, 217–19, 223, 229, 271
"Megrims" 61, 61n30
"Metamorphoses of the Moon" 66, 68n8
"Metaphors" 188
"Miss Drake Proceeds to Supper" 202
"Modern Tragedy in the Classic Tradition" 141
"The Moon and the Yew Tree" 70, 73, 79n9, 82, 82n13, 96, 179–82, 191–3, 207
"Morning Song" 41, 78, 87–8, 178, 180–1, 189
"The Mother's Union" 227
"Mrs. Cherry's Kitchen" 111–16, 112n2, n4, 118–22, 124
"The Munich Mannequins" 28, 100, 284
"Mushrooms" 21, 60
"Mystic" 28
"Natural History" 60n25
"A New Idiom" 200–1
"Nick and the Candlestick" 65n5, 178, 180–1
"The Night Dances" 25, 71
"November Graveyard" 80
"Ocean 1212-W" 72, 248
"Oregonian Original" 123n12
"Owl" 61
"Parliament Hill Fields" 188–9, 192
"Pearls of Dew" 155
"In Plaster" 19, 22–3, 96, 109
*The Poet Speaks: Interviews with Contemporary Poets Conducted by Hilary Morrish, John Press and Ian Scott-Kilvert* 256, 309

"Poppies in July" 28, 201
"Poppies in October" 65n5
"The Princess and the Goblins" 67
"Purdah" 95–6
"Pursuit" 157–9, 225
"The Rabbit Catcher" 178–9, 181, 276, 315
"To a Refractory Santa Claus" 61n30
"Resolve" 58, 60–1, 60n25–6
"Review: *The Stones of Troy* by C. A. Trypanis" 145n18
"The Rival" 69, 94, 179–81, 181n2
"Second Winter" 10, 203, 207
"A Secret" 179–81, 181n2
"The Shadow" 8, 233, 235, 241
"Sheen & Speck" 312
"Sheep in Fog" 60, 72, 170–1
"Soliloquy of the Solipsist" 66
"Sow" 99
"Spinster" 255
*The Spoken Word: Sylvia Plath* 256n2
"Stars over the Dordogne" 69–70
"Stillborn" 26, 189
"Stings" 71, 164, 179, 205–6
"Stone Boy with Dolphin" 41
"Stones of Troy" 145–6, 145n19, 146n20–2
"Stopped Dead" 179–80, 182
"Street Song" 60n25
"Suicide off Egg Rock" 28
"Sunday at the Mintons'" 224–5
"Superman and Paula Brown's New Snowsuit" 233–5, 241
"The Swarm" 163, 204, 267n2
*Sylvia Plath: Drawings* 56, 314n26
"Ten Poems by Sylvia Plath" 267n2
"Thalidomide" 28, 94, 235, 263n11, 267n2
"The Thin People" 28
"'Three Caryatids without A Portico,' by Hugo Robus. A Study in Sculptural Dimensions" 143n12
"Three Women" 6, 8–9, 95, 188, 191–4, 243–5, 247, 249–51, 253–4, 256–65
"Three Women: A Poem for Three Voices" 8, 255
"Tomorrow Begins Today" 241
"The Tour" 28
"Tulips" 21, 96
"Two Lovers and a Beachcomber" 53n2
"Two Views of Withens" 80
*The Unabridged Journals of Sylvia Plath 1950–1962: Transcribed from the Original Manuscripts at Smith College* 1–2, 4, 6, 12, 18, 35, 38–40, 42, 45, 54–5, 61, 63–4, 66, 68, 75, 94, 98–9, 105, 114–15, 118, 125–30, 139, 142, 151, 155, 157–8, 171, 194, 200, 216, 228–30, 237, 239, 283–4, 295–6, 300, 310, 314
"Virus TV" 236–7, 241
"A Walk to Withens" 80n10
"Watercolor of Grantchester Meadows" 56n14, 58, 60–1, 60n24
"The Weird Ones" 248
"Whiteness I Remember" 55n11
"Widow" 69
"Winter Landscape, with Rooks" 54–5, 55n9, 56n12, 58, 61
"A Winter Ship" 267n4
*Winter Trees* 249
"Wintering" 94, 96, 99, 160, 164, 179, 205–6, 295
"A Winter's Tale" 80n10
"The Wishing Box" 8, 238, 240
"Words" 96, 108, 161–2
"You're" 178, 180–1, 189
"Zoo Keeper's Wife" 78–9
"Plath and Television" (Presley, N.) 238
Plath, Warren 215, 248
*Plath's Incarnations: Woman and the Creative Process* (Bundtzen, L.) 205n6, 219n1
"Plath's Lives" (Hammer, L.) 9, 167n1, 171, 173n2
Plato 105, 140
*Playing in the Dark: Whiteness and the Literary Imagination* (Morrison, T.) 11
*The Pleasures of Children's Literature* (Nodelman, P.) 119
Poe, Edgar Allan 49, 50n9, 55n7
"The System of Dr. Tarr and Prof. Fether" 49, 50n9
*Poems* (Amichai, Y., tr. Gutmann, A.) 292
*Poems: Ruth Fainlight, Ted Hughes, Alan Sillitoe* (Fainlight, R.; Hughes, T.; Sillitoe, A.) 179
*The Poems of William Dunbar* (Dunbar, W., ed. Laing, D.) 125
*Poems from the Women's Movement* (ed. Moore, H.) 271
"The Poet Realized: An Interview with Ruth Fainlight" (Bush, K.) 190
*The Poet Speaks: Interviews with Contemporary Poets Conducted by Hilary Morrish, John Press and Ian Scott-Kilvert* (Plath, S., ed. Orr, P.) 256, 309

*The Poetics of Space* (Bachelard, G.) 79
"Poetry" (Moore, M.) 25
*Poetry from Cambridge 1958* (ed. Levenson, C.) 57
"Poetry and the Microphone" (Orwell, G.) 263
*The Poet's Voice* (Radio Show) 255, 256n2
*The Political Possibility of Sound: Fragments of Listening* (Voegelin, S.) 264
"Poppies in July" (Plath, S.) 28, 201
"Poppies in October" (Plath, S.) 65n5
Potter, Stephen 257
Pound, Ezra 160, 178
"A Prayer for my Daughter" (Yeats, W. B.) 188
pregnancy 94, 112n4, 131, 188–91, 250, 253–4, 261
*The Prelude* (Wordsworth, W.) 178
Prendergast, Catherine 48
Presley, Nicola 8
  "Plath and Television" 238
Price, Richard 246n6–7
  *British Poetry Magazines 1914–2000: History and Bibliography of "Little Magazines."* 246n6–7
"The 'Priestess' and Her 'Cult': Plath's Confessional Poetics and the Mythology of Women Readers" (Badia, J.) 276
"Priestesses of the Gold Comb" (Sitwell, E.) 204
"The Princess and the Goblins" (Plath, S.) 67
*Principles of Literary Criticism* (Richards, I. A.) 141
Prouty, Olive Higgins 54n3, 160, 213, 240, 312
  *Home Port* 213
"Public Archives, New Knowledge, and Moving beyond the Digital Humanities/Digital Pedagogy Distinction" (Konkol, M.) 280n6
*Punch* 312
"Purdah" (Plath, S.) 95–6
*Pursuing Privacy in Cold War America* (Nelson, D.) 64, 253n14
"Pursuit" (Plath, S.) 157–9, 225

Quayle, Edward 44
*The Queens and the Hive* (Sitwell, E.) 205
*Quick Hits for Service-Learning: Successful Strategies by Award-Winning Teachers* (eds Cooksey, M. A.; Olivares, K.) 296

"The Rabbit Catcher" (Plath, S.) 178–9, 181, 276, 315
Racine, Jean 141, 158
racism 3, 5, 10–12, 21, 24–6, 29, 93–105, 107–10, 269, 272, 274
Radford, Gary P.
  "The Library as Heterotopia: Michel Foucault and the Experience of Library Space" 89–90
Radford, Marie L.
  "The Library as Heterotopia: Michel Foucault and the Experience of Library Space" 89–90
*Radical Children's Literature: Future Visions and Aesthetic Transformations in Juvenile Fiction* (Reynolds, K.) 124
"Radio and Television Address to the American People on the Soviet Arms Build-up in Cuba, October 22, 1962" (Kennedy, J.) 57, 65
"The Radio Play" (Cleverdon, D.) 259
*The Radio Times* 248, 252, 260
*Radio Voices: American Broadcasting, 1922–1952* (Hilmes, M.) 244n2, 252n12, 253n13
Rafferty, Janet Wagner 31–2, 32n2
Raine, Kathleen 245, 250
Ranger, Holly 9
Rank, Otto 169
  "The Double as Immortal Self" 169
Rankine, Claudia 22
  *Citizen: An American Lyric* 22
Rankovic, Catherine 7, 213n5, 220–2, 220n2, 221n3
  "Aurelia Plath's Shorthand Transcriptions" 222
  "Dick Norton Knew Shorthand" 217n13
  "Studying Aurelia Plath" 221
"A Rare Bee" (Duffy, C.) 206
*RAT Subterranean News* 5, 267–77
Raymo, Judith G. 304
"Reading Plath Photographs: In and Out of the Museum" (Helle, A.) 293–4
"Red" (Hughes, T.) 80n11, 295
*Red Comet: The Short Life and Blazing Art of Sylvia Plath* (Clark, H.) 1n3, 48n6, 61n28, 98, 115n8, 140, 147n26, 153–60, 162, 201, 219–21, 258
Redgrove, Peter 246
Redpath, Theodore 54, 141n7
Rees-Jones, Deryn 208

*Consorting with Angels: Essays on Modern Women Poets* 208
*Modern Women Poets* 208
"Reforming the Law of Rape" (Schulhofer, S.) 268
"To a Refractory Santa Claus" (Plath, S.) 61n30
Reid, Christopher
   (ed.) *Letters of Ted Hughes* 56, 126, 168, 292, 313, 313n20
Reith, John 244
*Representing Sylvia Plath* (eds Bayley, S.; Brain, T.) 1n3
"Resolve" (Plath, S.) 58, 60–1, 60n25–6
"Revealing the Roots of Sylvia Plath" (Geevarghese, R.; Patel, U.) 280, 282, 284, 286
"Review: *The Stones of Troy* by C. A. Trypanis" (Plath, S.) 145n18
*Revising Life: Sylvia Plath's Ariel Poems* (Van Dyne, S.) 7
"Reviving the Journals of Sylvia Plath" (Kukil, K.) 300
Reynolds, Kimberley 114n6, 124
   *Children's Literature: A Very Short Introduction* 114n6
   *Radical Children's Literature: Future Visions and Aesthetic Transformations in Juvenile Fiction* 124
*Rhinocéros* (Ionesco, E.) 227
Rich, Adrienne 10, 130, 245, 290, 303
Richards, I. A. 140–1, 140n4, 141n6
   *Principles of Literary Criticism* 141
Riding, Laura 190, 245, 248
Riffaterre, Michel 262, 262n10
Riley, Denise 102
Rilke, Rainer Maria 158
   "The Panther" 158
*Rising Tides: Twentieth-Century American Women Poets* (eds Chester, L.; Barba, S.) 268
"The Rival" (Plath, S.) 69, 94, 179–81, 181n2
*River* (Hughes, T.) 179
Rivers, W. H. R. 170
"Robbing Myself" (Hughes, T.) 80n11
Roberts, David 112, 116, 123
Roberts, Neil 183
Robinson, Katherine 7–8
Robson, Catherine
   (ed.) *The Norton Anthology of English Literature* 127
Roche, Clarissa 134, 301

Roethke, Theodore 104, 161n4
Rombauer, Irma S 4, 127–9
   *Joy of Cooking* 4, 127–8, 131
Rose, Jacqueline 2, 2n6, 21n1, 63–4, 66, 90, 106, 113, 139n2, 143n12, 148n28, 173, 178, 178n1, 220, 225, 233
   *The Haunting of Sylvia Plath* 2, 2n6, 63–4, 66, 90, 106, 113, 148n28, 173, 178n1, 220, 225, 233
Ross, David 246
Ross, Karen
   *Media and Audiences: New Perspectives* 240
Rossetti, Christina 127, 202, 207
   "Goblin Market" 127, 202
Roth, Philip 283–4
Rovito, Maria 43
   "Toward a New Madwoman Theory: Reckoning the Pathologization of Sylvia Plath" 43
Rudd, Mark 272
"Rules of the Game" (Hughes, T.) 294
Russo, Linda 246
Ryan-Bryant, Jennifer 7

Sachar, Neva Nelson 35
Sackville-West, Vita 207
Sagar, Keith 143n12, 184
*Saint Botolph's Review* 8, 165–6, 246
"St Botolph's" (Hughes, T.) 58n18, 166
Saldívar, Toni 11
Salinger, J. D. 227
*Salt and Bitter and Good: Three Centuries of English and American Women Poets* (Kaplan, C.) 207
"Sam" (Hughes, T.) 55n11
Sampson, Fiona 176, 199
   "After Plath: The Legacy of Influence" 176
"Sapphic Moon" (Fainlight, R.) 6, 188, 193
Sassoon, Richard 54, 131n1, 157, 309n11, 310, 310n12
Saxton, Eugene F. 302
Schott, Webster 276
   "The Cult of Plath" 276
"On the Scope of Feature Programmes: Producing for the Third" (Cleverdon, D.) 257
Schulhofer, Stephen 268
   "Reforming the Law of Rape" 268
"The Second Coming" (Yeats, W. B.) 157
*The Second Wave* 268
"Second Winter" (Plath, S.) 10, 203, 207

Second World War 4, 7, 9, 32, 207, 234, 243
"A Secret" (Plath, S.) 179–81, 181n2
"Seize the Land" (Article in *RAT*) 272
*Selected Poems* (Amichai, Y., tr. Gutmann, A.) 292
*Selected Prose of T. S. Eliot* (Eliot, T. S., ed. Kermode, F.) 140–1, 144–6
Seuss, Dr. 123, 123n12
    *Horton Hatches the Egg* 123, 123n12
*Seventeen* 34, 269n5
Sexton, Anne 2, 6, 19, 95, 187, 192, 245, 303
    "The Abortion" 192
    *All My Pretty Ones* 192
    "The Barfly Ought to Sing" 187
    "Sylvia's Death" 187
"The Shadow" (Plath, S.) 8, 233, 235, 241
*The Shadow* (Radio Play) 235–6
*Shadow Archives: The Lifecycles of African American Literature* (Cloutier, J.) 3n8, 12, 287
Shakespeare, William 105, 128, 130, 161n4, 206–7, 281
    *Macbeth* 54, 55n7, 175
    *The Tempest* 89n13, 206
Shapley, Olive 252
"She Was Going Crazy—and She Knew It" (Martin, W.) 48
"Sheen & Speck" (Plath, S.) 312
"Sheep in Fog" (Plath, S.) 60, 72, 170–1
Shero, Jeff 270
shorthand 7, 97, 211–18, 221–2
"The Shot" (Hughes, T.) 40
Showalter, Elaine 102
    "Women and the Literary Curriculum" 102
Siddiqi, Asif A. 63n2, 68n7
    *Challenge to Apollo: The Soviet Union and the Space Race, 1945–1974* 63n2
Sidney, Philip 178
    *Astrophil and Stella* 178
Siggs, L. H. 312
Sigmund, Elizabeth (*née* Compton) 279n2, 304, 314n25
*The Silence of the Lambs* (Demme, J.) 49
*The Silent Woman: Sylvia Plath and Ted Hughes* (Malcolm, J.) 64, 219n1, 308
*The Silent World* (Cousteau, J.) 72
Sillitoe, Alan 189–90, 192, 194–6
    *The Loneliness of the Long-Distance Runner* 6, 190
    *Poems: Ruth Fainlight, Ted Hughes, Alan Sillitoe* 179
Simensky Bietila, Susan 270, 276

Simpson, Joan Murray 207
    *Without Adam: The Femina Anthology of Poetry* 202, 207
Singh, Amardeep 285
*Sinister Wisdom* 268
*Sisterhood Is Powerful: An Anthology of Writings from the Women's Liberation Movement* (Morgan, R.) 267–8
Sitwell, Edith 6, 10, 199–208, 245
    "Aubade" 202
    "Bee in the Spirit" 206
    "The Bee Oracles" 10, 200, 204–7
    "The Bee-Keeper" 204–5
    *Bucolic Comedies* 201
    *The Canticle of the Rose: Poems 1917–1949* 10, 200–3, 205
    "Dark Song" 200–1
    "Dirge for the New Sunrise" 203
    "Gold Coast Customs" 202
    "King Cophetua and the Beggar Maid" 201
    "Priestesses of the Gold Comb" 204
    *The Queens and the Hive* 205
    "Some Notes on My Own Poetry" 200
    "The Song of the Cold" 203
    "Still Falls the Rain" 208
    "Three Poems of the Atomic Age" 202
    "On the Vanity of Human Aspirations" 202
    "Waltz" 208
*The Sleeping Beauty* (Perrault, C.) 201
"Sleepwear in Hollywood Film and Television, and the US Sleepwear Industry, 1945–c.1977" (Tuite, R.) 33n4–6
Smith, Caroline 33
Smith, Carrie 1n2, 8
Smith College 4, 7–10, 17, 19, 32, 34–5, 37, 42, 48, 56, 76, 86, 102, 105, 126, 129–30, 140–1, 144–5, 154–5, 157, 159, 167, 170–1, 194, 200, 202, 206, 213–15, 220, 222–4, 227, 244, 283–4, 299–304, 309–10, 313
Smith, Richard Curson
    *Ted Hughes: Stronger Than Death* (Documentary) 292
Smith, Stevie 104, 199, 207–8, 248
*The Snake Pit* (Ward, M.) 4, 43–50, 49n8
*Snow White and the Seven Dwarfs* (Brothers Grimm) 241
"Soliloquy of the Solipsist" (Plath, S.) 66
"Some Notes on My Own Poetry" (Sitwell, E.) 200
"The Song of the Cold" (Sitwell, E.) 203

*The Song of Hiawatha* (Longfellow, H.) 178
*Song of Myself* (Whitman, W.) 178
"The Song of Wandering Aengus" (Yeats, W. B.) 156–7
"Songs to Joannes" (Loy, M.) 68
Sonnenberg, Ben 195
Sophocles 9, 129, 139–42, 148
   *Electra* 139, 142
   *Oedipus Tyrannus* 148
   *Philoctetes* 142, 149
Souffrant, Leah 256n3, 262
"Sow" (Plath, S.) 99
"Speaking the Space between Mother and Child: Sylvia Plath, Julia Kristeva, and the Place of Children's Literature" (Barai, A.) 111
*Speakout* 268
*Spectacular Confessions: Autobiography, Performative Activism, and the Sites of Suffrage, 1905–1938* (Green, B.) 5, 269–70
speedwriting 212–13, 213n5
Spender, Dale 106–7, 244n1
Spender, Stephen 227, 244n1
Spenser, Edmund 177
   *The Faerie Queen* 177
Spigel, Lynn 238
   *Welcome to the Dreamhouse: Popular Media and Postwar Suburbs* 238
"Spinster" (Plath, S.) 255
Spitz, Marc 17–18, 26
   *Twee: The Gentle Revolution in Music, Books, Television, Fashion, and Film* 17
Spivak, Gayatri Chakravorty 104, 110
*The Spoken Word: Sylvia Plath* (Plath, S.) 256n2
*Standing Female Nude* (Duffy, C.) 199
"The Stare's Nest by My Window" (Yeats, W. B.) 162–4
"Starfish Prime" 65–6, 71
Starr, Marlo 282–3
"Stars over the Dordogne" (Plath, S.) 69–70
Stein, Gertrude 280–1
   *Ida: A Novel* 280
Steinberg, Peter K. 1, 5, 12, 18, 75n1, 112, 112n4, 142n11, 144n15, 153n1, 193, 215n8, 220–1, 223, 226n4, 300–1
   (ed.) *The Letters of Sylvia Plath* 1–2, 4, 7, 12, 18, 56, 216–18, 220–3, 270, 300–4, 307–9, 312–14
   *Sylvia Plath* 112
*These Ghostly Archives: The Unearthing of Sylvia Plath* 5, 61n30, 75n1, 79, 221

Stephens, John 119
   "Ideology in Children's Books" 119
Sterling, Christopher H. 234
   *The Concise Encyclopedia of American Radio* 234–5
Stern, Marcia 300–2, 304; See also Marcia Brown
Stevenson, Anne 105, 134–6, 183, 191–2, 208, 282, 299, 308
   *Bitter Fame: A Life of Sylvia Plath* 134–6, 183, 282, 299, 308
   "Sylvia Plath: An Exchange" 283
Stevenson, Robert Louis
   *Dr. Jekyll and Mr. Hyde* 172–3
Stewart, Martha 125–6
*Stigma: Notes on the Management of a Spoiled Identity* (Goffman, E.) 43
"Still Falls the Rain" (Sitwell, E.) 208
*Still Mad: American Women Writers and the Feminist Imagination, 1950–2020* (Gilbert, S.; Gubar, S.) 4
"Stillborn" (Plath, S.) 26, 189
"Stings" (Plath, S.) 71, 164, 179, 205–6
"Stone Boy with Dolphin" (Plath, S.) 41
*The Stones of Troy* (Trypanis, C. A.) 145–6, 145n19, 146n20–1, 148n29
"Stones of Troy" (Plath, S.) 145–6, 145n19, 146n20–2
"Stopped Dead" (Plath, S.) 179–80, 182
Strangeways, Al 106
Stray, Christopher 140
   "A Parochial Anomaly: The Classical Tripos 1822–1900" 140
"Street Song" (Plath, S.) 60n25
Stubbs, Naomi J. 285
"Studying Aurelia Plath" (Rankovic, C.) 221
"Suicide off Egg Rock" (Plath, S.) 28
Sullivan, Shannon 104
"Sunday at the Mintons'" (Plath, S.) 224–5
*The Sunday Times* 300
"Superman and Paula Brown's New Snowsuit" (Plath, S.) 233–5, 241
*Surviving Literary Suicide* (Berman, J.) 17
"Swans" (Hughes, T.) 56n12
"The Swarm" (Plath, S.) 163, 204, 267n2
*Sylvia* (Film) (Jeffs, C.) 292
*Sylvia Plath* (Steinberg, P.) 112
"Sylvia Plath: *Ariel*" (Vice, S.) 178n1, 180
*Sylvia Plath: A Biography* (Wagner-Martin, L.) 32n2, 105, 258
"Sylvia Plath and the Costume of Femininity" (Bayley, S.) 34–5, 34n10

INDEX 365

*Sylvia Plath: A Critical Study* (Kendall, T.) 5, 17, 181, 183
*Sylvia Plath: Drawings* (Plath, S.) 56, 314n26
Sylvia Plath Estate 295
"Sylvia Plath: The Evolution of 'Sheep in Fog'" (Hughes, T.) 170
"Sylvia Plath: An Exchange" (Hughes, O.; Stevenson, A.; Alvarez, A.) 283
"Sylvia Plath and Her Journals" (Hughes, T.) 131
"Sylvia Plath: Letters, Words, and Fragments" (conference at Ulster University) 2n4, 85n5, 220n2, 307n
*Sylvia Plath: Method and Madness* (Butscher, E.) 148n27, 282
*Sylvia Plath and the Mythology of Readers* (Badia, J.) 18
*Sylvia Plath and the Theatre of Mourning* (Britzolakis, C.) 143n12, 148n28, 236–7
Sylvia Plath: Transitions 211
"Sylvia Plath and You" (Brain, T.) 21
*Sylvia Plath: The Wound and the Cure of Words* (Axelrod, S.) 2, 95, 101, 161n4, 256, 274–5
"Sylvia Plath's Anti-Psychiatry" (Farland, M.) 43
*Sylvia Plath's Fiction: A Critical Study* (Ferretter, L.) 43, 48n7, 113, 118, 233, 295
"Sylvia Plath's Letters and Journals" (Brain, T.) 219n1, 222, 294
"Sylvia Plath's Teaching and the Shaping of Her Work" (Golden, A.) 19, 200
"Sylvia Plath's Voice, Annotated" (Moses, K.) 243, 248
"Sylvia's Death" (Sexton, A.) 187
"The System of Dr. Tarr and Prof. Fether" (Poe, E.) 49, 50n9

*T. S. Eliot in Context* (Harding, J.) 160
*Talking Proper: The Rise and Fall of the English Accent as a Social Symbol* (Mugglestone, L.) 247
*Tao Te Ching: A New English Version* (Laozi, ed. Mitchell, S.) 68
*The Teaching Archive: A New History for Literary Study* (Buurma, R.; Heffernan, L.) 9n15, 141n6
Teasdale, Sara 160, 212, 214
  *Dark of the Moon* 212, 214
"Technologies of Reproduction: The Maternity Ward in Sylvia Plath's *Three Women* and Ingmar Bergman's *Brink of Life*" (Fraser, L.) 250n11

"Ted Hughes: *Crow*" (Brandes, R.) 183–4
*Ted Hughes: Stronger Than Death* (Documentary) (Smith, R.) 292
*Ted Hughes: The Unaccommodated Universe* (Faas, E.) 179
Teicher, Craig Morgan 27
*The Tempest* (Shakespeare, W.) 89n13, 206
"Ten Poems by Sylvia Plath" (Plath, S.) 267n2
"Thalidomide" (Plath, S.) 28, 94, 235, 263n11, 267n2
*The Theory of Psychoanalysis* (Jung, K.) 139
*These Ghostly Archives: The Unearthing of Sylvia Plath* (Crowther, G.; Steinberg, P.) 5, 61n30, 75n1, 79, 221
Thiher, Gary 270
"The Thin People" (Plath, S.) 28
"The Third Programme" (Newby, P. H.) 257, 263, 263n12
*The Third Programme: A Literary History* (Whitehead, K.) 246, 250
"This living hand" (Keats, J.) 23
Thomas, Dylan 105, 244, 258, 301
  "Do Not Go Gentle into that Good Night" 258
  *Under Milk Wood* 244, 258
Thompson, J. Walter (JWT) 292
"'Three Caryatids Without A Portico,' by Hugo Robus. A Study in Sculptural Dimensions" (Plath, S.) 143n12
"Three Legends" (Hughes, T.) 183
"Three Poems of the Atomic Age" (Sitwell, E.) 202
"Three Women" (Plath, S.) 6, 8–9, 95, 188, 191–4, 243–5, 247, 249–51, 253–4, 256–65
"Three Women" An Audience Research Report 263
"On *Three Women*" (Cleverdon, D.) 258–60, 262, 265
"Three Women: A Poem for Three Voices" (Plath, S.) 8, 255
*Three-Martini Afternoons at the Ritz: The Rebellion of Sylvia Plath & Anne Sexton* (Crowther, G.) 283, 303n5
"Tiger, Tiger" (Blake, W.) 158
*The Times* 66
"Tomorrow Begins Today" (Plath, S.) 241
"The Tour" (Plath, S.) 28
"Toward a New Madwoman Theory: Reckoning the Pathologization of Sylvia Plath" (Rovito, M.) 43
"The 'Tragedy' Paper at Cambridge" (Collini, S.) 140

*Transcription* (Atkinson, K.) 243
Trinidad, David 309n10–11, 314n23
Trotter, David 8, 252
    *Literature in the First Media Age: Britain between the Wars* 8
Trypanis, C. A. 145–8, 145n19, 146n20–2, 151
    *The Stones of Troy* 145–6, 145n19, 146n20–1, 148n29
Tucker, Beryl 38
    "Your Children Are Looking at You!" 38
Tucker, T. G 149, 149n30
    (tr.) *The Choephori of Aeschylus* 149, 149n30
Tuite, Rebecca 4, 33n4–5
    "Sleepwear in Hollywood Film and Television, and the US Sleepwear Industry, 1945–c.1977" 33n4–6
"Tulips" (Plath, S.) 21, 96
Tunstall, Lucy 19–20
*Twee: The Gentle Revolution in Music, Books, Television, Fashion, and Film* (Spitz, M.) 17
"The Twentieth-Century Long Poem" (Keller, L.) 177–8
Twiddy, Ian 206
"The Two *Ariels*: The (Re)Making of the Sylvia Plath Canon." (Perloff, M.) 101, 178n1
"Two Lovers and a Beachcomber" (Plath, S.) 53n2
*Two for the Money* (TV Show) 237
"Two Songs from a Play" (Yeats, W. B.) 158–9, 162
"Two Views of Withens" (Plath, S.) 80

"*Ulysses*, Order, and Myth" (Eliot, T. S.) 145, 145n17
*The Unabridged Journals of Sylvia Plath 1950–1962: Transcribed from the Original Manuscripts at Smith College* (Plath, S., ed. Kukil, K.) 1–2, 4, 6, 12, 18, 35, 38–40, 42, 45, 54–5, 61, 63–4, 66, 68, 75, 94, 98–9, 105, 114–15, 118, 125–30, 139, 142, 151, 155, 157–8, 171, 194, 200, 216, 228–30, 237, 239, 283–4, 295–6, 300, 310, 314
*Under Milk Wood* (Thomas, D.) 244, 258
*The Unraveling Archive: Essays on Sylvia Plath* (ed. Helle, A.) 2
"From 'Unruly Guest' to 'Good Companion': The Gendered Meanings of Early Radio in the Home" (Moores, S.) 251

"Up … in Ceylon" (Article in *RAT*)) 272
Uroff, Margaret Dickie 56n14, 59n22, 60n24
*The Use of Poetry and the Use of Criticism* (Eliot, T. S.) 59

van Dyne, Susan 7
    *Revising Life: Sylvia Plath's Ariel Poems* 7
vanDette, Emily 296
    "The Literature Classroom, College Library, and Reading Publics: Building Collaborative Critical Reading Networks" 296
"On the Vanity of Human Aspirations" (Sitwell, E.) 202
Vellacott, Philip 139n1, 148–51, 148n29, 149n30, n33, 150n35, 151n37
    (tr.) *Aeschylus, The Oresteian Trilogy* 139n1, 148–50, 151n38
    (tr.) *The Oresteian Trilogy* 139, 148–9, 151
Verma, Neil 261
"A Very Scary Light Show: Exploding H-Bombs in Space" (Krulwich, R.) 71
"Vessel of Wrath" (Merwin, D.) 134
Vice, Sue 178, 178n1, 180
    "Sylvia Plath: *Ariel*" 178n1, 180
Villa, José García
    (ed.) *A Celebration for Edith Sitwell* 200
"Virgil's Bees" (Duffy, C.) 206–7
*Virginia: A Play* (O'Brien, E.) 279
"Virus TV" (Plath, S.) 236–7, 241
*A Vision* (Yeats, W. B.) 155n2, 156–7, 161n4
Voegelin, Salomé 260, 264
    *Listening to Noise and Silence: Towards a Philosophy of Sound Art* 260
    *The Political Possibility of Sound: Fragments of Listening* 264
*Vogue* 34
Voyce, Stephen 268–9, 271
    "The Women's Liberation Movement: A Poetic for a Common World" 271
Vuong, Ocean 22
    *On Earth We're Briefly Gorgeous* 22

Wagner, Erica 173, 178
    *Ariel's Gift: Ted Hughes, Sylvia Plath and the Story of Birthday Letters* 170, 173
Wagner-Martin, Linda 32n2, 105, 258, 307n1, 314n1
    *Sylvia Plath: A Biography* 32n2, 105, 258
Wain, John 147
Walcott, Derek 104
Walde, Christine 3, 84, 88

"A Walk to Withens" (Plath, S.) 80n10
Walker, Andrew 247n8
Walpole, Horace 299
"Waltz" (Sitwell, E.) 208
"War: Weather Report" (Dohrn, B.) 272
Ward, Mary Jane 4, 43–51, 49n8
   *The Snake Pit* 4, 43–50, 49n8
Warner, Ahren 281, 283
   "Introduction: Poetry, Theory, Archives" 283
Warren, Robert Penn 141, 141n6, 215
*The Waste Land* (Eliot, T. S.) 59, 59n20–1, 86, 202–3
"Watercolor of Grantchester Meadows" (Plath, S.) 56n14, 58, 60–1, 60n24
Watling, Edward 139n1, 142n8
"Weather Report" (article in *RAT*) 272
"Weather Underground" (Lambert, L.) 272
*Wednesday Magazine* (TV Show) 237
"The Weird Ones" (Plath, S.) 248
*Welcome to the Dreamhouse: Popular Media and Postwar Suburbs* (Spigel, L.) 238
*West Country Fly Fishing* (Bark, A.) 179
Wevill, Assia 10, 78, 135, 181, 183, 289–96, 301, 314; *See also* Assia Gutmann
Wevill, Shura 183, 294
"What Is an Author?" (Foucault, M.) 90
"What Made You Stay?" (Radio Show) 248, 256n2
White, Gillian 3n9, 19
   *Lyric Shame: The "Lyric" Subject of Contemporary American Poetry* 3n9, 19
*The White Goddess* (Graves, R.) 174, 190
*White Women Writing White: H. D., Elizabeth Bishop, Sylvia Plath, and Whiteness* (Curry, R.) 11, 21, 101, 274
Whitehead, Kate 244, 246, 249–50
   *The Third Programme: A Literary History* 246, 250
"Whiteness I Remember" (Plath, S.) 55n11
Whitman, Walt 178
   *Song of Myself* 178
Whittington, Ian 256–7
"Whoever She Was" (Duffy, C.) 204
"Widow" (Plath, S.) 69
Wiese, Otis Lee
   "Live the Life of McCall's" 33
*Wife Dressing* (Fogarty, A.) 38
"The Wife of Bath's Tale" (Chaucer, G.) 58
Wilbur, Richard 6, 130, 303
Wilcox, Fred M.
   *Forbidden Planet* (Film) 67
Wilde, Oscar 204
Williams, Nerys 8–9
Williams, Tennessee 67n6, 311
   *The Glass Menagerie* 311
Williams, William Carlos 178
Willoughby, Vanessa 11
Wilson, Andrew 309n8, 310n12
   *Mad Girl's Love Song: Sylvia Plath and Life before Ted* 32n3, 35, 310n12
Wimsatt, William K. 140
   "The Concrete Universal" 140
Winder, Elizabeth 32n2, 35–6
   *Pain, Parties, Work: Sylvia Plath in New York, Summer 1953* 32n2, 35–6
*The Winding Stair* (Yeats, W. B.) 156
"Winter Landscape, with Rooks" (Plath, S.) 54–5, 55n9, 56n12, 58, 61
"A Winter Ship" (Plath, S.) 267n4
*Winter Trees* (Plath, S.) 249
"Wintering" (Plath, S.) 94, 96, 99, 160, 164, 179, 205–6, 295
"A Winter's Tale" (Plath, S.) 80n10
*The Wireless Past: Anglo-Irish Writers and the BBC, 1931–1968* (Bloom, E.) 8
"The Wishing Box" (Plath, S.) 8, 238, 240
*Without Adam: The Femina Anthology of Poetry* (Simpson, J.) 202, 207
Wolfe, Thomas 227
   "You Can't Go Home Again" 227
*Woman's Day* 133
*Women: A Journal of Liberation* 268
"Women and the Literary Curriculum" (Showalter, E.) 102
*Women's Hour* (Radio Show) 252
Women's Liberation Movement 5, 267–9
"The Women's Liberation Movement: A Poetic for a Common World" (Voyce, S.) 271
*Women's Poetry and Popular Culture* (Bryant, M.) 116, 226
Wood, Clement 157
   *The Complete Rhyming Dictionary and Poet's Craft Book* 106, 157
Woods, Marjorie Binford 48
   "Mary Jane Ward Declares Her Book Not Autobiography" 48
Woody, J. Melvin 310, 313
Woolf, Virginia 6, 61n31, 105–6, 118, 128, 142n9, 160, 279, 299, 302
"Words" (Plath, S.) 96, 108, 161–2
"Words" (Yeats, W. B.) 161
Wordsworth, William 178
   *The Prelude* 178

"The World Split Open: Feminism, Poetry, and Social Critique" (Berke, N.) 268
*The World Split Open: Four Centuries of Women Poets in England and America, 1552–1950* (Bernikow, L.) 207
World War II 17, 34, 234
*The Wound* (Hughes, T.) 247, 258
*The Writer* 106
*Writing Back: Sylvia Plath and Cold War Politics* (Peel, R.) 64–5, 65n5, 71, 95
"Writing for Radio" (Cleverdon, D.) 257
*Wuthering Heights* (Brontë, E.) 57, 80
"Wuthering Heights" (Hughes, T.) 70, 80, 96

"X" (Hughes, T.) 54, 54n4

*Yale Edition of Horace Walpole's Correspondence* (Lewis, W.) 300
*Yeats Collected Poems* (Yeats, W. B.) 157–9, 161–2, 166
"Yeats as an Example" (Auden, W. H.) 153–4
"Yeats as an Example?" (Heaney, S.) 162–4
"In Yeats' House: The Death and Resurrection of Sylvia Plath" (Gilbert, S.) 6, 160, 163, 238
Yeats, W. B. 6–7, 23, 105, 153–64, 166, 188, 196, 202–4, 227, 261, 301
  *Cathleen Ní Houlihan* 162
  "Easter 1916" 158, 162
  "Girl's Song" 156
  *The Green Helmet and Other Poems* 161
  *The Hour-Glass* 161–2
  "The Lake Isle of Innisfree" 163
  "Leda and the Swan" 261
  "The Man and the Echo" 162
  "Nineteen Hundred and Nineteen" 155, 202
  "No Second Troy" 166
  "A Prayer for my Daughter" 188
  "The Second Coming" 157
  "The Song of Wandering Aengus" 156–7
  "The Stare's Nest by My Window" 162–4
  "Two Songs from a Play" 158–9, 162
  *A Vision* 155n2, 156–7, 161n4
  *The Winding Stair* 156
  "Words" 161
  *Yeats Collected Poems* 157–9, 161–2, 166
"You Can't Go Home Again" (Wolfe, T.) 227
"You Hated Spain" (Hughes, T.) 94, 99
Young, Louise B.
  *Earth's Aura* 70
"Your Children Are Looking at You!" (Green, B.; Tucker, B.) 38
"You're" (Plath, S.) 178, 180–1, 189
"You're the Prettiest Mommy on Earth" (Article in *Good Housekeeping*) 38

"Zoo Keeper's Wife" (Plath, S.) 78–9

www.ingramcontent.com/pod-product-compliance
Lightning Source LLC
Chambersburg PA
CBHW080934300426
44115CB00017B/2807